MW00999863

UNDERSTANDING THE FAITH

A SURVEY OF CHRISTIAN APOLOGETICS

JEFF MYERS

UNDERSTANDING THE FAITH
Published by Summit Ministries
P.O. Box 207
Manitou Springs, CO 80829

In cooperation with
David C Cook
4050 Lee Vance Drive
Colorado Springs, CO 80918 U.S.A.
Integrity Music Limited, a Division of David C Cook
Brighton, East Sussex BN1 2RE, England

The graphic circle C logo is a registered trademark of David C Cook.

The website addresses recommended throughout this book are offered as a resource
to you. These websites are not intended in any way to be or imply an endorsement
on the part of David C Cook, nor do we vouch for their content.

Unless otherwise noted, all Scripture quotations are taken from the ESV® Bible (The Holy Bible, English
Standard Version®), copyright © 2001 by Crossway, a publishing ministry of Good News Publishers.
Used by permission. All rights reserved; Scripture quotations marked HCSB are taken from the Holman
Christian Standard Bible®, copyright © 1999, 2003 by Holman Bible Publishers. Used by permission.
Holman Christian Standard Bible®, Holman CSB®, and HCSB® are federally registered trademarks
of Holman Bible Publishers; NIV are taken from the Holy Bible, NEW INTERNATIONAL VERSION®,
NIV®. Copyright © 1973, 2011 by Biblica, Inc.® Used by permission. All rights reserved worldwide.
NEW INTERNATIONAL VERSION® and NIV® are registered trademarks of Biblica, Inc. Use of either
trademark for the offering of goods or services requires the prior written consent of Biblica, Inc.
The author has added italics to Scripture quotations for emphasis.

LCCN 2015949921
ISBN 978-0-7814-1360-2
eISBN 978-1-4347-0969-1

© 2016 Summit Ministries

Printed in the United States of America
First Edition 2016

5 6 7 8 9 10 11 12 13 14

041019

CONTENTS

ACKNOWLEDGMENTS

Writing a book on theology and the Bible is tricky, to say the least. I'm so grateful to our amazing Summit team for helping make it a life-shaping experience for so many people.

The Verdoorn family and many others gave sacrificially to help make it happen. Joey Amadee prepared a brilliant digital delivery system to significantly expand the book's vibrancy and its reach. Jason Graham, David Knopp, Amanda Bridger, Tosha Payne, and many others on the Summit team took personal ownership, gave detailed feedback, and kept the project moving along.

Our curriculum team, including Karl Schaller and Roy Faletti, along with our management team headed by Jeff Wood, somehow arranged the schedule so I could research and write several hours a day for the better part of a year. Thank you.

A "who's who" of subject matter experts checked various chapters for their accuracy and logic. These include Dr. Doug Groothuis, Dr. Gary Phillips, Dr. Ken Turner, Dr. Gene Fant, Dr. Wayne House, Dr. David K. Naugle, Dr. Michael W. Goheen, Dr. Mike Licona, Tom Gilson, Dr. Gary Habermas, Casey Luskin, professor Nancy Pearcey, Dr. Frank Beckwith, Dr. Garrett J. DeWeese, and Dr. Paul Copan. Along with Heather Peterson, who edited *Understanding the Faith*. They knew just how to steer me in the right direction and give significant input with a light touch. Nevertheless, if any deficiencies remain, that responsibility lies solely with me.

From brainstorming sessions to discussions about how to handle tough theological topics, John Stonestreet was an indispensable support in this project. I could not have written the book without his insightful input, deft editing, and timely encouragement.

Finally, I'm grateful for my family's support. May the words on these pages come alive in your minds and hearts as you seek to be a blessing to your generation.

Jeff Myers, PhD, President
Summit Ministries

*P*REFACE

How to Use the Summit Worldview Library

Noted Christian writer and teacher Del Tackett has said that the Summit Worldview Library needs to be the core in every high school, college, and seminary today. Colson Center president John Stonestreet has said that this series should have a place in every Christian's home library. Why is this series so important for Christian students and adults in all walks of life to use often in today's complex world? Perhaps seeing how the trilogy came together will help explain:

- *Understanding the Faith: A Survey of Christian Apologetics*—**the first book in the series enables Christians to better understand theology and apologetics.** *Understanding the Faith* is a fast-track, fast-paced theological education for those who want to understand God and his world in a profound way and share their faith intelligently with unbelievers. Theology and apologetics aren't just academic exercises for pastors and church leaders; we are all "ambassadors for Christ" (2 Cor. 5:20) charged with giving "reason[s] for the hope" we have in him (1 Pet. 3:15). Pressing questions about life and faith deserve thoughtful answers.

- *Understanding the Times: A Survey of Competing Worldviews*—**the second book in the series gives Christians insight into the battle other worldviews are waging against Christ and inspires newfound confidence in the breadth and depth of a biblical Christian worldview.** By providing trusted, documented insight into the six major worldviews that drive the global events of our day, *Understanding the Times* helps Christians "[understand] the times" in which they live so they can know what to do in response to the critical issues they're facing today (1 Chron. 12:32).

- *Understanding the Culture: A Survey of Social Engagement*—**the third book in the series shows Christians how to transform culture.** With a firm foundation in biblical theology, apologetics, and worldview, Christians have something vital to say about every significant issue of our day. The depth and creativity of Christian thought on today's events should inspire tremendous confidence in communicating biblical truth to friends, loved ones, and associates. In John 8:32, Jesus said we can "know the truth, and the truth will set [us] free." Entire nations are in bondage to bad ideas, but believers can proclaim the truth—boldly, intelligently, and practically—that can set people free.

As a result, the Summit Worldview Library is eminently useful for students, teachers, pastors, businesspeople, public leaders, and others who want their faith to make an impact on twenty-first-century society.

CHAPTER 1

INTRODUCTION

1. How to Figure Out Where You're Going

Let's say you parachute into the middle of New York City's Central Park. When you land, a mysterious stranger says to you, "There is a five-thousand-dollar diamond necklace waiting for you at Tiffany & Co. It's yours, free, on one condition: you have to claim it in the next twenty minutes."

Even if you care nothing for diamond necklaces, this would get your attention. You could always sell it and keep the cash.

"But what is Tiffany & Co., and how do I get there?" you ask.

"I can't tell you," says your anonymous source. "You'll have to find out on your own."

Of course, you suspect a trick. After all, you just parachuted in. You know nothing about your would-be benefactor. But the necklace is worth a lot, so you have a strong incentive to check it out.

Your heart begins pounding. You feel your pocket—smartphone must have fallen out during the jump. You've never been in New York City before. The time limit creates a sense of urgency—if you just wandered around for a few hours, you might eventually find Tiffany & Co. But you don't have hours. You have twenty minutes.

> **If you want the necklace, you're going to have to overcome your fear (and your embarrassment at dragging a parachute behind you) and start asking for directions.**

If you want the necklace, you're going to have to overcome your fear (and your embarrassment at dragging a parachute behind you) and start asking for directions. You will probably have three questions: Where am I? Where is Tiffany & Co.? What is the fastest way to get there?

But what kind of person do you ask? It must be someone who knows New York City generally and where certain stores are in particular. The homeless guy on the bench may know the layout of New York City, but he doesn't seem like the kind of guy who would know much about jewelry stores. The skateboarding teenager probably won't know either. Will the mom pushing the baby in a stroller?

Let's say you find a source you think might be credible. How do you know he or she is telling the truth? After all, people in New York act as if they know what they're doing, but some of them must be just as lost as you. *In fact, they might be wrong and not even know it.* Or worse, your source may have a sick sense of humor and think it's funny to send you running off in the wrong direction. Will you ask more than one person to get confirmation? What do you do if their answers conflict?

The middle of Central Park to Tiffany & Co. on Fifth Avenue on the southeast side of the park is less than a mile. You can easily make it there inside of twenty minutes, especially if you jog. But it will take a few minutes to get directions and to orient yourself. There's no time for mistakes.

If you want the necklace, you'll have only one chance.

2. GETTING DIRECTIONS FOR LIFE

Some things about the search for the Tiffany & Co. necklace are very much like real life.

People who figure out what works in life are rewarded. The rewards may be tangible (money or things) or intangible (peace of mind, satisfaction with a job well done). The rewards may be temporal (in this life) or eternal (beyond death). Either way, there is a time limit; one out of every one person dies (you've probably noticed). There is a real world with real rules. You can't set off to the north and expect to reach a southerly destination (except after a very long walk and swim around the earth).

This book was written to aid you in your exploration for God: Is he real? What is he like? Is what the Bible says about him authoritative and worthy of obedience? Many people question whether this is a valid pursuit. Some think it is irrelevant whether God exists. Others see belief in God and the Bible as an anesthetic that exists only to help those who have a low tolerance for pain cope. Still others see God and the Bible as fictions invented to help the powerful oppress the weak.

We should not be too quick to dismiss these assertions. There are undoubtedly people who claim to be Christians but live as if God is irrelevant. And we can easily imagine people embracing Christianity because they want a crutch to help them hobble through life or a club with which to bully others.

Skeptics, cynics, atheists, agnostics, and firm believers all have at least one thing in common: they don't know everything. Beyond general things (such as how to walk without falling down, how to feed ourselves, and so on), we need help. Think of all the confusing issues humans face:

> Skeptics, cynics, atheists, agnostics, and firm believers all have at least one thing in common: they don't know everything.

- Is there a God? And what do I understand to be true about him?

- How should I respond to those who believe differently, especially those whose understanding of God tells them to harm people like me?

- Where did we come from? Are we really a special creation of God, or are we the result of a random process of evolution? What does this mean for how we live together?

- What should I do for a job? What kinds of jobs are worth doing? How can we create more jobs?

- What does God want from me? How can I even know? What if people who have a different view of him try to stop me from doing what he wants?

- Should I get married? What is marriage anyway? If two people of the same sex want to marry each other, is that truly marriage?

- How can I live in harmony with those around me? Which political and economic policies are most harmonious with human flourishing? How should we respond when bad decisions made by leaders create disharmony?

It's tempting to dismiss these questions as trivial, but they matter. In the end, we have to act on what we know, and all our questions and actions will lead us to some destination. You might say, "I refuse to think about this—I'm not going anywhere," but you actually are. In this case, *nowhere* is surely as much a destination as *somewhere*.

> You might say, "I refuse to think about this—I'm not going anywhere," but you actually are. In this case, *nowhere* is surely as much a destination as *somewhere*.

All these questions about direction in life matter because we humans are not mere animals; we need to make sense of the world, not just survive in it. Among all living creatures, only human beings seem to wrestle with *why* we exist. In *A World without Heroes*, George Roche said:

> Man is a very *strange* animal.... Not that there is anything particularly queer about our physical equipment; this is all quite reasonable. But gorillas have hands as we do, yet use them for very little, and never to play the piano or skip stones or whittle or write letters. Dolphins have bigger brains than we do, but you seldom hear them discoursing on nuclear physics. Chihuahuas are more hairless than we, but have never thought to wear clothes.... Man alone weeps for cause, and "is shaken with the beautiful madness called laughter."[1]

The products of our musings and mental processing are called *ideas*, and our lives are full of them.[2] Some ideas accurately reflect our world. Many do not. Some help us; others cause harm. Are there clues we can use to figure out the difference?

3. Is One Direction Better Than Another?

Alice was completely overwhelmed by Wonderland and at an absolute loss for where to go. She asked the Cheshire Cat,

> "Would you tell me, please, which way I ought to walk from here?"
> "That depends a good deal on where you want to get to," said the Cat.
> "I don't much care where—," said Alice.
> "Then it doesn't matter which way you walk," said the Cat.
> "—so long as I get somewhere," Alice added as an explanation.
> "Oh, you're sure to do that," said the Cat, "if you only walk long enough."[3]

The dialogue between Alice and the Cat is more profound than it might appear. Even if we don't care enough to think deeply about truth and meaning, our ideas lead us somewhere. Of that we can be certain. But where do they lead?

Even if we don't care enough to think deeply about truth and meaning, our ideas lead us somewhere.

Our culture floods our senses with ideas—advertisements, programming, conversations, text messages. All this noise can seem like random, neutral bits of information, but if we look more closely, we realize that every bit of information contains proposals about how the world works. The ideas communicated might be true or false, but they are not neutral. They have the power, for better or worse, to change how we see the world. Over time, patterns emerge that hold certain ideas together and conform our lives to values and ways of living. The ideas we encounter may be complex, but they are not random.

The ideas we encounter may be complex, but they are not random.

We are influenced, even if only with tiny nudges, by this information. The average person makes a few big decisions every day (Should I study for this test?) and ten thousand to twenty thousand small ones (Should I eat the chips first or the sandwich?).[4] Taken together, that which influences our decisions affects the way we live and possibly even the direction of our lives.

Overwhelmed, many "tune out" and believe whatever they're told. History tells how unthinking people become the victims of ideas. A characteristic of those in the rising generation, however, is their dissatisfaction with the "That's just the way it is, so stop asking questions" approach to tough questions. They crave meaning and know they must go beyond seeing the world in "bits and pieces," as Francis Schaeffer put it, to seeing the big picture.[5]

What we need is a map. Maps provide clear mental models of the terrain we must navigate. A good map shows where the various towns, roads, and landmarks are situated in relation to one another. An "ideas map" would describe the contours of the world of thought and help us navigate the information we encounter. The more accurate our map, the more we'll understand. On the map of life, there are five major landmarks—five questions we must ask and answer whether we want to or not.

4. Five Questions Affecting Our Direction in Life

Obviously, mastering the world of ideas is a complex undertaking. I think of this every time I visit the Bodleian Library at the University of Oxford. "The Bod" is one of the world's great libraries and the repository of more than eleven million books and artifacts. As you imagine Oxford's majestic spires, recall the apostle Paul's statement "Take every thought captive to obey Christ" (2 Cor. 10:5). How many *thoughts* are in all those books? How could a person possibly master them all?

Thoughtful people have always felt overwhelmed by how much there is to know. Even King Solomon said, "Of making many books there is no end" (Eccles. 12:12). Think how many more books have been written in the centuries and millennia since he said that! Today the world of ideas is more complex than ever. Which ideas should we take seriously? Which should we dismiss as frivolous, incoherent, or patently ridiculous? And which should we actively oppose as dangerous?

> Which ideas should we take seriously? Which should we dismiss as frivolous, incoherent, or patently ridiculous? And which should we actively oppose as dangerous?

Maybe it will help to identify five landmarks on the "idea map" that form five questions every human must grapple with.

Origin. Where did we come from? Some say we were created by God to bear his image. Others say we evolved through random-chance processes. One American Indian creation story begins with "The woman and the man dreamed that God was dreaming them."[6] So were they already created and dreaming, or were they part of God's dream? Is the story intended to be taken literally, or is it poetry? The various creation stories contradict one another. They can't all be right, but which is wrong?

Identity. Who are we? What is a human being? Are we more than just animals? Does every human being have intrinsic worth and dignity, or are worth and dignity determined by external factors, skills, and attributes? Further, most people suspect that something is wrong with us. What exactly, if anything, is wrong, and how do we fix it?

Meaning. What is real and true, and how do we know? What is life all about? Is there purpose to our lives, or must we contrive it somehow? Is reality real or an illusion? Is there such a thing as "the good life," and if so, what is it? What makes life worth living at all? Why do humans not only exist but also wonder about why they exist? Will the answers we embrace determine what we ultimately live for and the lengths to which we should go to achieve it?

Morality. How should we live? Are there rules for the good life? Who makes them? Are they true for all times and all cultures, or do they depend on our circumstances? A study by Barna Group states that 83 percent of young adults said moral truth depends on the circumstances, and only 6 percent said moral truth is absolute.[7] Is morality based on feelings? Does morality change if our feelings change?

> A study by Barna Group states that 83 percent of young adults said moral truth depends on the circumstances, and only 6 percent said moral truth is absolute.

Destiny. What happens next? Where is history headed? Is there an afterlife? If so, what is it like? Clearly there is something wrong with the world: poverty, injustice, pain, and sickness exist. How do we explain this? And what do we do about it? Some say that bad things are just an illusion, while others say that bad things result from evolution and have no larger meaning. Still others blame sin. Some say there is a possibility of redemption, but there are many different ideas about what that means. Should we try to fix things or merely look forward to a life beyond this one?

And just when we think we've got everything figured out, one question continues to haunt us all: How do we know that our answers to these questions are right?

5. WHY WE MUST UNDERSTAND THE TIMES

The Bible tells of a tribe in ancient Israel called Issachar, whose men had an "understanding of the times to know what Israel ought to do" (1 Chron. 12:32). Those who understand the times aren't as likely to be tricked by wrong ideas. What's more, because they understand reality more clearly, they can come up with solutions to the problems that plague us all.

The Old Testament often uses the Hebrew word *derek* to describe a direction-filled life. *Derek* means "the way." According to seminary professor Joel Williams, the ancient Hebrews thought "to walk in the ways of God meant to live according to his will and commandments."[8] Deuteronomy 10:12 says that we should "walk in all his ways." Isaiah 40:3 says to "prepare the way of the LORD." In life, there is a right way to go and a wrong way to go. There is a way of wisdom and a way of foolishness. There is a right way and a wicked way. There is a way of life and a way of death.

> Those who understand the times aren't as likely to be tricked by wrong ideas.

If you can understand the right way, the wrong way will become evident. If you can know how to stay on the right way, you can discern when you (and others) deviate from the path.

The apostle Paul, for example, in his lengthy and complex letter to the Christians in Rome, begins with a summary of how humanity had lost its way:

> For the wrath of God is revealed from heaven against all ungodliness and unrighteousness of men, who by their unrighteousness suppress the truth. For what can be known about God is plain to them, because God has shown it to them. For his invisible attributes, namely, his eternal power and divine nature, have been clearly perceived, ever since the creation of the world, in the things that have been made. So they are without excuse. For although they knew God, they did not honor him as God or give thanks to him, but they became futile in their thinking, and their foolish hearts were darkened. (Rom. 1:18–21)

In this passage Paul describes what happens when people reject God. As a friend of mine puts it, when people do not think well of God in their minds, God gives them minds that do not think well.

Although it might sound broad-minded to argue that we should invite everyone to live as he or she pleases, the world does not change to fit our whims and desires. If Christianity is true, then it accurately describes the world *as it actually is*. Rejecting Christianity, then, is the same as rejecting reality itself. Inevitably, the real world crashes in, revealing the consequences of rejecting God's rules and patterns.

> If Christianity is true, then it accurately describes the world *as it actually is*. Rejecting Christianity, then, is the same as rejecting reality itself.

For more than fifteen years, British physician and psychiatrist Theodore Dalrymple cared for the poorest of the poor in London's slums. He observed in the process that the government's attempts to show compassion to the poor actually worsened their situations. Drunkenness, promiscuity, gluttony, and abuse were common, along with all the health consequences you might expect from such lifestyles.

As Dalrymple tried to heal people's wounds, he asked, "Why do you live like this?" Stunningly, he concluded that these vulnerable individuals had simply embraced—and practiced—the ideas about gender, sexual liberation, and meaning that were taught in theories at top universities and in the media.

In his book *Life at the Bottom*, Dalrymple turns his acerbic wit on twentieth-century intellectuals who "sought to free our sexual relations of all social, contractual, or moral obligations and meaning whatsoever, so that henceforth only raw sexual desire itself would count in our decision making." Dalrymple shows that the results of adopting these ideas "both literally and wholesale" are horrifying.

> If anyone wants to see what sexual relations are like, freed of contractual and social obligations, let him look at the chaos of the personal lives of members of the underclass....
>
> Here are abortions procured by abdominal kung fu; children who have children, in numbers unknown before the advent of chemical contraception and sex education; women abandoned by the father of their child a month before or a month after

delivery; insensate jealousy, the reverse of the coin of general promiscuity, that results in the most hideous oppression and violence; serial stepfatherhood that leads to sexual and physical abuse of children on a mass scale; and every kind of loosening of the distinction between the sexually permissible and the impermissible.[9]

After reading Dalrymple's graphic portrayal of the consequences of creating our own moral standards, we need to reevaluate the wisdom of the world in light of the wisdom of God; we need to rediscover the differences between right and wrong, good and evil.

6. CAN WE KNOW THE RIGHT WAY? CAN WE KNOW ANYTHING AT ALL?

When people make up worldviews, they tend to make up ones they believe they can successfully live out. The Christian worldview is not like that. Scripture reveals a God who does not change the rules and patterns of reality just because people do not like them. He does not adjust right or wrong according to the actions and philosophies of any particular community. As essayist Flannery O'Connor said, "Truth does not change by our ability to stomach it emotionally."[10] Conversely, God does not consider something to be true just because people do manage to stomach it or because it seems to give them success.

Epistemology: the branch of philosophy that seeks to understand the nature of knowledge.

But God does care that we know the truth he makes plain to us. He cares that we understand the consequences of turning a blind eye to his standards of righteous thought and behavior.

The study of what knowledge is, how we know, and how our knowledge relates to what is real is called **epistemology** (*episteme* is Greek for "knowledge").[11] What we believe about knowledge itself serves as a kind of greenhouse in which we nurture our ideas and transplant them into every area of life.

Relativism: the belief that truth, knowledge, and morality are relative to the individual, society, and historical context.

Although it may not be possible to know everything, surely it is possible to know something. Yet some disagree with even this, claiming that we can't know anything outside our own "personal" reality and must instead get in touch with consciousness—our "higher selves." Trying to search for knowledge outside ourselves wilts our true potential. New Spiritualist writer Shakti Gawain believes that "when we consistently suppress and distrust our intuitive knowingness, looking instead for [external] authority, validation, and approval from others, we give our personal power away."[12]

Secular Humanism: a religious and philosophical worldview that makes mankind the ultimate norm by which truth and values are to be determined; a worldview that reveres human reason, evolution, naturalism, and secular theories of ethics while rejecting every form of supernatural religion.

The idea that truth and morality depend on our personal or cultural situation is called **relativism**. If relativism is correct, one of the main goals in life should be to remove any barriers people might face in finding truth for themselves. But isn't this dangerous? Even Paul Kurtz, an atheist philosopher who helped develop a philosophy called "**Secular Humanism**," acknowledged that it can be:

The humanist is faced with a crucial ethical problem: Insofar as he has defended an ethic of freedom, can he develop a basis for moral responsibility? Regretfully, merely to liberate individuals from authoritarian social institutions, whether church or state, is no guarantee that they will be aware of their moral responsibility to others. The contrary is often the case. Any number of social institutions regulate conduct by some means of norms and rules, and sanctions are imposed for enforcing them.… Once these sanctions are ignored, we may end up with [a man] concerned with his own personal lust for pleasure, ambition, and power, and impervious to moral constraints.[13]

Kurtz understands that unless there is some revealed moral truth we are all obligated to obey, anything can be construed as good or bad relative to the situation in which we find ourselves. Even though we strive to do the right thing, if there is no absolute standard by which to judge, then we may honestly disagree among ourselves what the right thing is.

> If there are no absolute standards, how do we decide who is right and wrong when it comes to making societal decisions?

So if there are no absolute standards, how do we decide who is right and wrong when it comes to making societal decisions? According to Corliss Lamont, who donated the proceeds of his father's business fortune to build a library at Harvard University and in turn was able to serve as Harvard's "humanist chaplain," the answer is easy: intelligence. "For the Humanist," Lamont said, "stupidity is just as great a sin as selfishness; and 'the moral obligation to be intelligent' ranks always among the highest of duties."[14] The implication of this statement is that only intelligent people are capable of making correct moral choices, leading to the assumption that intelligent people are to act as the moral compass for the rest of society. The smartest people should be in charge, and the rest of us must follow.

But surely some intelligent people are evil, right? Should we believe what they "know" just because they're smart? There must be a better way. Christianity may have an answer, but it leads to a whole lot of other questions.

> Surely some intelligent people are evil, right? Should we believe what they "know" just because they're smart?

7. Is It Truly Godly to Seek Knowledge?

The Bible calls on Christians to have their minds and hearts renewed to discern right from wrong and good from evil (Rom. 12:2)[15] and to be renewed in the spirit of their minds (Eph. 4:17–22).[16]

But for some Christians, this mission is at odds with what they wrongly understand Christianity to be. Some say it is a waste of time and even sinful to talk about non-Christian ideas. We should just study the truth, they say. Many even quote the passage "Where is the one who is wise? Where is the scribe? Where is the debater of this age? Has not God made foolish the wisdom of the world?… For the foolishness of God is wiser than men, and the weakness of God is stronger than men" (1 Cor. 1:20, 25).

Closely read what the passage actually says. It doesn't say that philosophy or scholarship or debating is bad; it says that approaching life from a worldview not centered in God is a foolish thing to do. Studying is not bad; being taken captive by false ideas is. The Bible is full of examples of people who understood the truth from God's perspective and were better thinkers and leaders as a result. Daniel, for example, was even considered by a pagan king to be the wisest of men because his heart and mind were completely committed to God.

Similarly, some think Colossians 2:8 prohibits Christians from the study of philosophy when it says, "See to it that no one takes you captive by philosophy and empty deceit, according to human tradition, according to the elemental spirits of the world, and not according to Christ." Have philosophies deceived people? Certainly. But it does not follow that philosophy itself is deceptive and should not be studied. Rather, we should be wary of any idea based on human wisdom rather than Christ. Christian philosophers, then, must work hard to operate from a knowledge of Christ and a desire to serve their neighbors, helping them find release from their own captivity of heart and mind.

This leads us back to the idea of knowledge. To know something about a subject means to be acquainted with the facts and truths surrounding it. A close examination of Scripture shows that God cares very much about knowledge:

> The heavens declare the glory of God, and the sky above proclaims his handiwork. Day to day pours out speech, and night to night reveals knowledge. There is no speech, nor are there words, whose voice is not heard. Their voice goes out through all the earth, and their words to the end of the world. (Ps. 19:1–4)

> For the LORD gives wisdom; from his mouth come knowledge and understanding. (Prov. 2:6)

> An intelligent heart acquires knowledge, and the ear of the wise seeks knowledge. (Prov. 18:15)

> My people are destroyed for lack of knowledge. (Hosea 4:6)

> And it is my prayer that your love may abound more and more, with knowledge and all discernment. (Phil. 1:9)

So God does care about what we know. But does it really matter whether we understand the times and know what we ought to do? Can we even claim to know what people "ought" to do?

8. IF KNOWLEDGE IS IMPORTANT TO GOD, WHY ISN'T IT IMPORTANT TO CHRISTIANS?

Many people believe that Christianity can't contribute to the world's body of knowledge. A professor once told me, "You believe what you believe because you have faith.

I believe what I believe because I have the facts." Ouch. Was my professor's assessment correct?

Nancy Pearcey is a professor and author who has studied the Christian worldview for decades. She says that the confusion over what we can know stems from an uncertainty about "upper versus lower story truth." The problem, Pearcey says, is we have created an artificial separation between "fact" (what is demonstrably true) and "value" (what is important). She explains the idea as it was described by her mentor, Francis Schaeffer:

> **A professor once told me, "You believe what you believe because you have faith. I believe what I believe because I have the facts." Ouch.**

> Using the metaphor of a building, [Schaeffer] warned that truth had been split into two stories. The lower story consists of scientific facts, which are held to be empirically testable and universally valid. The upper story includes things like morality, theology, and aesthetics, which are now regarded as subjective and culturally relative. Essentially the upper story became a convenient dumping ground for anything that an empiricist worldview did not recognize as real. Schaeffer used a simple graphic, which we can adapt like this:

The two-story concept of truth

VALUES
Private, subjective, relative

FACTS
Public, objective, universal

> This dichotomy has grown so pervasive that most people do not even realize they hold it.[17]

In Pearcey's mind, people have come to accept this fact/value split and don't question it anymore, even though it pushes Christian thought to the fringes of society. Pearcey isn't the only one who has noticed this. J. P. Moreland, a respected philosopher and evangelical Christian, says,

> There has emerged a secular/sacred separation in our understanding of the Christian life with the result that Christian teaching and practice are privatized and placed in a separate compartment from the public or so-called secular activities of life. The withdrawal of the corporate body of Christ from the public sphere of ideas is mirrored by our understanding of what is required to produce an individual disciple. Religion has become personal, private, and too often, simply a matter of "how I feel about things." By contrast, the culture encourages me to invoke my intellect in my secular, public life. By way of example, I'm always encouraged to use my intellect in how I approach my vocation, select a house, or learn to use a computer. But within

the sphere of my private, spiritual life of faith, it is my heart, and my heart alone, that operates. The life of the mind is thus separated, broken off, and compartmentalized as a function of the "secular" life instead of more naturally being integrated with the spiritual. As a result, Sunday school classes, discipleship materials, and sermons too often address the heart and not the head, or focus on personal growth and piety and not on cultivating an intellectual love for God in my vocation.[18]

Clearly, both Pearcey and Moreland think it is incorrect to separate the world into the secular and sacred, into facts and values. The only way to overcome this artificial separation is to recover Christianity as a knowledge tradition. To do that, we have to believe that God is actually real and has authority as opposed to being just a figment of our imaginations. As it turns out, this question of authority is one of the trickiest questions of our day.

9. What Does It Mean to Have Authority?

Who has authority? Too often, we think *we* do. It's common to hear, "I don't think God would send anyone to hell" or "I would never worship a God who didn't allow people in love to get married." In these cases, the speaker claims authority on behalf of (or over) God. Is this legitimate? To answer this question, we need to understand what authority is all about in the first place.

Consider two definitions of the word *authority* from *The Concise Oxford Dictionary*: (1) "The power or right to give orders, make decisions, and enforce obedience" and (2) "the power to influence others, especially because of one's commanding manner or one's recognized knowledge about something."[19] Let's call the first definition "hard" authority, and let's call the second "soft" authority. Let's take a look at each in turn.

Hard Authority: the power or right to give orders and demand obedience with the threat of punishment.

Hard authority is the power to give orders and enforce obedience. In the military, the general has hard authority over the captain. If a captain disobeys the general's direct order, he or she can be court-martialed and imprisoned. On the road, a police officer has hard authority to enforce the speed limit and issue penalties for violations. Here are three characteristics of hard authority:

1. **Hard authority is *extrinsic*.** It resides in the *office* rather than in the *person*. The off-duty police officer may not be allowed to issue tickets. An army captain is no longer obligated to accept orders from a retired general.

2. **Hard authority is *hierarchical*.** Both parties understand that one has standing over the other. "Because I said so!" is a valid, though not necessarily winsome, argument when a general gives a command to a captain.

3. **Hard authority *commands* obedience because it is *punitive*.** It has "teeth"; if you resist, there will be consequences.

Soft authority, on the other hand, comes from the power of influence. People possess it because others respect who they are and what they know. Upon his retirement, the general in the example above may offer counsel, but not orders, to the military. A police officer may advise you on how to protect your home from burglars. A medical doctor may give you advice when you're sick. Soft authority, then, also has three identifying characteristics:

> **1. Soft authority is *intrinsic*.** It resides within the person. Others may be wise to follow it, but they are not compelled to do so.

> **2. Soft authority is *relational*.** A person who obeys it does so because the advice seems sound or because he or she trusts the source.

> *Soft Authority:* **the power to influence and persuade others because of a person's knowledge or out of an earned respect.**

> **3. Soft authority *persuades* obedience rather than *commands* it.** It is *nonpunitive*. Those who resist may face consequences, but they aren't breaking the law.

Unless you've joined the military or have agreed by contract to obey in certain ways, most of the authority in your life is probably soft authority. This is not to say there are no consequences for ignoring authority. In the situation of the military general or the off-duty police officer or the medical doctor, the law permits you to ignore the advice you've been given. Ignoring it may lead to a bungled military strategy or a higher risk of burglary or a longer duration of staying sick, even though you won't go to jail as a result.

Even so, the categories of hard and soft authority overlap more than you might think. If you take a stand for a certain political position, your college professor might grade you down. Sometimes people are denied job promotions because they refuse to commit unethical acts. Sometimes Christian actors are denied parts in movies because they refuse to use vulgar language or perform nude.

> **The law permits you to ignore the advice you've been given.**

As we will see in later chapters, Christianity is based on the authority of God as revealed both generally in nature and specifically in the Bible. Following Christ will lead to a life of peace with God that is not contingent upon your circumstances. And one day, according to the Bible, Jesus will return as "King of kings and Lord of lords" (Rev. 19:16).[20] On that day, he will render judgment, bestow rewards, and punish evil. God's authority is both hard *and* soft, extrinsic *and* intrinsic, obligatory *and* persuasive, hierarchical *and* relational.

10. Why Should We Submit to God's Authority?

Obviously, submitting to God's authority is a weighty matter. Some people have no problem doing it. Others intellectually know they should obey God but struggle to do so. Still others reject God's authority entirely. These different responses usually have something to do with a person's early experiences of authority.

Our earliest experience with authority involves believing and obeying our parents, teachers, and pastors. At first it doesn't even occur to us to doubt them. Over time we gradually learn that they are not expert authorities on everything; they are capable of being wrong. If we are rebellious, we might think this gives us the right to ignore them entirely. We no longer fear what they will do to us, so we no longer respond to their commands. Of course, in disobeying these authorities, we choose to obey someone else—usually our peers or, indirectly, popular-culture icons. We're selective, often unreasonably so, and refuse to respond to our parents' "Because I said so" but may unquestioningly obey a rock star whose best argument is "Because I said so."

Imagine a student we'll call Dalton. Dalton grows up in a strongly authoritarian ("hard") church and is so accustomed to being told "Because I said so" that he stops questioning it. His problem isn't unanswered questions but rather unquestioned answers.

When Dalton arrives at his History of Civilizations class at college, the professor says that the Bible is filled with nonhistorical myths, a claim illustrated with apparently compelling examples. His own lectures, the professor promises, will strive to reflect the consensus of today's best scholars, regardless of where they lead. The professor is popular and cheerful, not mean or angry. He's funny in class, and to disagree with him is to appear grumpy and humorless. In fact, he is a genuinely nice person, at one point taking the time to help Dalton figure out a complex registration schedule when nobody else would. Compared to the rigid voices from Dalton's past, the professor is very appealing.

> **Imagine a student we'll call Dalton. Dalton grows up in a strongly authoritarian ("hard") church and is so accustomed to being told "Because I said so" that he stops questioning it. His problem isn't unanswered questions but rather unquestioned answers.**

How should Dalton reconcile the authority of his church and the authority of his professor?

We evaluate authorities all the time. Should we believe the politician who tells us what we want to hear? Should we believe the weather person's forecast? Should we believe the friend who says, "You *have* to see this movie!"? Sometimes we believe what others say because we lack good reason not to. Plus, if we had to try to evaluate every claim—for example, asking three people instead of one what time it is—we would end up in gridlock. If I ask someone for directions, I don't know if the person is honest, sane, or knowledgeable, but my life experience tells me that people don't usually tell pointless lies to strangers. Similarly, if my history teacher says George Washington died December 14, 1799, or that John F. Kennedy was born May 29, 1917, I have no reason to doubt her.

Evaluating authority is much harder if we're filled with doubt. If you've ever engaged in online debates about faith, you know that many people are conspiracy theorists: "Your priest was *deceiving* you—it's a conspiracy to keep the church in power!" "You were *lied* to by your parents—it's a conspiracy to keep you from enjoying life!" Can you *prove* there is no conspiracy to deceive you? Probably not. But just because a skeptic (or cynic) raises questions does not mean his doubts should be considered "authoritative." Instead, we should gather reliable sources ("authorities") and life experiences, think and pray about them carefully, and then act on them.

Most people who have considered the claims of Christianity have doubts about those claims. How do I know that the Bible is true? If something is in the Bible, do I have to obey it? What does the Bible itself say about obeying authorities? Am I obligated to follow the Bible even if those who say they believe it are following it poorly? These are important questions, but in themselves they are not a strong basis for doubt. If the balance of evidence shows Christianity to be authoritative, it would be unreasonable to reject it. For those who confess Christianity (affirming that "Jesus is Lord"), Jesus's view of the world must become their view of the world.

11. But Isn't Christianity Based on Faith, Not Knowledge?

At this point, both believers and nonbelievers might have objections. Believers might say, "You're missing the point of Christianity. It isn't about facts; it's about faith." Nonbelievers could readily agree: "You Christians believe by faith; we non-Christians believe facts. Stop trying to tell us what to do."

Steven Pinker, a professor at Harvard University, defines faith as "believing something without good reasons to do so."[21] But this is far too simplistic if not downright misleading. Certainly, biblical faith is a gift of God (Eph. 2:8), and it involves trusting that God is who he says he is and will do all that he has promised to do.[22] But biblical faith is based on knowledge, not blind obedience. In Colossians 1:9–10, the apostle Paul says, "And so, from the day we heard, we have not ceased to pray for you, asking that you may be filled with the *knowledge* of his will in all spiritual *wisdom* and *understanding*, so as to walk in a manner worthy of the Lord, fully pleasing to him, bearing fruit in every good work and increasing in the *knowledge* of God." The more we know, the better able we are to walk by faith.

Biblical faith is not blind. As we will see, the Bible is unique among books because it includes so many specific details—details that can be observed to be true or not true. It practically *invites* scrutiny. The apostles were confident not that their faith would be interesting to others but that it would be seen to be factual. In 1 Corinthians 15:19, the apostle Paul tells his readers, in essence, "You can check out the evidence for the resurrection of Christ for yourself. You'll see that it actually happened. And if it didn't happen, everything else I'm telling you is false." Maybe it was based on the apostle Peter's own occasional doubting that he encouraged his readers to be prepared to give good reasons for the hope they placed in Christ (1 Pet. 3:15).[23]

> The Bible is unique among books because it includes so many specific details—details that can be observed to be true or not true. It practically *invites* scrutiny.

What makes faith valid is not that we have it but that the object of our belief is actually worthy of belief. Theologian David Clark says, "Faith derives its value not from the intensity of the believer but from the genuineness of the one she believes in. True faith is faith in the right object; faith in an unfaithful person is worthless or worse."[24] It is not enough to be sincere in our belief. We can sincerely believe that our parachutes will deploy as we jump out of a plane over Central Park, but all the sincerity in the world won't help if the parachutes turn out to be ordinary backpacks.

So what do we do with doubt, then? All of us experience doubt because all of us are limited in our knowledge. We have questions for which we have not gotten satisfactory answers. But doubt can actually be a healthy part of a Christ-centered, thoughtful life. Here's how pastor Tim Keller says it:

> A faith without some doubts is like a human body without any antibodies in it. People who blithely go through life too busy or indifferent to ask hard questions about why they believe as they do will find themselves defenseless against either the experience of tragedy or the probing questions of a smart skeptic. A person's faith can collapse almost overnight if she has failed over the years to listen patiently to her own doubts, which should only be discarded after long reflection.[25]

Dealing with doubt is part of what it means to mature in the faith. It takes courage to doubt. But here's a hugely important key: rather than just give up, you should be *specific* about what bothers you, and you should gather the *will* to look for answers. Learn to doubt your doubts so they will not overpower everything else in your life.

12. Coming of Age in the World of Ideas: Why This Book Is Important

Maybe it would be helpful if I illustrated this with some of my own story. My name is Jeff Myers. I grew up in a small town where everyone I knew was either Protestant or Catholic (or lapsed from one of the two). Other than by the one classmate who was a Jehovah's Witness, I was never confronted with other faiths in my town. I didn't even meet a Muslim or Hindu or Buddhist or true atheist until I went to college. There, however, my world expanded, and the choices stopped being simple.

Growing up, I never imagined that I might be a scholar, mostly because I could barely understand what was going on in class, even in elementary school. My teachers' instructions didn't make sense to me, leading to poor grades and a lot of running laps in gym class. I could feel my heart pounding when they issued instructions because I knew I would forget or misunderstand them. My greatest fear was that I would not understand what people wanted from me and that I would be punished, either by them or by life, as a result.

> Growing up, I never imagined that I might be a scholar, mostly because I could barely understand what was going on in class, even in elementary school.

I did love to read, though, and even in the middle of the school day, I would find myself tuning out the teacher and reading a book about whatever I was interested in at the time. I didn't necessarily learn what my teachers wanted me to learn, but I did enjoy learning about the topics I found interesting, such as philosophy and history.

Unfortunately, the more I learned about philosophy and history, the more at odds I felt with the faith of my parents. Our family attended a small conservative church. I remember one day the pastor gave a sermon on why women should wear dresses and not slacks or jeans. Why was this kindhearted, well-meaning pastor taking so much time to answer questions like this, which were of no concern to my classmates and me, and ignoring such questions as "Why does a good God allow pain and suffering?"

Fortunately, just after I graduated from high school, my father arranged for me to attend a two-week program in Colorado sponsored by the organization I now lead, Summit Ministries. Summit has been around for a long time (more than fifty years!) and was started by David Noebel.[26] Noebel and the other instructors helped me acquire answers to my difficult questions about God, the world, and life's purpose. It changed my life and led me into a personal relationship with Jesus Christ.

One of the most important gifts I received from Noebel was a mental model of worldviews. From this, he showed how the Christian worldview is more in tune with the way the world actually is than any other worldview we studied.

Summit gave me a vision for leadership. Noebel was the first to show me the reference to the tribe of Issachar from 1 Chronicles 12:32, who had an "understanding of the times" and would "know what Israel ought to do." Notice the connection: because the men of this tiny tribe understood the times, they knew how to lead Israel. Learning this made me want to focus my life on understanding the times so I could make a difference.

> Fortunately, just after I graduated from high school, my father arranged for me to attend a two-week program in Colorado sponsored by the organization I now lead, Summit Ministries.

Today I have the privilege of heading up that same ministry. Our mission hasn't changed: to cultivate young leaders to transform culture with a biblical worldview. Our headquarters is in a collection of Victorian buildings in Manitou Springs, Colorado, a little town the *New York Times* has described as a "hippie Mayberry."[27] I live there with my family. I went to school nearby at the University of Denver, where I had some great professors and earned a doctorate of philosophy in human communication studies.

Summit Ministries continues the wonderful tradition of cultivating rising generations to know the truth and to lead. Its instructors are world-class experts committed to living godly lives, communicating vibrantly, dialoguing, and mentoring others. They don't desire to impress people with how smart they are but rather want to prepare purposeful, resolute, articulate, and compassionate champions of the Christian worldview. Simply put, Summit helps high school and college students learn what they need to know in order to become our nation's most trusted leaders.

My goal for you is, first, that you will be a more thoughtful person when it comes to understanding the ideas that rule our world. But more than that, I want you to experience confidence in God and the Bible such that you are motivated to be a courageous, articulate, compassionate, completely sold-out follower of Jesus Christ who applies your faith to every area of life.

> My goal for you is, first, that you will be a more thoughtful person when it comes to understanding the ideas that rule our world. But more than that, I want you to experience confidence in God and the Bible such that you are motivated to be a courageous, articulate, compassionate, completely sold-out follower of Jesus Christ who applies your faith to every area of life.

13. Introduction to the Book Series

There are three books in this series, which is called Understanding the Times:

- *Understanding the Faith: A Survey of Christian Apologetics.* We'll explore the nature of God, what the Bible is all about, and how to answer the common challenges people pose in attempting to refute Christianity. Along the way, we hope you come to not only understand the importance of the Bible intellectually but also love God with all your heart, soul, mind, and strength.

- *Understanding the Times: A Survey of Competing Worldviews.* We'll compare the Christian worldview with five other worldviews that all want their truth claims to be believed in Christianity's place. We'll also learn to respond to those challenges in ten academic areas that most students will face in college—and in life.

- *Understanding the Culture: A Survey of Social Challenges.* We'll learn how to be intelligent, thoughtful Christians living in today's world. We will explore some of the most difficult issues of our day and apply to them our understandings of God, his revelation, and our insight into the other worldviews.

For most people, this series of books will serve as a clear, comprehensive, and compelling case for Christianity, which is good in and of itself. But if you're the kind of person who craves a sense of purpose, who longs for a noble cause, who has sensed that most people move through their lives unaware, then this series will mean so much more: it will be an essential part of your journey to becoming a champion for truth.

> But if you're the kind of person who craves a sense of purpose, who longs for a noble cause, who has sensed that most people move through their lives unaware, then this series will mean so much more: it will be an essential part of your journey to becoming a champion for truth.

The search for truth is not one we should fear. As Thomas Jefferson said, "Truth is great and will prevail if left to herself, that she is the proper and sufficient antagonist to error, and has nothing to fear from the conflict, unless by human interposition disarmed of her natural weapons, free argument and debate."[28] We're going to have plenty of debate and discussion. We approach each question honestly, deal with the doubts many experience while courageously doubting those doubts, and always move toward the truth.

14. Understanding the Faith So We Can Understand the Times

By picking up this book and deciding to study it, you join a long line of tens of thousands of leaders in business, politics, medicine, science, ministry, the arts, and dozens of other cultural channels of influence who have committed to knowing the facts and truth about

Christianity; their beliefs have become stronger, their values deeper, their convictions more firm, and their actions more likely to take them in the direction they should go.

At Summit, we've uncovered some convincing findings about why all this matters:

- Today's Christian young adults are unprepared for opposition. Only one out of six students understands the worldviews that set themselves up against the knowledge of God (Col. 2:8).[29]

- Today's Christian young adults cannot mount a defense. Although more than two out of three students are confident that the Christian worldview is true, only one in five feels prepared to defend it as such.

- Today's Christian young adults are failing at spiritual disciplines. Only one in three students claims to have a strong devotional or prayer life.

- Today's Christian young adults feel alienated from God. Imagine a youth group meeting at church: only one in two students assembled there actually feels close to God.[30]

Understanding the faith makes a big difference. An in-depth study of 1,591 students who studied with Summit showed a dramatic positive influence on their level of Christian commitment, feeling of closeness to God, devotional life, prayer life, church attendance, sharing of faith, understanding of a Christian worldview, understanding of other worldviews, confidence in the truth of a Christian worldview, ability to explain their beliefs, and ability to defend those beliefs when challenged. In fact, the average respondent says he or she is 85 percent better prepared—almost twice as prepared—for higher education.

This is great news for a struggling generation. Of today's young people in America ages twelve to twenty-two, only one in five possesses a sense of purpose in life,[31] while 25 percent are at "risk of not achieving 'productive adulthood.'"[32] Young Christians are disengaging from their faith, embracing instead what sociologist Christian Smith calls "liberal whateverism."[33] Yet fully 60 percent say they want to make a difference.[34] They just need guidance.

> Of today's young people in America, ages twelve to twenty-two, only one in five possesses a sense of purpose in life, while 25 percent are at "risk of not achieving 'productive adulthood.'"

Let's get ready to embark on a journey through the world of ideas. At points, it may be rough going. Don't give up! Some things might not make sense at first. You might realize flaws in your thinking or disagree with what you read. I'm fine with that as long as you're motivated to do something. C. S. Lewis observed, "If you are on the wrong road, progress means doing an about-turn and walking back to the right road; and in that case the man who turns back soonest is the most progressive man."[35] The study of ideas isn't just to find what "works for me." It's about expressing the truth publicly and persuasively. It's about leadership.

15. For Such a Time as This

For most of my life, I wished I lived in a *Lord of the Rings* moment—an age of defining battles and a clear difference between good and evil. Our world might not seem so clearly divided, but we do live in an epic time. What we do now will affect the world for hundreds of years, for evil as well as for good. In a world of change, small things often become great in consequence. Karl Marx, notorious founder of the world's most bloody and miserable worldview, did most of his work alone in a quiet library. When Marx died, only a handful attended his funeral. And still, as pastor and theologian Dave Breese memorably phrased it, his ideas "rule the world from the grave."[36]

The battle of our time isn't just a battle for territory or power; it's a battle for truth. It is your destiny to battle for truth against lies, for justice against injustice, and for good against evil. This is no accident in God's sovereign plan. It is time for us to be brave and stand up. C. S. Lewis said that Christians "are tempted to make unnecessary concessions to those outside the Faith." We give in too much, he said. "We must show our Christian colours, if we are to be true to Jesus Christ. We cannot remain silent and concede everything away."[37]

> The battle of our time isn't just a battle for territory or power; it's a battle for truth.

Of course, the need to understand the times as Christians does not mean we know everything. I have to confess, my greatest fear in writing this book is that if people read it and disagree with any given point, the dialogue between us will break down. Too often, Christians succumb to what political theorist and historian Russell Kirk called the "excommunication temptation," a belief that we all must agree on everything or else there is no truth and that those who "disagree with me" must be shunned.[38] What we're shooting for in this book is what C. S. Lewis called *mere* Christianity: agreement on the nonnegotiable basics of the faith while exercising charity in the areas where we disagree. For my part, I'll try to outline my assumptions and thinking as clearly as possible as well as what I understand to be the biblical basics. I encourage you to, as you read, think about how we can move forward together even where we disagree.

Several millennia ago, a young Jewish woman named Esther was pushed into marrying King Xerxes, one of the cruelest and most pompous kings of ancient history. Sometime afterward, Esther's uncle Mordecai uncovered a plot, hatched by one of the king's trusted advisers, to massacre the Jewish people. Mordecai urged Esther to intercede with the king. She informed him that the king, in his paranoia, would have anyone killed who came into his presence without invitation—including, presumably, his own queen. But Mordecai pressed her to act by saying, "Who knows but that you have come to a royal position for such a time as this?" (Esther 4:14 NIV). Perhaps we too have come to a royal position for such a time as this.

> Several millennia ago, a young Jewish woman named Esther was pushed into marrying King Xerxes, one of the cruelest and most pompous kings of ancient history.

16. Conclusion

We'll get started in the next chapter by examining what the Bible is and isn't. This is sure to be controversial. The Bible has been the most influential book in the history of the world, and it's not because—as some would claim—it is a love story from God, an instruction manual for life, a book of dos and don'ts, or even a book about admirable heroes. It is something much, much more. Interestingly, some famous skeptics and atheists have understood this even better than many Christians.

> **Get ready to think hard, because the following chapters will engage you at the *intellectual* level. More than that, though, be ready to wonder.**

So get ready to think hard, because the following chapters will engage you at the *intellectual* level. More than that, though, be ready to wonder. This book will engage you at the level of *imagination* as well: life is an art, not a science. If God is real and the Bible is authoritative, then truth is real and there is a sure way in which we should walk. We should be prepared to follow it.

Endnotes

1. George Roche, *A World without Heroes: The Modern Tragedy* (Hillsdale, MI: Hillsdale College Press, 1987), 103. Note: the words "is shaken with the beautiful madness called laughter" quoted within this text are from G. K. Chesterton.
2. Dictionary.com defines *idea* as "any conception existing in the mind as a result of mental understanding, awareness, or activity." Dictionary.com Unabridged, Random House, Inc., dictionary.reference.com/browse/idea.
3. Lewis Carroll, *Alice's Adventures in Wonderland* (Boston: Colonial Press Inc., 1865), 41.
4. Jim Clifton, *The Coming Jobs War: What Every Leader Must Know about the Future of Job Creation* (New York: Gallup Press, 2011), 51.
5. Francis A. Schaeffer, *A Christian Manifesto* (Wheaton, IL: Crossway, 2005), 17.
6. "American Indian Creation Myths: Creation," trans. Frank Thomas Smith, *Southern Cross Review*, www.southerncrossreview.org/19/creation.htm. (Myth originally published in Spanish in *Memoria del Fuego–1* by Eduardo Galeano. His source was Marc de Civrieux, *Watunna. Motología Makiritare*.)
7. "Americans Are Most Likely to Base Truth on Feelings," Barna Group, February 12, 2002, https://barna.org/component/content/article/5-barna-update/45-barna-update-sp-657/67-americans-are-most-likely-to-base-truth-on-feelings#.Vkz2hGSrRz8.
8. Joel F. Williams, "Way," in *Eerdmans Dictionary of the Bible*, ed. D. N. Freedman, A. C. Myers, and A. B. Beck (Grand Rapids, MI: Eerdmans, 2000), 1370–71. Williams says, "In the concrete sense, a road (Deut. 1:2; Ruth 1:7) or a movement along a particular path, i.e., a journey (Exod. 13:21; 1 Kgs. 19:4). However, Heb. *derek* was also employed more broadly. To walk in the ways of God meant to live according to his will and commandments (Deut. 10:12–13; 1 Kgs. 3:14). In Isaiah 'the way of the Lord' can refer to God's provision of deliverance from enslavement or exile (Isa. 40:3; 43:16–19). The word was often used to identify the overall direction of a person's life, whether righteous or wicked (Judg. 2:17–19; Ps. 1:6; cf. Matt 7:13–14), wise or foolish (Prov. 4:11; 12:15). In the NT Gk. *hodōs* has a similar range of meanings. In Mark's Gospel it is used repeatedly to present Jesus as 'on the way,' i.e., on his journey to Jerusalem (Mark 8:27; 9:33–34; 10:32). The broader context adds a deeper significance to these more literal references, since Jesus' willingness to go the way of suffering provides an example for his followers who must also prepare to suffer (Mark 8:31–34). In John 14:6 Jesus claims to be 'the way,' i.e., the only means of access to God (cf. Heb. 9:8; 10:19–20). In Acts 'the Way' functions as a title for the Christian message (Acts 19:9, 23; 22:4; 24:22) or the Christian community (9:2; 24:14)."
9. Theodore Dalrymple, *Life at the Bottom: The Worldview That Makes the Underclass* (Chicago: Ivan R. Dee, 2001), xi.
10. Flannery O'Connor, *The Habit of Being: Letters of Flannery O'Connor*, ed. Sally Fitzgerald (New York: Farrar, Straus and Giroux, 1979), 100.
11. Some philosophers posit the existence of categories of meaning that exist whether we know about them or not and that make knowledge possible (idealism). Others focus on what we can know through experience (empiricism). Still others focus on using abstract concepts such as logical arguments to create a structure through which we can know things (rationalism). The postmodern view that knowledge is constructed through our social experiences is called "constructivism."
12. Shakti Gawain, *Living in the Light: Follow Your Inner Guidance to Create a New Life and a New World* (San Rafael, CA:

New World Library, 1986), 69.

13. Paul Kurtz, "Does Humanism Have an Ethic of Responsibility?," quoted in Morris B. Storer, ed., *Humanist Ethics Dialogue on Basics* (Buffalo, NY: Prometheus Books, 1980), 15.

14. Corliss Lamont, *The Philosophy of Humanism* (New York: Frederick Ungar, 1982), 248.

15. Romans 12:2: "Do not be conformed to this world, but be transformed by the renewal of your mind, that by testing you may discern what is the will of God, what is good and acceptable and perfect."

16. Ephesians 4:17–22: "Now this I say and testify in the Lord, that you must no longer walk as the Gentiles do, in the futility of their minds. They are darkened in their understanding, alienated from the life of God because of the ignorance that is in them, due to their hardness of heart. They have become callous and have given themselves up to sensuality, greedy to practice every kind of impurity. But that is not the way you learned Christ!—assuming that you have heard about him and were taught in him, as the truth is in Jesus, to put off your old self, which belongs to your former manner of life and is corrupt through deceitful desires."

17. Nancy Pearcey, *Saving Leonardo: A Call to Resist the Secular Assault on Mind, Morals, and Meaning* (Nashville: B&H, 2010), 26–27.

18. J. P. Moreland, *Love Your God with All Your Mind: The Role of Reason in the Life of the Soul*, rev. ed. (Colorado Springs, CO: NavPress, 2012), 21–22.

19. *The Concise Oxford Dictionary*, main ed., s.v. "authority."

20. Revelation 19:16: "On his robe and on his thigh he has a name written, King of kings and Lord of lords."

21. Steven Pinker, "Less Faith, More Reason," *The Harvard Crimson*, October 27, 2006, www.thecrimson.com /article/2006/10/27/less-faith-more-reason-there-is/.

22. Ephesians 2:8: "By grace you have been saved through faith. And this is not your own doing; it is the gift of God."

23. 1 Peter 3:15: "In your hearts honor Christ the Lord as holy, always being prepared to make a defense to anyone who asks you for a reason for the hope that is in you; yet do it with gentleness and respect."

24. David K. Clark, *Dialogical Apologetics: A Person-Centered Approach to Christian Defense* (Grand Rapids, MI: Baker, 1993), 20.

25. Timothy J. Keller, *The Reason for God: Belief in an Age of Skepticism* (New York: Dutton, 2008), xvi–xvii.

26. David A. Noebel is also the author of the original text, *Understanding the Times*. He and I coauthored a revised version of the work, which in turn became the anchor of the Understanding the Times three-book series, of which the current volume, *Understanding the Faith,* is volume 1.

27. Andy Newman, "In Colorado, a Hippie Mayberry," *New York Times: Escapes*, October 19, 2007, www.nytimes .com/2007/10/19/travel/escapes/19american.html.

28. Quoted in Thomas S. Kidd, *God of Liberty: A Religious History of the American Revolution* (New York: Basic Books, 2010), 184.

29. Colossians 2:8: "See to it that no one takes you captive by philosophy and empty deceit, according to human tradition, according to the elemental spirits of the world, and not according to Christ."

30. This and many of the following findings are discussed at length in *Turning the Tide: Evidence of Impact*, a white paper produced by Summit Ministries, www.turningthetide.net.

31. See William Damon, *The Path to Purpose: How Young People Find Their Calling in Life* (New York: Free Press, 2009), 8.

32. J. Eccles and J. A. Gootman, eds., *Community Programs to Promote Youth Development* (Washington, DC: National Academy Press, 2002), quoted in Annette Bjorklund, *Strengthening Positive Youth Development Environments: Youth Development and Problem Prevention*. University of Wisconsin-Extension (Madison, WI, 2004). Also see Commission on Children at Risk, *Hardwired to Connect: The Scientific Case for Authoritative Communities* (New York: Institute for American Values, 2003).

33. Christian Smith, "Religious Tolerance: Karma, Christ, Whatever," *Huffington Post*, September 16, 2011, www.huffingtonpost .com/christian-smith/religious-tolerance-karma-christ-whatever_b_965072.html. Similarly, Gary Railsback found that between 30 and 50 percent of young adults who claim to be born-again Christians as college freshmen claim not to be born-again Christians when they graduate in "Faith Commitment of Born-again Students at Secular and Evangelical Colleges," *Journal of Research on Christian Education* 15, no. 1 (Spring, 2006): 39–60. In addition, Scott McConnell found that 75 percent of students who were significantly involved in church in high school are no longer even attending church as twentysomethings in "LifeWay Research Uncovers Reasons 18- to 22-Year-Olds Drop Out of Church," LifeWay Articles, www.lifeway.com/Article /LifeWay-Research-finds-reasons-18-to-22-year-olds-drop-out-of-church.

34. Ron Alsop, *The Trophy Kids Grow Up: How the Millennial Generation Is Shaking Up the Workplace* (San Francisco: Jossey-Bass, 2008), 226. From a 2006 survey by Cone Inc., a communications agency, and Amp Insights, a marketing agency.

35. C. S. Lewis, *Mere Christianity* (New York: HarperCollins, 1952), 28.

36. Dave Breese, *Seven Men Who Rule the World from the Grave* (Chicago: Moody, 1989), chaps. 4 and 5.

37. C. S. Lewis, *God in the Dock: Essays on Theology and Ethics* (Grand Rapids, MI: Eerdmans, 2002), 262.

38. See Peter Wehner, "Conservatives and the Excommunication Temptation," *Commentary Magazine*, September 27, 2013.

CHAPTER 2

2

WHAT THE BIBLE IS AND ISN'T

1. WHAT THE BIBLE IS REALLY ALL ABOUT

The Bible is the bestselling book in the world. It is printed (in part or in whole) in 2,800 languages worldwide.[1] On average, 85 percent of US households own a Bible; the average number of Bibles per household is 4.3.[2] Unfortunately, although the Bible is widely owned, it goes largely unstudied.

- Barely one-quarter of adults (27 percent) are confident that Satan exists, even though this is a key teaching of the Bible and something Jesus taught.[3]

- 47 percent of American Christians strongly agree or agree somewhat that the Book of Mormon, the Quran, and the Bible all express the same spiritual truths.[4]

- 69 percent believe they are knowledgeable about the Bible, but 58 percent are unable to correctly identify its first five books.[5]

- 45 percent of adults in the United States strongly—but erroneously—believe that the Bible teaches that God helps those who help themselves.[6]

- 60 percent of Americans can't name five of the Ten Commandments.[7]

- Only 52 percent of young adults know it is false to say that Sodom and Gomorrah were married.[8]

- 50 percent of Americans, including Christians, can't name any of the four gospels.[9]

The United States may be one of the most religious nations in the West, but the American people are quite ignorant of things they ought to know about religion.[10]

If the majority of Christians don't know what the Bible says, we can be sure they also don't realize what the Bible is *for*. "It's a rule book," some say. "It's a love letter," we've heard, "from God to just us."

> **Recognizing what the Bible is will affect how we read it and whether we understand it.**

However, the Bible doesn't *look* like a rule book, an instruction manual, or a love letter. It looks like something else altogether. Recognizing what the Bible is will affect how we read it and whether we understand it. The introduction to *The Jesus Storybook Bible*, a children's book written by author Sally Lloyd-Jones, simply sets forth what the Bible is really all about.

> God wrote, "I love you"—he wrote it in the sky, and on the earth, and under the sea. He wrote his message everywhere! Because God created everything in his world to reflect him like a mirror—to show us what he is like, to help us know him, to make our hearts sing....
>
> And God put it into words, too, and wrote it in a book called "the Bible."
>
> Now, some people think the Bible is a book of rules, telling you what you should and shouldn't do. The Bible certainly does have some rules in it. They show you how life works best. But the Bible isn't mainly about you and what you should be doing. It's about God and what he has done.
>
> Other people think the Bible is a book of heroes, showing you people you should copy. The Bible does have some heroes in it, but (as you'll soon find out) most of the people in the Bible aren't heroes at all. They make some big mistakes (sometimes on purpose). They get afraid and run away. At times they are downright mean.

No, the Bible isn't a book of rules, or a book of heroes. The Bible is most of all a Story. It's an adventure story about a young Hero who comes from a far country to win back his lost treasure. It's a love story about a brave Prince who leaves his palace, his throne—everything—to rescue the one he loves. It's like the most wonderful of fairy tales that has come true in real life!

You see, the best thing about this Story is—it's true.

There are lots of stories in the Bible, but all the stories are telling one Big Story. The Story of how God loves his children and comes to rescue them.

It takes the whole Bible to tell this Story. And at the center of the Story, there is a baby. Every Story in the Bible whispers his name. He is like the missing piece in a puzzle—the piece that makes all the other pieces fit together, and suddenly you can see a beautiful picture.[11]

The Bible is God's big story of the world and everyone in it. Being ignorant of the Bible is to miss the whole point of life itself! There are many complicated parts to the story, but as Lloyd-Jones points out, the plotline is simple enough for a child to understand: it's about Jesus.

There is another story worth knowing. There was a time when the Bible's influence was widespread, and everyone in the West was better off for it. This is another fascinating story in and of itself and one most people—even longtime believers—will find amazing. In this chapter, we'll explore this story. We'll discover what the Bible is and is not. Along the way, we'll take a look at concepts such as revelation, knowledge, and truth that can help us grasp the place of the Bible in our lives. If we're willing, we'll recover an understanding of why and how this one book—the Bible—changed the world.

> **We'll recover an understanding of why and how this one book—the Bible—changed the world.**

2. The Influence of the Bible

In his visit to America in the 1830s, French sociologist Alexis de Tocqueville discovered that "America is still the place where the Christian religion has kept the greatest real power over men's souls; and nothing better demonstrates how useful and natural it is to man, since the country where it now has widest sway is both the most enlightened and the freest."[12] If this was so, it was intentional. Here's what some of America's founders said about the Bible and Christianity:

- John Jay (the first chief justice of the Supreme Court) called the Bible the "best of Books" and told his daughter, "Do not omit reading in it daily; in it you will find the best rules for your Conduct in this life and the most elevated hopes for futurity."[13]

- Samuel Adams (founding father and Massachusetts governor): "The Rights of the Colonists as Christians may be best understood by reading and carefully studying the institutes of the great Law Giver and Head of the Christian Church, which are to be found clearly written and promulgated in the New Testament."[14]

- Noah Webster (author of the famous dictionary): "All of the miseries and evils which men suffer from vice, crime, ambition, injustice, oppression, slavery, and war, proceed from them despising or neglecting the precepts contained in the Bible."[15]

- Benjamin Rush (medical doctor and founding father): "The Bible contains more knowledge necessary to man in his present state than any other book in the world."[16]

A remarkable number of US presidents through history have concurred:

- John Adams: "The Bible is the best book in the world."[17]

- John Quincy Adams: "No book in the world deserves to be so unceasingly studied and so profoundly meditated upon as the Bible."[18]

- Abraham Lincoln: "The Bible is the best gift God has given to men. All the good the Savior gave to the world was communicated through this book. But for it, we could not know right from wrong."[19]

- Theodore Roosevelt: "The teachings of the Bible are so interwoven and entwined with our whole civic and social life that it would be literally—I do not mean figuratively, I mean literally—impossible for us to figure to ourselves what that life would be if these teachings were removed."[20]

- Woodrow Wilson: "The Bible is the one supreme source of revelation of the meaning of life, the nature of God, and spiritual nature and needs of men. It is the only guide of life which really leads the spirit in the way of peace and salvation."[21]

- Calvin Coolidge: "The strength of our country is the strength of its religious convictions. The foundations of our society and our government rest so much on the teachings of the Bible that it would be difficult to support them if faith in these teachings would cease to be practically universal in our country."[22]

- Franklin Roosevelt: "We cannot read the history of our rise and development as a nation without reckoning with the place the Bible has occupied in shaping the advances of the Republic. I suggest a nationwide reading of the Holy Scriptures."[23]

- Harry Truman: "The fundamental basis of this Nation's law was given to Moses on the Mount. The fundamental basis of our Bill of Rights comes from the teachings which we get from Exodus and St. Matthew, from Isaiah and St. Paul. I don't think we emphasize that enough these days."[24]

- Ronald Reagan: "Of the many influences that have shaped the United States of America into a distinctive Nation and people, none may be said to be more fundamental and enduring than the Bible."[25]

Of course, not all these men were what we would today call evangelical Christians. Even so, the significance of the Bible to their way of thinking was so important that America's first English-language Bible included a recommendation by the United States Congress: "Resolved that the United States in Congress assembled … recommend this edition of the Bible to the inhabitants of the United States."[26] Clearly, America's founders saw the Bible as essential to the basis of a free society.

> America's founders saw the Bible as essential to the basis of a free society.

The preservation of freedom is only one of many reasons for studying the Bible. In his lecture "Why Should We Study the Bible?" David A. Noebel, Summit Ministries' founder, offers compelling reasons for why *everyone* should take the Bible seriously. Here are four of his key points:

1. The Bible is part of world literature. In *Bartlett's Book of Quotations*, there are more quotations from the Bible than from any other source. Even atheist Richard Dawkins, who abhors the Bible as a source of morality, wrote a startling editorial proclaiming that all children should read the Bible. Dawkins said, "A native speaker of English who has never read a word of the King James Bible is verging on the barbarian."[27]

2. The Bible changed Western civilization. Alvin Schmidt's *How Christianity Changed the World* says the Bible's moral guidance influenced everything, including the abolition of slavery, the banning of child molestation, freedom and dignity for women, the formation of hospitals and schools, the securing of liberty and justice for all, the advance of science, the development of great art and architecture, and the sanctity of human life.[28]

3. Knowledge of the Bible is the mark of an educated person. William Lyon Phelps, a Yale professor for forty-one years, wrote in *Human Nature in the Bible*, "Everyone who has a thorough knowledge of the Bible may truly be called educated; and no other learning or culture, no matter how extensive or elegant, can, among Europeans and Americans, form a proper substitute.… I believe a knowledge of the Bible without a college education is more valuable than a college course without the Bible."[29]

4. Knowledge of the Bible is the mark of a moral person. To live successfully in this world, a person must be able to distinguish between right and wrong, good and evil, and choose to do what is right and good. The famous Golden Rule of morality, "Do unto others what you would have them do unto you," comes directly from the Bible. (See Matthew 7:12 and also Mark 12:29–31, in which Jesus references the Old Testament passages of Exodus 3:6, Deuteronomy 6:4–5, and Leviticus 19:18.[30]) Even famed British atheist Bertrand Russell understood the principle when he said, "What the world needs is Christian love or compassion."[31]

So knowing the Bible is important. But exactly *how* do we come to know it?

---

3. The Bible's Unique Call to Study

As Noebel points out, every worldview has a "Bible," a book of what we consider to be revealed truth. Muslims have the Quran, Secular Humanists have *The Humanist Manifesto*, Libertarians have *Atlas Shrugged*, Marxists have *The Communist Manifesto*, Hindus have the *Bhagavad Gita*. Among all others, the Bible is unique in its tremendous influence.

> Every worldview has a "Bible."

We come to know the Bible through careful study. The apostle Paul wrote to his protégé Timothy, "Do your best to present yourself to God as one approved, a worker who has no need to be ashamed, rightly handling the word of truth" (2 Tim. 2:15). Later in the same letter, he affirmed his own careful study with a request: "When you come, bring the cloak that I left with Carpus at Troas, also the books, and above all the parchments" (4:13). Even though Paul was an old man approaching his death, he intended to continue studying Scripture to his dying day.

The Bible encourages its readers to be deeply familiar with the Scriptures (Ps. 119) and not distort them (2 Pet. 3:16).[32] It applauds those who compared the apostle Paul's teachings to the Old Testament to see if they were true (Acts 17:1–4).[33] It is extraordinarily rare for a holy book to call for careful, rational examination of its own teachings to see if they are consistent with revealed truth. Nothing in the Quran, for example, says, "Check this out for yourself to see if the prophet Muhammad was correct" or "Study this to see if it is consistent with the rest of the Quran." In fact, Muhammad himself was told to consult the "people of the Book" (Christians and Jews) if he doubted that the message he was receiving from the angel Gabriel was correct.[34] Why? Because Christians and Jews had diligently studied the Bible (though, the Quran claims, to little effect).[35] As for the Quran, its message is much like the books of other religious worldviews: "Here it is, take it or leave it."[36]

> In addition to calling for careful examination, the Bible promises several benefits to believers who engage in its study.

In addition to calling for careful examination, the Bible promises several benefits to believers who engage in its study:

1. Blessing: Psalm 119 indicates that those who study Scripture will be blessed with delight, freedom from shame, wisdom, hope, and protection against doing evil.

2. Insight into how to bear spiritual fruit: "The fruit of the Spirit is love, joy, peace, patience, kindness, goodness, faithfulness, gentleness, self-control; against such things there is no law" (Gal. 5:22–23).

3. Freedom from spiritual bondage: Understanding God is the basis of freedom. "Now the Lord is the Spirit, and where the Spirit of the Lord is, there is freedom.… But we have renounced disgraceful, underhanded ways. We refuse to practice cunning or to tamper with God's word, but by the open statement of the truth we would commend ourselves to everyone's conscience in the sight of God" (2 Cor. 3:17–4:2).

4. Direction in life: "Trust in the LORD with all your heart, and do not lean on your own understanding. In all your ways acknowledge him, and he will make straight your paths" (Prov. 3:5–6).

5. The ability to grasp truth and defeat error: "Though we walk in the flesh, we are not waging war according to the flesh. For the weapons of our warfare are not of the flesh but have divine power to destroy strongholds. We destroy arguments and every lofty opinion raised against the knowledge of God, and take every thought captive to obey Christ" (2 Cor. 10:3–5; see also Eph. 6:10–19).

> We must first dispose of the common myth that the Bible is an "instruction manual" for life.

Why does the Bible call for careful examination, and how is it possible that such examination will lead to a profound sense of freedom and direction in life? To answer these questions, we must have a clear understanding of the concept of revelation. In order to grasp the concept of revelation, though, we must first dispose of the common myth that the Bible is an "instruction manual" for life.

4. Not Merely a Book of Instructions

A common acronym from the 1990s said that the Bible stands for "Basic Instructions Before Leaving Earth." To this view, the Bible's value is that of a checklist. When my sons were small, we enjoyed assembling Lego sets. Just follow the pictures, snap the right pieces together in the correct order, and you'll end up with an airplane, a ship, or an epic scene from *The Lord of the Rings*.

What makes Lego instruction manuals valuable is their simplicity. Each instruction is stated as a command: "Do this next." As long as you follow each step correctly and in the right order, everything works out. There is no depth, no explanation of why things work as they do, no higher-level thinking skills required, and no connection to anything else in life.

> [The Bible] is about God and what he has done, is doing, and will do in the world and for all eternity.... Studying it orients us to the world God both created and redeemed.

But the Bible, the whole Bible, complete with stories and poems and wisdom and prophecy—not just rules—is not even primarily about us at all. It is about God and what he has done, is doing, and will do in the world and for all eternity. It is *from* God and *for* humans. Studying it orients us to the world God both created and redeemed. This allows us to live wisely. The Bible, then, is less like an instruction manual and more like a compass. Theologian N. T. Wright puts it this way:

> Reading scripture, like praying and sharing in the sacraments, is one of the means by which the life of heaven and the life of earth interlock. (This is what older writers were referring to when they spoke of "the means of grace." It isn't that we can control

God's grace, but that there are, so to speak, places to go where God has promised to meet with his people, even if sometimes when we turn up it feels as though God has forgotten the date. More usually it's the other way around.) We read scripture in order to hear God addressing us—*us*, here and now, today.[37]

It makes very little sense to study the Bible over and over again if it is just a book of rules. Can you imagine a longtime driver dedicating time every day to studying a driver's education manual? Can you imagine an employee sitting down daily with a cup of coffee and his employment manual? If, however, the Bible is a compass, it will direct us to the right path on our daily journey. It will guide us toward a relationship with God and purpose in his kingdom, correcting us when we stray.

> **Can you imagine a longtime driver dedicating time every day to studying a driver's education manual?**

The compass analogy is important to me as one who has led many expeditions into the Colorado wilderness. With a compass and a topographical map, it is possible to find the way through any wilderness area. Without the compass, the map is of little use. All the mountains, trees, and streams become obstacles rather than landmarks.

A compass does its job by showing you magnetic north. It doesn't point to you. It doesn't seek to validate your direction. It just shows the fixed, unchanging truth. It offers a reference point outside of you. Deviating from it, even a little, means that the longer you travel, the more lost you'll be. The same is true with the Bible. Theologian Robert L. Plummer notes, "The person who reads Scripture and does not obey it is self-deceived (James 1:22). To claim to know God while consistently and consciously disobeying his Word is to demonstrate the falseness of one's claim."[38]

Therefore, the Bible-as-compass analogy helps us see God's Word less as a to-do list and more as a guide to wise living, which is important in this fallen world where beauty and ugliness, safety and danger exist side by side.

On a recent ski trip, my son and I found ourselves at the top of a mountain in extreme terrain and taking in a spectacular vista. Above and behind us, though, we could see snow cliffs eroding in the unseasonably warm afternoon. Of course, they *looked* awesome, but experience in the mountains told us they were nonetheless unstable and might quickly collapse, triggering an avalanche. We found a safe area as quickly as we could. Wisdom about mountain conditions enabled us to both enjoy the view and take measures to protect our safety.

> **Wisdom about mountain conditions enabled us to both enjoy the view and take measures to protect our safety.**

But perhaps you're wondering why we should trust the Bible as life's compass. Many religions and philosophies offer direction. Why not trust one of those instead?

This question brings us to a significant point: Christianity is a *revealed* religion. It claims that God exists and that he alone has the authority to speak into our lives. If the Bible's revelation about God is accurate, then what it says is authoritative. This is serious and warrants a closer look at the idea of revelation, what it means to know something, what is true, and how we might be confident that the Bible is indeed God's Word.

WHAT THE BIBLE IS AND ISN'T

5. What Does It Mean to Call the Bible "Revelation"?

Revelation means to make known something that was previously unknown. Revelation's Hebrew word (*galah*) and the Greek word (*apokalypto*) "express the idea of uncovering what was concealed."[39] Professor Gordon R. Lewis writes, "Revelation is an activity of the invisible, living God making known to finite and sinful people His creative power, moral standards, and gracious redemptive plan."[40]

> *Revelation:* the act of making something known that was previously hidden or unknown.

There are really only two options when it comes to the origins of religion: revelation or evolution. Either God exists and has spoken and is *discovered* by humanity, or religion and religious texts are *invented* (not revealed) and therefore our concepts of the divine evolve over time.

Christianity claims that an infinite yet personal God exists and that he has spoken. He wants to be known. Erik Thoennes says,

> Knowing God is the most important thing in life. God created people fundamentally for relationship with himself. This relationship depends on knowing who he is as he has revealed himself. God is personal, which means he has a mind, will, emotions, relational ability, and self-consciousness. Because he is personal, and not merely an impersonal object, God must personally reveal himself to us.[41]

This is clear from the very first book of the Bible: "And *God said to them*, 'Be fruitful and multiply and fill the earth and subdue it, and have dominion'" (Gen. 1:28). He didn't talk *at* our first parents, Adam and Eve; he spoke *to* them in a way they could understand. New Testament scholar D. A. Carson puts it this way:

> *God is a talking God....* He *speaks* to them. So the God of the Bible in the very first chapter [of Genesis] is not some abstract "unmoved mover," some spirit impossible to define, some ground of all beings, some mystical experience. He has a personality and dares to disclose himself in words that human beings

> There in the garden of Eden, the man and woman knew exactly what to *do* not because he sent word but because he was *with* them.

> understand. Right through the whole Bible, that picture of God constantly recurs. However great or transcendent he is, he is a talking God.[42]

There in the garden of Eden, the man and woman knew exactly what to *do* not because he sent word but because he was *with* them.

6. That All May Know: Two Ways God Reveals His Nature and Character

Would people be able to know about God even if they did not have the Bible? To a certain extent, yes. There are many aspects of his character they would not understand, but through his creation, many things about him would be clear. Psalm 19:1–4 says, "The heavens declare

---

the glory of God, and the sky above proclaims his handiwork. Day to day pours out speech, and night to night reveals knowledge. There is no speech, nor are there words, whose voice is not heard. Their measuring line goes out through all the earth, and their words to the end of the world."

Chuck Colson, the founder of Prison Fellowship, which brought Bible-based reform to prisons all over the world, described in his book *Born Again* a particular experience he had as a marine captain leading a battalion to quell a communist rebellion in Guatemala. Shortly before the action commenced, Colson stood apprehensively on the deck of his ship staring at the stars:

> That night I suddenly became as certain as I had ever been about anything in my life that out there in that great starlit beyond was God. I was convinced that He ruled over the universe, that to Him there were no mysteries, that He somehow kept it all miraculously in order. In my own fumbling way, I prayed, knowing that He was there, questioning only whether He had time to hear me.[43]

Colson did not enter into a personal relationship with Jesus Christ at that moment, but his recognition of God's creation laid a foundation on which God would build, through godly mentors and twenty years in the future, to make himself completely known.

> *General Revelation:* God's universal revelation about himself (Ps. 19:1–6; Rom. 1:18–20) and morality (2:14–15) that can be obtained through nature.

This kind of revelation (i.e., God showing himself in creation, revealing his existence to our hearts) is called **general revelation**. Bruce Demarest describes the content of what can be known through general revelation: "While not imparting truths necessary for salvation—such as the Trinity, the incarnation, or the atonement—general revelation conveys the conviction that God exists and that he is transcendent, immanent, self-sufficient, eternal, powerful, good and a hater of evil."[44]

Like the unveiling of a famous painting, general revelation is a silent unveiling in which God's work speaks for itself. As I write this, an exhibit of Dutch Golden Age paintings is making its way across the United States for the first time in at least three decades. The most anticipated piece is probably Johannes Vermeer's *Girl with the Pearl Earring*. Imagine the scene as the opening night crowd gathers and the curator parts the curtain, revealing Vermeer's beloved work to many who are seeing it in person for the first time. A few people murmur their approval, but no one says a word. There is no need. This is the actual painting, the one Vermeer personally labored over almost four hundred years ago. Nothing of the moment is lost on the crowd: this is the real thing, and everyone knows it.

Because God's general revelation is clear, ignorance of reality is no excuse. Romans 1:19–20 says, "What can be known about God is plain to them, because God has shown it to them. For his invisible attributes, namely, his eternal power and divine nature, have been clearly perceived, ever since the creation of the world, in the things that have been made. So they are without excuse."

General revelation is written on our hearts as well as in our observation of creation. Later in his letter to the Romans, the apostle Paul wrote,

When Gentiles, who do not have the law, by nature do what the law requires, they are a law to themselves, even though they do not have the law. They show that the work of the law is written on their hearts, while their conscience also bears witness, and their conflicting thoughts accuse or even excuse them on that day when, according to my gospel, God judges the secrets of men by Christ Jesus. (2:14–16)

But general revelation reveals God's work in only its broadest strokes. The finer details about what we need to be united with God in Christ fit into what theologians call **special revelation**. Christian theologian Millard J. Erickson says, "By special revelation we mean God's manifestation of himself to particular persons at definite times and places, enabling those persons to enter into a redemptive relationship with him."[45] Scripture speaks of this in Hebrews 1:1–2, which says, "Long ago, at many times and in many ways, God spoke to our fathers by the prophets, but in these last days he has spoken to us by his Son, whom he appointed the heir of all things, through whom also he created the world."

A few years ago I was privileged to attend an advanced screening of a movie called *Amazing Grace*, the story of William Wilberforce's battle to end the British slave trade. The director, writer, and producer were all on hand to introduce the movie and answer questions. The movie spoke for itself, but having the filmmakers present enabled us to receive special insight into how the movie was made, why it was made, and how we could help spread the word about it.

> *Special Revelation:* God's unique revelation about himself through the Scriptures (Ps. 19:7–11; 2 Tim. 3:14–17), miraculous events (dreams, visions, prophets, prophecy), and Jesus Christ (John 1:1–18).

Similarly, when we call Christianity a revealed religion, we are pointing out something more than the general existence of a creator-God. We are proclaiming God's special revelation through the Bible—like having spoken to the movie director himself!—which is knowable and true and thus has a legitimate claim to authority over our lives. As N. T. Wright puts it, "The authority of Scripture is the authority of God exercised through Scripture."[46] Most important, the Bible is essential to knowing God truly through Jesus Christ. All of this is involved when we say the Bible is God's Word, but what exactly this means and how we know it to be true requires closer examination.

7. What Does It Mean to Say the Bible Is "the Word of God"?

How do we know the Bible is God's Word? As you investigate the evidence, you will discover, as my friend Jonathan Morrow puts it, that "the Bible did not magically fall from heaven leather bound; its composition was a divine and human process consistent with the natural limitations associated with writing documents in the ancient world."[47]

So when we say the Bible is the revealed Word of God, we're making several claims:

- There is an external world that can be known.

- Truth about this world can be discovered.

- The Bible describes this world objectively, as it is for everyone.

- The Bible makes claims that opens itself up for scrutiny and can thus be examined for truth.

Christians need to be prepared to understand and defend the Bible's "true truth" and not just how they feel about it. As author Nancy Pearcey phrases it, "When Christians are willing to reduce religion to noncognitive [feelings rather than thoughts] categories, unconnected to questions of truth or evidence, then we have already lost the battle."[48]

There is a growing confusion over what people mean when they say the Bible is God's Word.

> **There is a growing confusion over what people mean when they say the Bible is God's Word.**

Some people say the Bible *contains* God's Word, which is a very different thing from saying it *is* God's Word. To say that the Bible merely contains God's Word implies that it contains some other things too. But who is to decide which parts of the Bible contain God's Word and which do not? Claiming that the Bible *contains* God's Word places the decision in human hands: God's Word is what *we* say it is. Presumably, for people who hold this view, the Bible is God's Word only insofar as it rings true in our experience. Bluntly put, the compass of the Bible is God's Word only if it points to us. This is contrary to the whole point of biblical revelation. The traditional, historical argument for the Bible being God's Word acknowledges that the Bible's words ring true, but it clearly asserts that even if they didn't, the Bible itself *is* still true.

Following are some reasons to be confident that the Bible is God's Word.

The Bible is rooted in history and has been accurately transmitted. The Bible isn't just a random holy book proceeding from the imagination of a spiritual person. It is based on actual events in history. As philosopher William Lane Craig says,

> Christianity … is rooted in real events of history. To some people this is scandalous because it means that the truth of Christianity is inexplicably bound up with the truth of certain historical facts, such that if those facts should be disproved, so would Christianity. But at the same time, this makes Christianity unique because, unlike most other world religions, we now have a means of verifying its truth by historical evidence.[49]

From the beginning, those charged with transmitting God's Word through time sensed the need to conduct their work with great care. As we will see, the more that archaeologists examine the Bible's historical evidence, the more confirmation they find of its accuracy. The meticulous care with which scribes copied the text was seen in a special way with the 1947 discovery of the **Dead Sea Scrolls** in caves near Qumran in Israel. Among the documents was a stunning scroll containing nearly the complete text of the book of Isaiah nearly one thousand years older than the next oldest copy. In spite of the hundreds of times it must have been copied, between the old and the newer

> *Dead Sea Scrolls:* the oldest surviving collection of Jewish canonical texts written three hundred to four hundred years before the birth of Christ.

versions there was a variation of less than 5 percent, most of which was spelling variations.[50] This is no secret: the amazing Isaiah scroll may be seen today at the Israel Museum in Jerusalem.

The accuracy of the New Testament is similarly demonstrated by manuscript evidence, the presence of early texts, the number of witnesses testifying to its truth, and archaeological discoveries confirming what the text actually says.[51] We'll look at some of this evidence in greater detail in coming chapters.

The Bible is inspired by God. Theologian David Clark says we must distinguish between our *recognition* of the Bible's authority and its *inherent possession* of authority. If we start by recognizing the Bible's truth and admit that our recognition is not what makes it true, we can respond with full confidence to the way its truths resonate in our lives. As Clark says, "The objective authority of the Bible rooted in God's inspiring action stands against allowing any contemporary agendas to gain control over the theology. The subjective recognition of the Bible as authoritative guards against a dead orthodoxy that pays lip service to divine truth even as it pursues other agendas."[52] In this statement, Clark uses the term *inspiring* not as a synonym for *motivational* but in its literal meaning, "to breathe." It is a reference to the Greek word *pneuma* used in 2 Timothy 3:16, which says, "All Scripture is *breathed out* by God and profitable for teaching, for reproof, for correction, and for training in righteousness."

There is also much confusion regarding what theologians mean when they talk about the inspiration of Scripture, and I certainly do not expect to settle the matter with a few brief comments. At the very least, to say that God *inspired* the Bible means, according to Gordon Lewis, that "the Holy Spirit supernaturally motivated and superintended the prophetic and apostolic recipients of revelation in the entire process of writing their scriptural books."[53] Second Peter 1:20–21 says, "No prophecy of Scripture comes from someone's own interpretation. For no prophecy was ever produced by the will of man, but men spoke from God as they were carried along by the Holy Spirit." In fact, more than three thousand times the writers of the Bible claim to have received messages by the Holy Spirit.[54] In other words, the authors of the books of the Bible clearly believed they were led by God's Spirit to write what they did. The Holy Spirit "*breathed into*" (the literal meaning of *inspired*) God's intentions into their minds and hearts so that what they wrote accurately displayed his nature and character.

> The authors of the books of the Bible clearly believed they were led by God's Spirit to write what they did.

The product of the Holy Spirit's work is stunning: one completely coherent book made up of sixty-six separate books written over the course of fifteen hundred years by forty different writers. Some were kings and philosophers, yes, but others were fishermen and tentmakers. As biblical scholar Robert Saucy put it, "They lived in diverse cultures, and wrote in a variety of literary styles. But the message of the Bible is one great drama in which all of the parts fit together."[55]

The Bible is inerrant. Many theologians go beyond *inspiration* to say the Bible is inerrant (that is, without error). Theologian Carl F. H. Henry makes an extended argument about **inerrancy** in his six-volume work, *God,*

> *Inerrancy:* the doctrine that the Bible is without error.

Revelation and Authority, explaining that God used the writers to communicate exactly what he wanted and yet did so without overriding their personalities. And because God cannot lie, the Bible is accurate in the original writings.[56]

Is this a reasonable claim? Yes, as long as we clearly understand what we mean by inerrancy. David Dockery, president of Trinity International University, explains it as follows: "When all the facts are known, the Bible (in its original writings) properly interpreted in light of which culture and communication means had developed by the time of its composition will be shown to be completely true (and therefore not false) in all that it affirms, to the degree of precision intended by the author, in all matters relating to God and his creation."[57] If a personal, infinite God exists, such a God could inspire writers to say what he wants them to say.[58]

Here is another way of arriving at an understanding of Scripture's reliability. The text of the New Testament has been reliably transmitted and, as we will see, passes the test of being reliable in the historical information it provides. In these writings, Jesus's claims and deeds present him as the incarnation of God. Because Jesus endorses the divine authority of the Old Testament and authorized the apostles to carry on his ministry and preserve his teachings, we can have confidence in all sixty-six books of the Bible.[59]

> **Jesus's claims and deeds present him as the incarnation of God.**

This does not mean there have been no errors in transmitting the text through time. But we can say that the essential doctrines of the faith have been transmitted reliably and that the best translations today will not mislead us on anything to which they speak.[60]

The doctrine of inerrancy says that the truth of the Bible does not depend on how we understand it, on the skill of the people who translated it from one language to another, or even on the care with which various people transmitted its words through time. It depends entirely on the truth of God's revelation.

But is this truth something we human beings can actually know?

8. DOES BIBLICAL REVELATION LEAD TO TRUE KNOWLEDGE?

> **Knowledge: justified true belief.**

To speak of *knowing the truth* about God, we must first define both knowledge and truth. **Knowledge** is justified true belief. It isn't enough to believe. We must feel certain that our beliefs are true, and we must be justified in holding those beliefs. Jonathan Morrow explains the definition of knowledge this way: "For something to count as knowledge, (1) you must believe it; (2) the belief you hold must be true (that is, it accurately describes the way things actually are); and (3) this true belief must be justified or supported by adequate evidence based on thought and experience."[61]

The Bible assumes that true belief is possible and justified. In fact, a medical doctor named Luke mentioned this exact thing in the account we know today as the gospel of Luke:

> Inasmuch as many have undertaken to compile a narrative of the things that have been accomplished among us, just as those who from the beginning were eyewitnesses and ministers of the word have delivered them to us, it seemed good to me also, having followed all things closely for some time past, to write an orderly

account for you, most excellent Theophilus, that you may have certainty concerning the things you have been taught. (1:1–4)

Luke's testimony wasn't based on wishes or strong feelings but on a careful investigation that included interviews with eyewitnesses. Knowledge led to truth, which in turn led to confidence. Similarly, the apostle John wrote, "This is the testimony, that God gave us eternal life, and this life is in his Son" (1 John 5:11).

Knowledge is vitally important. As we saw in chapter 1, the lack of it destroys people (Hosea 4:6).[62] Philosopher Dallas Willard explains, "People perish for lack of knowledge, because only knowledge permits assured access to reality; and reality does not adjust itself to accommodate our false beliefs, errors, or hesitations in action. Life demands a steady hand for good, and only knowledge supplies this. This is as true in the spiritual life as elsewhere."[63] The analogy of a steady hand is an important one. The captain of a sailing vessel must have such a hand, provided by knowledge of the seas and of his craft, to navigate safely to the proper destination. Lack of knowledge, then, is disastrous. Theologian J. I. Packer agrees:

> **Knowledge is vitally important.**

> We are cruel to ourselves if we try to live in this world without knowing about the God whose world it is and who runs it. The world becomes a strange, mad, painful place, and life in it a disappointing and unpleasant business, for those who do not know about God. Disregard the study of God, and you sentence yourself to stumble and blunder through life, blindfolded, as it were, with no sense of direction and no understanding of what surrounds you.[64]

In the absence of knowledge we are lost, and being lost terrorizes us. Going through life lost turns what might otherwise be beautiful and meaningful into an experience of progressive horror and chaos.

No one relishes the idea of being lost in the cosmos, but where that person turns for knowledge depends on what he or she believes about the nature and character of God. As we will see, many people are "naturalists." They believe that everything that happens has a natural cause and explanation—that there is no supernatural revelation and we're on our own for guidance.

But is naturalism a plausible theory about how knowledge develops? If naturalism is true, everything that has ever happened or occurs now—including our cognitive abilities—must be explained through natural processes, such as evolution. However, according to philosopher Alvin Plantinga, one of the most respected philosophers of the twentieth century, naturalism and evolution do not provide a sufficient basis for knowledge. Plantinga's reasoning is as follows. Evolution selects the fittest organisms. It doesn't select for truth because it is interested only in survival, and truth is not necessary for survival. It is possible that false beliefs enable survival as much as true ones, as with, for example, a group of witches who become more fit for survival because they treat every threat as something that might hold

> **Is naturalism a plausible theory about how knowledge develops?**

magical powers over them; thus, they avoid everything that might kill them. Evolution might allow these witches to flourish, but it doesn't deliver true beliefs about the world.

Though evolution may give us faculties that help us survive, there is no guarantee that those faculties deliver truth. In other words, if everything that has come about has occurred through natural processes, there is no good reason to believe we have received true ideas about the world. In fact, we have no good reason to believe that naturalism itself is actually true. Actually, we have good reason to *doubt* it because, as Plantinga phrases it, "if naturalism and evolution were both true, our cognitive faculties would very likely not be reliable."[65]

As opposed to naturalism, Christian theism says that a rational God *created* us to be knowers. "God has endowed humans with a structure of rationality patterned after the ideas of His own mind: we can know truth because God has made us like himself [i.e., in his image]," philosopher Ronald Nash states.[66] Not only do we bear God's image as knowers, Nash says, but we do so through communication as well: "Language is a divinely given gift to facilitate communion between God and humans that is both personal and cognitive."[67]

When we say we're searching for knowledge, what we're actually looking for is "adequate reasons" for our beliefs. Some kinds of knowledge require more and better reasons than others. If I want to go skiing, I can look online for snow reports at the various ski resorts. Making a wrong choice usually isn't a big deal. After all, for those who like to ski, a bad day of skiing is better than a good day doing most other things.

> **A rational God *created* us to be knowers.**

When it comes to something like deciding which church to join, however, we need a much deeper level of knowledge. We need to study the church's doctrine, interview the pastor, and discern whether it is the kind of place in which we can serve effectively. If we make a thoughtless choice, we risk becoming dissatisfied and a source of discouragement to others in the church. We need a greater amount of evidence to satisfy the "adequate reasons" condition.

> **100 percent certainty is not a necessary condition for knowledge.**

Here is something you may find surprising: 100 percent certainty is not a necessary condition for knowledge. If we wait around for 100 percent certainty, we would never go skiing or join a church or get married or anything else. This is especially true in considering spiritual claims, as philosopher J. P. Moreland points out:

> One can know something without being certain about it and in the presence of doubt or the admission that one might be wrong.... When Christians claim to have knowledge of this or that, for example, that God is real, that Jesus rose from the dead, that the Bible is the Word of God, they are not saying that there is no possibility that they could be wrong, that they have no doubts, or that they have answers to every question raised against them.[68]

In a world of uncertainty, it is comforting to know that God has given us minds to think, consider arguments rationally, and reason toward conclusions, even when we do not possess all the world's information.

WHAT THE BIBLE IS AND ISN'T

Often when Dr. Moreland talks about knowledge and certainty, someone in his audience will say, "You can't know something unless you can prove it scientifically." Of course, although this claim is self-defeating—because it could not itself be scientifically proven—Moreland's response goes a bit further:

> This assertion—known as scientism—is patently false and, in fact, not even a claim of science but rather a philosophical view about science. Nevertheless, once this view of knowledge was widely embraced in the culture, the immediate effect was to marginalize and privatize religion by relegating it to the back of the intellectual bus. To verify this, one need only compare the number of times scientists, as opposed to pastors or theologians, are called upon as experts on the evening news. If knowledge and reason are identical with what can be tested scientifically or with scientific theories that a majority of scientists believes to be correct, then religion and ethics will no longer be viewed as true, rational domains of discourse because, supposedly, religious or ethical claims are not scientifically testable.[69]

Scientism is the belief that all knowledge comes through science. However, science is not the only way of knowing. In fact, in volume 2 of this series, David Noebel and I will examine nine additional ways of knowing—theological, philosophical, ethical, psychological, sociological, political, legal, economical, and historical. The scientific method gives us a disciplined way of examining the evidence of the physical world, but it cannot reasonably claim to be the source of *all* truth.

Scientism: the philosophical belief that reliable knowledge is obtained solely through the scientific method.

Not everyone agrees with the definition of *knowledge as justified true belief*. Postmodern critics wonder how we can say we have objective knowledge when we all have our own personal, subjective perspectives and biases. "Whose way of thinking is right?" they challenge. Yes, people do have biases and perspectives, but does this mean that no truth can be known? Isn't it possible to *acknowledge* that no one is "purely neutral" even while we *affirm* that knowledge of the truth is possible?

Christianity makes many truth claims. Some can be tested by looking at the evidence from history or archaeology; others cannot be tested this way. As we have seen, Christianity's claims do open themselves up to rational inquiry. They can be known to be true or false. Reasonable people who seriously investigate Christianity's claims will see this to be so, according to Jonathan Morrow:

Christianity makes many truth claims.

> If Christianity is relegated to the realm of fairy tales, which may provide personal significance or meaning but not knowledge, then people will continue not taking the claims of Jesus or the Christian worldview seriously. If, however, people are invited to consider the claims of Christianity as a knowledge tradition, then chances are good that they may come to know the living God and live life according to the knowledge provided in his Word.[70]

The Bible claims to be revelation from God. Knowledge is possible. We have minds to understand it. But we must connect these dots or else God's Word will remain senseless to us. As Christian apologist Greg Koukl phrases it, "We cannot grasp the authoritative teaching of God's Word unless we use our minds properly."[71]

But there is one objection we haven't dealt with yet: Does the Bible actually *claim* to speak the truth?

9. Does the Bible Actually Claim to Be True?

John 18:37–38 records a conversation between the Roman leader of Jerusalem, Pontius Pilate, and Jesus, as part of Jesus's trial: "Then Pilate said to him, 'So you are a king?' Jesus answered, 'You say that I am a king. For this purpose I was born and for this purpose I have come into the world—to bear witness to the truth. Everyone who is of the truth listens to my voice.' Pilate said to him, 'What is truth?'"

The question "What is truth?" hangs in the air even today. It is likely that Pilate was familiar with the intellectual contortions that ancient philosophers had performed around the question of truth. Aristotle, for example, had come up with this head-scratcher: "To say of what is that it is not, or of what is not that it is, is false, while to say of what is that it is, and of what is not that it is not, is true; so that he who says of anything that it is, or that it is not, will say either what is true or what is false; but neither what is nor what is not said to be or not to be."[72]

Correspondence Theory of Truth: the view that the truth of a proposition is determined by how accurately it describes the facts of reality.

Most people, when they hear definitions such as Aristotle's, dissolve into confusion. But at root, Aristotle is saying something fairly self-evident: *a belief, thought, or statement is true if it corresponds to reality.* This is called the **correspondence theory of truth**. Philosopher Douglas Groothuis explains,

> A belief or statement is true only if it matches with, reflects or corresponds to the reality it refers to. For a statement to be true it must be factual. Facts determine the truth or falsity of a belief or a statement. It is the nature and meaning of truth to be fact dependent. In other words, for a statement to be true, there must be a *truth-maker* that determines its truth. A statement is never true simply because someone thinks it or utters it. We may be entitled to our own opinions, but we are not entitled to our own facts. Believing a statement is one thing; that statement being true is another.[73]

According to Groothuis, the Bible implicitly advances the correspondence view of truth—that truth is that which relates to reality. He lists many examples:

> The Bible does not set forth a technical view of truth, but it does implicitly and consistently advance the correspondence view in both Testaments. ... The Hebrew and Greek words for truth are rich in meaning but have at their core the idea of conformity to fact. Scripture also emphasizes that God is true to his

truth, meaning that he is faithful and will not lie (Hebrews 6:18). God is a God of truth, whose word is truth (John 17:17). The Holy Spirit is "the Spirit of truth" (John 14:17; 15:26; 16:13) and so will teach us true things. Jesus, the Son of God, is "full of grace and truth" (John 1:14), and declared himself to be "the way and the truth and the life" and that no one could come to the Father apart from him (John 14:6). The prophets (Jeremiah 8:8), Jesus (Matthew 24:24) and the apostles (1 John 4:1–6) warn of those who pervert the truth of God through errors and lies. Hence, all of Scripture puts God's revealed objective truth at the solid center of spiritual and ethical life and faithfulness. God's truth must be learned (Acts 17:11), meditated upon (Psalm 119) and defended (1 Peter 3:15–17; Jude v. 3). Error must be addressed in love (2 Corinthians 10:3–5; 2 Timothy 2:24–26), whether it is theological or moral, and whether it concerns the false beliefs of unbelievers or the false beliefs of errant Christians.[74]

The Christian beliefs that reality can be known and that it is honorable to seek truth set Christianity apart from many world religions. It helps explain why Christianity led to the development of philosophy, science, history, and so forth, while far older religious traditions did not in other parts of the world.

Often people distinguish between **objective truth claims** (those that do not depend on one's beliefs) and **subjective truth claims** (those that say truth changes according to one's beliefs). The Bible clearly makes objective truth claims whose truth does not rely on whether people believe them. The Bible is a compass pointing north even when we wish it would point another way.

> *Objective Truth Claim:* a claim regarding an independent fact about the world.

> *Subjective Truth Claim:* a claim regarding a dependent fact about a subject.

10. Why Truth Matters

Understanding of absolute, objective truth is largely lost today. Spend just a few minutes discussing issues such as politics and religion and you'll hear someone say, "There is no truth!" or "That may be true for you, but it is not true for me." This view, **relativism**, says that truth is relative to each individual person or culture.

> *Relativism:* the belief that truth, knowledge, and morality are relative to the individual, society, and historical context.

The silliness of relativism dawned on me in a conversation I had with one of my college professors, who had indicated to our class that there are no absolute truths.

I asked, "Are you sure?"

He replied, "Yes."

"Are you *absolutely* sure there are no absolutes?" I pressed.

Smiling, the professor replied, "You're a very clever young man. If I say there are no absolutes, I've made an absolute statement. Let me rephrase. There is one absolute: there are no absolutes."

I'm sure the professor was trying to make a joke, but most of my classmates were bewildered, as was I. Playing along, I said, "Thank you for admitting that there is one absolute. But is it possible or conceivable that there are *two* absolutes?"

"No."

To which I replied, "Are you *sure*?"

By this point, the professor and my classmates were all chuckling. They probably still embraced relativism, but they also realized their doing so could not be sustained philosophically.

> **Self-Refuting Claim:** a statement that attempts to affirm two opposite propositions at the same time and in the same sense.

You might try something similar. If someone says, "There is no truth," ask, "Is *that statement* true?" If someone says, "That may be true for you, but not for me," ask, "Is that statement true for both of us?" A **self-refuting claim** cannot possibly be true—it is a statement that commits suicide!

Truth is the only foundation on which to build a life, but as Jonathan Morrow points out, "We live at a time in which Christians are more consumer-driven than truth-driven."[75] If believers are to bear redemption effectively to a needy world, this must change. As author Kelly Monroe Kullberg puts it,

> Truth yields life. If we are sailors lost at sea, we need true north. If we're branches on [a] tree hoping to bear fruit, which we are, we need connection to a true vine. Truth tells us where we are, who we are, to whom we belong, and the real story in which we can fully live. It seems to me that our American culture, in its present condition, is both lost and starving for truth, and therefore vulnerable to the deception of power politics, marketing schemes, and politically correct slogans of professors, politicians, and media that often lead to the death of the soul and the body. Lies lead to death and a culture of death, but the truth sets people free for life.[76]

> **These claims are revolutionary and, as you can imagine, controversial, because if the Bible's claim to reveal God is authoritative, then it extends to every area of life—to everyone in the world, at all times.**

The world is desperate for truth, but without knowing God's Word, through which he reveals his nature and character, our attempts to communicate it will be nothing more than the offering of an opinion.

11. CONCLUSION

So let's review. Christianity says the Bible is God's Word. Through it, the almighty God, creator of the universe, speaks to humankind; that is, the Bible is God's revelation. As theologian Darrell Bock says,

> The Bible is not a book like any other. It makes a claim that God spoke and speaks through its message. It argues that as his creatures, we are accountable to him for what he has revealed. The trustworthiness of Scripture points to its authority as well. Scripture is far more than a history book, as good and trustworthy as that history is.

It is a book that calls us to examine our lives and relationship to God. Beyond the fascinating history, it contains vital and life-transforming truths about God and us.[77]

These claims are revolutionary and, as you can imagine, controversial, because if the Bible's claim to reveal God is authoritative, then it extends to every area of life—to everyone in the world, at all times. And there are many who are determined not to let that happen. In the next chapter, we'll wade right into the middle of the controversy and consider whether the Bible's claims to authority are actually authoritative for our lives today.

ENDNOTES

1. For more on Bible translation efforts around the world, see "What's Been Done, What's Left to Do: Latest Bible Translation Statistics," Wycliffe Bible Translators, wycliffe.org.uk/wycliffe/about/vision-whatwedo.html.

2. Lamar Vest, "Does the Bible Still Matter in 2012?," *Fox News*, April 29, 2012, www.foxnews.com/opinion/2012/04/29/does-bible-still-matter-in-2012/.

3. "Barna Studies the Research, Offers a Year-in-Review Perspective," Barna Group, December 18, 2009, www.barna.org/barna-update/article/12-faithspirituality/325-barna-studies-the-research-offers-a-year-in-review-perspective#.UnJ3mvkWL3g.

4. *The State of the Bible, 2013: A Study of U. S. Adults* (New York: American Bible Society, 2013), www.americanbible.org/uploads/content/State%20of%20the%20Bible%20Report%202013.pdf.

5. *State of the Bible.*

6. *State of the Bible.*

7. Cathy Lynn Grossman, "Americans Get an 'F' in Religion," *USA Today*, March 14, 2007, usatoday30.usatoday.com/news/religion/2007-03-07-teaching-religion-cover_n.htm.

8. *State of the Bible.*

9. Kevin Roose, "Quick, Can You Name a Gospel?," *Forbes*, April 8, 2009, www.forbes.com/2009/04/08/unlikely-disciple-roose-bible-opinions-contributors-christian-easter.html.

10. See Stephen Prothero, *Religious Literacy: What Every American Needs to Know—and Doesn't* (New York: HarperOne, 2008), chap 1.

11. Sally Lloyd-Jones, *The Jesus Storybook Bible: Every Story Whispers His Name* (Grand Rapids, MI: ZonderKids, 2007), 12–17.

12. Alexis de Tocqueville, *Democracy in America*, ed. J. P. Mayer, trans. George Lawrence (New York: Harper Perennial, 1969), 291.

13. John Jay to Maria, October 21, 1794, in *Selected Letters of John Jay and Sarah Livingston Jay* (Jefferson, NC: McFarland, 2005), 235.

14. John Adams, "The Rights of the Colonists: The Report of the Committee of Correspondence to the Boston Town Meeting: November 20, 1772," Constitution Society, last modified March 8, 2015, www.constitution.org/bcp/right_col.htm.

15. Noah Webster, *History of the United States* (New Haven, CT: Durrie and Peck, 1832), 339.

16. Benjamin Rush, "A Defense of the Use of the Bible in Schools," in *The American Museum, or, Universal Magazine* 9, from January to June 1791 (Philadelphia: Carey, Stewart, 1791): 129.

17. John Adams, "Letter from John Adams to Thomas Jefferson: December 25, 1813," Beliefnet, www.beliefnet.com/resourcelib/docs/72/Letter_from_John_Adams_to_Thomas_Jefferson_1.html.

18. John Quincy Adams, *Letters by John Quincy Adams to His Son on the Bible and Its Teachings* (Auburn, ME: James A. Alden, 1850), 119.

19. Abraham Lincoln, "Reply to Loyal Colored People of Baltimore upon Presentation of a Bible: September 7, 1864," *Collected Works of Abraham Lincoln*, vol. 7, quod.lib.umich.edu/l/lincoln/lincoln7/1:1184?rgn=div1;singlegenre=All;sort=occur;subview=detail;type=simple;view=fulltext;q1=September+7%2C+1864.

20. Theodore Roosevelt, "On Reading the Bible," *The Christian Century* 36, no. 13 (March 27, 1919): 8.

21. James Kearney, *The Political Education of Woodrow Wilson* (New York: The Century Company, 1926), 273.

22. Calvin Coolidge, "Religion: Our Nation's Strength," *The Delineator*, vol. C, no. 6 (July 1922): 2.

23. Franklin D. Roosevelt, *The Public Papers and Addresses of Franklin D. Roosevelt* (New York: Random House, 1938), 420.

24. Harry S. Truman, *Harry S. Truman: Containing the Public Messages, Speeches, and Statements of the President, 1945–53* (Washington, DC: US Government Printing Office, 1961), 157.

25. Ronald Reagan, "Proclamation 5018 of February 3, 1983, 'Year of the Bible,'" in Federal Code of Regulations, 1983 Compilation (Washington, DC: Office of the Federal Register, 1984), 9.

26. For a photograph of the proclamation, see www.loc.gov/exhibits/religion/vc006473.jpg.

27. Richard Dawkins, "Why I Want All Our Children to Read the King James Bible," *The Guardian*, May 19, 2012, www.guardian.co.uk/science/2012/may/19/richard-dawkins-king-james-bible.

28. See Alvin J. Schmidt, *How Christianity Changed the World* (Grand Rapids, MI: Zondervan, 2004).

29. William Lyon Phelps, *Human Nature in the Bible* (New York: Charles Scribner's Sons, 1922), ix.

30. Matthew 7:12: "Whatever you wish that others would do to you, do also to them, for this is the Law and the Prophets"; Mark 12:29–31: "Jesus answered, 'The most important is, "Hear, O Israel: The Lord our God, the Lord is one. And you shall love the Lord your God with all your heart and with all your soul and with all your mind and with all your strength." The second is this: "You shall love your neighbor as yourself." There is no other commandment greater than these"; Exodus 3:6: "He said, 'I am the God of your father, the God of Abraham, the God of Isaac, and the God of Jacob.' And Moses hid his face, for he was afraid to look at God"; Deuteronomy 6:4–5: "Hear, O Israel: The Lord our God, the Lord is one. You shall love the Lord your God with all your heart and with all your soul and with all your might"; Leviticus 19:18: "You shall not take vengeance or bear a grudge against the sons of your own people, but you shall love your neighbor as yourself: I am the Lord."

31. Bertrand Russell, *Human Society in Ethics and Politics* (New York: Mentor, 1962), viii.

32. 2 Peter 3:16: "As he does in all his letters when he speaks in them of these matters. There are some things in them that are hard to understand, which the ignorant and unstable twist to their own destruction, as they do the other Scriptures."

33. Acts 17:1–4: "Now when they had passed through Amphipolis and Apollonia, they came to Thessalonica, where there was a synagogue of the Jews. And Paul went in, as was his custom, and on three Sabbath days he reasoned with them from the Scriptures, explaining and proving that it was necessary for the Christ to suffer and to rise from the dead, and saying, 'This Jesus, whom I proclaim to you, is the Christ.' And some of them were persuaded and joined Paul and Silas, as did a great many of the devout Greeks and not a few of the leading women."

34. See the Quran 10:94; 16:43; 21:7.

35. See, for example, Quran 2:40–44; 2:121.

36. See the Quran 2 in its entirety for insight into how the Quran is to be believed and not questioned.

37. N. T. Wright, *Simply Christian: Why Christianity Makes Sense* (New York: HarperCollins, 2006), 188.

38. Robert Lewis Plummer, *40 Questions about Interpreting the Bible* (Grand Rapids, MI: Kregel, 2010), 99.

39. Millard Erickson, *Christian Theology*, 2nd ed. (Grand Rapids, MI: Baker Academic, 2001), 201.

40. Gordon R. Lewis, "What Is Divine Revelation?," in Ted Cabal et al., eds., *The Apologetics Study Bible* (Nashville: B&H, 2007), 1823.

41. Erik Thoennes, *Life's Biggest Questions: What the Bible Says about the Things That Matter Most* (Wheaton, IL: Crossway), 41–42.

42. D. A. Carson, *The God Who Is There: Finding Your Place in God's Story* (Grand Rapids, MI: Baker Books, 2010), 20.

43. Charles W. Colson, *Born Again* (Grand Rapids, MI: Chosen, 1976), 26–27, quoted in Eric Metaxas, *Seven Men: And the Secret to Their Greatness* (Nashville: Thomas Nelson, 2013), 167.

44. Bruce Demarest, "General Revelation," in *Evangelical Dictionary of Theology*, ed. Walter A. Elwell (Grand Rapids, MI: Baker Academic, 2001), 1019–21.

45. Erickson, *Christian Theology*, 201.

46. N. T. Wright, *The Last Word: Scripture and the Authority of God—Getting beyond the Bible Wars* (New York: HarperOne, 2005), 25.

47. Jonathan Morrow, *Welcome to College: A Christ-Follower's Guide for the Journey* (Grand Rapids, MI: Kregel, 2008), 88.

48. Nancy Pearcey, *Total Truth: Liberating Christianity from Its Cultural Captivity* (Wheaton, IL: Crossway, 2004), 178.

49. William Lane Craig, *Reasonable Faith: Christian Truth and Apologetics*, 3rd ed. (Wheaton, IL: Crossway, 2008), 207.

50. Garry K. Brantley, "The Dead Sea Scrolls and the Biblical Integrity," Apologetics Press, www.apologeticspress.org/apcontent.aspx?category=13&article=357.

51. Morrow, *Welcome to College*, 88.

52. David K. Clark, *To Know and Love God: Method for Theology* (Wheaton, IL: Crossway, 2003), 65.

53. Gordon R. Lewis, "What Does It Mean That God Inspired the Bible?," in Ted Cabal et al., eds., *The Apologetics Study Bible* (Nashville: B&H, 2007), 1812.

54. Lewis, "What Does It Mean," 1812.

55. Robert Saucy, *Scripture: Its Power, Authority, and Relevance* (Nashville: Word, 2001), 78. See also Carl F. H. Henry's chapter "The Lost Unity of the Bible," in *God, Revelation and Authority*, vol. 4, *God Who Speaks and Shows: Fifteen Theses, Part Three*, 2nd ed. (Wheaton, IL: Crossway, 1999).

56. Henry, *God, Revelation and Authority*.

57. David S. Dockery, *Christian Scripture: An Evangelical Perspective on Inspiration, Authority, and Interpretation* (Nashville: Broadman & Holman, 1995), 64, quoted in Morrow, *Welcome to College*, 81.

58. The term *personal-infinite* comes from Francis Schaeffer in *He Is There and He Is Not Silent* (Carol Stream, IL: Tyndale, 1972).

59. For an extended, documented version of this argument, see Douglas R. Groothuis, *Christian Apologetics: A Comprehensive Case for Biblical Faith* (Downers Grove, IL: IVP Academic, 2011), especially chaps. 19 and 20.

60. In addition to Groothuis, *Christian Apologetics*, see also John R. Stott, *The Authority of the Bible* (Downers Grove, IL: InterVarsity, 1974).

61. Jonathan Morrow, *Think Christianly: Looking at the Intersection of Faith and Culture* (Grand Rapids, MI: Zondervan, 2011), 95.

62. Hosea 4:6: "My people are destroyed for lack of knowledge; because you have rejected knowledge, I reject you from being a priest to me. And since you have forgotten the law of your God, I also will forget your children."

63. Dallas Willard, *Knowing Christ Today: Why We Can Trust Spiritual Knowledge* (New York: HarperOne, 2009), 39.

64. J. I. Packer, *Knowing God*, 20th anniv. ed. (Downers Grove, IL: InterVarsity, 1993), 19.

65. Alvin Plantinga, *Where the Conflict Really Lies: Science, Religion, and Naturalism* (Oxford: Oxford University Press, 2011), 314. A PDF of Plantinga's paper "Naturalism Defeated" may be found online at www.calvin.edu/academic /philosophy/virtual_library/articles/plantinga_alvin/naturalism_defeated.pdf.

66. Ronald Nash, *The Word of God and the Mind of Man: The Crisis of Revealed Truth in Contemporary Theology* (Phillipsburg, NJ: P&R, 1992), 81, 132.

67. Nash, *The Word of God,* 81, 132.

68. J. P. Moreland, *Love Your God with All Your Mind: The Role of Reason in the Life of the Soul,* rev. ed. (Colorado Springs, CO: NavPress, 2012), 56–57.

69. Moreland, *Love Your God,* 29.

70. Morrow, *Think Christianly,* 101.

71. Gregory Koukl, *Tactics: A Game Plan for Discussing Your Christian Convictions* (Grand Rapids, MI: Zondervan, 2009), 32.

72. Aristotle, *Metaphysics,* ed. Roger Bishop Jones, trans. W. D. Ross, 58–59, texts.rbjones.com/rbjpub/philos/classics /aristotl/mbook_draft.pdf.

73. Groothuis, *Christian Apologetics,* 124.

74. Groothuis, *Christian Apologetics,* 126.

75. Morrow, *Think Christianly,* 13.

76. Quoted in Morrow, *Think Christianly,* 50.

77. Darrell L. Bock, *Can I Trust the Bible? Defending the Bible's Reliability* (Norcross, GA: RZIM, 2001), 52.

CHAPTER 3

DOES THE BIBLE HAVE AUTHORITY?

1. MASTERS OF OUR FATE

At 8:00 a.m., hospital personnel strapped the patient to a gurney at the federal penitentiary in Terre Haute, Indiana. The doctor calmly administered a dose of sodium thiopental, rendering the patient unconscious, followed by a dose of pancuronium bromize to stop his breathing and paralyze his body.

Finally, the doctor injected a dose of potassium chloride, stopping his heart. At 8:14 a.m., June 11, 2001, the doctor pronounced him dead.

His name was Timothy McVeigh. A young man in his early thirties, McVeigh had parked a moving truck loaded with five thousand pounds of explosives in front of the Alfred P. Murrah Federal Building in Oklahoma City and lit the fuse. In the blast 171 people, including three unborn children, were killed.

When asked what he would say to the families of his victims, McVeigh snapped, remorselessly, "To these people in Oklahoma who have lost a loved one, I'm sorry but it happens every day. You're not the first mother to lose a kid, or the first grandparent to lose a grandson or a granddaughter. It happens every day, somewhere in the world."[1] Just before his execution, he was asked for his final words. He silently handed the prison warden a handwritten copy of a poem.

> Out of the night that covers me,
> Black as the Pit from pole to pole,
> I thank whatever gods may be
> For my unconquerable soul.
>
> In the fell clutch of circumstance
> I have not winced nor cried aloud.
> Under the bludgeonings of chance
> My head is bloody, but unbowed.
>
> Beyond this place of wrath and tears
> Looms but the Horror of the shade,
> And yet the menace of the years
> Finds and shall find me unafraid.
>
> It matters not how straight the gate,
> How charged with punishments the scroll,
> I am the master of my fate:
> I am the captain of my soul.

Anarchy: a society that exists without government control.

Authority: the power to command or the expertise to influence others.

You might recognize the poem. It is titled "Invictus" (Latin for "unconquered"), and it was written by William Ernest Henley (1849–1903) during a difficult illness as an anthem of perseverance. McVeigh, however, transmuted it into a paean to **anarchy**: *I am my own authority. I answer to none.*

Authority comes from a Latin word meaning "influence" or "command." It answers the question "Who is in charge?" Growing up, I saw the statement "Question Authority" plastered on bumper stickers and buttons and spray-painted on subway cars. There is, of course, a warranted democratic sentiment to it: don't believe everything you hear, especially from the government. This is probably what

DOES THE BIBLE HAVE AUTHORITY?

Benjamin Franklin had in mind when he said, "It is the first responsibility of every citizen to question authority."[2]

Today, however, the statement "Question Authority" usually expresses radical individualism. "No one has the right to tell me what to do," people say. Few enjoy being told what to do or how to think. Yet the insolent rejection of authority sweeps away the baby with the bathwater, removing both illegitimate and legitimate forms of authority: both unthinking rhetoric *and* public reason, both manipulation *and* persuasion are cast away. When all authority is banished, civil society becomes impossible. But as the iconic musician Bob Dylan sang, "You're gonna have to serve somebody." How can we know when to submit and when to oppose?

For Christians, the lines of authority are clear: to confess "Jesus is Lord" is to proclaim one's submission to Jesus's authority.[3] Refusal to acknowledge God's authority is serious business, for we are all accountable to him. In both Romans 14:10–12 and Philippians 2:9–11, the apostle Paul quotes Isaiah 45:23[4] in claiming that every knee shall bow and every tongue confess to God.

> For Christians, the lines of authority are clear: to confess "Jesus is Lord" is to proclaim one's submission to Jesus's authority.

The New Testament word for "obey" in Greek literally means "to hear under" (that is, to place oneself under authority). Embracing Jesus's worldview—believing what he believed and obeying his teaching—is an invitation to "a long obedience in the same direction," a journey toward conformity to Christ.[5] Romans 8:29 says, "Those whom he foreknew he also predestined to be conformed to the image of his Son."

Mindless mimicry is not the goal of our conformity to Christ. Jesus said we are to love the Lord God with our entire *minds* (Matt. 22:37).[6] Paul said we are to be transformed by the renewing of our *minds* (Rom. 12:2).[7] You do not have to be brilliant to be Christ-like, but you cannot be blissfully mindless either.

> You do not have to be brilliant to be Christ-like, but you cannot be blissfully mindless either.

Of course, even if we are mindful, we may find ourselves baffled by God's commands. For example, forgiving our enemies seems counterintuitive, as does patiently enduring suffering. Still, the Bible regularly invades personal space: it tells us how to treat our friends, our parents, our spouses, and our children. It tells us how to think about politics and entertainment, how to use money, and how to act toward others. Saying "Jesus is Lord" commits us to a certain way of seeing—and living in—the world.

Although there is much we will not understand, Christians for millennia have maintained that what God wants is not unknowably mysterious. Authors W. Gary Phillips, William E. Brown, and John Stonestreet explain:

> If God's Person is such that He can function with human language (certainly being greater than man!), then God *could* condescend to communicate verbally to man. If God's character is such that He is both a truthful and loving Creator who is concerned about His creatures, then God *would* condescend to communicate verbally to man. No loving God would play cosmic hide-and-seek with His beloved ones.[8]

Christians throughout the ages have maintained that God makes himself known most clearly through Scripture. If this is true, obedience to what the Bible says is of paramount importance. We'll explore this idea in the coming pages, assuming the following precepts:

- The Bible is authorized by God and uses human language to communicate heavenly principles to earthly society.

- The Bible is trustworthy in this communication because it is God himself who is the ultimate communicator, speaking through the authors of each of its books.

- The Bible is clear in this communication. You don't have to be a highly trained expert to understand it.

- The Bible, being in written form, can be accurately transmitted from generation to generation.

- If the Bible is authorized by God, trustworthy, and clearly communicated in written form, then it is reasonable to regard it as having authority.

In this chapter, we will examine the Bible's claim to authority both internally and externally and deal with common objections, such as "The Bible was written only by men," "The Bible has been corrupted," and "Important books have been left out of the Bible." At the end, we'll look at what sort of commitment this authority calls for. We will begin with what the Bible says about itself.

2. Internal Evidence for the Bible's Authority

The Bible is divided into two sections, usually called the Old Testament and the New Testament. The Old Testament includes thirty-nine books of history, poetry, and prophecy. The New Testament contains twenty-seven books that are history (Gospels, Acts), letters (the epistles), and the apocalyptic book of Revelation. The Old Testament narrative begins with Genesis and ends with 2 Chronicles, around four hundred years before Christ. Other documents gathered in the Apocrypha (from the Greek word for "hidden") cover the gap in time, but many Christians do not consider them authoritative with the rest of the biblical **canon** (from the Greek word for "standard"; a common word used for the accepted list of books in the Bible).

> *Canon:* from the Greek word for "standard"; the collection of biblical writings commonly accepted as genuine and authoritative.

The Bible claims authority for itself, internally. To nonbelievers, choosing to submit to such authority sounds crazy, but the Bible claims it nonetheless. Throughout the Old Testament, phrases such as "Thus says the Lord" and "The Word of the Lord came to me saying" occur over two thousand times. The writers claimed to communicate God's authoritative revelation.

We'll discuss the authority the Bible claims for itself in three parts: Jesus's assertion of authority, Jesus's trust of the Bible's authority, and Jesus's conferring of authority on his disciples.

Jesus asserted authority. Jesus claimed to be not only God's spokesman but also God in the flesh. In contrast to the Old Testament prophets who said, "Thus says the Lord" or "The Word of the Lord came to me," Jesus said, "You have heard it said, but I say to you ..." and "Truly, truly, I say unto you ..." He claims divine authority to reveal what God wants us to understand. Here are two examples:

> And when Jesus finished these sayings, the crowds were astonished at his teaching, for he was teaching them as one who had authority, and not as their scribes. (Matt. 7:28–29)

> And immediately Jesus, perceiving in his spirit that they thus questioned within themselves, said to them, "Why do you question these things in your hearts? Which is easier, to say to the paralytic, 'Your sins are forgiven,' or to say, 'Rise, take up your bed and walk'? But that you may know that the Son of Man has authority on earth to forgive sins'—he said to the paralytic—'I say to you, rise, pick up your bed, and go home.' And he rose and immediately picked up his bed and went out before them all, so that they were all amazed and glorified God, saying, 'We never saw anything like this!'" (Mark 2:8–12)

Jesus's authority was not part of his office as rabbi but part of his nature as God. He claimed to be the "I Am" of the Old Testament (John 8:58).[9] He said he and God are "one" **essence** (10:30)[10] and that those who had seen him had seen God (14:7–9).[11] Jesus claimed authority over heaven and earth, including the power of all judgment (5:22),[12] astonishing his audience, enemies, and disciples.[13]

> *Essence:* defining attributes that give an entity its fundamental identity.

In chapter 2, we talked about Scripture being written through the inspiration of the Holy Spirit. But Jesus's disciples also witnessed Jesus's authority in the flesh and were commissioned by him to be apostles and carry his authority to the world. As twentieth-century theologian Carl F. H. Henry put it,

> The apostles, to be sure, did not rest the case for Christian realities wholly upon divine inspiration, that is, upon the Spirit's supernatural guidance in ... written teaching. First and foremost they were eyewitnesses of the historical facets of Jesus's life and ministry ... [which] preceded their apostolic authorization.... Without the resurrection eyewitnessing there would be no commission for world witnessing. Without the Spirit's guidance there would be no divinely authoritative teaching.[14]

The biblical account is clear: Jesus claimed authority. But that's not all.

Jesus trusted the Bible's authority. Many people like Jesus's *decency*, not his *divinity*; they approve of his teachings but not of the commotion regarding his claims to be God. As we have seen, though, Jesus claimed authority far beyond the goodness of his moral teachings. In fact, he claimed far more than that: he considered all of Scripture to be authoritative. One cannot consistently embrace as authoritative some of Jesus's teaching while rejecting his teaching about the Bible itself.[15]

Theologian and pastor W. Gary Phillips summarizes Jesus's trust in Scripture:[16]

- Jesus consistently refers to the Old Testament (in both quotation and allusions) as the present and eternal truth of God. When he quotes Scripture, he uses the present tense ("it says" or "it is saying") or the perfect tense ("it is written" or "it stands written"). These teachings are not in the *past*; they are for *now*.

- Jesus always assumes that Scripture is final in authority and that each part is of equal authority, whether it is an obscure reference to how King David referred to God (Matt. 22:41–45 in reference to Ps. 110:1)[17] or the Pharisees' objection to him calling himself the Son of God (John 10:34–36 in reference to Ps. 82:6).[18]

- Jesus always assumes that Old Testament prophecies must be fulfilled as given (Matt. 5:17).[19] He refers to them as that which "must be fulfilled" (Luke 24:44).[20]

- Jesus always treats the miraculous events of the Old Testament as if they occurred exactly as written. This is true even for the ones thought to be scientifically "embarrassing" today, such as Adam and Eve's literal existence, Noah's flood, Sodom's judgment, Moses's burning bush, the miracle of manna in the wilderness, and the story of Jonah and the great fish.

- Jesus leans on the Old Testament in his personal spiritual anguish. He does this during his temptation in the wilderness (Matt. 4:1–10) and in his crucifixion when he quotes Psalm 22 (Matt. 27:46).[21]

- Jesus never hesitates to confront error, but he says absolutely nothing about problems in the Scriptures. Apparently, at least in the parts of his ministry recorded in the Gospels, Jesus found nothing to confront in the Old Testament. If anything, he builds on the foundation of the Old Testament by clarifying the profound extent to which its teachings must be applied. (For example, in Matthew 5:27–28, he says, "You have heard that it was said, 'You shall not commit adultery.' But I say to you that everyone who looks at a woman with lustful intent has already committed adultery with her in his heart.")

Summarizing Jesus's teachings, Carl F. H. Henry said, "All four Gospels evidence the truth that Jesus affirmed the authority of Scripture. Luke 24:25 records Christ's view of the authority of the Old Testament, and this, in correlation with John 14:26, implies his similar view of the New Testament."[22]

Jesus conferred authority on his disciples. Jesus's disciples were eyewitnesses to his authority, and before the completion of his earthly ministry, Jesus conferred his own authority upon them.

DOES THE BIBLE HAVE AUTHORITY?

He called to him his twelve disciples and gave them *authority* over unclean spirits, to cast them out, and to heal every disease and every affliction. (Matt. 10:1)

All things have been handed over to me by my Father, and no one knows the Son except the Father, and no one knows the Father except the Son and *anyone to whom the Son chooses to reveal him*. (Matt. 11:27)

This conferred authority extended beyond the time boundaries of Jesus's earthly ministry:

These things I have spoken to you while I am still with you. But the Helper, the Holy Spirit, whom the Father will send in my name, he will teach you all things and bring to your remembrance all that I have said to you. (John 14:25–26)

When the Helper comes, whom I will send to you from the Father, the Spirit of truth, who proceeds from the Father, he will bear witness about me. And you also will bear witness, because you have been with me from the beginning. (John 15:26–27)

I still have many things to say to you, but you cannot bear them now. When the Spirit of truth comes, he will guide you into all the truth, for he will not speak on his own authority, but whatever he hears he will speak, and he will declare to you the things that are to come. He will glorify me, for he will take what is mine and declare it to you. All that the Father has is mine; therefore I said that he will take what is mine and declare it to you. (John 16:12–15)

On the night before going to the cross, Jesus imparted authority to his disciples, praying, "I do not ask for these only, but also for those who will believe in me through *their* word" (John 17:20). And after his resurrection, Jesus issued a clear and powerful statement of conferred authority that we call the Great Commission:

> After his resurrection, Jesus issued a clear and powerful statement of conferred authority that we call the Great Commission.

And Jesus came and said to them, "All authority in heaven and on earth has been given to me. Go therefore and make disciples of all nations, baptizing them in the name of the Father and of the Son and of the Holy Spirit, teaching them to observe all that I have commanded you. And behold, I am with you always, to the end of the age." (Matt. 28:18–20)

The disciples obeyed. They went proclaiming this message "in Jesus's name" (Acts 3:6, 16; 4:7, 10, 12, 17–18, 30). Even Jesus's enemies recognized the authority with which Jesus's disciples spoke: "Now when they saw the boldness of Peter and John, and perceived that they were uneducated, common men, they were astonished. And they recognized that they had been with Jesus" (Acts 4:13).

Jesus had authority, the disciples were given authority by him, and their work was authoritative *because he said it would be*. Peter classified Paul's collected writings with the "Scriptures" (2 Pet. 3:16);[23] Paul even quoted Luke's gospel and called it "Scripture" (1 Tim. 5:18).[24]

Is there any evidence *outside* Scripture offering credibility to the Bible's authority?

Let's review. Jesus claimed authority for his own ministry, the Scriptures, and the ministry of his disciples. Skeptics might still be skeptical, though. Is there any evidence *outside* Scripture offering credibility to the Bible's authority? The answer is an emphatic yes. Let's take a look at some of this evidence now.

3. EXTERNAL EVIDENCE FOR THE BIBLE'S AUTHORITY

A person's testimony about him- or herself constitutes *internal* evidence for authority. But the claims of others *external* to the person can add a different kind of credibility. So far we've examined Jesus's authority based on the words of the Bible itself, but is there any testimony about the Bible's truthfulness from outside sources? If a longtime basketball player said, "My career three-point shot percentage was 65 percent," we might scoff in doubt. If, however, we uncovered an old record book verifying the claim, we might reasonably say, "It sounds too good to be true, but I must give this player's claim the benefit of the doubt."

The absence of external evidence, though, would not mean the player is lying. He might be telling the truth, but, for one reason or another, we choose not to believe him. In the same way, lack of external evidence would not be proof of the Bible's falsity. Kenneth A. Kitchen says, "Absence of evidence is not evidence of absence."[25]

Professor emeritus of biblical studies Philip R. Davies provides an example of why we should not assume that a biblical source is untrustworthy just because we haven't yet found evidence. A professor at the University of Sheffield in

"Absence of evidence is not evidence of absence."

England, Davies wrote the following in a book called *In Search of 'Ancient Israel'*: "There are no literary criteria for believing David to be more historical than Joshua, Joshua more historical than Abraham, and Abraham more historical than Adam. There is no non-literary way of making this judgment either, since none of these characters has left a trace outside the biblical text!"[26] But just a year after Davies's book was published, an inscription referring to the house of David was found at the Tel Dan archaeological dig. Such an inscription implies the existence of not only David but also a kingly dynasty named after him. Israel Finkelstein, professor of archaeology at Tel Aviv University, remarked, "Biblical nihilism collapsed overnight with the discovery of the David inscription."[27] And more recently, archaeologists have discovered what they believe to be a palace or temple of David, providing additional evidence for David as a historical person.[28]

The presence of historically verifiable external evidence, such as the David inscription and discovery of a Davidic temple, adds weight to the Bible's truthfulness. It provides the kind of converging evidence one would expect a divinely authoritative book to possess. Not all discoveries are as dramatic as the David inscription, but as television correspondent and religion writer Jeffery Sheler observed,

We have discovered an abundance of evidence—both direct and indirect—that sheds light on the historical claims and the context of the Scriptures. … As we have examined that evidence and considered the scholarly arguments drawn from it, and as we have compared the Scriptures to other written histories from the ancient Near East, we have found the Bible consistently and substantially affirmed as a credible and reliable source of history.[29]

Dennis Ingolfsland, a professor at Crown College, has compiled a lengthy list of archaeological discoveries from each of several centuries before Christ verifying the accuracy of many of the Bible's claims. These discoveries do not establish the inspiration, inerrancy, and authority of the Bible, but they do point to the reasonableness of belief in Scripture's truthfulness. Here are some examples.

- Eleventh century BC—Most of the cities mentioned from Genesis through the book of Joshua have been discovered: Ur (Gen. 11:28) and Erech (Gen. 10:10);[30] Shechem (Gen. 12:6);[31] Gerar (Gen. 20:1);[32] Pithom and Raamses (Exod. 1:11);[33] Arad, Jericho, Lachish, Bethel, Gezer, Ashdod, Bethshan, Megiddo, Hazor, and Eglon (Josh. 2–17);[34] Shiloh, Joppa, and Hammath (Josh. 18–21).[35]

- Tenth century BC—Some of the building projects of Solomon have been unearthed at Megiddo and Gezer. At tenth-century Megiddo levels, there was a palace fortified by a massive wall and defensive towers, as well as stables.[36]

- Ninth century BC—The Monolith Inscription of Shalmaneser mentions "Ahab the Israelite" as having the most powerful military elements in the Israelite and Syrian coalition.[37]

- Eighth century BC—The Khorsabad Annals give the account of Sargon II's captivity of Samaria in 722: "I besieged and captured Samaria, carrying off 27,290 of the people who dwelt therein."[38]

- Seventh century BC—The tunnel Hezekiah built to bring water into Jerusalem has been found (2 Kings 20:20; 2 Chron. 32:30). It even had an inscription written in eighth-century script.[39]

- Sixth century BC—The Annals of Nebuchadnezzar II mention the taking of "the city of Judah" (Jerusalem) by Nebuchadnezzar (2 Kings 24:10).[40] It says that he appointed a new king (v. 17)[41] and that he carried great amounts of treasure from Jerusalem to Babylon (vv. 13–16).[42]

- Fifth century BC—Critics once denied many aspects of the book of Ezra on the basis that the Aramaic segment it contains was late. They dated it to the third century BC, after the time of Alexander the Great. The discovery of the Elephantine papyri (legal contracts, deeds, official documents, agreements, diplomatic texts, and private letters) shows that Aramaic was the language of trade and diplomacy in the time of Ezra and that the Aramaic used in the book of Ezra was characteristic of the fifth century BC.

This is remarkable external evidence. Volumes of such evidence have been collected. If you would like to read more, I recommend *On the Reliability of the Old Testament*, by Kenneth A. Kitchen (professor emeritus of Egyptology and honorary research fellow at the School of Archaeology, Classics, and Egyptology, University of Liverpool, England).[43]

What about the historical reliability of the New Testament? First, several documents outside the Bible support the basic outlines of the story told in the Gospels. Historian Edwin Yamauchi says,

> Even if we did not have the New Testament or Christian writings, we would be able to conclude from such non-Christian writings as Josephus, the Talmud, Tacitus, and Pliny the Younger that … Jesus was a Jewish teacher; many people believed he performed healings and exorcisms; he was rejected by the Jewish leaders; he was crucified under Pontius Pilate in the reign of Tiberius; despite this shameful death, his followers, who believed that he was still alive, spread beyond Palestine so that there were multitudes of them in Rome by AD 64; all kinds of people from the cities and countryside—men and women, slave and free—worshipped him as God by the beginning of the second century.[44]

This kind of evidence does not *prove* Jesus's life and actions, but a reasonable person, in view of how this evidence converges with the biblical testimony, should give Scripture the benefit of the doubt.

> This kind of evidence does not *prove* Jesus's life and actions, but a reasonable person, in view of how this evidence converges with the biblical testimony, should give Scripture the benefit of the doubt.

The book of Acts in the New Testament is an interesting place to look for confirming evidence because it is a story line within which most of the writings of the apostle Paul are embedded. Written by Luke, the medical doctor mentioned earlier, Acts of the Apostles gives a number of historical details for which we might be able to find archaeological evidence. New Testament scholar F. F. Bruce, in his book *The New Testament Documents: Are They Reliable?*, collected a remarkable listing of historical affirmations (having to do with terminology and titles) that begin with the first missionary journey in Acts 13, all of which validate the historical accuracy of the only "history book" of the early church.[45]

For example, skeptics have challenged the reference to "proconsuls" (plural) in Acts 19:38 because elsewhere there was only one proconsul at a time.[46] But proconsul Junius Silanus had been assassinated a few months before the Ephesian riot by "messengers" from Agrippina, mother of the recently installed emperor Nero. These two "messengers" assumed the reins of government until their successor arrived from Rome. If the events of Acts 19 took place (as it seems) within this window of time, then this serves as a remarkable case of historical accuracy.[47]

We can learn two things from this example. First, the person who wrote the Acts of the Apostles accurately recorded verifiable details, making him a credible witness. Second, in the ancient world, there is really no way someone would have known these details unless he had actually traveled to the cities that are described. The various verified accounts provide evidence that the journeys took place the way the author said they did.

The evidence provided here just scratches the surface. There is much more evidence affirming the basic historical truthfulness of the Bible in those areas that can be verified, even with accounts of miracles that people today find unbelievable. John P. Meier, a professor at the University of Notre Dame, rigorously studied the gospel miracles and reported his findings in a volume more than 1,100 pages in length. He found that almost half of them included enough detail to conclude that the historical scene they described could, in fact, have occurred as reported.[48] Graham Twelftree, a professor at Regent University School of Divinity, thinks the percentage is even higher: possibly three-fourths of the miracle accounts in the Gospels included historical details that could be verified.[49]

> The various verified accounts provide evidence that the journeys took place the way the author said they did.

Such evidence gives skeptics good reason to acknowledge the basic truthfulness of the Bible. For the Christian, the motivation is even stronger: the testimony of Jesus about the Bible, about himself, and about his disciples is powerful evidence of the Bible's claim for an authority that extends to every aspect of our lives.

Even so, many questions remain: How could the Bible, written by men, actually claim to be authoritative over our lives? Wasn't the Bible corrupted over time? What about other "gospels" and ancient texts ignored by the early church fathers—don't those disprove some of the things in the Bible? Let's take a look at each of these objections.

> The testimony of Jesus about the Bible, about himself, and about his disciples is powerful evidence of the Bible's claim for an authority that extends to every aspect of our lives.

4. Answering Objections to the Authority of the Bible

People are skeptical of the Bible for all sorts of reasons, some good and some bad. Here are the three most common objections.

Objection 1: The Bible was written by human beings. Obviously, the Bible did not descend from heaven in its complete form. It was penned by about forty authors over a time span of approximately 1,500 years. Even so, the Bible describes the origin of Scripture as a process that is both fully human and fully divine:

- The apostle Peter: "Knowing this first of all, that no prophecy of Scripture comes from someone's own interpretation. For no prophecy was ever produced by the will of man, but men spoke from God as they were carried along by the Holy Spirit" (2 Pet. 1:20–21).

- The apostle Paul: "As for you, continue in what you have learned and have firmly believed, knowing from whom you learned it and how from childhood you have been acquainted with the sacred writings, which are able to make you wise for salvation through faith in Christ Jesus. All Scripture is breathed out by God and profitable for teaching, for reproof, for correction, and for training in righteousness, that the man of God may be complete, equipped for every good work" (2 Tim. 3:14–17).

Here's the rub. We know that people are capable of lying (either on purpose or by letting mistaken impressions stand) or writing untrue things because they were deceived into believing them. A skeptic might insist, at some point in the course of the 1,500 years it took to compile the Bible, this must have happened, right? So how can we trust the authority of Scripture?

To answer this objection, we must first decide whether humans are capable of saying or writing *anything* that is true. If so, would they not be capable of truthfully writing down what God told them to? Author and speaker Greg Koukl makes this point through a series of questions: "Do you have any books in your library? Were those books written by humans? Do you find any truth in them? Is there a reason you think the Bible is less truthful or reliable than other books you own? Do people always make mistakes in what they write? Do you think that if God did exist, he would be capable of using humans to write down exactly what he wants? If not, why not?"[50] In the end, the person who insists that the authors of the Bible must have lied or been deceived is often objecting to the Bible as a way to indirectly cast doubt on God's existence. Well-placed questions such as these are good ways to dislodge threadbare slogans and get to the heart of the issue.

If you assume that God does not exist, then of course the authority of his Word seems like nonsense. However, if it is reasonable to believe that God does exist (and we will examine such evidence in subsequent chapters), then the "written by men" objection begs the question. If someone brings it up, ask, "Before we talk about the objection of the Bible being written by men, can I ask you this: Do you find the evidence of God's existence persuasive? Why or why not?"

Here's something else to consider. The Bible contains many fulfilled prophecies. Some of these are so specific that it defies imagination to think that they could have been written merely by human sources with no knowledge of the future. Evangelist D. James Kennedy tells a story about an encounter he had about fulfilled prophecy in the life of Jesus:

> The Bible contains many fulfilled prophecies. Some of these are so specific that it defies imagination to think that they could have been written merely by human sources with no knowledge of the future.

Some time ago I had the opportunity to speak to a man who had no belief whatsoever in the Scriptures as any sort of divine revelation from God. He was a writer who was articulate and well-educated. While he was well-read, he was completely ignorant of any evidences for the truthfulness of the Christian faith and the Scriptures which reveal it. He said the Bible was simply a book written by men, just like any other book. I said, "That's very interesting. I would like to read some statements to you about someone and have you tell me, assuredly, without question, about whom I am reading."[51]

DOES THE BIBLE HAVE AUTHORITY?

From that point, Kennedy listed out twenty-four scriptural texts, including Isaiah 50:6, Zechariah 11:12–13, Psalm 22:16, Psalm 69:21, Isaiah 53:9, Exodus 12:46, Psalm 34:20, and Psalm 22:18.[52] He then continues his story:

> I said to him, "About whom did I read?" He replied, "Well, you obviously read of the life and ministry and suffering and death and resurrection of Jesus of Nazareth." I said, "Is there any question in your mind about that?" He answered, "No, that could refer to no one else." I replied, "Well then, I would want you to understand that all of the Scriptures I just read to you are taken from the Old Testament, which was completed some four hundred years before Jesus was born. No critic, no atheist, no agnostic has ever once claimed that any one of those writings was written after His birth. In fact, they were translated from Hebrew into Greek in Alexandria some 150 years before He was born. If this is merely a book written by men, would you please explain to me how these words were written?"[53]

A note of caution: a number of the prophecies Kennedy references were general in nature and had meaning at the time but in retrospect could also be applied to Jesus. Yet, even with this consideration in mind, the sheer weight of evidence has convinced many Bible scholars that it could not have been an accident. The Old Testament writers were led to write about something that could have made complete sense only when viewed backward through the lens of Jesus's life and work.

> The Old Testament writers were led to write about something that could have made complete sense only when viewed backward through the lens of Jesus's life and work.

Objection 2: The Bible has been corrupted. This objection is sometimes called the Telephone Game objection. Maybe you've played the game in which a person whispers a statement into a second person's ear, who then whispers it to a third, and so forth, until the last person says aloud what he was told. It's usually hilariously wrong, even bizarre. If we can't communicate one simple statement around a room with any accuracy, how is it possible for the Bible to have been transmitted accurately by hundreds of people over the course of thousands of years?

This objection is particularly important to Muslims who contend for the validity of the Quran based largely on the argument that the modern-day Bible has been

> Paul is not so easily dismissed. He both introduces and concludes his letter to the Romans by noting how the gospel he proclaims stems from the Old Testament. In fact, all throughout the New Testament we see affirmations of the Old Testament as inspired by God.

cleansed of Islamic teachings and is therefore corrupted. Unfortunately for scholars of Islam, large portions of Old Testament texts, dating to and before the first century AD, illustrate that the texts we have are substantially the same as those Jesus and Paul had, making it difficult for Muslim scholars to argue that the Old Testament was corrupted sometime after Jesus's death.[54] If you get into a conversation with a Muslim acquaintance about this, ask, "If God can sustain the Quran throughout the ages, can he not sustain the biblical texts?" The evidence shows that he has preserved his Word.[55]

Muslim critics also like to argue that there are differences between the teachings of Jesus, whom they consider to be a prophet, and the apostle Paul, who they think corrupted Jesus's teachings.[56] Paul, however, is not so easily dismissed. He both introduces and concludes his letter to the Romans by noting how the gospel he proclaims stems from the Old Testament.[57] In fact, all throughout the New Testament we see affirmations of the Old Testament as inspired by God.[58] Paul also noted that "the Law and the Prophets" testified to the heart of the gospel—the righteousness of God (Rom. 3:21).[59] He taught that his ministry and message about Christ confirmed God's promises to the patriarchs: "I tell you that Christ became a servant to the circumcised to show God's truthfulness, in order to confirm the promises given to the patriarchs, and in order that the Gentiles might glorify God for his mercy" (Rom. 15:8–9).[60]

It is in fact true that we have no original manuscripts of the Old or the New Testaments. According to Jonathan Morrow, however, this isn't a serious objection to the validity of the texts we do possess.

> To begin with, you need to know that none of the original manuscripts of either the Old or New Testaments are still in existence—all that remain are imperfect copies. But this is exactly the same situation of all the other ancient works of literature as well. No one has the originals. While this may come as a surprise, this fact should not turn us into skeptics regarding ancient texts. But we do need to recognize how the composition and transmission of ancient documents worked.[61]

> Other writings from antiquity are not seriously doubted (e.g., Aristotle, Livy, and so on), so why should the Bible be held to a different standard?

Other writings from antiquity are not seriously doubted (e.g., Aristotle, Livy, and so on), so why should the Bible be held to a different standard?

Here's a more important question, though. In the absence of original manuscripts, do scholars have enough evidence to reconstruct the text? The authors of *Reinventing Jesus* say yes.

> The wealth of material that is available for determining the wording of the original New Testament is staggering: more than fifty-seven hundred Greek New Testament manuscripts, as many as twenty thousand versions, and more than one million quotations by patristic writers. In comparison with the average ancient Greek author, the New Testament copies are well over a thousand times more plentiful. If the average-sized manuscript were two and one-half inches thick, all the copies of the works of an average Greek author would stack up four feet high, while the copies of the New Testament would stack up to over a mile high! This is indeed an embarrassment of riches.[62]

Scholars of other ancient texts would love to have the "problem" New Testament scholars have.

Still, if all these copies were duplicated over and over again, wouldn't mistakes accumulate over time, corrupting the text? To answer this question, we must understand the nature of copy mistakes. When scholars examine multiple manuscripts, they can compare them word by word, sentence by sentence. Often differences arise, called **textual variants**. And because we have so many manuscripts, the number of textual variants among the manuscripts is quite high. Skeptic Bart Ehrman refers quite often to four hundred thousand textual variants, so we will go with that number.

> *Textual Variants:* differences between particular words, phrases, or passages within multiple copies of the same ancient manuscript.

Essentially there are four kinds of textual variants:

1. Spelling and unclear readings

2. Changes that can't be translated, such as words that do not have an equivalent meaning in the language being translated into, or word order (e.g., "Christ Jesus" versus "Jesus Christ")

3. Meaningful variants that are not viable (i.e., variants that are just not plausible and occur in questionable manuscripts)

4. Meaningful and viable variants (i.e., variants that both are plausible and affect the meaning of the text)

The only variants of serious concern to biblical scholars are those in the fourth group because they are in trusted manuscripts and affect the meaning of the text. As Darrell Bock and Daniel Wallace summarize, though, "Less than one percent of all textual variants are both meaningful and viable, and by 'meaningful' we don't mean to imply earth-shattering significance but rather, almost always, minor alterations to the meaning of the text."[63] This comes out to fewer than four thousand of the original four hundred thousand variants having any real significance at all for the meaning of a verse. And none of these affects any core doctrines, according to Bock and Wallace.[64]

> The bottom line is this: what we have in the New Testament today, with 99 percent accuracy, is essentially what was written then.

The bottom line is this: what we have in the New Testament today, with 99 percent accuracy, is essentially what was written then. If this is so, the Telephone Game objection simply doesn't apply to New Testament texts. Wallace explains why:

> In the telephone game the goal is to garble an original utterance so that by the end of the line it doesn't resemble the original at all. There's only one line of transmission, it is oral rather than written, and the oral critic (the person who is trying to figure out what the original utterance was) only has the last person in line to interrogate. When it comes to the text of the NT, there are multiple lines of transmission, and

the original documents were almost surely copied several times (which would best explain why they wore out by the end of the second century). Further, the textual critic doesn't rely on just the last person in the transmissional line, but can interrogate many scribes over the centuries, way back to the second century. And even when the early manuscript testimony is sparse, we have the early church fathers' testimony as to what the original text said. Finally, the process is not intended to be a parlor game but is intended to duplicate the original text faithfully—and this process doesn't rely on people hearing a whole utterance whispered only once, but seeing the text and copying it. The telephone game is a far cry from the process of copying manuscripts of the New Testament.[65]

Still, those who uphold the Telephone Game objection have played a valuable role in apologetics, pressing biblical scholars carefully to examine the evidence, which in turn has served to reinforce the Bible's trustworthiness.

Lost Gospels: a collection of fifty-two gnostic texts discovered in 1945 in Nag Hammadi, Egypt, and written sometime between the second and fourth centuries AD.

Objection 3: Important books have been left out of the Bible. In 1945, fifty-two papyri were discovered at Nag Hammadi in Lower Egypt. Some of these texts had the word *gospel* in the title. Scholars have known about these and other second- through fourth-century documents for a long time, but in a culture that loves conspiracy theories and cover-ups, these so-called **Lost Gospels** make an irresistible story for investigative reports on television.

Why are these Lost Gospels excluded from the biblical canon? Generally speaking, there were three criteria used to decide which books were received as authoritative (that is, as Scripture):

1. **Apostolicity:** Was a book written by an apostle or an associate of an apostle? Mark was accepted because he was an associate of Peter, and Luke was accepted because of his relationship to Paul. Or to put it another way, if the book was not from the first century, it was not Scripture because it could not be historically connected to the apostles who were taught and commissioned by Jesus (who was crucified in AD 30–33).

2. **Orthodoxy:** Did this book conform to the teachings and theology of other books known by the apostles?[66]

3. **Pedigree:** Was the book accepted early on in the life of the church and by the majority of churches across the region? It was important that a book wasn't just accepted in one location but that lots of Christians in different cities and regions accepted it.[67]

Based on these criteria, the Lost Gospels, while historically interesting, are inferior to the canonical writings contained in the New Testament. The New Testament writings all date to the first century, when the apostles—or those who could have interviewed them—would have been alive.

Here's something else of interest: there was a collection of texts *already* functioning as Scripture in the early church, long before the emperor Constantine could have decreed them as Scripture (as books such as Dan Brown's *The Da Vinci Code* claim). New Testament scholars Andreas Köstenberger and Michael Kruger summarize as follows:

> The concept of canon not only existed before the middle of the second century, but … a number of New Testament books were already received and being used as authoritative documents in the life of the church. Given the fact that such a trend is evident in a broad number of early texts—2 Peter, 1 Timothy, 1 Clement, the Didache, Ignatius, Polycarp, Barnabas, and Papias—we have good historical reasons to think that the concept of a New Testament canon was relatively well established and perhaps even a widespread reality by the turn of the century. Although the borders of the canon were not yet solidified by this time, there is no doubt that the early church understood that God had given a new set of authoritative covenant documents that testified to the redemptive work of Jesus Christ and that those documents were the beginning of the New Testament canon. Such a scenario provides a new foundation for how we view the historical evidence after c. AD 150. For example, the Muratorian Fragment reveals that by c. AD 180 the early church had received all four Gospels, all thirteen epistles of Paul, the book of Acts, Jude, the Johannine epistles (at least two of them), and the book of Revelation. Yet, in light of the evidence viewed here, some of these books had already been received and used long before the middle of the second century and viewed as part of the revelation of the new covenant (though we do not know how many). Thus, the Muratorian Fragment does not appear to be establishing or "creating" a canon but is expressly affirming what has already been the case within the early church.[68]

All of the extant "Lost" or "Missing" Gospels are from the second century or later; therefore, they are not our earliest and best sources. They fail the test of having been written by an apostle or produced through a direct interview with one.

Most important, the worldviews and theology of many of the Lost Gospels—such as the gospels of Thomas, Mary, Philip, and many others—are inconsistent with the teachings of earliest Christianity. Their theology is based on **gnosticism**, not orthodox Christianity.[69] Gnosticism taught that the world was made by a lesser divine being and that the material world and body were intrinsically evil. Because Jesus's appearing in a body would have corrupted his ministry, gnostics believed that Jesus was merely a spirit who *appeared* to be human. Gnostics taught that our main problem is ignorance, not sin, and that it is possible to gain "special knowledge" leading to salvation for those clever enough to decode it.[70] In short, these Lost Gospels teach a false gospel. The early church fathers therefore rejected them after careful study.[71] In spite of

Gnosticism: a second-century heretical Christian movement that taught that the material world was created and maintained by a lesser divine being, that matter and the physical body are inherently evil, and that salvation can be obtained only through an esoteric knowledge of divine reality and the self-denial of physical pleasures.

...sationalist claims in the media, these Lost Gospels were known in the early centuries after Christ's ministry and rejected for very good reasons.[72]

5. How Far Does God's Authority Extend?

If God actually exists and if the revelation about him is trustworthy, then he has authority. How far does this authority extend? The often neglected third verse of Isaac Watts's "Joy to the World" might help us here:

No more let sins and sorrows grow,
Nor thorns infest the ground;
He comes to make His blessings flow
Far as the curse is found,
Far as the curse is found,
Far as, far as, the curse is found.

How far did Watts think God's authority extends? As far as the curse is found, which is everywhere, as nothing in the world is untouched by human sin. South African scholar J. Norval Geldenhuys wrote,

> As Creator and Sustainer of the universe he has the absolute right over all created beings and an all-embracing authority in heaven as on earth. This final and supreme authority gives him the unlimited prerogative to command and enforce obedience, to unconditionally possess and absolutely govern all things at all times in all places of the universe.[73]

Derived Authority: authority that has been ordained or permitted by God.

Because God created and sustains the universe, his authority is supreme over all. That means that all other legitimate authorities have **derived authority** (ordained or permitted by God).

If what we've seen so far is accurate, the authority of the Bible does not rest on the ponderous decision of some church council; its authority comes from God. Carl F. H. Henry explains,

> The classical view of inspiration refuses to ground the authority of Scripture in the common life of the community of faith; it correlates that authority instead with a divinely imparted property of the scriptural texts. Nor does it, as frequently charged, in any way reduce the issue of religious authority to a circular argument. The classic view discussed divine authority in the contexts of the authority of God, self-revealed in Christ, attested by general and special revelation, including scriptural authority, as objective factors.[74]

If the Bible is indeed from God to us, there is nothing that exists that escapes the authority of Scripture. Cultures, governments, life, death, family, entertainment—all are to be subjected to God's authority.

Let's take a look at several areas subject to God's authority as revealed in Scripture.

God has authority over the limits of reason. Our worldview determines the limits and standards for what we would consider reasonable. A biblical worldview commits us to a view of reality larger than our ability to explain every-thing it contains. A biblical worldview means that God determines what is reasonable and what is not. For example, Abraham was willing to sacrifice his son Isaac because Abraham believed that God could raise Isaac from the dead, even though no miracles of resurrection had yet occurred in history.[75] Abraham's worldview was *enlarged* because "reasonable" for Abraham no longer merely included only natural possibilities but grew to also include the realm of supernatural. If God exists, then our definition of what is reasonable must expand by its very nature.

> If God exists, then our definition of what is reasonable must expand by its very nature.

God has authority over our understanding of reality. A biblical worldview commits us to a view of reality larger than our capacity to understand it. We tend to believe only what we can see or prove, but a biblical worldview includes spiritual entities (including God himself). Being finite and limited, we cannot see or touch some of the things Scripture describes, such as Satan, angels, and demons. Yet the Bible describes these as utterly real. Second Corinthians 4:18 says, "We look not to the things that are seen but to the things that are unseen. For the things that are seen are transient, but the things that are unseen are eternal." In talking about the armor of God, Ephesians 6:12 says, "We do not wrestle against flesh and blood, but against the rulers, against the authorities, against the cosmic powers over this present darkness, against the spiritual forces of evil in the heavenly places." The Old Testament tells of the prophet Elisha, who had so angered his enemies that they sent an army to capture him. Elisha's servant, Gehazi, was terrified until Elisha prayed that God would open his eyes to see the greater reality: that the king of Aram's mighty army was completely outnumbered by much more powerful spiritual forces (2 Kings 6:17).[76]

God has authority over culture. Time and again, in both testaments, believers are tempted to embrace the values and morals of the surrounding cultures, whether they were the Canaanites in the Old Testament or the Corinthians in the New Testament. Contrary to the practices of many cultures, though, following God meant obeying him. The prophets and apostles regularly confronted evil practices within their own cultures. These practices are not legitimized by them as "true for the culture that practiced them." Instead, the truths of Scripture are true for *all* cultures at *all* times. Postmodernists may say this is impossible, that cultures are too different, but Carl F. H. Henry disagrees: "Russians, Chinese, Koreans, and others have no problem learning the formulas of modern physics and the foreign languages in which implications are expounded for nuclear bombing and space shuttling. If scientists can communicate their ideas across cultural barriers, God certainly can do so."[77]

God has authority over entertainment. The voices of entertainers speak authoritatively over such wide-ranging issues as abortion, the environment, and spirituality—topics about which those entertainers have rarely been educated. And yet these voices are considered to be authoritative because millions of people listen to them and watch their videos on YouTube. Popularity, however, is not the same as authority. The number of people who believe an idea is rarely an indication in itself of the idea's truth. In a world where popularity is equated with being right, God claims authority over what voices we pay attention to and insists that we filter out what is not true or not worth thinking about (Phil. 4:8).[78]

God has authority over our senses. We've all been to enough magic shows to know that our senses can be deceived. We may see and hear things we think are true but are not. The Bible values our senses, given to us by God, as ways to know truth. The authority of the Bible extends beyond what we are able to verify with our senses. The Bible claims to be a reality check when our senses fail us. The apostle John wrote, "What was from the beginning, what we have heard, what we have *seen* with our eyes, what we have looked at and *touched* with our hands … testify and proclaim to you the eternal life" (1 John 1:1–3). Peter, for example, described being both an eyewitness and an "ear-witness" to the transfiguration of Jesus. These observations did not prove to him the truth of what he had seen but only served to "have the prophetic word more fully confirmed."[79]

> The Bible claims to be a reality check when our senses fail us.

God has authority over our emotions. God repeatedly expresses his authority over the emotional life. He commands that we love him and love others (Luke 10:27).[80] He even commands that we love our enemies and pray for them (Matt. 5:44).[81] Truth is not determined by our feelings. Truth is not determined by what makes us comfortable. Truth does not depend on how many people agree with us. Feelings can guide us to truth, but they can also mislead us. We may feel good about things that are untrue and bad about things that are true. As Flannery O'Connor said, "Truth does not change according to my ability to stomach it."[82]

> God repeatedly expresses his authority over the emotional life.

God has authority over knowledge. It is common for people to say, "I won't believe something unless it can be proven scientifically." They assume science to be the most reliable means of knowing. Later in this volume we will explore the topic of science and the Bible, but for now it is worth noting that to believe only what science can prove excludes anything that cannot be empirically demonstrated, including principles of origins, supernatural truths, any universally applicable truth, and even the underlying principles of science itself.[83] Half a century ago, Martyn Lloyd-Jones observed,

> If you study the history of science you will have much less respect for its supposed supreme authority than you had when you began. It is nothing but a simple fact of history to say that a hundred years ago and less, scientists were teaching dogmatically and with extreme confidence that the thyroid gland, the pituitary gland, and other glands were nothing but vestigial remains. They said that they had no value and no function whatsoever.… But today we know that these glands are essential to life.[84]

The truth is, biblical writers were enabled by the Holy Spirit at times to "write better than they knew" and better than the science of that day could grasp.[85]

God has authority over governments. Psalm 2:1–6 says,

> Why do the nations rage,
>   and the peoples plot in vain?
> The kings of the earth set themselves,
>   and the rulers take counsel together,
> against the LORD and against his Anointed, saying,
>   "Let us burst their bonds apart
> and cast away their cords from us."
>   He who sits in the heavens laughs;
> the Lord holds them in derision.
>   Then he will speak to them in his wrath,
> and terrify them in his fury, saying,
>   "As for me, I have set my King
> on Zion, my holy hill."

Even the authority of nations is derived from and dependent on God (whether that authority is acknowledged or not) and, as revealed in the Bible, will accomplish God's purpose for all nations. In response to Pilate, Jesus said, "You would have no authority over me at all unless it had been given you from above" (John 19:11). Romans 13:1–2 says there is no authority except that which is from God.[86] Jesus specifically instructed his followers not to fear human authorities because they have only the capacity to destroy the body (Luke 12:4–5).[87] In Acts 5:29, when confronting unjust governmental authority, Peter and the other apostles say, "We must obey God rather than men." When governing authorities conflict with the authority of God, obedience is rendered to God alone. Why? As Psalm 22:27–28 says, "All the ends of the earth shall remember and turn to the LORD, and all the families of the nations shall worship before you. For kingship belongs to the LORD, and he rules over the nations."

> **When governing authorities conflict with the authority of God, obedience is rendered to God alone.**

6. CONCLUSION

If every area of life falls under God's authority, God has the right to tell us what to do. We are told by Scripture to be stewards of our minds (Rom. 12:2; Eph. 4:23; Col. 3:2, 10),[88] our physical bodies (1 Cor. 6:12–20), our spouses (Eph. 5:18–33), and our children (Deut. 6:4–8).[89] We are told to be truthful and loving and not to gossip (Eph. 4:15, 25; James 1:19, 26)[90] and to be generous and hospitable to all people (Rom. 12:1–21). Biblical truth is not relative but absolute (John 17:17),[91] and Jesus is the only way to it (John 14:6; Acts 4:12).[92] Nothing is excluded. God's authority extends beyond what we can perceive with our senses to all areas of knowledge and over all human authority. God's worldview is bigger than ours. Will we live small, or will we live big?

In the end, all people must decide where they will place their faith. When I get on an airplane, I put my faith in the pilots, the air traffic control system, physics, engineering, the

> **In the end, all people must decide where they will place their faith.**

maintenance crew, the integrity of the airplane's structure, the quality of the fuel company that refined and delivered the jet fuel, and an endless number of other people and factors. This is not blind faith, however; based on extensive experience, I trust the system designed to put airplanes safely in the air. Is it possible that my faith is misplaced? Yes. But no one can live apart from ongoing faith in the truths and systems we have come to trust as reliable.

Trust in the authority of Scripture is like trust in the airline system. It is not blind. God expresses his authority in Scripture, which, we have good reason to believe, is both internally

> **God expresses his authority in Scripture, which, we have good reason to believe, is both internally and externally trustworthy.**

and externally trustworthy. Jesus claims authority, and the accuracy of biblical documents lends credence to his claim. Jesus also shows trust in the Old Testament revelation and lends his authority to those who later write the New Testament. Common objections to this trustworthiness only strengthen the Bible's claim to authority.

And so we have come full circle. Bob Dylan was right: you gotta serve somebody. But whom? Some find they have a problem with authority. Others don't want to accept the lifestyle the Bible says is best for human flourishing. Others honestly search, but they doubt whether anyone can properly understand God's message as communicated through his Word. To grapple with these difficulties, we must understand more clearly what God is like. This is what we will discuss in chapter 4.

ENDNOTES

1. "Timothy James McVeigh: Executed June 11, 2001 at 7:14 a.m. CDT by Lethal Injection by U.S. Government at Terre Haute, Indiana," Clark Prosecutor, www.clarkprosecutor.org/html/death/US/mcveigh717.htm.
2. Often attributed to Benjamin Franklin.
3. See Romans 10:9: "If you confess with your mouth that Jesus is Lord and believe in your heart that God raised him from the dead, you will be saved"; Philippians 2:9–11: "God has highly exalted him and bestowed on him the name that is above every name, so that at the name of Jesus every knee should bow, in heaven and on earth and under the earth, and every tongue confess that Jesus Christ is Lord, to the glory of God the Father."
4. Romans 14:10–12: "Why do you pass judgment on your brother? Or you, why do you despise your brother? For we will all stand before the judgment seat of God; for it is written, 'As I live, says the Lord, every knee shall bow to me, and every tongue shall confess to God'"; Philippians 2:9–11: "God has highly exalted him and bestowed on him the name that is above every name, so that at the name of Jesus every knee should bow, in heaven and on earth and under the earth, and every tongue confess that Jesus Christ is Lord, to the glory of God the Father"; Isaiah 45:23: "By myself I have sworn; from my mouth has gone out in righteousness a word that shall not return: 'To me every knee shall bow, every tongue shall swear allegiance.'"
5. The phrase "long obedience in the same direction" comes, ironically, from Friedrich Nietzsche, *Beyond Good and Evil* (New York: Millennium, 2014), 46. For his usage see *The Selected Writings of Friedrich Nietzsche* (Radford, VA: Wilder, 2008), 471. Eugene Peterson appropriates the term in his book *A Long Obedience in the Same Direction: Discipleship in an Instant Society* (Downers Grove, IL: InterVarsity, 2000) as a figure of speech for following Christ.
6. Matthew 22:37: "He said to him, 'You shall love the Lord your God with all your heart and with all your soul and with all your mind.'"
7. Romans 12:2: "Do not be conformed to this world, but be transformed by the renewal of your mind, that by testing you may discern what is the will of God, what is good and acceptable and perfect."
8. W. Gary Phillips, William E. Brown, and John Stonestreet, *Making Sense of Your World: A Biblical Worldview* (Salem,

DOES THE BIBLE HAVE AUTHORITY?

WI: Sheffield, 2008), 113.

9. John 8:58: "Jesus said to them, 'Truly, truly, I say to you, before Abraham was, I am.'"

10. John 10:30: "'I and the Father are one.'"

11. John 14:7–9: "'If you had known me, you would have known my Father also. From now on you do know him and have seen him.' Philip said to him, 'Lord, show us the Father, and it is enough for us.' Jesus said to him, 'Have I been with you so long, and you still do not know me, Philip? Whoever has seen me has seen the Father. How can you say, "Show us the Father"?'"

12. John 5:22: "The Father judges no one, but has given all judgment to the Son."

13. Specifically, Jesus claimed authority over the Sabbath (Mark 2:27–28), to forgive sin (Mark 2:5), to perform miracles (Mark 2:8–12), to raise himself from the dead (John 2:19), over the angels (Matt. 13:41), over the kingdom of God (Matt. 13:41), over the prophets throughout the centuries (Matt. 23:34), and over judgment of all the world (Matt. 25:31–46; 26:63–65; John 5:22, 27).

14. Carl F. H. Henry, *God, Revelation and Authority*, vol. 4 (Wheaton, IL: Crossway, 1999), 68–69.

15. A popular movement called Red Letter Christians would probably take issue with this approach. The leader of the movement, a retired sociology professor named Tony Campolo, said in a response to an article in *Christianity Today*, "While we, like you, have a very high view of the inspiration of Scripture and believe the Bible was divinely inspired, you are correct in accusing Red Letter Christians of giving the words of Jesus priority over all other passages of Scripture. What is more, we believe that you really cannot rightly interpret the rest of the Bible without first understanding who Jesus is, what he did, and what he said." Campolo goes on to distinguish between the teachings of Jesus and the teachings of the Old Testament. Sam Guthrie, "When Red Is Blue: Why I Am Not a Red-Letter Christian," *Christianity Today*, October 11, 2007, www.christianitytoday.com/ct/2007/october/33.100.html. My point is that this is a distinction Jesus himself did not make.

16. W. Gary Phillips, research provided to the author, April 16, 2013.

17. Matthew 22:41–45: "Now while the Pharisees were gathered together, Jesus asked them a question, saying, 'What do you think about the Christ? Whose son is he?' They said to him, 'The son of David.' He said to them, 'How is it then that David, in the Spirit, calls him Lord, saying, "The Lord said to my Lord, sit at my right hand, until I put your enemies under your feet"? If then David calls him Lord, how is he his son?'" In reference to Psalm 110:1, "The LORD says to my Lord: 'Sit at my right hand, until I make your enemies your footstool.'"

18. John 10:34–36: "Jesus answered them, 'Is it not written in your Law, "I said, you are gods"? If he called them gods to whom the word of God came—and Scripture cannot be broken—do you say of him whom the Father consecrated and sent into the world, "You are blaspheming," because I said, "I am the Son of God"?'" In reference to Psalm 82:6, "I said, 'You are gods, sons of the Most High, all of you.'"

19. Matthew 5:17: "'Do not think that I have come to abolish the Law or the Prophets; I have not come to abolish them but to fulfill them.'"

20. Luke 24:44: "Then he said to them, 'These are my words that I spoke to you while I was still with you, that everything written about me in the Law of Moses and the Prophets and the Psalms must be fulfilled.'"

21. Matthew 27:46: "About the ninth hour Jesus cried out with a loud voice, saying, 'Eli, Eli, lema sabachthani?' that is, 'My God, my God, why have you forsaken me?'"

22. Henry, *God, Revelation and Authority*, vol. 4, 51.

23. 2 Peter 3:16: "As he does in all his letters when he speaks in them of these matters. There are some things in them that are hard to understand, which the ignorant and unstable twist to their own destruction, as they do the other Scriptures."

24. 1 Timothy 5:18: "For the Scripture says, 'You shall not muzzle the ox when it treads out grain,' and, 'The laborer deserves his wages.'"

25. Kenneth A. Kitchen, *Ancient Orient and the Old Testament* (Downers Grove, IL: InterVarsity, 1975), 30–32. Kitchen's particular point had to do with archaeological evidence, but the principle he stated so cleverly applies generally to the investigation of historical claims, too.

26. Philip R. Davies, *In Search of 'Ancient Israel': A Study in Biblical Origins* (Sheffield, England: Sheffield Academic Press, 1992), 12.

27. Quoted in Jeffery Sheler, *Is the Bible True? How Modern Debates and Discoveries Affirm the Essence of the Scriptures* (San Francisco: Harper Collins, 1999), 96.

28. Edward Lane, "King David's Temple Found by Archaeologists in Israel," *The Examiner*, July 20, 2013, www.examiner.com/article/king-david-s-temple-found-by-archaeologists-israel.

29. Sheler, *Is the Bible True?*, 254.

30. Genesis 11:28: "Haran died in the presence of his father Terah in the land of his kindred, in Ur of the Chaldeans"; Genesis 10:10: "The beginning of his kingdom was Babel, Erech, Accad, and Calneh, in the land of Shinar."

31. Genesis 12:6: "Abram passed through the land to the place at Shechem, to the oak of Moreh. At that time the Canaanites were in the land."

32. Genesis 20:1: "From there Abraham journeyed toward the territory of the Negeb and lived between Kadesh and Shur; and he sojourned in Gerar."

33. Exodus 1:11: "They set taskmasters over them to afflict them with heavy burdens. They built for Pharaoh store cities,

Pithom and Raamses."

34. As one example, Joshua 10:34–35: "Then Joshua and all Israel with him passed on from Lachish to Eglon. And they laid siege to it and fought against it. And they captured it on that day, and struck it with the edge of the sword. And he devoted every person in it to destruction that day, as he had done to Lachish."

35. As one example, Joshua 19:35: "The fortified cities are Ziddim, Zer, Hammath, Rakkath, Chinnereth."

36. R. K. Harrison, *Introduction to the Old Testament* (Peabody, MA: Hendrickson, 2004), 125.

37. Harrison, *Introduction to the Old Testament,* 127.

38. Harrison, *Introduction to the Old Testament,* 128. See also Victor Matthews, *Old Testament Parallels: Laws and Stories from the Ancient Near East,* 3rd ed. (Mahwah, NJ: Paulist, 2007), 137–38.

39. Harrison, *Introduction to the Old Testament,* 128. See also Matthews, *Old Testament Parallels,* 137–38.

40. 2 Kings 24:10: "At that time the servants of Nebuchadnezzar king of Babylon came up to Jerusalem, and the city was besieged."

41. 2 Kings 24:17: "The king of Babylon made Mattaniah, Jehoiachin's uncle, king in his place, and changed his name to Zedekiah."

42. 2 Kings 24:13–16: "… and carried off all the treasures of the house of the LORD and the treasures of the king's house, and cut in pieces all the vessels of gold in the temple of the LORD, which Solomon king of Israel had made, as the LORD had foretold. He carried away all Jerusalem and all the officials and all the mighty men of valor, 10,000 captives, and all the craftsmen and the smiths. None remained, except the poorest people of the land. And he carried away Jehoiachin to Babylon. The king's mother, the king's wives, his officials, and the chief men of the land he took into captivity from Jerusalem to Babylon. And the king of Babylon brought captive to Babylon all the men of valor, 7,000, and the craftsmen and the metal workers, 1,000, all of them strong and fit for war." See Matthews, *Old Testament Parallels,* 141–43.

43. K. A. Kitchen, *On the Reliability of the Old Testament* (Grand Rapids, MI: Eerdmans, 2003).

44. Quoted in Michael J. Wilkens and J. P. Moreland, *Jesus Under Fire: Modern Scholarship Reinvents the Historical Jesus* (Grand Rapids, MI: Zondervan, 1995), 221–22.

45. Second, consider the book of Acts, our best source to aim at historical and archaeological authentication. New Testament scholar F. F. Bruce, in his book *The New Testament Documents: Are They Reliable?* (Grand Rapids, MI: Eerdmans, 1981), collected a remarkable listing of historical affirmations (having to do with terminology and titles) that begin with the first missionary journey in Acts 13, all of which validate the historical accuracy of the only "history book" of the early church. The reason these examples are significant is that there is no way someone would have known these details unless they had traveled to the cities that are described.

- Acts 13:7—Cyprus became a senatorial province (as opposed to "imperial" province) in 22 BC, and thus the governor was rightly called "proconsul" Sergius Paulus.
- Acts 16:12, 20ff, 35ff.—"Praetors" (magistrates of Philippi) were attended by "Lictors" (sergeants, with whose rods Paul and Silas were beaten—these titles are confirmed by the Roman writer Cicero).
- Acts 17:6, 9—at Thessalonica, the term *politarchs* (found in no other city) was corroborated by an inscription discovered at Thessalonica.
- Acts 18:12—Achaia had been a senatorial province only since AD 44, thus the term *proconsul* for Gallio, who had arrived in July of AD 51, is entirely accurate.
- Acts 19:31—At Ephesus, the term *town clerk* referred to a local official who acted as a link between municipal government and Roman administration; also, the term *Asiarchs* also is accurate, referring to chief priests of the "Rome and the Emperor" cult from throughout the province, who would have been in Ephesus to represent the emperor during the festival of Artemis.
- Acts 19:35—Also at Ephesus, the term *Warden of the Temple* is confirmed in an inscription describing the city of Ephesus as the "Temple-Warden" of Artemis.
- Acts 19:38—Finally at Ephesus, the term *proconsuls* (plural) was challenged by liberal critics because elsewhere there was only one proconsul at a time. But proconsul Junius Silanus had been assassinated a few months before the Ephesian riot by messengers from Agrippina, the mother of Nero. Nero had just become emperor in AD 54, and these two messengers/assassins had assumed the reins of government until the successor arrived from Rome. Within this window of time, the events in Acts 19 took place.
- Acts 28:7—The title of the ruler of Malta was "first man of the island," which is corroborated by both Greek and Latin inscriptions. Dr. Bruce cites the confusing way an Oxford University student refers to the heads of Oxford colleges by their proper titles: Provost of Oriel, Master of Lalliol, Rector of Exeter, President of Magdalen, and so on. These titles are very difficult for someone in another part of academia even within the United Kingdom, and these don't change on you every decade or so, the way they did in the Greco-Roman Empire.

Historically, the events of the Old Testament and the events of the New Testament (Gospels—the life of Christ; Acts—the historical account of the spread of the church) took place just as the authoritative words of the Word of God claim.

46. Acts 19:38: "If therefore Demetrius and the craftsmen with him have a complaint against anyone, the courts are open, and there are proconsuls. Let them bring charges against one another."

DOES THE BIBLE HAVE AUTHORITY?

47. Bruce, *New Testament Documents*, 84.

48. John P. Meier, *A Marginal Jew: Rethinking the Historical Jesus, vol. 2, Mentor, Message, and Miracles* (New York: Doubleday, 1994).

49. Graham H. Twelftree, *Jesus the Miracle Worker: A Historical and Theological Study* (Downers Grove, IL: IVP Academic, 1999), chaps. 1–2.

50. Gregory Koukl, *Tactics: A Game Plan for Discussing Your Christian Convictions* (Grand Rapids, MI: Zondervan, 2009), 44.

51. D. James Kennedy, "Christ: The Fulfillment of Prophecy," in Ted Cabal et al., eds., *The Apologetics Study Bible* (Nashville: B&H, 2007), xxviii–xxix.

52. Isaiah 50:6: "I gave my back to those who strike, and my cheeks to those who pull out the beard; I hid not my face from disgrace and spitting"; Zechariah 11:12–13, "Then I said to them, 'If it seems good to you, give me my wages; but if not, keep them.' And they weighed out as my wages thirty pieces of silver. Then the LORD said to me, 'Throw it to the potter'—the lordly price at which I was priced by them. So I took the thirty pieces of silver and threw them into the house of the LORD, to the potter"; Psalm 22:16: "Dogs encompass me; a company of evildoers encircles me; they have pierced my hands and feet"; Psalm 69:21: "They gave me poison for food, and for my thirst they gave me sour wine to drink"; Isaiah 53:9: "They made his grave with the wicked and with a rich man in his death, although he had done no violence, and there was no deceit in his mouth"; Exodus 12:46: "It shall be eaten in one house; you shall not take any of the flesh outside the house, and you shall not break any of its bones"; Psalm 34:20: "He keeps all his bones; not one of them is broken"; and Psalm 22:18: "They divide my garments among them, and for my clothing they cast lots."

53. Kennedy, "Christ: The Fulfillment of Prophecy."

54. See Walter C. Kaiser, *Are the Old Testament Documents Reliable and Relevant?* (Downers Grove, IL: InterVarsity, 2001).

55. See Norman L. Geisler and William E. Nix, *A General Introduction to the Bible*, rev. ed. (Chicago: Moody, 1986).

56. See, for example, Mohd Elfie Nieshaem Juferi, "Paul of Tarsus: The False Apostle according to Islam," Bismika Allahuma, www.bismikaallahuma.org/archives/2005/paul-of-tarsus-the-false-apostle-according-to-islam/. In response, see David Wenham's books *Paul: Follower of Jesus or Founder of Christianity?* (Grand Rapids, MI: Eerdmans, 1995) and *Paul and Jesus: The True Story* (Grand Rapids, MI: Eerdmans, 2002).

57. See Romans 1:1–2: "Paul, a servant of Christ Jesus, called to be an apostle, set apart for the gospel of God, which he promised beforehand through his prophets in the holy Scriptures"; Romans 16:25–27: "Now to him who is able to strengthen you according to my gospel and the preaching of Jesus Christ, according to the revelation of the mystery that was kept secret for long ages but has now been disclosed and through the prophetic writings has been made known to all nations, according to the command of the eternal God, to bring about the obedience of faith—to the only wise God be glory forevermore through Jesus Christ! Amen"; Galatians 3:6–8: "Just as Abraham 'believed God, and it was counted to him as righteousness'? Know then that it is those of faith who are the sons of Abraham. And the Scripture, foreseeing that God would justify the Gentiles by faith, preached the gospel beforehand to Abraham, saying, 'In you shall all the nations be blessed.'"

58. See 2 Timothy 3:14–17: "As for you, continue in what you have learned and have firmly believed, knowing from whom you learned it and how from childhood you have been acquainted with the sacred writings, which are able to make you wise for salvation through faith in Christ Jesus. All Scripture is breathed out by God and profitable for teaching, for reproof, for correction, and for training in righteousness, that the man of God may be complete, equipped for every good work." The Old Testament prophets are acknowledged to have been inspired (1 Pet. 2:21; cf. 2 Sam. 23:2). Furthermore, both the Old and New Testaments contain divine declarations that God's Word will not pass away (Isa. 40:6–8; 1 Pet. 1:24–25). Jesus confirmed the truthfulness of the Old Testament in the Sermon on the Mount (Matt. 5–7, especially 5:17–18) and elsewhere (Luke 16:31; 24:27; John 10:35; 17:17). For more information and examples, see John W. Wenham, *Christ and the Bible* (Grand Rapids, MI: Baker, 1984).

59. Romans 3:21: "Now the righteousness of God has been manifested apart from the law, although the Law and the Prophets bear witness to it."

60. Even though some of his contemporaries charged Paul with being unlawful (Rom. 3:8; 6:1, 15), he denied their accusations: "Do we, then, nullify the law by this faith? Not at all! Rather, we uphold the law" (Rom. 3:31). He even viewed himself and his congregations as accountable to the Old Testament Scriptures, noting that they have a continuing validity for the church as the people of God: "Whatever was written in former days was written for our instruction, that through endurance and through the encouragement of the Scriptures we might have hope" (Rom. 15:4; also 4:23–24; 1 Cor. 10:1). Paul's dependence on the Old Testament is amply verified by the many explicit quotations he culled from the law, the writings, and the prophets (Rom. 3:10–18; 10:5–21; 15:8–12) as well as his innumerable allusions to the Old Testament. For more information, see Gerald F. Hawthorne and Ralph P. Martin, eds., *Dictionary of Paul and His Letters* (Downers Grove, IL: InterVarsity, 1993), 630–42; Ben Witherington, *Paul's Narrative Thought World: The Tapestry of Tragedy and Triumph* (Nashville: Westminster/John Knox, 1994); and the relevant discussions in Gregory K. Beale, ed., *Right Doctrine from the Wrong Texts? Essays on the Use of the Old Testament in the New* (Grand Rapids, MI: Baker, 1996).

61. Jonathan Morrow, *Welcome to College: A Christ-Follower's Guide for the Journey* (Grand Rapids, MI: Kregel, 2008), 83.

62. J. Ed Komoszewski, M. James Sawyer, and Daniel B. Wallace, *Reinventing Jesus: How Contemporary Skeptics Miss the Real Jesus and Mislead Popular Culture* (Grand Rapids, MI: Kregel, 2006), 82.

63. Darrell L. Bock and Daniel B. Wallace, *Dethroning Jesus: Exposing Popular Culture's Quest to Unseat the Biblical Christ* (Nashville: Thomas Nelson, 2007), 60.

64. Bock and Wallace, *Dethroning Jesus*, 60–72.

65. Daniel B. Wallace, "An Interview with Daniel B. Wallace on the New Testament Manuscripts," by Justin Taylor, The Gospel Coalition, March 21, 2012, thegospelcoalition.org/blogs/justintaylor/2012/03/21/an-interview-with-daniel-b-wallace-on-the -new-testament-manuscripts/.

66. Strikingly, the apostle Paul applied his strict criterion for biblical knowledge and truth to his own writings. In fact, he proclaimed that if his own future writings deviated from the inspired truth already received from God, they should be rejected. In his letter to the Galatians, Paul wrote, "I would have you know, brothers, that the gospel that was preached by me is not man's gospel. For I did not receive it from any man, nor was I taught it, but I received it through a revelation of Jesus Christ" (1:11–12). This is significant because Paul had just made this declaration: "Even if we or an angel from heaven should preach to you a gospel contrary to the one we preached to you, let him be accursed!" (v. 8).

67. This is summarized from Jonathan Morrow's article "How Do We Know the Bible Includes the Right Books?" in *The Apologetics Study Bible for Students*, ed. Sean McDowell (Nashville: B&H, 2010), 1230.

68. Andreas J. Köstenberger and Michael J. Kruger, *The Heresy of Orthodoxy: How Contemporary Culture's Fascination with Diversity Has Reshaped Our Understanding of Early Christianity* (Wheaton, IL: Crossway, 2010), 149–50.

69. See Marvin Meyer, *The Gnostic Gospels of Jesus: The Definitive Collection of Mystical Gospels and Secret Books about Jesus of Nazareth* (New York: HarperOne, 2005).

70. See, for example, Dan Graves, "Gnosticism," Christianity, www.christianity.com/church/church-history/timeline/1-300 /gnosticism-11629621.html.

71. The writings of many of the church fathers are still available in printed form if you would like to study their arguments in more detail. For example, see *Against Heresies* by St. Irenaeus of Lyons, Project Gutenberg, self.gutenberg.org/article /WHEBN0000015414/Irenaeus#Scripture.

72. For detailed information on how the books of the Bible were carefully selected, see F. F. Bruce, *The Canon of Scripture* (Downers Grove, IL: IVP Academic, 1996).

73. J. Norval Geldenhuys, "Authority and the Bible," in *Revelation and the Bible: Contemporary Evangelical Thought*, ed. Carl F. H. Henry (Grand Rapids, MI: Baker, 1958), 371–86.

74. Henry, *God, Revelation and Authority*, vol. 4, 93–94.

75. See Hebrews 11:17–19: "By faith Abraham, when he was tested, offered up Isaac, and he who had received the promises was in the act of offering up his only son, of whom it was said, 'Through Isaac shall your offspring be named.' He considered that God was able even to raise him from the dead, from which, figuratively speaking, he did receive him back."

76. 2 Kings 6:17: "Then Elisha prayed and said, 'O LORD, please open his eyes that he may see.' So the LORD opened the eyes of the young man, and he saw, and behold, the mountain was full of horses and chariots of fire all around Elisha."

77. Henry, *God, Revelation and Authority*, vol. 4, 115.

78. Philippians 4:8: "Finally, brothers, whatever is true, whatever is honorable, whatever is just, whatever is pure, whatever is lovely, whatever is commendable, if there is any excellence, if there is anything worthy of praise, think about these things."

79. 2 Peter 1:16–21: "We did not follow cleverly devised myths when we made known to you the power and coming of our Lord Jesus Christ, but we were eyewitnesses of his majesty. For when he received honor and glory from God the Father, and the voice was borne to him by the Majestic Glory, 'This is my beloved Son, with whom I am well pleased,' we ourselves heard this very voice borne from heaven, for we were with him on the holy mountain. And we have the prophetic word more fully confirmed, to which you will do well to pay attention as to a lamp shining in a dark place, until the day dawns and the morning star rises in your hearts, knowing this first of all, that no prophecy of Scripture comes from someone's own interpretation. For no prophecy was ever produced by the will of man, but men spoke from God as they were carried along by the Holy Spirit." See also Acts 22:9; John 12:27–30.

80. Luke 10:27: "He answered, 'You shall love the Lord your God with all your heart and with all your soul and with all your strength and with all your mind, and your neighbor as yourself.'"

81. Matthew 5:44: "I say to you, Love your enemies and pray for those who persecute you."

82. Flannery O'Connor, *The Habit of Being: Letters of Flannery O'Connor*, ed. Sally Fitzgerald (New York: Farrar, Straus and Giroux, 1979), 100.

83. On this, Carl F. H. Henry says, "Only on the basis of the scriptural witness … do we know that God is creator ex nihilo of heaven and earth and is lord of the whole universe; no view of origins or principle of universal applicability can be established empirically. Since its teaching centers in supraempirical realities, much of what the Bible teaches cannot be empirically demonstrated. To replace scriptural authority with some rival authority-principle abridges historic Christian commitments in respect to Scripture as the supreme rule of faith and practice" (*God, Revelation and Authority*, vol. 4, 43).

84. David Martyn Lloyd-Jones, *Authority* (Downers Grove, IL: InterVarsity, 1958), 40.

85. A good example, proposed by Alva J. McClain, is of God's revelation to Abram that his offspring would be as numerous

as the stars in the sky (Gen. 15:5). To us, because we know there are billions of stars, that claim would be a good example of hyperbole that communicates a vast number of descendants. But for Abram, in that day, the promise would have seemed lame. There are only about four thousand stars visible to the naked eye even on a level horizon on the clearest night. But later when the same promise was repeated, Abram was told that his descendants would be as the stars in the sky and "as the sand which is on the seashore" (Gen. 22:17). To Abram that would have seemed a much greater promise; to us a few hundred years after Galileo invented the telescope, we know the comparisons to be equivalent. God spoke (and that promise was recorded for us) better than any scientist of his day could have understood. See Alva J. McClain, *The Greatness of the Kingdom: An Inductive Study of the Kingdom of God* (Winona Lake, IN: BMH Books, 2001).

86. Romans 13:1–2: "Let every person be subject to the governing authorities. For there is no authority except from God, and those that exist have been instituted by God. Therefore whoever resists the authorities resists what God has appointed, and those who resist will incur judgment."

87. Luke 12:4–5: "I tell you, my friends, do not fear those who kill the body, and after that have nothing more that they can do. But I will warn you whom to fear: fear him who, after he has killed, has authority to cast into hell. Yes, I tell you, fear him!"

88. Romans 12:2: "Do not be conformed to this world"; Ephesians 4:23: "To be renewed in the spirit of your minds"; Colossians 3:2: "Set your minds on things that are above, not on things that are on earth"; Colossians 3:10: "Have put on the new self, which is being renewed in knowledge after the image of its creator."

89. Deuteronomy 6:4–8: "'Hear, O Israel: The LORD our God, the LORD is one. You shall love the LORD your God with all your heart and with all your soul and with all your might. And these words that I command you today shall be on your heart. You shall teach them diligently to your children, and shall talk of them when you sit in your house, and when you walk by the way, and when you lie down, and when you rise. You shall bind them as a sign on your hand, and they shall be as frontlets between your eyes.'"

90. Ephesians 4:15: "Speaking the truth in love, we are to grow up in every way into him who is the head, into Christ"; Ephesians 4:25: "Having put away falsehood, let each one of you speak the truth with his neighbor, for we are members one of another"; James 1:19: "Know this, my beloved brothers: let every person be quick to hear, slow to speak, slow to anger"; James 1:26: "If anyone thinks he is religious and does not bridle his tongue but deceives his heart, this person's religion is worthless."

91. John 17:17: "Sanctify them in the truth; your word is truth."

92. John 14:6: "Jesus said to him, 'I am the way, and the truth, and the life. No one comes to the Father except through me'"; Acts 4:12: "There is salvation in no one else, for there is no other name under heaven given among men by which we must be saved."

CHAPTER 4

4

WHAT THE BIBLE SAYS ABOUT GOD

1. GOD IS "BACK"

Despite the mockery from **New Atheism** and some comedians and despite having been exiled from public schools, strong faith in God is making a comeback. "Almost everywhere you look, from the suburbs of Dallas to the slums of Sao Paulo to the back streets of Bradford," say John

Micklethwait and Adrian Wooldridge, editors of *The Economist* magazine, "you can see religion returning to public life."[1]

New Atheism: a contemporary form of atheism that not only denies the existence of God but also contends that religion should be vehemently criticized, condemned, and opposed.

In fact, the religions and denominations requiring commitment to stringent doctrines are growing faster than the "easy" religions, even among the upwardly mobile, educated middle classes.[2] Even among younger people or political liberals, who typically proclaim higher levels of unbelief, the percentage of those who claim belief in God is around 85 percent.[3] It's enough to give New Atheists such as Richard Dawkins indigestion.

What people mean when they say they believe in God, though, requires some teasing out. As Baylor University sociologists Paul Froese and Christopher Bader have discovered, Americans usually fall into one of four God-belief categories based on whether they understand God to be engaged or disengaged in the world, and judgmental or nonjudgmental.

- 31 percent believe in an *authoritative* God who is both engaged and judgmental. These Americans see God as a caring father figure who can also become angry and act on his anger.[4]

- 24 percent believe in a *benevolent* God who is engaged and nonjudgmental. These Americans see God as "a kind of all-powerful and ever-present life coach."[5]

- 16 percent believe in a *critical* God who is disengaged and judgmental. Say Froese and Bader, "These believers think that God's displeasure will be felt in another life but that divine justice will not be meted out in this world."[6]

- 24 percent believe in a *distant* God who is disengaged and nonjudgmental. "They view God as a cosmic force that set the laws of nature in motion but does not really 'do' things in the world or hold clear opinions about our activities or world events."[7]

How people view God both affects and is affected by the way they live. Conservatives are more likely to believe in an authoritative God, whereas liberals are more likely to believe in a distant God.[8] Those who believe in an authoritative God are more likely to say that adultery, gay marriage, and abortion are always wrong, whereas those who believe in a distant God are more likely to say that such activities are not wrong at all.[9] People who believe that God is authoritative or benevolent are less likely to believe that science can solve human problems and less likely to believe that humans evolved from primates but also more likely to view science as revealing God's glory.[10]

How people view God is a reflection of how they view life. As Froese and Bader put it, "It is when a person talks about God, instead of herself, that she reveals the most."[11] We can truly say that everyone is, in a sense, a theologian. We all have thoughts about who God is, and those thoughts affect our lives.

WHAT THE BIBLE SAYS ABOUT GOD

What are these thoughts based on, though? If Scripture has authority, as we discussed in the previous chapter, then we need to see what Scripture reveals about who God is. In this chapter, we'll talk first about what it means that we are all theologians and whether there is even a point in trying to discover who an infinite God is. We'll then look at who God reveals himself to be, his attributes, and his nature as Father, Son, and Holy Spirit. This is a lot to study. I pray that rather than being overwhelmed by details and rationalistic thoughts about God, you'll be captivated by his awesomeness and how he cares for us personally.

2. WHAT IT MEANS TO BE A THEOLOGIAN

Although we are all theologians, we might be good ones or bad ones. Still, all of us, even atheists, think about God. We cannot *not* contemplate life's biggest questions. We are curious beings, hungry for answers, and we somehow know that these answers do not come merely from our physical circumstances. As the Preacher said, God "has put eternity into man's heart" (Eccles. 3:11).

We shouldn't make our goal, however, merely thinking accurately about God or avoiding disobedience. Instead, we should *love* him with all of our minds and hearts, as Jesus stated in Matthew 22:37.[12] Loving God, we will want to know his thoughts and values. We ought to think God's thoughts after him and turn our hearts toward what he says. The best theology is more than an academic discipline; it is a way of loving, knowing, and cherishing God.[13] Good theology is an act of worship, and of the very highest sort.

Good theology also reminds people of what is really true. Prominent Christian cleric Richard John Neuhaus is spot-on:

> It is the responsibility and the opportunity of Christians to communicate to the world what is aptly called "the world's own story." The world does not know its own story. The story of God's creating love; His preparing redemption for the world; His calling a chosen people and from this people raising up a Redeemer, the Messiah; His establishing an Apostolic community of faith, the Church, that would then reach out through all times and all places and all languages and cultures. This story bearing the promise of the *telos*—of the end—the destiny of the Cosmos itself and God's loving purposes for the world that He so loved that He gave His only begotten Son. This is the story of the world. It is the story of everybody in the world. Our job is to alert people to their own story and to help them understand that everything that goes on in this world, all the dimensions of human activity—if they are rightfully ordered, if they are rightfully understood—are sacred, for they are all endowed with the presence of the God of creating and redeeming love who continues to be disposed to His creation, of which He once said, "Behold it is very good." So also He invites a return to that goodness and a fulfillment of that goodness in Jesus Christ. We have to share God's love for the world. To have a Christian world view is to love the world.[14]

God's story—this incredibly good news—straightens what sin has bent, uncovers the treasure of meaning that often goes buried and forgotten, and assures us of love that we, fearing disappointment, dared not hope for.

God is really God, his goodness is really good, and his truth is really true.

But as we've already seen, people disagree about what God is like, and their beliefs about him affect everything. Preacher and author A. W. Tozer once said, "What comes into our minds when we think about God is the most important thing about us."[15] If God is who he claims to be in the Bible, the Bible's answers to life's biggest questions are worth paying attention to. A true picture of God will lead to real life and help us avoid the counterfeit gods vying for our affections.

What do people imagine when they think of God? Well, for 53 percent of people surveyed, God is not a person but a "cosmic force."[16] Obviously, people could mean by this that God has no human form. But we must be careful about what terms we employ. Cosmic forces cannot tell you what to do or judge you, but neither can they love or rescue you. They can't even really be a "they." A person who thinks God is a cosmic force will likely never grasp what it means to bear God's image. It may seem innocuous enough to be mistaken about who God is, but these mistakes can lead to crippling doubt. As English author Os Guinness states,

> Believers get into their heads such a wrong idea of God that it comes between them and God or between them and their trusting God. Since they do not recognize what they are doing, they blame God rather than their faulty picture, little realizing that God is not like that at all. Unable to see God as he is, they cannot trust him as they should, and doubt is the result.[17]

> **Properly understanding God can help us find answers to life's big questions.**

Properly understanding God can help us find answers to life's big questions. Humans wrestle with where we come from, the meaning of life, our purpose on earth, how we should live, and where we are going. If God "is there and he is not silent,"[18] as Francis Schaeffer put it, we might actually find trustworthy answers to these perplexing questions. But this can happen only if we discover and come to know the present, communicating creator of life and the good news he proclaims.

But can we actually *know* him?

3. Can Finite Human Beings Really Know an Infinite God?

Before we get too far ahead of ourselves, though, let's define what we mean when we use the word *God*. This is tricky because our ability to understand God is limited; surely, then, he is greater than our definitions. It is a paradox considered by a Benedictine monk and philosopher nearly a thousand years ago, Anselm of Canterbury. Anselm defined God as "that than which none greater can be conceived."[19] This **Perfect Being Theology** says we must think of God as "the greatest possible being, an individual exhibiting maximal perfection."[20] God is, by his very nature, everything it is better to be than not to be.

> *Perfect Being Theology:* a view of God formulated by Anselm of Canterbury that defines God as "the greatest possible being" and "that than which none greater can be conceived."

WHAT THE BIBLE SAYS ABOUT GOD

Believers often fall into the trap of thinking that because they don't know *everything* about God that therefore they cannot know *anything* about God. It isn't true. One commonly used thought exercise that I've conducted with students is to draw a circle representing everything that can be known. Then draw a circle inside the circle representing what you personally know. Everyone reaches the same conclusion. They draw a very big circle for everything that can be known and a very tiny circle representing what they personally know. As Jonathan Morrow phrases it,

> While we cannot know God *exhaustively*, we can know him *truly*. The finite human mind cannot fully comprehend the nature of an infinite God (even in heaven), but we can grow in our understanding and experience of God as he has *revealed* himself in Creation, Scripture, and through Jesus Christ.[21]

In order to grow in this kind of understanding, obviously, we must humbly acknowledge the truth: we simply don't have the *capacity* to understand God exhaustively. As this famous passage from Augustine reminds us,

> **We must humbly acknowledge the truth: we simply don't have the *capacity* to understand God exhaustively.**

> We are speaking of God. Is it any wonder if you do not comprehend? For if you comprehend, it is not God you comprehend. Let it be a pious confession of ignorance rather than a rash profession of knowledge. To attain some slight knowledge of God is a great blessing; to comprehend him, however, is totally impossible.[22]

Augustine is not saying that we cannot know anything about God; he's saying that what we actually know about him pales in comparison to what he actually is. This is similar to what the apostle Paul says in Romans 11:33: "Oh, the depth of the riches and wisdom and knowledge of God! How unsearchable are his judgments and how inscrutable his ways!"

Yet while we marvel at how far God is above our understanding, Scripture also assumes we can know God well enough to bring him delight:

> Thus says the LORD: "Let not the wise man boast in his wisdom, let not the mighty man boast in his might, let not the rich man boast in his riches, but let him who boasts boast in this, that he understands and knows me, that I am the LORD who practices steadfast love, justice, and righteousness in the earth. For in these things I delight," declares the LORD. (Jer. 9:23–24)

Not only can we know God to his satisfaction, but we can know him well enough to obey: "The secret things belong to the LORD our God, but the things that are revealed belong to us and to our children forever, that we may do all the words of this law" (Deut. 29:29).

We can be confident that we can know God truthfully only because he has chosen to reveal himself. Had God intended to remain hidden from us, we would be unable to know him at all. Instead, however, God wants to be known and, through *revelation*, enables us to know him.

God has chosen to reveal himself in how he created the world and by giving us the Scriptures. However, the fullest way we know God, according to Hebrews 1:1–2, is through Jesus Christ: "Long ago, at many times and in many ways, God spoke to our fathers by the prophets, but in these last days he has spoken to us by his Son, whom he appointed the heir of all things, through whom also he created the world."

> **God reveals himself both by what he does and who he is: he wants to be known.**

God reveals himself both by what he does and who he is: he wants to be known. With this in mind, let's search the Scriptures to understand more clearly some of God's nature and characteristics. Although an infinite God is ultimately beyond reason, our understanding of him can still be reasonable, and Scripture can show us how to understand him as he wants to be understood. We'll need to define our terms and shun sloppy thinking, but in the end we will be able to understand more of who God is—and worship him better—as a result.

4. Who God Reveals Himself to Be

In Scripture, God reveals three aspects of his nature that we'll now examine. God is self-existent, God is spirit, and God is personal.

1. God is self-existent. Theologians use the word **aseity** (from the Latin *a se*, "from oneself") to describe God's self-sufficiency. As philosopher William Lane Craig describes, "God

> *Aseity:* **from the Latin word meaning "from oneself"; God's self-existent and self-sufficient nature.**

doesn't just happen to exist, as if by accident. Rather God exists by a necessity of his own nature; it is impossible for him not to exist. Moreover, God does not depend upon any other being for his existence. God alone is self-existent, and everything else depends on Him."[23]

God is life, and the source of all life. God is a necessary being. Everything that exists does so only because he exists first. We humans *have* life. But God *is* life.

God's aseity also means he is completely free. As theologian John Feinberg puts it, "Absolute self-determination means that God's choices depend on his own desires and purposes alone and that he has the power to actualize those choices."[24]

We see evidence for these points throughout Scripture. Jesus said in John 5:26, "As the Father has life in himself, so he has granted the Son also to have life in himself." It's a clear statement of self-determination. The apostle Paul further affirms God's self-existence in his speech to a religious society in Athens: "The God who made the world and everything in it, being Lord of heaven and earth, does not live in temples made by man, nor is he served by human hands, as though he needed anything, since he himself gives to all mankind life and breath and everything" (Acts 17:24–25).

As a self-existent being, God alone has the power to cause everything else to exist and to sustain its existence. In his letter to the church at Colossae, Paul reiterates this point: "By him all things were created, in heaven and on earth, visible and invisible, whether thrones or dominions or rulers or authorities—all things were created through him and for him. And he is before all things, and in him all things hold together" (Col. 1:16–17).

God's existence, as a completely necessary, free, and self-sufficient being, makes sense of the origin of the universe because, in order to create, a creator must be outside of creation. It also makes sense of the universe's design. Design, after all, must have a designer. Further, God's self-existent nature grounds objective moral values, duties, human dignity, and purpose. Objective truths actually exist, and all people and cultures are bound to them at all times. God's self-existence also grounds the idea of consciousness. He is why there is something rather than nothing and why we *know* there is something rather than nothing.

> He is why there is something rather than nothing and why we *know* there is something rather than nothing.

In short, God is the ultimate provider of all things. He doesn't need us; we need him! Unless God invites or permits it, nothing can influence his sovereign choices. We cannot manipulate him.

2. God is spirit. God is pure spirit. He has no material nature and is not bound by space or time. He is ultimate reality. As an immaterial spirit, God is not composed of pieces or separable parts.[25]

The Bible affirms this. Jesus said in John 4:24, "God is spirit, and those who worship him must worship in spirit and truth." God is not "seeable" by us, according to the gospel of John: "No one has ever seen God; the only God, who is at the Father's side, he has made him known" (1:18). Because God is spirit, we are instructed not to make images of him (Exod. 20:4),[26] or we wind up worshipping our own impressions rather than God himself.

Some worldviews contend that only the physical universe exists (materialism). The Bible's teaching on God as spirit, though, describes ultimate reality as not merely physical. Reality is physical but also spiritual. To not worship God as spirit is to not worship him truly.

3. God is personal. God is a person, not a cosmic force. As theologian Millard J. Erickson phrases it, "God is personal. He is an individual being, with self-consciousness and will, capable of feeling, choosing, and having a reciprocal relationship with other personal and social beings."[27]

We do not really need to cite specific Scripture passages about the personhood of God because the entirety of the Bible is the story of God interacting personally. In Genesis chapter 1, God talked to the people he had created, instructing them on how to steward creation. In Genesis chapter 2, God told Adam how to steward the garden he had prepared. In Genesis 3, God spoke to the man and the woman about their sin. And so it goes. A simple word search for "the Lord said" in the English Standard Version of the Bible yields 247 results.

Scripture reveals God as personal to the point that people who think God is *disengaged* can maintain such a belief only by drawing from a source of revelation other than the Bible. Not only is God engaged but his engagement is good. He doesn't just show up for spankings. As Millard Erickson says,

> Because God is a person, the relationship we have with him has a dimension of warmth and understanding. God is not a machine or a computer that automatically supplies the needs of people. He is a knowing, loving, good Father.... He is not merely one of whom we hear, but one whom we meet and know. Accordingly, God is to be treated as a being, not an object or force. He is not something to be used or manipulated.[28]

God is a person to be known rather than a force to be used. As a person, he made humans in his image and gave them value and dignity. Because the very idea of personhood comes from God, the value and dignity he imparts cannot be changed by any other person or circumstance.

To review, God is self-existent, spirit, and personal. These three points emphasize God's *nature*. But as the writers of Scripture recorded God's words and observations about him, they attributed to him several characteristics. Let's take a look at ten of these.

5. THE ATTRIBUTES OF GOD

Incommunicable Attributes: qualities that belong to only God, such as being holy, eternal, omniscient, omnipotent, omnipresent, and unchanging.

Communicable Attributes: qualities that God and human beings share, such as wisdom, righteousness, love, mercy, and grace.

Scripture gives many identifiable attributes, or characteristics, of God. Some belong to only God (such as eternality) and are called **incommunicable attributes**. Attributes God shares with people (such as wisdom) are called **communicable attributes**.

Because of the fall, our human attributes are sometimes at odds with one another. For example, we might think it is unloving to confront a person who is behaving unjustly. God is not like this. God perfectly embodies all of his attributes at the same time, without conflict. For example, he perfectly loves while also being perfectly just.

Let's look at ten attributes of God along with scriptural evidence for each attribute. The first six of these are *incommunicable* attributes, true of God alone and not shared with his creation.

1. God is holy. To be **holy** means to be set apart. God is set apart from everything and everyone. No one is like him. He is absolutely pure. Professor Gordon Lewis says, "God is morally spotless in character and action, upright, pure, and untainted with evil desires, motives, thoughts, words, or acts. God is … the source and standard of what is right."[29] In his holiness, God is unique from all creation. As Millard Erickson phrases it, "God not only is personally free from any moral wickedness or evil. He is unable to tolerate the presence of evil. He is, as it were, allergic to sin and evil."[30]

Holy: to be set apart.

Scripture affirms the holiness of God. Exodus 15:11 says, "Who is like you, O LORD, among the gods? Who is like you, majestic in holiness, awesome in glorious deeds, doing wonders?" Revelation 4:8 says, "The four living creatures, each of them with six wings, are full of eyes all around and within, and day and night they never cease to say, 'Holy, holy, holy, is the Lord God Almighty, who was and is and is to come!'" Habakkuk says of God, in frustration at God's silence in the face of wickedness, "You who are of purer eyes than to see evil and cannot look at wrong, why do you idly look at traitors and are silent when the wicked swallows up the man more righteous than he?" (Hab. 1:13).

Habakkuk was a prophet whose book is a "call and response" with God. In it, the prophet asks questions of God and God replies. God, though perfectly capable of ending injustice, was not doing so to Habakkuk's satisfaction, yet Habakkuk knew that God was infinitely powerful, holy, and good. God could be trusted to use his power consistently with his perfect holiness and moral perfection. We might suffer under the power of evil, but Scripture tells us God will not tolerate evil forever. He cannot. He is holy.

2. God is eternal.[31] To say that God is **eternal** is to say that he has always existed. There never was a time when he was not, and there never will be a time when he will not be. He acts within time but is not contained within time. His ability to care for us and save us is never exhausted. Life with God (or apart from him) never ends because God himself will never end. God does not need to meet our time frame. He's not in a hurry.

> *Eternal:* always existing or existing outside of time; everlasting.

Psalm 90:2 says, "Before the mountains were brought forth, or ever you had formed the earth and the world, from everlasting to everlasting you are God." Deuteronomy 33:27 says, "The eternal God is your dwelling place, and underneath are the everlasting arms." Jude verses 24–25 give a benediction acknowledging God's eternal attributes: "Now to him who is able to keep you from stumbling and to present you blameless before the presence of his glory with great joy, to the only God, our Savior, through Jesus Christ our Lord, be glory, majesty, dominion, and authority, before all time and now and forever. Amen."

3. God is all-knowing. We use the word **omniscient** to describe God's unique and unbounded capacity for knowledge. He knows everything possible and actual. God possesses complete knowledge of the past, present, and future.[32] Knowing all truths and believing no falsehoods, he is perfect in knowledge. As Gordon Lewis puts it, "God's intellectual capabilities are unlimited, and God uses them fully and perfectly."[33]

> *Omniscient:* God's unique ability to know everything that can be known.

A passage we looked at earlier, Romans 11:33, affirms this: "Oh, the depth of the riches and wisdom and knowledge of God! How unsearchable are his judgments and how inscrutable his ways!" Isaiah 46:8–11 says,

> Remember this and stand firm,
> recall it to mind, you transgressors,
> remember the former things of old;
> for I am God, and there is no other;
> I am God, and there is none like me,
> declaring the end from the beginning
> and from ancient times things not yet done,
> saying, "My counsel shall stand,
> and I will accomplish all my purpose,"
> calling a bird of prey from the east,
> the man of my counsel from a far country.
> I have spoken, and I will bring it to pass;
> I have purposed, and I will do it.

Although humans cannot see the full scope of history and how our own lives fit into it, God has no such limitation. He sees everything in context, enabling him to do all he wants to do without mistake. Hebrews 4:13 says, "No creature is hidden from his sight, but all are naked and exposed to the eyes of him to whom we must give account." God is never caught off guard, surprised, or outflanked by evil. Says professor Erik Thoennes, "All God's thoughts and actions are perfectly informed by perfect knowledge, so he is perfectly trustworthy."[34]

Omnipotent: God's unique ability to do anything that can be done.

4. God is all-powerful. We use the word **omnipotent** to say that God is perfect in power. Being untamed and completely free, God possesses the power to do anything he desires. This does not mean, however, that God can do *anything*. God cannot do the logically impossible (such as make a squared circle or a married bachelor), nor can he act contrary to his nature (such as lie or act unjustly). These impossibilities are hardly limitations, however. As Millard Erickson explains,

> He can do only those things which are proper objects of his power. Thus, he cannot do the logically absurd or contradictory. He cannot make square circles or triangles with four corners. He cannot undo what happened in the past, although he may wipe out its effects or even the memory of it. He cannot act contrary to his nature—he cannot be cruel or unconcerned. He cannot fail to do what he has promised.[35]

Every once in a while you might hear the age-old village atheist question "If God is so powerful, can he make a rock so big he can't lift it?" It may sound like an irrefutable argument against God's omnipotence but only because it is based on a faulty assumption. You should reply, "God can make the biggest possible rock, and God can lift the biggest possible rock. I don't see the problem."

God can make the biggest possible rock, and God can lift the biggest possible rock.

In the end, though, God is not interested in our word games. What must be remembered, Thoennes says, is this: "God is able to do all his holy will."[36]

The Bible is full of passages about God's powerfulness. Jeremiah 32:17 says, "Ah, Lord GOD! It is you who has made the heavens and the earth by your great power and by your outstretched arm! Nothing is too hard for you." In Mark 10:27, Jesus said, "With man it is impossible, but not with God. For all things are possible with God." Isaiah 46:9–10, which we quoted earlier, ends with God saying, "My counsel shall stand, and I will accomplish all my purpose."

One problem with God's omnipotence is called the problem of evil: If God is powerful enough to stop evil but does not, isn't he then evil? Or, if God is willing to stop evil but *not* powerful enough to stop evil, how can we say he is all-powerful? We will devote an entire chapter to responding to this question later in this volume, but perhaps for now we might make a simple observation: every worldview must grapple with the problem of evil. The biblical answer is that we know in our hearts that evil is wrong because we have a sense of what is *right*; we know further that God is not captive to evil. As Thoennes states, "God's ultimate will

WHAT THE BIBLE SAYS ABOUT GOD

is never frustrated by evil, so there is peace and confidence in the face of suffering for those who trust God."[37]

5. God is everywhere present. We use the word **omnipresent** is to say that God is eternally present—in all places, at all times. There is nowhere that God is not. This is not to say God is identical to space; he transcends space. Nor does it mean God has no substance. God is everywhere present *in the sense* that wherever space and matter exist, he is at that place. He knows what is happening there (omniscience) and is causally active there (omnipotence).[38]

> *Omnipresent:* God's unique ability to be present in all places and at all times.

Once again, we can turn to Scripture to affirm the omnipresence of God. Jeremiah 23:23–24 says, "Am I a God at hand, declares the LORD, and not a God far away? Can a man hide himself in secret places so that I cannot see him? declares the LORD. Do I not fill heaven and earth? declares the LORD." Psalm 139:7–10 says,

> Where shall I go from your Spirit?
>   Or where shall I flee from your presence?
> If I ascend to heaven, you are there!
>   If I make my bed in Sheol, you are there!
>
> If I take the wings of the morning
>   and dwell in the uttermost parts of the sea,
> even there your hand shall lead me,
>   and your right hand shall hold me.

As Solomon dedicated the temple he had built, he prayed, "Will God indeed dwell on the earth? Behold, heaven and the highest heaven cannot contain you; how much less this house that I have built!" (1 Kings 8:27).

Knowledge of God's *everywhere-ness* comforts us greatly. A child of God is never out of reach of his providential care. The wicked are never safe because God knows of their wicked acts.

Some people get confused about this. How can God be simultaneously *with* us and *removed from* us? As Rick Cornish states, "God is independent from the universe and removed from us, called transcendence; yet He is active in the universe and accessible to us, called immanence."[39] Scripture affirms God as *both* **immanent** and **transcendent**. Isaiah 57:15 says, "Thus says the One who is high and lifted up, who inhabits eternity, whose name is Holy: 'I dwell in the high and holy place, and also with him who is of a contrite and lowly spirit, to revive the spirit of the lowly, and to revive the heart of the contrite.'"

> *Immanent:* an attribute of God that describes him as being both within and among his creation.

> *Transcendent:* an attribute of God that describes him as being both above and outside of his creation.

To say God is immanent and not transcendent is **pantheism** (i.e., the universe is God). To say God is transcendent and not immanent is **deism** (i.e., God set the universe in motion and is known by nature and reason but is not known personally). Recognizing God as both transcendent and immanent, based on Scripture, helps us understand God as great enough to create all things but humble enough to enter into his own creation.

Pantheism: the belief that everything in the universe is ultimately divine.

Of course, some Christians are "functional deists": they believe that God enters creation but act as though he does not. Charles H. Kraft puts it this way:

> Deists believe that God created the universe and set up unchangeable, universal laws that preclude him from getting directly involved in the running of the universe in any way.... Though we Evangelicals would contend that deism embodies an unacceptable, even heretical understanding of God's relation to the universe, I'm afraid we may have been infected.[40]

Deism: the belief that God exists and created the world but currently stands completely aloof from his creation; the belief that reason and nature sufficiently reveal the existence of God but that God has not revealed himself through any type of special revelation.

If God is everywhere present, as he's revealed in the Bible, he can be both Creator and Redeemer. In his nature as the infinite Creator, he exists within creation and is present with us in the person of Jesus (Acts 17:24–27).[41] He is the Alpha and the Omega—the beginning and the end (Rev. 22:13).[42] He is the very definition of reason, yet we are invited to reason with him (Isa. 1:18).[43] He is high and lifted up (Isa. 6:1),[44] yet he answers when we call out in distress (Jon. 2:1–2).[45]

6. God is unchanging. God's character is constant and unchangeable. He is the same yesterday, today, and forever. He cannot lie. Everything he says he will do, he does. Scripture says in Numbers 23:19, "God is not man, that he should lie, or a son of man, that he should change his mind. Has he said, and will he not do it? Or has he spoken, and will he not fulfill it?" Psalm 33:11 concurs: "The counsel of the LORD stands forever, the plans of his heart to all generations." God does not change, which is a source of protection for his people. Malachi 3:6 says, "I the LORD do not change; therefore you, O children of Jacob, are not consumed."

God confirms his unchanging character by binding himself to his promises. Hebrews 6:17 says, "When God desired to show more convincingly to the heirs of the promise the unchangeable character of his purpose, he guaranteed it with an oath." God's unchanging perfection is solid ground for assurance of salvation: God does not change his standards. What he expects of us remains the same. As author Bruce Milne says, "God's changelessness is expressed in his faithfulness and dependability in his relationships with his people."[46]

While we're on the subject of God's unchanging character, we need to point out the fact that there are passages in Scripture that seem to contradict the claim that God is unchanging. For example, Genesis 6:6[47] says that in view of the wickedness of people, God "regretted"

WHAT THE BIBLE SAYS ABOUT GOD

having made humans. In Exodus 32:14,[48] the Lord "relented" from his plan to destroy the children of Israel after an appeal by Moses. There are many more examples, and they all seem to be quite clear that God considered what he had done and changed his planned course. How can we say that God is "unchanging" in view of these passages?

The Bible includes a narrative of a prophet named Jonah that may help us make sense of this apparent contradiction. God sent Jonah to a city called Nineveh to preach to the people so they would repent of their sins and avoid destruction. Jonah tried to run away from God's plan and ended up in the belly of a big fish, where he regretted his rebellion and decided to go to Nineveh after all. This much of the narrative is familiar to most people. When Jonah finally did make it to Nineveh, the people listened to his message and repented. Jonah 3:10 says, "When God saw what they did, how they turned from their evil way, God relented of the disaster that he had said he would do to them, and he did not do it."

Ironically, Jonah became quite angry about God's act of mercy. He assumed God was unchanging in the sense that he would never reverse anything he had set in motion. Jonah seemed to anticipate Nineveh's destruction with some delight, perhaps because it would allow him to say, "I told you so." But then God reversed his planned destruction, and Jonah felt like a fool.

So what did Jonah fail to understand about God? As we have seen, God is all-knowing. Therefore, he knows how things occurred in the past, how they occur now, and how they will occur in the future. He is also all-powerful, which means he is able to change how things will turn out. Jonah felt bitter because he failed to accept that God would not change according to Jonah's whims. He told God, in a whiny spirit, "I knew that you are a gracious God and merciful, slow to anger and abounding in steadfast love, and relenting from disaster" (4:2).

From Jonah's perspective, God had apparently changed his mind. But as theologian John Frame has pointed out, this so-called change is actually an indication of the deeper unchanging nature of God's character: his love. He always has loved and always will love. To act out of love is not a change of his character but an affirmation of it.

To understand this, we should return to God's transcendence and immanence. As a transcendent being, God is outside of time. But as a God who is immanent, he also acts in time so we can understand. Frame puts it this way:

> Within time, he sees time as we do, the past as past, the future as future. He responds appropriately to each moment, each day, as it comes: with rejoicing or grief. When his rejoicing turns to grief, or vice versa, we can say as the biblical writers do that he changes. But these changes are not changes to his eternal plan. Rather they represent his changing relationships to creatures, as he executes his eternal plan through history.[49]

So God does not change his mind or his character, and because of this consistency, he changes his actions as a character-driven act of mercy, love, justice, or any of the other aspects of his character.

All right. So we've taken a brief glimpse at six incommunicable attributes of God, attributes that are true of God alone. There are also four *communicable attributes*, exemplified by God perfectly and infinitely and yet also available for humans to exhibit, however imperfectly. Let's take a look at these.

7. God is wise. To say God is wise is to say he knows all the implications of his actual and potential actions, bringing about no unintended consequences. The wisdom of God means, according to Millard Erickson,

> when God acts, he takes all of the facts and correct values into consideration. Knowing all things, God knows what is good…. God has access to all information. So his judgments are made wisely. He never has to revise his estimation of something because of additional information. He sees all things in their proper perspective; thus he does not give anything a higher or lower value than what it ought to have. One can therefore pray confidently, knowing that God will not grant something that is not good.[50]

Our perspective is always limited. Like a child who thinks he *needs* a new toy or more candy, we often think we know what we need to make life work. But God knows better. He knows when we don't *want* what we *think* we want, or don't *need* what we *think* we need. He is wisdom itself. We can be wise but are often foolish. God is never foolish.

> [God] knows when we don't *want* what we *think* we want, or don't *need* what we *think* we need.

Scripture affirms that God is wisdom more than two hundred times. "Oh, the depth of the riches and wisdom and knowledge of God! How unsearchable are his judgments and how inscrutable his ways!" says Romans 11:33. Psalm 104:24 says, "O LORD, how manifold are your works! In wisdom have you made them all; the earth is of your creatures."

As Gordon Lewis puts it, "History is the product of God's eternally wise planning, creative purpose, providential perseverance, and common grace. God fills space and time with his presence, sustains it, and gives it purpose and value."[51] People are seen to be wise when God's wisdom is in them and to be fools when knowledge of him is absent. We ought to pursue wisdom all our lives, and its ultimate source is God.

8. God is righteous. God's righteousness, according to Millard Erickson, means that "his actions are in accord with the law which he himself has established."[52] God is always right, and his decisions are always just. God's justice, to Erickson, is God's "official righteousness, his requirement that other moral agents adhere to the standards as well. God is, in other words, like a judge who as a private individual adheres to the law of society, and in his official capacity administers that same law, applying it to others."[53]

Deuteronomy 32:4 says, "The Rock, his work is perfect, for all his ways are justice. A God of faithfulness and without iniquity, just and upright is he." Psalm 89:14 affirms, "Righteousness and justice are the foundation of your throne; steadfast love and faithfulness go before you." Many people think God's judgment is a cause for terror, but Psalm 98:8–9 says that joy should be our response instead: "Let the hills sing for joy together before the LORD, for he comes to judge the earth. He will judge the world with righteousness, and the peoples with equity."

God's righteousness and justice express his holiness and moral purity. This is good news in a corrupt world where authorities too often act unjustly. God will always do right. He can't be bribed and he won't lie. He is in the business of righting wrongs.

9. God is loving. God is Trinity, or more accurately, Tri-unity. Three in one. We'll talk more about God as Trinity soon, but a key attribute of God that flows out of this peculiar but profound teaching is *love*. We see God's relationship within his own being as Father, Son, and Holy Spirit, and this relationship is expressed through love. Gordon Lewis defines love in this respect as "a settled purpose of will involving the whole person in seeking the well-being of others."[54] God, whose perfect expression of self-giving love is not selfish, doesn't just put up with us; he really *loves* us. His love seeks our highest good, drives out fear, and does not change based on how good we are.

Erik Thoennes says, "God freely and eternally gives of himself. The ultimate historical demonstration of God's love is seen in the cross of Christ."[55] Ephesians 2:4–5 says, "God, being rich in mercy, because of the great love with which he loved us, even when we were dead in our trespasses, made us alive together with Christ—by grace you have been saved." Before suffering on the cross, Jesus prayed for his disciples to experience oneness "so that the world may know that you sent me and loved them even as you loved me" (John 17:23).

> The Bible describes love as so central to God's character that to misunderstand it is to *not even know God.*

Some people grow weary of "Jesus loves me" and "Oh, how he loves me" kinds of songs. Perhaps they see talk of love as a touchy-feely, insubstantial part of Christian theology. But the Bible describes love as so central to God's character that to misunderstand it is to *not even know God.* The apostle John says this quite clearly:

> Anyone who does not love does not know God, because God is love. In this the love of God was made manifest among us, that God sent his only Son into the world, so that we might live through him. In this is love, not that we have loved God but that he loved us and sent his Son to be the propitiation for our sins. (1 John 4:8–10)

The centrality of God's love is not just a New Testament understanding of God. Deuteronomy 33:12 says, "The beloved of the LORD dwells in safety. The High God surrounds him all day long, and dwells between his shoulders." Even Jeremiah the prophet, who had many strong things to say about God's judgment, affirmed, "The LORD appeared to him from far away. I have loved you with an everlasting love; therefore I have continued my faithfulness to you" (Jer. 31:3).

Keep this firmly in mind: God does not love us because we are lovable. If we were cuddly and innocent, we might be excused for thinking this way, but we're not. We know in our hearts we are self-serving, double-dealing, mass-manipulating, pity-party-throwing whiners. There's little in us for an infinitely wise, all-knowing, and all-powerful God to love. He loves us anyway *because of who he is.*

It is God's nature to love. And here's some stunning news: because of the power of the Holy Spirit, we can love this way too. In *Harper's Bible Dictionary*, we read,

> *Agape:* from the Greek word *agapé* for "selfless love."

> **Agape** (ah-gah´pay), the principal Greek word used for 'love' in the NT. Of the three words for love in the

Hellenistic world, it was the least common. The other two words were **eros**, which meant sexual love, and **philos**, which meant friendship, although their meanings could vary according to the context in which they appeared. Agape, because it was used so seldom and was so unspecific in meaning, could be used in the NT to designate the unmerited love God shows to humankind in sending his son as suffering redeemer. When used of human love, it means selfless and self-giving love.[56]

Eros: the Greek word for "sexual love."

Philos: the Greek word for "brotherly, familial love."

Romans 5:5 says that God's love (agape) has been "poured into our hearts through the Holy Spirit who has been given to us." It is this kind of love of which the Paul speaks in his famous passage on love:

> Love [agape] is patient and kind; love [agape] does not envy or boast; it is not arrogant or rude. It does not insist on its own way; it is not irritable or resentful; it does not rejoice at wrongdoing, but rejoices with the truth. Love [agape] bears all things, believes all things, hopes all things, endures all things. (1 Cor. 13:4–7)

Whether in friendship, in family relationship, or in a romantic sense, we should pray for the Holy Spirit to pour love into our hearts, enabling us to love truly, as God loves, rather than just through fuzzy sentimentality.

Mercy: not receiving what one deserves.

Grace: receiving what one does not deserve.

10. God is merciful and gracious. Mercy and **grace** are two sides of a coin. In his mercy, God *doesn't* give us what we *do* deserve. In his grace, God *does* give us what we *don't* deserve. Millard Erickson says, "God's mercy is his tenderhearted, loving compassion for his people. It is his tenderness of heart toward the needy. If grace contemplates humans as sinful, guilty, and condemned, mercy sees them as miserable and needy."[57]

Just as God loves because it is his character to do so, God also dispenses grace not based on our worthiness but because grace is *who he is*. Erickson says,

> Grace is another attribute which is part of the manifold of God's love. By this we mean that God deals with his people not on the basis of their merit or worthiness, what they deserve, but simply according to their need; in other words, he deals with them on the basis of his goodness and generosity.[58]

Grace and mercy are enduring characteristics of God. Some look at the differences between the Old and the New Testaments to conclude that God must have changed at some point, from being judgmental to being gracious. Scripture itself refutes this, however. The Old Testament passage Psalm 103:8 says, "The Lord is merciful and gracious, slow to anger and abounding in steadfast love." Nehemiah, the leader who rescued Jerusalem, said in his leading of corporate praise at God's provision,

WHAT THE BIBLE SAYS ABOUT GOD

They refused to obey and were not mindful of the wonders that you performed among them, but they stiffened their neck and appointed a leader to return to their slavery in Egypt. But you are a God ready to forgive, gracious and merciful, slow to anger and abounding in steadfast love, and did not forsake them. (Neh. 9:17)

As Nehemiah recognized, God's character, not people's goodness, was the basis of his grace and mercy. Titus 3:5 says, "He saved us, not because of works done by us in righteousness, but according to his own mercy, by the washing of regeneration and renewal of the Holy Spirit." In case we somehow missed the point, Ephesians 2:8–9 emphasizes, "By grace you have been saved through faith. And this is not your own doing; it is the gift of God, not a result of works, so that no one may boast."

The common thread of God's grace and mercy runs through all of human history. God's justice demands atonement for sin and his mercy provides a savior to take the penalty, making way for our salvation. Consider all of God's attributes together and you get a picture of him as consistent, trustworthy, good, generous, and loving though we deserve none of it.

For most Christians, everything we've talked about so far makes sense. But one doctrine presented in Scripture has confused people for centuries and still confuses people today: *God as Trinity*. For some, it is a barrier to accepting God's mercy and grace. A close examination, though, reveals how the Trinity affirms and makes sense of every other aspect of God's nature and character.

6. God Is Trinity

The **doctrine of the Trinity** teaches that God in his being is Trinity or, as some put it, Tri-unity. He is three in one: Father, Son, and Holy Spirit. In the Trinity, as seminary professor Scott Horrell phrases it, "One divine Being eternally exists as three distinct centers of consciousness, wholly equal in nature, genuinely personal in relationships, and each mutually indwelling the other."[59]

Say what?

> *Doctrine of the Trinity:* the orthodox Christian belief that God is one being in three persons: Father, Son, and Holy Spirit.

The doctrine of the Trinity is perhaps the most confusing aspect of God's nature. How can three persons have one **essence**? It seems unreasonable. And the word *Trinity* isn't even in the Bible. Can we say that the Bible even teaches it?

> *Essence:* defining attributes that give an entity its fundamental identity.

On the other hand, if the Trinity is biblical, failing to uphold it will leave us with an inaccurate view of God. This does not mean that we'll be able to make perfect sense of it or that God is simple to understand.

Let's dig in and see if we can grasp at least the essential nature of what it means to say that God is Trinity. Erik Thoennes states it this way:

The biblical teaching on the Trinity is summarized with four essential affirmations: (1) There is one—and only one—true and living God, (2) This one God eternally exists in three persons—God the Father, God the Son, and God the Holy Spirit, (3) These three persons are completely equal in attributes, each having the same divine nature, and (4) While each person is fully and completely God, the persons are not identical.[60]

Tritheism: the belief that the Trinity is composed of three separate and distinct Gods.

Heresy: any belief that is contrary to orthodox Christian doctrine.

Modalism (aka Sabellianism): the belief that the Trinity is composed of one God who has presented himself in different modes, or forms (the Father in the Old Testament, the Son in the New Testament, and the Holy Spirit today) throughout time.

The Trinity is *not* claiming there is *one* God *and three* Gods; the Trinity teaches that there is one *God* who exists as three distinct *persons* (one *What* and three *Whos*). It's hard to illustrate this by way of analogy. Some people say the Trinity is like an egg with a shell, a white, and a yolk, all together. But this is incorrect. Each part of an egg is a separate and distinct part. To say the Trinity is like an egg is to flirt with **tritheism**: three Gods. Others say the Trinity is like the three states of water: liquid, solid, and gas. But water is still water. Saying the Trinity is like water gets close to a **heresy** called **modalism**, which denies the "three-ness" of the Trinity.

Here's what we can know from examining Scripture:

God is one essence. Deuteronomy 6:4 says, "Hear, O Israel: The LORD our God, the LORD is one." Isaiah 45:5 says, "I am the LORD, and there is no other, besides me there is no God; I equip you, though you do not know me." Ephesians 4:4–6 says, "There is one body and one Spirit—just as you were called to the one hope that belongs to your call—one Lord, one faith, one baptism, one God and Father of all, who is over all and through all and in all."

The Father is God. First Corinthians 8:6 says that "for us there is one God, the Father, from whom are all things and for whom we exist." John 6:27 says, "Do not work for the food that perishes, but for the food that endures to eternal life, which the Son of Man will give to you. For on him God the Father has set his seal." Second Peter 1:17 says, "He received honor and glory from God the Father."

Jesus is God. Titus 2:13 talks about "waiting for our blessed hope, the appearing of the glory of our great God and Savior Jesus Christ." Hebrews 1:3 says, "He is the radiance of the glory of God and the exact imprint of his nature, and he upholds the universe by the word of his power." John 1:1 says, in introducing Jesus, "In the beginning was the Word, and the Word was with God, and the Word was God." Jesus manifests many of the incommunicable attributes of God such as eternality (John 17:5),[61] omniscience (Matt. 9:4),[62] and omnipotence and omnipresence (28:18–20).[63] He is God over all (Rom. 9:5).[64]

The Holy Spirit is God. The book of Acts recounts a conversation between the apostle Peter and Ananias, the man who lied about his offering to the Lord. Peter says, "Ananias, why has Satan filled your heart to lie to the Holy Spirit?... You have not lied to man but to God"

WHAT THE BIBLE SAYS ABOUT GOD

(Acts 5:3–4). First Corinthians 3:16 says, "Do you not know that you are God's temple and that God's Spirit dwells in you?" First Corinthians 6:11 says, "You were washed, you were sanctified, you were justified in the name of the Lord Jesus Christ and by the Spirit of our God." Scripture also shows the Holy Spirit manifesting several attributes of God: omnipresence (Ps. 139:7),[65] omniscience (1 Cor. 2:10–11),[66] and omnipotence (Job 33:4).[67]

The word *Trinity* is used by theologians to describe this "three and yet one" nature of God. The word itself is not used in Scripture. It was first used by a third-century theologian named Tertullian. Still, there are many passages in which all three persons of the Trinity are mentioned together:

> The grace of the *Lord Jesus Christ* and the love of *God* and the fellowship of the *Holy Spirit* be with you all. (2 Cor. 13:14)

> Go therefore and make disciples of all nations, baptizing them in the name of the *Father* and of the *Son* and of the *Holy Spirit*, teaching them to observe all that I have commanded you. And behold, I am with you always, to the end of the age. (Matt. 28:19–20)

> Peter, an apostle of Jesus Christ … according to the foreknowledge of *God the Father*, in the sanctification of the *Spirit*, for obedience to *Jesus Christ* and for sprinkling with his blood: May grace and peace be multiplied to you. (1 Pet.1:1–2)

> How much more will the blood of *Christ*, who through the eternal *Spirit* offered himself without blemish to *God*, purify our conscience from dead works to serve the living God. (Heb. 9:14)

One of the clearest accounts of all three persons in the Trinity being present together is the baptism of Jesus. Matthew 3:16–17 describes the event this way: "When Jesus was baptized, immediately he went up from the water, and behold, the heavens were opened to him, and he saw the Spirit of God descending like a dove and coming to rest on him; and behold, a voice from heaven said, 'This is my beloved Son, with whom I am well pleased.'" In this passage, God the Son is in the water as God the Father speaks and God the Spirit descends; in this one scene we see the distinct persons of the Trinity, as well as their unity of purpose. The Father blesses the work of the Son even as the Son obeys the Father and while the Spirit endorses both the will of the Father and the obedience of the Son. It is an amazing display of unifying love.

Far from being an esoteric doctrine that only pointy-headed theologians care about, the doctrine of God as Trinity affects everything. God is both eternally personal and in relationship. Thus, because of the relationship of the godhead, we understand what it means to be persons in relationship. As pastor Tim Keller puts it, "God did not create us to *get* the cosmic, infinite joy of mutual love and glorification, but to *share* it."[68]

Further, the Trinity enables us to know God through Christ. *Atonement* becomes possible: the blood of Christ was offered through the Spirit so we can serve God. *Love* becomes possible: the relationship among the Father, Son, and Holy Spirit shows us what our relationships in the body of Christ should be like (Eph. 4:4–7).[69] *Unity* becomes possible: we understand what harmony in relationships looks like because of the Trinity. No wonder Erik Thoennes says that "biblical Christianity stands or falls with the doctrine of the Trinity."[70]

The doctrine of the Trinity clearly distinguishes Christian theism from other theistic views, such as Islam. As Muslims see it, the idea that God eternally exists as three persons in one essence is polytheism, the belief in more than one God, and it's blasphemy.

So how do Muslims understand the Trinity? First, they see Jesus as a prophet but not as God.[71] Second, Muslims take Jesus's prophecy of the coming of "another counselor" to be a prophecy about the coming of Muhammad, not the coming of the Holy Spirit. Muslim theologian A. Yusuf Ali makes the case in a footnote to surah 3:81 in the Quran, using the word *Comforter* from an older Bible translation:

> You (People of the Book) are bound by your own oaths, sworn solemnly in the presence of your own Prophets. In the Old Testament as it now exists, Muhammad is foretold in Deut. xviii. 18; and the rise of the Arab nation in Isaiah, xlii. 11, for Kedar was a son of Ismail and the name is used for the Arab nation: in the New Testament as it now exists, Muhammad is foretold in the Gospel of St. John, xiv. 16, xv. 26, and xvi.7: the future Comforter cannot be the Holy Spirit as understood by Christians, because the Holy Spirit already was present helping and guiding Jesus. The Greek word translated "Comforter" is "Paracletos", which is an easy corruption from "Periclytos", which is almost a literal translation of "Muhammad" or "Ahmad."[72]

But absolutely no evidence supports the claim of *parakletos* being a corruption of *periclytos*. Of the more than five thousand manuscripts now available, not one witnesses to *periclytos*.[73] Ali's charge of textual corruption in this example is without historical or textual support.

Additionally, just a few verses after John 14:16, Jesus clearly identifies the counselor to whom he refers as the Holy Spirit: "The Counselor, *the Holy Spirit*, whom the Father will send in my name, will teach you all things and will remind you of everything I have said to you" (John 14:26 NIV). Muslims claim that later Christians made up this statement, but such an accusation requires at least *some* evidence. There is none.

7. CONCLUSION

Our lengthy discussion of God's nature and character in this chapter can be summarized in this statement from Gordon Lewis:

> God is an invisible, personal, and living Spirit, distinguished from all other spirits by several kinds of attributes: metaphysically, God is self-existent, eternal, and unchanging; intellectually, God is omniscient, faithful, and wise; ethically, God is just, merciful, and loving; emotionally, God detests evil, is longsuffering, and is compassionate; existentially, God is free, authentic, and omnipotent; relationally, God is transcendent in being, immanent universally in providential activity, and immanent with his people in redemptive activity.[74]

These attributes of God are unified in his nature. God doesn't *become* these things by doing them, nor does any aspect of his character take second place to any other aspect.

As humans, we have a hard time seeing how we can be both just and merciful at the same time. God does not evidence this conflict. The Bible reveals him to be both perfectly just and perfectly merciful. We see this in the person of Christ. Judaism denies Jesus Christ as the Messiah and the incarnation of God: God may care about us, but he has not yet entered into our suffering to redeem us. The same is true of Muslim theology. As Timothy George observes, "In the Quran, God's love is conditional and accidental. Love is something God *does*, not that which God *is*…. In the Christian faith, God's love is neither conditional nor accidental."[75] Contrast surah 19:96 of the Quran: "As to those who believe and work righteousness, Allah will pay them (in full) their reward; but Allah loveth not those who do wrong"[76] with Romans 5:8 "God demonstrates his own love for us in this: While we were still sinners, Christ died for us" (NIV).

The only proper response to the scriptural understanding of God is worship. We bow down in humble awe and reverence to the perfect, utterly trustworthy, only wise, self-existent, personal, completely unselfish, great, good God: Father, Son, and Holy Spirit. Amen.

> The only proper response to the scriptural understanding of God is worship.

ENDNOTES

1. John Micklethwait and Adrian Wooldridge, *God Is Back: How the Global Revival of Faith is Changing the World* (New York: Penguin, 2009), 12.

2. Micklethwait and Wooldridge, *God Is Back*, 18.

3. Frank Newport, "More than 9 in 10 Americans Continue to Believe in God," Gallup, June 3, 2011, www.gallup.com/poll/147887/americans-continue-believe-god.aspx.

4. Paul Froese and Christopher Bader, *America's Four Gods: What We Say about God—and What That Says about Us* (New York: Oxford, 2010), 27–29.

5. Froese and Bader, *America's Four Gods*, 31.

6. Froese and Bader, *America's Four Gods*, 32.

7. Froese and Bader, *America's Four Gods*, 33–34. It should be noted that *authoritative* and *judgmental* are loaded terms in today's world. God certainly does have authority in his universe, but his love and authority work in concert, not in opposition. The Bible proclaims God to be a completely balanced being, exercising grace, mercy, and loving kindness alongside authority and judgment, without contradiction. God does judge humans but does so as a just and all-knowing deity who has a right to judge and does so with understanding and mercy.

8. Froese and Bader, *America's Four Gods*, 60.

9. Froese and Bader, *America's Four Gods*, 66.

10. Froese and Bader, *America's Four Gods*, 90–91, 104.

11. Quoted in Froese and Bader, *America's Four Gods*, 10.

12. Matthew 22:37: "He said to him, 'You shall love the Lord your God with all your heart and with all your soul and with all your mind.'"

13. See David K. Clark, *To Know and Love God: Method for Theology*, Foundations of Evangelical Theology Series, ed. John S. Feinberg (Wheaton, IL: Crossway, 2003).

14. Richard John Neuhaus, "Telling the World Its Own Story," The Wilberforce Forum, July 2001, www.colsoncenter.org/search-library/search?view=searchdetail&id=21199.

15. A. W. Tozer, *The Knowledge of the Holy: The Attributes of God and Their Meaning in the Christian Life* (New York: HarperSanFrancisco, 1992), 1.

16. Froese and Bader, *America's Four Gods*, 5.

17. Os Guinness, *God in the Dark: The Assurance of Faith beyond a Shadow of Doubt* (Wheaton, IL: Crossway, 1996), 58–59.

18. Francis A. Schaeffer, *He Is There and He Is Not Silent* (Carol Stream, IL: Tyndale, 1972), chap. 1.

19. Quoted in Thomas V. Morris, *Our Idea of God: An Introduction to Philosophical Theology* (Downers Grove, IL:

InterVarsity, 1991), 35.

20. Anselm, quoted in Morris, *Our Idea of God*, 35.

21. Jonathan Morrow, "Can We Truly Know an Infinite God?," *Think Christianly* (blog), December 29, 2012, www .thinkchristianly.org/can-we-truly-know-an-infinite-god/.

22. Augustine, *Lectures on the Gospel of John*, tract XXXIV. A Select Library of Nicene and Post-Nicene Fathers of the Christian Church (1), VII, 217–21. As quoted in Herman Bavinck, *Reformed Dogmatics: Abridged in One Volume*, ed. John Bolt (Grand Rapids, MI: Baker, 2011), 154.

23. William Lane Craig, *God Is Self-Sufficient*, Dr. Craig's What Is God Like?, no. 4 (La Mirada, CA: Biola University, 2012).

24. John S. Feinberg, *No One Like Him: The Doctrine of God*, Foundations of Evangelical Theology Series, ed. John S. Feinberg (Wheaton, IL: Crossway, 2001), 240.

25. There is a significant controversy among evangelical theologians today over the doctrine of the simplicity of God. It's a complicated issue, but by the simplicity of God, theologians usually mean that all of God's attributes/properties are numerically identical with each other and his existence. The philosophical problems for metaphysical simplicity are significant (that God's omniscience is not different from his love or that God cannot do or know any different than he knows or does). Leading Christian philosophers such as Alvin Plantinga and William Lane Craig have critiqued this view along with evangelical theologian John Feinberg: "These philosophical problems plus the biblical considerations raised earlier lead me to conclude that simplicity is not one of the divine attributes. This doesn't mean that God has physical parts, but that the implications of the doctrine of metaphysical simplicity are too problematic to maintain the doctrine." *No One Like Him*, 325–37. See also Jay Wesley Richards, *The Untamed God: A Philosophical Exploration of Divine Perfection, Immutability, and Simplicity* (Downers Grove, IL: InterVarsity, 2003). On the other side, see Norman Geisler and H. Wayne House, *The Battle for God: Responding to the Challenge of Neotheism* (Grand Rapids, MI: Kregel, 2001). A "third way" might be to talk of the unity of God instead, focusing on the way in which none of God's attributes is in conflict with another.

26. Exodus 20:4: "You shall not make for yourself a carved image, or any likeness of anything that is in heaven above, or that is in the earth beneath, or that is in the water under the earth."

27. Millard J. Erickson, *Introducing Christian Doctrine*, 2nd ed. (Grand Rapids, MI: Baker Academic, 2001), 83.

28. Erickson, *Introducing Christian Doctrine, 83*.

29. Gordon R. Lewis, "Attributes of God," in *Evangelical Dictionary of Theology*, ed. Walter A. Elwell (Grand Rapids, MI: Baker Academic, 2001), 496.

30. Erickson, *Introducing Christian Doctrine*, 89.

31. The Bible unanimously teaches that God is everlasting but is agnostic as to whether God exists in time or timelessly. For a great discussion of this, see William Lane Craig, *Time and Eternity: Exploring God's Relationship to Time* (Wheaton, IL: Crossway, 2001). This is a coherence/conceptual question about what the nature of time is and what is necessary for a living God who relates personally to his people entails (for example, prayer, incarnation), not an orthodoxy question.

32. In recent years, some theologians and preachers such as John Sanders, Greg Boyd, and Winkie Pratney have advocated something called Open Theism. Open Theists think it is impossible for God to know future events because such events have not yet occurred. Open Theists maintain that God knows everything logically possible to know but think the future isn't logically possible to know. One motivation for Open Theism is that saying God does not know the future makes the problem of evil less painful: God is doing the best he can in light of not knowing what choices we will make and what will result from those choices. But this diminishes God and makes the problem worse; not only is God now without knowledge, but he is also powerless against bad things happening. (Later in this volume, we'll examine a very different argument about why God allows evil and suffering.) Many passages of Scripture indicate that God knows the future (Isa. 41:21–23; 42:9; 43:9–12; 44:7; 48:3–7). These verses, however, indicate that God can know the future. If we understand the verses correctly, then we must conclude that Open Theism is inconsistent with biblical teaching. Although it is beyond the scope of this chapter, for a biblical defense of God's foreknowledge in light of the challenge of Open Theism, see Bruce A. Ware, *God's Lesser Glory: The Diminished God of Open Theism* (Wheaton, IL: Crossway, 2000). For a philosophical treatment of the relevant issues, see William Lane Craig, *The Only Wise God: The Compatibility of Divine Foreknowledge and Human Freedom* (Eugene, OR: Wipf and Stock, 2000). A shorter, simpler treatment may be found in William Lane Craig, *What Does God Know? Reconciling Divine Foreknowledge and Human Freedom* (Norcross, GA: RZIM, 2002).

33. Lewis, "Attributes of God," 494.

34. Erik Thoennes, *Life's Biggest Questions: What the Bible Says about the Things That Matter Most* (Wheaton, IL: Crossway, 2011), 66.

35. Erickson, *Introducing Christian Doctrine*, 86.

36. Thoennes, *Life's Biggest Questions*, 65.

37. Thoennes, *Life's Biggest Questions*, 65.

38. J. P. Moreland and William Lane Craig, *Philosophical Foundations for a Christian Worldview* (Downers Grove, IL: InterVarsity, 2003), 515. See also Craig, *God Is Self-Sufficient*.

39. Rick Cornish, *Five Minute Theologian: Maximum Truth in Minimum Time* (Colorado Springs, CO: NavPress, 2004), 99.

40. Charles H. Kraft, *Christianity with Power: Your Worldview and Your Experience of the Supernatural* (Eugene, OR: Wipf

and Stock, 1989), 28.

41. Acts 17:24–27: "The God who made the world and everything in it, being Lord of heaven and earth, does not live in temples made by man, nor is he served by human hands, as though he needed anything, since he himself gives to all mankind life and breath and everything. And he made from one man every nation of mankind to live on all the face of the earth, having determined allotted periods and the boundaries of their dwelling place, that they should seek God, and perhaps feel their way toward him and find him. Yet he is actually not far from each one of us."

42. Revelation 22:13: "I am the Alpha and the Omega, the first and the last, the beginning and the end."

43. Isaiah 1:18: "Come now, let us reason together, says the LORD: though your sins are like scarlet, they shall be as white as snow; though they are red like crimson, they shall become like wool."

44. Isaiah 6:1: "In the year that King Uzziah died I saw the Lord sitting upon a throne, high and lifted up; and the train of his robe filled the temple."

45. Jonah 2:1–2: "Jonah prayed to the LORD his God from the belly of the fish, saying, 'I called out to the LORD, out of my distress, and he answered me; out of the belly of Sheol I cried, and you heard my voice.'"

46. Bruce Milne, *Know the Truth: A Handbook of Christian Belief*, 3rd ed. (Downers Grove, IL: IVP Academic, 2009), 86.

47. Genesis 6:6: "The LORD regretted that he had made man on the earth, and it grieved him to his heart."

48. Exodus 32:14: "The LORD relented from the disaster that he had spoken of bringing on his people."

49. John Frame, "Does God Change His Mind?," Frame-Poythress.org, May 17, 2012, www.frame-poythress.org/does-god-change-his-mind/.

50. Erickson, *Introducing Christian Doctrine*, 85.

51. Lewis, "Attributes of God," 494.

52. Erickson, *Introducing Christian Doctrine*, 90.

53. Erickson, *Introducing Christian Doctrine*, 90.

54. Lewis, "Attributes of God," 497.

55. Thoennes, *Life's Biggest Questions*, 67.

56. Paul J. Achtemeier, *Harper's Bible Dictionary* (San Francisco: Harper & Row and the Society of Biblical Literature, 1985), 14.

57. Erickson, *Introducing Christian Doctrine*, 93.

58. Erickson, *Introducing Christian Doctrine*, 93.

59. J. Scott Horrell, "The Eternal Son of God in the Social Trinity," in *Jesus in Trinitarian Perspective: An Introductory Christology*, ed. Fred Sanders and Klaus Issler (Nashville: B&H Academic, 2007), 47–48.

60. Thoennes, *Life's Biggest Questions*, 71–72.

61. John 17:5: "Father, glorify me in your own presence with the glory that I had with you before the world existed."

62. Matthew 9:4: "Jesus, knowing their thoughts, said, 'Why do you think evil in your hearts?'"

63. Matthew 28:18–20: "Jesus came and said to them, 'All authority in heaven and on earth has been given to me. Go therefore and make disciples of all nations, baptizing them in the name of the Father and of the Son and of the Holy Spirit, teaching them to observe all that I have commanded you. And behold, I am with you always, to the end of the age.'"

64. Romans 9:5: "To them belong the patriarchs, and from their race, according to the flesh, is the Christ, who is God over all, blessed forever. Amen."

65. Psalm 139:7: "Where shall I go from your Spirit? Or where shall I flee from your presence?"

66. 1 Corinthians 2:10–11: "These things God has revealed to us through the Spirit. For the Spirit searches everything, even the depths of God. For who knows a person's thoughts except the spirit of that person, which is in him? So also no one comprehends the thoughts of God except the Spirit of God."

67. Job 33:4: "The Spirit of God has made me, and the breath of the Almighty gives me life."

68. Timothy J. Keller, *The Reason for God: Belief in an Age of Skepticism* (New York: Dutton, 2008), 219 (emphasis mine).

69. Ephesians 4:4–7: "There is one body and one Spirit—just as you were called to the one hope that belongs to your call—one Lord, one faith, one baptism, one God and Father of all, who is over all and through all and in all. But grace was given to each one of us according to the measure of Christ's gift."

70. Thoennes, *Life's Biggest Questions*, 78–79.

71. For more information on the difference between Islam and Christianity on who Jesus is, see Nabeel Qureshi, *Seeking Allah, Finding Jesus* (Grand Rapids, MI: Zondervan, 2014). Here is a summary of the issue. The weight of the evidence supports Jesus's claim that "if you believed Moses, you would believe me; for he wrote of me" (John 5:46). This is a reference to Deuteronomy 18:15–18 (that God would "raise up for them a prophet … from among their brothers"). Muslims say this prophecy couldn't have been about Jesus because Jesus did not proclaim the law as Moses did. But Jesus did seek to restore the people of God to the purity of the law. We see this in Jesus's statement in Matthew 5:17–20: "Do not think that I have come to abolish the Law or the Prophets; I have not come to abolish them but to fulfill them. For truly, I say to you, until heaven and earth pass away, not an iota, not a dot, will pass from the Law until all is accomplished. Therefore whoever relaxes one of the least of these commandments and teaches others to do the same will be called least in the kingdom of heaven, but whoever does them and teaches them will be called great in the kingdom of heaven. For I tell you, unless your

righteousness exceeds that of the scribes and Pharisees, you will never enter the kingdom of heaven." Later New Testament authors even speak of "the law of Christ" (Gal. 6:2; 1 Cor. 9:21). Muslims also say the phrase "from among their brothers" must refer to a non-Israelite. The reference to "brothers" is repeatedly used in Deuteronomy 17 and 18, though, and the context is always to a fellow Israelite (see, for example, Deuteronomy 17:15, which uses the same phrase to refer to the installment of a king over Israel, saying that he must be "from among your brothers," not "a foreigner"). Muhammad definitely was a foreigner to Israel. Jesus was an Israelite, and the whole testimony of the New Testament is that Old Testament prophecy was fulfilled in him.

72. A. Yusuf Ali, *The Holy Qur'an*, p. 85, n. 416. Yusuf Ali goes further in a footnote to Quran 61:6: "'Ahmad,' or 'Muhammad,' the Praised One, is almost a translation of the Greek word Periclytos. In the present Gospel of John, xiv. 16, xv. 26, and xvi. 7, the word 'Comforter' in the English version is for the Greek word 'Paracletos,' which means 'Advocate,' 'one called to the help of another, a kind friend' rather than 'Comforter.' Our doctors contend that Paracletos is a corrupt reading for Periclytos, and that in their original saying of Jesus there was a prophecy of our holy Prophet Ahmad by name." See A. Yusuf Ali, *The Holy Qur'an*, p. 1540, n. 5438.

73. The Greek *kappa* (κ) is usually transliterated with a *k*, so the spelling would ordinarily be *parakletos*, not *paracletos*.

74. Lewis, "Attributes of God," 492.

75. Timothy George, *Is the Father of Jesus the God of Muhammad? Understanding the Differences between Christianity and Islam* (Grand Rapids, MI: Zondervan, 2002), 82.

76. A. Yusuf Ali, *The Holy Qur'an*.

5

The Bible: God's Big Story, Part 1

1. The Cameras Are Rolling

All the best fairy tales begin, "Once upon a time." Then comes a description of the world of the story, of the way that world goes, of where the story is happening, and of why—because if we know the story's world, we can appreciate fully both the rising conflict's true horror and the hero whose sacrifice sets everything right.

The Bible treats God's story as the true story that makes sense of all the other stories. The world it describes is his world. As poet Gerard Manley Hopkins put it, "The world is charged with the grandeur of God."[1] Yet humanity has fallen under evil's assault and has been catapulted into vast spiritual and moral darkness. But—as in *The Hobbit* when daylight broke just in time, turning the cannibal trolls into stone—Paul tells us that hope broke through this world, just in time. "When the fullness of time had come, God sent forth his Son" (Gal. 4:4).

> The Bible treats God's story as the true story that makes sense of all the other stories.

What's different about God's story is that we are in it. It's being filmed right now. The cameras are rolling. We are on the set. In fact, we are among its actors.

Now, we know how the story ends. If we've looked ahead, we know that God is, in Christ, "making all things new" (Rev. 21:5). But what happens in the meantime? What's our next line? What role are we playing in the story? There's only one way to know: read the script.

That script, of course, is the Bible. As we've seen, the Bible, this diverse collection of writings by many different authors who span a millennia and a half, linked together by the inspiration of the Holy Spirit, addresses distinct audiences and historical circumstances. Yet the Bible possesses an overarching unity centered on *God's working in and through his people*. Its story's climax is in the work of the God-man, Jesus Christ: his birth, death, resurrection, and ascension.

In all of this, the Bible tells the story of the world, to which God's very existence is the prelude. It is therefore God's story. In the Bible, we learn not of ourselves, at least not at first, but about the God who lives and reigns and who is not silent.

God is the first speaker in the Bible: "Let there be light" (Gen. 1:3). A simple sentence. No hammering, no sawing. Just the sound of God's voice turning *nothing* into *something*. As Paul David Tripp puts it, "God reveals himself, his plan, and his purpose in words.... All of his other means of self-revelation were explained and defined by this one central means."[2]

When God commanded it to, impenetrable murkiness became brilliantly illuminated. Plants and animals came to life. And then God created humans, his image bearers, and spoke to them: "Be fruitful and multiply and fill the earth and subdue it, and have dominion over the fish of the sea and over the birds of the heavens and over every living thing that moves on the earth.... And God saw everything that he had made, and behold, it was very good" (Gen. 1:28–31).

It wasn't just what God said but more so how he said it that is important. Lots of people think the God of the Bible is like the gods of other stories: distant, inaccessible, and contemptuous of humanity. They might imagine God speaking like this:

> It is to be considered an axiomatic imperative for you to consummate your consanguinity and proliferate through the Diaspora, acclimating your autonomous ego to the vicinity which you must tenaciously subjugate, and exercise prepotency over the ichthyoids of the oceanica and the columbiformes of the caelum and of the animated quadrupeds that traverse the terra firma. (And all the people heard God's voice and said, "Huh?")

But it didn't happen like that. God spoke so that people could understand him.

And what God spoke of is a *very good* plan for human beings. "God saw everything that he had made, and behold, it was very good" (Gen. 1:31). In Hebrew, the phrase *very good* is *tob meod* (pronounced Tōve MAY-owed). It means exceedingly, heartbreakingly, abundantly, richly, loudly, immeasurably good in a festive, generous, happy, intelligent, charming, splendid way.[3] God's plan is not only good, but it is *very* good. To those who think Christianity is basically a dismal set of perplexing rules, this may come as a surprise. Still, it's true!

In studying God's very good plan, it helps to know about **metanarrative**, the idea that an overarching story can explain the world and everything in it. In its flow and coherence, the Bible offers a metanarrative. In this chapter, we'll look at the concept of metanarrative and dig into Act 1 of the drama: creation of the story that Scripture

> *Metanarrative:* a single, overarching interpretation, or grand story, of reality.

presents. In the next chapter, we'll look at the rest of the story: the fall of humanity, from which we still suffer today, and God's plan for redemption. First, let's see if we can better grasp the idea of metanarrative.

2. Metanarrative: The Story of Scripture

When we say the Bible is a story, some people may think we are demoting it to the level of, say, Dr. Seuss's *Horton Hears a Who.* "There are lots of stories," someone might say. "How could you relegate the Bible to nothing more than one of those?"

First, we need to distinguish between good stories and bad stories. A story is not good just because it is long and complex. There's more to it. Look closely and you'll find the following elements in all well-written stories:

- **A theme.** There may be many subplots, but there will be one overarching plot that brings everything else into focus.

- **Tension rising and being resolved.** A good story features competing voices and counterpoints that get worked out within the larger story line.

- **Diversity within unity.** Like a fascinating painting, unity is not a stark oneness but rather a coming together of a multitude of details. In a good story, the reader is able to see how all of the details weave together by the end.

We find each of these elements in the Bible. The Bible, at heart, tells a story that is diverse but unified, with tensions that are resolved and an overarching plot that holds the story together. Even a quick glance shows that it doesn't resemble a textbook, an encyclopedia, or other books whose primary purpose is to list facts. The Bible is telling a story, but it's a particular type of story.

About half of the Bible can be classified as **historical narrative,**[4] while the rest—including wisdom literature, poetry, prophecies, and letters to churches—are books

> *Historical Narrative:* a story of historical events.

written from within that narrative. All together, the books of the Bible unfold the story of human history from beginning to end.

To best understand how the diverse books of the Bible come together in one coherent story, we must grasp the kind of story a metanarrative is. *Narrative* means "story," and *meta* means "beyond." A metanarrative is the *story beyond the story*—the story by which we make sense of all stories.

All worldviews offer a metanarrative. Here are some examples:

- The Marxist idea that all history can be explained by the conflict of economic classes of people leading to an inevitable communist utopia

- The Secularist idea that all living organisms evolve gradually through natural selection

- The Mormon idea that God has revealed his final will through the Book of Mormon and that following its precepts enables a person to become God and secure a celestial kingdom

> ***Ummah:*** **from the Arabic word for "nation"; the collective community of Muslims around the world.**

- The Islamic idea that the spread of the ***ummah***, or the Muslim community, is universal and inevitable

- The New Age idea that we are all progressing toward inner enlightenment on our journey to joining the universal spirit of the universe

- The Postmodernist idea that all metanarratives are inescapably and universally used to oppress others

Similarly, the Christian worldview offers a metanarrative, which helps us make sense of the Bible. If God is the ultimate divine author of Scripture, it would make sense that the details and subplots of the Bible come together, telling one story. However, the Bible's story is not just any story: it is true.

When theologians speak of the Bible being true, they first describe the Bible as *comprehensive*, in that it accounts for all the information of which it speaks. Second, despite its diversity, the Bible is *coherent*. The fact that the details from so many human authors cohere suggests that God was the ultimate author superintending its writing. Finally, it is *normative* because as it encompasses all of reality, it calls for a response from all its participants (i.e., the actors: you and me).[5]

3. CAN METANARRATIVES BE TRUE?

Of course, a metanarrative is not true just because it exists or merely because people believe it. A narrative must meet the tests of reality we examined in chapter 2. Not all metanarratives are equally valid: some were imagined and others actually happened. We are claiming that the Bible is, as J. R. R. Tolkien persuaded a reluctant C. S. Lewis, the great myth that became fact. Tolkien, it must be noted, was using the term *myth* in a different way than we use it today: Tolkien meant a "narrated worldview." All cultures, in this sense, have myths or stories that create their worldview; even the Bible, according to Tolkien's definition, qualifies as myth. But the biblical myth, in *having become fact*—in *having actually happened*—explains how other myths might ring true, because they, though incomplete and imperfect, are actually grasping for fulfillment through Christianity.[6]

Many postmodern scholars believe, however, that all metanarratives should be regarded with suspicion—that no overarching story of life actually moves us closer to the truth about all reality. French philosopher Jean-François Lyotard even defined Postmodernism as an "incredulity toward metanarratives."[7] To Lyotard, broad explanations are arrogant: How can we assume that what is true in our experience is true for everyone in the world?

Lyotard's starting assumption is that people who write about the past are biased. They might write what is factual to them, but for everyone else whose cultural experiences are different, their writing is mere fiction.

Historians do have worldviews just like everyone else. They have a set of answers to life's ultimate questions that affect how they see the world and what they think ought to happen in the future. And, like everyone else, they are emotionally invested in their beliefs. But does this mean that all writing about history is hopelessly biased?

Professional historians once attempted to eliminate personal biases in their writing.[8] In today's culture clashes, though, many believe no such escape is possible. Take, for instance, the widespread belief in the Middle East that the terrorist attacks of September 11, 2001, were a Jewish plot to encourage America to pursue a more aggressive policy against Muslims.[9] Is this true or false? Can it be true for some and false for others?

Whether "the Jews" orchestrated the 9/11 attacks is either true for everyone in the world or it is false.[10] It is not just a matter of intellectual curiosity, as it would determine how justice is pursued, how nations interact with one another, and so forth.

So although Postmodernism helps us to be appropriately wary about "just so" stories and alerts us to how our cultural biases can affect how we read, it is going too far to suggest that all historical accounts are fictional.[11] In fact, saying that all historical accounts are fictional commits two serious errors. First, it dismisses the fact that some historical accounts *reveal* the truth and others *conceal* it. The former Soviet Union, for instance, concealed the truth by teaching through its government-sanctioned history textbooks that Joseph Stalin was the epitome of virtue. In reality, he was a mass murderer.[12] Eyewitnesses revealed the truth, describing the atrocities and mass graves of the slaughtered. Continued research reveals the historical truth about Stalin, as well as Lenin and China's Mao Tse-tung.[13]

Second, lumping all historical accounts together as fiction minimizes the significance of such atrocities. Historians telling about these crimes are doing far more than just socially constructing reality or manifesting a political bias. Real people died. It is ludicrous to pretend we don't know why. Hard-core Postmodernists may not be willing to admit this, but we must be sensible about it.

We examined in previous chapters some of the many good reasons to trust the Bible, focusing mainly on evidence external to the biblical account. In this chapter and in the next, we focus on the internal consistency of the Bible and show that its sheer coherence makes it very unlikely that it was manufactured for someone's selfish purposes. Viewing the Bible as a metanarrative helps us see how this is so.

---

4. WHY APPROACH THE BIBLE AS A METANARRATIVE?

Humans think in stories. We see our lives as stories and remember stories told by others. When it comes to answering questions such as *Where did I come from? Who am I? What is my purpose in life? What is wrong with this world? What is the solution? Where am I going after I die?* we find answers from within a narrative. It's like a jigsaw puzzle. We're more likely to believe that the picture being created is actually meaningful if we can see how the pieces fit together.

Although the Bible is embedded with propositions, as we recognized in previous chapters, it is not organized as a "Frequently Asked Questions" list. Instead, we discover the truth about God as we contemplate the Bible's historical narratives, poetry, prophecy, and letters. The Bible's metanarrative is thorough yet accessible to readers of all ages and levels of education.[14]

It's also worth noting that the *Bible* understands the Bible within its metanarrative! Biblical authors seem overwhelmingly conscious of the fact that they are operating within a larger story. For example, the gospel of Mark says, "The beginning of the gospel of Jesus Christ, the Son of God.... Now after John was arrested, Jesus came into Galilee, proclaiming the gospel of God, and saying, 'The time is fulfilled, and the kingdom of God is at hand; repent and believe in the gospel'" (1:1, 14–15). Mark actually *tells* us he is writing about the gospel of Jesus *and* that this gospel participates in the larger story of life *and* that the climax of the story is the ministry of Jesus.

The apostle Paul also recognized the historical significance of his ministry. Romans 1:1–6 says,

> Paul, a servant of Christ Jesus, called to be an apostle, set apart for the gospel of God, which he promised beforehand through his prophets in the holy Scriptures, concerning his Son, who was descended from David according to the flesh and was declared to be the Son of God in power according to the Spirit of holiness by his resurrection from the dead, Jesus Christ our Lord, through whom we have received grace and apostleship to bring about the obedience of faith for the sake of his name among all the nations, including you who are called to belong to Jesus Christ.

The story began long before Paul was born and before Jesus came to earth, and Paul sees his own ministry in light of the big story we all take part in.

The people in Jesus's life also knew they were part of something special. Jesus's mother, Mary, sensing her part in a bigger story, sang a song we now know as the Magnificat, a beautiful statement of faith in God for his deliverance (Luke 1:46–55). Zechariah, the father of John the Baptist, also knew he was part of God's grand narrative (Luke 1:5–25), and so did the prophetess Anna (Luke 2:36–38).[15] When Jesus was a baby, a devout man named Simeon came into the temple and blessed him, having been informed by the Holy Spirit that Jesus was the Christ. In his blessing he said, "Lord, now you are letting your servant depart in peace, according to your word; for my eyes have seen your salvation that you have prepared in the presence of all peoples, a light for revelation to the Gentiles, and for glory to your people Israel" (Luke 2:29–32). All throughout Scripture, the biblical characters come to life as people who sense that they are part of something bigger than themselves—of something God is doing all over the world. So how does that bigger story play out?

5. Outlines of the Biblical Metanarrative

There are several ways to understand the metanarrative of Scripture. Church of England cleric Vaughan Roberts describes it concisely as "the kingdom of God: God's people in God's place under God's rule and blessing."[16] For Roberts, the Old Testament gives the pattern of the kingdom, shows how it perished, envisions the promise of a coming restoration, shows that restoration partially, and prophesies about its completion. The New Testament describes the present kingdom, proclaims its presence, and describes what it will be like when perfected.

Authors Craig Bartholomew and Michael Goheen summarize the biblical story as a six-act drama of the kingdom of God.[17] In Act 1, God establishes his kingdom through creation. In Act 2, humans rebel. In Act 3, God the king initiates redemption by choosing the nation of Israel. In Act 4, Christ comes as king and accomplishes redemption. In Act 5, the news of the king's redemption spreads, and this forms the church, first from Jerusalem to Rome and then into the entire world. Act 6 describes the return of the king and completion of God's plan of redemption.

Kenneth Turner, a Bible professor at Bryan College, provides a synthesized approach that focuses on both the flow of Scripture and God's kingdom work.[18] Here's a summary chart, adapted from Bartholomew and Goheen's outline of the drama, that we'll unpack in a moment.

ACT	KINGDOM	CREATION–FALL–REDEMPTION	PRIMARY TEXTS
1	*God Creates His Kingdom*	*Creation*	*Genesis 1–2*
2	*Rebellion in God's Kingdom*	*Fall*	*Genesis 3–11*
3	*Promise of Restoration: Israel's Mission*	*Redemption Initiated: Promise and God's Plan for Israel (and the World)* *Redemption Complicated: Israel's Failure and God's Covenant Faithfulness [Israel's Kingdom]* *Redemption Predicted: The Rise of the Prophets*	*Pentateuch (Genesis 12; Exodus 19; Deuteronomy 4)* *Historical Books, Wisdom Literature (2 Samuel 7)* *Prophets, Postexilic & Intertestamental Literature (Jeremiah 31)*
4	*Kingdom Restored: Jesus's Mission*	*Redemption Accomplished*	*Gospels*
5	*Kingdom Displayed: Church's Mission*	*Redemption Applied: The Church*	*Acts; Epistles*
6	*Consummation of God's Kingdom*	*Redemption Completed: New Creation*	*Revelation*

Understanding the big picture of Scripture is how we understand the ways in which God has revealed himself. In a previous chapter, we discussed the fact that God has both **incommunicable attributes** (those he does not share with people) and **communicable attributes** (attributes that humans share and embody). For example, only God is holy (set apart), eternal (has always existed), omniscient (all-knowing), omnipotent (all-powerful), omnipresent (everywhere present), and unchanging. On the other hand, God allows humanity to have wisdom, righteousness, love, mercy, and grace. But with the exception of such passages as Exodus 34:6–7,[19] God's attributes are not usually presented in Scripture in list form. Typically, God instead reveals himself as characters are formed in a novel, through a progression of seeing him act and speak.

> *Incommunicable Attributes:* qualities that belong to only God, such as being holy, eternal, omniscient, omnipotent, omnipresent, and unchanging.

> *Communicable Attributes:* qualities that God and human beings share, such as wisdom, righteousness, love, mercy, and grace.

Rather than relying on selective verses or personal hunches, if people instead allowed the metanarrative of Scripture to inform their views of God, they would be less confused about him, his world, and how he relates to his creation. As it is, confusion abounds. Television personality Oprah Winfrey, for instance, once stated that the Bible described a God who was jealous of her.[20] In typical English usage, jealousy is a petty characteristic. Winfrey concluded that God, if he is jealous of her success (to her way of thinking, God was trying to get her to *not* be successful), must be a petty person. But there is another sense in which jealousy is a good thing, not a bad thing, such as a mother being protective of a child threatened with attack or a husband being protective of his wife being stalked by a stranger. If Winfrey had understood what the term *jealous* means biblically—that God is jealous for his glory ("You shall have no other gods before me," Exod. 20:3) and that this jealousy is part of God's "showing steadfast love to thousands" of those who love him and keep his commandments (Exod. 20:5–6)[21]—perhaps she would not have been so quick to reject God.

Understanding the big picture of Scripture also helps us resolve apparent contradictions, such as where God's immutability (unchangeableness) seems to contradict passages in which God changes his mind (e.g., 1 Sam. 15:11, 35; Jon. 3:10)[22] or passages where God's goodness, justice, and perfection seem to contradict Old Testament laws permitting slavery or commanding the Israelites to wipe out the Canaanites.

Our goal should not be to explain away the more troubling texts; we cannot assume that our limited understanding can perfectly judge the Scriptures. In future chapters, we will discuss how to approach these apparent contradictions. There *are* good answers. Still, God doesn't always seem interested in resolving all of our questions. Like all great stories, there is more to be understood as the narrative unfolds.

Understanding the metanarrative of Scripture also helps us understand ourselves as image bearers of God, even if we never make it past the first three chapters of Genesis. Recall that in Genesis 1:26–28,[23] we see that God is personal and relational. The "let us" phrase (v. 26) is an early indicator that God is triune and therefore in an eternal relationship *within himself*. His desire to relate to his creation, especially human beings, is seen in how he created humans as

THE BIBLE: GOD'S BIG STORY, PART 1

image bearers. Instead of merely putting up statues of himself, as kings in the Near East were known to do, he creates image bearers who serve as stewards of his creation (Gen.1:26–28; Gen. 2).[24] He relates with these image bearers, even walking with them in the garden (Gen. 3:8).[25] Throughout Genesis and the rest of the Bible, we learn that this sovereign creator-king chooses human beings over the rest of creation, and Israel over the other nations of the world, through which to initiate his plan of redemption. He is not removed from his creation but, having established a special relationship with them, serves with them as a partner.

Recognizing how God is wise and knowledgeable and patiently instructs, chastens, delivers, and restores his people; how he is faithful to his promises; and how he protects his people against their enemies even while also using them to bring discipline and restoration provides a strong counterpoint to the common impression that God is brooding, grumpy, mean, and distant.

Let's see how this is so by looking at the first act in his great story: creation.

6. ACT 1: CREATION

Most of the creation account is found from Genesis 1:1 to Genesis 2:3 and somewhat in Genesis 2:4–25, but aspects of God's creation are revealed throughout the Scriptures, giving us deeper insight into God's motives and methods. Psalm 8, for example, celebrates creation's wonders:

> O LORD, our Lord,
>   how majestic is your name in all the earth!
> You have set your glory above the heavens.
>   Out of the mouth of babies and infants,
> you have established strength because of your foes, to
>   still the enemy and the avenger.
>
> When I look at your heavens, the work of your fingers,
>   the moon and the stars, which you have set in place,
> what is man that you are mindful of him,
>   and the son of man that you care for him?
>
> Yet you have made him a little lower than the heavenly beings
>   and crowned him with glory and honor.
> You have given him dominion over the works of your hands;
>   you have put all things under his feet,
> all sheep and oxen,
>   and also the beasts of the field,
> the birds of the heavens, and the fish of the sea,
>   whatever passes along the paths of the seas.
>
> O LORD, our Lord,
>   how majestic is your name in all the earth!

Other passages offer insight into the process of God's creation, including Job 38–39, which chronicles everything from the making of the stars to the breath of life. Psalms 19 and 104 ascribe glory to God for the creative work he has done. Proverbs 8 says that wisdom was God's companion during the creation. New Testament passages such as Romans 8, Colossians 1, and Hebrews 1 add further insight.[26]

Literary Context: the genre, structure, and grammar of a text.

Historical Context: the time, place, culture, and audience of a text.

Theological Context: the theological purpose of a text.

Much of what has been written about Genesis in the past fifty years has focused on scientific questions about origins, but to fully grasp what Scripture is teaching, we need to understand the literary, historical, and theological contexts as well.[27] The **literary context** includes such things as genre, structure, grammar, and a text's place within the larger perspective of all of Scripture. The **historical context** considers the time and place in which the author wrote and what the author and audience would have assumed to be true about life and the world. For instance, the Israelites to whom this account was written would certainly have known creation stories from neighboring countries and, of course, those from Egypt. How would this knowledge affect their understanding of the creation account in Genesis and what the author chose to communicate? The **theological context** includes the balance provided by the whole Bible. How did other authors of the Bible speak of creation, and how did this affect the way their hearers lived their lives and spread the gospel?

Keep the literary, historical, and theological contexts in mind as we seek to understand what God did in creation. It will help us resolve a common question about Genesis: Do the first two chapters of Genesis present contradictory creation accounts?

Are There Two Creation Accounts in Genesis?

Recapitulation: a storytelling technique in which an overview of a story is given before the story is laid out in specific detail.

Once when I was describing the differences between men and women in the biblical account, a person said to me, "You think this only because you choose to believe the second creation account rather than the first, which says men and women were created at the same time." It's a common misperception if we don't understand the Hebrew mind-set. The Hebrews employed a storytelling technique scholars call **recapitulation**, in which the overview is given first and followed by zooming in on key actors.[28] You've seen this in movies. In the same way, Genesis 1 offers the big picture of what God did, while Genesis 2 focuses on how God created and relates to the first humans.

Although Genesis 1 and Genesis 2 do not present contradictory creation accounts, they do offer different angles from which to see God's creation (see chart that follows).[29] In literary style, Genesis 1 is formal and dignified, whereas Genesis 2 is informal and earthy. In Genesis 1, the word for "man," *ădām* in Hebrew, represents both male and female. In Genesis 2, the man represents the 'ādām role. In Genesis 1, God speaks creation into existence. In Genesis 2, the man and woman are handmade. The climax of creation in Genesis 1 is the creation of 'ādām, and the woman is the crowning glory of creation, 'iššâ ("from man"), in Genesis 2.

And God reveals different aspects of his nature in Genesis 1 and 2. In Genesis 1, God is **transcendent**, or *above* and *outside* of creation. In Genesis 2, God is **immanent**, or *in* the created garden *with* the man and woman.

In some ways, the differences between Genesis 1 and 2 help resolve these two attributes of God's nature that may seem at odds. Only the Christian concept of God holds these two together. Other non-Christian views of God tend to emphasize one or the other.

> *Transcendent:* an attribute of God that describes him as being both above and outside of his creation.

> *Immanent:* an attribute of God that describes him as being both within and among his creation.

TOPIC	GENESIS 1:1–2:3	GENESIS 2:4–25
Literary Style	*Formal, dignified, catechetical*	*Informal, earthy, historiographic*
Place of 'ādām in Creation	*Climax of creation*	*Focus of creation*
Meaning of 'ādām	*Generic—both male and female*	*Male—"the Man"*
Creation of 'ādām	*Special creation (bārā')— as image of God by divine word*	*"Made" as "living being"; "formed" from dust*
Relationship between 'ādām and God	*Royal imagery (i.e., "image" as king)*	*Priestly imagery*
Relationship between 'ādām and Creation	*Emphasizes distance ("image of God" versus "according to their kind")*	*Emphasizes affinity (made from "ground" [ădāmâ]); as "living being" [nephesh haya])*
Climax of Creation	*Creation of 'ādām*	*Creation of the "woman" ('iššâ) from "man" ('îš) as helper and complement*

So what are we to learn about God, humans, and the world from the biblical creation account? Here are some important takeaways.

---

1 | The Creation Account Showcases God's Glory

As we noted earlier, the creation account is first and foremost *about God*. Although Christians might disagree about the "how" and the "when" of creation, we should all agree on the who and the why. God is "who," and his glory is "why."

> **Elohim:** from the Hebrew for "deity"; the generic name used in the Old Testament for the creator-God.

> **Yahweh:** from the Hebrew for "I Am"; the personal and covenantal name of God used in the Old Testament.

> **Doxology:** a liturgical or poetic narrative of praise to God.

The two most common Hebrew words for God demonstrate who he is:

- **Elohim** ("God") is a generic designation for deity and focuses on God as the creator of the whole world.

- **Yahweh** ("the LORD") is the personal and covenantal name of God. Preeminently, he is the God who redeemed his people from Egypt and brought them into covenant relationship with himself.

In Genesis 1, God is referred to as *Elohim*. He is the great creator of the world. Genesis 1 is a **doxology**, a hymn of praise about the only one awesome enough to pull off the creation of the universe.

In Genesis 2:4, God is introduced using both names as *Yahweh Elohim* ("the LORD God"). Together, these two titles showcase God as both the awesome creator and the one who is personally revealed to his people.

2 | The Creation Account Establishes Order

The Genesis account of creation goes like this: At the beginning of creation, the world was formless, empty, and dark. For the first three days, God formed, filled, and prepared the universe for life. On day one he created light to fill the darkness and separated day from night. On day two he created the upper and lower waters and separated them from the land. Then for the next three days, God made vegetation and filled the world with living creatures. On day six he put living creatures on the land and made human beings to be stewards of them. On day seven he rested and appreciated his work.

Seven days. One week.

Why is this worth noting? Think of this: the *year* (the time it takes the earth to orbit the sun) is a natural part of creation. A *month* (the time it takes the moon to orbit the earth) is also a natural part of creation, as is a *day* (the time it takes the earth to complete its rotation).

But a week? A week is different. It isn't built naturally into the cosmos, as are the year, month, and day. Instead, the concept of a seven-day week exists in the mind of God, drawing our attention to him each time we rest at the end of our labors.[30]

Atheists throughout history have sought to abolish the idea of the seven-day week and the setting apart of one day as the Sabbath. Voltaire, the deistic French revolutionary, declared, "If you want to kill Christianity, you must abolish Sunday."[31] So in 1795, the committee governing the French Revolution decreed a new calendar in which each month would have three ten-day weeks (with five extra days at the end of the year). This eliminated Sundays and holidays (holy days), but after ten years, the system was abolished. People longed for the traditional system of religious observances, which also, according to many historians, was healthier for people and animals and had beneficial effects on commerce.[32]

In 1929 another atheistic government, the USSR, tried to abolish the seven-day week by decreeing a week of five days. This time the experiment lasted eleven years before the seven-day week was once again acknowledged.[33]

Perhaps, then, we ought to reconsider. Although not as obvious as the year, the month, or the day, the week *is* a natural part of creation—but *deeply* so, built not into the orbits of Earth and moon but into our sense of work and rest. To ignore a weekly Sabbath is to ignore the way God created the world to work.

God himself set the precedent for a day of rest after working hard for six days. The idea of a day to rest, renew, and reflect is known as the *Sabbath* in Jewish and Christian traditions. Jews rest on Saturday to commemorate God's rest from creation, and Christians rest on Sunday to commemorate the resurrection.[34]

3 *The Creation Account Confronts Paganism*

The portrayal of God in Genesis 1 confronts the pagan gods and popular creation stories with which the Hebrews would have been familiar. Two of these creation myths include the *Enuma Elish* (the Egyptian Memphite Creation text) and the Phoenician cosmogony of Philo of Byblos. Some secular scholars have argued that the Hebrew account stole from these. However, though the Old Testament shares some commonalities with other creation stories (for example, a three-tiered universe), there are far more differences than similarities. The Hebrew account is distinctive: Yahweh is an altogether different kind of God, far superior to his would-be rivals.

Turner points out some of the major differences:[35]

1. There is one God, not many. The sun, moon, and sea were viewed as gods in the ancient Near East creation stories. In the biblical narrative, they are just creations.[36]

2. The universe has a divine origin. The universe had a beginning and has not existed eternally.[37]

3. Creation is perfect. God's Spirit hovered over the waters, superintending every aspect of creation. The pagan stories offer up a creation full of imperfections.[38]

4. Creation resulted from God speaking. Many creation stories are of a divine power struggle. For example, in the *Enuma Elish*, Marduk creates the heavens and earth from the body of the defeated goddess Tiamat. The God of the Bible spoke creation into existence *ex nihilo* (out of nothing).[39]

5. God is spirit. The pagan gods featured in other ancient Near East creation stories were not only embodied but were sexually active, power hungry, and petty.[40]

---

6. God organized creation in a structured and orderly way. In Genesis 1, plants and animals are created "according to their kinds." This is far different from the birth of bizarre forms in the pagan omen texts.[41]

7. Humanity has a special place. In the biblical narrative, human beings are divinely created to bear the *imago Dei*, the Latin term for "image of God." This is far different from pagan creation stories in which humans are slaves of the gods and only special classes of people (such as pharaohs) bear God's image. Even in Islam, which is theistic (belief in one God) and largely affirms the biblical account of creation, humans are viewed as slaves of God rather than his image bearers.[42] Imagine the Israelites' amazement at learning, after four hundred years of captivity in Egypt, that their identity was fundamentally that of bearing God's image rather than being slaves to their masters and the gods.[43]

8. God rests. God enjoys and takes pleasure in his creation and even creates space and time in which to enjoy it. This is in stark contrast to the perpetual restlessness of the pagan gods.[44]

In other words, Genesis chapters 1 and 2 present a creation account that deliberately clashes with the cosmology (nature of God and origin of the universe) of ancient Israel's neighbors and many of the ideas developed since then as well. The biblical creation account

- affirms the direct hand of one God in every phase of creation;

- rejects **atheism** (no God), **polytheism** (more than one God), and **naturalism** (everything that exists can be explained through natural processes);

- affirms the distinction between creation and the creator;

- rejects **pantheism** (God is creation), **panentheism** (God is *in* creation), and **astrology** (creation controls God);

THE BIBLE: GOD'S BIG STORY, PART 1

- affirms that creation is purposeful and good;

- rejects **deism** (God and creation do not interact), **gnosticism** (the material world is evil), **agnosticism** (uncertainty about God's existence and purpose), and **nihilism** (total purposelessness);

- affirms the special creation of humanity;

- rejects evolutionary theories that propose that all life arose merely through random chance processes, without God's guiding hand to ordain and classify it according to his purpose.

4 *The Creation Account Establishes Humans as the Climax of Creation*

That human beings were given God's image exposes a false picture many have of God—that he is stern, ever disapproving. Genesis 1:26–27 says,

> Then God said, "Let us make man in our image, after our likeness. And let them have dominion over the fish of the sea and over the birds of the heavens and over the livestock and over all the earth and over every creeping thing that creeps on the earth." So God created man in his own image, in the image of God he created him.

The word *image* appears dozens of times in the Bible. Almost all the other occurrences than this first one refer to graven images (carved idols). Rarely does the word *image* refer directly to the image of God or the image of Christ. Three of those rare occurrences are in this one passage. This ought to get our attention.

So what does *image* mean? Genesis 1 uses two words that reinforce one another, making God's perspective clear:

- Image: *Tselem*—shape, resemblance

- Likeness: *Demooth*—model, shape, bodily resemblance

Image was a very important concept in the ancient Near Eastern culture in which the Bible was written.

Deism: the belief that God exists and created the world but currently stands completely aloof from his creation; the belief that reason and nature sufficiently reveal the existence of God but that God has not revealed himself through any type of special revelation.

Gnosticism: a second-century heretical Christian movement that taught that the material world was created and maintained by a lesser divine being, that matter and the physical body are inherently evil, and that salvation can be obtained only through an esoteric knowledge of divine reality and the self-denial of physical pleasures.

Agnosticism: the belief that knowledge of God is ultimately inaccessible or unknowable.

Nihilism: the view that the world and human existence are without meaning, purpose, comprehensible truth, or essential value.

Kings set up images of themselves in conquered cities to remind people who was in charge. An image symbolized authority over a certain domain.[45]

God's domain is the entire universe, but he didn't set up a statue of himself on the earth. He took the dust of earth, breathed into it, and created a living, moving representation of his image. In fact, whenever people tried to make statues of God (or other gods), he condemned them. Jeremiah 51:17 says, "Every man is stupid and without knowledge; every goldsmith is put to shame by his idols, for his images are false, and there is no breath in them."

People make images of gods as a way of trying to control the divine. Images compress the grandeur, power, and eternality of God into a little statue to be displayed or hidden as needed. Idols of any kind strangle aliveness into stillness.

As image bearers of God, we don't give shape to ourselves. Instead, we take on God's "shape." As sons and daughters resemble their parents, we resemble God. His view of humanity directly contradicts scientists who merely view human beings as highly functioning blobs of protoplasm or radical environmentalists who place animals on par with people. The way God created humanity is a profound statement about what it means to be human, so profound that all other insights and understanding of our lives come forth from it.

Here are some significant ways the Bible emphasizes the special place humans have in creation:

- Humans were created last; all of creation seemed to be preparation for humanity's arrival.

- Humans were the product of divine deliberation (God said, "Let us make man in our image" in Gen. 1:26).[46]

- The creation of humans is described as more intensive and extensive than any other creative act.

- Scripture uses a special word for "create" (*bara‘*), which always involves a special creative act of God (Gen. 1:1, 21, 27; 2:3).[47]

- Although each act of creation was described as "good," the creation of humanity was evaluated by God with the superlative "*very* good" (Gen. 1:31).[48]

Cosmology: the study of the structure, origin, and design of the universe.

Anthropology: the study of humanity's origins, cultures, and behavior.

- Humans possess exalted status over other creatures, as bearers of God's image (Gen. 1:26–27).[49]

Just as Genesis 1 and other passages about creation confront pagan ideas of God and the universe (**cosmology**), Genesis 2 and other passages about the creation of humanity confront pagan ideas about humanity (**anthropology**). For example, the biblical creation account

- affirms the direct hand of God in the creation of humanity; all humans came from a single pair;

- rejects theories claiming that all life arose from a single self-replicating molecule, or even the evolution of humans from several sources (**polygenesis**), which gave rise to **eugenics**, the pseudoscience that supported racist views in the nineteenth and twentieth centuries;

- affirms the superiority of humanity over other creatures;

> *Polygenesis:* the evolution of species from several independent sources.

- rejects the "Who are we to say we are any better than any other creature?" claims from radical environmentalist and animal rights groups;

- rejects neopagan and New Spiritualist theories claiming that humans are no more an expression of the divine than any other living thing;

- rejects the postmodern view that humans are nothing more than social constructions;

- affirms the dignity of all humans;

- rejects the devaluation of persons based on gender, race, intelligence, physical form, or circumstances of conception;

> *Eugenics:* a social movement advocating the genetic improvement of the human race through such practices as selective breeding, compulsory sterilization, forced abortions, and genocide.

- affirms the male/female distinction;

- rejects the splintering of male/female sexual differences into socially constructed gender preferences;

- affirms the honoring of human procreation;

- rejects the devaluation of sex by denying its proper context of man/woman marriage; affirms the wholeness of human personhood;

- rejects the devaluation of humans as either solely material (**materialism**) or immaterial (**asceticism**);

> *Materialism:* the belief that reality is composed solely of matter.

- affirms the sanctity of human life;

- rejects elective abortion and infanticide;

> *Asceticism:* the practice of avoiding all forms of indulgence.

- affirms the sanctity of work;

- rejects laziness;

- affirms gender equality;

Misandry: the hatred or dislike of men.

- rejects the devaluation of either men or women (**misandry** *or* **misogyny**).

Misogyny: the hatred or dislike of women.

Making humans responsible for such a vast domain pleased God. Genesis 1:31 says, "God saw everything that he had made, and behold, it was very good. And there was evening and there was morning, the sixth day." As we saw earlier, the Hebrew phrase for "very good" is *tob meod*, which communicates great awe and wonder—goodness so good that it makes one want to burst from sheer joy.

We should stand amazed by this. God created the planets and the stars and called them good. He created the fish and the animals and called them good. But when he created human beings and gave them dominion, he pronounced his plan "very good." We bear God's image as rulers of creation. We do not rule for ourselves. Rather, we are stewards, or "viceroys" (vice-regents ruling on the king's behalf). God owns it all but is pleased for us to produce and initiate to increase creation's value.

5 *The Creation Account Gives Meaning to Humanity's Mission*

"And God blessed them" (Gen. 1:28a). The creation of man and woman was not a curse; it was something great and exciting. "And God said to them, 'Be fruitful and multiply and fill the earth and subdue it, and have dominion'" (Gen. 1:28b). God was interested in abundance. Not scarcity, not just enough to get by, not just make-do. Abundance. As author and public speaker Andy Crouch puts it in his book *Culture Making*, God wanted "teeming 'swarms of living creatures.'"[50]

The words for "work" and "keep" in Hebrew mean to work or serve, to teach, to exercise great care over. Adam was to teach the earth what to do. In essence, God was saying, "See that peach tree? I want more peaches out of that. See that wheat field? I want a higher yield out of it. I want more of everything. I want more *quality* and I want more *quantity*."

The word *dominion* makes people nervous, but it shouldn't. It simply means having responsibility for a certain domain. If you have a family, you have responsibility in the family domain; if you have a job, you have responsibility in the vocational domain. The domain God gave humans is

> "over the fish of the sea and over the birds of the heavens and over every living thing that moves on the earth." And God said, "Behold, I have given you every plant yielding seed that is on the face of all the earth, and every tree with seed in its fruit. You shall have them for food. And to every beast of the earth and to every bird of the heavens and to everything that creeps on the earth, everything that has the breath of life, I have given every green plant for food." (Gen. 1:28–29)

Then "God said to them, 'Be fruitful and multiply and fill the earth and subdue it" (Gen. 1:28). The word *subdue* means to force into submission. God created the earth with work that needed to be done. It was perfect yet incomplete. That there were unfinished tasks, including both maintenance and further creative work to be accomplished, was not a sign of imperfection.

6 The Creation Account Gives Meaning to Sexuality

Before even the first person was made, God designed and announced the categories of "male" and "female" (Gen. 1:27).[51] In other words, *they were male and female before they were embodied.* We may think we are male or female because we have male or female parts, but we were male or female before that. We have been given male or female identities that go beyond our bodies.

This could lead to a lot of interesting theological discussions. I hope it does, but at the very least if God is spirit and does not have a body as we do, and if there is something about us that is spirit as well as body, we're not just matter in motion as Karl Marx said. We're something more than that. We bear God's image in ways that go far beyond the physical.

If you've ever seen a dead person, you know exactly what I mean. You realize, "That's a *body*, but it's not *them* anymore." Their spirit is gone. The part of them that bore God's image is no longer there.

Our spirits make us recognizable.

It is also at the spiritual level that we recognize the meaningfulness of our relationships to one another. Genesis 2:20 says, "The man gave names to all livestock and to the birds of the heavens and to every beast of the field. But for Adam there was not found a helper fit for him." This was a teachable moment. How many animal pairs would Adam name before he realized that "one of these things was not like the others"?

This is the cow—Mr. Cow, Mrs. Cow.

This is the giraffe—Mr. Giraffe, Mrs. Giraffe.

This is the bear—Mr. Bear, Mrs. Bear.

This is the donkey—Mr. Donkey, Mrs. Donkey.

At some point Adam surely looked around and realized that there was a Mr. Adam but no Mrs. Adam.

Then it gets even better. Verse 21 says, "So the LORD God caused a deep sleep to fall upon the man, and while he slept took one of his ribs and closed up its place with flesh." The rib he had taken "he made into a woman and brought her to the man. Then the man said, 'This at last is bone of my bones and flesh of my flesh; she shall be called Woman, because she was taken out of Man'" (vv. 22–23).

Do you see what Adam just did? He named her "Woman." He identified her characteristics and took responsibility for her. God gave her to the man, and he instantly realized his bond and his relationship to her and how unique their relationship would be.

Hebrew scholars point out that Adam's statement is an explosive cry of surprise and joy—a love poem.[52]

This at last is bone of my bones
   and flesh of my flesh;
she shall be called Woman,
   because she was taken out of Man. (v. 23)

Adam's poem foreshadows the love song of the Song of Solomon, which expresses the romance of God-given, marital love. Then the Scripture commentary says, "A man shall leave his father and his mother and hold fast to his wife, and they shall become one flesh" (v. 24).

That's interesting because Adam and Eve did not have parents; they were made directly by God. The father and mother were mentioned because God was establishing a prototype. The creation of this man and this woman, the uniting of the two of them together to be one flesh, began a pattern to be adopted by all subsequent human beings.

> **The creation of this man and this woman, the uniting of the two of them together to be one flesh, began a pattern to be adopted by all subsequent human beings.**

The one-flesh relationship is especially important. It doesn't just mean the man and woman were sexually united, though it does have that connotation. The idea of one flesh is one *clan*. God created them as a *family government*. Were Adam and the woman married? Yes, they were. They were made a family by God himself.

Thus, the story of creation begins not with a birth but with a wedding. This is pure beauty. The man and woman were together in a completely trusting relationship, made perfectly for each other, and engrossed in work so profoundly meaningful that it was worshipful. It is a picture of grace, enjoyment, pleasure, fulfillment, work, accomplishment, and satisfaction. All of these went together in creation. And it's worth noting that, at the end of all things, the finale of God's redemptive story is the wedding feast!

7. CONCLUSION

Four word pairs give shape to the biblical creation narrative. God is a God of both *creation* and *covenant*. He was *transcendent* above the world but also *immanent* in it. He made humans to do in creation just as he had done: to *fill* and *form* it. Humans were both *material* and *immaterial*; that is, they had bodies and lived in the physical world, but they also had souls that made their experiences spiritual as well. The biblical narrative presents these not as "either/or" but as "both/and." The complexity is not contradiction, the Bible insists, but rather a healthy tension in the way two pitches of a roof lean on one another and create strength.

Christians, too, have often set things up in a false "either/or" fashion:

- You can't focus on both improving the world and preparing people for eternity.

- You can't celebrate valued contributions of humans unless they have a personal relationship with Christ.

- The church has nothing to do with the world.

- Now that we have the **special revelation** of the Bible, we no longer need general revelation.

- Making arguments for Scripture based on evidence is bad; we have moved beyond that into a postmodern era.

> **Special Revelation:** God's unique revelation about himself through the Scriptures (Ps. 19:7–11; 2 Tim. 3:14–17), miraculous events (dreams, visions, prophets, prophecy), and Jesus Christ (John 1:1–18).

What would happen if we invited the tension into the discussion rather than trying to eliminate it? Is it possible to focus on "inside" (covenant) issues and on "outside" (creation) concerns at the same time?

After all, even after the fall, the goodness of creation remains, pointing the way to redemption:

- God is still sovereign and in control. Neither his character nor his purposes have changed.

- Creation still reveals God's glory, power, care, and order (Pss. 8; 19; 104; Rom. 1:18–23).

- The creation is still considered "good" (1 Tim. 4:4).[53]

- Human beings are still fully made in God's image (Gen. 9:6; James 3:9),[54] and the creation mandate is still intact (Gen. 9:1–7; James 3:7).[55]

Creation was very good, and it still is. But it is marred by something so horrifying that even today, so many thousands of years later, it still gives us a sick feeling. That's what we'll talk about in the next chapter.

ENDNOTES

1. See "God's Grandeur," by Gerard Manley Hopkins, Poetry Foundation, www.poetryfoundation.org/poem/173660.

2. Paul David Tripp, *War of Words* (Phillipsburg, NJ: Presbyterian and Reformed, 2000), 8.

3. See *meod*, Strong's Hebrew reference number 3966, and *tob*, Strong's Hebrew reference number 2896a, in Robert L. Thomas, *New American Standard Exhaustive Concordance of the Bible/Hebrew-Aramaic and Greek Dictionaries*, updated ed. (Nashville: Holman, 1981).

4. Statistics vary. Robert L. Plummer, in *40 Questions about Interpreting the Bible* (Grand Rapids, MI: Kregel, 2010), 191, cites "about 60 percent" for OT and NT combined. Gordon D. Fee and Douglas Stuart, in *How to Read the Bible for All Its Worth*, 3rd ed. (Grand Rapids, MI: Zondervan, 2003), 89, suggest that "over 40 percent" of the OT is narrative.

5. The focus on comprehensive and normative is discussed in Craig G. Bartholomew and Michael W. Goheen, *The Drama of Scripture: Finding Our Place in the Biblical Story* (Grand Rapids, MI: Baker, 2004), 20.

6. Alister McGrath, "A Contemporary Philosophy of Persuasion," (lecture, Summit Oxford C. S. Lewis Conference, Oxford, UK, October 7, 2013); http://www.kevinbywater.com/lewis-persuasion-mcgrath.

7. Jean-François Lyotard, *The Postmodern Condition: A Report on Knowledge* (Minneapolis: University of Minnesota Press, 1984), xxiv.

8. See Tom Dixon's essay "Postmodern Method: History," in *The Death of Truth*, ed. Dennis McCallum (Minneapolis: Bethany, 1996), 138–39.

9. Among the conspiracy claims are one asserting that four thousand people of Israeli origin, and presumably Jewish, were absent from the World Trade Center on September 11, 2001. The claim apparently originated with a Syrian newspaper

and has been roundly refuted. See web.archive.org/web/20070211085836/http://usinfo.state.gov/media/Archive/2005/Jan/14-260933.html and www.snopes.com/rumors/israel.asp.

10. We are assuming, of course, that the words *true* and *false* are distinct terms with identifiable essences or properties that present themselves consistently, enabling rational people to distinguish between them. This is disputed by some hardcore Postmodernists, but the fact that they expect their disputations to be taken seriously, even though they are made in words, proves the inherent absurdity of their argument.

11. This is important today because many people, ignorant of what actually happened in history, can fall for the agenda filmmakers want to promote. Films such as *Braveheart*; *Good Night, and Good Luck*; *The Last Temptation of Christ*; and *The Da Vinci Code* leave viewers with a compelling story of the past yet with no way to decipher where history ends and embellishment begins. By weaving together fact and fiction in entertaining ways with attractive actors and engaging story lines, screenwriters, directors, and producers can manipulate the understanding of the average viewer because most are ill-equipped to sort out historical events from imaginative interpretations. See Ben Witherington III, *The Gospel Code: Novel Claims about Jesus, Mary Magdalene and Da Vinci* (Downers Grove, IL: InterVarsity, 2004).

12. Stephane Courtois et al., *The Black Book of Communism: Crimes, Terror, Repression* (Cambridge, MA: Harvard University Press, 1999).

13. For example, Jung Chang and Jon Halliday's *Mao: The Unknown Story* (New York: Knopf, 2005) is a definitive study and story of Mao's life and times along with his crimes.

14. Bartholomew and Goheen discuss the reality of competing metanarratives in *The Drama of Scripture*, 18–21. One of the implications is that we (Western Christians) are already confronted with "the humanistic story of Western culture," which seeks to dominate us and even incorporate the Bible within it. Therefore, we must challenge this other story with the biblical story. This is how metanarrative and worldview are intricately connected. To make the point, Bartholomew and Goheen cite works of Lesslie Newbigin, Eugene Peterson, and N. T. Wright.

15. Luke 2:36–38: "There was a prophetess, Anna, the daughter of Phanuel, of the tribe of Asher. She was advanced in years, having lived with her husband seven years from when she was a virgin, and then as a widow until she was eighty-four. She did not depart from the temple, worshipping with fasting and prayer night and day. And coming up at that very hour she began to give thanks to God and to speak of him to all who were waiting for the redemption of Jerusalem."

16. See the full chart and diagram in Vaughan Roberts, *God's Big Picture: Tracing the Storyline of the Bible*, deluxe ed. (Downers Grove, IL: InterVarsity, 2003), 149, 157. Roberts's approach is influenced by Graeme Goldsworthy, *Gospel and Kingdom* (Exeter, UK: Paternoster, 1981).

17. See the outline in Bartholomew and Goheen, *The Drama of Scripture*, 27. Their outline (and use of drama) expands upon N. T. Wright, *The New Testament and the People of God* (London: SPCK, 1992), 139–43.

18. The rest of this outline will follow the Creation–Fall–Redemption pattern.

19. Exodus 34:6–7: "The LORD passed before him and proclaimed, 'The LORD, the LORD, a God merciful and gracious, slow to anger, and abounding in steadfast love and faithfulness, keeping steadfast love for thousands, forgiving iniquity and transgression and sin, but who will by no means clear the guilty, visiting the iniquity of the fathers on the children and the children's children, to the third and the fourth generation.'"

20. *Oprah & Eckhart Tolle: A New Earth—Chapter 1*, Episode 101, aired 3/23/14, www.oprah.com/own-a-new-earth/Chapter-1-Episode-Guide-for-Oprah--Eckhart-Tolle-A-New-Earth.

21. Exodus 20:5–6: "You shall not bow down to them or serve them, for I the LORD your God am a jealous God, visiting the iniquity of the fathers on the children to the third and the fourth generation of those who hate me, but showing steadfast love to thousands of those who love me and keep my commandments."

22. 1 Samuel 15:11: "'I regret that I have made Saul king, for he has turned back from following me and has not performed my commandments.' And Samuel was angry, and he cried to the LORD all night"; 1 Samuel 15:35: "Samuel did not see Saul again until the day of his death, but Samuel grieved over Saul. And the LORD regretted that he had made Saul king over Israel"; Jonah 3:10: "When God saw what they did, how they turned from their evil way, God relented of the disaster that he had said he would do to them, and he did not do it."

23. Genesis 1:26–28: "God said, 'Let us make man in our image, after our likeness. And let them have dominion over the fish of the sea and over the birds of the heavens and over the livestock and over all the earth and over every creeping thing that creeps on the earth.' So God created man in his own image, in the image of God he created him; male and female he created them. And God blessed them. And God said to them, 'Be fruitful and multiply and fill the earth and subdue it, and have dominion over the fish of the sea and over the birds of the heavens and over every living thing that moves on the earth.'"

24. While the plural reference in "let us" (Gen. 1:26; cf. 3:22; 11:7) is open to interpretation, polytheism is not an option. All the verbs in Genesis 1 with God as subject are singular in the Hebrew.

25. Genesis 3:8: "They heard the sound of the LORD God walking in the garden in the cool of the day, and the man and his wife hid themselves from the presence of the LORD God among the trees of the garden."

26. Hugh Ross provides a list of some of these texts in "The Major Biblical Creation Texts/Creation Accounts," Reasons to Believe, August 1, 2008, www.reasons.org/articles/the-major-biblical-creation-texts-creation-accounts.

27. See Kenneth J. Turner, "Teaching Genesis 1 at a Christian College," in *Reading Genesis 1–2: An Evangelical Conversation,* ed. J. Daryl Charles (Peabody, MA: Hendrickson, 2013), chapter 6.

28. Gleason Archer, *A Survey of Old Testament Introduction* (Chicago: Moody, 2007), 135.

29. Chart courtesy of Kenneth Turner, Bryan College. Used by permission.

30. This is based on a teaching by Gregg Harris. For more information, see www.nobleinstitute.org/.

31. Voltaire, *The International Standard Bible Encyclopedia,* vol.1: *A–D,* ed. Geoffrey William Bromily (Grand Rapids, MI: Eerdmans, 1986), 159.

32. See chapter 2, "The Seven Day Wars," in Eviatar Zerubavel, *The Seven Day Circle: The History and Meaning of the Week* (Chicago: University of Chicago Press, 1985).

33. See chapter 2, "The Seven Day Wars," in Zerubavel, *The Seven Day Circle.*

34. For an excellent essay on the Sabbath, see Abraham Joshua Heschel, "From the Sabbath," in *Leading Lives That Matter: What We Should Do and Who We Should Be,* ed. Mark R. Schwehn and Dorothy C. Bass (Grand Rapids, MI: Eerdmans, 2006), 216–21.

35. See Kenneth J. Turner, "The Kind-ness of God: A Theological Reflection of Mîn, 'Kind,'" in *Genesis Kinds: Creationism and the Origin of Species,* ed. Todd C. Wood and Paul A. Garner, Center for Origins Research in Creation (Eugene, OR: Wipf & Stock, 2009), 31–64; Turner, "Teaching Genesis 1."

36. Turner, "Kind-ness of God," 31–64.

37. Turner, "Teaching Genesis 1."

38. Turner, "Teaching Genesis 1."

39. Turner, "Kind-ness of God," 31–64.

40. Turner, "Kind-ness of God," 31–64.

41. Turner, "Kind-ness of God," 31–64.

42. The Quran consistently refers to people as slaves of Allah. See, just as a starting point, 2:23, 2:90, 2:186, 2:207, 3:15, 3:20, 3:30, 3:61, 3:79, 3:182, 4:172, 6:18, 6:88, 7:128, 7:194, 8:51, 9:104, 10:107, 14:11, and 15:49. The Arabic word is *abd,* which means one who is totally subordinated. Badru Kateregga says, "The Christian witness, that man is created in the 'image and likeness of God,' is not the same as the Muslim witness." See Badru D. Kateregga and David W. Shenk, "Islam and Christianity: A Muslim and a Christian in Dialogue," electronically available on *The World of Islam: Resources for Understanding* (Colorado Springs, CO: Global Mapping International, 2000), CD-ROM, 5350.

43. See Turner, "Teaching Genesis 1."

44. Turner, "Teaching Genesis 1."

45. See D. J. A. Clines, "The Image of God in Man," *Tyndale Bulletin* 19 (1968): 53–103, 98.131.162.170//tynbul/library /TynBull_1968_19_03_Clines_ImageOfGodInMan.pdf.

46. The "us" is a matter of interest to theologians, some of whom see it as God meeting with a divine counsel, others as a plural of majesty, and others a pre-announcement of the Trinity of Father, Son, and Holy Spirit.

47. Genesis 1:1: "In the beginning, God created the heavens and the earth"; Genesis 1:21: "God created the great sea creatures and every living creature that moves, with which the waters swarm, according to their kinds, and every winged bird according to its kind. And God saw that it was good"; Genesis 1:27: "God created man in his own image, in the image of God he created him; male and female he created them"; Genesis 2:3: "God blessed the seventh day and made it holy, because on it God rested from all his work that he had done in creation."

48. Genesis 1:31: "God saw everything that he had made, and behold, it was very good. And there was evening and there was morning, the sixth day."

49. Genesis 1:26–27: "God said, 'Let us make man in our image, after our likeness. And let them have dominion over the fish of the sea and over the birds of the heavens and over the livestock and over all the earth and over every creeping thing that creeps on the earth.' So God created man in his own image, in the image of God he created him; male and female he created them."

50. Andy Crouch, *Culture Making: Recovering Our Creative Calling* (Downers Grove, IL: InterVarsity), 106.

51. Genesis 1:27: "God created man in his own image, in the image of God he created him; male and female he created them."

52. R. Kent Hughes, *Genesis: Beginning and Blessing* (Wheaton, IL: Crossway, 2004), 61.

53. 1 Timothy 4:4: "Everything created by God is good, and nothing is to be rejected if it is received with thanksgiving."

54. Genesis 9:6: "Whoever sheds the blood of man, by man shall his blood be shed, for God made man in his own image"; James 3:9: "With it we bless our Lord and Father, and with it we curse people who are made in the likeness of God."

55. James 3:7: "Every kind of beast and bird, of reptile and sea creature, can be tamed and has been tamed by mankind."

CHAPTER 6

6

THE BIBLE: GOD'S BIG STORY, PART 2

1. THE REST OF THE STORY

Far too often, the beauty ascribed to creation in Genesis seems like a distant dream. Bad news is everywhere. Every day, headlines betray the cruelty and anguish all too common in the human story:

- "Long-Running US-Russian Feud Reignited"

- "Syrian Troops Ambush Rebels, Kill 62"

- "Father of Missing Daughter Pleads for Abductor to Release Her"

- "School Shooting Stuns Community"

Doctrine of Original Sin: the orthodox Christian belief that Adam's first sin corrupted the nature of his descendants, leading to humanity's present propensity toward committing sin.

That humans do evil should not shock Christians. The **doctrine of original sin** says humans are so *thoroughly* fallen that nothing remains unaffected by our fallenness. It also says we are so *absolutely* fallen that there's nothing we can do to fix ourselves. None of this is hidden from view. Christian apologist G. K. Chesterton thought that original sin was "the only part of Christian theology which can really be proved."[1]

All worldviews recognize that something is wrong about the world, but they disagree about what precisely is wrong and what ought to be done about it. The scriptural metanarrative showcases life in a world of sin. Bad people don't just do very bad things and make life miserable for the rest; *each of us* falls short of God's glory. Sin affects all of creation. The proper response is to admit this and be reconciled to God. In Chesterton's reply to a newspaper query about what is wrong with the world, he got straight to the truth: "What's wrong with the world? I am. Yours truly, G. K. Chesterton."[2]

Scripture, however, does not leave it there. It points to a way out: God's plan for ending sin's dominion altogether. In the previous chapter, we dove deep into the first act in this story: creation. In this chapter, we'll unflinchingly examine Act 2: The fall and then burrow deep into Scripture to see how God patiently moves us into Act 3: Promise of Restoration, Act 4: Kingdom Restored, Act 5: Kingdom Displayed, and Act 6: Kingdom Consummated.

So you can see where we've been and where we're going, here's the chart from chapter 5 representing Craig Bartholomew and Michael Goheen's "drama of Scripture." (I've simplified their act titles for our purpose in this book.)

ACT	KINGDOM	CREATION–FALL–REDEMPTION	PRIMARY TEXTS
1	*God Creates His Kingdom*	*Creation*	*Genesis 1–2*
2	*Rebellion in God's Kingdom*	*Fall*	*Genesis 3–11*
3	*Promise of Restoration: Israel's Mission*	*Redemption Initiated: Promise and God's Plan for Israel (and the World)* *Redemption Complicated: Israel's Failure and God's Covenant Faithfulness [Israel's Kingdom]* *Redemption Predicted: The Rise of the Prophets*	*Pentateuch (Genesis 12; Exodus 19; Deuteronomy 4)* *Historical Books, Wisdom Literature (2 Samuel 7)* *Prophets, Postexilic & Intertestamental Literature (Jeremiah 31)*

THE BIBLE: GOD'S BIG STORY, PART 2

4	Kingdom Restored: Jesus's Mission	Redemption Accomplished	Gospels
5	Kingdom Displayed: Church's Mission	Redemption Applied: The Church	Acts; Epistles
6	Consummation of God's Kingdom	Redemption Completed: New Creation	Revelation

2. ACT 2: THE FALL

God originally created human beings and his world in a state of *shalom*. This Hebrew word for "peace," "prosperity," and "welfare" implies that in creation, everything was good and in order. The existence of our first parents was one of wholeness in their relationship with God, one another, and creation. But in the fall, each of these relationships was ruptured. The world is now, as author Cornelius Plantinga puts it, "not the way it's supposed to be."[3]

What happened? As the creation narrative moves from Genesis 2 to Genesis 3, the focus abruptly changes. A new character, the serpent, comes into the picture. He is "crafty," a word in Hebrew (*ārûm*) that forms a wordplay with the word for "naked" (*ārôm*) in Genesis 2:25.[4] In English, it would read something like this: Adam and Eve were "nude" but the serpent was "shrewd."[5] The serpent is clearly more than just a reptilian member of the animal kingdom. It is intelligent, it speaks, it asks thought-provoking questions, and it is antagonistic toward both humans and God.

Right away the serpent challenges Eve's understanding of what God has said: "Did God actually say, 'You shall not eat of any tree in the garden'?" It's a simple question, but Eve's response is revealing: "We may eat of the fruit of the trees in the garden, but God said, 'You shall not eat of the fruit of the tree that is in the midst of the garden, *neither shall you touch it*, lest you die.'" But God hadn't said anything about touching it. He merely told them not to eat of it. This is our first indication that something is very wrong. Has Eve misrepresented the truth on purpose? Has she misunderstood? Has Adam given her wrong information?[6] Either way, this confrontation is what scriptwriters call an inciting incident. Once it occurs, things can never go back to the way they were before.

The Genesis 3 account of the fall of humanity calls forth several perplexing questions.

Who was the serpent? The serpent is referred to as one of the wild creatures God made (v. 1),[7] which would be consistent with the curse about crawling on the belly (v. 14).[8] Many indicators, including the serpent's actions and the curse against him in verse 15,[9] support the New Testament identification of the serpent with Satan (Rev. 12:9; 20:2; Rom. 16:20).[10]

What was the nature of the temptation? The man and woman are tempted with "the knowledge of good and evil." The meaning of this phrase is hard to nail down. It seems that the serpent is offering something to the man and woman that is proper for only God to know (Gen. 3:22).[11] Perhaps it has something to do with claiming for themselves the authority to *define* "good" and "evil." If so, then the temptation to eat from this tree is the temptation to replace God.

What was the nature of sin? This first act of sin helps us understand four things about sin's nature:

> **1. Sin is an act of unbelief.** It is a refusal to trust God and even a desire to believe the opposite of what he says.

> **2. Sin is a desire for autonomy.** The man and woman want to be wise on their own terms rather than on God's.

> **3. Sin is an act of irresponsibility.** Although Adam knew the serpent's nature (he had observed its characteristics and named it), he failed to intervene when his wife was under spiritual attack. He needed to be a warrior, and instead he was a wimp.

> **4. Sin is an act of rebellion.** Sin is not just the bad things others do to us; it is an active choice to go against what God says is best.

In the end, it's less about the fruit than about the man and woman saying, "God, we don't think your plan is as good as you think it is. *We want what we want, and we want it now.*"

What were the consequences of sin? God himself breaks the bad news, first to the serpent and then to Adam and Eve. In Genesis 3:14–15, he tells the "more crafty" (*ʿārûm*) serpent that he will be "more cursed" (*ʿārûr*), crawling in humiliation and being regarded with fear and contempt. Further, his relationship with Eve will be hostile. This is far more than distrust between humans and animals; it is a picture of the eternal spiritual struggle between humans and Satan.

> **What had previously been a relationship of complete oneness and trust would in the future be a grappling for power and control.**

The consequences of sin for the woman are twofold. Genesis 3:16[12] says she would experience increased pain in childbearing, adding great pain to an event of great blessing. Second, men and women would experience frustration in their relationships. Genesis 3:16b refers to the woman's "desire" to usurp the man's headship, but he will "rule" over her, presumably harshly. What had previously been a relationship of complete oneness and trust would in the future be a grappling for power and control.[13]

To the man the curse is on the ground (Gen. 3:17–19).[14] The earth would rebel against Adam as he had rebelled against God, and only through painful toil would he wring productivity out of the soil.

What happened as a result of sin? Genesis 4–11 runs through early human history at a rapid pace, slowing down only for a closer look when Abram comes on the scene in chapter 12. Even though it is a broad overview, the subsequent chapters tell the early history of humanity as one of ever-increasing arrogance, abuse, and death. The impact of the fall multiplies. In Genesis 4:8,[15] Cain murders his brother and is terrorized by his punishment. By the end of the chapter, Lamech murders a man and boasts about *being* a terrorist (vv. 23–26).[16] Before long, people crave evil (Gen. 6:5).[17]

Bracketed by moments of hope, humanity's deterioration continues unabated to this day. "Everyone did what was right in his own eyes" (Judg. 17:6). Humanity's spiritual genes have mutated in such a way that the cell division that keeps us alive is the very thing that kills us. As the saying goes, we are not sinners because we sin; we sin because we are sinners. Sin is in our blood. Death looks to win.

COUNTERFEIT IDEAS ABOUT THE FALL

In order to understand the world rightly, we must understand the fall; we can fix something only if we first know what is wrong with it. The secular perspective, though, is that nothing (permanently, at least) is wrong. What Christians call sin, Secularists say, is "nothing but a flesh wound" (to quote a reference from comic troupe Monty Python's movie *The Holy Grail*)[18] caused by momentary clumsiness. This false belief is not trivial. Secularists almost universally reject the doctrine of original sin, distorting the Christian story to make their denial seem more plausible. German social psychologist Erich Fromm claims,

> The Christian interpretation of the story of man's act of disobedience as his "fall" has obscured the clear meaning of the story. The biblical text does not even mention the word "sin"; man challenges the supreme power of God, and he is able to challenge it because he is potentially God.[19]

Author Wendell W. Watters writes, "The Christian is brainwashed to believe that he or she was born wicked, should suffer as Christ suffered, and should aspire to a humanly impossible level of perfection nonetheless."[20] To Watters, the confusion and guilt heaped on Christians promotes mental illness: "A true Christian must always be in a state of torment, since he or she can never really be certain that God has forgiven him or her."[21] According to this view, though, the biblical God either doesn't exist or is evil. Human flourishing comes by escaping belief in God; Adam and Eve become heroes.

Secularists stray from the truth because of three false assumptions about the self, mind, and mental processes:

- **Humans are good by nature.** Secular psychologists emphatically proclaim our lack of fallenness. Abraham Maslow wrote, "As far as I know we just don't have any intrinsic instincts for evil."[22] Atheist philosopher Paul Kurtz saw humans as "perfectible."[23]

- **Society and its institutions are responsible for the evil we do.** Carl Rogers said, "I see members of the human species, like members of other species, as essentially constructive in their fundamental nature, but damaged by their experience."[24] In other words, humanity as a whole doesn't have a destructive bent.

- **Mental health can be restored to those who can overcome psychological guilt.** Because only society is truly evil, Secularists think people's guilt feelings are a false psychological guilt. When people rid themselves of this false guilt, they presumably will be healthy again.[25]

Broken Beyond Self-Repair

Christianity disputes the contention that humans are good by nature, that our evil is the responsibility of society and not ourselves, and that all guilt is false guilt. Without question, humanity's fallenness has become embedded in society's institutions. It can be deeply hurtful, and this hurt can include false guilt over things we had no control over. But to conclude that therefore we have no sin nature is to let ourselves off the hook in an unbiblical way. The fall actually happened, Christians say, and it affects us so deeply—both physically and psychologically—that our attempts at self-repair highlight how disgusting our condition really is.

A gentle translation of Isaiah 64:6 says, "All our righteous deeds are as a polluted garment." The actual phrase in Hebrew for "polluted garment" means a rag soaked in menstrual blood. This metaphor—blood—makes us seem worse than we would like to think. And we are worse. Our feeble protests of innocence—"I'm not that bad ... it was just a little mistake ... it's only a white lie"—do nothing more than deaden our crippled limbs. Our effort to disguise sinful impulses by embracing trendy causes merely spreads the virus of disfiguring superficiality. We are in a million pieces; the more we glue together, the more we disintegrate.

> What appears to be humanity's unraveling may be, from God's perspective, the beginning of restoration.

But in another way, what appears to be humanity's unraveling may be, from God's perspective, the beginning of restoration. Perhaps, as in a tapestry viewed from the back, we see incoherence and depravity and rot, but when we view it from the front, we see the intricacy and beauty and hope that has always been there. We long for it to be so. We are beyond desperate. There must be a third act or we die.

3. ACT 3: PROMISE OF RESTORATION, ISRAEL'S MISSION

Act 3, beginning in Genesis 12 and moving through the Old Testament period and the nation of Israel, is our introduction to God's plan of redemption toward a New Testament fulfillment. Act 3 is subdivided into three scenes according to Bartholomew and Goheen: (1) God initiates redemption, (2) Israel's failure complicates things, and (3) redemption continues through the "intertestamental period" (the four-hundred-year gap between the Old Testament's end and the birth of Christ).

As we've seen, Secularists believe that redemption is unnecessary because there is no such thing as a fall.[26] Interestingly, though, many Secularists still speak in the language of "becoming," as if humans fall short of their true potential at the present time. This does not mean in their thinking, though, that humanity's state can be described as evil, as Ellis G. Olim takes pains to note: "Man is constantly becoming," he says. "What we want, then, is not to encourage a static type of personality based on traditional notions of right and wrong, but the kind of person who is able to go forward into the uncertain future."[27]

Secularists say that if we are sufficiently enlightened, we can look inward and determine what is right.[28] From a biblical perspective, though, people cannot heal themselves; sin is a parasite on humanity. We cannot rid ourselves of it without help. Promising wisdom and freedom, sin worms itself into our lives, and once inside it reproduces uncontrolled. The measures we take to sustain our lives sustain the parasite, giving it more and more strength, more and more power.[29]

Humanity's natural response to sin is denial, then guilt, then fear, followed by a terrible aloneness. Who could ever love us in such a condition?

But in reality, humanity has never been alone. God's plan of healing began immediately after the sin of our first parents in the garden of Eden. As Act 2 ended, we saw things go from bad to worse: Adam and Eve rejected God's plan and saw tragic results. Sin plagued them and plagues us yet today. It all makes us want to cry out with the apostle Paul, "Wretched man that I am! Who will deliver me from this body of death?" (Rom. 7:24).

> In reality, humanity has never been alone. God's plan of healing began immediately after the sin of our first parents in the garden of Eden.

Grace Is Our Hope

As sad and painful as the Genesis account of sin looks, its discordant notes and lurching rhythms give way to a faint but clear melody of grace. The double feature of Genesis 4, murder (Cain and Lamech) and polygamy (Lamech), is met by the grace of cultural development (vv. 17–22). The continuation of Adam's sinful seed (offspring) is met by the grace of people calling upon the name of Yahweh (vv. 25–26).[30] Even in the judgment of the flood (Gen. 6), we see grace in Noah's rescue (v. 8)[31] and in the covenant renewal and re-creation that immediately follows (9:1–19). In one sense, Noah serves as a new or second Adam.

But the cycle continues. Noah's drunkenness and Ham's sin (vv. 20–25) are followed by God's grace in the continuation of the human race in the table of nations (the listing of the clans of the sons of Noah, Gen. 10). Genesis 11 tells the sad story of the tower of Babel and also the genealogy of Shem (leading to Abram). And so it goes, all throughout Scripture: grace, sin, grace. Humanity simply cannot exile itself from the presence of the one who is everywhere and who plants an act of grace down the road from every sinful act.

Grace Is the Subtle Subtext of the Curse

God's grace first appears in the middle of sin—in Genesis 3:15—as God announces the consequences of the first disobedience. The defeat of the serpent is promised, as is humanity's victory. This is known as a **protevangelium**, the first announcement that God would provide redemption through the One who would ultimately and finally crush Satan. This is the first promise of Jesus Christ.

> *Protevangelium*: the first gospel or God's first promise of coming redemption through Jesus Christ (Gen. 3:15).

We'll divide this cryptic announcement into four lines so we can examine each more carefully (Gen. 3:15 HCSB):

1. I will put hostility between you and the woman,

2. and between your seed and her seed.

3. He will strike your head

4. and you will strike his heel.

Based on two grammatical oddities in the text, we can see that God is up to something monumental. First is the imbalance in the description of the opponents through the lines of the verse. Lines 1–2 show same-generation opponents: the serpent versus the woman (line 1), then the serpent's seed versus the woman's seed (line 2). But lines 3–4 switch things up: the woman's seed ("He") does not battle the serpent's seed but rather the *serpent himself*. The serpent is doomed to live through the ages and be met in every generation by fresh reinforcements springing forth from the woman.

> **It seems that God is communicating that although there will ultimately come *one* who is the seed of the woman and will destroy evil forever, in the meantime all human offspring have the potential to be destroyers of Satan's work.**

The second oddity stems from the word translated "seed" (Hebrew *zéra'*). This Hebrew word is a collective noun. Like the English word *sheep*, it is grammatically singular but can be used as both singular and plural. To discern whether a collective noun is to be singular or plural, we must understand the context. If a farmer says, "I'm going to shear my sheep," we don't know whether he has one sheep or a flock of sheep. But if he follows that sentence by saying, "It won't be easy because she's a little ornery," then we know he's talking about just one animal.

The context of Genesis 3:15 indicates that *both* singular and plural meanings are intended. The most natural reading is to take the serpent's "seed" and the woman's "seed" as plural—multiple offspring. But the singular "he/his" in lines 3–4 suggests the possibility that a true singular is intended. It seems that God is communicating that although there will ultimately come *one* who is the seed of the woman and will destroy evil forever, in the meantime all human offspring have the potential to be destroyers of Satan's work.[32]

Grace Is Not Merely a New Testament Phenomenon

If we had only Genesis 3:15, all we could do is scratch our heads and wonder what God is saying. Looking back from the progression of revelation through the rest of Scripture, though, we can see that at the precise moment of sin's entrance into the world, God began unfolding his plan of redemption as big as a canvas covering the sky.

The picture revealed as this canvas unfolds takes our breath away. It is of a man on a cross who, in his dying, condemns humanity's tormentor and, in his resurrection, secures forever the victory God planned from the beginning. Jesus ultimately and finally defeats Satan. In the meantime, Eve's descendants—such as Abraham (Gen. 22:17–19; Gal. 3:16–17)[33] and David (2 Sam. 7:12–15),[34] with whom God initiated covenantal relationships—are the "seed" through whom God carries out his Satan-crushing work. Ultimately, all those who believe in Jesus also participate in defeating Satan. As Paul said in Romans 16:20, "The God of peace will soon crush Satan under *your* feet."

Grace Is the Basis of Covenant

To see this, we need to understand how God interacts with his people through covenant. This is a critically important concept, and most of the rest of this chapter will be confusing unless we grasp it clearly, so let's get started.

Throughout the story of Scripture, God makes agreements with his people. The word for these agreements is **covenant**. The English word *cove-nant* connotes a legal agreement between two parties that involves both rights and responsibilities.

> *Covenant:* an agreement between two parties that involves both rights and responsibilities.

A covenant is different from a contract. Although both involve a commitment between two parties, in a contract each party is *self-centered* ("What's in it for me? What are my rights? What can I demand?"). A contract focuses on the obligations of the other party, looking for specific, concrete results. "Do this or else!" If a contract is broken, the signers can seek recourse through courts of law. A professional football team, for instance, may choose to release a player after three years, but if it has agreed to pay the player for four years, it must, even if the player doesn't play.

A covenant, on the other hand, is *other-centered*. Take marriage. When two people marry, each makes a vow that clarifies what he or she will do, not what he or she expects the other to do: "I take you to be my wife (or husband), to have and to hold from this day forward, for better, for worse, for richer, for poorer, in sickness and in health, to love and to cherish, till death us do part, according to God's holy law, and this is my solemn vow." High expectations? You bet: marriage is for life. It generates love based on commitment, not just feelings.

The foundation of a marriage covenant is a common vision, not a bullet list of perfor-mance-oriented results. The question in a covenant is not "What specifically will you do?" but rather "Will I be faithful to you as a person?" Person, not to-do list; love, not obligation. If one spouse acts in an unloving fashion, he or she can remedy it by humbly asking for forgiveness and thus restoring the relationship.

When God made covenants with people, the typical covenantal structure was to list the *authority* of the one making the covenant, outline the *terms* of the covenant, and then announce the *blessings* and *curses*. There were clear consequences, good or bad, that those making the covenant would call down on themselves if they followed the covenant or refused to do so (Lev. 26; Deut. 28). The prophets were well aware of these blessings and curses, and they referenced them repeatedly. The ultimate covenantal curse was exile.   X

God has a covenant relationship with his creation. Sometimes God's covenant part-ner is all of creation, sometimes it is a select group of people, and sometimes it is an individual and his future descendants (seed). Covenants provide the backbone of the Bible's metanarrative. Without understanding covenants, we will miss much of the way God works.

Here's a brief description of the major covenants in the Bible and how each one is ultimately secured by Jesus Christ himself.

1. Creation covenant. This covenant was made with Adam to establish an environment of *shalom* (wholeness) with those made in God's image. Jesus fulfills this covenant. The New Testament says that Jesus was the ultimate image of God (Col. 1:15),[35] the Second Adam (1 Cor. 15:45),[36] and the "Seed" of the woman who ultimately crushes Satan (Rev. 21–22).

2. Noahic covenant. This covenant, made with Noah in Genesis 9, describes how Noah and his family were rescued from judgment and tasked to preserve creation. The sign of the covenant was the rainbow. Jesus ultimately fulfilled this covenant by ushering in the new creation (Gal. 6:12–16, 2 Cor. 5:17).[37]

3. Abrahamic covenant. This covenant, made with Abraham, established a new nation that would be a blessing to all the other nations (Gen. 12). The sign of the covenant was the circumcision of Abraham. The apostle Paul talked about Jesus's fulfilling this covenant: all who are in Christ are the "seed" of Abraham (Gal. 3:29).[38]

4. Mosaic (or Sinaitic) covenant. Through Moses, God made a covenant with the people of Israel, setting them apart, giving them the mission to reach the world (Exod. 6:1–8, Exod. 19). The sign of the covenant was the Sabbath (Exod. 31:13).[39] Jesus fulfilled this covenant as the Son of God, the true Israel,[40] the true tabernacle (Heb. 9:1–15), and the ultimate sacrifice (Phil. 2:1–11, Heb. 10:11–13).[41]

5. Davidic covenant. God's covenant with David was the promise of an eternal dynasty (2 Sam. 7:8–13). Jesus fulfilled this covenant by being the "Son of David" (Matt. 1:1)[42] and the eternal king (1 Tim. 1:17–20).[43]

6. New covenant. God established a new covenant with Israel (Jer. 31), promising a new heart and *shalom* and forgiveness for their sins. The sign of this covenant would be the circumcision of the heart (Jer. 4:4)[44] and baptism (Col. 2:8–15). Jesus fulfilled this covenant by inaugurating all these things, which began in him (Heb. 10:11–14).[45]

Here is one highly important point to keep in mind. The English word *covenant* suggests an agreement between two consenting people. The biblical covenants, however, are one-sided. In each case, God chooses his covenant partner and sets out the expectations without human input. In this sense, "covenant" is similar to the notion of "vow" or "promise." God's covenants both *declare* promises of God's commitment and express *expectations* of human faithfulness. Of course, only Jesus was perfectly faithful to each covenant's conditions. Thus, he is the ultimate fulfillment of each covenant.

4. ACT 3A: REDEMPTION INITIATED

God's plan to redeem the world includes his election of one nation, Israel. We know this because of God's covenants with Abraham (Gen. 12; 15; 17) and Israel (Exod. 19; Deut. 4).

The Abrahamic Covenant

The Abrahamic covenant begins in Genesis 12:1–3[46] but is expanded on in later chapters. God chose Abraham to be the conduit of his blessings to humankind. Contrary to what one might expect in an ancient Near East culture (in which the firstborn had all the rights), God never seemed to act according to expectations. Of Abraham's sons he chose Isaac, not Ishmael. Of Isaac's sons he chose Jacob, not Esau. Even among Jacob's twelve sons, only two (Judah and Joseph) were selected for special ministries.

In any event, God chose Abraham and made five promises to him that draw a contrast between how God dealt with Adam, Eve, and their descendants and how he dealt with Abraham and his descendants:

> God chose Abraham to be the conduit of his blessings to humankind. Contrary to what one might expect in an ancient Near East culture (in which the firstborn had all the rights), God never seemed to act according to expectations.

- **Relationship.** Whereas Adam and Eve had experienced the curse of constant battle with Satan (Gen. 3:15),[47] God established a covenant to protect Abraham and his descendants.

- **Nationhood.** Whereas Adam and Eve had been evicted from the garden of Eden (Gen. 3:23),[48] God told Abraham that his descendants would form into a great nation.

- **Seed.** Whereas God had told Eve that childbirth would be painful and that her descendants would be attacked by Satan (Gen. 3:15–16),[49] God promised Abraham that his descendants would be as numerous as the stars in heaven and the sand on the seashore.[50]

- **Land.** Whereas Cain was cursed to be a wanderer and fugitive (Gen. 4:12),[51] God promised to escort Abraham to a land where he could settle down and prosper (Gen. 12:1).[52]

- **Blessing to Others.** Whereas Canaan was cursed to be a slave to the nations (Gen. 9:25),[53] God promised Abraham that his descendants would be a blessing to all the families of the earth (Gen. 12:3).[54]

Through one man, God would reach the nations. This is a common characteristic of how God operates. When he wants to do something *really big* (such as spread his blessing to the world), he starts *really small* (with a nomadic sheepherder rather than a prominent king). In response, Abraham and his descendants were to have faith (Gen. 15:6),[55] obey God's call and command (Gen. 12:1–4; 22:1),[56] enter into God's presence (Gen. 17:1), lead blameless lives (Gen. 17:1),[57] and be circumcised (Gen. 17:9–14, 22–27). Using royal imagery, the author makes it clear that Abraham's descendants would be missionaries to the world, spreading the word of God's covenant promises.[58]

> God's covenant with Abraham is so important throughout Scripture that we cannot understand the flow of Scripture unless we grasp how central this aspect of God's revelation is.

In the New Testament, Matthew saw the connection. Jesus was the "seed" of Abraham (Matt. 1:1).[59] The apostle Paul saw it too (Gal. 3). Paul even called Abraham the paragon of faith (Rom. 4:1–20). God's covenant with Abraham is so important throughout Scripture that we cannot understand the flow of Scripture unless we grasp how central this aspect of God's revelation is.

The Mosaic Covenant

The most significant historical and theological event in Israel's history is the exodus of the children of Israel from Egypt (Exod. 1–15). The Bible connects the exodus to the Abrahamic covenant (Exod. 2:24; 6:4–8),[60] showing that the covenant God made with Moses at Mount Sinai is a continuation of the covenant he made with Abraham some six hundred years earlier.

Through Moses, God made a covenant with the children of Israel. Contrary to what many people think, the Mosaic covenant was not a way for the children of Israel to earn righteousness through good works. In making the covenant, God reminded them that he is the one who brought them to himself (Exod. 19:4; 20:2).[61] Obedience to the law is a *response* to God's grace; the exodus is the image of salvation. The children of Israel understood this clearly and sang a victory hymn: "I will sing to the LORD, for he has triumphed gloriously; the horse and his rider he has thrown into the sea. The LORD is my strength and my song, and he has become my salvation" (Exod. 15:1–2).

The exodus is so central in the biblical narrative that trying to understand *anything* in Scripture without grasping its significance is like trying to understand, without reference to bees, how honey is made. The exodus appears throughout the Old Testament as what film story consultant Bobette Buster calls a "gleaming detail"—a motif that appears repeatedly and orients viewers to the film's central message.[62] The exodus is everywhere in the Old Testament: in the historical narrative,[63] the psalms,[64] and the prophets.[65] Many of these passages refer to the future restoration of the nation in terms of a "new exodus."

The exodus shows up in the New Testament as well, such as in 2 Corinthians 6:16, when the apostle Paul applies God's promise to the church: "I will make my dwelling among them and walk among them, and I will be their God, and they shall be my people."[66]

5. ACT 3B: REDEMPTION COMPLICATED

The bulk of the Old Testament shows God's sustained faithfulness to Israel, despite Israel's unfaithfulness to him. This tension is seen in the historical narrative, in the wisdom literature, and especially in the writings of the prophets.[67]

The Davidic Covenant

In the Davidic covenant (2 Sam. 7), God promised an eternal dynasty to David and his seed. The Abrahamic covenant included promises of royalty (Gen. 17:6; 49:10).[68] Judah, David's tribe, was prominent from Israel's early days. The historical books discussed the need for a king (Judg. 21:25).[69]

Clearly, the prophet Samuel saw the connection and focused on identifying David's line through the amazing and providential story of David's great-grandmother Ruth, through Samuel's mother's (Hannah's) prayer for the birth of Samuel (who would eventually anoint David king), and through the foreshadowing events displaying Saul's badness and David's goodness (1 Sam. 9–15). All of these point to David's reign as something extraordinary. But most extraordinary is that Jesus comes from David's line. David's psalms focus strongly on the *idea* of God's anointed one. Another word for "anointed one" is *messiah*.

> Most extraordinary is that Jesus comes from David's line. David's psalms focus strongly on the *idea* of God's anointed one. Another word for "anointed one" is *messiah*.

Israel had a wrong desire for a king (1 Sam. 8; 12), yet God was faithful. Saul was an utter failure as Israel's first king, yet God was faithful. David was a disappointment as well, his life marked by sin and failure, yet God was faithful. Solomon began as a wise king but ultimately caused the kingdom to divide (1 Kings 11:11)[70] as he became the antithesis of the godly idea of kingship. He developed a private army, took many wives, taxed people heavily to accumulate wealth for himself, and considered himself to be better than the people he ruled (each of these was specifically prohibited in Deuteronomy 17:14–20). And yet God was faithful.

After Solomon's death, the kingdom split. As 1 Kings 12 to 2 Kings 25 records, the northern kingdom had a terrible track record: twenty bad kings and no good ones. The southern kingdom was hardly better; only eight of its twenty kings were good.

And yet God was faithful.[71]

6. Act 3C: Redemption Predicted

In most movies, a point comes when things can't get any worse. And then things get worse. The Old Testament period ends this way: with frustration, uncertainty, and a four-hundred-year silence. In this part of Act 3, when people think God has abandoned them, prophets arise to urge the people to return to faithfulness to God. Typically, God raised up prophets when leaders, the kings and priests, failed to do their jobs or when they led the people into unfaithfulness.

So what do prophets do? Mainly their job is to call people back to faithfulness to God's law and God's mission. Some of what they say involves predictions for the future, but essentially they are to highlight God's covenant promises: if the people will repent of their wicked ways, God will forgive them.

> What do prophets do? Mainly their job is to call people back to faithfulness to God's law and God's mission.

Two categories of sin concern the prophets most: idolatry and social injustice. Idolatry, attempting to replace the one true God, is the focus of the first half of the Ten Commandments.

Vertical Commands: commandments relating to humanity's relationship with God.

These **vertical commands**, emphasizing people's relationship with God, include having no other gods, not making idols, not taking the Lord's name in vain, and so forth. The second half of the Ten Commandments, the **horizontal commands**, emphasizing people's relationship with each other, provide justice by prohibiting such things as bearing false witness, committing adultery, stealing, and killing. This is why Jesus summed up the law as loving God with all of our hearts, souls, minds, and strength and loving our neighbors as ourselves.

Horizontal Commands: commandments relating to humanity's social relationships.

The prophets' denunciations of idolatry and injustice boil down to this: you have turned away from bearing God's image; you must turn back or, just as surely as thunder follows lightning, you will experience the consequences. The prophets' message was essentially a divorce decree; because of the people's unfaithfulness, God was sending them into exile.[72]

The prophets realized, though, that exile is not the last word. After exile comes restoration (Deut. 4:29–31;[73] 30:1–10). Although people might see prophets as preaching judgment, their ultimate message is salvation. Take a look at this much-quoted (and often misquoted) portion from Jeremiah:

> I know the plans I have for you, declares the LORD, plans for welfare and not for evil, to give you a future and a hope. Then you will call upon me and come and pray to me, and I will hear you. You will seek me and find me, when you seek me with all your heart. I will be found by you, declares the LORD, and I will restore your fortunes and gather you from all the nations and all the places where I have driven you, declares the LORD, and I will bring you back to the place from which I sent you into exile. (29:11–14)

The prophetic writings—which feature powerful promises of material blessing, defeat of enemies, restoration of reputation, and a willingness and desire to obey God—show a God who restores broken people.[74] Here we also find promises of a coming messiah. The prophecies promise the following:

- the coming king (Zech. 9:9–13; 12:10–14)[75]

- the day of the Lord and his appearing (Zech. 9:14–17; 12:1–9; 14:1–21; Mal. 4:1–3)[76]

- the restoration of Judah and Israel (Zech. 10)

- the coming of the Lord's messenger (Mal. 3:1–4)[77]

- the coming of Elijah (Mal. 4:5–6)[78]

THE BIBLE: GOD'S BIG STORY, PART 2

The book of Psalms is also a rich source of prophecy. Most psalms are written from David's point of view, describing his experiences and emotions. David's dynasty was secured through all time by direct promise from God. The so-called royal psalms (e.g., Psalms 2, 18, 20, 21, 45, 72, 101, 110, 132, 144) cause us to think of the coming Son of David through whom God will restore everything completely.[79]

We can imagine these promises sounding fantastical to their original hearers. *Have these prophets lost their minds? Why are they so focused on the distant future? We need help now!* To some extent, though, the people took the prophets at their word. Persia's defeat of Babylon (539 BC) allowed exiled Jews to return home. The returning exiles must have been filled with hope. The prophets' words were coming true: a glorious restoration was at hand! But as the books of Ezra, Nehemiah, Esther, Haggai, Zechariah, and Malachi show, the actual experience of the returning exiles failed to reach the rhetorical heights seemingly promised by the prophets' writings. The people avoided wholesale idolatry but were instead plagued by apathy, self-interest, infighting, divorce, and failure to follow the Mosaic law.[80] Plus, the exiles never regained political independence, so David's dynasty was never reestablished. No wonder people doubted God's promises.

At this time of uncertainty and doubt, the call was dropped, so to speak. For four hundred years, the people heard nothing from God.

Intertestamental Silence

After the writings of the prophets, the Old Testament ends. The four-hundred-year silence theologians call the **intertestamental period** was, outside of Palestine, anything but silent. Revelation from God to Israel had ceased, but the world was on the move. Geopolitically, Greece under Alexander the Great conquered Persia (around 333 BC) to become the new world empire, and then in the first-century BC, Rome took over.

Through a movement to universalize Greek culture, called **Hellenization** (from the Greek word *ellinismos*, which refers to the Greek language and values), the Jews were pressured to change their language, dress, and other basic ways of living, and they splintered into factions over how to respond to these pressures. **Zealots** wanted to overthrow foreign rulers. **Sadducees** wanted to accommodate them.

> *Intertestamental Period:* the four-hundred-year period between the completion of the Old Testament and the writing of the New Testament.

> *Hellenization:* the spread of Greek culture (language, arts, ideas, religion, government) throughout the conquered ancient world.

> *Zealots:* a first-century Jewish faction that militantly opposed the Roman occupation of Palestine.

> *Sadducees:* a first-century Jewish faction of priests and aristocrats who expressed complacency toward the Roman occupation, denied the concept of an afterlife, rejected the Talmud, and believed that only the first five books of the Torah were authoritative.

Essenes wanted to separate themselves by moving into the wilderness. **Pharisees** thought an obsessive attention to God's law would bring the messiah. Whatever theological differences existed, each group hoped to be seen as the "remnant" referred to in Isaiah 10 and 11—the devoted believers who would hold on despite the circumstances. This caused more infighting and tension, as you can imagine. Who would be called unfaithful, and who was the "true Israel"?

> *Essenes:* a first-century Jewish faction that lived a monastic and communal life in the desert, shared everything in common, practiced ritual cleansing, and produced the oldest known copies of the Old Testament (for instance, the Dead Sea Scrolls).

God's silence was, in reality, the dark before the dawn. When the dawn arrived, it revealed something so stunning that the theological elite couldn't fathom it. As songwriter Michael Card writes, "For a thousand years the dreamers dreamt, and hoped to see his love. But the Promise showed their wildest dreams had simply not been wild enough."[81] What the dawning light revealed is the subject of the New Testament narrative. Let's look at it through the redemptive ministry of Jesus (Act 4), the redemptive ministry of the church (Act 5), and consummation of God's plan at the end of time.

> *Pharisees:* a first-century Jewish faction that practiced a legalistic interpretation of the Torah, accepted the Talmud as authoritative, believed in the concept of an afterlife, and opposed the Roman occupation of Palestine.

7. ACT 4: KINGDOM RESTORED, REDEMPTION ACCOMPLISHED

The prophets envisioned a messiah who would drive death and humiliation further and further from the field of battle until they disappeared altogether. In fact, the very last statement of the Old Testament, Malachi 4:5–6, says, "Behold, I will send you Elijah the prophet before the great and awesome day of the LORD comes. And he will turn the hearts of fathers to their children and the hearts of children to their fathers, lest I come and strike the land with a decree of utter destruction."

After a four-hundred-year downbeat, the orchestral sounds of redemption arose as though the prolonged silence were an intentional part of the musical score. According to Luke 1:17,[82] John the Baptist was the one prophesied about in Malachi—the one who would come in the wild spirit of Elijah to prepare the way of the Lord. And as John the Baptist testified, the "Lord" was Jesus Christ, sent to earth to "re" everything: to *re*new, to *re*store, to *re*deem, to *re*concile.[83]

These "re" words belong today to our theological vocabulary because the music never really stopped, and God, the composer and conductor, never left the podium. Rather, he weaved pain, confusion, and doubt into the music so that with the resounding redemption, he might express the harmony of creation more profoundly than creation itself could have. We can see this in three major themes reflected in the gospel accounts of Matthew, Mark, Luke, and John.

First Theme: Gospel

Jesus came to proclaim and become God's gospel (good news). From the beginning, we see that Jesus Christ was the recipient of both the Abrahamic and Davidic covenants, he was of a kingly dynasty, he would save people, his coming was the fulfillment of prophecy, and he was bringing God's kingdom.

So what is the gospel? The letters of the apostle Paul clarify the term, so we'll get a clearer sense of it in Act 5. For now, though, the gospel accounts make clear that the "the gospel of Jesus Christ" (Mark 1:1) is part of a larger story line called "the gospel of God" (Mark 1:14). For example:

Matthew

The book of the genealogy of Jesus Christ, the son of David, the son of Abraham ... (1:1)

You shall call his name Jesus, for he will save his people from their sins. (1:21)

All this took place to fulfill what the Lord had spoken by the prophet. (1:22)

[John the Baptist said,] "Repent, for the kingdom of heaven is at hand." (3:2)

Mark

The beginning of the gospel of Jesus Christ, the Son of God. As it is written in Isaiah the prophet ..." (1:1–2)

Now after John was arrested, Jesus came into Galilee, proclaiming the gospel of God, and saying, "The time is fulfilled, and the kingdom of God is at hand; repent and believe in the gospel." (1:14–15)

Luke

[In the synagogue, Jesus] unrolled the scroll and found the place where it was written, "The Spirit of the Lord is upon me, because he has anointed me to proclaim good news to the poor. He has sent me to proclaim liberty to the captives and recovering of sight to the blind, to set at liberty those who are oppressed, to proclaim the year of the Lord's favor." (4:17–19)

Today this Scripture has been fulfilled in your hearing. (4:21)

I must preach the good news of the kingdom of God to the other towns as well; for I was sent for this purpose. (4:43)

John

The Word became flesh and dwelt among us, and we have seen his glory, glory as of the only Son from the Father, full of grace and truth. (1:14)

The law was given through Moses; grace and truth came through Jesus Christ. (1:17)

Behold, the Lamb of God, who takes away the sin of the world! (1:29)

I have seen and have borne witness that this is the Son of God. (1:34)

The gospel writers were unified: Jesus is the Messiah. But there is a second theme as well: Jesus is the *prophesied* Messiah.

Second Theme: Prophetic Fulfillment

The Gospels connect the dots between the Old Testament and Jesus.[84] Very often, Jesus is said to "fulfill" something from the prophets. For example, five different prophetic fulfillments are mentioned in just the first two chapters of Matthew alone:

- Jesus's virgin birth (Matt. 1:23 / Isa. 7:14)[85]

- Bethlehem as the birthplace of the Messiah (Matt. 2:6 / Mic. 5:2)[86]

- Jesus's return from Egypt (Matt. 2:15 / Hosea 11:1)[87]

- Herod's killing of children (Matt. 2:18 / Jer. 31:15)[88]

- Jesus's home of Nazareth (Matt. 2:23 / [no clear OT text])[89]

When we turn back and look at the specific Old Testament passages, however, we may become confused. Many of these prophecies were clearly in reference to a localized event occurring at the time of the writing. Only one prophecy, that from Micah 5:2, is a simple prediction-fulfillment passage. Isaiah 7:14 should probably be read as having a double fulfillment: one in Isaiah's day and then Jesus's. The other three Old Testament passages aren't predictions at all, strictly speaking. Clearly, if we are to take the biblical text at its word, we need to have a larger notion of "fulfill" than anything akin to a sportscaster predicting the win of a sports team.

> Clearly, if we are to take the biblical text at its word, we need to have a larger notion of "fulfill" than anything akin to a sportscaster predicting the win of a sports team.

If we began with the assumption, however, that prophecy is straightforward, that each prediction comes with a onetime fulfillment, then we would miss seeing how Jesus's fulfillment of prophecy is part of the deep structure of the Gospels. For example, Matthew intentionally talks of Jesus in a way that shows a clear parallel to the journey of Israel itself.

ISRAEL'S JOURNEY	JESUS'S JOURNEY
Prehistory—Abraham	Genealogy—Abraham, David, Exile
"Birth" in Egypt	Birth
Plagues	Flight to Egypt Death of Firstborn
Exodus	Baptism
Mount Sinai	Wilderness Temptation
Wilderness	Sermon on Mount
Kingdom in Land	Kingdom Ministry
Exile	Death
Restoration	Resurrection

The one sense in which Jesus does *not* equal Israel is that where Israel failed, Jesus succeeded. The Old Testament is filled with tension and confusion to which Jesus brings clarity and resolution. At the moment of despair, Jesus brings hope. The Old Testament raises questions. In Christ, we have answers.

Third Theme: The Kingdom of God

The kingdom of God (or kingdom of heaven) blankets the pages of the New Testament. Taken together, the references to the kingdom of God are not about a *place* but about a *reality*: God is king. This has always been true, of course, but the New Testament shows how the reality of God-as-king over time, space, and history—just as the Old Testament writers anticipated—should affect everything we do. We rejoice in the kingdom of God, anticipating and participating in the removal of everything that plagues us presently: sin, sickness, death, and unfaithfulness. We become vessels of the kingdom by becoming vessels of the Spirit.

But the way in which the New Testament fulfills the Old Testament did not always align with Jewish expectations. For example, Jews expected a *messiah*, but they did not anticipate the *Messiah*, one person who would be both the human messiah and God. This is the culmination of the biblical narrative: God appeared in human flesh as the savior of the world. One person. One reality.

> Taken together, the references to the kingdom of God are not about a *place* but about a *reality*: God is king. This has always been true, of course, but the New Testament shows how the reality of God-as-king over time, space, and history—just as the Old Testament writers anticipated—should affect everything we do.

There are many theories about how the transition from the "kingdom-established" to the "kingdom-realized" will take place, but all agree that it is a two-stage process. The first stage was Jesus's incarnation, death, resurrection, and ascension and the advent of the new covenant. The second stage is known as Jesus's second coming. The return of Christ will lead to the full consummation of the kingdom of God. The kingdom is both *already* and *not yet*.

8. ACT 5: KINGDOM DISPLAYED, REDEMPTION APPLIED: THE CHURCH

As we have seen, the word *gospel* literally means "good news." But good news about what? First, the gospel found in the Scriptures is the good news of Jesus's life and work. Any gospel that does not focus on Jesus as Lord and Messiah and does not proclaim his death and resurrection is not the gospel of God. Second, the gospel of God is the *announcement* that God's kingdom is "at hand" (Matt. 4:17)[90] to bring blessing to the nations of the earth (Gal. 3:6–9).[91]

> **Gospel:** from the Old English for "good news"; the message of Jesus's saving work and God's present kingdom.

The word **gospel** was certainly not new to New Testament times. Isaiah 40–66 is a major part of the biblical background for the gospel. The **Septuagint** (one of the major original sources from which the Bible is translated) uses the Greek root for "gospel" as the word for heralding good news (Isa. 41:27; 52:7; 60:6; 61:1).[92] What good news? That God will rescue his covenant people from exile, demonstrating that he is their King and the one and only Lord over creation.

> **Septuagint:** the Greek translation of the Hebrew Scriptures.

Those of Jewish faith were not the only ones to talk about spreading the gospel. The Roman emperors of the first century used the word *gospel* to describe official reports that made them happy, such as military victories or the birth of an heir. In fact, the emperor was known as "Lord." Rome even had certain heralds who were to spread the good news about its successes. Undoubtedly, when the apostles announced the gospel and that Jesus is Lord, it would have been understood as a political statement about the king.

The apostle Paul, Jewish by birth and until his miraculous conversion a persecutor of Christians, is the biblical author who most prolifically articulates the message of the gospel. Paul's apostolic gospel has received much attention from biblical scholars, many of whom believe that Paul's gospel was different from Jesus's. But as theologian N. T. Wright has taken pains to show, Paul understood the gospel in light of his Jewish upbringing—indeed in light of all of Jewish history—and was faithful to spread the gospel of Jesus, not his own.[93]

What Is the Church?

The apostle Paul wrote most of his letters to entire churches—churches formed through the spread of the good news about Jesus. The book of Acts records how the church, the *ecclesia*, was a community united by God's Spirit and charged with proclaiming the reality of Christ's kingdom to the whole world. This community, based on the new covenant, was made up of both Jews and non-Jews (Gentiles). It defied all the old categories about who was the true Israel and which sect was best serving God's will.

In fact, the church created an entirely new identity. The new covenant articulated by Jesus, through which people could become a "new creation" (2 Cor. 5:17),[94] was unprecedented in the world. So how would people who joined this new church describe it? The New Testament uses many metaphors with which people are familiar. The church is described as a bride, army, nation, body, family, team, temple, flock, and hospital.

Many of the metaphors describing the church come from Old Testament descriptions of Israel. The apostle Peter, a constant companion of Jesus, gave one of the clearest statements about the church's mission in light of Israel's history:

> You are a chosen race, a royal priesthood, a holy nation, a people for his own posses-
> sion, that you may proclaim the excellencies of him who called you out of darkness
> into his marvelous light. Once you were not a people, but now you are God's people;
> once you had not received mercy, but now you have received mercy. (1 Pet. 2:9–10)

Very simply, the church would spread the good news about God, just as Israel had been instructed to do.

What Place Do We Have in the Metanarrative?

Earlier in this chapter, I hinted that Christians have a place in the biblical metanarrative *today*. The "filming" is still taking place; we are actors on the set as the story resolves. True, Scripture is no longer being written, and we don't have apostles who carry the full weight of God's authority. However, Scripture does include future believers in its narrative, and we do have a place in the story of God.

Earlier I quoted Erich Fromm and Wendell Watters, both of whom see Christians as brain-washed and tormented by sin. Now we can see that their account is precisely the opposite of the truth. Because of redemption, Christians can see themselves as image bearers of God with great worth and potential but suffering from sin's parasitical infestation. Redemption through Christ frees us from confusion and guilt. It is no wonder, then, that Christians (and even people of other religions) are more likely than those without religious belief to be mentally healthy.[95]

Although the New Testament certainly provides detailed instructions for the church that translate to today, it isn't primarily a "church manual"; rather, the story itself guides us. The rich metaphors used about the church in the New Testament help us see our connection to the earliest followers of God, even as far back as the garden of Eden. And we will also soon glimpse our future. These big-picture realities ought to guide us as we make corporate and personal decisions about our identity and mission, particularly regarding issues that the Bible does not address in a simple chapter-and-verse citation.

9. ACT 6: KINGDOM CONSUMMATED, REDEMPTION COMPLETED: NEW CREATION

Many Christians have the impression that their eternal destiny is "up there" some-where. According to Revelation 21–22, however, we do not go to God at the end of all things; rather, God comes to us, "tabernacling" among us. The experience of his presence

---

will be even better than Adam and Eve's in the original creation because sin will have been conquered once and for all. Everyone—even God's enemies—will at that time realize that a world that was created, fallen, and redeemed is a greater testament to God's glory than creation itself.

We cannot fully comprehend the description of the new creation pictured in the book of Revelation. There will be no sun and no sea, for example, and no sin. But what we can comprehend is very exciting: we won't just be floating around on clouds, playing harps. We'll be able to watch God at work—and we'll work alongside him—making all things new.

Bible professor and pastor W. Gary Phillips has shared an exciting insight he found about the unity of the Bible that shows remarkable parallels between the first three chapters of the Bible and the last three.[96]

GENESIS 1–3	REVELATION 20–22
"In the beginning, God created the heavens and the earth" (1:1)	*"I saw a new heaven and a new earth" (21:1)*
"The darkness he called Night" (1:5)	*"There will be no night there" (21:25)*
"God made the two great lights" (sun and moon, 1:16)	*"The city has no need of sun or moon" (21:23)*
"In the day that you eat from it you shall surely die" (2:17)	*"Death shall be no more, neither shall there be mourning" (21:4)*
Satan appears as deceiver of mankind (3:1)	*Satan disappears forever (20:10)*
Shown a garden, into which defilement entered (3:6–7)	*Shown a city, nothing that defiles shall ever enter it (21:27)*
Walk of God with man interrupted (3:8–10)	*Walk of God with man resumed (21:3)*
Initial triumph of the serpent (3:13)	*Ultimate triumph of the Lamb (20:10; 22:3)*
"I will surely multiply your pain" (3:16)	*There shall be no more pain (21:4)*
"Cursed is the ground because of you" (3:17)	*There shall be no more curse (22:3)*
Man's dominion broken in the fall of the first man, Adam (3:19)	*Man's dominion restored in the rule of the new man, Christ (22:5)*
First paradise closed (3:23)	*New paradise opened (21:25)*
Access to the tree of life disinherited in Adam (3:24)	*Access to the tree of life reinstated in Christ (22:14)*
They were driven from God's presence (3:24)	*They shall see his face (22:4)*

Christ will renew all things. There will be a great reversal of sin, suffering, and broken-ness. The Bible offers a complete story, from the beginning of time to the end, from the original creation to the new creation, from age to age—a testimony to God's faithfulness.

10. Conclusion

So how do we live in the meantime? Jesus's sacrifice is *already* complete, but we are *not yet* home with him. Our bodies are like a tent: they're temporary. But God clothes us in his glory and gives us his Spirit to enable us to live as redeemed people now, not just when we get to heaven. So what does this life look like? Here's how Paul puts it:

> The Bible offers a complete story, from the beginning of time to the end, from the original creation to the new creation, from age to age—a testimony to God's faithfulness.

We are always of good courage. We know that while we are at home in the body we are away from the Lord, for we walk by faith, not by sight. Yes, we are of good courage, and we would rather be away from the body and at home with the Lord. So whether we are at home or away, we make it our aim to please him. For we must all appear before the judgment seat of Christ, so that each one may receive what is due for what he has done in the body, whether good or evil. Therefore, knowing the fear of the Lord, we persuade others. (2 Cor. 5:6–11)

This is what the redeemed life looks like. We know we're not home yet, but in God's power we live courageously, seeking to please him, walking by faith, and persuading others that his story is the story of the whole world—the true story of the world and everyone in it.

Endnotes

1. Gilbert Keith Chesterton, *Orthodoxy* (New York: John Lane Company, 1909), 24.
2. Quoted in Ravi Zacharias, "Existential Challenges of Evil and Suffering," in *Beyond Opinion: Living the Faith We Defend*, ed. Ravi Zacharias (Nashville: Thomas Nelson, 2007), 206.
3. Cornelius Plantinga Jr., in one of the best resources on sin and the fall, *Not the Way It's Supposed to Be: A Breviary of Sin* (Grand Rapids, MI: Eerdmans, 1995).
4. Genesis 2:25: "The man and his wife were both naked and were not ashamed."
5. John C. Holbert, "Back to the Beginning as Lent Begins: Reflections on Genesis 2:15–17; 3:1–7," Patheos, March 4, 2011, www.patheos.com//Resources/Additional-Resources/Back-to-the-Beginning-as-Lent-Begins-John-Holbert-03-07-2011.html.
6. The apostle Paul said in Romans 5:12: "Sin came into the world through one man," implying that the man was the first to sin, even though he was not the first to eat of the forbidden fruit. Perhaps his misleading of the woman was that sin.
7. Genesis 3:1: "Now the serpent was more crafty than any other beast of the field that the Lord God had made. He said to the woman, 'Did God actually say, "You shall not eat of any tree in the garden"?'"
8. Genesis 3:14: "The Lord God said to the serpent, 'Because you have done this, cursed are you above all livestock and above all beasts of the field; on your belly you shall go, and dust you shall eat all the days of your life.'"
9. Genesis 3:15: "I will put enmity between you and the woman, and between your offspring and her offspring; he shall bruise your head, and you shall bruise his heel."
10. Revelation 12:9: "The great dragon was thrown down, that ancient serpent, who is called the devil and Satan, the deceiver of the whole world—he was thrown down to the earth, and his angels were thrown down with him"; Revelation 20:2: "He seized the dragon, that ancient serpent, who is the devil and Satan, and bound him for a thousand years"; Romans 16:20: "The God of peace will soon crush Satan under your feet. The grace of our Lord Jesus Christ be with you."
11. Genesis 3:22: "Then the Lord God said, 'Behold, the man has become like one of us in knowing good and evil. Now, lest

he reach out his hand and take also of the tree of life and eat, and live forever."'

12. Genesis 3:16: "To the woman he said, 'I will surely multiply your pain in childbearing; in pain you shall bring forth children. Your desire shall be for your husband, and he shall rule over you.'"

13. Scholars disagree about the meaning of the words *desire* and *rule* and thus whether Genesis 3:15b is a positive or negative statement. The negative seems more likely because of its immediate context (that is, among other curses) and the parallel of *desire* and *rule* in an obvious negative context in other places such as Genesis 4:7b ("[Sin's] desire is for you [Cain], but you must rule over it.").

14. Genesis 3:17–19: "To Adam he said, 'Because you have listened to the voice of your wife and have eaten of the tree of which I commanded you, "You shall not eat of it," cursed is the ground because of you; in pain you shall eat of it all the days of your life; thorns and thistles it shall bring forth for you; and you shall eat the plants of the field. By the sweat of your face you shall eat bread, till you return to the ground, for out of it you were taken; for you are dust, and to dust you shall return.'"

15. Genesis 4:8: "Cain spoke to Abel his brother. And when they were in the field, Cain rose up against his brother Abel and killed him."

16. Genesis 4:23–26: "Lamech said to his wives: 'Adah and Zillah, hear my voice; you wives of Lamech, listen to what I say: I have killed a man for wounding me, a young man for striking me. If Cain's revenge is sevenfold, then Lamech's is seventy-sevenfold.' And Adam knew his wife again, and she bore a son and called his name Seth, for she said, 'God has appointed for me another offspring instead of Abel, for Cain killed him.' To Seth also a son was born, and he called his name Enosh. At that time people began to call upon the name of the LORD." See Cornelius Plantinga Jr.'s discussion of this in *Not the Way It's Supposed to Be: A Breviary of Sin* (Grand Rapids, MI: Eerdmans, 1995), chap. 9.

17. Genesis 6:5: "The LORD saw that the wickedness of man was great in the earth, and that every intention of the thoughts of his heart was only evil continually."

18. *Monty Python and the Holy Grail*, directed by Terry Gilliam and Terry Jones (1975; Culver City, CA: Sony Pictures Home Entertainment, 2006), DVD.

19. Erich Fromm, *You Shall Be as Gods: A Radical Interpretation of the Old Testament and Its Tradition* (New York: Holt, Rinehart and Winston, 1966), 7.

20. Wendell W. Watters, "Christianity and Mental Health," *The Humanist* (Nov./Dec., 1987): 32.

21. Watters, "Christianity and Mental Health," 10.

22. Abraham Maslow, *Humanistic Psychology*, eds. I. David Welch, George A. Tate, and Fred Richards (Buffalo, NY: Prometheus Books, 1978), 11.

23. Paul Kurtz et al., "Credo," *The Humanist* (July/Aug. 1968): 18.

24. Carl Rogers, "Notes on Rollo May," *Journal of Humanistic Psychology* (Summer, 1982): 8.

25. In making his point about psychological guilt, Christian theologian Francis Schaeffer admitted that "psychological guilt is actual and cruel" but that the Christian view is more textured than the secular one because "Christians know that there is also real guilt, moral guilt before a holy God." Francis Schaeffer, *The Complete Works of Francis A. Schaeffer: A Christian Worldview*, 5 vols. (Westchester, IL: Crossway, 1982), 3:322. Schaeffer goes on to say, "When a man is broken in these [moral and psychological] areas, he is confused, because he has the feelings of real guilt within himself, and yet he is told by modern thinkers that these are only guilt-'feelings.' But he can never resolve these feelings, because … [he] has true moral awareness and the feeling of true guilt. You can tell him a million times that there is no true guilt, but he still knows there is true guilt."

26. This does not mean that Secularists have no conception of good and evil. But good and evil, from a secular viewpoint, need to be seen from the perspective of who humans have the potential to be, from what so-called "self-actualized" people (the most highly evolved) would think they are. As Abraham Maslow, the psychologist who coined the term *self-actualization,* admits, self-actualized people (those who are most highly evolved) have "notions of right and wrong and of good and evil [that] are often not the conventional ones." *Motivation and Personality*, 3rd ed., ed. Robert Frager et al. (London: Longman, 1987), 140–41.

27. Ellis G. Olim, *Humanistic Psychology*, eds. I. David Welch, George A. Tate, and Fred Richards (Buffalo, NY: Prometheus Books, 1978), 219.

28. Erich Fromm believed that "values are rooted in the very conditions of human existence; hence that our knowledge of these conditions—that is, of the 'human situation'—leads us to establishing values which have objective validity; this validity exists only with regard to the existence of man; outside of him there are no values." *Man for Himself: A Radical Interpretation of the Old Testament and Its Tradition* (New York: Holt, Rinehart and Winston, 1964), 17.

29. We will discuss the idea that sin is a parasite in greater depth in chap. 8.

30 Genesis 4:25–26: "Adam knew his wife again, and she bore a son and called his name Seth, for she said, 'God has appointed for me another offspring instead of Abel, for Cain killed him.' To Seth also a son was born, and he called his name Enosh. At that time people began to call upon the name of the LORD."

31. Genesis 6:8: "Noah found favor in the eyes of the LORD."

32. This is how the Septuagint, the Greek translation of the Old Testament, interprets the Hebrew text. The Greek *sperma*, "seed," is not a collective noun, so the singular "he/his" is clearly interpretive.

THE BIBLE: GOD'S BIG STORY, PART 2

33. Genesis 22:17–19: "'I will surely bless you, and I will surely multiply your offspring as the stars of heaven and as the sand that is on the seashore. And your offspring shall possess the gate of his enemies, and in your offspring shall all the nations of the earth be blessed, because you have obeyed my voice.' So Abraham returned to his young men, and they arose and went together to Beersheba. And Abraham lived at Beersheba"; Galatians 3:16–17: "Now the promises were made to Abraham and to his offspring. It does not say, 'And to offsprings,' referring to many, but referring to one, 'And to your offspring,' who is Christ. This is what I mean: the law, which came 430 years afterward, does not annul a covenant previously ratified by God, so as to make the promise void."

34. 2 Samuel 7:12–15: "When your days are fulfilled and you lie down with your fathers, I will raise up your offspring after you, who shall come from your body, and I will establish his kingdom. He shall build a house for my name, and I will establish the throne of his kingdom forever. I will be to him a father, and he shall be to me a son. When he commits iniquity, I will discipline him with the rod of men, with the stripes of the sons of men, but my steadfast love will not depart from him, as I took it from Saul, whom I put away from before you."

35. Colossians 1:15: "He is the image of the invisible God, the firstborn of all creation."

36. 1 Corinthians 15:45: "Thus it is written, 'The first man Adam became a living being'; the last Adam became a life-giving spirit."

37. Galatians 6:12–16: "It is those who want to make a good showing in the flesh who would force you to be circumcised, and only in order that they may not be persecuted for the cross of Christ. For even those who are circumcised do not themselves keep the law, but they desire to have you circumcised that they may boast in your flesh. But far be it from me to boast except in the cross of our Lord Jesus Christ, by which the world has been crucified to me, and I to the world. For neither circumcision counts for anything, nor uncircumcision, but a new creation. And as for all who walk by this rule, peace and mercy be upon them, and upon the Israel of God"; 2 Corinthians 5:17: "If anyone is in Christ, he is a new creation. The old has passed away; behold, the new has come."

38. Galatians 3:29: "If you are Christ's, then you are Abraham's offspring, heirs according to promise."

39. Exodus 31:13: "You are to speak to the people of Israel and say, 'Above all you shall keep my Sabbaths, for this is a sign between me and you throughout your generations, that you may know that I, the LORD, sanctify you.'"

40. We get a glimpse of this in Matthew 2:14, when Mary and Joseph flee from Herod to Egypt. Matthew says this happens to fulfill the words of the prophet: "Out of Egypt I called my son." This is a reference to Hosea 11:1, in which Israel is referred to as God's son. Now Jesus himself is referred to in this way, making him the true Israel.

41. Hebrews 10:11–13: "Every priest stands daily at his service, offering repeatedly the same sacrifices, which can never take away sins. But when Christ had offered for all time a single sacrifice for sins, he sat down at the right hand of God, waiting from that time until his enemies should be made a footstool for his feet."

42. Matthew 1:1: "The book of the genealogy of Jesus Christ, the son of David, the son of Abraham."

43. 1 Timothy 1:17–20: "To the King of the ages, immortal, invisible, the only God, be honor and glory forever and ever. Amen. This charge I entrust to you, Timothy, my child, in accordance with the prophecies previously made about you, that by them you may wage the good warfare, holding faith and a good conscience. By rejecting this, some have made shipwreck of their faith, among whom are Hymenaeus and Alexander, whom I have handed over to Satan that they may learn not to blaspheme."

44. Jeremiah 4:4: "Circumcise yourselves to the LORD; remove the foreskin of your hearts, O men of Judah and inhabitants of Jerusalem; lest my wrath go forth like fire, and burn with none to quench it, because of the evil of your deeds."

45. Hebrews 10:11–14: "Every priest stands daily at his service, offering repeatedly the same sacrifices, which can never take away sins. But when Christ had offered for all time a single sacrifice for sins, he sat down at the right hand of God, waiting from that time until his enemies should be made a footstool for his feet. For by a single offering he has perfected for all time those who are being sanctified."

46. Genesis 12:1–3: "The LORD said to Abram, 'Go from your country and your kindred and your father's house to the land that I will show you. And I will make of you a great nation, and I will bless you and make your name great, so that you will be a blessing. I will bless those who bless you, and him who dishonors you I will curse, and in you all the families of the earth shall be blessed.'"

47. Genesis 3:15: "I will put enmity between you and the woman, and between your offspring and her offspring; he shall bruise your head, and you shall bruise his heel."

48. Genesis 3:23: "The LORD God sent him out from the garden of Eden to work the ground from which he was taken."

49. Genesis 3:15–16: "'I will put enmity between you and the woman, and between your offspring and her offspring; he shall bruise your head, and you shall bruise his heel.' To the woman he said, 'I will surely multiply your pain in childbearing; in pain you shall bring forth children. Your desire shall be for your husband, and he shall rule over you.'"

50. See Genesis 22:17a; cf. Genesis 15:5. In addition to the multitude of descendants, an individual "seed" is also hinted at. Genesis 22:17b says, "Your offspring [seed] shall possess the gate of *his* enemies." In other words, God was hinting to Abraham of a promise we now know to have been fulfilled in David and ultimately David's greater Son, Jesus.

51. Genesis 4:12: "When you work the ground, it shall no longer yield to you its strength. You shall be a fugitive and a wanderer on the earth."

52. Genesis 12:1: "The LORD said to Abram, 'Go from your country and your kindred and your father's house to the land that I will show you.'"

53. Genesis 9:25: "He said, 'Cursed be Canaan; a servant of servants shall he be to his brothers.'"

54. Genesis 12:3: "I will bless those who bless you, and him who dishonors you I will curse, and in you all the families of the earth shall be blessed."

55. Genesis 15:6: "He believed the LORD, and he counted it to him as righteousness."

56. Genesis 12:1–4: "The LORD said to Abram, 'Go from your country and your kindred and your father's house to the land that I will show you. And I will make of you a great nation, and I will bless you and make your name great, so that you will be a blessing. I will bless those who bless you, and him who dishonors you I will curse, and in you all the families of the earth shall be blessed.' So Abram went, as the LORD had told him, and Lot went with him. Abram was seventy-five years old when he departed from Haran"; Genesis 22:1: "After these things God tested Abraham and said to him, 'Abraham!' And he said, 'Here I am.'"

57. Genesis 17:1: "When Abram was ninety-nine years old the LORD appeared to Abram and said to him, 'I am God Almighty; walk before me, and be blameless.'"

58. An older but still helpful resource on the progression of the messianic promise in the Old Testament is Walter C. Kaiser Jr., *Toward an Old Testament Theology* (Grand Rapids, MI: Zondervan, 1978).

59. Matthew 1:1: "The book of the genealogy of Jesus Christ, the son of David, the son of Abraham."

60. Exodus 2:24: "God heard their groaning, and God remembered his covenant with Abraham, with Isaac, and with Jacob"; Exodus 6:4–8: "I also established my covenant with them to give them the land of Canaan, the land in which they lived as sojourners. Moreover, I have heard the groaning of the people of Israel whom the Egyptians hold as slaves, and I have remembered my covenant. Say therefore to the people of Israel, 'I am the LORD, and I will bring you out from under the burdens of the Egyptians, and I will deliver you from slavery to them, and I will redeem you with an outstretched arm and with great acts of judgment. I will take you to be my people, and I will be your God, and you shall know that I am the LORD your God, who has brought you out from under the burdens of the Egyptians.'"

61. Exodus 19:4: "You yourselves have seen what I did to the Egyptians, and how I bore you on eagles' wings and brought you to myself"; Exodus 20:2: "I am the LORD your God, who brought you out of the land of Egypt, out of the house of slavery."

62. Bobette Buster, *Do Story: How to Tell Your Story So the World Listens* (London: The Do Book, 2013).

63. For example, Joshua 2:9–11; Judges 6:8–13; 1 Samuel 12:6–8; 1 Kings 8:51; 2 Chronicles 7:22; Nehemiah 9:9.

64. For example, Psalm 77:14–20; 78:12–55; 80:8; 106:7–12; 114; 136:10–22.

65. For example, Jeremiah 7:21–24; 11:1–18; 16:14–21; 34:13; Ezekiel 37:24–28 (affirming God's covenant in language like that used in the exodus); Hosea 11:1.

66. There *are* differences between the Abrahamic and Mosaic covenants. Kenneth Turner points out that "some discontinuity does exist. The Sinaitic covenant puts a lot of stress on conditionality—'*if* you will indeed obey my voice and keep my covenant, you shall be…' (Exod. 19:5). But there is conditional language in the Abrahamic covenant as well (see Genesis 12:1; 15:6; 17:1–2, 9–14; 18:19; 22:16–18; 26:2–5). Restoration following Israel's breaking of the (Sinaitic) covenant is consistently based on the Abrahamic promises. This is true in Exodus 32:13 following the golden calf incident and in Deuteronomy 4:31 following the exile, which means the Abrahamic covenant remained valid despite Israel's failure (cf. Galatians 3:15–29)."

67. When it comes to the wisdom literature—Job, Psalms, Proverbs, Song of Solomon, and Ecclesiastes—it's a little harder to see the flow of Scripture's metanarrative. The idea of the sage, the officially recognized wise man, was a whole new type of leader, different from a priest or prophet. The sage drew wisdom more from what we call "general revelation," from observation, experience, and tradition. The book of Proverbs presents life as straightforward: you reap what you sow. If you make right choices, you'll succeed; if you're a fool, you'll fail. This is called *normative* wisdom. But the books of Job and Ecclesiastes challenge the idea that life is so straightforward. Things don't always work out like you want them to. Bad things happen to good people. This is called *speculative* wisdom. The tension between normative wisdom (what life is always like under creation) and speculative wisdom (what life is often like under the fall) pictures the tension between God's faithfulness and Israel's lack of faith.

68. Genesis 17:6: "I will make you exceedingly fruitful, and I will make you into nations, and kings shall come from you"; Genesis 49:10: "The scepter shall not depart from Judah, nor the ruler's staff from between his feet, until tribute comes to him; and to him shall be the obedience of the peoples."

69. Judges 21:25: "In those days there was no king in Israel. Everyone did what was right in his own eyes."

70. 1 Kings 11:11: "The LORD said to Solomon, 'Since this has been your practice and you have not kept my covenant and my statutes that I have commanded you, I will surely tear the kingdom from you and will give it to your servant.'"

71. In actuality, the whole of the Old Testament is a story of God's covenant faithfulness. In Genesis, we see sibling rivalry, murder, arrogance, mistreatment of wives, lying, and perversion. And yet, God was faithful. In Exodus, the children of Israel can hardly make it out of Egypt before grumbling and building a golden calf to worship. And yet, God was faithful. In Leviticus, priests misbehave and Israel's leaders—Moses, Aaron, and Miriam—can't seem to stay out of trouble. And yet,

God was faithful. In Deuteronomy, which specifically predicts Israel's inability to be faithful to God, which will lead to exile, God promises to be with them (Deut. 4:29–31). The ray of light provided by Joshua's leadership was extinguished as soon as he died. Israel became increasingly wicked and idolatrous. "In those days there was no king in Israel," says Judges 21:25. "Everyone did what was right in his own eyes."

72. See Isaiah 50; Jeremiah 3.

73. Deuteronomy 4:29–31: "From there you will seek the LORD your God and you will find him, if you search after him with all your heart and with all your soul. When you are in tribulation, and all these things come upon you in the latter days, you will return to the LORD your God and obey his voice. For the LORD your God is a merciful God. He will not leave you or destroy you or forget the covenant with your fathers that he swore to them."

74. See also Jeremiah 30–33; Ezekiel 36–37; Isaiah 40–66; Hosea 14; Amos 9:11–15; Micah 4–5.

75. Zechariah 9:9–13: "Rejoice greatly, O daughter of Zion! Shout aloud, O daughter of Jerusalem! Behold, your king is coming to you; righteous and having salvation is he, humble and mounted on a donkey, on a colt, the foal of a donkey. I will cut off the chariot from Ephraim and the war horse from Jerusalem; and the battle bow shall be cut off, and he shall speak peace to the nations; his rule shall be from sea to sea, and from the River to the ends of the earth. As for you also, because of the blood of my covenant with you, I will set your prisoners free from the waterless pit. Return to your stronghold, O prisoners of hope; today I declare that I will restore to you double. For I have bent Judah as my bow; I have made Ephraim its arrow. I will stir up your sons, O Zion, against your sons, O Greece, and wield you like a warrior's sword"; Zechariah 12:10–14: "I will pour out on the house of David and the inhabitants of Jerusalem a spirit of grace and pleas for mercy, so that, when they look on me, on him whom they have pierced, they shall mourn for him, as one mourns for an only child, and weep bitterly over him, as one weeps over a firstborn. On that day the mourning in Jerusalem will be as great as the mourning for Hadad-rimmon in the plain of Megiddo. The land shall mourn, each family by itself: the family of the house of David by itself, and their wives by themselves; the family of the house of Nathan by itself, and their wives by themselves; the family of the house of Levi by itself, and their wives by themselves; the family of the Shimeites by itself, and their wives by themselves; and all the families that are left, each by itself, and their wives by themselves."

76. Zechariah 9:14–17: "The LORD will appear over them, and his arrow will go forth like lightning; the Lord GOD will sound the trumpet and will march forth in the whirlwinds of the south. The LORD of hosts will protect them, and they shall devour, and tread down the sling stones, and they shall drink and roar as if drunk with wine, and be full like a bowl, drenched like the corners of the altar. On that day the LORD their God will save them, as the flock of his people; for like the jewels of a crown they shall shine on his land. For how great is his goodness, and how great his beauty! Grain shall make the young men flourish, and new wine the young women"; Malachi 4:1–3: "Behold, the day is coming, burning like an oven, when all the arrogant and all evildoers will be stubble. The day that is coming shall set them ablaze, says the LORD of hosts, so that it will leave them neither root nor branch. But for you who fear my name, the sun of righteousness shall rise with healing in its wings. You shall go out leaping like calves from the stall. And you shall tread down the wicked, for they will be ashes under the soles of your feet, on the day when I act, says the LORD of hosts."

77. Malachi 3:1–4: "Behold, I send my messenger, and he will prepare the way before me. And the Lord whom you seek will suddenly come to his temple; and the messenger of the covenant in whom you delight, behold, he is coming, says the LORD of hosts. But who can endure the day of his coming, and who can stand when he appears? For he is like a refiner's fire and like fullers' soap. He will sit as a refiner and purifier of silver, and he will purify the sons of Levi and refine them like gold and silver, and they will bring offerings in righteousness to the LORD. Then the offering of Judah and Jerusalem will be pleasing to the LORD as in the days of old and as in former years."

78. Malachi 4:5–6: "Behold, I will send you Elijah the prophet before the great and awesome day of the LORD comes. And he will turn the hearts of fathers to their children and the hearts of children to their fathers, lest I come and strike the land with a decree of utter destruction."

79. For example, see Psalms 2 (especially vv. 2, 6, 12); 45:6–9; 110:1–7.

80. All of these sins may be seen in the book of Malachi, a prophetic book written in the period after the exiles had returned. See also Nehemiah 5 and 13.

81. Michael J. Card, vocal performance lyrics from "The Promise," on *The Promise: A Celebration of Christ's Birth* (Sparrow Records, 1994).

82. Luke 1:17: "He will go before him in the spirit and power of Elijah, to turn the hearts of the fathers to the children, and the disobedient to the wisdom of the just, to make ready for the Lord a people prepared."

83. For more on the importance of "re" words, see John Stonestreet, "Introducing ReEngage," *Breakpoint: Two-Minute Warning*, online radio program, January 30, 2013, www.colsoncenter.org/twominutewarning/entry/33/21383.

84. A good resource for the things discussed in this section is Christopher J. H. Wright, *Knowing Jesus through the Old Testament* (Downers Grove, IL: InterVarsity, 1992), 55–102.

85. Matthew 1:23: "'Behold, the virgin shall conceive and bear a son, and they shall call his name Immanuel' (which means, God with us)"; Isaiah 7:14: "The Lord himself will give you a sign. Behold, the virgin shall conceive and bear a son, and shall call his name Immanuel."

86. Matthew 2:6: "You, O Bethlehem, in the land of Judah, are by no means least among the rulers of Judah; for from you

shall come a ruler who will shepherd my people Israel"; Micah 5:2: "You, O Bethlehem Ephrathah, who are too little to be among the clans of Judah, from you shall come forth for me one who is to be ruler in Israel, whose coming forth is from of old, from ancient days."

87. Matthew 2:15: "… and remained there until the death of Herod. This was to fulfill what the Lord had spoken by the prophet, 'Out of Egypt I called my son'"; Hosea 11:1: "When Israel was a child, I loved him, and out of Egypt I called my son."

88. Matthew 2:18: "A voice was heard in Ramah, weeping and loud lamentation, Rachel weeping for her children; she refused to be comforted, because they are no more"; Jeremiah 31:15: "Says the LORD: 'A voice is heard in Ramah, lamentation and bitter weeping. Rachel is weeping for her children; she refuses to be comforted for her children, because they are no more.'"

89. Matthew 2:23: "He went and lived in a city called Nazareth, so that what was spoken by the prophets might be fulfilled, that he would be called a Nazarene."

90. Matthew 4:17: "From that time Jesus began to preach, saying, 'Repent, for the kingdom of heaven is at hand.'"

91. Galatians 3:6–9: "… just as Abraham 'believed God, and it was counted to him as righteousness'? Know then that it is those of faith who are the sons of Abraham. And the Scripture, foreseeing that God would justify the Gentiles by faith, preached the gospel beforehand to Abraham, saying, 'In you shall all the nations be blessed.' So then, those who are of faith are blessed along with Abraham, the man of faith."

92. Isaiah 41:27: "I was the first to say to Zion, 'Behold, here they are!' and I give to Jerusalem a herald of good news"; Isaiah 52:7: "How beautiful upon the mountains are the feet of him who brings good news, who publishes peace, who brings good news of happiness, who publishes salvation, who says to Zion, 'Your God reigns'"; Isaiah 60:6: "A multitude of camels shall cover you, the young camels of Midian and Ephah; all those from Sheba shall come. They shall bring gold and frankincense, and shall bring good news, the praises of the LORD"; Isaiah 61:1: "The Spirit of the Lord GOD is upon me, because the LORD has anointed me to bring good news to the poor; he has sent me to bind up the brokenhearted, to proclaim liberty to the captives, and the opening of the prison to those who are bound."

93. For a summary of much of this discussion, see N. T. Wright, *What Saint Paul Really Said: Was Paul of Tarsus the Real Founder of Christianity?* (Grand Rapids, MI: Eerdmans, 1997), 77–111.

94. 2 Corinthians 5:17: "If anyone is in Christ, he is a new creation. The old has passed away; behold, the new has come."

95. Peter C. Hill and Kenneth I. Pargament, "Advances in the Conceptualization and Measurement of Religion and Spirituality: Implications for Physical and Mental Health Research," *American Psychologist* 58, no. 1 (2003): 64–74.

96. W. Gary Phillips, research provided to the author.

7

HOW TO READ THE BIBLE

1. THE DYSFUNCTIONAL BIBLE STUDY

Sophia: "Guys, I was reading the book of Jeremiah and came across the most amazing passage! It says, 'For I know the plans I have for you, declares the LORD, plans for welfare and not for evil, to give you a future and a hope. Then you will call upon me and come and pray to me, and I will hear you. You will seek me and find me, when you seek me with all your heart.'"[1]

Mason: "Wow, that's cool!"

Sophia: "Yeah, I think I'm going to make this my life verse. It gives me hope because it shows that God wants to bless me and give me a good job and an awesome husband someday."

Mason: "Uh-huh. I'm not a Christian, but I really like that verse. What it means to me is, God is cool with where I am in life and he wants me to feel good and have a great life."

Noah: "Guys, are you sure that's what it means? I'm not sure we're supposed to read it in such a personal way."

Mason: "Who are you to say what Sophia's verse means to me? It means one thing to her and something else to me. If God is telling you something different, that's cool."

Susannah: "Well, that can't be what it means because I've always been taught that God has plans for you only if you are a Christian."

Sophia: "But that sounds really cruel. A good God wouldn't ignore people just because they don't fit your definition of Christianity!"

Susannah: "I don't think we need to argue. We can all be right. Maybe we should just pray about it."

Mason: "What good will *that* do? It means what it means to me, and it means what it means to you. There's no point in praying about it."

Aiden: "Not pray? But I like praying. I feel different when I pray. It makes me feel like God is my best friend."

Noah: "You pray because of how it makes you feel?"

Aiden: "Sure. When Jesus walked along the road to Emmaus, the guys he was with said the same thing."

Noah: "What thing?"

Aiden: "That their hearts burned within them when they were with him."[2]

Noah: "But that's because his teaching was true, not because he made them feel good about themselves."

Chloe: "Well, I hate to interrupt, but even if we don't all agree, God has still met us here today. You know, the Bible says, 'Where two or three are gathered in my name, there am I among them.'"[3]

Jacob: "I love having studies like this. It's like God is showing us things from the Bible that no one has ever noticed before!"

Noah: "Guys, I just have this bad feeling that we're making it about us and how we feel rather than about God."

Jacob: "Well, isn't it about us? I mean, God loves us, so isn't that the whole point?"

2. WHAT IS SCRIPTURE ALL ABOUT, EXACTLY?

Have you ever been in a discussion like this? Or has someone ever forwarded you an email or shared a Facebook meme that uses some part of a Bible verse completely out of context? Maybe you've heard a speaker or seen a Christian book using a Bible story to illustrate some unrelated point (the story of David and Goliath is often used this way). It's common. Without really even thinking about it, we have probably all done it.

Although we may be convinced of the Bible's authority as God's revelation to human beings, we might sometimes have interpreted the Bible improperly. Most of the students in the above-mentioned scenario want to know God personally, and that's good. But rather than try to understand the text's true meaning, they are reading through the filter of their own desires and cultural understandings, as though desires give rise to meaning; others assume that the meaning of Scripture is flexible, making context irrelevant.

But the Bible is about God, not us. It does not bend to our thoughts or desires; rather, it expresses what God thinks and has planned.

It is hard to blame these students, though; their approaches seem almost natural, given the times we live in. In order to raise interest in the Bible, publishers have customized it for many people's life situations, leaving the impression that the Bible's importance somehow depends on its immediate impact on us. There's an all-weather outdoor Bible, an army Bible, a cowboy Bible, a Bible for brides, a biker Bible—even a Bible published for teen girls, formatted like a magazine, with "Are you dating a godly guy?" on the cover; a boy's Bible promises "gross and gory Bible stuff," and a "pink and sparkly" *God's Little Princess Devotional Bible* offers girls the fantasy fun of playing pretend.[4]

> The Bible is about God, not us. It does not bend to our thoughts or desires; rather, it expresses what God thinks and has planned.

The endless stream of customized Bibles, while perhaps nothing more than an amusing example of mostly harmless free-market excess, runs the risk of disguising the Bible's true intent, which is to reveal the One who alone is worthy of our trust. If we truly desire to see the authority of God's Word elevated in our world, we must learn how to read—and *live*—the Bible so that others come to know God and become Jesus's disciples.

The impulse to make Christianity easy and user friendly can come back to bite us. As Francis Chan notes,

> We have done everything humanly possible to make church "easy." We kept the services short and entertaining, discipleship and evangelism optional, and moral standards low. Our motives were not bad. We figured we could attract more people by offering Jesus with minimal commitment. But we ended up producing nominal Christians whose unchanged lives have deterred others from being interested.[5]

> If we truly desire to see the authority of God's Word elevated in our world, we must learn how to read—and *live*—the Bible so that others come to know God and become Jesus's disciples.

Reading the Bible poorly both *causes* and *is symptomatic of* "easy" Christianity. Learning to handle Scripture properly, on the other hand, can help us think more carefully about the Christian faith, which in turn can lead to better Christian lives. In this chapter, we'll approach the Bible as a book God intends us to read, understand, ponder, pray over, and live out. The Bible serves as a fixed point in a world overrun by postmodern skepticism, but in order for us really to grasp its power, we must first learn how to read it well and truly.

> Most believers over the centuries did not have Bibles of their own, nor did they know much about the Bible's contents. Most couldn't even read!

3. TOLLE LEGE: PICK UP AND READ

Most believers over the centuries did not have Bibles of their own, nor did they know much about the Bible's contents. Most couldn't even read! The only way to get a Bible was to go to a church or synagogue and beg to see one. But Johannes Gutenberg's printing press, employing movable type, planted the seeds of change. In fact, historian Elizabeth Eisenstein argues, the mass production of Martin Luther's writings (more than three hundred thousand books and pamphlets sold just from 1517 to 1520) is what gave life to the Protestant Reformation, establishing a Christian tradition embraced by nearly a billion people in the world today. According to Eisenstein, the Reformation was a movement "shaped at the very outset (and in large part ushered in) by the new powers of the press."[6]

As a result, the Bible has profoundly affected every aspect of Western culture. Today the ready availability of the Bible is leading to such rapid evangelism in the global south that South America and Africa may soon become the continents with the greatest number of Christians.[7]

Let's be honest, though. Although there is no book so popular and available as the Bible, still it is little read. It's like a pile of kindling without a match: unless it is lit, it can provide neither heat nor light. As Mark Twain said, "A person who won't read has no advantage over a person who can't read."[8]

> Although there is no book so popular and available as the Bible, still it is little read. It's like a pile of kindling without a match: unless it is lit, it can provide neither heat nor light.

Illiteracy by choice is not a new problem. More than a millennia and a half ago, a young playboy complained, "We have no leisure to read. Where are we to find the books? How or when could I get ahold of them? From whom could I borrow them?"[9] Even 1,500 years ago, this was a false complaint. The young man's problem wasn't a lack of books; it was lack of interest. But one day he heard a child in a neighboring home chanting, "Pick it up and read it. Pick it up and read it" (in Latin: "*Tolle lege*"). Taking this as a sign from God, the young man picked up the Bible and began reading. When he encountered the apostle Paul's letter to the Romans—"Let us walk properly as in the daytime, not in orgies and drunkenness, not in sexual immorality and sensuality, not in quarreling and jealousy. But put on the Lord Jesus Christ, and make no provision for the flesh, to gratify its desires" (Rom. 13:13–14)—this young man, Augustine of Hippo, recognized his own sinfulness, committed his life to Christ, and ultimately became one of the world's most revered and influential theologians.[10] You can read his story in his book *Confessions*.

Just as the Bible changed everything for Augustine, it can change us today, but only if we approach it properly. Says theologian N. T. Wright,

> [G]od intends that we should have this book and should read and study it, individually and corporately; and that this book, by the power of the Spirit, bears witness in a thousand ways to Jesus himself, and to what God has accomplished through him.… [T]he Bible isn't simply a repository of true information about God, Jesus, and the hope of the world. It is, rather, part of *the means by which*, in the power of the Spirit, the living God rescues his people and his world, and takes them forward on the journey toward his new creation, and makes us agents of that new creation even as we travel.[11]

HOW TO READ THE BIBLE

The Bible has tremendous power. If we read it poorly or self-centeredly, however, we might not sense its power or see that power at work in our lives and culture. Let's talk about that next.

4. Why Is It So Common to Read the Bible with a Self-Centered Focus?

If you've ever found yourself reading the Bible and asking yourself, *What does this mean to me?* you're not alone. We're all searching for answers to our most pressing questions, and we naturally hope the Bible, like aspirin, will relieve life's everyday pains.

This hope, though, seems to have grown into a kind of narcissism, part of a larger cultural mood that promotes a hyperpersonalized approach to *all* of life. This cultural mood has a name: **Postmodernism**.

Academically, Postmodernism developed as scholars responded to the failure of modern science and technology to produce a utopian existence. As a response, Postmodernists turned their attention away from "capital T truth" to small, localized truths that were constructed through people's individual and cultural experiences.

> *Postmodernism:* a skeptical worldview, founded as a reaction to modernism, that is suspicious of metanarratives and teaches that ultimate reality is inaccessible, that knowledge is a social construct, and that truth claims are political power plays.

Culturally, Postmodernism affects how we think about everything, including the Bible.

Postmodernists say that we can really know only our *descriptions* of the world, not the world itself. Our talk about the world, they say, isn't really about the world at all but about us. In 1968, French literary theorist Roland Barthes wrote "The Death of the Author," a short essay in which he argued that we should not value the *origin* of a text (i.e., the author's intentions) as much as its *destination* (i.e., the reader's experience). Readers should free themselves from the author's single intended meaning and invent new meanings.[12]

If we cannot really know the world truly, then we certainly cannot learn anything about the world from a written work. For Postmodernism, texts claiming to speak the truth must undergo a **deconstruction** to reveal their underlying assumptions and intentions.[13] Even as you read this chapter, Postmodernists would say that you are not learning to understand the world as it actually is but rather you are merging together the concepts in this text with your experiences and your culture's influences.

> *Deconstruction:* a method of literary analysis that questions the ability of language to represent reality adequately and seeks to discern and expose the purported underlying ideologies of a text.

There is no real world "out there" for us to know.[14] They believe that what you think is true may be true for you but that it does not mean it is true for anyone else.[15] Once someone embraces assumptions like these, it becomes difficult to properly interpret the Bible. Even so, many Christians today embrace Postmodernist assumptions.

Today there is a significant discussion among Christians whether Postmodernism is compatible with orthodox Christianity.[16] Theologian D. A. Carson is one bothered by the postmodern impulse, primarily because of its focus on self. In *Becoming Conversant with the Emerging Church*, he makes the following observation:

> An omniscient, talking God changes everything. It does not change the fact that I will always be finite and that my knowledge of him and about him will always be partial. But once I know that he exists, that he is the Creator and my Savior and Judge, it is improper, even idolatrous, to try to think of my knowing things without reference to him. All of my knowledge, if it is true knowledge, is necessarily a subset of his.[17]

In other words, the Bible's authoritative revelation is about what God actually communicates, whether we feel good about it or not. Our part is learning to respond appropriately.

Unfortunately, well-meaning people read the Bible poorly, leading them to misunderstand and misapply it in their lives or even to manipulate others. Fortunately, however, we can learn to study Scripture carefully. To get started, let's look at some commonly made mistakes and see if we can find correctives, restoring the excitement and joy of actually reading—and grasping—God's Word.

5. Ten Common Mistakes in Reading the Bible and How to Fix Them

Hermeneutics: **from the Greek for "interpret"; the process of devising the best methods for understanding and interpreting Scripture.**

The mistakes people make—and I have certainly made my share—can be corrected through a little intellectual discipline. This begins with a strong *hermeneutic*. The term **hermeneutics** (from the Greek word *hermeneuo*, "to interpret") describes the process of devising correct methods of interpreting Scripture.[18] As we look at each mistake and how to correct it, we'll put in place hermeneutic building blocks that increase the accuracy of our interpretations and thus our knowledge of God.

Mistake 1: We assume that the Bible doesn't need to be interpreted. Some believe that the Bible does not need interpretation—that it speaks for itself. Some pastors even reject listing out their beliefs, saying instead, "The Bible is our doctrinal statement." It sounds noble, but what does it mean, exactly? Does it mean that everything people did in Bible times (slaughtering enemies, taking multiple wives, living in tents) should be done by us today? If the answer is "No, that's not what the Bible means to us today," that pastor has just engaged in an act of interpretation.

We cannot escape the fact that even though the Bible is the authoritative, inspired, inerrant Word of God, it still must be interpreted. As theologians Gordon Fee and Douglas Stuart point out,

> The first reason one needs to learn *how* to interpret is that, whether one likes it or not, every reader is at the same time an interpreter. That is, most of us assume as we

read that we also understand what we read. We also tend to think that *our understanding* is the same thing as the Holy Spirit's or human author's *intent*. However, we invariably bring to the text all that we are, with all of our experiences, culture, and prior understandings of words and ideas. Sometimes what we bring to the text, unintentionally to be sure, leads us astray, or else causes us to read all kinds of foreign ideas into the text.[19]

We need interpretation when reading the Bible for the same reason that we need interpretation when trying to communicate something to people in another language. When I travel to countries where another language is spoken, I don't just want a translator who tells the audience what is being *said*; I want an interpreter to help them understand what is *meant*. Similarly, with Scripture, if we don't have a proper interpretation, we can easily delude ourselves into thinking we know what God means when, in fact, we do not.

> With Scripture, if we don't have a proper interpretation, we can easily delude ourselves into thinking we know what God means when, in fact, we do not.

Mistake 2: We assume that the Bible applies uniquely to us. As they connect with the text, some people make the mistake of *individualizing* it, which means supposing that any or all parts apply to them in a unique way, outside of their original context. Examples of personalizing would be "The story of Balaam's talking donkey reminds me that I talk too much" or "The story of the building of the temple is God's way of telling us that we have to construct a new church building."[20]

In the dysfunctional Bible study at the opening of this chapter, Sophia stumbled into precisely this problem. She imagined Jeremiah 29:11—"For I know the plans I have for you, declares the LORD, plans for welfare and not for evil, to give you a future and a hope"—to be a personal promise of blessing, from God to *her*. However, these words were not written to her. They served as a prophecy to the nation of Israel at a particular point in time based on its own particular circumstances.

Another example is 2 Chronicles 7:14: "If my people who are called by my name humble themselves, and pray and seek my face and turn from their wicked ways, then I will hear from heaven and will forgive their sin and heal their land." This does not mean that God promises to make *our* nation godlier if citizens pray. We may love 2 Chronicles 7:14, but misapplying this verse to our own nation ignores the passage's original, intended audience: the nation of Israel, addressed at a specific time, for a specific reason. It should not be immediately applied to another country, at another time, for a different reason.

To approach the text well, before we focus on ourselves or our current circumstances, we should first focus on God—how to deepen and enrich our understanding of him. Is God the kind of deity who cares about our people's welfare? Yes! Does he have the future in mind? Yes! Is he the proper object of hope? Yes! Does he want us to be in communication with his image bearers? Yes! Does

> To approach the text well, before we focus on ourselves or our current circumstances, we should first focus on God—how to deepen and enrich our understanding of him.

he want us to call on him? Yes! By looking at the full context of the text, we learn more about who God shows himself to be and how he has dealt with his people in the past. From this we get insight into his unchanging nature and character and can better understand how we might more fully bear his image.

Mistake 3: We ignore passages that don't fit our theology. When people try to make sense of all of Scripture, they often create a *system*, or a sort of file cabinet into which everything in Scripture fits neatly. This **systematic theology** is not bad in and of itself, but it can go bad if people choose to highlight some verses rather than others as a way to make artificial space for their developed theology. For example, some people empha-size passages that call for believers to separate from the culture and they ignore passages that call believers to engage culture. Or they choose one set of verses about salvation and then minimize others. Scratch just about any controversial issue that separates Christians and it will bleed selective application.

> *Systematic Theology:* a form of theological inquiry that aims to arrange and categorize religious truths into an internally consistent system.

We must value all Scripture, not just the sections that serve our agendas. The Bible should not merely tell us what we already know or only the things we want to hear. The apostle Paul said in 2 Timothy 3:16–17, "All Scripture is breathed out by God and profitable for teaching, for reproof, for correction, and for training in righteousness, that the man of God may be competent, equipped for every good work."

When we ignore or minimize or explain away sections of the Bible that we don't like or understand, we commit a serious error. Theologian Wayne Grudem warns,

> It must be noted that these words [the Bible] are still considered to be God's own words, even though they are written down mostly by human beings and always in human language. Still they are absolutely authoritative and absolutely true: to dis-obey them or to disbelieve them is a serious sin and brings judgment from God (1 Cor. 14:37; Jer. 36:29–31).[21]

The corrective to ignoring the parts of the Bible that don't fit our theology is simple: we must approach it with a posture of humility, making *ourselves* fit *it* rather than trying to make *it* fit *us*.

Mistake 4: We treat the Bible allegorically. For much of church history, theologians have treated **alle-gory** as a legitimate way to read the Bible. The biblical narratives can help us understand how to live better. But when the main use of Scripture is to, for example, employ the story of David and Goliath to show that we need to be courageous or the story of Noah to show what it looks like to fight for our family's survival or the story of Jonah to display the consequences of being "swallowed up" because of our disobedience, it becomes little more than a bedtime storybook, such as *Aesop's Fables*.

> *Allegory:* a fictional narrative in which characters and events are presented as symbols for moral and spiritual truths.

HOW TO READ THE BIBLE

Certainly, we can learn from the life experiences of others, including those who lived in biblical times, and draw lessons that help us live better lives. Rather than view it as merely allegorical, though, we must see the entire Bible as the whole counsel of God, a comprehensive narrative that tells God's story in the world, not as a repository or "greatest hits" of favorite stories. Anglican theologian Graeme Goldsworthy states, "It is important to see that all human history from creation to new creation belongs to God's sovereign work and purpose. While the biblical focus is on the history of a specifically chosen people of God, the whole of human history is indirectly included."[22]

Mistake 5: We feel that our study is fruitless if we have not discovered a new truth. I love the "Aha!" moment—such as the sun breaking through the clouds—of grasping something I haven't understood before. It makes me feel clever. But my desire to be clever can stand in the way of grasping God's truth. As Gordon Fee and Douglas Stuart note, "Let it be said at the outset—and repeated throughout—that the aim of good interpretation is not uniqueness; one is not trying to discover what no one else has ever seen before."[23] The problem, they say, is pride:

> We need to see that Scripture doesn't exist to make us feel smart or to cause other people to think well of us. It exists to reveal God's nature and character, and we are to devote ourselves to its—even apparently mundane—"old" truths.

> Interpretation that aims at, or thrives on, uniqueness can usually be attributed to pride (an attempt to "outclever" the rest of the world), a false understanding of spirituality (wherein the Bible is full of deeply buried truths waiting to be mined by the spiritually sensitive person with special insight), or vested interests (the need to support a theological bias, especially in dealing with texts that seem to go against that bias). Unique interpretations are usually wrong. This is not to say that the correct understanding of a text may not often seem unique to someone who hears it for the first time. But it is to say that uniqueness is *not* the aim of our task.[24]

Instead, we need to see that Scripture doesn't exist to make us feel smart or to cause other people to think well of us. It exists to reveal God's nature and character, and we are to devote ourselves to its—even apparently mundane—"old" truths.

Mistake 6: We focus on what the text "means to me." What the text means to someone personally is not of first importance. Many readers today are confused by this. They wonder, *Aren't I supposed to apply this to my life*? Of course they are, but not until they understand what the text actually says. Postmodernists, such as Jacques Derrida, say that statements about meaning are not meaningful. We should be suspicious of this claim for one simple reason: Derrida and others who make the claim all assume that their *own* statements about meaning are meaningful. Meaning *does* exist. Knowing our own frailty should make it easier to give the benefit of the doubt to the meaning intended by the author (the human writer operating under the inspiration of the Holy Spirit) rather than to ourselves.

Mistake 7: We assume the Bible isn't relevant to us today. Some people, miffed at not being able to make Scripture fit their expectations, go to the opposite extreme and assume it has no relevance to them at all. This is an immature approach. Reading Scripture is like going to a dance: you can't really enjoy it just leaning against the wall. God intends for us to *connect* with the text. As theologian Gene Fant states,

> What I ask my students to consider is the hermeneutics of optimism, a way of looking at the text in a way that is critical but not cynical, probing but not suspicious, that is a way that seeks connection rather than isolation. This is why I stress the communal nature of narrative. The reader participates in the process not through the creation of subgroups (which end up spiraling into subjective/individualistic ramblings that are solipsistic or egomaniacal) that randomly assign meaning but by entering into an agreement with the writer that there *is* meaning in the text and that the author and the audience can connect with one another, creating a relationship of sorts that not only identifies meaning but carries it directly into the hearts, minds, and souls of the readers, applying it to their own lives in ways that are life-changing.[25]

Connecting to the text calls for a posture of prayer. Theologian Rob Plummer says, "As we approach the Bible, we need to realize that sin affects all of our being—our emotions, wills, and rational faculties. We can easily deceive ourselves or be deceived by others. We need the Holy Spirit to instruct and guide us. Thus, prayer is the essential starting point for any study of the Bible."[26] We might begin with the prayer of King David: "Open my eyes, that I may behold wondrous things out of your law" (Ps. 119:18).

> Christians also commonly misapply verses to their contemporary institutions that were originally intended in a specific way for a specific audience.

Mistake 8: We take the Bible out of context. Similar to overpersonalizing Scripture, Christians also commonly misapply verses to their contemporary institutions that were originally intended in a specific way for a specific audience. A common example is Matthew 18:19–20, which says, "Again I say to you, if two of you agree on earth about anything they ask, it will be done for them by my Father in heaven. For where two or three are gathered in my name, there I am among them." This is often taken as a promise that whenever believers get together to pray in the name of Jesus, God will do whatever they ask. But if you back up just four verses, it is clear that Jesus is referring to bringing two or three witnesses in to help resolve a conflict. In fact, the phrase "two or three witnesses," although used several times in Scripture, is never used except in reference to the testimony of witnesses in establishing justice.[27]

Rather than focusing on our present circumstances, we must instead approach the text focused on God: Does how he called out to his people *then* apply to us *today*? Perhaps, but probably not in the way most people think. We cannot assume, or "compute," that God, acting formulaically, will act with our nation as he acted with Israel. He hasn't made us that promise. We can say, however, that this passage reveals some consistent aspects of God's nature and character that have always been true, such as God's calling people to himself, his honoring humility, his desire for us to pray, and his hope that we turn from wickedness. If we stop trying to claim promises as belonging to us in ways they may not, we might be free to focus on God, on what he wants, rather than on whether our nation is failing to receive blessings.

Mistake 9: We interpret the Bible based on contemporary moral standards. The Bible is *eternally relevant* in that "it speaks to all humankind, in every age and in every culture."[28] Yet the Bible was communicated in certain languages, times, and cultures. It has *historical particularity*. Scripture's eternal relevance and its historical particularity are in tension.[29] This tension, though, is good, like the tension we might experience when we exercise, so do the heavy lifting if you want to grow stronger!

But some pastors and commentators don't like this tension. They want the Bible to be easy for both Christians and non-Christians to embrace. For example, when people object to the Bible's operating assumption—and clear teaching—on a sexual relationship being appropriate only between a man and woman married to each other, they might do so by arguing that the Bible's teaching on sexuality was related to a particular historical practice and is not relevant today.

Instead, we should ask, "How does the Scripture describe us, our world, and God?" Dismissing the Bible's teachings to accommodate contemporary views robs God's Word of its immense power, which in turn robs us of the power to live full, healthy lives that glorify God.

> Dismissing the Bible's teachings to accommodate contemporary views robs God's Word of its immense power, which in turn robs us of the power to live full, healthy lives that glorify God.

Mistake 10: We try to make the Bible fit contemporary standards for political correctness. It is embarrassing for some Christians that the Bible says "man" when these days we say "person" and that the Bible says "he" when we say "they." Surely these can be changed without changing the fundamental meaning, right? Unfortunately, in an effort to make translations clearer regarding gender inclusion, some translators have actually distorted the meaning of passages. Pastor Tim Keller offers an example in his book *Galatians for You*. In Galatians 3, the apostle Paul uses an analogy about the inheritance of "sons." Some translators, wanting to be more inclusive, have changed the wording to "children." This, according to Keller, is a mistake:

> Many take offense at using the masculine word "sons" to refer to all Christians, male and female. Some would prefer to translate verse 26: "You are all children of God" (as the NIV 2011 does). But if we are too quick to correct the biblical language, we miss the revolutionary (and radically egalitarian) nature of what Paul is saying. In most ancient cultures, daughters could not inherit property. Therefore "son" meant "legal heir,"' which was a status forbidden to women. But the gospel tells us we are *all* sons of God in Christ. We are *all* heirs. Similarly, the Bible describes all Christians together, including men, as the "bride of Christ" (Revelation 21:2). God is even-handed in His gender-specific metaphors. Men are part of His son's bride; and women are His sons. His heirs. If we don't let Paul call Christian women "sons of God," we miss how radical and wonderful a claim this is.[30]

Before we bow to the current way of seeing things, we must keep in mind that what is new is not necessarily true.

In the end, the big mistakes people make when reading the Bible can be remedied by trusting God to be bigger than culture and interpreting biblical texts more faithfully. As Gordon Fee and Douglas Stuart counsel, "*A text cannot mean what it never meant.* Or to put it in a positive way, the true meaning of the biblical text for us is what God originally intended it to mean when it was first spoken. This is the starting point."[31]

Now that we have examined ten common mistakes in reading the Bible and offered correctives for them, let's go one step further and look at ten principles of how to read the Bible in a way that unleashes its true power.

6. Ten Steps to Reading the Bible Well and Truly

The ten mistakes we discussed focus on what we should *not* do. But what *should* we do? How might we read Scripture *well*, avoiding pitfalls?

Earlier, we used the term *hermeneutics* to describe the general principles of interpreting Scripture. Good hermeneutics begins first and foremost with another technical term theologians use, *exegesis*, which refers to the proper interpretation of a particular passage of Scripture.[32] That is, large-scale interpretation (hermeneutics) must begin with the small-scale, difficult-but-rewarding work of wrestling with each chapter, verse, line, and word (**exegesis**) (we must also be careful of the danger of *eisegesis*, which means reading our own biases and cultural assumptions into the text).

> **Exegesis: from the Greek for "lead out"; the exposition or explanation of a biblical text based on careful study and analysis.**

How do we proceed? To Fee and Stuart, "the key to good exegesis, and therefore to more intelligent reading of the Bible, is *to learn to read the text carefully and to ask the right questions of the text*."[33] You should note that attention must be paid to both the details and the big picture. As N. T. Wright states,

> How then is scripture to be interpreted?… We take account of the nature of each book, each chapter, each syllable. Contexts, meanings within particular cultures, the overall place of a book, a theme, a line within the culture and time and within the scope and sweep of scripture itself—all these things matter. Exploring them with the rigor and attention they deserve constitutes a massive task, though there are today all kinds of encouragements and helps in undertaking it.[34]

We can easily see, then, how massive and comprehensive interpreting Scripture can become. To make it easier, let's take a look at a ten-step process that positions us to ask the right questions of the text and get meaningful answers.

Step 1: Commit to reading the Bible and studying it. Too often, when learning about the Bible, people wrongly assume that pastors' and commentators' words and arguments should replace their own personal study of the Bible. But Gene Fant chides,

For people who call themselves "The People of the Book," most Christians do not read the Bible very much. We talk about it, we sermonize about it, we even read other books about it, but we spend precious little time actually reading it. Worse, we rarely read the Bible's actual stories once we reach adulthood. In fact, professional Christians such as pastors may be the guiltiest about this. Reading secondary texts about the Bible is no substitute for reading the Bible itself.[35]

As a young Christian, I also fell into the habit of reading books *about* the Bible rather than reading the Bible itself. The authors I read were so brilliant and witty that my own reading of the Bible felt clumsy and inefficient.

But Bible reading is not something that should be "left to the pros." Imagine if only professionals played sports, or told jokes, or played music, or wrote poetry. How much emptier the world would be! In effect, though, this is what I was doing with the Bible. It never occurred to me that, while I should certainly care what "the pros" said, I should also read and study the Bible myself.

Take the time, then, to *really* read the Bible. You can't get in shape by watching other people exercise, nor can you grasp the Bible just by reading *about* it. You have to get seriously into the text.

> You can't get in shape by watching other people exercise, nor can you grasp the Bible just by reading *about* it. You have to get seriously into the text.

Step 2: Read the Bible in context. The best understanding comes from reading Scripture in chunks. Never content yourself with reading a single Bible verse. Verses belong to paragraphs, paragraphs belong to chapters, chapters belong to books, and books fit into the Bible as a whole. Understanding context helps us avoid straying from the text's plain meaning.[36] A good foreign-language interpreter does not insert his own meanings or render what "should have been" said. Instead, he renders his source faithfully. If he has questions, he asks the source. The same goes for a written text. As professor Michael Bauman says, "A text means what its author intends it to mean, not what a reader wants it to mean."[37]

Bible study is whole-life engagement. It always has been, even in Bible times. As the children of Israel were about to enter into the Promised Land, Moses told them,

> You shall therefore lay up these words of mine in your heart and in your soul, and you shall bind them as a sign on your hand, and they shall be as frontlets between your eyes. You shall teach them to your children, talking of them when you are sitting in your house, and when you are walking by the way, and when you lie down, and when you rise. You shall write them on the doorposts of your house and on your gates, that your days and the days of your children may be multiplied in the land that the LORD swore to your fathers to give them, as long as the heavens are above the earth. For if you will be careful to do all this commandment that I command you to do, loving the LORD your God, walking in all his ways, and holding fast to him, then the LORD will drive out all these nations before you, and you will dispossess nations greater and mightier than you. (Deut. 11:18–23)

Step 3: Choose a translation. It is important to begin your study of God's Word with a solid translation reflecting the realities of the original ancient texts. There are three types of translations, according to Fee and Stuart.

> It is important to begin your study of God's Word with a solid translation reflecting the realities of the original ancient texts.

Formal equivalence translations. "These translations … attempt to keep as close to the 'form' of the Hebrew or Greek, both words and grammar, as can be conveniently put into understandable English. The closer one stays to the Hebrew or Greek idiom, the closer one moves toward a theory of translation often described as 'literal.' Translations based on formal equivalence will keep historical distance intact at all points."[38] Examples are the King James Version (KJV), the New King James Version (NKJV), the New American Standard Bible (NASB), and the English Standard Version (ESV).[39]

Functional equivalence translations. These translations "attempt to keep the meaning of the Hebrew or Greek but to put their words and idioms into what would be the normal way of saying the same thing in English."[40] Examples are the New American Bible (NAB), the New Jerusalem Bible (NJB), the New Living Translation (NLT), and the New Revised Standard Version (NRSV). The New International Version (NIV) and Today's New International Version (TNIV) are somewhere in the middle between formal equivalence and functional equivalence.

Free translations. These translations "attempt to translate the *ideas* from one language to another, with less concern about using the exact words of the original. A free translation, sometimes also called a paraphrase, tries to eliminate as much of the historical distance as possible and still be faithful to the text."[41] Examples are the New English Bible (NEB), the Living Bible (TLB), and *The Message* (THE MESSAGE).

The Message has been particularly popular in the last fifteen years or so. It was written by a pastor named Eugene Peterson as a way of helping his congregants see the relevance of Scripture in a new light. While it is an interesting read, we must keep in mind that it is a *paraphrase* of the original Hebrew and Greek.

So which one should you choose? Perhaps, as Fee and Stuart suggest, "It is far better to use several translations, note where they differ, and then check out these differences in another source."[42] This is fairly easy with online Bible programs such as www.biblegateway.com, which offers several translations at the click of a mouse, or biblehub.com, which shows various translations side by side at a glance.

If you have the opportunity to pick out a Bible, look for one that's a study Bible. Even with this, one must be careful, though. Robert Plummer counsels,

> A study Bible provides extensive notes on the text of Scripture…. For a young Christian, a study Bible can be very helpful by providing brief summaries and historical backgrounds for each book of the Bible, supplying discussion of difficult and debated texts, and offering cross-references and indices. Wrongly used, a study Bible can provide a crutch that discourages Christians from thinking about and wrestling

with texts for themselves. Also, if a person purchases a study Bible from an avowed theological perspective, one faces the danger of letting theological predilections take priority over the text of Scripture.[43]

Step 4: Understand the genre. Next, to understand a specific Bible passage, identify its **biblical genre**, or type. Just as there are musical genres, such as country, hip-hop, and classical, there are several different genres of literature present in the Bible. These include poetry, historical narratives (of which the Gospels and Acts are subcategories), legal prescriptions, prophecies, psalms, proverbs (and other forms of wisdom literature), parables, epistles ("letters"), and apocalyptic literature (e.g., Daniel and Revelation).

> ***Biblical Genre:*** a classification of literary styles used in Scripture, including poetry, historical narratives, legal prescriptions, prophesies, psalms, proverbs, parables, epistles, and apocalyptic literature.

Understanding the genre helps us determine how to interpret a passage properly. For example, psalms are a kind of poetry, full of figurative and symbolic language, and we ought to take this into account as we approach the text. We understand, for example, the highly figurative and symbolic nature of Psalm 17:8, "Keep me as the apple of your eye; hide me in the shadow of your wings." Obviously, this does not literally mean God's eye has an apple in it or that he has wings. But we wouldn't (or shouldn't) read the report about manna falling from heaven (Exod. 16) or one of the Ten Commandments (Exod. 20; Deut. 5) so figuratively. Rather, these texts are more straightforward, and the principles of their genres help us understand them more clearly.

Each genre comes with its own set of interpretive principles. Says Graeme Goldsworthy, "The issue is not that of giving a piece of text a precise name of genre identification, but rather that of understanding the variety of ways that literature can be used to communicate."[44] For example, a proverb, by definition, is *not* a prophecy or promise. To misunderstand this point can create great damage. Just imagine how heartbroken a parent would be if she had taken Proverbs 22:6—"Train up a child in the way he should go; even when he is old he will not depart from it"—as a promise, only to have her child leave the faith. Sadly, far too many people have abandoned Christianity precisely because of misunderstandings like this.

Understanding genres also helps us grapple with some of the uncomfortable things the Bible's historical narrative records. Historical narratives report what happened, whether good or bad. They are not commands for how we ought to live; they are descriptive, not prescriptive (more on this in step 10). Thus, we do not need to explain away why some biblical character had two wives, for example, or why Jephthah committed the immoral act of sacrificing his daughter (Judg. 11:39–40).[45]

> ***Context:*** the discourse surrounding a passage that gives meaning to the content; the historical background and literary setting of a text that helps clarify meaning.

Step 5: Understand the context. By **context** we mean the historical and literary basis for a text as well as the discourse surrounding a passage that gives meaning to the content. **Historical context** refers to "the time and culture of the author and his readers, that is the geographical, topographical, and political factors that are relevant to the author's

setting; and the occasion of the book, letter, psalm, prophetic oracle, or other genre."[46] Two questions to ask are "What occasioned the writing?" and "What is the purpose of the writing?"[47]

Paul T. Penley, a theologian who loves studying the culture of Bible times, offers an interesting strategy for understanding context. In his book *Reenacting the Way (of Jesus)*, Penley suggests asking, "What is the biblical author or character in the story doing? What cultural norm is being challenged or borrowed by the biblical author? How does the Bible direct its ancient readers to take on that cultural norm?"[48]

For example, Penley says, in Matthew 5:39 Jesus says to "turn the other cheek." What is the context of this? In the time of Jesus, Roman soldiers could be quite abusive. Most were right-handed, which means if they struck you on the right cheek, it is because they backhanded you—a gesture of insult as well as of abuse. To turn your left cheek to them also, then, is to force the soldier to strike you with his fist, the way he might if in a fight with a peer. Offering the left cheek, according to Penley, might not be the act of subservience it has often been portrayed to be; rather, it may be an invitation to "hit me like a man." Penley explains, "[Jesus] wants to make each attacker stop and think about how they are mistreating another human being."[49] In this case, "'turning the other cheek' is not blanket acceptance of brutality or immorality. It is a plan for change. It is a strategy for motivating others toward lasting repentance."[50]

Penley's explanation is certainly compelling. Is he right? Well, to find out you'd have to talk to scholars of that time period, examine other historical sources, and look at the interpretation others have given of this passage. This is the work of understanding the historical context.

Literary context, though, is different from historical context. Literary context refers to the genre, structure, and grammar of a text. As Fee and Stuart phrase it, the "biblical sentences for the most part only have clear meaning in relation to preceding and succeeding sentences." They continue, "The most important contextual question you will ever ask—and it must be asked over and over of every sentence and every paragraph—is, 'What's the point?'"[51] In Genesis 22, the struggle and pathos of the story of Abraham's attempted sacrifice of Isaac is understood more clearly when we realize what Abraham himself realized only after the fact: that this is a test from God ("After these things God tested Abraham," Gen. 22:1). Understanding Jesus's discussion of the Sabbath in Matthew 12 makes better sense in light of his statement at the end of Matthew 11: "Come to me, all who labor and are heavy laden, and I will give you rest" (v. 28). The overall structure and progression of the book of Acts hinges on Jesus's promise and mention of increased geographical regions in Acts 1:8: "You will receive power when the Holy Spirit has come upon you, and you will be my witnesses in Jerusalem and in all Judea and Samaria, and to the end of the earth."

Paying attention to the literary context in the smaller stories can help us also understand the overarching story of the Bible: the metanarrative. The Bible is not just a collection of great stories that express our shared heritage; it is connected to the present as well, which means we cannot read it as just an account of past events. As Gene Fant says, "Learning from stories requires us to read in a way that is active, that seeks to find connection between even the most ancient of authors and the challenges of our own circumstances."[52] Michael Goheen expands ever further:

> When we speak of the biblical story as a narrative we are making an ontological claim. It is a claim that this is the way God created the world; the story of the Bible tells us the way the world really is. There is no more fundamental way to speak about the nature of God's world than to speak of it in terms of a story. Nor is the biblical story to be understood simply as a local tale about a certain ethnic group or religion. It makes a *comprehensive* claim about the world: it is public truth. The biblical story encompasses all of reality—north, south, east, west, past, present, and future. It begins with the creation of all things and ends with the renewal of all things. In between it offers an interpretation of the meaning of cosmic history. It, therefore, makes a comprehensive claim; our stories, our reality must find a place in this story.[53]

Step 6: Understand the content. The term **content** refers to the meaning of words or the subject matter of a written work. According to Fee and Stuart, it has to do with "the meanings of words, the grammatical relationships in sentences, and the choice of the original text where the manuscripts have variant readings. It also includes a number of the items [such as] the meaning of denarius, or a Sabbath day's journey, or 'high places,' etc."[54]

> *Content:* the meaning of words or passages; the subject matter of a written work.

Sometimes the most fascinating insights come from understanding the robust meaning of the words Scripture uses. For example, the word often translated "peace" in the Old Testament is actually the Hebrew word *shalom*. But *shalom* means much more than the mere absence of conflict. Says Elmer Martens, professor emeritus of Old Testament, *shalom* "embraces concepts of harmony, security, serenity, right relationships, wholeness, health, prosperity, and even success. The term may refer to a condition or a relationship, and in the latter designates a right relationship to God."[55] In this instance, understanding the meaning of the word adds depth to the understanding of "peace" in the Old Testament.

One helpful tool in understanding both the context and the content of Scripture is a **Bible commentary**, a kind of book written by a theologian to help people better understand Scripture, passage by passage. Of commentaries, Fee and Stuart say,

> *Bible Commentary:* a verse-by-verse exposition of scriptural passages written to help people better understand the Bible.

> What you want a commentary for is basically to supply three things: (1) helps on sources and information about the historical context, (2) answers to those manifold content questions, and (3) thorough discussions of difficult texts as to the possibilities of meaning, along with the supporting arguments.[56]

A *good* commentary digs into the theological issues rather than merely sharing the author's experiences, offering balanced discussions of several possible meanings of the text rather than proposing only what the author prefers. The best commentaries give insights into the cultures, specific points of interest regarding the Hebrew and Greek words used, and the historical background of the book.[57]

Step 7: Look for relationships. Matthew 4:2–4 describes Jesus's being led into the wilderness and tempted by the Devil: "After fasting forty days and forty nights, he was hungry. And the tempter came and said to him, 'If you are the Son of God, command these stones to become loaves of bread.' But he answered, 'It is written, "Man shall not live by bread alone, but by every word that comes from the mouth of God."'" There is no way to understand this text without looking at the Old Testament passage Jesus was quoting: Deuteronomy 8, in which Moses gave instruction to the children of Israel in the wilderness. The parallels are stunning and worth several hours of careful study. Every verse is significant:

- Careful obedience to God's commandments precedes the possession of the Promised Land (v. 1).[58]

- The time in the wilderness had been a test of the Israelites' hearts (v. 2).[59]

- God fed the Israelites with manna so they would know that provision does not come from bread alone but from God's words (vv. 3–4).[60]

- God disciplined the children of Israel in the wilderness to prepare them to hold fast to his commandments and not forget his provision when they entered the land of abundance (vv. 5–16).

- The temptation, Moses said, would be for the Israelites to say in their hearts, "My power and the might of my hand have gotten me this wealth" (vv. 17–18).[61]

- If the Israelites went after other gods and stopped listening to the voice of the Lord, they would perish (vv. 18–20).[62]

By comparing and contrasting Jesus's forty days in the wilderness in Matthew 4 with the Israelites' forty years in the wilderness in Deuteronomy 8, we can see God's nature more clearly, making proper connections between passages and taking seriously how they relate to one another and illuminate one another in relationship. We might otherwise have seen Jesus's time in the wilderness as a random incident in his life.

> The key is careful study of *all* Scripture, as well as study of the relationships that emerge between different texts.

The key is careful study of *all* Scripture, as well as study of the relationships that emerge between different texts. We must be like those commended by the apostle Paul in Acts 17:11–12 who "received the word with all eagerness, examining the Scriptures daily to see if these things were so." The people in this passage, as Jews, were commended for comparing everything Paul was teaching to the words of the Old Testament.

HOW TO READ THE BIBLE

Step 8: Study words. Because the Bible is a unified whole, we might expect words and concepts to be woven throughout in the way individual threads weave throughout a tapestry to create a meaningful picture. And they are.

To get started with a word study, just type the word you're studying into a Bible program, note every verse where it occurs, and study the verses, in context, one by one. You might use a book that explains the words of Scripture, called a **lexicon**; you might also use a **theological dictionary** to develop a deeper understanding of each word and each *use* of each word.

An example of a word study from the New Testament is the word *abundance*. The Greek word used in the original language is *perisseuo*. It means "to abound" or to have "a great deal of."[63] It's the word used in Mark 8:8[64] when the disciples, after feeding a great multitude through a miracle of Jesus, took up seven baskets full of pieces left over. It's also the word used in 2 Corinthians 9:8[65] when Paul talks about God's abundant provision for us through grace so we may be able to abound in every good work. Studying the word *abundance* helps us see God's focus on abundant grace in the New Testament, reminding us of God's focus on abundance in creation itself, with his command to be fruitful and multiply.

> *Lexicon:* an alphabetical dictionary that translates and defines words from another language, particularly Greek, Hebrew, and Latin.

> *Theological Dictionary:* a reference book of words and phrases found in the Bible.

Words are important. Words have meaning. Examining how they are used in Scripture can fascinate us, but, moreover, word study opens us up to seeing God's consistently loving message throughout the ages.

Step 9: Bring your experience to bear. At first this advice seems to contradict our earlier principle about not imposing our own meanings and cultural assumptions on Scripture. But sometimes we are *invited* to do so by the Bible's use of examples from everyday life. When the psalmist tells us that he hides in the shadow of God's wings, people who know something about chickens are invited to picture the way a mother hen shelters her chicks in times of danger. When Hebrews 12 uses the figure of speech of an athletic competition to describe how we should act in view of the faith lived out by biblical characters, scriptural principles are here anchored in our everyday experiences. Similarly, when Paul in Ephesians 6:10–12[66] talks about the whole armor of God, we have a way to think about "spiritual soldiering" when we see military soldiers in action.

The use of metaphors and allusions enables us to understand Scripture more deeply and connect it to our human experiences. Our understanding does not change the meaning of the text, but seeing how God inspired the writers of Scripture to provide touch points for key concepts enables us to more deeply grasp its key principles.

Step 10: Courageously pursue a response. We are "to be doers of the word, and not hearers only" (James 1:22).[67] To hear God's Word and do nothing about it is to deceive ourselves into thinking we are free to do nothing.

However, not every passage in the biblical text is meant to be read as a command or point the reader must act upon. We may be admonished in sermons to "be a Ruth" or think of David's five smooth stones as the basis of a five-point outline, but this isn't really the best use of Scripture. Most of the Bible is *descriptive* in nature. It tells of past events, explores the lives of our ancestors (the good, the bad, and the ugly), and provides a record of God's active plan of redemption. A **descriptive passage** teaches us through inference and example, giving us a sense of where the people of God have been, so that we might discern our future more clearly.

> **Descriptive Passage:** a biblical passage that describes specific events.

For example, when the book of Nehemiah describes how Nehemiah studied the problem of the broken city walls of Jerusalem and rallied the people to fix them, we can gain insight into how a man committed to glorifying God was able to lead and how we might also be able to lead in difficult situations.

> **Prescriptive Passage:** a biblical passage that prescribes how people ought to live.

A **prescriptive passage**, on the other hand, provides specific hallmarks of how we *ought* to live, how we *ought* to make decisions, and how we *ought* to think. There are many "prescriptive passages" in the Bible, passages that reflect something of God's nature and the created order and, thus, form commands to be obeyed or values to be adopted:

- Exodus 20:2–17 (the Ten Commandments)

- Matthew 5:1–16 (the Sermon on the Mount)

- Matthew 28:16–20 (the Great Commission)

Prescriptive passages have a particular use in our being discipled to be more like Christ. Take, for example, this rich passage from the apostle Paul's letter to the church at Colossae:

> Put on then, as God's chosen ones, holy and beloved, compassionate hearts, kindness, humility, meekness, and patience, bearing with one another and, if one has a complaint against another, forgiving each other; as the Lord has forgiven you, so you also must forgive. And above all these put on love, which binds everything together in perfect harmony. And let the peace of Christ rule in your hearts, to which indeed you were called in one body. And be thankful. Let the word of Christ dwell in you richly, teaching and admonishing one another in all wisdom, singing psalms and hymns and spiritual songs, with thankfulness in your hearts to God. And whatever you do, in word or deed, do everything in the name of the Lord Jesus, giving thanks to God the Father through him. (Col. 3:12–17)

This is clearly prescriptive: *do this; don't do that.* Both descriptive and prescriptive passages must be studied and learned from, but in different ways.

What kinds of specific actions should we pursue? I suggest three things, for starters:

First, journal what you are learning. You can buy inexpensive paper journals at any discount store. It's great to get "off-line" for a bit and actually write things down. These chronicle our growth, and we can refer to our writing for the rest of our lives. Our past writing may even be of spiritual benefit to us in later years or to those who come after us.

Second, share what you are learning. Talk to people. "May I share with you something I learned from Scripture today? It would help me if I could talk about it aloud."

> Talk to people. "May I share with you something I learned from Scripture today? It would help me if I could talk about it aloud."

Third, live what you are learning. God's Word is powerful, and often he meets us with specific promptings about how we should live differently. In college, after reading a certain passage, I was particularly convicted about feeding the hungry. It was quite cold outside. I gathered up some food and old sweatshirts and headed out to an abandoned house a few blocks away where I suspected a homeless man lived. Inside I found the man quite uncomfortable in the cold. Because of an injury, he had not been able to make it to the warmth of the homeless shelter. He shivered under a pile of blankets. Because I had listened to the Spirit's prompting, I was able to help him find the aid he needed. I wish I could say I've always obeyed in this way. The apostle Paul seems to have felt the same way. Rather than chastising himself for past failures, though, he wrote, "Forgetting what lies behind and straining forward to what lies ahead, I press on toward the goal for the prize of the upward call of God in Christ Jesus" (Phil. 3:13–14).

The key is acting on what you know. Jesus said in John 13:17, "If you know these things, blessed are you if you do them." To not *do* them is to not *know* them.

7. CONCLUSION

I'd like to close this chapter with some thoughts about doubt. In chapter 1, I counseled you to "doubt your doubts." This applies in reading the Bible, too. Some people read Scripture and steadily increase in faith. Others read and grow doubtful: "How can this possibly be true?" If you've experienced doubt, you are not alone. Very godly people have doubts. John the Baptist—the forerunner of Jesus, a prophet of the Lord—even experienced doubt (Matt. 11:2–3).[68] Peter denied Christ three times. Thomas wouldn't believe that Jesus had risen until he placed his hands in Jesus's wounds.

Earlier we talked about the Protestant Reformation. Many people do not realize that the Reformation's most celebrated figure, a monk named Martin Luther, experienced grave doubts. Ten years after posting his Ninety-Five Theses on the church door at Wittenberg, Luther wrote of an agonizing experience of doubt: "For more than a week I was close to the gates of death and hell. I trembled in all my members. Christ was wholly

> Many people do not realize that the Reformation's most celebrated figure, a monk named Martin Luther, experienced grave doubts.

lost. I was shaken by desperation and blasphemy of God."[69] Reflecting on the experience, Luther emphasized the importance of being anchored in truth in the middle of such experiences: "All this is written for our comfort that we should see how deeply God hides his face and how we must not go by our feeling but only by his Word."[70]

When you experience doubt or have questions, don't bury them. Share them with a trusted pastor, teacher, or mentor. Find a trained theologian and take him or her out for coffee. And remember, the steadiest growth happens in the context of a church. God never intended for humans to grow up spiritually alone. The apostles speak frequently of spiritual growth in their letters. Almost all these letters were written to groups of people, not individuals. Spiritual growth takes place in community. The church is a team, an army, a body, a family, a hospital. No church is perfect, of course, and many people have been involved with one for a long time and still have not grasped what the Bible is all about. Maybe part of your role is to help them grow too.

> Remember this: God is shaping you into the image of his Son, a process more like the making of a painting than like the manufacturing of a machine.

In the end, remember this: God is shaping you into the image of his Son, a process more like the making of a painting than like the manufacturing of a machine. John Ortberg vividly explains:

> God always knows what each person needs. He had Abraham take a walk, Elijah take a nap, Joshua take a lap, and Adam take the rap. He gave Moses a forty-year time out, he gave David a harp and a dance, and he gave Paul a pen and a scroll. He wrestled with Jacob, argued with Job, whispered to Elijah, warned Cain, and comforted Hagar. He gave Aaron an altar, Miriam a song, Gideon a fleece, Peter a name, and Elisha a mantle. Jesus was stern with the rich young ruler, tender with the woman caught in adultery, patient with the disciples, blistering with the scribes, gentle with the children, and gracious with the thief on the cross. God never grows two people the same way. God is a hand-crafter, not a mass-producer. And now it is your turn.[71]

It is your turn indeed. Start now. Pick up the Bible. Read it! As you do, you'll learn that the Bible carries many significant implications for our understanding of God and ourselves. We'll look at the implications of the Bible on our understanding of God in chapter 8 and the implications of the Bible on loving our neighbors in chapter 9.

ENDNOTES

1. Jeremiah 29:11–13.
2. Luke 24:32.
3. Matthew 18:20.
4. John Micklethwait and Adrian Wooldridge, *God Is Back: How the Global Revival of Faith Is Changing the World* (New York: Penguin, 2009), 273–77.
5. Quoted in David Kinnaman, *You Lost Me: Why Young Christians Are Leaving Church ... and Rethinking Faith* (Grand Rapids, MI: Baker, 2011), 215.
6. Elizabeth Eisenstein, *The Printing Revolution in Early Modern Europe* (Cambridge, UK: Cambridge University Press, 1983), 148.

7. See Philip Jenkins, *The Next Christendom: The Coming of Global Christianity* (New York: Oxford University Press, 2011).

8. Often attributed to Mark Twain.

9. Saint Augustine, *Confessions of St. Augustine* (Mineola, NY: Dover, 2002), 98.

10. Augustine, *Confessions*, 146.

11. N. T. Wright, *Simply Christian: Why Christianity Makes Sense* (New York: Harper-Collins, 2006), 191.

12. Glen Ward, *Postmodernism: Teach Yourself* (Chicago: McGraw-Hill, 2003), 162.

13. Jacques Derrida, a French philosopher and literary critic, even argued that because there is no meaning in a text, the reader's interpretation is more important than what the author intended. Kevin J. Vanhoozer, *Is There a Meaning in This Text? The Bible, the Reader, and the Morality of Literary Knowledge* (Grand Rapids, MI: Zondervan, 1998), 158.

14. Occasionally, you'll hear Postmodernists use the term *anti-realism* to describe this skeptical approach to the so-called real world. For a more complete definition of *anti-realism*, see Robert Audi, ed., *The Cambridge Dictionary of Philosophy*, 2nd ed. (Cambridge, UK: Cambridge University Press, 1999), 33, which reads in part, "Rejection, in one form or another form or area of inquiry, of realism, the view that there are knowable mind-independent facts, objects, or properties."

15. Postmodernists see the idea of a "metanarrative," a grand story explaining the whole world, as just a way to gain power and command others' obedience. Jean-François Lyotard urged his followers to free themselves from the grip of powerful people by exercising "incredulity towards metanarrative." To Lyotard, any broad explanations deserve skepticism because people's experiences are so varied and are all we really have to pay attention to. Jean-François Lyotard, *The Postmodern Condition: A Report on Knowledge* (Minneapolis: University of Minnesota Press, 1984), xxiv.

16. Many Christian theologians are more comfortable with a postmodern approach to biblical studies than I am. They range from unabashedly enthusiastic to somewhat sympathetic in their embrace of Postmodernism. Some names you'll see along this spectrum of people who have embraced Postmodernism's assumptions or written approvingly about them include Brian McLaren, Stanley Grenz, Nancey Murphy, Roger Olson, Robert Webber, James K. A. Smith, and Merold Westphal. We need to be careful not to confuse their version of Postmodernism with that of atheistic thinkers such as Nietzsche, Derrida, Foucault, Lyotard, and Rorty. For a more "pro" postmodern view, see Merold Westphal, *Overcoming Onto-Theology: Toward a Postmodern Christian Faith*, Perspectives in Continental Philosophy 21 (New York: Fordham University Press, 2001), xi, and Roger E. Olson, "Post-Conservative Evangelical Theology and the Theological Pilgrimage of Clark Pinnock," in *Semper Reformandum: Studies in Honour of Clark H. Pinnock*, ed. Stanley E. Porter and Anthony R. Cross (Carlisle, PA: Paternoster, 2003), 20. For a more "con" view, see D. A. Carson, *Becoming Conversant with the Emerging Church: Understanding a Movement and Its Implications* (Grand Rapids, MI: Zondervan, 2005). Also, see Millard J. Erickson, Paul Kjoss Helseth, and Justin Taylor, eds., *Reclaiming the Center: Confronting Evangelical Accommodation in Postmodern Times* (Wheaton, IL: Crossway, 2004).

17. Carson, *Becoming Conversant*, 123.

18. Wayne Grudem, *Systematic Theology: An Introduction to Biblical Doctrine* (Grand Rapids, MI: Zondervan, 1994), 108.

19. Gordon D. Fee and Douglas K. Stuart, *How to Read the Bible for All Its Worth* (Grand Rapids, MI: Zondervan, 2003), 18.

20. Fee and Stuart, *How to Read the Bible*, 104.

21. Grudem, *Systematic Theology*, 50.

22. Graeme Goldsworthy, *Christ-Centered Biblical Theology: Hermeneutical Foundations and Principles* (Downers Grove, IL: InterVarsity, 2012), 59–60.

23. Fee and Stuart, *How to Read the Bible*, 17.

24. Fee and Stuart, *How to Read the Bible*, 17–18.

25. Gene C. Fant, *God as Author: A Biblical Approach to Narrative* (Nashville: B&H Academic, 2010), 32.

26. Robert Lewis Plummer, *40 Questions about Interpreting the Bible* (Grand Rapids, MI: Kregel, 2010), 96.

27. See Deuteronomy 17:6, 19:15; also the apostle Paul's use in 2 Corinthians 13:1 and 1 Timothy 5:19. The author of Hebrews also uses the term in Hebrews 10:28.

28. Fee and Stuart, *How to Read the Bible*, 21.

29. Fee and Stuart, *How to Read the Bible*, 21.

30. Timothy Keller, *Galatians for You: For Reading, for Feeding, for Leading*, God's Word for You (Purcellville, VA: The Good Book Company, 2013), 90.

31. Fee and Stuart, *How to Read the Bible*, 30.

32. Grudem, *Systematic Theology*, 108–9.

33. Fee and Stuart, *How to Read the Bible*, 26 (emphasis mine).

34. Wright, *Simply Christian*, 191.

35. Fant, *God as Author*, 140.

36. Fee and Stuart, *How to Read the Bible*, 17–18.

37. Michael Bauman, "The Ethics of Meaning," in *Pilgrim Theology: Core Doctrines for Christian Disciplines* (Manitou Springs, CO: Summit Press, 2007), 141.

38. Fee and Stuart, *How to Read the Bible*, 41–42.

39. You have probably noticed that I tend to use the English Standard Version (ESV) throughout this volume. The ESV

updates and corrects the Revised Standard Version (RSV) and was translated by theologians such as Wayne Grudem and J. I. Packer, whom I know and trust.

40. Fee and Stuart, *How to Read the Bible*, 41–42.

41. Fee and Stuart, *How to Read the Bible*, 41–42.

42. Fee and Stuart, *How to Read the Bible*, 52.

43. Plummer, *40 Questions*, 118.

44. Goldsworthy, *Christ-Centered Biblical Theology*, 51.

45. Judges 11:39–40: "At the end of two months, she returned to her father, who did with her according to his vow that he had made. She had never known a man, and it became a custom in Israel that the daughters of Israel went year by year to lament the daughter of Jephthah the Gileadite four days in the year."

46. Fee and Stuart, *How to Read the Bible*, 26.

47. Fee and Stuart, *How to Read the Bible*, 27.

48. Paul T. Penley, *Reenacting the Way (of Jesus)* (Colorado Springs, CO: Re-enacting the Way, 2013), 22.

49. Penley, *Reenacting the Way*, 55.

50. Penley, *Reenacting the Way*, 55.

51. Fee and Stuart, *How to Read the Bible*, 27.

52. Fant, *God as Author*, 32.

53. Michael W. Goheen, "Reading the Bible as One Story," *Biblical Theology*, www.biblicaltheology.ca/blue_files/Reading%20the%20Bible%20as%20One%20Story.pdf.

54. Fee and Stuart, *How to Read the Bible*, 28.

55. Elmer A. Martens, *Believers Church Bible Commentary: Jeremiah* (Scottsdale, PA: Herald Press, 1986), 308.

56. Fee and Stuart, *How to Read the Bible*, 266.

57. Fee and Stuart, *How to Read the Bible*, 266–67.

58. Deuteronomy 8:1: "The whole commandment that I command you today you shall be careful to do, that you may live and multiply, and go in and possess the land that the LORD swore to give to your fathers."

59. Deuteronomy 8:2: "You shall remember the whole way that the LORD your God has led you these forty years in the wilderness, that he might humble you, testing you to know what was in your heart, whether you would keep his commandments or not."

60. Deuteronomy 8:3–4: "He humbled you and let you hunger and fed you with manna, which you did not know, nor did your fathers know, that he might make you know that man does not live by bread alone, but man lives by every word that comes from the mouth of the LORD. Your clothing did not wear out on you and your foot did not swell these forty years."

61. Deuteronomy 8:17–18: "Beware lest you say in your heart, 'My power and the might of my hand have gotten me this wealth.' You shall remember the LORD your God, for it is he who gives you power to get wealth, that he may confirm his covenant that he swore to your fathers, as it is this day."

62. Deuteronomy 8:18–20: "You shall remember the LORD your God, for it is he who gives you power to get wealth, that he may confirm his covenant that he swore to your fathers, as it is this day. And if you forget the LORD your God and go after other gods and serve them and worship them, I solemnly warn you today that you shall surely perish. Like the nations that the LORD makes to perish before you, so shall you perish, because you would not obey the voice of the LORD your God."

63. J. P. Louw and Eugene A. Nida, *Greek-English Lexicon of the New Testament: Based on Semantic Domains*, 2nd ed., vol. 1 (New York: United Bible Societies, 1996), electronic edition, 599.

64. Mark 8:8: "They ate and were satisfied. And they took up the broken pieces left over, seven baskets full."

65. 2 Corinthians 9:8: "God is able to make all grace abound to you, so that having all sufficiency in all things at all times, you may abound in every good work."

66. Ephesians 6:10–12: "Be strong in the Lord and in the strength of his might. Put on the whole armor of God, that you may be able to stand against the schemes of the devil. For we do not wrestle against flesh and blood, but against the rulers, against the authorities, against the cosmic powers over this present darkness, against the spiritual forces of evil in the heavenly places."

67. James 1:22: "Be doers of the word, and not hearers only, deceiving yourselves."

68. Matthew 11:2–3: "When John heard in prison about the deeds of the Christ, he sent word by his disciples and said to him, 'Are you the one who is to come, or shall we look for another?'"

69. Quoted in Ruth A. Tucker, *Walking Away from Faith: Unraveling the Mystery of Belief and Unbelief* (Downers Grove, IL: InterVarsity, 2002), 91.

70. Quoted in Tucker, *Walking Away from Faith*, 91.

71. John Ortberg, quoted in Kinnaman, *You Lost Me*, 216–17.

CHAPTER 8

8

WHAT THE BIBLE SAYS ABOUT LOVING GOD

1. FROM HOPELESSNESS TO HOPE

Christmas holiday songs can be trite and even silly, but one that has stood the test of time is Frank Sinatra's rendering of "I Heard the Bells on Christmas Day."[1] It was originally a poem by Henry Wadsworth Longfellow called "Christmas Bells."

> *I heard the bells on Christmas Day*
> *Their old, familiar carols play,*
> *And wild and sweet*
> *The words repeat*
> *Of peace on earth, good-will to men!*
>
> *And thought how, as the day had come,*
> *The belfries of all Christendom*
> *Had rolled along*
> *The unbroken song*
> *Of peace on earth, good-will to men!*

These verses reflect both a tender reminiscence and an awestruck realization that people all around the earth celebrate the birth of Christ. Just beneath these beautiful words, however, lies a story of a very broken man struggling to hold on to his belief in God and humanity.

"Christmas Bells" was composed Christmas morning, 1863, while Longfellow walked alone down a frosty street in Cambridge, Massachusetts. Not too long before, his second wife, Frances Appleton, had succumbed to injuries she suffered after her dress had caught on fire.[2]

> **Just beneath these beautiful words lies a story of a very broken man struggling to hold on to his belief in God and humanity.**

Longfellow had, years before, lost his first wife and his daughter. And now *this*?

But Longfellow's confusion wasn't just personal. The Northern and Southern armies were at that time locked in combat in a vicious Civil War. The nation Abraham Lincoln had called "the last best hope of earth" seemed daily to be dissolving into an era of unprecedented slaughter: neighbor against neighbor, brother against brother.

Utter loneliness. Hopelessness. The third verse of Sinatra's "I Heard the Bells on Christmas Day" or the sixth verse of the original "Christmas Bells" expresses Longfellow's sorrow:

> *And in despair I bowed my head;*
> *"There is no peace on earth," I said:*
> *"For hate is strong,*
> *And mocks the song*
> *Of peace on earth, good-will to men!"*

The temptation to hopelessness confronts every generation and every culture. A few years ago, the news reported that a famous diplomat, Richard Holbrooke, passed away after an unsuccessful surgery to repair a torn aorta. Holbrooke's last words were, "You've got to stop this war in Afghanistan."[3] He died, literally and figuratively, of a broken heart. For decades he had traveled the world pleading for peace, yet on his deathbed, he found

WHAT THE BIBLE SAYS ABOUT LOVING GOD

himself grappling with the awful recognition that peace is one thing human effort alone can never bring.

Yet we hope for—long for—things to be right-side up rather than upside down. We crave **shalom**. Psalm 78 counsels the people of Israel to teach God's principles to children "so that they should set their hope in God and not forget the works of God, but keep his commandments; and that they should not be like their fathers, a stubborn and rebellious generation, a generation whose heart was not steadfast, whose spirit was not faithful to God" (vv. 7–8).

> **Shalom: from the Hebrew for "peace, prosperity, and wellness"; implies harmony in creation and with one's neighbors as well as a right relationship with God.**

And not only should we have hope, but we should also proclaim it. First Peter 3:15 says "always" to be "prepared to make a defense to anyone who asks you for a reason for the hope that is in you." Our hope ought to turn heads, and we must be ready to explain its source.

In this way, Longfellow's final stanza is a shout of rescue to the despairing poet meandering down that wintry lane:

> *Then pealed the bells more loud and deep:*
> *"God is not dead; nor doth he sleep!*
> *The Wrong shall fail,*
> *The Right prevail,*
> *With peace on earth, good-will to men!"* [4]

This is hope: that God is alive and awake; that he stepped into his own creation, entering the world stage as a helpless baby; that Immanuel, God with us, lived among us and willingly gave himself over to death on the cross, paying the penalty for our sin; that he was resurrected, overcoming death; and that he promises life of the ages to all with ears to hear.

Longfellow's poem expresses the sorrow of a fallen world but also the metamorphosis of *shalom*: the repairing, rebuilding, renewing, and refreshing of the relationships that so violently ruptured in the fall. God's redemption brings restoration and reconciliation—to God, self, others, and the creation. This is the most significant development in human history, as Richard John Neuhaus eloquently expresses:

> We have not the right to despair, for despair is a sin. And finally we have not the reason to despair, quite simply because Christ has risen. And this is the strength of a Christian world view, the strength of the Christian way of telling the story of the world: it has no illusions about it. All the other stories are built upon delusions, vain dreams, and utopias.[5]

In this chapter, we'll look at "you and God" to ask what it means to be image bearers of God in a created, fallen, and redeemed world. We'll talk openly about the nature of sin and idolatry and explore what it means to live righteously, wisely, lovingly, and mercifully as God's image bearers in an age of redemption. In the following chapter, we'll look at "you and the world" to see the implications of the Bible's metanarrative for how our loving God transforms our relationships with those around us. Let's begin with a brief review of who God is and what it means that we bear his image.

2. WHO IS GOD?

As we saw in our study of the biblical metanarrative, there are two most common names for God in the language of God's covenant people:

Elohim: from the Hebrew for "deity"; the generic name used in the Old Testament for the creator-God.

Yahweh: from the Hebrew for "I Am"; the personal and covenantal name of God used in the Old Testament.

- **Elohim** ("God") is a generic designation for "deity" or "powerful" and focuses on God as the creator of the whole world.

- **Yahweh** ("I Am Who I Am") is the personal and covenantal name of Israel's God. Preeminently, he is the God who redeemed his people from Egypt and brought them into covenant relationship with himself. Translators usually render Yahweh as "the LORD," which, while accurate, does not capture for most readers God's deeply personal nature.

In Genesis 1, God is referred to as *Elohim*, the great creator of the world. The narrative that describes his creative work is a doxology, a hymn of praise to the only one powerful enough to form and fill the entire universe. In Genesis 2:4, God is introduced with both names as *Yahweh Elohim* ("the 'I Am Who I Am' Lord God"). Together, these two titles showcase God as both the awesome creator and the loving redeemer who is Israel's covenant God.

We have seen that no aspect of his character takes second place to any other aspect. For example, God doesn't cease to be loving when he judges sin.

We have also seen in our study that God reveals many of his attributes to his human creation. For example, God is holy (set apart), eternal (has always existed), omniscient (all-knowing), omnipotent (all-powerful), omnipresent (everywhere present), and unchanging. God is also righteous (always just in his decisions), loving (the perfect expression of self-giving), wise (generates no unintended consequences), and merciful (gives us what we don't deserve). God doesn't *become* these things by doing them; he *embodies* them. Further, we have seen that no aspect of his character takes second place to any other aspect. For example, God doesn't cease to be loving when he judges sin.

These attributes give us insight into how God designed us, how we humans are affected by the fall, and how we are being redeemed in our image-bearing capacity.

3. WHO ARE WE?

Christians believe in an identifiable human nature. We are embodied persons, made to bear the image of a personal God. The properties most important to our personhood are shared with him.[6] We are composed of immaterial entities: soul, spirit, mind, heart, will, consciousness, and intuition.[7] Our bodies maintain their identifiable form, but our identity, our consciousness, continues undisrupted.[8]

Possessing both bodies and souls, we humans exist and are sentient beings (that is, we are aware of our existence).[9] Humans are, by our nature, religious. We sense that there is "something more" to the universe. We intuitively know that somehow our lives are lived in response to that greater reality.

Of course, many people claim not to be religious. Some further claim that their non-religious state is actually the true, natural state of human beings, as if somehow religious people are defective or, as the criticism often goes, delusional. One such group calls themselves "Brights," implying that those who disagree are dull.[10] But the evidence is not that humans are nonreligious by nature. In fact, it is the opposite. University of Notre Dame sociologist Christian Smith has studied the religious nature of humans and concluded that the non-religious have deactivated a natural tendency in transferring the object of their worship to knowledge, possessions, or themselves:

> This not only helps to explain religion's primordial, irrepressible, widespread, and seemingly inextinguishable character in the human experience, it also suggests that the skeptical Enlightenment, secular humanist, and New Atheist visions for a totally secular human world are simply not realistic—they are cutting against a very strong grain in the nature of reality's structure and so will fail to achieve their purpose. But that is not the whole story. Taking the concept of "being religious by nature" in a properly critical sense also helps us interpret the data that tells us that human beings and societies often are not religious. This view tells us that nonreligious people possess the natural capacities and tendencies toward religion but that those capacities and tendencies have not been activated by environmental, experiential triggers or else have been activated but then neutralized or deactivated by some other social forces.[11]

Of course, in order to have a religious nature, we must have a human nature first. It cannot be, as Postmodernism insists, that humans do not have an identifiable nature or essence, a "singular and unique 'I.'"[12] If Postmodernism is true, we might be subjects, bodies, or units, but we are not beings or persons. There is only an ever-evolving, highly sexual, social animal with multiple subjective interests crying out for recognition and acceptance.[13] We are like onions: when you're done peeling away the layers of culture, nothing remains.

Not everyone thinks Postmodernism has it all figured out. In his textbook on Postmodernism, Glenn Ward points out that the highly respected philosopher Jürgen Habermas, for one, "disputes the claims of some postmodern thinkers that human identity is unstable, fragmented, or 'in process'.... For him we all, deep down, share eternal human needs and desires. The failure of the Postmodernists is that they refuse to propose a route towards the fulfillment of these."[14]

We sense that we have an enduring nature because we actually do, the biblical account insists. Rather than being like onions, we are more like peaches with a hard seed in the middle.

God made us in his image and fashioned us for his glory. Let's take a look at what image bearing means, how the fall affected it, and how God redeems it.

4. IMAGE BEARING: CREATED

As we saw in earlier chapters, image was a very important concept in the ancient Near Eastern culture in which the Bible was written. Kings set up images of themselves in conquered cities to remind people who was in charge. An image symbolized authority over a certain domain.

But when God decided to set up his image, he didn't do it by carving statues; he formed living, breathing humans. God did not merely want his creation to acknowledge his sovereignty; he wanted his creation to reflect it by living with purpose, trust, confidence, decisiveness, creativity, and responsibility.

> When God decided to set up his image, he didn't do it by carving statues; he formed living, breathing humans. God did not merely want his creation to acknowledge his sovereignty; he wanted his creation to reflect it by living with purpose, trust, confidence, decisiveness, creativity, and responsibility.

We see this in Genesis 2:18, when God announced, "It is not good that the man should be alone; I will make him a helper fit for him." He then created the animals and brought them to the man so he could name them. After the animals were named, the man was led to realize that none of the creatures was the complete kind of helper he needed. He needed a helper with whom he could walk and share love, someone who would help him accomplish his massive mission.

Even before God created woman, though, we can see how having lots of animals to take care of helped Adam, deepening his appreciation for God's creativity, expanding his awareness of nature, and, most important, helping him grow in responsibility. With every act of naming, Adam became more like the thoughtful, whimsical, hardworking, proactive, artistic, "can-do," responsibility-taking, abundance-minded God in whose image he was made.

Giving us jobs to do—*very big* jobs—is one way God shapes us into his image. But what exactly does it mean to bear God's image? If, as the Bible teaches, we are fallen creatures, does humanity resemble God *less* today than we resembled him before the fall? Or do Christians perhaps bear God's image differently than those who remain in rebellion against him? These are important and difficult questions about God's image in us. Over time, three different views of the *imago Dei* have emerged:

- **Resemblance.** The most popular view says we are "like God" with respect to certain attributes such as intelligence, rationality, emotions, free will, morality, and ability to communicate. Because this view focuses on "how we are" (our being or nature) instead of "what we do" (our function), it's called an *ontological* view.

- **Relationship.** This view expands on the idea of resemblance, saying we are like God by our being relational. We relate to God and one another. In our relational capacity, we can even relate to false gods—to idols.

WHAT THE BIBLE SAYS ABOUT LOVING GOD

- **Rule.** Some connect their understanding of "image of God" to his commanding humanity to rule and have dominion over the rest of creation (Gen. 1:28).[15] This view, which as opposed to our *being* is focused on our *function*, gains strength when we remember that in ancient Near East literature, "image" and "likeness" signified one's rule, one's function. In this sense, humans are fully images of God even after the fall. We all bear God's image equally, and we do this uniquely as humans.

These are three very different views, but Old Testament professor Kenneth Turner thinks they can be synthesized.[16] Perhaps we are "like God" in our function as rulers on the earth, but we also possess the God-given tools needed to carry out that function, such as intelligence, ability to communicate, and so forth. Even in our fallen state, we are able to use these tools, however imperfectly, to carry out our mission and relate to one another and even to God. Humans were created to bear God's image, and all do, even when only faint traces of the family resemblance persist.

5. Image Bearing: Fallen

The **doctrine of the fall** teaches us that things are not as God originally intended. As we saw while examining the biblical metanarrative, our first parents tried to slough off their image-bearing capacity but found underneath only nakedness and shame, not the shiny skin of wisdom they'd hoped for. Irresponsibility, paranoia, and blame replaced responsibility, trust, and purpose. God then pronounced a curse on the serpent, the woman, and the man.

> *Doctrine of the Fall:* the orthodox Christian belief that sin entered the natural world when Adam and Eve chose to disobey God and ate from the Tree of Knowledge of Good and Evil.

A God who curses people forever because they ate some fruit fits the Secularist portrayal of God as a mean-spirited judge whose punishments do not fit the crime. But this stereotype misrepresented what really happened. The curse was not God saying, "I'm angry, so I'm going to ruin your lives!" Rather, it was the man and woman calling down upon themselves the natural consequences of their actions. They said, in essence, "We can handle it from here. Leave us alone." Without God's presence, what once had been pleasurable became painful. Without God's touch, what once had been obedient became rebellious. Without God's wisdom, what once had been fruitful became barren. God's constant presence does not merely comfort us pleasantly but also holds everything together; the garment of nature, however, by our rebellion, unravels at the seams. It's easier to see this if we understand sin's nature and how it affects human nature. Let's examine that next.

> *Parasite:* an organism that survives at the expense of a host (for example, viruses, bacteria, tapeworms, flukes, fleas, ticks, and louses).

6. What Sin Does to Us

As professor emeritus of religion Albert Wolters explains, sin is like a parasite on human nature.[17] **Parasite** is the generic name for any organism that survives at the expense of the host. Viruses and bacteria are parasites, for example, as are tapeworms, flukes, fleas, ticks, and louses. They survive only by living off a life-generating host organism.

In other words, parasites can survive only if the host organism off which they are surviving is really alive—if it contains a high degree of order, is responsive to stimuli, maintains stable internal conditions, can acquire the energy it needs to stay alive, grows, reproduces, and changes through time without changing its basic genetic characteristics.[18] Most parasites do not kill their host, at least not right away. Tapeworms don't kill your dog, at least directly; they just steal the nutrients your dog needs to sustain life.

Here's what we know about parasites:

- Everyone is at risk. Parasites are everywhere in the environment and are difficult to avoid.

- Parasites are opportunistic. They thrive in sick bodies.

- Parasites are often difficult to detect.

- It is difficult to get rid of parasites.[19]

Sin is like this. It is parasitical. Take lying, for example. Lying couldn't exist unless we humans had the capacity to tell the truth. When we distort this truth-telling capacity to mislead others, to get them to believe that what is *not* actually true is in fact the way things really are, we have invited a parasite into our lives. Our relationship with others is broken. Not only do our words invite skepticism if we are discovered to have lied, but our natures are such that we assume that others are lying to us just as we are to them. The parasite of lying continues to eat away at both truth and relationship.

7. What We Can Do about Sin

So what do we do about sin? When a creature is afflicted with parasites, the goal is to remove them, not to kill the host. If the host is unhealthy, restoring it to health must be part of the prescription. To do this with the parasite of sin, though, we must know something of the state to which we wish to restore people.[20] This means first seeking a clear picture of physical and spiritual health.

If we consider health from only a physical point of view, we'll miss very important insights about how to be truly healthy. We might look at a physically vibrant twentysomething and see only a picture of health, or we might believe that an elderly person, stooped and wheelchair bound, is merely a product of time and gravity. But if we are more than our bodies—if we are something soulish, mindful, and spirited—then what from the body's perspective appears to be healthy could actually be an advanced state of decay, and what appears to be the cruelty of aging could be a reflection of wisdom and grace. People have different perspectives about the effects of sin, but it is fair to say that all views agree on this one thing: sin diminishes or covers up the *imago Dei*, but it doesn't kill it. We may be fallen image bearers, but we never stop being image bearers.

WHAT THE BIBLE SAYS ABOUT LOVING GOD

To really restore people to health, we must know about the spiritual parasites afflicting us all. The most vicious parasite, because it goes directly to the heart of humanity's bearing of God's image, is idolatry.

8. Idolatry: Attacking God's Image

Without a sense of who God is, we can never grasp what true health looks like. The Bible has a word for anything that diverts us from perceiving God clearly: *idolatry*. Idolatry is so much more than making graven images. If that's all it was, we would probably be off the hook. Most of us don't make carvings and worship them. But when it comes to wrong ideas about God, none of us is off the hook. A. W. Tozer explains:

> The essence of idolatry is the entertainment of thoughts about God that are unworthy of Him. It begins in the mind and may be present where no overt act of worship has taken place.… Wrong ideas about God are not only the fountain from which the polluted waters of idolatry flow; they are themselves idolatrous. The idolater simply imagines things about God and acts as if they were true.[21]

Bizarrely, this is what happened after God led the children of Israel out of Egypt. While Moses received the Ten Commandments, his brother Aaron fashioned a golden calf and other idols and announced, "These are your gods, O Israel, who brought you up out of the land of Egypt!" (Exod. 32:4). A *golden calf* had brought them out of Egypt? How had they become so stupid this quickly?

You Become What You Worship

We might think we are superior to a tribe of refugees who danced around a golden calf, but we share with those ancient Israelites the same core problem. In our fear and arrogance, we construct things to worship only to end up resembling the idols we have created. This is one of the direst consequences of idolatry, according to Psalm 135. Not only do idols steal the worship of which God alone is worthy but they actually transmute the worshipper into the image of what is being worshipped:

> The idols of the nations are silver and gold, the work of human hands. They have mouths, but do not speak; they have eyes, but do not see; they have ears, but do not hear, nor is there any breath in their mouths. Those who make them become like them, so do all who trust in them. (vv. 15–18)

So when we idolize any part of the created world, we take on its attributes and in a sense "become" what we worship. If we worship things rather than the creator, we end up becoming like things: we can't see or hear or think about what is true, and we begin seeing others as objects to be used for our own benefit rather than as image bearers of God.

So when we idolize any part of the created world, we take on its attributes and in a sense "become" what we worship. If we worship things rather than the creator, we end up becoming like things: we can't see or hear or think about what is true, and we begin seeing others as objects to be used for our own benefit rather than as image bearers of God.

If God had not made us living, breathing representations of his authority, we might occasionally worship the created thing rather than the creator. But God's image is at the heart of everything, as even the Old Testament law in Leviticus reflects: the two things that called for the death penalty were crimes against God's covenant, and crimes that distort his image, as in, say, graven images or abuse or murder of people. If the Creator actually exists, worshipping the created thing rather than the Creator is absurd, like believing that the football itself—rather than football players—scores winning touchdowns.

Not only is it absurd to replace life-giving persons with lifeless objects, but it is also offensive. Imagine how ripped off you would feel to tour the world-famous San Diego Zoo and find that the animals had been replaced with inanimate models. Similarly, trying to off-load our image-bearing capacity onto lifeless objects is to rip off God. It would be like knocking out a priceless Chagall stained-glass window to put up a bedsheet or trading the Hope Diamond for Mardi Gras beads.

Still, in this sense, we all have much in common with the children of Israel, who traded the presence of almighty God for a golden calf, and with Judas, who traded the life of his friend and teacher for thirty pieces of silver. People make these kinds of bad trades all the time: trading a lifelong marriage for a night with a prostitute, or a God-given talent for a shaky crack high, or a deep friendship for the pleasure of a snarky social media post. We become shallow, unstable, unthinking, and uncaring, just like the things we worship.

What can save us from our moldy, withered, shuffling, drooling imitation of God's goodness? Only one thing.

The More We Understand God, the Less We Will Worship Ourselves

We are rescued from idolatry only by understanding once again who God is. When we encounter him, we see what our nature without him is like. He is holy and we are not. Moses and Isaiah were two men who saw God. Both were pretty good guys trying to do what God wanted, yet their first reaction to their sin was being overcome with a renewed sense of its seriousness. Let's take a look at each.

"Please show me your glory," Moses asked God. The narrative then reads as follows:

> He said, "I will make all my goodness pass before you and will proclaim before you my name 'The LORD.' And I will be gracious to whom I will be gracious, and will show mercy on whom I will show mercy. But," he said, "you cannot see my face, for man shall not see me and live." And the LORD said, "Behold, there is a place by me where you shall stand on the rock, and while my glory passes by I will put you in a cleft of the rock, and I will cover you with my hand until I have passed by. Then I will take away my hand, and you shall see my back, but my face shall not be seen." (Exod. 33:19–23)

So God in all his goodness passed before Moses, proclaiming the full meaning of his name, the Lord:

The LORD, the LORD, a God merciful and gracious, slow to anger, and abounding in steadfast love and faithfulness, keeping steadfast love for thousands, forgiving iniquity and transgression and sin, but who will by no means clear the guilty, visiting the iniquity of the fathers on the children and the children's children, to the third and the fourth generation. (34:6–7)

Moses, out of reflex, hit the deck: "And Moses quickly bowed his head toward the earth and worshipped. And he said, 'If now I have found favor in your sight, O Lord, please let the Lord go in the midst of us, for it is a stiff-necked people, and pardon our iniquity and our sin, and take us for your inheritance'" (vv. 8–9). In experiencing the full goodness of the Lord, Moses grasped that his own sin—not just the sin of his people—was also the problem.

For the second example, we fast-forward a few hundred years to Jerusalem just prior to the exile of the tribe of Judah. The prophet Isaiah, in Isaiah 6:1–4, vividly describes a vision:

In the year that King Uzziah died I saw the Lord sitting upon a throne, high and lifted up; and the train of his robe filled the temple. Above him stood the seraphim. Each had six wings: with two he covered his face, and with two he covered his feet, and with two he flew. And one called to another and said: "Holy, holy, holy is the LORD of hosts; the whole earth is full of his glory!" And the foundations of the thresholds shook at the voice of him who called, and the house was filled with smoke.

Isaiah reacted similarly to Moses: "Woe is me! For I am lost; for I am a man of unclean lips, and I dwell in the midst of a people of unclean lips; for my eyes have seen the King, the LORD of hosts!" (v. 5). In the light of God's glory, Isaiah saw himself as an unclean man leading an unclean people.

Only in the all-seeing light of God's glory do we see ourselves correctly. We realize how ridiculous it is to worship ourselves or other people or things. God's glory points with laser-like precision, revealing our hidden idols of self-doubt and low expectations as nothing more than masked pride. God's glory instantly scours away any illusion that we are superior to anyone else. The white-hot hum of God's glory also ignites within us a burning determination to declare war against *anything* standing in the way of fully bearing the image of the always-good, always-merciful, and always-faithful God.

God's glory reveals how fallen our condition is, like the examining room light that fully exposes all the damage done by the parasites that have tried to destroy us. God does not merely try to make the best of a bad situation; he is a redeemer at war with anything that wars against his image bearers.

> Only in the all-seeing light of God's glory do we see ourselves correctly. We realize how ridiculous it is to worship ourselves or other people or things. God's glory points with laser-like precision, revealing our hidden idols of self-doubt and low expectations as nothing more than masked pride.

9. Image Bearing: Redeemed

Romans 8:29 says, "Those whom he foreknew he also predestined to be conformed to the image of his Son." Beneath the theological debate over the doctrine of predestination, a deeper point reveals itself: what it means to be conformed to the image of Jesus. God aims to restore us to the place where we can bear his image righteously, wisely, lovingly, and mercifully. In each of these four communicable attributes of God, we can discern how we ought to live in light of Christ's redemption.

Righteousness

The first of the four communicable attributes we will explore is **righteousness**, which means for us humans a strong personal desire to understand and embody the character of Christ.

> *Righteousness:* the quality of being morally and spiritually right with God.

> *Identity:* the set of characteristics, giftings, and convictions that uniquely define who a person is.

Understand your identity in Christ. A person's **identity** is the set of characteristics, gifting, and convictions that make him "who" he is. One's identity develops through time and experience. Psychologist James E. Marcia, based on the work of psychologist Erik Erikson, developed a series of tests to examine Erikson's thought about how young adults form a sense of identity.[22] He found that people go through four phases as their sense of identity develops:

- **Identity Diffusion:** Diffusion is when people flounder but are unconcerned about it. They have not yet arrived at their purpose in life or understood who they are. They have no answers and few, if any, questions.

- **Identity Foreclosure:** Foreclosure is when people embrace a certain identity by ignoring any questions or thoughts that might challenge it. Usually they just follow the dictates of those in authority over them. They might have answers, but they have not questioned them.

- **Identity Moratorium:** Moratorium is a full-blown identity crisis. People in this stage struggle, concerning themselves with finding answers to unanswered questions.

- **Identity Achievement:** When a person has a stable sense of identity—committed to certain goals, beliefs, and values—that person has reached identity achievement. He has asked the right questions and has settled on answers.

Some people never make it out of phase one, *diffusion*. Their own identities are so poorly developed that they find themselves unable to know God or care about spiritual things and life purpose. Others make it into the second phase, *foreclosure*, because they were raised in families that made clear the values they ought to embrace but may find themselves dangerously

WHAT THE BIBLE SAYS ABOUT LOVING GOD

relying on too much certainty or too much doubt, and rather than *actually* knowing, they only *think* they know.

The third phase, *moratorium*, is common in our culture among college students. Their beliefs have been challenged by new views and information, and they don't know what to do. They're struggling. The fourth phase, *achievement*, is the most stable place to be. Having wrestled with the difficult issues and having emerged with a sense of identity and purpose, a person in this phase is more prepared to move confidently into the next season of life.

From a biblical perspective, we can never really know ourselves properly without first knowing God through Jesus Christ. In the gospel of Matthew, we see an example of one of the disciples, Peter, being moved to identity achievement through acknowledging God through Christ. It took place in the district of Caesarea Philippi, which was a center of both religious and political worship.

> **From a biblical perspective, we can never really know ourselves properly without first knowing God through Jesus Christ.**

> Now when Jesus came into the district of Caesarea Philippi, he asked his disciples, "Who do people say that the Son of Man is?" And they said, "Some say John the Baptist, others say Elijah, and others Jeremiah or one of the prophets." He said to them, "But who do you say that I am?" Simon Peter replied, "You are the Christ, the Son of the living God." And Jesus answered him, "Blessed are you, Simon Bar-Jonah! For flesh and blood has not revealed this to you, but my Father who is in heaven. And I tell you, you are Peter, and on this rock I will build my church, and the gates of hell shall not prevail against it. I will give you the keys of the kingdom of heaven, and whatever you bind on earth shall be bound in heaven, and whatever you loose on earth shall be loosed in heaven." (16:13–19)

Notice how Simon's identifying of the established work of Christ is nested in Christ's establishment of Simon's identity. By renaming Simon "Peter," which means "rock," Jesus takes what from a human standpoint would be an offense—"You're as dumb as a rock"—and transforms it into a picture of strength, steadfast to the point where not even the gates of hell can dislodge what God is accomplishing.

Peter's identity achievement did not make him perfect. It did not place him beyond the reach of doubt. In fact, during Jesus's trial, Peter denied even knowing him. But when restored by Jesus, Peter learned to "doubt his doubts." He became a man on a death-defying mission to proclaim the gospel.

> **The New Testament is full of passages that describe what it would mean to trust Christ with your identity.**

The New Testament is full of passages that describe what it would mean to trust Christ with your identity:

- You have the right to be a child of God (John 1:12).[23]

- By abiding in Christ, you will bear much fruit (John 15:5).[24]

- You are free from spiritual condemnation (Rom. 8:1).[25]

- You are heirs with Christ of whatever God has to give (Rom. 8:16–17).[26]

- You are one spirit with Christ (1 Cor. 6:17).[27]

- You are able to glorify God in your body (1 Cor. 6:19–20).[28]

- You are a new creation (2 Cor. 5:17).[29]

- You have become God's kind of righteous (2 Cor. 5:21).[30]

- Christ lives in you (Gal. 2:20).[31]

- You have been blessed with every spiritual blessing (Eph. 1:3).[32]

- You are holy and blameless before God (Eph. 1:4).[33]

- You are rooted in Christ and built up in him (Col. 2:7).[34]

- You have been filled with Christ in whom all authority resides (Col. 2:10).[35]

- You need not fear, as you have the capacity for power, love, and self-control (2 Tim. 1:7).[36]

- You are a recipient of mercy and grace when you need it (Heb. 4:16).[37]

- You have escaped the bondage to corruption that comes through sinful desire (2 Pet. 1:4).[38]

- The evil one cannot touch you (1 John 5:18).[39]

Repent and be restored. The Scriptures reveal how Christ's righteousness is available to operate in us. For most, though, such promises are abstractions they have not personally experienced. At Summit Ministries, we once surveyed students from our leadership conferences. Even among committed Christians, before they attended the program, only one-third reported feeling close to God. Something stood in the way of a close relationship with their Creator.[40]

Repentance: from the Greek for "changing one's mind"; the process of reviewing, regretting, and then changing direction with one's thoughts and actions.

God has a way of knocking down the barrier to spiritual victory. It is called **repentance**. The New Testament word for "repentance" is the Greek word *metanoia*, which means "changing one's mind." The word *metanoia* was often used in a philosophical sense, referring to changing one's mind-set: rejecting an inferior way of life and setting off on the path of enlightenment. This kind of change comes only from a radical shift to a far-superior way of life. As pastor Tim Keller has said, "Fear-based

WHAT THE BIBLE SAYS ABOUT LOVING GOD

repentance makes us hate ourselves. Joy-based repentance makes us hate the sin."[41] According to Scripture, God's kindness leads us to repentance of the right sort (Rom. 2:4).[42]

Repentance almost never takes place on our own. The Holy Spirit leads us to repentance by what Proverbs 27:6 calls "the wounds of a friend." We need accountability, someone who will confront us with our sin, someone in whom we can confide. In fact, for much of church history, repentance was part of the public act of worship. Because sin is not merely a private act but has public implications, repentance ought also be done, at least in part, in a public manner.

The Book of Common Prayer, for example, offers a beautiful and humbling prayer of repentance that would be a good model for anyone who wants to be restored to right relationship with God:

> Almighty and most merciful Father; We have erred, and strayed from Thy ways like lost sheep. We have followed too much the devices and desires of our own hearts. We have offended against Thy holy laws. We have left undone those things which we ought to have done; And we have done those things which we ought not to have done; And there is no health in us. But Thou, O Lord, have mercy upon us, miserable offenders. Spare Thou those, O God, who confess their faults. Restore Thou those who are penitent; According to Thy promises declared unto mankind in Christ Jesus our Lord. And grant, O most merciful Father, for His sake; That we may hereafter live a godly, righteous, and sober life, To the glory of Thy holy Name. Amen.[43]

For Anglicans, this prayer is usually said at home in the morning, when the members of a household have not had many opportunities to commit sins! It reminds us that sin is a *state of being*, not just a *set of actions*, and it causes us to humbly rely on God's grace to remove sin's parasite and restore the joy of *shalom*.

Develop a proper view of sin: structure and direction. A second part of having our identity in Christ is having a proper view of sin. Sin does not morph us into genetic mutants incapable of bearing God's image. Rather, as we saw earlier, sin is a parasite that sucks away vital nutrients and grows itself at the expense of a healthy body. With each aspect of creation, we must think of both the "structure" of creation and the "direction" we move. Sin does not destroy the structure but hijacks it to wrong purposes.[44]

Take, for example, the idea of "ambition." Many Christians think ambition is sinful in structure. They believe that it is never right to purposefully try to get the things we want. For support of their position, they turn to Scripture.[45] But the Bible condemns *selfish ambition*, not *ambition* itself. Ambition is not the problem; the problem is ambition put to selfish uses. The structure of ambition is fine, but its *direction* is often corrupted.

> With each aspect of creation, we must think of both the "structure" of creation and the "direction" we move. Sin does not destroy the structure but hijacks it to wrong purposes.

In our redeemed image bearing, for example, we might even think of ambition as a virtue that can be used to spread the gospel. The apostle Paul says in Romans

15:20, "I make it my ambition to preach the gospel, not where Christ has already been named, lest I build on someone else's foundation." He seemed to think that ambition was good when it came to spreading the gospel. The *structure* of ambition is good. The difference between fallen image bearing and redeemed image bearing is the use to which ambition is put.

> If the structure of creation is still good but we humans hijack it and take it in the wrong direction, discerning the *right* direction is part of redemptive image bearing.

We can approach each of the "seven deadly sins"—wrath, greed, sloth, pride, lust, envy, and gluttony—in a similar way. Wrath takes the structure of righteousness and moves in the direction of self-righteousness. Sloth takes the structure of contentment and turns it into laziness. Pride takes the confidence we feel knowing we bear God's image and turns it toward self-worship. Lust distorts the goodness of intimacy. Envy takes the structure of protectiveness and turns it into obsessiveness. Gluttony abuses the goodness of enjoyment.

If the structure of creation is still good but we humans hijack it and take it in the wrong direction, discerning the *right* direction is part of redemptive image bearing. This skill in discerning the right direction from the many competing alternatives is called *wisdom*.

Wisdom

A second communicable attribute of God, **wisdom**, does not come from how we think or feel but rather by how we act. As philosopher Mortimer Adler puts it, "We have seen artistic skill and scientific knowledge put to evil use. But we do not ordinarily think a man wise unless he acts wisely. To act wisely is to act well, even as to have wisdom is to use it."[46]

> *Wisdom:* the ability of thinking and acting with good judgment.

In ancient times, there were two very different concepts of wisdom and they were not equally good. The first concept of wisdom was that it is an otherworldly state that one can reach only by detaching from the things of this world. Plato (428–348 BC), for example, saw wisdom as an unattainable form about which we could know enough to want and love it.[47] Alcinous, a pagan philosopher of the second-century AD who followed Plato in claiming that God is "eternal, ineffable, self-sufficient, without need ... and perfect in every respect," taught that the only way to know such a God was to ascend from earthly things to higher realities:

> First one contemplates the beauty found in bodies, after this one passes on to the beauty of the soul, then to the beauty in customs and laws, then to the vast ocean of beauty; after this one conceives of the good itself ... which appears as light and shines on the soul as it makes its ascent. Then one comes to the idea of God because of his preeminence in honor.[48]

The Greek philosopher Lucretius (99–55 BC) agreed. He thought absorbing the teachings of the wise separated people from the striving masses so they could live a life free from pain, fear, or struggle.[49] Plotinus (AD 205–270) concurred but added an intellectual component—that wisdom is the state of rest or repose that comes from having reasoned your way to a satisfactory solution.[50]

The second type of wisdom, the Hebrew conception, rejected the idea that wisdom was an otherworldly state attained through restful repose. The Hebrews were focused instead on making good decisions in everyday circumstances. In Hebrew, the dominant word for "wisdom" is *chokmah*, which means "skill in living."[51] Although the Greeks thought that wisdom appeared in party clothes and looked a lot like leisure, the Hebrews thought it appeared in overalls and looked a lot like work.

Early Christians, drawing from the Jewish heritage of their faith, embraced the Hebrew rather than the Greek concept of wisdom. While the Romans stayed true to the Greek tradition of trying to perfect their own images, Christians focused on becoming like Christ. Such a life featured feasts and physical gatherings, and it involved healing sick people and the poor. It was very earthy. This Christian focus on the here and now so concerned the Romans that some of their writers called Christians atheists! Author and minister Peter J. Leithart explains, "Instead of ascending past sensible things to the intellectual realm, Christians said that God had made Himself known in flesh, and continues to give Himself in water and wine, bodies and bread. Christians were so earthly-minded that they could be no heavenly good."[52]

The phrase "so earthly-minded that they could be no heavenly good" is the opposite of what many Christians today are accused of being, but it is the redeemed response to Scripture. If the one who established and maintains the moral order is a *person*, then wisdom is not just a fanciful guide to better manners or winning the praise of others; it is the key to understanding the very best ways for people to live well with nature, one another, and God. It is true both now and for all eternity.

So how does one acquire wisdom? Fortunately, advanced age is not a precondition. Proverbs 10:1 says, "A wise son makes a glad father." Proverbs 13:1 says, "A wise son hears his father's instruction." Job 32:9 says, "It is not the old who are wise, nor the aged who understand what is right." Wisdom-related knowledge and judgment are, like language learning, more natural for those who are young; the optimal age for wisdom development is between adolescence and the midtwenties.[53] Preparing for a life of wisdom while young moves people toward what scholars call **gerotranscendence**: *away* from superficial social engagement *toward* concern for others, meaningful relationships, and contribution to society.[54]

> *Gerotranscendence:* the stage in life when a person makes the shift from self-interest toward a genuine concern for others and society.

But failing to make the pursuit of wisdom a lifelong search leads people to plateau in their maturity. You've probably heard of a "midlife crisis," in which people wonder whether their life contributions have made any difference and whether they have undersold their potential. In his song "Why, Georgia?" singer/songwriter John Mayer wonders about "the outcome of a still verdictless life" and muses, "It might be a quarter-life crisis."[55]

Picked up by sociologists, the term *quarter-life crisis* has become descriptive of the transition to adulthood in which so many young adults with so much potential nonetheless feel lost, afraid, and confused.

Those focused on wisdom, on the other hand, are more likely to live with a sense of anticipation that turns obstacles into opportunities. For the wise, joy replaces fear. Growing wise is a process, not a state of being. A person can't live most of his or her life as a fool and expect to flip a switch and become wise. To grow wise, one must

- know the difference between wisdom and foolishness;

- understand the essence of true success;

- find wise people and get them to invest in you;

- gain enriching experiences;

- discover how to tell the truth about yourself;

- identify potential in others and help them learn and grow;

- work with people in spite of differences; and

- avoid the behaviors that cause wise people to become fools.

As you can see, the task of growing wise is larger than an intellectual exercise; it is a spiritual one. The evidence shows that the more you focus on spirituality while you're young, the more likely you are to be wise in *later* adulthood.[56] So what does spiritual exercise look like? Let's talk about that now.

Love

Love is the third of God's attributes he has measured out to his image bearers. Contrary to what most people think based on what they see in the popular culture, love isn't just a feeling; it takes work. It is a commitment to do hard things *regardless* of how you feel. When you promise to love your spouse until death, you are not promising to always feel a certain way toward him or her but to always *act* in a caring manner. Luke 10:25–28 records an exchange between Jesus and a lawyer that does away with the notion that love is nothing more than a warm feeling:

> **Love:** a commitment to cherish others regardless of how one feels about them.

> A lawyer stood up to put him to the test, saying, "Teacher, what shall I do to inherit eternal life?" He said to him, "What is written in the Law? How do you read it?" And he answered, "You shall love the Lord your God with all your heart and with all your soul and with all your strength and with all your mind, and your neighbor as yourself." And he said to him, "You have answered correctly; do this, and you will live."

Many people are concerned that they don't really love God because they seldom have warm feelings for him during times of worship. But loving God is obeying him even when you are mad at him, confused by his actions, or lacking in feeling toward him. In the same way, loving our neighbors means doing right by them even when we are upset with them.

Love for God is a barometer for all other loves. If we love God richly and fully, this will spill out into a life of love for our neighbors. So how do we cultivate a life of love for God? Like with a tree that produces delicious fruit, it happens in its time, with careful attention. It is formed through what we habitually do. It is not just Christians who see this. The ancient Greek philosopher Aristotle believed that *habits* connected belief and action. Only good habits can keep us from living just for our next meal. They rule our bellies and build our chests—our sense of determination and will—and give us something worth pursuing in life.

To Aristotle, the purpose for human existence was to live the "good life."[57] In his book *Nicomachean Ethics*, he used the term **eudaimonia** to describe a life of flourishing and happiness.[58] Nicomachus was Aristotle's son, so many readers see the book, which outlines much of his thinking, as similar to Solomon's writing of the book of Proverbs to give guidance to his offspring.

> *Eudaimonia:* a term used in ancient Greek philosophy to describe a life of flourishing and happiness.

In *Nicomachean Ethics*, Aristotle says that people can find happiness in living the good life by practicing "virtues": good habits that allow them to flourish. Virtues are the "golden mean" between excess and defect. For example, it is not virtuous to be a coward and run away from trouble, but nor is it virtuous to unthinkingly rush into trouble. To Aristotle, true courage is measured; it does not turn away, nor does it mindlessly engage. He believed that the most important virtues to practice are as follows:

Justice: "What is right?"

Temperance: "What is the reasonable course?"

Prudence: "What is wise in a practical sense?"

Fortitude: "How will I push forward in spite of obstacles?"

Although early Christians thought a great deal about Aristotle's ideas, they recognized that they were based on a Greek conception of God that taught that God was a **prime mover** but could not really be personally known. To Greeks, "God" is really just pure thought that exists apart from the world. Christianity goes much further than this. It says that God can be truly known.[59]

That God can be known is what transforms our understanding of him from something we respect to some*one* we love. This love animates our love for others and, in turn, draws out the beauty in us. As the church father Augustine said, "Beauty grows in you to the extent that love grows, because charity itself is the soul's beauty."[60]

> *Prime Mover (aka Unmoved Mover):* Aristotle's conception of an utterly transcendent, impersonal, immortal, immaterial, necessary, and unchanging being that set the universe into motion.

Speaker John Stonestreet, from the Chuck Colson Center, has adopted a set of questions from Australian thought leader Rod Thompson. Stonestreet recommends asking these questions to connect our love for God and the life habits that lead to flourishing:

- **What are my loves?** With what or whom am I intimate? What causes me to offer my intimacy? (Do I love the right things? Are my loves properly ordered?)

- **What are my loyalties?** Who or what gets the real me? What causes me to commit my time and energy?

- **What are my longings?** Toward what am I aiming my life? What is success? If I continue where I have aimed, where will I end up? (Our imagination shapes our actions. What are we thinking about in our private moments?)

- **What are my liturgies?** What do I worship? What are the habits of my life? (Liturgies are a fancy theological term for the rhythms of life.)[61]

These four questions are important because if we are not intentional, we'll be swept along thinking about what everyone else is thinking about, focused on what everyone else is focused on, loving what everyone else loves, and doing what everyone else is doing.

What specific habits should Christians pursue? Two are properly basic, in that without them it is difficult to keep our attention focused on God and his glory. We'll look at more habits in the next chapter when we look at how redeemed image bearing affects the way we love our neighbors as ourselves, but the following two habits are scripturally prescribed means of connecting with and loving God.

Explore God's Word. Charles Colson described the Bible this way:

> The Bible—banned, burned, beloved. More widely read, more frequently attacked than any other book in history. Generations of intellectuals have attempted to discredit it, dictators of every age have outlawed it and executed those who read it. Yet soldiers carry it into battle believing it more powerful than their weapons. Fragments of it smuggled into solitary prison cells have transformed ruthless killers into gentle saints.[62]

In view of the incredible impact of the Bible through human history, we should take time each day to study it, embracing the opportunity to dip into the river of history itself, as nearly all great persons in the last two thousand years have. Skeptics and nonbelievers cannot figure out how their mockery and scorn shade the truth. As the famous theologian J. I. Packer said, "One of the many divine qualities of the Bible is this: that it does not yield its secrets to the irreverent and censorious."[63] Read the Bible not to defend or attack it but as a means of learning to love God.

Pray. The character of C. S. Lewis in the movie *Shadowlands*, when confronted with why he engaged in such an ineffectual and primitive practice as prayer, said, "I pray because I can't help myself. I pray because I'm helpless. I pray because the need flows out of me all

WHAT THE BIBLE SAYS ABOUT LOVING GOD

the time—waking and sleeping. It doesn't change God—it changes me."[64] If you aren't sure what to pray, begin by turning to the book of Psalms, which includes many prayers, and pray them back to God. This will help you learn to cultivate, as David did, a heart after God.

Mercy

The fourth communicable attribute of God is **mercy**. Agents of mercy bring blessing wherever they go. And because the gospel aims to bless all nations, those who embrace God's story are agents of mercy, embodying the gospel of grace and moving into the world as though arriving at a disaster with the gifts of a life-giving and truly healing remedy. We bring true *shalom*: peace, well-being, restoration. We bring more than rescue; we bring transformation. This is how we love our neighbors, and we will invest all of chapter 9 exploring how to do it better.

10. Conclusion

The gospel of God is not merely a plan by which we avoid hell but also a way to live differently now. Jesus said in Matthew 28:18–20 that all authority in heaven and on earth had been given to him and that, in response, his disciples would teach the nations to obey God. It's a clear covenantal statement of what the gospel is about: making disciples of the nations, baptizing them into the Trinity, and preparing them to obey God wherever Jesus has authority, which is to say *every area of life*. As Abraham Kuyper, a theologian who became prime minister of the Netherlands, famously stated, "There is not one square inch of the entire creation about which Jesus Christ does not cry out, 'This is mine! This belongs to me!'"[65]

C. S. Lewis, for one, grasped how profound of a shift the earthly ministry of Christ truly was in reconciling us with God and preparing us for an altogether different kind of life. As the Christ figure Aslan said in *The Lion, the Witch and the Wardrobe*, "When a willing victim who had committed no treachery was killed in a traitor's stead … even death itself would turn backwards."[66] It is like that in fact, not just in fiction: in Christ, death itself has turned backwards.

That death itself would turn backward is the hope in which Henry Wadsworth Longfellow rested in proclaiming that "God is not dead; nor doth he sleep." God wins. Death loses.

> Jesus said in Matthew 28:18–20 that all authority in heaven and on earth had been given to him and that, in response, his disciples would teach the nations to obey God. It's a clear covenantal statement of what the gospel is about: making disciples of the nations, baptizing them into the Trinity, and preparing them to obey God wherever Jesus has authority, which is to say *every area of life*.

Endnotes

1. Frank Sinatra, "I Heard the Bells on Christmas Day," recorded (1983), original lyrics by Henry Wadsworth Longfellow (1863), music by John Baptiste Calkin (1872).
2. Charles C. Calhoun, *Longfellow: A Rediscovered Life* (Boston: Beacon Press, 2004), 215.
3. Lucy Madison, "Holbrooke's Last Words: 'You've Got to Stop This War in Afghanistan,'" CBS News, December 14, 2010,

www.cbsnews.com/8301-503544_162-20025587-503544.html.

4. Frank Sinatra's lyrics are only slightly different.

5. Richard John Neuhaus, "Telling the World Its Own Story" (lecture, The Wilberforce Forum, July 2001).

6. Alvin Plantinga, "Advice to Christian Philosophers," *Faith and Philosophy* 1 (July 1984): 264–65, cited in J. P. Moreland and Scott B. Rae, *Body and Soul: Human Nature and the Crisis in Ethics* (Downers Grove, IL: InterVarsity, 2000), 24.

7. See Moreland and Rae, *Body and Soul.*

8. J. R. Smythies, "Some Aspects of Consciousness," in *Beyond Reductionism: New Perspectives in the Life Sciences*, ed. Arthur Koestler and J. R. Smythies (London: Hutchinson Publishers, 1969), 251–52. For an updated discussion of identity, see J. P. Moreland and William Lane Craig, *Philosophical Foundations for a Christian Worldview* (Downers Grove, IL: InterVarsity, 2003), 290.

9. Moreland and Rae, *Body and Soul*, 17.

10. For more on "Brights," see www.the-brights.net.

11. Christian Smith, "Man: The Religious Animal," *First Things*, April 2012, www.firstthings.com/article/2012/03/man-the-religious-animal.

12. David F. Ruccio and Jack Amariglio, *Postmodern Moments in Modern Economics* (Princeton, NJ: Princeton University Press, 2003), 167.

13. Ruccio and Amariglio, *Postmodern Moments*, 134.

14. Glenn Ward, *Teach Yourself Postmodernism*, 2nd ed. (Chicago: McGraw-Hill, 2003), 179.

15. Genesis 1:28: "God blessed them. And God said to them, 'Be fruitful and multiply and fill the earth and subdue it, and have dominion over the fish of the sea and over the birds of the heavens and over every living thing that moves on the earth.'"

16. BreakPoint interview with Drs. Kenneth Turner and Kathy Koch on "In His Image," June 21, 2013, www.breakpoint.org/features-columns/discourse/entry/15/22584.

17. Albert Wolters is professor emeritus at Redeemer University College, Ontario, Canada. His book is *Creation Regained: Biblical Basics for a Reformational Worldview* (Grand Rapids, MI: Eerdmans, 2005), 46.

18. Barbara Christopher et al., *Modern Biology* (New York: Holt, Reinhart and Winston), 6–9.

19. Go to www.webmd.com and search "parasites" to find out everything you never wanted to know.

20. Wolters, *Creation Regained*, 46.

21. A. W. Tozer, *The Knowledge of the Holy* (New York: HarperCollins, 1961), 3–4.

22. James E. Marcia, "Identity in Adolescence" in *Handbook of Adolescent Psychology*, ed. J. Adelson (New York: Wiley, 1980), 159–87.

23. John 1:12: "To all who did receive him, who believed in his name, he gave the right to become children of God."

24. John 15:5: "I am the vine; you are the branches. Whoever abides in me and I in him, he it is that bears much fruit, for apart from me you can do nothing."

25. Romans 8:1: "There is therefore now no condemnation for those who are in Christ Jesus."

26. Romans 8:16–17: "The Spirit himself bears witness with our spirit that we are children of God, and if children, then heirs—heirs of God and fellow heirs with Christ, provided we suffer with him in order that we may also be glorified with him."

27. 1 Corinthians 6:17: "He who is joined to the Lord becomes one spirit with him."

28. 1 Corinthians 6:19–20: "Do you not know that your body is a temple of the Holy Spirit within you, whom you have from God? You are not your own, for you were bought with a price. So glorify God in your body."

29. 2 Corinthians 5:17: "If anyone is in Christ, he is a new creation. The old has passed away; behold, the new has come."

30. 2 Corinthians 5:21: "For our sake he made him to be sin who knew no sin, so that in him we might become the righteousness of God."

31. Galatians 2:20: "I have been crucified with Christ. It is no longer I who live, but Christ who lives in me. And the life I now live in the flesh I live by faith in the Son of God, who loved me and gave himself for me."

32. Ephesians 1:3: "Blessed be the God and Father of our Lord Jesus Christ, who has blessed us in Christ with every spiritual blessing in the heavenly places."

33. Ephesians 1:4: "He chose us in him before the foundation of the world, that we should be holy and blameless before him."

34. Colossians 2:7: "… rooted and built up in him and established in the faith, just as you were taught, abounding in thanksgiving."

35. Colossians 2:10: "You have been filled in him, who is the head of all rule and authority."

36. 2 Timothy 1:7: "God gave us a spirit not of fear but of power and love and self-control."

37. Hebrews 4:16: "Let us then with confidence draw near to the throne of grace, that we may receive mercy and find grace to help in time of need."

38. 2 Peter 1:4: "He has granted to us his precious and very great promises, so that through them you may become partakers of the divine nature, having escaped from the corruption that is in the world because of sinful desire."

39. 1 John 5:18, "We know that everyone who has been born of God does not keep on sinning, but he who was born of God protects him, and the evil one does not touch him."

40. To sign up for a free copy of this report, go to turningthetide.net/.

41. Timothy Keller, *Counterfeit Gods: The Empty Promises of Money, Sex, and Power, and the Only Hope That Matters* (New York: Riverhead, 2011), 172.

42. Romans 2:4: "Do you presume on the riches of his kindness and forbearance and patience, not knowing that God's kindness is meant to lead you to repentance?"

43. Thomas Church Brownell, *The Family Prayer Book, or* the Book of Common Prayer (New York: Sydney's Press, 1823), 7.

44. Wolters, *Creation Regained*, 88.

45. For example, Philippians 1:17: "The former proclaim Christ out of selfish ambition, not sincerely but thinking to afflict me in my imprisonment"; Philippians 2:3: "Do nothing from selfish ambition or conceit, but in humility count others more significant than yourselves"; James 3:14: "If you have bitter jealousy and selfish ambition in your hearts, do not boast and be false to the truth"; James 3:16: "Where jealousy and selfish ambition exist, there will be disorder and every vile practice."

46. Mortimer Adler, "Chapter 101: Wisdom," in *The Great Ideas: A Syntopicon of Great Books of the Western World*, ed. Robert Maynard Hutchins and Mortimer Adler (Chicago: Benton, 1971), vol. 3 of 60 volumes, 938.

47. Plato, *The Republic*, trans. Benjamin Jowett (full text), classics.mit.edu/Plato/republic.mb.txt. See especially book 7 on the allegory of the cave.

48. Quoted in Robert Louis Wilken, *The Spirit of Early Christian Thought: Seeking the Face of God* (New Haven, CT: Yale University, 2003), 9.

49. Titus Lucretius Carus, *On the Nature of Things*, bk. 2, trans. William Ellery Leonard (full text), classics.mit.edu/Carus/nature_things.mb.txt.

50. Plotinus, "On Virtue," *The Six Enneads*, third tractate, trans. Stephen Mackenna and B. S. Page (full text), classics.mit.edu/Plotinus/enneads.mb.txt.

51. This is seen throughout the Old Testament. *Chokmah* is used in reference to the skilled craftsmen who built the temple in Exodus 35, those skilled in music (1 Kings 4:31–32) and performance (Jer. 9:17), strength of leadership (Deut. 34:9), magicians and soothsayers are considered wise men (Gen. 41:8; Isa. 44:25), and those who could make difficult judicial decisions (2 Sam. 14:17, 20; 19:27).

52. Peter J. Leithart, "No Heavenly Good," Leithart.com, June 25, 2007, www.leithart.com/archives/003113.php.

53. Ursula M. Stuadinger and Monisha Pasupathi, "Correlates of Wisdom-Related Performance in Adolescence and Adulthood: Age-Graded Differences in 'Paths' toward Desirable Development," *Journal of Research on Adolescence* 13, no. 3 (2003): 240.

54. Lars Tornstam, "Gerotranscendence: The Contemplative Dimension of Aging," *Journal of Aging Studies 11*, no. 2 (1997): 143–54.

55. John Mayer, "Why, Georgia?," on *Room for Squares*, Columbia Records, 2001, compact disc.

56. Thao N. Le, "Age Differences in Spirituality, Mystical Experiences and Wisdom," *Aging & Society* 28 (2008): 383–411.

57. There are two main categories of ethical theories. Aristotle's focus on human flourishing is called a "teleological" theory, the end of which is a good life. A second category is the "deontological" theory, which focuses on "oughtness," or duty. For more, see John Deigh, *An Introduction to Ethics, Cambridge Introductions to Philosophy* (New York: Cambridge University Press, 2010), 14. As my coauthor David Noebel and I point out originally in *Understanding the Times*, a true theory of ethics ought to be able to be lived by human beings in a sinful world where the right is not always obvious and not always easy to live out. A true theory of ethics must give us a way to decide, without guidance from the authorities, that not everything legal is right and that an unjust law has no purpose if it defies the law of God. A true theory of ethics must take into account a higher law if lower laws are not to tyrannize us. Christianity, though not fitting neatly into either teleological or deontological categories, helps resolve these dilemmas.

58. Aristotle, *Nicomachean Ethics*, trans. W. D. Ross (full text), classics.mit.edu/Aristotle/nicomachaen.mb.txt.

59. Despite its inadequacies, Aristotle's philosophy was very compelling to early Christian thinkers. One of them, Thomas Aquinas (1227–1274), wrote extensively on how to apply Aristotelian logic to Christian principles.

60. John Burnaby, ed., *Augustine: Later Works, The Library of Christian Classics* (Philadelphia: Westminster, 1956), 336.

61. "A Worldview That's Big Enough," *Christian Worldview Journal*, www.colsoncenter.org/the-center/columns/changepoint/15359-a-worldivew-thats-qbig-enoughq.

62. Charles Colson, *Loving God* (Grand Rapids, MI: Zondervan, 1996), 55.

63. J. I. Packer, *God Has Spoken: Revelation and the Bible* (Grand Rapids, MI: Baker, 1979), 44.

64. *Shadowlands*, directed by Richard Attenborough (Price Entertainment, 1993), DVD.

65. Abraham Kuyper, *Near unto God: Daily Meditations Adapted for Contemporary Christians by James C. Schaap* (Grand Rapids, MI: CRC Publications, 1997), 7.

66. C. S. Lewis, *The Chronicles of Narnia: The Lion, the Witch and the Wardrobe* (New York: HarperCollins, 1994), 94.

CHAPTER 9

WHAT THE BIBLE SAYS ABOUT LOVING OUR NEIGHBORS

1. GOD'S PRINCIPLES CHANGE EVERYTHING

Imagine what would happen if humanity decided to follow God's order and walk in God's way. Loren Cunningham, founder of Youth with a Mission, spent a few pages imagining this in *The Book That Transforms Nations*. Here's part of his list:

- A majority would honor God and respect each other, viewing life as God's gift.

- Every mother would treasure her unborn child, and every father would provide the loving stability his child needs.

- Racism would be rare. Reconciliation and unity would bring all races and ethnic groups together.

- We wouldn't have to fear violence or theft.

- People would keep the streets clean. No one would intentionally litter in neighborhoods or scrawl graffiti on walls, freeway overpasses, or buildings.

- Most people would protect the environment, practicing good stewardship over God's creation.

- Child abuse and spousal abuse would all but disappear.

- Divorce would be extremely rare.

- Broken relationships would be restored as people repented and forgave one another.

- Businesses would seek to outdo one another with initiatives of compassion and productivity for the good of the community.

- Politicians, officials, and judges would be public servants, not abusers of power.

- Worker productivity would soar as addiction to alcohol, illegal drugs, and pornography declined.

- People would work with vision, diligence, purpose, and skill.

- Empty prisons would be demolished or repurposed for other uses.

- People would speak the truth in love.

- Profanity and slander would become the exception, not the norm.

- Road rage would be a peculiar phenomenon for history scholars to ponder.[1]

WHAT THE BIBLE SAYS ABOUT LOVING OUR NEIGHBORS

Many have chosen to take God at his word and pursue economic productivity, concern for the welfare of others, volunteerism, and just government. They've alleviated human suffering and made it possible for more people all over the world to experience transformation. By contrast, if the underlying assumptions of other prominent world-views are taken seriously, inaction and **fatalism** result. As international relief expert Darrow Miller writes in *Discipling Nations*,

> *Fatalism:* **the belief that all events are predetermined and inevitable.**

> Members of animistic cultures see the fates or spirits (often demonic) as all-powerful. In Islamic culture the common phrase "it is written" creates a crushing framework of fatalism. In Thailand peasants are labeled *jaak-con*: "destined to poverty." Hinduism sees perfection as a state of resignation. Better to withdraw from the world than attack its evils. Secularism, for its part, sees man as little more than a complex machine, just one more component of the physical universe. There is little more motivation to fight hunger and poverty or protect the preborn, disabled, and elderly.[2]

But Christianity teaches that humans are made in God's image. There is no such thing as fate. We are responsible to do justly, love mercy, and walk humbly with our creator (Mic. 6:8).[3]

If the Bible is, in fact, the true story of the world and its revelation of God trustworthy, then how should we love our neighbors? In this chapter, we'll look at God's intent for neighborliness in creation, how it was lost in the fall, and how God's plan for redemption transforms the whole idea of neighborliness in character, calling, conversation, community, and citizenship.

One quick note: sometimes we're tempted to place our own participation in God's plan for redemption above our worship of him. It is easy to be grandiose and think, *Why just focus on our neighborhood? We're going to change the whole world!* Although truly loving our neighbors has global implications, we must act faithfully in a local way first. As theology professor Gary Badcock says, "The will of God … is close to home: one finds it simply in loving God and, crucially, in loving one's neighbor."[4]

> **Although truly loving our neighbors has global implications, we must act faithfully in a local way first.**

2. NEIGHBORLINESS: CREATED

As we have seen, God's plan for humans to bear his image and have dominion is "very good," or, in Hebrew, *tob meod*: abundantly and richly good, enabling humans to live in an environment of *shalom*, of completeness, peace, wellness, prosperity, tranquility, and contentment. At the very heart of *shalom* is neighborliness; we should wish peace and harmony for others as well as for ourselves. In fact, God told the Israelites in captivity that their *shalom* would be secured as they worked to secure *shalom* for those around them, even their captors (Jer. 29:7).[5]

The creation account of Genesis 1 and 2 describes God's plan for his image bearers. It radically differs from the creation stories told by the other ancient Near East religions. According to the biblical account, the universe had a divine origin at the hands of one God (not many), who is spirit and who organized creation in an orderly fashion, giving humans a special place in it. A thoughtful reading of Genesis in comparison to, say, the *Enuma Elish* or the Phoenician cosmogony of Philo of Byblos, makes it clear: Yahweh is altogether different from, and far superior to, his would-be rivals.

In fact, as we have already noted, the accounts in Genesis 1 and 2 deliberately clash with the worldviews of ancient Israel's neighbors. The biblical account affirms God's direct hand in creation, distinguishes the Creator from the creation, and highlights the good, purposeful nature of creation at the center of which is humanity. It therefore rejects all other popular "isms," such as atheism, polytheism, naturalism, pantheism, panentheism, gnosticism, agnosticism, nihilism, and even **evolutionism**.[6]

We call people human *beings*, not human *doings*; our worth comes from who we are, not what we do. That humans specially bear God's image most distinguishes the Judeo-Christian conception of God from all others. This view says that human beings are actually distinct and inherently valuable persons regardless of size, age, gender, ethnicity, ability, level of development, or intelligence.[7] They have a definable essence.[8] As America's founders proclaimed, everyone has an unalienable right to life, liberty, and the pursuit of happiness. The founders rejected, *in principle*, anything that prevented people from exercising their God-given design. I stress *in principle* because, sadly, it took eighty-seven years before our nation's leaders aligned principle and practice regarding the issue of slavery.[9]

> *Evolutionism:* the belief that all life arose through random chance processes starting with the first self-replicating molecule.

Even so, humans must *do*—we must work. Many mistakenly believe that work is troublesome toil resulting from human sin.[10] But according to Genesis, work *preceded* the fall. Of course, having to get up early when we don't want to, having to work with other flawed humans, not getting paid as much as we wish to or deserve, and having work fall apart before our eyes—these surely are consequences of the fall. Still, work itself is good.[11]

God told Adam to "work and keep" the garden (Gen. 2:15), beginning with naming the animals. Verse 19 says, "Out of the ground the LORD God had formed every beast of the field and every bird of the heavens and brought them to the man." We saw in an earlier chapter that the animals helped Adam by displaying the beauty, purpose, and order of creation. Although he could harness some animals for work, Adam more importantly cared for the animals, enabling him to grow in responsibility and more fully bear God's image. It was work, and it was good.

> *Abad:* from the Hebrew for "to serve"; to work and worship.

The Hebrew word for "work," *abad*, means "to serve." Interestingly, it is the same word used for *worship*.[12] Work is worship, and worship is work. Apparently, for Adam, going into the garden to work was a worshipful experience: work drew him closer to God.

This idea that work is worship and worship is work challenges the theology of those who imagine the garden of Eden to be a place of mindless leisure where God did all the work until after the fall, when Adam and Eve had to finally get busy and do something. Even a cursory glance at the text shows this to be misguided. God didn't just bring the animals to Adam and say, "I'll tell you the name of all of the animals; I hope you can remember them all." Rather, he gave

WHAT THE BIBLE SAYS ABOUT LOVING OUR NEIGHBORS

them to the man to *see what the man would call them*. Adam's identification of them became their identities. The Hebrew word for "name" is *sem*, which mean two things: (1) the object's identity, and (2) the object's place in relation to the one doing the naming. To name something is to identify its characteristics and take responsibility for it.[13]

Among other things, this kind of naming is an intellectual task, leading to a strong impression that our first parents were not the intellectually undeveloped cave dwellers depicted in science textbooks or the leisurely, listless beings depicted in romantic paintings. They were thinking, creative, hardworking image bearers of God.

Today, brain research provides an interesting parallel to the creation account, demonstrating that the human brain is designed physiologically to connect deep thought, decision making, and pleasure. Dr. Caroline Leaf, a neuropsychologist and Christian, believes that human beings are designed for deep intellectual thought.[14] Research is also showing a connection between the decision-making part of the human brain and the pleasure center of the brain, indicating that hard work can actually bring us satisfaction.[15] Other research has shown that when people worship deeply or work very hard at something, the part of their brains that is sensitive to space and time goes dim. They experience bliss, almost as if they are touching eternity.[16]

Some researchers call this phenomenon **flow** and describe it as a state in which a person works intently on something fascinating and is able to exert effort in a smooth rhythm, be creative, and recognize afterward that it was a pleasurable experience.[17]

> *Flow:* a state in which a person works intently on something fascinating and is able to work in a smooth rhythm, be creative, and recognize afterward that it was a pleasurable experience.

Of course, brain research is limited in what it can show us about how the mind works, and it offers little help in showing us what God wants us to do. But to the Christian, it makes perfect sense that God would design us to humbly and obediently connect with him in work as well as worship.

There was also a community aspect to life in creation. With all the animals named, something was still missing; what Adam had been given to do could not be done alone. So God created woman. We noted earlier that Adam's reaction was poetic: "This at last is bone of my bones and flesh of my flesh; she shall be called Woman, because she was taken out of Man" (Gen. 2:23). The text continues, "Therefore a man shall leave his father and his mother and hold fast to his wife, and they shall become one flesh. And the man and his wife were both naked and were not ashamed" (vv. 24–25). The term *flesh* in Hebrew is **basar**, which implies the idea of "clan." A reasonable rendering of this phrase would be "*Adam and Eve*

> *Basar:* from the Hebrew for "flesh"; implies the idea of clan or family.

became one family." They were married. It was *not* good that the man was alone. The goodness of companionship was not merely a cure for loneliness; it was the realization of the "very good" aspect of God's plan for humankind.

Adam's family ultimately expanded to include the whole human race. Acts 17:26 says, "He made from one man every nation of mankind to live on all the face of the earth, having determined allotted periods and the boundaries of their dwelling place." Every person on this spinning globe is actually family, from those who live next door to those who live halfway around the world. We know all this by the time we finish reading the second chapter of the first book of the Bible.

By cultivating the garden and caring for the animals, Adam bore God's image as a worker. And through God's plan for his helper-completer, Adam became a neighbor.

3. NEIGHBORLINESS: FALLEN

Down the chute came a new Snoodle with wings and a backpack full of paints, paintbrushes, and a kazoo. That's where the VeggieTales production *A Snoodle's Tale* begins. The older residents of Snoodleburg despise Snoodle Doo, as the new Snoodle is named. They ridicule him and force him to carry around their pictures of his failures, which drag him down and make him feel foolish. Only a meeting with his Creator enables Snoodle Doo to really soar as he was created to do.

On the surface, *A Snoodle's Tale* is a cute story of an easily remedied self-esteem problem. Beneath the surface, though, we know the deeper sadness of people using their words to, in a sense, *uncreate* each other. The words we speak have the power to make others and ourselves wrongly believe that all of us are worthless. More than our feelings get hurt. Humans have shown throughout history a tendency to identify a group of people and deny their personhood—and sometimes even their lives—as long as that group is some "other" kind, whether "Jew" or "fetus" or "greedy capitalist."[18]

> Beneath the surface we know the deeper sadness of people using their words to, in a sense, *uncreate* each other. The words we speak have the power to make others and ourselves wrongly believe that all of us are worthless.

In the fall of humankind, the "very good" relationships of creation disintegrated. Adam and Eve set themselves at odds with God. They experienced a loss of trust and struggled with one another for power. Internally, they dealt with shame and embarrassment that led them to hide from their image bearing rather than live in harmony with it. Even their relationship with nature was disrupted. The "filling and forming" tasks became corrupted with pain and toil.

From *shalom* to shame. From wellness to worry. From contentment to contempt. From wholeness to brokenness. Sin was like a blast of graffiti on the face of the *Mona Lisa*. Trust was betrayed. Purity decayed into perversity. The pristine was polluted. Integrity disintegrated. Author Cornelius Plantinga calls this the "vandalism of shalom" that leads to "a partly depressing, partly ludicrous caricature of genuine human life."[19] Sin scalps us of dignity and leaves us as cartoonish versions of ourselves.

It is human nature, post-fall, to mutiny against God, only to find ourselves marooned from meaning. As theologian D. A. Carson says,

> People do not drift toward Holiness. Apart from grace-driven effort, people do not gravitate toward godliness, prayer, obedience to Scripture, faith, and delight in the Lord. We drift toward compromise and call it tolerance; we drift toward disobedience and call it freedom; we drift toward superstition and call it faith. We cherish the indiscipline of lost self-control and call it relaxation; we slouch toward prayerlessness

WHAT THE BIBLE SAYS ABOUT LOVING OUR NEIGHBORS

and delude ourselves into thinking we have escaped legalism; we slide toward god-lessness and convince ourselves we have been liberated.[20]

Some also drift toward spite, godlessly and in the name of philosophy. The revered atheistic scientist Edward O. Wilson mused that a commitment to naturalism, the belief that everything can be explained through natural processes without reference to God, means that "no species, ours included, possesses a purpose beyond the imperatives created by its genetic history."[21]

If human life is nothing special, then how do we secure our right not to be treated with cruelty? How do we defend the most vulnerable among us? To some philosophers, the only thing that gives us such a right is **sentience**, the ability to feel pain and understand what is causing it. Authors Kenneth L. Feder and Michael Alan Park write,

> *Sentience:* the ability to feel and experience sensations.

> There is no objective rationale for elevating our species into a category separate from the rest of the animals with whom we share the presence of a nervous system, the ability to feel pain, and behaviors aimed at avoiding pain. Thus, the fundamental rights we accord ourselves must be equally applicable to any other organism with these same characteristics.[22]

This erasing of the distinction between humans and other sentient beings leads to a lot of vibrant discussions on college campuses. Should we permit lions to pursue happiness at the expense of antelope, knowing we have the power to stop it? What about the antelope's feelings? Feder and Park and others like them may have been well intentioned, trying to expand the meaningfulness of human rights by extending them to animals, but in the end they simply justify the animalistic treatment of humans. If we humans have no more rights than the cows and pigs killed to feed us, what is the inherent harm in killing humans?

In the end, naturalism cannot *raise* the rights of animals without *lowering* the rights of humans. If there is no transcendent moral truth, what we call human rights depend solely on the whims of powerful people. If they decide to stop protecting rights or change the rights protected or sacrifice one group on behalf of another, there is nothing we can do.

The fall carries profound implications for neighborliness on personhood, everyday relationships, relationships between ethnic groups, sexual ethics, technology, leisure, and life in the modern world.

> If there is no transcendent moral truth, what we call human rights depend solely on the whims of powerful people.

The fall has implications for personhood. Fallenness destroys neighborliness starting with the very definition of what it means to be a person. In the infamous *Roe v. Wade* decision in 1973, Justice Harry Blackmun opined, "We need not resolve the difficult question of when life begins. When those trained in the respective disciplines of medicine, philosophy, and theology are unable to arrive at any consensus, the judiciary, at this point in the development of man's knowledge, is not in a position to speculate."[23] But, of course, the Supreme Court actually *did* speculate and by default concluded that unborn children do not meet the criteria for human personhood.

The Supreme Court's capitulation to those favoring legalized abortion continues to echo through the canyons of time. By embracing a **functional view of personhood**—that humans only *become* persons by, say, engaging in higher-level thinking processes or having a self-concept—the court left without protection those who are too young to actualize their human abilities or who are too old or disabled to exercise them. It is disconcerting to realize how many people in the world think a human's value is found only in what they do. Those with a waning ability to function must realize that a *very* high percentage of people consequently no longer see them as persons. They had better hope their doctors and nurses are not among them.[24] From a biblical viewpoint, humans have value because they are image bearers of God, not because society recognizes their usefulness. We might call this the **intrinsic view of personhood**. According to philosopher Francis Beckwith, "What is crucial morally is the being of a person, not his or her functioning. A human person does not come into existence when human function arises, but rather, a human person is an entity who has the natural inherent capacity to give rise to human functions, whether or not those functions are ever attained."[25]

Functional View of Personhood: **the belief that human beings become persons only after gaining particular abilities, such as sentience, higher-level thinking, and self-awareness.**

Intrinsic View of Personhood: **the belief that human beings are inherently persons.**

The fall has implications for everyday relationships. In their fallenness, humans reject neighborliness by becoming self-centered and forfeiting their sense of their public responsibility. In his book *Shop Class as Soulcraft*, political philosopher and motorcycle mechanic Matthew Crawford relates the story of an author, Robert Pirsig, who took his motorcycle to the shop of a careless mechanic who proceeded to ruin it. Based on what happens, Crawford considers the mechanic an **idiot**, but not just because he lacks rudimentary knowledge of motorcycles. Here's how he describes it:

Idiot: **from the Greek for "private"; a person who fails to be active in society.**

> Pirsig's mechanic is, in the original sense of the term, an idiot. Indeed, he exemplifies the truth about idiocy, which is that it is at once an ethical and cognitive failure. The Greek *idios* means "private," and an *idiotes* means a private person, as opposed to a person in their public role—for example, that of motorcycle mechanic. Pirsig's mechanic is idiotic because he fails to grasp his public role, which entails, or should, a relation of active concern to others, and to the machine. He is not involved. It is not his problem. Because he is an idiot.[26]

A brief tour to nearly any university in the country will reveal something similar. There might be twenty thousand people on campus, but most are listening to music on headphones or texting and ignoring everyone else. There is no sense of community because no

WHAT THE BIBLE SAYS ABOUT LOVING OUR NEIGHBORS

one feels compelled to take responsibility to create it. *Idios* has replaced **koinonia** (the Greek word for "community").

Although traumatic events such as terrorist attacks and national disasters can pull people together in community, the general trend is toward incoherence, manipulation, miscommunication, deceit, pride, flattery, and greed. The problems multiply because "hurt people hurt people." For example, they shoot out nasty remarks through social media; they spread the kind of gossip that ruins reputations.

> *Koinonia:* from the Greek for "community"; the role of fellowship within the Christian church.

This problem has a name: anger. People today seem *proud* of their anger, which justifies their flying off the handle at the most minor slight. In his book *A Bee in the Mouth*, Peter Wood says this problem is worse now than it has ever been:

> The anger we see and hear around us differs in character from the anger of previous epochs, and it is no illusion. The anger of the present is, among other things, more flamboyant, more self-righteous, and more theatrical than anger at other times in our history. It often has the look-at-me character of performance art.[27]

Wood concludes, "We have become, without really noticing it, a culture that celebrates anger."[28] This destroys neighborliness because neighbors no longer view one another as persons. Instead, we see each other as uncultured bipedal organisms that we have the right not to see, hear noise from, smell the cooking of, or otherwise take into account.

The fall has implications for relationships between ethnic groups. Another way fallenness affects neighborliness is in accepting human value as being based on race or skin color rather than on people being image bearers of God. In an article on the civil rights movement, theologian Russell Moore notes the cross-cultural impact of dehumanizing others:

> The struggle for civil rights for African-Americans in this country wasn't simply a "political" question. It wasn't merely the question of, as Martin Luther King Jr. put it from before the Lincoln Memorial, the unfulfilled promises of the Declaration of Independence and the U.S. Constitution (although it was nothing less than that). At its root, Jim Crow (and the spirit of Jim Crow, still alive and sinister) is about theology. It's about the question of the "Godness" of God and the humanness of humanity.[29]

As Martin Luther King Jr. phrased it, "The arc of the moral universe is long, but it bends towards justice."[30] Race relations have certainly improved over the last two centuries, but we need reconciliation now as much as ever. The global acceptance of slavery and discrimination has demonstrated how difficult it is for humans to see one another as human and love one another fully.

The fall has implications for sexual ethics. Fallenness also destroys neighborliness through the culture of pornography, which thinks nothing of distributing images that reduce human value to sexual behavior. The effects of widespread porn use are frightening:

- Of the 2.2 billion Internet users in the world, 42.7 percent view porn. That's nearly one billion people regularly looking at pornography.[31]

- 70 percent of 18- to 24-year-old men visit pornographic websites in a typical month.[32]

- 40 percent of 8- to 15-year-olds have viewed pornography online.[33]

- Pornography propagates rape culture, the belief that sexual assault victims are to blame or that rape is not a serious crime.[34]

- 46 percent of child molesters have said that pornography directly led to their molestations.[35]

- Approximately 1.2 million children are exploited annually through child pornography and prostitution in the United States.[36]

A Princeton University study showed that viewing pictures of scantily clad women activated the "tool use" part of men's brains, causing them to view women as objects to be used.[37] Porn leads to the destruction of personhood at the level of creation's most basic distinction, being male or female.

The fall has implications for technology. Fallenness also destroys neighborliness by diverting technology from its good purposes toward that which damages community and individual purpose. In one startling study by the Barna Group, half of the young people surveyed said they use email and text even while they eat and as they fall asleep, and half said they never intentionally "disconnect from or turn off technology so they can have a break from it."[38] *Time* magazine, in an issue devoted to the study of happiness, found a decade-long increase in unhappiness from 2004 to 2013. In 2004, 79 percent of people said they were optimistic. Fewer than 50 percent say so now. People reported spending less time than before doing things to improve their mood. At the same time, there is one area of significant growth in time usage: social media, and this in spite of the fact that 60 percent of people said they have *never* had the experience of feeling better about their lives after spending time on a social media website.[39] For many, digital technology has led to a whole new class of addictions.

> Fallenness also destroys neighborliness by diverting technology from its good purposes toward that which damages community and individual purpose.

The fall has implications for leisure. After the fall, people have seen work as a way to survive, not as a way to grow and glorify God. Those who are clever or lucky will figure out how to get out of work, we think. But this does not mean that the alternative is pleasurable. In the late 1990s, a researcher named Mihaly Csikszentmihalyi (pronounced Chick-SENT-me-high) conducted a groundbreaking study in which people wore a device that alerted them, at random intervals, to complete a notebook of their activities. In their notebooks,

WHAT THE BIBLE SAYS ABOUT LOVING OUR NEIGHBORS

one thing they wrote was how much *flow*—a heightened sense of enjoyment—they were experiencing at the moment.

Csikszentmihalyi stumbled on an odd finding: people spend most of their leisure time doing things they do *not* find enjoyable. One such activity that we gravitate toward is watching television. Studies show that even among teenagers, who watch television less than adults, the average number of hours watched per week is around twenty.[40] Yet, as Csikszentmihalyi reports,

> After the fall, people have seen work as a way to survive, not as a way to grow and glorify God.

> Hobbies are about two and a half times more likely to produce a state of heightened enjoyment than TV does, and active games and sports about three times more. Yet these same teenagers spend at least four times more of their free hours watching TV than doing hobbies or sports. Similar ratios are also true for adults. Why would we spend four times more time doing something that has less than half the chance of making us feel good?[41]

Csikszentmihalyi concludes that "each of the flow-producing activities requires an initial investment of attention before it begins to be enjoyable."[42] Is that not one of the saddest implications of the fall? People too apathetic to get up and do something they find enjoyable?

The fall has implications for life in the modern world. Fallenness destroys neighborliness by convincing us that the way things are now is better. I remember hearing a self-proclaimed futurist revel in how much computing power is in a digital watch (enough to send a rocket to the moon) and how much information was in a Sunday edition of the *New York Times* (as much information as someone in the late seventeen hundreds would have had in an entire lifetime). But does having more information really constitute progress? Back in 1934, T. S. Eliot wrote a poem about this very thing, that progress:

> Fallenness destroys neighborliness by convincing us that the way things are now is better.

> Brings knowledge of motion, but not of stillness;
> Knowledge of speech, but not of silence;
> Knowledge of words, and ignorance of The Word.
> . . . .
> Where is the knowledge we have lost in information?[43]

In the beginning God defined humans as made in his image. Then humanity defined God in *its* image. Finally humanity got rid of the idea of image altogether. As Henry Grunwald, once the managing editor of *Time* magazine, observed, "The great religious heresy used to be making man the measure of all things; but we have come close to making man the measure of nothing."[44]

What ought we to do? It doesn't take a Christian to see the answer. Douglas Coupland—the novelist who coined the term *Generation X*, and a self-proclaimed cynical, angry, narcissistic, sexually broken person—lets the reader of his book *Life after God* into a very private place in his confused life:

> Now—here is my secret: I tell it to you with an openness of heart that I doubt I shall ever achieve again, so I pray that you are in a quiet room as you hear these words. My secret is that I need God—that I am sick and can no longer make it alone. I need God to help me give, because I no longer seem to be capable of giving; to help me be kind, as I no longer seem capable of kindness; to help me love, as I seem beyond being able to love.[45]

This is where we are. All of us. The only questions remaining are whether or not we realize it and are prepared to accept the redemption we desperately long for.

4. NEIGHBORLINESS: REDEEMED

Sitting in the grass, I felt the breeze whip up waves, a relief from the afternoon heat. Seventy-five yards away, our Holy Land tour guide recited the Sermon on the Mount, and I heard every word clearly. I wondered whether Jesus uttered those famous words at this exact spot. Somehow the thought caused me to attend to the familiar passage in a way I hadn't for years, and it occurred to me just how radical Jesus's words were. As N. T. Wright puts it, the Sermon on the Mount was Jesus's way of saying, "God's future is arriving in the present, in the person and work of Jesus, and you can practice, right now, the habits of life which will find their goal in that coming future."[46]

The Sermon on the Mount is neighborliness in action: *here's what it looks like to live well, with one another, in the new reality of redemption.* Neighbors seek peace, resolve anger, tell the truth in a straightforward way, resist retaliation for personal offenses, love their enemies, and give to those in need. This is not a static reality; it is a journey whose pathway is not a set of rules but a person, leading to a God who is not a slave-owner but a father (John 1:12).[47]

That the way to God is not through the law but through the One the law points to both deeply confused and shocked the disciples. They asked Jesus about it, and he said, "I am the way, and the truth, and the life. No one comes to the Father except through me. If you had known me, you would have known my Father also. From now on you do know him and have seen him" (John 14:6–7).

Derek: from the Hebrew for "the way"; refers to the overall direction of a person's life.

Jesus's Hebrew-speaking audience—his disciples in this context—would have recognized the term "the way," calling to mind the Hebrew word **derek**, which we saw earlier refers to the overall direction of a person's life.[48] It's all throughout Scripture:

- Deuteronomy 10:12 says we should "walk in all his ways."

- Isaiah 40:3 says to "prepare the way of the LORD."

WHAT THE BIBLE SAYS ABOUT LOVING OUR NEIGHBORS

- Jeremiah 6:16 says, "Thus says the LORD: 'Stand by the roads, and look, and ask for the ancient paths, where the good way is; and walk in it, and find rest for your souls.' But they said, 'We will not walk in it.'"

There is a good way to go and a bad way to go. There is a way of truth and a way of deception. There is a way of life and a way of death. And the good, the true, and life-giving are known by knowing Jesus.

Most Christians intellectually understand that God gave his Son to save people to everlasting life (John 3:16).[49] They know that following Jesus's teachings brings rest to their souls (Matt. 11:29)[50] and that being a disciple of Jesus is the way to know the kind of truth that sets people free (John 8:30–32).[51] What they may not know, however, is that the gospel is not just a mysterious set of disciplines or secret rules to live an enlightened life. The hope found in the gospel is not due to our own actions; rather, it presents humans as criminals, guilty beyond a shadow of a doubt, who are offered complete pardon by the judge of the universe. What's more, those who accept Christ's offer of pardon are deputized to proclaim his offer of pardon throughout the world. That's the gospel: the good news.

> The good news does not end with our pardoned guilt but expands into a promise of renewed abundance to "restore to you the years that the swarming locust has eaten" (Joel 2:25). The famine has ended; the feast is set. And you're invited.

The good news does not end with our pardoned guilt but expands into a promise of renewed abundance to "restore to you the years that the swarming locust has eaten" (Joel 2:25). The famine has ended; the feast is set. And you're invited. As author Thomas Howard puts it,

> The Incarnation takes all that properly belongs to our humanity and delivers it back to us, redeemed. All of our inclinations and appetites and capacities and yearnings and proclivities are purified and gathered up and glorified by Christ. He did not come to thin out human life; he came to set it free. All the dancing and feasting and processing and singing and building and sculpting and baking and merrymaking that belong to us, and that were stolen away into the service of false gods, are returned to us in the Gospel.[52]

> We share abundance—and abundance is best when shared—by teaching others to obey God wherever Jesus has authority (Matt. 28:18–20), by persisting in spite of hardship (2 Tim. 2:1–13), and by serving as the channel through which God blesses the nations (Gal. 3:6–9).

We share abundance—and abundance is best when shared—by teaching others to obey God wherever Jesus has authority (Matt. 28:18–20),[53] by persisting in spite of hardship (2 Tim. 2:1–13), and by serving as the channel through which God blesses the nations (Gal. 3:6–9).[54] As Nancy Pearcey phrases it,

> We have to reject the division of life into a sacred realm, limited to things like worship and personal morality, over against a secular realm that includes science,

politics, economics, and the rest of the public arena. This dichotomy in our own minds is the greatest barrier to liberating the power of the gospel across the whole of culture today.[55]

The gospel, good news for all the world, applies everywhere, to every area of life. Let's look at five ways it affects neighborliness: character, calling, conversation, community, and citizenship.

The Gospel of Redemption Applies to Character

Rick Rescorla, once vice president of security for Morgan Stanley, was a decorated Vietnam veteran memorialized in the remarkable book and movie *We Were Soldiers*. In fact, Rick appears on the cover of the book.

As a veteran, Rick handled his job at Morgan Stanley with military precision. In his gut he knew that Morgan Stanley's headquarters, housed in the World Trade Center towers, was at risk. He predicted both the 1993 and the 2001 terrorist attacks. When Morgan Stanley refused his recommendation to move out of the building, Rick instituted regular surprise fire drills and instructed people on the basics of life safety.

On September 11, 2001, when the first plane struck World Trade Center Tower 1, an announcement was made in Tower 2 for everyone to stay calm and resume their work. Rick immediately ignored the announcement and evacuated his employees, standing in the stairwell with his bullhorn, singing "God Bless America," and shouting, "Today is a day to be proud to be an American!"

Having grown up in Cornwall, England, Rick inspired the fleeing employees by belting out a battle hymn he had learned as a child calling the men of Cornwall to "stop your dreaming" and "stand and never yield." He was last seen in a Tower 2 stairwell, heading back up to look for others. His body was never recovered. Because of Rick's preparation and his bravery, all but six of Morgan Stanley's 2,700 employees in the World Trade Center buildings survived the attack. Rick's widow, Susan, said, "He lived by a code. He had his own philosophy and he used to say to me, 'You declare what you're about when you're young, and you try to stay on that road so that at the end of your life you knew you did the very best you could.'"[56]

> **Character is far more than merely an intellectual posture; knowing *about* good character is of little use unless good character is embodied.**

Rick Rescorla, heroically embodying redeemed neighborliness, understood that character is not something we are born with, such as brown hair or blue eyes. It must be cultivated. Further, character is far more than merely an intellectual posture; knowing *about* good character is of little use unless good character is embodied. In *The Abolition of Man*, C. S. Lewis said,

Without the aid of trained emotions the intellect is powerless against the animal organism. I had sooner play cards against a man who was quite skeptical about ethics, but bred to believe that "a gentleman does not cheat," than against an irreproachable moral philosopher who had been brought up among sharpers [card cheats]. In battle it is not syllogisms that will keep the reluctant nerves and muscles to their post in the third hour of the bombardment.[57]

The phrase "without the aid of trained emotions" is telling. We can train our emotions. We are not victims of how we feel. We can cultivate our wants to want what is worth cultivating.

The Gospel of Redemption Applies to Calling

If the time we spend is any indication, our *work* connects to neighborliness more than any other thing we do. Often, we interact with others through our work more than we do with our own family members. Christian thinkers have invested a lot of time contemplating the value of work, with vastly different perspectives. William Law, a respected eighteenth-century minister, believed that Christians should work only to earn a living, with the rest of their time being dedicated to preparing for life after death:

> If the time we spend is any indication, our *work* connects to neighborliness more than any other thing we do.

> Most of the employments of life are in their own nature lawful, and all those that are so may be made a substantial part of our duty to God, if we engage in them only so far, and for such ends, as are suitable to beings that are to live above the world, all the time that they live in the world. This is the only measure of our application to any worldly business, let it be what it will, where it will; it must have no more of our hands, our hearts, or our time than is consistent with a hearty, daily, careful preparation of ourselves for another life.[58]

Perhaps Law meant that we should work well but remain unattached to our jobs, because they are only worldly concerns. Unfortunately, his statement also implies that we should give only the bare minimum of our efforts to our work and that spending one minute more at work than absolutely necessary would be sinful.

This approach to work has always confused me because I enjoy my work. Whether on the debate team in high school and college or in my academic studies or in my professorship or in various entrepreneurial activities, I have liked my work. By "like" I mean that I feel a sense of *flow* while working; I find work meaningful and fun. Some Christians openly condemn this. "But I *like* my work," I remember telling one person. "Then you're a workaholic," he confidently asserted.

The word **vocation** comes from the Latin word *vocare*, which means "to call." Redeemed neighborliness calls for transforming our understanding of work from a troublesome toil to a God-given vocation. As we saw earlier, work was part of God's plan for humans bearing his image. Therefore, in many ways, work is a thread running from creation straight to the cross. As poet and essayist Dorothy Sayers puts it,

> *Vocation:* from the Latin for "to call"; the work to which a person is drawn or well suited.

> The whole of Christian doctrine centers round the great paradox of redemption, which asserts that the very pains and sorrows by which fallen man is encompassed can become the instruments of his salvation, if they are accepted and transmuted by

love.... The first Adam was cursed with labor and suffering; the redemption of labor and suffering is the triumph of the second Adam—the Carpenter nailed to the cross.[59]

Christ did not crush Satan's work merely to produce warm spiritual feelings. As authors Ralph T. Mattson and Arthur F. Miller Jr. say, "This is not the plot of some delicate love affair. This is the God who has smashed the wall of partition between Himself and us, who has spent blood and somehow entered spaces of horror to bring about reconciliation with us at a gruesome price."[60] God did not ignore the wall between the secular and the sacred; he blew it up.

Through vocation, we step through the gap where the secular/sacred wall used to be. No one can make us do this. We must choose, and it is a deeply personal choice. Others may not understand, and we may find ourselves fumbling for words to express our calling. As author and educator Parker Palmer says, "Vocation at its deepest level is, 'This is something I can't not do, for reasons I'm unable to explain to anyone else and don't fully understand myself but that are nonetheless compelling.'"[61]

Even though it is a personal process, how we live out our vocation is intimately related to loving our neighbors:

- Every time we see the unique contributions others make, it gives us a better glimpse into their personhood.

- Every time we use our gifts to provide a service or good for others that they cannot provide for themselves, we are expressing for others the love Jesus shows to us.

- Every time we see our own weaknesses and the strengths of others, we realize that true success comes through each person doing his or her part, as if in a body.

- Every time we see true talent, it should remind us that our every vocational act is a culture-creating act and that culture is the sum total of all the things all of us do.

Following are some of the ways calling, work, and culture creation combine.

Gifting. Some believe that people are born *tabula rasa* (as a "blank slate") and with proper training can be made to do just about anything. A growing number of researchers, though, are learning that people seem to have a kind of motivated ability that cannot simply be explained by naturalistic factors. Many refer to this as gifting, which appropriately recognizes that it isn't something we give to ourselves. When we do the sorts of things that return energy to us and make us feel more alive, patterns emerge. After half a century of researching gifting and helping people discover their motivated abilities, Arthur F. Miller Jr. believes these patterns are highly significant. He says, "Every time people do something well that they find satisfying, they make use of some or all of the same behavior pattern and achieve one special purpose of unsurpassed personal worth."[62]

We are wise to pay attention to these patterns and think about how we might pursue our gifting rather than just trying to overcome our weaknesses. English author and

WHAT THE BIBLE SAYS ABOUT LOVING OUR NEIGHBORS

speaker Ken Robinson tells the story of a girl named Gillian, who at age eight was already a failure in school. This was the 1930s, before anyone had thought of names for various learning disabilities, but Gillian's concerned mother had the sense to take her to a psychologist. After talking with Gillian and her mother, the psychologist thanked Gillian for her patience and asked for just a little more time to talk with her mother privately. Just before leaving the room, he turned on the radio. The psychologist and Gillian's mother stood outside the room, looking through a window in a way that Gillian would not see them. Almost immediately Gillian began to gracefully twirl around the room, transfixed by the music. The psychologist said to Gillian's mother, "You know, Gillian isn't sick. She's a dancer. Take her to a dance school." This is the story of Gillian Lynne, a dancer who performed with the Royal Ballet and choreographed many highly successful productions, including *Cats* and *The Phantom of the Opera*.[63] One wonders what would have happened if Gillian's mother had ignored this advice and merely tried to fit Gillian into the mold of what society says is important.

Attitude. Although work is good, some jobs do not feel fulfilling. Faithfully doing them is a test of character. A number of years ago, I was doing a workshop about the nature of work and someone raised his hand and said, "I'm a delivery driver. I hate my job. I only do it to pay the bills." We were in the middle of a group and I didn't want to say anything negative, but I felt like saying, "You need to meet Buddy, the delivery driver who brings packages to our house." I order a lot of books, so Buddy comes to the house almost every day. He loves his job, and he's good at it. Our kids love Buddy. One time we were going to be away at Buddy's usual delivery time. The children wrote, "Hi, Buddy!" in sidewalk chalk on the driveway. They returned to find a huge sidewalk chalk message in reply: "UPS rocks." When compared to Buddy, it's hard not to conclude that the man who said he hated his job was displaying a disturbing attitude of entitlement. He seemed to think that when God did not give him a job he found easy to enjoy, he felt justified in expressing bitterness. Your job might not be glamorous, but it does have the potential to display God's glory on earth. You can use your job to love your neighbor by aligning your attitude with God's redemptive view of work.

> Although work is good, some jobs do not feel fulfilling. Faithfully doing them is a test of character.

Rigor. Talent is distressingly common; hard work is rare. In his book *Talent Is Overrated,* Geoff Colvin says that "deliberate practice" is what moves talented people to high performance and that deliberate practice has five characteristics:

1. **Deliberate practice is designed specifically to improve performance.** *Designed* is the key word. The best athletes in the world still go to teachers because others have the ability to see things about them that they cannot see themselves.

2. **Deliberate practice can be repeated a lot.** World-renowned pianist Van Cliburn practiced six hours a day, including two hours of scales. Scales are boring, but it was

not Cliburn's goal to get good enough to avoid doing them. Repetition was a major part of what made him good.

3. Deliberate practice seeks continuous feedback. Colvin compares practicing without feedback to bowling through a curtain that hangs down to knee level. You can never know if you're meeting the standard or getting better.

4. Deliberate practice is mentally demanding. Hours of sustained practice every day is the minimum requirement for true expertise. Some studies have shown that people approach expertise only when they have collected ten thousand hours of rigorous, focused practice![64]

5. Deliberate practice is hard. It isn't much fun. That's why most people don't do it. Those who do, though, move into the category of people whose talent results in high performance.[65]

In the end, a proper understanding of calling helps us see God's redemptive power at work. If we ask, "What do I *want*?" then we risk the kind of self-centered perspective that is more characteristic of fallenness. If we instead ask, "What should I do with my life?" then it is easier to keep the focus on our God-given design. It doesn't mean that sin has no sway over our lives, but it opens the door for living in a way that inspires purpose and displays God's glory.

The Gospel of Redemption Applies to Conversation

Dialogue: from the Greek for "through words"; the process of talking through thoughts.

The proper response to the communication breakdown caused by fallen neighborliness—whether through anger, lack of caring, or the disruption of technology—isn't more *talk* but more **dialogue**, a word that comes from two Greek words: *dia* (through) and *logos* (word/thoughts). In other words, to dialogue is to talk through thoughts.

William Isaacs has thought a lot about dialogue since his dissertation adviser asked, "What do you want to be known for?" Isaacs decided to be known for opening up a deeper way for people to talk about what is really important. In his lectures at MIT's Sloan School of Management, Isaacs defines dialogue as "a *conversation with a center, not sides*."[66] He continues, "The intention of dialogue is to reach new understanding and, in doing so, to form a totally new basis from which to think and act."[67]

In fallen neighborliness, talking is aimed toward showing how right you are, how worthy, how superior your ideas are, and how seriously you feel you ought to be taken. But these aims strip away neighborliness and understanding. Isaacs explains:

There is a deeply communal dimension to speaking together that is typically lost on us. If I speak, it is often to make *my* point, to indicate my superiority, to claim

WHAT THE BIBLE SAYS ABOUT LOVING OUR NEIGHBORS

my ground. Often I lie in wait in meetings, like a hunter looking for his prey, ready to spring out at the first moment of silence. My gun is loaded with preestablished thoughts. I take aim and fire, the context irrelevant, my bullet and its release all that matter to me.[68]

We are meant to live in peace with one another (Rom. 12:18)[69] and avoid conceit, provocation, and envy (Gal. 5:26).[70] But how do we do this, especially in high-pressure environments?

It is easier said than done. One college student shared that she dreaded going to a particular class because her professor was a difficult person who seemed easily angered. Trying to be respectful seemed to make him even madder, she told me. Can someone like this student live peaceably with people like that professor? Here are some of the things I shared to help her engage rather than escape this difficult situation and do so without sin:

1. **Give up rights.** I realized years ago that I became incensed when I felt my "rights" were being violated. For instance, when I give up my right to get a full night's sleep or to have my plane arrive on time or to be in a short line, my stress level decreases dramatically.

2. **Choose to be joyful.** My *feelings* of anger hurt me more than the hurt that originally caused my anger. Anger is destructive, and I can simply refuse to collect it by developing a grateful spirit.

> I realized years ago that I became incensed when I felt my "rights" were being violated. For instance, when I give up my right to get a full night's sleep or to have my plane arrive on time or to be in a short line, my stress level decreases dramatically.

3. **Take people seriously.** In a conflict, it's especially important to concentrate on the message being delivered. Taking others seriously does not obligate me to do what they say or to appreciate how they said it. But it *does* show that I want to treat them with dignity as persons.

4. **Respond sincerely.** In conflict, I might want to respond sarcastically or angrily or to become doormat-submissive. Instead, I am learning to respond honestly and seriously: "I can see that I've done something that really ticks you off. I want to make it right. Please tell me specifically what I should do differently next time."

5. **Apologize for your wrongs.** A meaningful apology doesn't say, "I'm sorry, *but* …" In justifying my actions, I negate the value of the apology. Now I am learning to say, "Here's what I did. I was wrong and I'm sorry. Will you forgive me?"

6. **Turn the tide.** Former police officer George Thompson says in *Verbal Judo*, "Never use words that rise readily to your lips or you'll make the greatest speech you'll ever live to regret." Thompson suggests a "sword of insertion," such as "Whoa …" or "Listen …" or "Wait a second …" (earnestly, not in anger), and then, "Let me be sure I heard what

you just said." This interrupts the harangue, shows empathy, and helps the other person reframe emotions more thoughtfully.

7. Plan your words. In his excellent book *The Peacemaker*, Ken Sande suggests writing out our thoughts before a conversation, focusing on the issues needing to be addressed, words and topics that should be avoided, words that describe feelings, a description of the effect the problem is having, suggestions for a solution, and the benefits of the solution. *Don't accuse; describe.*

8. Accept the blessing God has for you. Jesus said, "Blessed are the peacemakers." Being able to put up with unfair treatment is a character quality called "long-suffering." Lots of people have grown in patience, humility, and compassion because of the guff they took. I pray that God gives you and me this ability as well.

The Gospel of Redemption Applies to Community

It is God's nature to love, and because of the power of the Holy Spirit, we can love too. We've seen that the most common Greek word for "love" is *phileo*, or "brotherly, familial love." But the most common New Testament word for "love" is *agape*, which means "selfless love." Romans 5:5 says that God's agape has been "poured into our hearts through the Holy Spirit who has been given to us." We should pray for the Holy Spirit to pour love into our hearts so we can love as God loves.

> We should pray for the Holy Spirit to pour love into our hearts so we can love as God loves.

Community is more than just having a group of friends; it means building the intermediate institutions that help kids learn to read and have positive role models, keep the community clean and free from crime, and so much more. The prophet Jeremiah wrote to the captives in Babylon and told them not to insulate themselves from others: "Seek the welfare of the city where I have sent you into exile, and pray to the Lord on its behalf, for in its welfare you will find your welfare" (Jer. 29:7).

John Stonestreet, from the Chuck Colson Center, asks four questions to identify where to jump into community involvement:

- What's good that we can protect?

- What's broken that we can fix?

- What's evil that we can stop?

- What's missing that we can contribute?

This involves everything from helping the people in our communities flourish to stopping consumption of things that encourage mistreatment of others (pornography, for example). There are always children who need help. There are always liberties that need to be defended.

There is always cleanup that needs to take place. We can all do something, big or small, to build community.

Here are four positive results stemming from community involvement:

Abundance. If we're weighed down by a distorted view of God's plan, we won't be able to glorify him and influence others: "For while there is jealousy and strife among you, are you not of the flesh and behaving only in a human way?" (1 Cor. 3:3). If we focus on things we want to acquire and protect, we become selfish. When we display a willingness to share the gifts and opportunities God has given us, though, we open the door to a mind-set of abundance that transforms community. That's the principle behind Asset-Based Community Development, a movement that enables everyone in a community to apply his or her gifts to make everything better for all.[71]

Cooperation. Working with others requires cooperation. Cooperation is necessary for getting things done effectively and efficiently, but it is also a good in and of itself. Unfortunately, in bringing people together, conflicts arise. God, in his infinite wisdom and with his sense of humor, has arranged things so that the only way to maximize our gifts is to cooperate with others whose gifts complement our own. Because of our sin natures and differing perspectives, we disagree over how to pursue our goals, who gets credit for what, who's abusing their power, who's lording it over whom, and an endless array of other concerns. Instead, we ought to pray for an "abundance mentality." We can and should ask the One who owns everything to help us develop a finely tuned vision of togetherness.

> God, in his infinite wisdom and with his sense of humor, has arranged things so that the only way to maximize our gifts is to cooperate with others whose gifts complement our own.

Reconciliation. Being close to others is difficult, or impossible, without a spirit of reconciliation. When we come together for a common goal, we are going to step on one another's toes. Living in the spirit means being forgiving and seeking always to be reconciled to others. Jesus laid it out very soberly in Matthew 6:14–15: "If you forgive others their trespasses, your heavenly Father will also forgive you, but if you do not forgive others their trespasses, neither will your Father forgive your trespasses." The underlying problem is that from God's perspective, we're steeped in sin. If we choose not to forgive, it's because we underestimate the seriousness of our offenses before God. I once saw a gracious leader handle an unfair personal attack in the following way: "I'm afraid I'm really much worse than you think. I'm just a flawed person God has chosen to advance this vision. I'm glad it isn't about me; it is about the vision. Let's focus on accomplishing the vision."

Blessing. In Genesis 12:2–3, God told Abraham, "I will make of you a great nation, and I will bless you and make your name great, so that you will be a blessing.… All the families of the earth shall be blessed." This applies to all Christ-followers. In Galatians 3:7–9, the apostle Paul said, "Know then that it is those of faith who are the sons of Abraham.… *Those who are of faith are blessed along with Abraham, the man of faith.*" You can be a blessing by meeting physical and spiritual needs. James 2:17 says, "Faith by itself, if it does not have works, is dead." Start where you are. A woman named Amber Cannon serves as an example. Struggling with suicidal thoughts, Amber often felt that life didn't seem worth living. Based on her mayor's call for community involvement, though, Amber organized a block party. More than one hundred people came. In the process of planning for the event, Amber met a neighbor who had some great idea for games for the event but struggled with anxiety and did not want to leave her home.[72] The community event broke the spell of depression and anxiety and enabled these neighbors to be a blessing to one another.

The Gospel of Redemption Applies to Citizenship

In an earlier chapter, I quoted A. W. Tozer, the theologian who noted that what we think about when we think about God is the most important thing about us. To Tozer, this is true for nations as well as for people: "The history of mankind will probably show that no people has ever risen above its religion, and man's spiritual history will positively demonstrate that no religion has ever been greater than its idea of God."[73] If people in a nation have a big view of God, society will thrive. Societies with a small view of God, on the other hand, wither. This does not mean that Christians should step in and take things over; rather, it means we should be good citizens who focus on establishing orderly and just governance.

> If people in a nation have a big view of God, society will thrive. Societies with a small view of God, on the other hand, wither.

Order. Nothing happens in our communities without laws that establish order. Even things as simple as providing clean drinking water and properly disposing of sewage result from such laws. The Mosaic law, one of the earliest sources of administrative regulations, still forms the basis for law today. Take for example Exodus 21:33–34: "When a man opens a pit, or when a man digs a pit and does not cover it, and an ox or a donkey falls into it, the owner of the pit shall make restoration. He shall give money to its owner, and the dead beast shall be his." These laws about neighborliness are the basis of what is called **tort law**. We are obligated to act in a way that will not harm our neighbors' interests and to make restitution when we do.[74]

> *Tort Law:* the area of law governing remedies for those wronged by others, such as through negligence.

Justice. The Constitution of the United States is representative of the way America's founding fathers thought about justice. When forming our government, they focused on *securing* liberties, not *establishing* them. They believed that laws are discovered, not developed. What constitutes just laws? As a lifelong scholar of justice, Yale University's Nicholas Wolterstorff has found that justice is not that which makes people happy but that which creates space for living virtuously.[75] The goal of a just life is to remove barriers to liberty not so people can do whatever they want but so they may secure the freedom to do what they ought.

WHAT THE BIBLE SAYS ABOUT LOVING OUR NEIGHBORS

The American founders' idea of justice has been corrupted through the years into a focus on equality of outcome rather than equality of opportunity, and this has hurt people by removing from them a desire to improve themselves. After all, why go to the trouble to pursue a college degree if you can have an income guaranteed by the government?

A lot of people think we can wash our hands of the need to pursue justice by voting for government policies that advocates say will help the poor. From a Christian view, it is much more than that. It isn't just about money; it's about loving our neighbors.

Involvement. Get to know your elected officials and their office staff personally. Find ways to help them in areas of agreement. Not only will this promote the common good, but it will give you credibility in persuading them in areas where you disagree. "People are policy," the political strategist Morton Blackwell is fond of saying. The worldview of those with influence becomes the law in practice, regardless of what the letter of the law says. Rather than try to go around them, perhaps we should reach out to them. Political figures are real people struggling with real issues. Helping them makes a genuine difference.

Study. At Summit Ministries, we believe (and say often), "If you want to be a leader, you've got to be a reader." You can't truly understand political issues merely by reading Internet snippets or watching television. If you want to do everything you can to exercise your rights and privileges as a citizen, you've got to develop a clear and purposeful reading strategy. Read Christian publications such as *World Magazine*, a local newspaper, and at least one substantial book a month. This will leave much less time for television viewing, social media, and gaming. Consider this, though: citizenship is a right that is hard to win and easy to lose. Be part of the solution, not part of the problem.

> At Summit Ministries, we believe (and say often), "If you want to be a leader, you've got to be a reader."

Voting. For many years, I taught political communication at a Christian college where students in my class complained incessantly about their elected officials, yet the day after the election, I discovered that only two of my students had voted. Most weren't even *registered* to vote! I told them, "For the rest of the semester, if you didn't vote, you have lost your right to complain." Years later, one still calls me every time she votes. Let's face it: voting is a simple act, the most basic act a citizen can take. To fail to vote is to abandon your most basic responsibility as a citizen. In a government where the authority rests with the people, voting is a clear way of submitting to the governing authorities.

Speaking. Like the ancient Israelite tribe of Issachar, we owe it to our fellow citizens to understand the times in which we live (1 Chron. 12:32).[76] Further, we owe it to our fellow citizens to speak the truth as we understand it. To not do so is to violate at least three scriptural principles, all from the book of Proverbs:

- 3:27: "Do not withhold good from those to whom it is due, when it is in your power to do it."

- 31:8: "Open your mouth for the mute, for the rights of all who are destitute."

- 24:11–12: "Rescue those who are being taken away to death; hold back those who are stumbling to the slaughter. If you say, 'Behold, we did not know this,' does not he who weighs the heart perceive it? Does not he who keeps watch over your soul know it, and will he not repay man according to his work?"

These are deeply challenging verses we should take with utmost seriousness. If we don't speak up, who will?

5. Conclusion

Remember the old saying "A man convinced against his will is of the same opinion still." By *engaging* rather than *escaping*, by developing good character, dialogue skill, and making a commitment to be a productive member of a community, we win twice. We clarify our own views, and we help bring truth back into the public sphere.

This can change the world. In the seventeen hundreds, a Quaker farmer, John Woolman, came to realize that owning slaves was wrong. He freed his slaves and set about trying to persuade his Quaker neighbors to do the same. Woolman didn't lecture or preach to them. Instead, he asked questions: What does it mean to be a person? What does it mean to *own* a person? What does it mean to *will* a person to your descendants as a piece of property? By the time Woolman finished his crusade, all the Quakers in American had released their slaves, and a good number had joined the abolitionist cause.[77]

Woolman, through simple persuasion, played the part of a caring neighbor and brought freedom to thousands. Just imagine what you could do if you loved God so much with your heart, soul, mind, and strength that this love spilled over in an abundance of love for your neighbor, whether he lives next door or around the world.

This chapter concludes the first section of this book, which has focused on who God is, how Scripture reveals him, how he should be viewed as having authority, what the narrative flow of the Bible is, how we can study it, and how we can respond to Scripture's call to love God and our neighbors. Now we transition to a new section focused on challenges to Scripture's truth, beginning with how we can even know that God exists.

Endnotes

1. Loren Cunningham, *The Book That Transforms Nations: The Power of the Bible to Change Any Country* (Seattle, WA: YWAM, 2007), 44–45.
2. Darrow Miller and Stan Guthrie, *Discipling Nations: The Power of Truth to Transform Culture* (Seattle, WA: YWAM, 1998), 33–34.
3. Micah 6:8: "He has told you, O man, what is good; and what does the LORD require of you but to do justice, and to love kindness, and to walk humbly with your God?"
4. Gary D. Badcock, *The Way of Life: A Theology of Christian Vocation* (Grand Rapids, MI: Eerdmans, 1998), 83.
5. Jeremiah 29:7: "Seek the welfare of the city where I have sent you into exile, and pray to the LORD on its behalf, for in its welfare you will find your welfare."
6. Each of these terms briefly defined: *atheism* (no God), *polytheism* (more than one God), *naturalism* (everything that exists can be explained through natural processes), *pantheism* (God and creation are the same thing), *panentheism* (God is in creation), *Gnosticism* (the material world is evil), *agnosticism* (uncertainty about God and purpose), and *nihilism* (no

purpose). By *evolutionism*, I am referring not to such things as change through natural selection, which we can observe, but rather to the belief that all life arose through random chance processes starting with the first self-replicating molecule.

7. See www.prolifetraining.com/ for how these four points—size, level of development, environment, and degree of dependenc—form an acronym, S.L.E.D., which in turn forms an extremely strong argument against elective abortion.

8. See chapter 9 of R. Scott Smith's *In Search of Moral Knowledge: Overcoming the Fact-Value Dichotomy* (Downers Grove, IL: IVP Academic, 2014), in which he reviews the sometimes-complicated but deeply compelling arguments of philosopher Edmund Husserl about how we can know reality because people and ideas have definable essences that present themselves in a consistent way that can be understood by others.

9. America's founders believed that if a nation based its actions on commonsense principles rooted in natural law, its actions would be self-correcting. This thinking was based, in part, on the writing of Scottish economist Adam Smith (author of *Wealth of Nations*). See Samuel Fleischacker, "Adam Smith's Reception among America's Founders, 1776–1790," in *The William and Mary Quarterly 59*, third series, no. 4 (October 2002). It was perhaps this belief in self-correcting government that encouraged them to proceed with forming a nation without resolving the slavery question. Certainly, they would have been horrified to think that the cost would be hundreds of thousands of lives and the near destruction of the nation in a civil war. Yet the fact remains that various cultures have opposed slavery in certain circumstances, or for themselves, but opposing slavery in all its forms because it was sinful arose only because of Christian theology and remains a uniquely Christian impulse to the present time. Rodney Stark, *For the Glory of God: How Monotheism Led to Reformations, Science, Witch-Hunts, and the End of Slavery* (Princeton, NJ: Princeton University Press, 2003), 291. The entirety of Stark's fourth chapter, "God's Justice: The Sin of Slavery," should be carefully studied by all Christians.

10. See Ecclesiastes 1 and 2.

11. See Ecclesiastes 3:22 and Colossians 3:23–24, for example.

12. See *abad*, Strong's Hebrew reference number 5646, in Robert L. Thomas, *New American Standard Exhaustive Concordance of the Bible/Hebrew-Aramaic and Greek Dictionaries*, updated ed. (Nashville: Holman, 1981).

13. *The Zondervan Pictorial Encyclopedia of the Bible* says, "The Hebrew term which comes closest to our modern occidental concept of 'personality,' i.e. the total picture of man's organized behavior, is sem, 'name.' Thus the sum total of a person's internal and external pattern of behavior was gathered up into his name" (p. 363). And also this: "When one gives a name to another, he thereby establishes a relation of dominion or possession to him. Already in Eden, Adam demonstrated that part of the imago Dei (image of God) which promised to him the subjugation and rulership over all things upon the earth by naming the animals (Gen. 2:19f.). This right is held on loan from God who already has not only made the world, but named it as well (Gen. 1:5, 8, 10). Man in turn names his wife 'Woman' (Gen. 2:23).... Linked with the concept of authority is the idea of protection. What God or man owns, they must thereby protect, e.g. 1 Kings 8:43; 2 Chronicles 7:14, Jeremiah 7:10, 11, 14, 30; 14:9; 34:15; Daniel 9:18; Amos 9:12" (363–64). Merrill C. Tenney, *Zondervan Pictorial Encyclopedia of the Bible*, vol. 4 (Grand Rapids, MI: Zondervan, 2010).

14. Caroline Leaf, "We Are Designed for Deep Intellectual Thought—It Keeps Us Healthy," *Dr. Leaf* (blog), March 26, 2012, drleaf.com/blog/we-are-designed-for-deep-intellectual-thought-it-keeps-us-healthy/.

15. There is a significant amount of medical research on this point. One simple and helpful summary is by medical doctor and psychologist Leonard Sax in *Boys Adrift: The Five Factors Driving the Growing Epidemic of Unmotivated Boys and Underachieving Young Men* (New York: Basic Books, 2009), 91.

16. See the research of Andrew Newberg, University of Pennsylvania School of Medicine. In measuring blood flow as people meditate or pray, he has found that during prayer and meditation, the parietal lobe goes dim and the frontal lobe and limbic system are more active, providing feelings of rapture. Andrew Newberg, Michael Pourdehnad, Abass Alavi, and Eugene G. d'Aquili, "Cerebral Blood Flow during Meditative Prayer: Preliminary Findings and Methodological Issues," *Perceptual and Motor Skills* 97 (2006): 625–30.

17. Mihaly Csikszentmihalyi, *Finding Flow: The Psychology of Engagement with Everyday Life* (New York: Basic Books, 1998).

18. William Brennan parallels the word games used by Hitler and those used by abortion advocates against the unborn. He demonstrates that propaganda is not a thing of the past but rather a current reality; we must always be on guard. See William Brennan, *Dehumanizing the Vulnerable: When Word Games Take Lives* (Fort Collins, CO: Life Cycle Books, 2000).

19. Cornelius Plantinga Jr., *Not the Way It's Supposed to Be: A Breviary of Sin* (Grand Rapids, MI: Eerdmans, 1995), 5. Plantinga's chapter titles are an excellent summary of how the Bible depicts sin: "Vandalism of Shalom"; "Spiritual Hygiene and Corruption"; "Perversion, Pollution, and Disintegration"; "The Progress of Corruption"; "Parasite"; "Masquerade"; "Sin and Folly"; "The Tragedy of Addiction"; "Attack"; and "Flight."

20. D. A. Carson, *For the Love of God: A Daily Companion for Discovering the Riches of God's Word* (Wheaton, IL: Crossway, 1999), 23.

21. Edward O. Wilson, *On Human Nature* (Cambridge, MA: Harvard University Press, 2004), 2.

22. Kenneth L. Feder and Michael Alan Park, "Animal Rights: An Evolutionary Perspective," *The Humanist* (July/August 1990): 44.

23. *Roe v. Wade* 410 U.S., 113, 160 (1973).

24. Obviously, human beings change through time, but our essence remains the same. Most of our body's cells are regularly

dying and being replaced, but we do not because of this say, "Well, I don't have to pay my mortgage because the guy who signed that document was a completely different person." As Francis Beckwith puts it, "In fact, this same you was also once a fetus, an embryo, and a zygote. To be sure, you have changed. But it is you who has changed." Francis J. Beckwith, "Abortion, Bioethics, and Personhood: A Philosophical Reflection," *The Southern Baptist Journal of Theology 4*, no. 1 (2000): 16–25.

25. Francis J. Beckwith, "Abortion, Bioethics, and Personhood," 16–25.

26. Matthew Crawford, *Shop Class as Soulcraft: An Inquiry into the Value of Work* (New York: Penguin, 2009), 98.

27. Peter Wood, *A Bee in the Mouth: Anger in America Now* (New York: Encounter Books, 2006), 2.

28. Wood, *Bee in the Mouth*, 4.

29. Russell Moore, "Racial Justice and the Goodness of God," *Moore to the Point* (blog), July 14, 2013, www.russellmoore com/2013/07/14/racial-justice-and-the-goodness-of-god-2/.

30. This quotation from Martin Luther King Jr. is a paraphrase of a statement by abolitionist Theodore Parker (1810–1860). It is quoted in Tony Evans's *Oneness Embraced: Through the Eyes of Tony Evans, A Fresh Look at Reconciliation, the Kingdom and Justice* (Chicago: Moody, 2011), 21. Evans points out that although Americans in the white majority ignore their nation's history of proclaiming justice for all while denying it for many, minority Americans too often foster "a victim mentality that reinforces a pathology of dependency." He is an evangelical pastor whose passionate look at race issues in the church is a very important read.

31. See this statistic and many other statistics about pornography at "Pornography Statistics," Family Safe Media, familysafemedia.com/pornography_statistics.html.

32. David Roach, "Pastors: Porn a Big Problem among Members," *Baptist Press*, November 10, 2011.

33. The actual figure is said to be as high as 90 percent. See this statistic and many other statistics about pornography at "Pornography Statistics," Family Safe Media, familysafemedia.com/pornography_statistics.html.

34. Mike Allen, "Exposure to Pornography and Acceptance of Rape Myths," *Journal of Communication* 45, no. 1 (Winter 1995): 5–14; Shawn Corne, "Women's Attitudes and Fantasies about Rape as a Function of Early Exposure to Pornography," *Journal of Interpersonal Violence* 7, no. 4 (December 1992): 454–61.

35. William L. Marshall, "Revisiting the Use of Pornography by Sexual Offenders: Implications for Theory and Practice," *Journal of Sexual Aggression* 6, no. 1–2 (2000): 67–77. The latest statistics are available at en.wikipedia.org/wiki/Relationship _between_child_pornography_and_child_sexual_abuse.

36. International Labor Organization, "Training Manual to Fight Trafficking in Children for Labour, Sexual and Other Forms of Exploitation" (2009), www.unicef.org/protection/Textbook_1.pdf.

37. Doug Eshleman, "Men View Half-Naked Women as Objects, Study Finds," *The Daily Princetonian*, February 17, 2009, dailyprincetonian.com/news/2009/02/men-view-half-naked-women-as-objects-study-finds/.

38. Chap Clark, *When Kids Hurt: Help for Adults Navigating the Adolescent Maze* (Ada, MI: Baker, 2009), 104.

39. "Got Joy?," Time/ABT SRBI Poll, *Time*, July 8–15, 2013, 34.

40. "Media Literacy: Fast Facts," *Teen Health and the Media*, depts.washington.edu/thmedia/view.cgi?section=medialiteracy &page=fastfacts. See also the "Generation M2" report from the Kaiser Family Foundation, www.kff.org/entmedia/upload /8010.pdf.

41. Csikszentmihalyi, *Finding Flow*, 67.

42. Csikszentmihalyi, *Finding Flow*, 68.

43. T. S. Eliot, *The Complete Poems and Plays: 1909–1950* (New York: Harcourt-Brace, 1950), 96.

44. Henry Grunwald, "The Year 2000," *Time*, March 30, 1992, 50–51.

45. Douglas Coupland, *Life after God* (New York: Pocket Books, 1995), 359, quoted in Brian J. Mahan, *Forgetting Ourselves on Purpose* (San Francisco, CA: Jossey-Bass, 2002), 31.

46. N. T. Wright, *After You Believe: Why Christian Character Matters* (New York: HarperOne, 2010), 103.

47. John 1:12: "To all who did receive him, who believed in his name, he gave the right to become children of God."

48. See Joel F. Williams, "Way," in *Eerdmans Dictionary of the Bible*, ed. D. N. Freedman, A. C. Myers, and A. B. Beck (Grand Rapids, MI: Eerdmans, 2000), 1370–71. Williams says, "In the concrete sense, a road (Deut. 1:2; Ruth 1:7) or a movement along a particular path, i.e., a journey (Exod. 13:21; 1 Kgs. 19:4). However, Heb. *derek* was also employed more broadly. To walk in the ways of God meant to live according to his will and commandments (Deut. 10:12–13; 1 Kgs. 3:14). In Isaiah 'the way of the Lord' can refer to God's provision of deliverance from enslavement or exile (Isa. 40:3; 43:16–19). The word was often used to identify the overall direction of a person's life, whether righteous or wicked (Judg. 2:17–19; Ps. 1:6; cf. Matt 7:13–14), wise or foolish (Prov. 4:11; 12:15). In the NT Gk. *hodós* has a similar range of meanings. In Mark's Gospel it is used repeatedly to present Jesus as 'on the way,' i.e., on his journey to Jerusalem (Mark 8:27; 9:33–34; 10:32). The broader context adds a deeper significance to these more literal references, since Jesus' willingness to go the way of suffering provides an example for his followers who must also prepare to suffer (Mark 8:31–34). In John 14:6 Jesus claims to be 'the way,' i.e., the only means of access to God (cf. Heb. 9:8; 10:19–20). In Acts 'the Way' functions as a title for the Christian message (Acts 19:9, 23; 22:4; 24:22) or the Christian community (9:2; 24:14)."

49. John 3:16: "For God so loved the world, that he gave his only Son, that whoever believes in him should not perish but have eternal life."

50. Matthew 11:29: "Take my yoke upon you, and learn from me, for I am gentle and lowly in heart, and you will find rest

WHAT THE BIBLE SAYS ABOUT LOVING OUR NEIGHBORS

for your souls."

51. John 8:30–32: "As he was saying these things, many believed in him. So Jesus said to the Jews who had believed him, 'If you abide in my word, you are truly my disciples, and you will know the truth, and the truth will set you free.'"

52. Thomas Howard, *Evangelical Is Not Enough: Worship of God in Liturgy and Sacrament* (San Francisco, CA: Ignatius Press, 1984), 36–37.

53. Matthew 28:18–20: "Jesus came and said to them, 'All authority in heaven and on earth has been given to me. Go therefore and make disciples of all nations, baptizing them in the name of the Father and of the Son and of the Holy Spirit, teaching them to observe all that I have commanded you. And behold, I am with you always, to the end of the age.'"

54. Galatians 3:6–9: "... just as Abraham 'believed God, and it was counted to him as righteousness'? Know then that it is those of faith who are the sons of Abraham. And the Scripture, foreseeing that God would justify the Gentiles by faith, preached the gospel beforehand to Abraham, saying, 'In you shall all the nations be blessed.' So then, those who are of faith are blessed along with Abraham, the man of faith."

55. Nancy Pearcey, *Total Truth: Liberating Christianity from Its Cultural Captivity* (Wheaton, IL: Crossway, 2005), 20.

56. William Bennett, *The Book of Man: Readings on the Path to Manhood* (Nashville: Thomas Nelson, 2011), 28–31.

57. C. S. Lewis, *The Abolition of Man* (New York: HarperCollins, 1944), 14.

58. William Law, *The Works of the Reverend William Law, Vol. 4: A Serious Call to a Devout and Holy Life* (London: J. Richardson, 1729), 33–34.

59. Dorothy L. Sayers, "Vocation in Work," *Callings: Twenty Centuries of Christian Wisdom on Vocation*, ed. William Carl Placher (Cambridge, UK: Eerdmans, 2005), 406.

60. Ralph Mattson and Arthur F. Miller Jr., *Finding a Job You Can Love* (Phillipsburg, NJ: Presbyterian and Reformed, 1982), 36–37.

61. Parker Palmer is a Quaker author who would probably not agree with much of the theology of this book. Nevertheless, his work on vocation and calling is thoughtfully helpful. See *Let Your Life Speak: Listening for the Voice of Vocation* (San Francisco: Jossey-Bass, 2000), 25.

62. Arthur F. Miller Jr., *Designed for Life: Hardwired—Empowered—Purposed, The Birthright of Every Human Being* (Charlotte, NC: Life[n] Media, 2006), 39.

63. Ken Robinson, *The Element: How Finding Your Passion Changes Everything* (New York: Viking, 2009), 3.

64. For more information, see Malcolm Gladwell, *Outliers: The Story of Success* (New York: Little, Brown, and Company, 2008).

65. Geoff Colvin, *Talent Is Overrated: What Really Separates World-Class Performers from Everyone Else* (New York: Penguin, 2008), 66–72.

66. William Isaacs, *Dialogue: And the Art of Thinking Together* (New York: Currency, 1999), 19 (emphasis in the original).

67. Isaacs, *Dialogue*, 19.

68. Isaacs, *Dialogue*, 165.

69. Romans 12:18: "If possible, so far as it depends on you, live peaceably with all."

70. Galatians 5:26: "Let us not become conceited, provoking one another, envying one another."

71. See the Asset-Based Community Development website at www.abcdinstitute.org/ and read stories of how this approach transforms communities at www.abundantcommunity.com/.

72. Michelle Strutzenberger, "What's Possible When Two Women Step Up to Connect Their Neighbourhood?," *Abundant Community*, January 13, 2015, www.abundantcommunity.com/home/stories/parms/1/story/20150113_whats_possible_when_two_women_step_up_to_connect_their_neighbourhood.html.

73. A. W. Tozer, *The Knowledge of the Holy: The Attributes of God and Their Meaning in the Christian Life* (New York: HarperSanFrancisco, 1992), 1.

74. Baron Lord Atkin, from the nineteenth century, said, "The rule that you are to love your neighbor becomes in law you must not injure your neighbor; and the lawyer's question: Who is my neighbor? receives a restricted reply. You must take reasonable care to avoid acts or omissions which you can reasonably foresee would be likely to injure your neighbor. Who, then, in law, is my neighbor? The answer seems to be—persons who are so closely and directly affected by my act that I ought reasonably to have them in contemplation as being so affected when I am directing my mind to the acts or omissions that are called into question." James Richard Atkin, quoted in Carol Harlow, *Understanding Tort Law*, 3rd ed. (London: Sweet and Maxwell, 2005), 47–48.

75. See chapter 7, "Why Eudaimonism Cannot Serve as a Framework for a Theory of Rights," in Nicholas Wolterstorff, *Justice: Rights and Wrongs* (Princeton, NJ: Princeton University Press, 2008).

76. 1 Chronicles 12:32: "... of Issachar, men who had understanding of the times, to know what Israel ought to do, 200 chiefs, and all their kinsmen under their command."

77. Robert Greenleaf and Larry Spears, *Servant Leadership: A Journey into the Nature of Legitimate Power and Greatness* (Mahwah, NJ: Paulist, 2002), 43–44.

CHAPTER 10

IS GOD CHRISTIAN?

1. GOD: A CULTURAL PHENOMENON?

Bishop Desmond Tutu, one of the most respected religious leaders in the world, is known primarily for his work in South Africa to end *apartheid* ("apartness"), South Africa's bungled and painful attempt to resolve racial tension. After **apartheid** was abolished, Tutu headed the Truth and Reconciliation Commission to bring healing among racial groups.

> *Apartheid:* government-enforced racial segregation.

Although Tutu is an Anglican bishop, his most recent thinking shows that he has real doubts about whether Christianity is true for all people, at all times, and in all cultures. In *God Is Not a Christian*, he writes,

> The accidents of birth and geography determine to a very large extent to what faith we belong.… Perhaps … we should not succumb too easily to the temptation to exclusiveness and dogmatic claims to a monopoly of the truth of our particular faith. You could so easily have been an adherent of the faith that you are now denigrating, but for the fact that you were born here rather than there.[1]

In other words, Tutu is saying that because people can't help which religion they were raised in, we cannot say it would be better for them to be Christian instead of the way they were raised. By using such words as *exclusiveness* and *dogmatic* and *monopoly*, Tutu implies that to believe otherwise is unthinking, rude, and perhaps even cruel.

For many, Tutu's insight is self-evidently true. A person growing up in Thailand is likely to be Buddhist and would therefore reject the idea of a personal creator. But does this mean that no such personal creator exists or that his existence depends on our understanding? And if he does in fact exist, are all people in all cultures at all times bound to acknowledge and respond to him?

These questions are not to be taken lightly, nor are the concerns of such a respected figure as Bishop Tutu. In this chapter, we'll explore whether it's reasonable to believe that God, as he is described in the Bible, actually exists. We'll ask, Can we know that he is more than just a human invention, born out of cultural and environmental forces? Is there sufficient evidence for the God of the Bible available to those who seek it?

The Bible suggests that God has revealed himself in a way that goes beyond our cultural biases and perspectives. But many people resist understanding. They raise objections, such as, If God made everything, who made God? Why do we need God when unbelievers can live just as moral lives as believers (or even better)? Isn't religious truth just a cultural preference?

In this chapter, we'll take a look at some of the evidence for God's existence, and then we'll examine each of these objections in turn to see whether it is reasonable to deny God's existence as he is revealed in the Bible.

2. Evidence of God Is Clearly Seen

The Bible says that certain things about God can be known outside of the Bible, through **general revelation**, which refers to ways God has made himself known through creation. It includes:

> **General Revelation:** God's universal revelation about himself (Ps. 19:1–6; Rom. 1:18–20) and morality (2:14–15) that can be obtained through nature.

- **God is great in power; he is deity.** Romans 1:19–20 says, "What can be known about God is plain to them, because God has shown it to them. For his invisible attributes, namely, his eternal power and divine nature, have been clearly perceived, ever since the creation of the world, in the things that have been made. So they are without excuse."

- **God is a designer.** Psalm 19:1 speaks of his universal craftsmanship: "The heavens declare the glory of God, and the sky above proclaims his handiwork."

- **God has written his law on our hearts.** Romans 2:14–15 says, "When Gentiles, who do not have the law, by nature do what the law requires, they are a law to themselves, even though they do not have the law. They show that the work of the law is written on their hearts, while their conscience also bears witness, and their conflicting thoughts accuse or even excuse them."

As Bruce Demarest says, "While not imparting truths necessary for salvation—such as the Trinity, the incarnation, or the atonement—general revelation conveys the conviction that God exists and that he is transcendent, immanent, self-sufficient, eternal, powerful, good and a hater of evil."[2]

In other words, people who have never read a Bible can know a great deal about God, the same God who is revealed in the Bible. This makes the argument that it is culturally insensitive to speak of God as being both real and really important less than convincing.

No one needs to be 100 percent certain of God's existence; complete certainty is impossible. All it takes is good reason to believe he exists. So are there good reasons to believe there is a God? Let's begin by looking at the evidence of the physical universe.

3. COSMOLOGICAL ARGUMENT: EXPLAINING THE EXISTENCE OF THE UNIVERSE

Cosmology is the study of the order, structure, and design of the universe. There is more than one version of the **cosmological argument** for God, but they all say that the universe could not be without God. Everything that exists has an explanation for its existence. The universe obviously exists. The only sufficient explanation for its existence is God.

> *Cosmology:* the study of the structure, origin, and design of the universe.

Philosopher Gottfried Wilhelm von Leibniz (1646–1716) was an early modern proponent of the cosmological argument. His brilliance was unquestionable. The co-discoverer of calculus, Leibniz also made major contributions in physics, philosophy, probability theory, medicine, psychology, linguistics, and even geology. In addition to science, he wrote books in fields as diverse as theology and law, and wrote fluently in Latin as well as in German and French. It was Leibniz who refined the binary number system and thus prepared the way for the invention of computers—three hundred years before it actually happened.

> *Cosmological Argument (aka Casual Argument):* an argument for God's existence that begins with the premise that something caused the universe to exist and ends with the conclusion that God is the best explanation for the existence of the universe.

Leibniz thought a lot about how we can make statements such as "God exists." For such a statement to be thinkable, there must be a concept of existence with actual, identifiable properties. It occurred to Leibniz that whether or not the statement "God exists" is true, the very fact that we can think such concepts means that something exists, as concepts are something rather than nothing. But why is there something rather than nothing?[3] There's no reason this had to be the case. Someone must have made it happen intentionally.

To be a little more detailed, the cosmological argument says that God is a necessary being—a being that exists by necessity of his own nature. The universe, on the other hand, has a contingent existence: it could have failed to exist and so needs a cause external to itself to explain why it exists.[4] The cosmological argument for God says that all existence has an explanation and that this explanation is God.

Furthermore, in God's nature, we must find an explanation of what we know to exist. Thought, creativity, and personality exist; therefore, God must be something more than a thoughtless, impersonal force.[5]

William Lane Craig offers a helpful analogy:

> Imagine that you're hiking through the woods and you come across a translucent ball lying on the forest floor. You would naturally wonder how it came to be there. If one of your hiking partners said to you, "Hey, it just exists inexplicably. Don't worry about it!" you'd either think that he was crazy or figure that he just wanted you to keep moving. No one would take seriously the suggestion that the ball existed there with literally no explanation. Now suppose you increase the size of the ball in this story so that it's the size of a car. That wouldn't do anything to satisfy or remove the demand for an explanation. Suppose it were the size of a house. Same problem. Suppose it were the size of a continent or a planet. Same problem. Suppose it were the size of the entire universe. Same problem. Merely increasing the size of the ball does nothing to affect the need of an explanation.[6]

The universe needs an explanation. Christians say that the explanation must be outside of the universe itself because things can't cause themselves to come into being. The cosmological argument says that the universe exists, that everything that exists has an explanation of its existence, and that the explanation of the universe's existence is God. The cosmological argument says that only God's existence can explain why there is something rather than nothing.

4. Kalam Cosmological Argument: Explaining the Cause of the Universe

Kalam Cosmological Argument: an argument for God's existence that begins with the premise that something caused the universe to exist and ends with the conclusion that God is the best explanation for that cause.

The **kalam cosmological argument** was developed by Islamic philosophers in the twelfth century who sought to explain how they could know about the supernatural when our tools of understanding seem to work only inside of nature.[7] The argument says that whatever begins to exist has a cause, the universe began to exist, so therefore it must have a cause. That cause is God.

For most of recorded history, most philosophers and scientists have believed that the universe is eternal, having no cause. It has simply always existed, they believed, just like God himself. Aristotle believed this. He thought that everything that comes into existence had to have come from something and that if we were to go back in time, we would find that everything came from something else, all the way back. There was never a beginning to this: the universe is static and unchanging and has always been this way.[8]

In the twentieth century, though, new advances made it possible to study the universe's origin from a scientific standpoint. Albert Einstein, in developing his **general theory of relativity**, began to realize that the universe was not static but was either expanding or contracting. If it was doing either of these things, it would point strongly to a moment in time in which the universe actually began.

Much of Einstein's thinking was affirmed by the work of astronomer Edwin Hubble, who showed that galaxies are moving farther away from Earth and that the farther they are from Earth, the faster they're moving. This is known as **Hubble's Law**, which he discovered through the phenomenon of **red shift**, in which the light from an object moves toward the red end of the color spectrum as it moves away from us and its wavelengths lengthen. The implication that the universe is expanding led to the development of what we call the **big bang theory**.

Think of an expanding balloon, and then think of what its expansion would look like played in reverse. At some point, it had to have started expanding. The expanding universe, played backward, leads to the same conclusion, except scientists think that at its earliest moment it was much, much smaller (and way more energy filled!) than a balloon.

Many Christians view the big bang as hostile to Christianity, but others are more accepting. Christian apologist Frank Turek, for example, says, "I don't have a problem with the Big Bang because I know who 'banged' it."[9] Interestingly, the famous atheist philosopher Antony Flew, who became a theist later in life, said it was his understanding of the big bang that made him realize that the universe probably had a beginning and that if it had a beginning, it probably had a cause: God. Here's how Flew phrased it:

> When I first met the big-bang theory as an atheist, it seemed to me the theory made a big difference because it suggested that the universe had a beginning and that the first sentence in Genesis ("In the beginning, God created the heavens and the earth")

General Theory of Relativity: Albert Einstein's geometric theory of gravitation, which proposes that space and time are interwoven and can be curved by the presence of massive objects, such as planets and black holes.

Hubble's Law: based on Edwin Hubble's astronomical observations; the law that states that the universe is expanding, i.e., the galaxies within the universe are moving away from one another at a rate directly proportional to the distances between galaxies.

Red Shift: the expansion of the frequency of light toward the red end of the electromagnetic spectrum.

Big Bang Theory: the theory that the universe arose around fourteen billion years ago from an extremely dense state that rapidly expanded and continues to expand today.

was related to an event in the universe. As long as the universe could be comfortably thought to be not only without end but also without beginning, it remained easy to see its existence (and its most fundamental features) as brute facts. And if there had been no reason to think the universe had a beginning, there would be no need to postulate something else that produced the whole thing. But the big-bang theory changed all that. If the universe had a beginning, it becomes entirely sensible, almost inevitable, to ask what produced this beginning.[10]

Today, virtually every scientist, or at least almost every physicist, believes that the universe had a beginning.[11] The kalam cosmological argument builds on this understanding and speculates about what brought the universe into existence. Here's how the argument goes, as Craig states it:

> Whatever begins to exist has a cause.
> The universe began to exist.
> Therefore, the universe has a cause.[12]

The claim "Whatever begins to exist has a cause" seems pretty solid. After all, it's self-evident that physical objects don't just pop into existence without a cause. If they did, we wouldn't be able to conduct successful scientific experiments because we would never know whether our experiment or some random factor caused the effects we observe. It's also clear that nothing can cause itself to begin to exist; in order to do that, it would have to exist before it existed! There are, of course, people who deny that everything that begins has a cause, but they have to pay a high rational price for this belief. They are denying the logic we use to make sense of the material universe.

Second Law of Thermodynamics: a scientific law that states that the amount of usable energy in a closed system will decrease over time.

The second premise, "The universe began to exist," rests on solid ground as well. Einstein's general theory of relativity (that the universe isn't static) and Hubble's red shift (the galaxies are all moving away from each other in every direction) offer evidence for it. Moreover, as J. P. Moreland observes, there is evidence from the **second law of thermodynamics**, which

> in one form states that the amount of useful energy in the universe is being used up. If the universe were infinitely old, it would already have used up all its useful energy and have arrived at a temperature of absolute zero. Since there are many pockets of useful energy (for example, the sun), the universe must be finite in duration. Therefore, there was a beginning when the universe's useful energy was put into it "from the outside."[13]

To be sure, such evidence doesn't prove that the Bible or Christianity is true or that Jesus is God. But it does indicate that the universe was made and that there was a maker.

As authors Sean McDowell and Jonathan Morrow put it,

The Kalam helps narrow the range of possible causes to a being that is nonphysical, spaceless, timeless, changeless, and powerful: If matter began to exist at the moment of creation, then the matter's cause must be nonphysical, or spiritual. Since space itself came into existence at the big bang, space's cause must be spaceless. Since time began at the moment of the big bang, time's cause must be timeless. Since change is a product of time, time's cause must also be changeless.[14]

The amount of energy in the universe is powerful. The amount of matter in the universe is immense. The cause of this power and immensity must be immensely powerful. The kalam cosmological argument says the cause is God.

An Objection to Cosmological Arguments

"If God made the universe, who made God?" You can respond to this common objection by pointing out that the cosmological argument does not claim that *everything* has a cause but that everything that had a *beginning* had a cause. That simply doesn't apply to God, who is a necessary being and therefore without beginning.

Besides that, the one who raises that objection is putting himself into a quandary: if everything needs a cause, and if there is no God, what caused the universe? To say that *everything* had a cause leads to an infinite cycle of cause and effect that could never have a beginning. If there never was a beginning, we could never have reached the point in which you are currently reading this sentence. There must be one eternal uncaused causer, or nothing would have ever come into existence.

Some scientists today, though, are saying that physics tells us that the universe can create itself. Stephen Hawking, whom some consider the greatest scientist alive, says that certain laws of gravity are all that's necessary for the universe to have created itself from nothing.[15] **Quantum physics** shows that it's possible for particles—real atomic matter—to emerge out of a pure vacuum.

The problem, though, is that a vacuum isn't really "nothing," and neither are the laws of physics. It takes energy in a vacuum to produce particles, and that's not nothing. Plus, a vacuum requires space, which isn't nothing either. All of these, including the laws of physics, are as contingent (depending for their existence on things they cannot themselves explain) as everything else in the universe. None of them could be the ultimate explanation that has to stand behind and before every contingent thing.

Quantum Physics: the branch of physics dealing with physical phenomena on the subatomic level, where particles behave in a fashion difficult to quantify and understand using the scientific method.

Design Argument (aka Teleological Argument): an argument for God's existence that begins with the premise that design requires an intelligent designer and ends with the conclusion that God is the best explanation for the observable design within the universe.

5. The Design Argument: Explaining the Physical Order of the Universe

The **design argument** says the world appears to be the product of design and that a designed universe requires an intelligent designer. That designer is God. One important early version of this, from Thomas Aquinas, takes the very simple approach of pointing out that design is apparent to everyone everywhere in almost everything we see. To deny that the world is designed is to deny the obvious, Aquinas said.[16]

> *Intelligent Design:* the study of information, complexity, and design in life and the cosmos; the theory that life could not have arisen by chance and random natural processes but was designed by an intelligent being.

More recently, the design argument has come up in another form, **intelligent design** (ID). Before getting to the particular evidence, it will be helpful to discuss what ID is. Perhaps William Dembski, one of ID's founders, has the best explanation. Dembski is a scientist and philosopher who holds master's degrees in statistics, mathematics, philosophy, and theology and doctoral degrees in mathematics and philosophy. He has conducted postdoctoral research at Princeton University and the Massachusetts Institute of Technology. About ID, Dembski asks and answers,

> Is that radio signal from outer space just random noise or the result of an alien intelligence? Is that chunk of rock just a random chunk of rock or an arrowhead? Is Mount Rushmore the result of wind and erosion or the creative act of an artist? We ask such questions all the time, and we think we can give good answers to them. Yet, when it comes to biology and cosmology, scientists balk at even raising such questions, much less answering them in favor of design. This is especially true of biology. According to well-known evolutionist Francisco Ayala, Darwin's greatest achievement was to show how the organized complexity of organisms could be attained without a designing intelligence. By contrast, ID purports to find patterns in biological systems that signify intelligence. ID therefore directly challenges Darwinism and other materialistic approaches to the origin and evolution of life.[17]

When we look around, we see things that exist, such as rocks, trees, and water. We see events occur, such as the sun rising and rain falling. We notice that some things are constant, such as the law of gravity and, given certain conditions, the point at which water freezes. What are we to make of such observations? How could they happen? First, they could be the result of law, that is, they had to be this way; second, they could be the result of chance accident; or third, they could be the product of design.

Imagine standing at the bottom of the Grand Canyon, gazing at the many eerily beautiful rock formations. You would recognize these formations as the outworking of natural laws resulting in certain water flows and environmental conditions that erode some of the rock, leaving unusual shapes. Now imagine standing at the base of Mount Rushmore, noticing how the rock formation bears a definite resemblance to four US presidents: George Washington, Thomas Jefferson, Teddy Roosevelt, and Abraham Lincoln. You would immediately realize that this was not caused by erosion. Except by design, faces do not appear on mountainsides in such recognizable detail.

So how can we tell whether something has resulted from law, chance, or design? Thomas Aquinas's answer would be something like, "Do you even need to ask if Mount Rushmore was designed? Isn't it obvious?" Still, when it comes to biological systems, evolutionary scientists have asked the question anyway. According to Dembski, the test for design is **specified complexity**.

> *Specified Complexity:* any event that is contingent and complex, and exhibits an independently given pattern.

> An event exhibits specified complexity if it is contingent and therefore not necessary, if it is complex and therefore not readily reproducible by chance, and if it is specified in the sense of exhibiting an independently given pattern. Note that a merely improbable event is not sufficient to eliminate chance—flip a coin long enough and you'll witness a highly complex or improbable event. Even so, you'll have no reason not to attribute it to chance. The important thing about specifications is that they be objectively given and not just imposed on events after the fact. For instance, if an archer fires arrows into a wall, and then we paint bull's-eyes around them, we impose a pattern after the fact. On the other hand, if the targets are set up in advance ("specified"), and then the archer hits them accurately, we know it was by design.[18]

Let's take a look at three ways specified complexity manifests itself: fine-tuning, the privileged planet, and biological information.

Fine-Tuning

The physical constants in the universe are extremely fine-tuned. Fine-tuning is not the same thing as design; it just means that if any of the variables that permit life to exist were, as Craig puts it, "to be altered by a hair's breadth, the delicate balance required for the existence of life would be upset and the universe would be life-prohibiting instead."[19]

Robin Collins, a professor at Messiah College, is trained in both physics and philosophy. In *The Case for a Creator*, Lee Strobel relates a conversation with Collins about fine-tuning:

> "Let's talk about gravity," [Collins] said. "Imagine a ruler, or one of those old-fashioned linear radio dials, that goes all the way across the universe. It would be broken down into one-inch increments, which means there would be billions upon billions upon billions of inches. The entire dial represents the range of force strengths in nature, with gravity being the weakest force and the strong nuclear force that binds protons and neutrons together in the nuclei being the strongest, a whopping ten thousand billion billion billion billion times stronger than gravity. The range of possible settings for the force of gravity can plausibly be taken to be at least as large as the total range of force strengths. Now, let's imagine that you want to move the dial from where it's currently set. Even if you were to move it by only one inch, the impact on life in the universe would be catastrophic."[20]

In a different location, Collins continued,

> Each of the four fundamental forces of nature had to be carefully fine-tuned for life: gravity, electromagnetism, the strong nuclear force, and the weak nuclear force. In particular, the ratio of the electromagnetic force to the gravitational force must be delicately balanced to one part in 10^{40} (that's one part in 10,000,000,000,000,000,000,000,000,000,000,000,000,000). If the ratio varied even slightly, then our universe would not have small and large stars, which are both necessary for a planet to sustain life. How delicate a balance is this? Imagine covering one billion continents the size of North America with coins. Stack the coins in columns that reach to the moon. Paint one coin red and place it in one of the columns. Blindfold a friend and have her attempt to pick it out. The odds are roughly 1 in 10^{40} that she will.[21]

These probabilities are so infinitesimal that it is very hard to imagine such things occurring by chance. In fact, if you think you can imagine them happening by chance, that means you haven't understood how small the probabilities are. Even Paul Davies, a physicist who claims not to be a Christian, says, "It is hard to resist the impression that the present structure of the universe, apparently so sensitive to minor alterations in numbers, has been rather carefully thought out.... The seemingly miraculous concurrence of these numerical values must remain the most compelling evidence for cosmic design."[22]

The Privileged Planet

We seem to live on a "privileged planet," according to authors Guillermo Gonzalez and Jay W. Richards. The planet itself, to paraphrase physicist Freeman Dyson, seems to have known we were coming. As Gonzalez and Richards put it,

> If you were a cosmic chef, your recipe for cooking up a habitable planet would have many ingredients. You would need a rocky planet large enough to hold on to a substantial atmosphere and oceans of water and to retain internal heat for billions of years. You would need the right kind of atmosphere. You would need a large moon to stabilize the tilt of the planet's rotation on its axis. You would need the planet to have a nearly circular orbit around a main sequence star similar to our sun. You would need to give that planet the right kind of planetary neighbors within its star system. And you would need to put that system far from the center, edges, and spiral arms of a galaxy like the Milky Way. You would need to cook it during a narrow window of time in the history of the universe. And so on. This is a partial list, but you get the idea.[23]

And not only is our planet fine-tuned for life but, as Gonzalez and Richards go on to say, we also seem to have been placed in an excellent location for making observations about the rest of the universe. It appears that the Creator wanted us to be discoverers.

Biological Information

Biological information appears to have been designed. When we look at the complexity of DNA, we see that it is full of information. Only rational minds produce information. Francis Collins, the scientist who led the team to map the human genome, delightfully explains the awesome complexity of DNA:

> Bacteria have DNA. Yeast have DNA. So do porcupines, peaches, and people. It is the universal language of all living things.... All of the DNA of an organism is called its genome, and the size of the genome is commonly expressed as the number of base pairs it contains. Think of the twisted helix of DNA as a ladder.... The simplest free-living single-cell organism, such as bacteria, generally pack all their information into a genome of a few million base pairs. Fancier multicellular organisms with more complex body plans require larger genomes to specify those functions. Our own genome stacks up as 3.1 billion rungs of the DNA ladder.[24]

Philosopher Douglas Groothuis further points out that DNA contains genetic information, an example of specified complexity. And only intelligence, not chance, can produce such information.[25] Because DNA isn't a product of necessity (that is, it's scientifically and logically conceivable to think of a world without it) and because DNA could not have been produced by mere chance, it is therefore reasonable to infer design.

Whether we're talking about design on a very large or very small scale, the formal argument for design is the same:

- Design requires a designer.

- The universe exhibits design.

- Therefore, the universe was designed by an intelligent designer.

Two Objections to the Design Argument

"The multiverse would explain away fine-tuning." Scientists such as Max Tegmark and Brian Greene have proposed what they consider to be a possible solution to the incredible odds against life arising from chance processes in this universe: the **multiverse theory**. If there were, in fact, many universes rather than just one, then the chances of life arising in at least one of them would seem to be much greater. Some theories in physics seem to say there might actually be a vast number of different universes, each of them with different histories and even different physical laws. But as William Lane Craig points out,

Multiverse Theory: a theoretical reality that postulates an infinite set of parallel and diverse universes, of which our own universe is just one instantiation.

In order to be scientifically credible, some plausible mechanism must be suggested for generating the many worlds. But if the many worlds hypothesis is to be successful in attributing fine-tuning to chance alone, then the mechanism that generates the many worlds had better not be fine-tuned itself! For if it is, then the problem arises all over again: How do you explain the fine-tuning of the multiverse?[26]

Not only that, but no scientist has ever proposed a way we could check and find out if those other universes actually exist. The physical theories behind them are very far from being proved, and many people are quite sure they could never be proved, at least by any science anyone can imagine. That means that multiverse theory is little more than a guess, and it almost looks like a guess that some people have made in order to avoid believing in a designer. One cosmologist said it clearly: "If there is only one universe you might have to have a fine-tuner. If you don't want God, you'd better have a multiverse."[27]

"Design does not require a designer." Scientists keep on proposing new theories, attempting to explain how things that appear to be designed could have arisen by chance processes. But multiverse theory makes assumptions about the world and about information that are reasonable only if, in fact, things that appear to be designed actually are.

The other major objection to the design argument comes through evolutionary theory. In his 1996 book *The Blind Watchmaker: Why the Evidence of Evolution Reveals a Universe without Design*, famed atheist Richard Dawkins admits that everything in biology appears designed, but he says that whether something appears designed is something we can ascertain only after the fact, like detectives coming upon a crime scene.[28] Yet every time Dawkins attempts his own detective work—namely, to try to prove that such design could have emerged from natural selection and random mutations—he does so, as advocate for intelligent design Stephen Meyer points out, by smuggling in "the guiding hand of an intelligent agent."[29]

For example, when Dawkins tries to show that a computer program could randomly come up with a phrase from Shakespeare, he ignores the fact that he himself has designed the program and that the statement the program "arrived" at is a meaningful one.[30] Dawkins, in effect, accuses creationists of stacking the deck by stacking the deck himself.

Evolutionary theory still faces formidable obstacles, however, in explaining the specified complexity found in living things everywhere. It has not yet actually shown in any detail, either, how one species can evolve into another, more complex one. Evolutionary theorists assume it must happen, but after decades of work, they have never shown that it does or how it could.[31]

> **Moral Argument (aka Axiological Argument):** an argument for God's existence that begins with the premise that objective morality exists and ends with the conclusion that God is the best explanation for the existence of an objective morality.

6. THE MORAL ARGUMENT: EXPLAINING THE MORAL ORDER OF THE UNIVERSE

The **moral argument** for God's existence says that the existence of **objective morality** provides good evidence for the existence of God. Not everyone agrees with this, obviously. Science-fiction writer Glen Cook writes, "More evil gets done in the name of righteousness than any other way."[32] But in order to know this, he must first have a sense of what good and evil, righteousness and unrighteousness, actually are. Where does such a sense come from? Cook denies the existence of God and revelation, but he still recognizes that things are not as they ought to be, that injustice occurs, that bad things happen.

> *Objective Morality:* the belief that morality has a universal and unchanging standard that is independent from human opinion, culture, and sentiment.

But is this sense of oughtness just personal preference? Imagine a person saying, "It's not wrong to torture puppies for fun; it's just not my thing, so I prefer to not do it." Would we consider this to be a valid viewpoint? What would we think of the idea that it's just a matter of personal preference? Most of us would say that's the wrong way to see it. We have a firm and confident sense that torturing puppies is wrong and that personal preference doesn't decide the answer.

Everyone engages in moral thinking. Everyone seems to have a sense of what's right and wrong, of what's good and evil. Everyone seems to view right and wrong as being objectively real. "Objectively real," in this case, means that rightness and wrongness depend on something far deeper and more solid than human opinion.

Therefore, there seems to be a firm foundation for an argument for God's existence that goes like this:

- If objective moral values and duties exist, then God exists.

- Objective moral values and duties exist.

- Therefore, God exists.

Let's look at premise one first: If objective moral values and duties exist, then God exists. The moral law (another way of speaking about moral values and duties) makes sense in the light of God's existence in the same way that speed-limit signs make sense in light of the existence of lawmakers and police. As Sean McDowell and Jonathan Morrow put it, "If God exists, then objective morality is a natural and reasonable inference to make. There seems to be a natural connection between the idea of God as a moral lawgiver and the fact that there is an objective moral law that humans can either violate or obey."[33]

Some people reject God's necessary connection to moral principles, proposing instead a Darwinian explanation for human morality. But this is problematic for several reasons. First, morality is about how we *should* behave. Even if it adequately explains why we behaved a certain way in the past, it cannot explain how we *ought* to behave in the future. In other words, it *describes* but can't *prescribe*. It doesn't even provide a sound basis for saying that it's good that we got to this point in our history!

A morality that is descriptive but not prescriptive could be ignored. Who *cares* what helped people evolve in the past? Why shouldn't we just do what we want and then work to be sure we survive anyway? When it comes to morality, we need prescription, not just description. Plus, moral principles that came about through evolution would always be arbitrary. William Lane Craig explains:

> The most popular form of atheism is naturalism, which holds that the only things that exist are the things described by our best scientific theories. But science is morally neutral; you can't find moral values in a test tube. It follows immediately that moral values don't really exist; they're just illusions of human beings. Even if the atheist is willing to go beyond the bounds of science, why think, given an atheistic worldview, that human beings are morally valuable? On a naturalistic view moral values are just the by-product of biological evolution and social conditioning. Just as a troop of baboons exhibit cooperative and even self-sacrificial behavior because natural selection has determined it to be advantageous in the struggle for survival, so their primate cousins Homo sapiens exhibit similar behavior for the same reason. As a result of sociobiological pressures there has evolved among Homo sapiens a sort of "herd morality," which functions well in the perpetuation of our species. But on the atheistic view there doesn't seem to be anything about Homo sapiens that makes this morality objectively true. If we were to rewind the film of human evolution back to the beginning and start anew, people with a very different set of moral values might well have evolved.[34]

A second objection to the idea that evolution explains morality is the existence of strong similarities in moral codes across cultures. If cultures and societies evolved independently of each other, it is difficult to imagine how countless cultures could have all independently evolved the same moral code. Yet this is precisely what we have: moral commonality across time and societies.

Third, evolution is interested in survival. Yet actions that yield the best chances for survival are not the same as moral actions. Consider altruistic acts. We've all seen people take actions that risk their own survival in order to rescue someone whose survival does not affect their own in any way. Such unselfish acts diminish the rescuer's chance of survival, yet are considered moral.

Now let's look at premise two: Objective moral values and duties do exist. Whenever we claim that someone's action is right or wrong, we are making a moral judgment. Often our judgment is just expressing a preference: "It's wrong of you to hum while you're doing your homework because you are distracting me from doing mine." On the other hand, the statement "It's wrong to steal a person's homework and turn it in to the professor claiming it as one's own" proposes an objective moral value that should be applied, even if stealing is fashionable these days or even if professors don't think it's a big deal. The Nazi Holocaust in Germany, in which millions of innocent people were slaughtered by men wanting to "purify" the nation, was objectively wrong even while many Germans were in agreement that it was just fine.

Still, some reject the idea of objective moral truths by claiming that morality is relative to one's personal or cultural situation. Not only non-Christians make this claim. According to pollster George Barna, more than half of born-again Christians are moral relativists.[35] But **moral relativism** is a breathtakingly naive view to hold. Doug Groothuis explains:

> **Moral Relativism:** the belief that morality is relative to, or defined by, the individual or culture.

IS GOD CHRISTIAN?

Relativism, both cultural and individual, entails that no human act is intrinsically and always wrong. Yet consider these statements: 1. It is always wrong to torture the innocent merely for pleasure. 2. Rape is always wrong. 3. Female genital mutilation is always wrong. If relativism is true, then statements 1–3 cannot be true, since they make absolute, universal and objective moral claims. Therefore, relativism is refuted by a simple modus tollens argument, which can be illustrated by using any one of the previous three statements.[36]

What kind of world would it be, Groothuis wonders, if moral relativism were true? Francis Beckwith and Gregory Koukl respond,

It would be a world in which nothing was wrong—nothing is considered evil or good, nothing worthy of praise or blame. It would be a world in which justice and fairness are meaningless concepts, in which there would be no accountability, no possibility of moral improvement, no moral discourse.[37]

No one would want to live in a world like that. But the only way for moral values to be timeless and absolute is if they have a timeless and absolute source. A timeless, absolute moral lawgiver is just what God is described to be in the Bible. This is how the moral argument comes to the conclusion that God must exist.

But there is more. Objective moral values must also derive from a personal source. Let's say I have a program that causes my computer to shout, "Get back to work!" when it senses a five-minute pause in my typing. It would be irrational to think of the computer as having generated the program on its own. It would be equally irrational to think I owed my computer a duty to type. A person would have had to have programmed it, and if there were any duty to keep typing, it would be a duty I owed to some person. Moral values, in order to be personal and thoughtful, must have a personal and thoughtful source. As professor of philosophy Paul Copan puts it,

A personal, self-aware, purposeful, good God provides the natural and necessary context for the existence of valuable, rights-bearing, morally responsible human persons. That is, personhood and morality are necessarily connected; moral values are rooted in personhood. Without God (a personal being), no persons—and thus no moral values—would exist at all: no personhood, no moral values. Only if God exists can moral properties be realized.[38]

Two Objections to the Moral Argument

"Objective morality doesn't exist." It's easy to say there's no objective morality, but very few people would deny that horrifying acts of evil, such as the Nazi Holocaust, were objectively wrong. Very few people would let a stranger walk out of the coffee shop with their computer without saying, "Hey, stealing is wrong." Very few people would deny that giving loving care and nurture to one's children is the right way to treat them.

Occasionally, you'll run into stubborn people who continue to insist—even when given such examples as the Holocaust, caring for children, or even the theft of their own computer—that even though we *like* the idea of objective morals, they simply do not exist. Usually, though, such people hold to moral relativism, not because they actually believe it but because it helps them feel more comfortable with their disbelief in God. When push comes to shove, though, if someone walks out of the coffee shop with their laptop, they're still going to shout, "That's wrong!"

"Atheists can live good lives without believing in God." Skeptics and atheists often raise this objection, but it only shows that they've misunderstood the moral argument. The issue isn't whether atheists can be moral but whether atheism can *explain* morality. Of course atheists can live according to objectively good moral values while denying God's existence. Atheists can obey traffic laws, love their children, care for their neighbors, and stand against injustice. But as William Lane Craig notes, "The question is not about the necessity of belief in God for objective morality but about the necessity of the *existence* of God for objective morality."[39] Atheists may deny God's existence and live moral lives, but they can do so only in a world of objective morality explained by God's existence. It's like denying the existence of bakers while stuffing one's mouth with delicious puff pastry.

There are people who believe that the cosmological, design, and moral arguments persuasively demonstrate God's existence and yet still feel uncomfortable accepting the Bible's more specific claim that what it says about who God is and what he wants us to be is true for everyone. How do we respond to this objection?

7. But Isn't Religious Belief Just a Cultural Phenomenon?

The arguments questioning whether the Bible's truth is for everyone typically come in one of two forms. First, the prescriptive form of religious pluralism says that all religions are true to those who believe them. Second, the postmodern form says that talk about God isn't expressing truth but rather that it's merely using language based on our own cultural interpretations. In its most extreme form, Postmodernism says that trying to change the beliefs of others does violence to their cultures, which is wrong. Let's take a look at each of these in turn.

> *Religious Pluralism:* the acknowledgment that many different religions exist in today's diverse society.

> *Descriptive Pluralism:* the belief that we should be tolerant of competing religions in order to get along with one another.

Religious Pluralism

"Isn't religious preference just an artifact of where one grows up?" Someone born in Saudi Arabia, say, is much more likely to be a Muslim than a Christian. So doesn't this mean that everyone who believes does so on account of how he or she was brought up rather than on account of what's true? And if so, doesn't that cast doubt on any religion's claim to being true or at least on our ability to *know* if a religion is true?

Religious pluralism is the recognition that different religions exist. Two common forms of religious pluralism are **descriptive pluralism,** which says that the competing claims of various religions cannot all be true, so we must tolerate those with whom we disagree; and **prescriptive pluralism**, which claims that we cannot know any one religion to be exclusively true. One prominent religious pluralist was the philosopher John Hick (1922–2012). Superbly educated, with two doctoral degrees and prestigious teaching positions at Cornell, Cambridge, and Princeton Theological Seminary, Hick became one of the most influential philosophers of religion in our time.

> *Prescriptive Pluralism:* the belief that we should be tolerant of other religions because no single religion can be universally true for everyone.

During his fifteen-year stint at the University of Birmingham in England, Hick met people who were immigrating from all over the world. As he befriended Hindus, Sikhs, and Muslims, he realized that many of them were better people than he judged himself to be. How could these saintly people be ruled out from salvation?

In an effort to help create understanding among religions, Hick helped start a group called All Faiths for One Race (AFFOR). Along the way, he also began questioning the evangelical faith he had embraced as a teenager. Just as the Copernican Revolution overturned the Ptolemaic view that Earth was the center of the solar system, Hick came to believe that we also needed to overturn the idea that Christianity is objectively true for everyone. He wrote,

> The different religious traditions, with their complex internal differentiations, have developed to meet the needs of the range of mentalities expressed in the different human cultures. So long as mankind is gloriously various—which, let us hope, will be always—there will be different traditions of religious faith with their associated forms of worship and lifestyle.[40]

Hick's argument does not, in and of itself, defeat Christianity, but it does seem to undercut the validity of its claim to be true for everyone at all times. How could Christianity be true when most cultures in the world today—indeed, most people in history—never knew about it and never had the opportunity to become Christians?

As an alternative view, Hick developed the idea of **the Real**. The Real, Hick said, represents ultimate reality and is the source of all world religions. Each religion views the Real differently because of its unique cultural understandings.[41] This difference can even cause various

> *Real, the:* defined by John Hick to be ultimate reality and the source of all world religions.

religions to arrive at contradictory conclusions about the Real: "[The Real] cannot be said to be one or many, person or thing, conscious or unconscious, purposive or nonpurposive, substance or process, good or evil, loving or hating," Hick said. "None of these descriptive terms apply literally to the unexperienceable reality that underlies that realm."[42]

As Douglas Groothuis points out, though, if the attributes of the Real are unknowable, how can we know that it explains anything at all, especially the variety of world religions? And if it has no moral properties, how could it reveal to us whether anyone from a given religion is truly saintly?[43]

Alvin Plantinga, an American contemporary of John Hick and a respected philosopher and Christian, insightfully observed that people all over the world seem to have always

---

assumed that their own religion is the true one, and it is only in our own age that people began to widely embrace the idea that all religions are equally valid. If Hick had been born in another culture or time, Plantinga observed, it probably never would have occurred to him to be a religious pluralist. So if our religious beliefs are culturally and historically situated, Hick's belief that no religion has a legitimate claim on ultimate truth is simply a religious viewpoint based on his cultural or historical situation and not actually knowable as true.[44]

At a practical level, though, Hick's argument makes sense to a lot of people. We've all known people who adhered to other religions who seemed genuinely good, and people who adhered to Christianity who seemed genuinely bad. And we've also known people who, while claiming Christianity, mix in so many other religious, cultural, and political assumptions that it's hard to tell what the foundation of their worldview actually is.

Because the particular people we know—Christian or non-Christian—are all over the map in terms of the goodness they manifest, we should probably refrain from judging any given religious system by the particular people who hold to it. Questions such as "Is a particular person living this religion in a holy way?" and "Have there ever been people who lived this religion in a harmful way?" are not as helpful as such questions as "Is this religion livable by everyone?" and "Does this religion describe the contours of the world as it actually exists?"

Hick believed that a genuinely saintly person could be identified by anyone. But this could be so only if some things are true regardless of time and culture and if it is possible for all of us to recognize these things as true (provided our judgment is not clouded by self-deception). In other words, Hick's argument could be true only if "the Real" could truly be known as it actually is. This would require *special* access to some source of truth that lies outside of God and the Bible. But this is to claim that religious truth can be reliably known, which contradicts the pluralist claim to begin with. It's a bewildering but important point to keep in mind.

The central question, then, goes back to chapters 2 and 3 of this volume. Christians are not arguing that other religions are devoid of truth; rather, they claim that biblical Christianity more accurately describes the contours of the world than other religious systems. Christians source this claim based on what the Bible says about God, human beings, and the world, and how this understanding has worked itself out in culture since the time the Bible was written.

> **Modernism:** a broad term used to describe a range of arts, attitudes, philosophies, and cultural moods that emerged following the eighteenth-century Enlightenment. It is characterized by a strong belief in rationalism, empiricism, science, and technological progress as well as skepticism toward the supernatural, special revelation, and the authority of religion.

Postmodernism

"Isn't talk about God just … talk?" Postmodernists don't like to be categorized or defined, but still they have some things in common. One of those points in common is a kind of weariness with **modernism**, especially the use of science and rationalism to seek absolute truth. **Postmodernism** typically says that when we claim to know objective reality, we are just using language to construct our own meaning based on our culture and life experiences.

Postmodernist professor Jacques Derrida proposed a way to deconstruct any text or statement to uncover how it is culturally bound and therefore not tied to any truth. Derrida's theory of **deconstruction** influenced a group of theologians in 1960s England. Among them was a bishop named John A. T. Robinson, who wrote a book called *Honest to God*. In it, Robinson tried to reform Christianity to be consistent with postmodern assumptions.[45] Those who agreed with Robinson's thinking started a movement known as the **Death of God theology**. According to theologian Graham Ward, they saw "the potential of [Derrida's] deconstruction for furthering their project of announcing the end of theology [the death of God]."[46]

According to Derrida's theory of deconstruction, books are just words connected with words, flowing out of subjective experiences and not connected with any actual reality. Another influential Postmodernist, Jean-François Lyotard, said that communication is really just "language-games."[47] That includes the Bible: it's just another book written by mere men who were locked in their own cultures, experiences, and languages. The biblical authors may have thought they were communicating eternal truths about God and humanity, but the Death of God theologians said they were just writing about their own subjective experiences.

Now, if the words of the Bible refer only to other words in a textual setting and do not actually describe external realities such as God, then God is not the Supreme Being who is literally "up there" in heaven somewhere; rather, he comes into existence when we talk about him. Christianity is not about God, sin, and redemption. If it's about anything (which some Postmodernists aren't even sure of), then it's about something such as loving people, but on the whole, God, sin, and redemption are culturally bound concepts that have no ultimate meaning.[48]

> *Postmodernism:* a skeptical worldview, founded as a reaction to modernism, that is suspicious of metanarratives and teaches that ultimate reality is inaccessible, knowledge is a social construct, and truth claims are political power plays.

> *Deconstruction:* a method of literary analysis that questions the ability of language to represent reality adequately and seeks to discern and expose the purported underlying ideologies of a text.

> *Death of God Theology:* a theological movement that believes in a god who transcends all being and thus technically does not exist.

Although Derrida's thinking is popular in some academic circles, many notable philosophers have made good arguments to the contrary. German philosopher Edmund Husserl, for example, argues that thoughts are about things, and they are intended to be about things. Objects and thoughts have qualities that present themselves consistently to the mind, no matter who is thinking about them. If love has no definable essence, people who try to "love" their neighbors might end up killing them—and there would be no objective way to know whether this kind of "love" was right or wrong, true or twisted.

Whatever your thoughts about Postmodernism in general, it is clear that Scripture views talk about God in a different way than other kinds of talk. It isn't just chatty conversation to pass the time; rather, it's intended to communicate truth that applies to all people at all times in all cultures.

Some, though, see any attempt to bring about change in other cultures as "cultural genocide," implying that it is always negative. This extreme form of Postmodernism implies that trying to bring Jesus into a culture that doesn't know about him would be harmful by definition. Is this the case? Extreme Postmodernists often focus on instances of Christian missionaries who, even though their intentions may have been good, did things that brought harm to the people and cultures they were trying to reach.[49] Scholars have found, however, that most of the blame laid at the feet of Christian missionaries for cultural clashes and oppressive behavior lies with colonial or trading activity, not with missions.[50] In the Age of Enlightenment, European colonists and traders, convinced of their superiority in securing human progress, thought it was their special duty to "help" the "natives" become as good as they believed themselves to be.

When Charles Darwin came along, his ideas about the survival of the fittest were like peanut butter to the Enlightenment's jelly. The Enlightenment's "sweetness" was now "sticky" because it was thought to be scientifically accurate to say that the European races were more highly evolved than other races. Such a view is unbelievable to us today, but Darwin believed it, and many others did as well.

It is no secret that one of Darwin's intentions was to show that Europeans were, in fact, superior. After all, the subtitle of his most famous book, *Origin of Species*, is *The Preservation of Favored Races in the Struggle for Life*. Scholars such as Stewart Gill now believe that such Darwinian thinking is largely responsible for the oppressive policies of aboriginal people in Australia, for example.[51] To the extent that missionary societies were involved, it was because they were co-opted by traders and governments to carry out policies of cultural supremacy. Even into the twentieth century, atheists such as Bertrand Russell thought it was a duty to "civilize" native peoples, and, importantly, he saw Christianity as an obstacle in doing this.[52] In fact, the use of the word *civilize*, from an Enlightenment view, means making progress stripped of religious faith.[53] There may have been racist missionaries, but racism in the form of **cultural imperialism** is more properly laid at the feet of Enlightenment rationalism than of Christian missions.

Cultural Imperialism: the belief that one's culture or race is superior to others.

In our fallen world, it should not surprise us to find that some Christian missionaries acted abusively toward those they set out to reach. But we should not let this obscure the fact that Christian missionaries have done a great deal of good in bringing freedom, health, and peace to cultures around the world. In fact, it is now widely known that Christian missionaries were the only ones to consistently work to stop the systematic enslavement of native populations, even to the point of, as in the case of medical missionary David Livingston, trying to find alternative, legitimate business activity for slave traders so they would stop their hideous work.[54] Moreover, contrary to accounts of missionaries forcing natives to act like Europeans, it was missionaries who helped preserve native music, culture, and language.[55]

Why then all this nasty opposition to missionaries? One historical reason is that missionaries stood against the sexual and economic exploitation of natives to which the "civilized" European colonists and traders thought they were entitled.[56] For all his faults, even Charles

Darwin blamed opposition to missionary efforts on the licentiousness of those who wished to exploit native women.[57]

8. WHAT SHOULD CHRISTIANS DO?

Wow. We've covered a lot of ground in this chapter, from philosophical arguments for God's existence to how morality proceeds from God's nature and character to responses to arguments about how the religions of different cultures disprove biblical revelation about God. The question now is what to *do* with all this information.

True north is true north for everyone, regardless of culture. God's revelation represents true north in a spiritual and cultural sense. C. S. Lewis showed that despite their differences, cultures all over the world largely seem to operate by the same moral laws, with similar understandings of the need to do good to others, duties to family and leaders, justice, duties to future generations, good faith, truth telling, and mercy.[58] What explains this? Because God created all humans in his own image, Christianity says, an ethical system based on his character will be resident in every soul, across all cultures, at all times. Calvin D. Linton, onetime professor at George Washington University, found that, in fact, such a basic pattern of ethical codes exists:

> Because God created all humans in his own image, Christianity says, an ethical system based on his character will be resident in every soul, across all cultures, at all times.

> There is a basic pattern of similarity among [ethical codes]. Such things as murder, lying, adultery, cowardice are, for example, almost always condemned. The universality of the ethical sense itself (the "oughtness" of conduct), and the similarities within the codes of diverse cultures indicate a common moral heritage for all mankind which materialism or naturalism cannot explain.[59]

If Christianity alone can explain objective morality, are we not obligated to try to spread it? Do we have any right to withhold good from those who haven't heard? Of course, we ought to act in a culturally sensitive way, but the good news about Jesus is what the world truly needs and desperately seeks. Here are two practical implications as we draw this chapter to a close.

Truth Is True in Practical Ways, Not Just in the Spiritual Realm

As authors Darrow Miller, Bob Moffitt, and Scott D. Allen say, "All nations, to some degree, hold to destructive, false beliefs, even nations where the church is active and prosperous."[60] When God's principles are brought to bear, humans flourish, even when those promoting God's principles lack a full understanding of their implications.

For example, Japanese immigrants to the Dominican Republic are doing far better and are far more prosperous than native farmers, after just a few decades. Their belief that hard work and perseverance lead to success was superior to the fatalistic belief system of the local farmers who believed that they would always be poor and that they could never succeed because of the hardships they faced.[61]

Health care in America, where people are more likely to hold to a belief that human life is valuable, is better than in India, where it is believed that humans are dispensable.[62] The teachings of the Bible have ended cycles of revenge and blood feuding in the remote jungles of Papua New Guinea.[63] Air and water pollution is far worse in China, cutting the life span in some parts of the country by more than five years, than in nations that have embraced a biblical value of caring for the environment.[64]

As an American, I must also be willing to look at my own nation through a biblical lens. In my country, abortion policies have led to the murder of tens of millions of tiny persons, all in the pursuit of sexual activity without consequences.[65] If humans are truly made in God's image, and if, as Dr. Seuss's Horton so wisely said, "A person's a person no matter how small," then this is nothing short of a holocaust. Part of spreading the good news is working to establish the dignity and value of all people, no matter how small.

Discipleship Is a Command, Not a Suggestion

People are incalculably devious in finding ways to suppress the truth (Rom. 1). If we knew of a coming tsunami, though, how could we justify failing to warn people to leave the beach? Similarly, if we know spiritual truth and fail to share it with people caught in the grip of false religions and philosophies, wouldn't that be wrong?

> If we knew of a coming tsunami, how could we justify failing to warn people to leave the beach? Similarly, if we know spiritual truth and fail to share it with people caught in the grip of false religions and philosophies, wouldn't that be wrong?

In Matthew 28:18–20, Jesus told his disciples, "All authority in heaven and on earth has been given to me. Go therefore and make disciples of all nations, baptizing them in the name of the Father and of the Son and of the Holy Spirit, teaching them to observe all that I have commanded you." In Luke 24:47, Jesus said, "Repentance and forgiveness of sins should be proclaimed in his name to all nations." In Acts 1:8, he told believers, "You will receive power when the Holy Spirit has come upon you, and you will be my witnesses in Jerusalem and in all Judea and Samaria, and to the end of the earth."

Jesus is good news for everyone, everywhere. Scripture says Satan has deceived the nations into believing what is untrue (Rev. 20:1–3),[66] but the gospel promises that God, in Christ, has made a way of freedom. John 8:36 says, "If the Son sets you free, you will be free indeed." The good news is good news for everyone, even the most vulnerable. Jesus said, "Let the little children come to me and do not hinder them, for to such belongs the kingdom of heaven" (Matt. 19:14). The disabled are also welcome (Luke 5:18–20)[67] as are outcasts (Luke 5:12–14).[68]

According to English Christian leader John Stott, God is a God of mission. God is fulfilling the promise given to Abraham that through his revelation, all nations of the earth would be blessed. Stott says this understanding

> condemns all our petty parochialism and narrow nationalism, our racial pride (whether white or black), our condescending paternalism and arrogant imperialism. How dare we adopt a hostile or scornful or even indifferent attitude to any person of

another color or culture if our God is the God of "all the families of the earth?" We need to become global Christians with a global vision, for we have a global God.[69]

So is God Christian? Not in the sense that humans are (or can be) by becoming saved and forgiven followers of Jesus Christ. But is the God of Christianity the real God of all reality? As we have seen, there are very good reasons to believe he exists as the Bible reveals him. His truth—made known through Jesus Christ, the Word of God made flesh—changes people and sets them free in every way a person can be set free. This is good news for all of eternity, and it is good news every day, everywhere, throughout all the earth.

ENDNOTES

1. Desmond Tutu, *God Is Not a Christian: And Other Provocations* (New York: HarperOne, 2011), 6.

2. Bruce Demarest, "General Revelation," in *Evangelical Dictionary of Theology*, ed. Walter A. Elwell (Grand Rapids, MI: Baker Academic, 2001), 1019–21.

3. William Lane Craig, *On Guard: Defending Your Faith with Reason and Precision* (Colorado Springs, CO: David C Cook, 2010), 53.

4. Craig, *On Guard*, 55.

5. For a thorough explanation of this complicated argument, see Lois Frankel, "From a Metaphysical Point of View: Leibniz and the Principle of Sufficient Reason," *The Southern Journal of Philosophy* 24, no. 3 (1986): 321–33; and other essays reprinted in *Gottfriend Wilhelm Leibniz: Critical Assessments*, ed. Roger S. Woolhouse (New York: Routledge, 1994).

6. Craig, *On Guard*, 56–57.

7. Norman L. Geisler, *Baker Encyclopedia of Christian Apologetics* (Grand Rapids, MI: Baker, 1999), 399. *Kalam* is the Arabic word for "discourse."

8. Aristotle developed a version of the cosmological argument, as mentioned above, but his version doesn't depend on when things are first caused. It says instead that there has to be an uncaused cause operating at all times. Interestingly, Einstein's equations pointed to a universe that was not static. However, because this contradicted the scientific consensus of his day, Einstein added the "cosmological constant" to his theory to make it fit the prevailing assumption. Many years later, Edwin Hubble showed that the universe was not static. Einstein realized his error: instead of trusting his numbers, he had altered his theory. He later called his cosmological constant the biggest mistake of his career.

9. Frank Turek makes this statement in his lecture at the Summit Student Conferences. He discusses this issue of the big bang in chap. 3 of a book he coauthored with Norman Geisler, *I Don't Have Enough Faith to Be an Atheist* (Wheaton, IL: Crossway, 2004).

10. Antony Flew and Roy Abraham Varghese, *There Is a God: How the World's Most Notorious Atheist Changed His Mind* (San Francisco: HarperOne, 2007), 136.

11. In a January 2012 issue of *New Scientist*, Lisa Grossman reports that every model of the universe assumes a beginning, "Why Physicists Can't Avoid a Creation Event," www.newscientist.com/article/mg21328474.400-why-physicists -cant-avoid-a-creation-event.html. In a December 2012 issue of the same publication, Marcus Chown reviews research from cosmologists Alex Vilenkin and Audrey Mithani, offering three reasons the universe cannot have existed forever, "Before the Big Bang: Something or Nothing," www.newscientist.com/article/mg21628932.000-before-the-big-bang -something-or-nothing.html.

12. William Lane Craig, "Must the Beginning of the Universe Have a Personal Cause? A Rejoinder," Reasonable Faith, www.reasonablefaith.org/must-the-beginning-of-the-universe-have-a-personal-cause-a-rejoinder.

13. J. P. Moreland, "Does the Cosmological Argument Show There Is a God?," in Ted Cabal et al., eds., *The Apologetics Study Bible* (Nashville: B&H, 2007), 806.

14. Sean McDowell and Jonathan Morrow, *Is God Just a Human Invention? And Seventeen Other Questions Raised by the New Atheists* (Grand Rapids, MI: Kregel, 2010), 78–79.

15. This is obviously a simplification of Hawking's argument. If you'd like to go into detail, see Stephen Hawking and Leonard Mlodinow, *The Grand Design* (New York: Bantam, 2010), especially chap. 6, 121–46, "Choosing Our Universe."

16. See Thomas Aquinas, *Summa Theologica*, trans. Fathers of the English Dominican Province (Benziger Bros. ed., 1947), Treatise on the Creation. Access online at www.ccel.org/ccel/aquinas/summa.

17. William A. Dembski, "Intelligent Design: A Brief Introduction," in *Evidence for God: 50 Arguments for Faith from the Bible, History, Philosophy, and Science*, ed. William A. Dembski and Michael R. Licona (Grand Rapids, MI: Baker, 2010), 104.

18. Dembski, "Intelligent Design: A Brief Introduction," 105.

19. Craig, *On Guard*, 109.

20. Lee Strobel, *The Case for a Creator: A Journalist Investigates Scientific Evidence That Points toward God* (Grand Rapids, MI: Zondervan, 2004), 131–32.

21. Hugh Ross, *The Creator and the Cosmos* (Colorado Springs, CO: NavPress, 1995), 117, quoted in McDowell and Morrow, *Is God Just a Human Invention?*, 96.

22. Paul Davies, *God and the New Physics* (New York: Simon & Schuster, 1983), 189, quoted in Lee Strobel, *The Case for a Creator: A Journalist Investigates Scientific Evidence That Points toward God* (Grand Rapids, MI: Zondervan, 2004), 125.

23. Guillermo Gonzalez and Jay W. Richards, "Designed for Discovery," in *Evidence for God: 50 Arguments for Faith from the Bible, History, Philosophy, and Science*, ed. William A. Dembski and Michael R. Licona (Grand Rapids, MI: Baker, 2010), 102.

24. Francis Collins, *The Language of Life: DNA and the Revolution in Personalized Medicine* (New York: Harper Perennial, 2011), 6.

25. Douglas R. Groothuis, *Christian Apologetics: A Comprehensive Case for Biblical Faith* (Downers Grove, IL: IVP Academic, 2011), 312–13.

26. Craig, *On Guard*, 117–18.

27. Bernard Carr, quoted in Tim Folger, "Science's Alternative to an Intelligent Creator: The Multiverse Theory," *Discover Magazine*, December, 2008, discovermagazine.com/2008/dec/10-sciences-alternative-to-an-intelligent-creator.

28. Richard Dawkins, *The Blind Watchmaker: Why the Evidence of Evolution Reveals a Universe without Design* (New York: Norton, 1996). See especially chap. 1, "Explaining the Very Improbable."

29. Stephen C. Meyer, *Darwin's Doubt: The Explosive Origin of Animal Life and the Case for Intelligent Design* (New York: HarperOne, 2013), 185.

30. Meyer, *Darwin's Doubt*, 185–86.

31. For obvious reason, this point is a tender spot for those who believe that all life arose spontaneously and in an unguided fashion from a common ancestor. Those who say new species can and do evolve from other species do so by shifting the definition of species. An interesting essay on the topic written by James Tours, one of the most respected chemists in the world (and a believing Christian, though not a proponent of intelligent design), may be found at www.jmtour.com/personal-topics/the-scientist-and-his-"theory"-and-the-christian-creationist-and-his-"science"/. Tours says he does not understand macroevolution and has not found anyone else who understands it either, even though that person might not be willing to admit it in public.

32. Glen Cook, *Dreams of Steel, The Chronicles of the Black Company*, bk. 5 (New York: Tor Books, 1990), 123.

33. McDowell and Morrow, *Is God Just a Human Invention?*, 206.

34. Craig, *On Guard*, 131–32.

35. "Barna Survey Examines Changes in Worldview among Christians over the Past 13 Years," March 6, 2009, www.barna.org/barna-update/article/21-transformation/252-barna-survey-examines-changes-in-worldview-among-christians-over-the-past-13-years#.UfFolo0snTY.

36. Groothuis, *Christian Apologetics*, 340. *Modus tollens* is an argument form that says that if a statement is true, its opposite is untrue. So if there are valid examples of acts we know to be always morally wrong, then it is by definition untrue to say that no moral act is always wrong.

37. Francis Beckwith and Gregory Koukl, *Relativism: Feet Firmly Planted in Mid-Air* (Grand Rapids, MI: Baker, 1998), 69.

38. Paul Copan, "The Moral Argument for God's Existence," in *Evidence for God: 50 Arguments for Faith from the Bible, History, Philosophy, and Science*, ed. William A. Dembski and Michael R. Licona (Grand Rapids, MI: Baker, 2010), 22.

39. Craig, *On Guard*, 134.

40. John Hick, *God Has Many Names* (Philadelphia: Westminster, 1982), 21.

41. Groothuis, *Christian Apologetics*, 578–86.

42. John Hick, *An Interpretation of Religion: Human Responses to the Transcendent* (New York: Oxford University Press, 1989), 350, quoted in Groothuis, *Christian Apologetics*, 580.

43. Groothuis, *Christian Apologetics*, 581, 584. As a side note, like Kant, Hick believed that the world, in and of itself, was ultimately inaccessible. Humans are sensory beings. We can have sensory experiences of the world, but as sensory beings, it is impossible to get beyond our sensory perceptions about the world and get at the world as it actually is. Hick thought that the reason we have different, even contradictory, views about God is because none of us have direct access (that is, access apart from sensory perception) to ultimate reality. We all have mitigated access to the divine, but none of us have unmitigated access. There is a "god," but no one can say if that god is personal or impersonal, one or many, substance or process, good or evil. All interpretations are valid. Every expression is a manifestation of the Real.

44. Alvin Plantinga, "Pluralism: A Defense of Religious Exclusivism," in *The Philosophical Challenge of Religious Diversity*, ed. Kevin Meeker and Philip Quinn (New York: Oxford University Press, 1999), 172–92.

45. Besides Robinson, other "Death of God" theologians include William Hamilton, Thomas J. J. Altizer, Mark C. Taylor, Robert Scharlemann, Charles Winquist, Max Meyer, and Carl Raschke.

IS GOD CHRISTIAN?

46. Graham Ward, "Deconstructive Theology," in *The Cambridge Companion to Postmodern Theology*, ed. Kevin J. Vanhoozer (Cambridge, UK: Cambridge University Press, 2003), 76.

47. Jean-François Lyotard, *The Postmodern Condition: A Report on Knowledge* (Minneapolis: University of Minnesota, 1984). If you're interested in exploring this idea further, Lyotard's ideas on language games find their genesis in the work of another philosopher, Ludwig Wittgenstein.

48. A good example of "Death of God theology" can found in Mark C. Taylor, "A Postmodern Theology," in *From Modernism to Postmodernism: An Anthology*, ed. Lawrence E. Cahoone, 2nd ed. (Malden, MA: Blackwell, 2003), 435–46.

49. Among examples cited of the abuses of native populations were the practice of forcing native children into mission schools (which then forbade the use of their native language in favor of English), compelling converts to wear European-style clothing, and prohibiting many cultural rituals and practices. It is fair to ask, however, whether this was actually an attempt to spread Christianity or to force conformity to Western cultural norms. Not all missionaries were engaged in trying to Westernize their converts. Notable examples, such as the Jesuit "reductions" in Paraguay and the work of Bartolomé de Las Casas in advocating for native populations against Spanish abuse, show how European missionaries were engaged in defending the rights of native peoples.

50. Philip J. Sampson, *6 Modern Myths about Christianity and Western Civilization* (Downers Grove, IL: InterVarsity, 2001), 94. The entirety of chap. 4, "The Missionaries," should be examined carefully.

51. Sampson, *6 Modern Myths*, 96–97. See also Stewart Gill, "Conquerors or Saviours?," in *Kategoria* 7 (1997): 9–26, available online at tgc-documents.s3.amazonaws.com/kategoria/kategoria7.pdf.

52. Sampson, *6 Modern Myths*, 96.

53. Sampson, *6 Modern Myths*, 96.

54. Sampson, *6 Modern Myths*, 102–3.

55. Sampson, *6 Modern Myths*, 109.

56. For a specifically documented firsthand account, read about how missionaries helped the native Dani people in Papua New Guinea protect their possessions from Dutch soldiers who otherwise felt free to plunder the native populations in David L. Scovill, *The Amazing Danis: A Hidden Mountain Tribe Becomes a Modern Day People of Faith* (Maitland, FL: Xulon, 2007).

57. Charles Darwin, *The Voyage of the "Beagle"* (Geneva: Heron, 1845), 414–15.

58. C. S. Lewis, *The Abolition of Man* (San Francisco: HarperSanFrancisco, 1974), 83–102.

59. Carl F. H. Henry, ed., *Baker's Dictionary of Christian Ethics* (Grand Rapids, MI: Baker, 1973), 620.

60. Darrow L. Miller, Bob Moffitt, and Scott D. Allen, *The Worldview of the Kingdom of God* (Seattle: YWAM, 2005), 104.

61. Miller, Moffitt, and Allen, *The Worldview of the Kingdom of God*, 103.

62. See Visha Mangalwadi, *India: The Grand Experiment* (Farnham, UK: Pippa Rann Books, 1997), available online at www.revelationmovement.com/learn/pdf/india/india-the-grand-experiment.pdf.

63. See David L. Scovill, *The Amazing Danis: A Hidden Mountain Tribe Becomes a Modern Day People of Faith* (Maitland, FL: Xulon, 2007). See especially 17, "Enemies Reconciled."

64. Calum Mcleod, "In China, Air Pollution Report Brings Despair, Humor," *USA Today*, July 9, 2013, www.usatoday.com/story/news/world/2013/07/09/china-air-pollution-study-fujian/2503319/.

65. Daniel W. Kucera, O.S.B, "Abortion and the Unraveling of American Society," Priests for Life, www.priestsforlife.org/magisterium/kucera.htm.

66. Revelation 20:1–3: "I saw an angel coming down from heaven, holding in his hand the key to the bottomless pit and a great chain. And he seized the dragon, that ancient serpent, who is the devil and Satan, and bound him for a thousand years, and threw him into the pit, and shut it and sealed it over him, so that he might not deceive the nations any longer, until the thousand years were ended. After that he must be released for a little while."

67. Luke 5:18–20: "Behold, some men were bringing on a bed a man who was paralyzed, and they were seeking to bring him in and lay him before Jesus, but finding no way to bring him in, because of the crowd, they went up on the roof and let him down with his bed through the tiles into the midst before Jesus. And when he saw their faith, he said, 'Man, your sins are forgiven you.'"

68. Luke 5:12–14: "While he was in one of the cities, there came a man full of leprosy. And when he saw Jesus, he fell on his face and begged him, 'Lord, if you will, you can make me clean.' And Jesus stretched out his hand and touched him, saying, 'I will; be clean.' And immediately the leprosy left him. And he charged him to tell no one, but 'go and show yourself to the priest, and make an offering for your cleansing, as Moses commanded, for a proof to them.'"

69. John R. W. Stott, "The Living God Is a Missionary God," in *You Can Tell the World: A Mission Reader*, ed. James E. Berney (Downers Grove, IL: InterVarsity, 1979), 32. Read the essay online at www.worldevangelicals.org/resources/rfiles/res3_425_link_1342020737.pdf.

CHAPTER 11

11

SUPERNATURAL GOOD AND EVIL

1. OTHERWORLDLY BELIEFS

"I very much believe in ghosts. There is no question in my mind that they exist," said my classmate emphatically. I was shocked. This wasn't grade school. We were both enrolled in a PhD program, and my classmate had made it clear that as a skeptic and liberal political activist, she had no use for spiritual things, at least those of the Christian variety.

It seemed odd, though: How could my classmate believe in supernatural beings but express skepticism about God or miracles? Even though she was very smart, my classmate did not have a coherent belief system. She was not alone. Many modern people struggle with biblical accounts of the supernatural: angelic appearances, unexplainable and timely divine interventions in the physical world, demon possession, and, most incredible of all, the resurrection of the dead. They wonder, *Haven't accounts such as the Red Sea parting and Lazarus returning to life been disproved by science?*

Age of Enlightenment: an eighteenth-century intellectual movement that emphasized reason, science, and individualism over tradition and religious authority.

Since the **Age of Enlightenment**, some have tried to present a Christianity minus the supernatural. With good intention and respect for Jesus of Nazareth, they wanted to champion the moral teaching of Christianity to those who were skeptical of the supernatural. For example, Thomas Jefferson wrote a "Bible," titled *The Life and Morals of Jesus of Nazareth*, consisting of the Gospels with all references to miracles and Jesus's deity removed. In a letter to John Adams, Jefferson trumpeted his achievement as "forty-six pages, of pure and unsophisticated doctrines," saying, "In extracting the pure principles which he taught, we should have to strip off the artificial vestments in which they have been muffled."[1]

If what we have seen so far in this volume has any merit, though, Christianity without the supernatural is like a symphony with no instruments or like snow skiing without snow: the supernatural is a central ingredient that brings out the flavor of everything else. The apostle Paul, for example, stakes the validity of the Christian faith on whether Christ bodily rose from the dead (1 Cor. 15). Without this miraculous event, we are still in our sins, he said.

Further, the Bible describes miraculous events not just to impress people with God's power but also to display how God uses his power to restore all things to himself. As pastor Tim Keller puts it,

> We modern people think of miracles as the suspension of the natural order, but Jesus meant them to be the restoration of the natural order. The Bible tells us that God did not originally make the world to have disease, hunger, and death in it. Jesus has come to redeem where it is wrong and heal the world where it is broken. His miracles are not just proofs that he has power but also wonderful foretastes of what he is going to do with that power. Jesus' miracles are not just a challenge to our minds, but a promise to our hearts, that the world we all want is coming.[2]

Jesus's healing of sick people showed his desire to restore things to rights. His turning of barrels of water into wine showed an attitude of abundance; Jesus lavished the wedding feast with barrel after barrel of the finest wine, showing up the Greek god of wine and son of Zeus, Dionysius (John 2:1–11). And Jesus's walking on the water showed that he, not Baal, was the master of nature (Matt. 14:22–33).

The Bible does not seem interested in offering just a moral philosophy; it tells of a God who displayed his power in creation and continues to show it today. In this chapter, we'll journey into the heart of the Bible's supernatural claims, focusing on how God relates to the world. We'll then tackle the main arguments used to deny the supernatural, explore the question of miracles (most notably, the resurrection of Christ), and delve briefly into the reality

SUPERNATURAL GOOD AND EVIL

of supernatural evil (Satan, demons, and demon possession). Our goal is twofold: first, to explore evidence of the Bible's truth, and second and most important, to restore our amazement at how the Bible demonstrates Christ's transformative power to this very day.

2. The Materialist/Naturalist Challenge to the Supernatural

Christianity is quite different from other faiths in that it relies heavily on miracles to provide proof of faith in ways other religions, such as Islam, do not. The story of Islam begins with Muhammad receiving divine visions and communicating with the angel Gabriel, and the Quran affirms that prophets of old performed many miracles.[3] The Quran acknowledges Jesus's miracles too,[4] but Muhammad was a prophet, not a miracle worker.[5] Professor of philosophy Oliver Leaman observes, "Islam as a religion does not make much use of miracles."[6] Muhammad claimed to be greater than Jesus, but as the Christian philosopher Blaise Pascal puts it, "Any man can do what Muhammad has done; for he performed no miracles.… No man can do what Christ has done."[7]

In the Greek language, the word for "**miracle**," *simaios*, means "sign." As author and speaker Eric Metaxas phrases it, "Miracles are signs, and like all signs, they are never about themselves; they're about whatever they are pointing toward. Miracles point to something *beyond* themselves. But to what? To God himself."[8]

> **Miracle:** a supernatural sign or event that is intended to highlight the power and goodness of God.

Author Stephen Davis points out that Scripture shows God's relating to the world in four primary ways: (1) bringing the world into existence, (2) sustaining its existence, (3) acting through natural causes in the world, and (4) acting miraculously or outside of natural causes in the world.[9] In other words, God is more than the fuse lighter of the big bang; he shapes, sustains, and cares for the world he made.

With today's mind-set of scientific investigation, many claim that faith simply cannot be proved. "Faith is believing what you know ain't so," Mark Twain famously said.[10] Many today follow Twain's dictum in conceiving of religion as that which relies on unsubstantiated belief or even ignorance, and science as the systematic, impartial application of reason. Science, according to this narrative, rescues the world from superstition and backward thinking.

To atheists, disproving miracles is an important strategy in getting people to give up their God beliefs. But atheists have their beliefs too. In fact, underlying arguments against the supernatural in this common way of thinking are two interrelated assumptions:

(1) **Materialism**, which focuses on *being*, says that everything that exists is purely material and that nothing that is immaterial (such as God) exists, and

> **Materialism:** the belief that reality is composed solely of matter.

(2) **Naturalism**, which focuses on *knowing*, says that everything that exists is composed of natural entities that

can be explained and justified through scientific investigation. Anything said to exist outside of nature (such as God) is thought by naturalists to either not exist or to be unknowable.[11]

Those who embrace materialist/naturalist assumptions find it impossible to believe in any supernatural world. In fact, they define reality in such a way as to exclude the supernatural by definition. Harvard paleontologist Richard Lewontin admits, "Materialism is absolute, for we cannot allow a Divine Foot in the door."[12] Everything is material, the famed Edward O. Wilson asserted, "including the mind and all its spiritual products."[13] It is important to remember that materialists/naturalists do not prove that the supernatural does not exist; they *assume* it does not exist and build their worldview on that assumption. And if nothing supernatural exists, then the Christian conception of God vaporizes as well, like the clearing away of a thick fog, revealing what is real, to the minds of materialists/naturalists.

Believing that all life evolved from nonlife, that only the material world exists, and that everything has a natural cause can lead people to look down on those who believe in the supernatural as people who just don't "get it" and ought not be taken seriously. For example, Richard Dawkins offered a crowd at an atheist rally the following advice: "Mock them, ridicule them, in public ... with contempt."[14]

To support their convictions, materialists/naturalists often turn to the arguments of philosopher David Hume (1711–1776), who objects to the existence of miracles both "in principle" and "in fact." His primary "in principle" objection concerns humanity's alleged uniform experience against miracles. Nature, he suggests, develops in a uniform fashion. Such a world leaves no room for miracles, and so therefore they most likely have not occurred.[15]

Hume then made four "in fact" arguments against miracles:

> First, no historical miracle has been sufficiently attested by honest and reliable men who are of such social standing that they would have a great deal to lose by lying. Second, people crave miraculous stories and will gullibly believe absurd stories, which is evidenced by the sheer number of false tales of miraculous events. Third, miracles only occur among barbarous people. And fourth, miracles occur in all religions and thus cancel each other out, since they espouse contradictory doctrines.[16]

Materialists/naturalists consider these arguments to be a tour de force of intellectual reasoning and therefore irrefutable evidence of Christianity's deep flaws. Is there a response?

3. RESPONDING TO THE MATERIALIST/NATURALIST CHALLENGE

In this short space, we'll focus on five responses to the materialist/naturalist challenge.

Hume's Arguments against Miracles Are Flawed

Our first response to the materialist/naturalist challenge is that Hume's reasonable-sounding arguments are not, in fact, reasonable. Let's take each argument in turn. First, in reference to Hume's "in principle" argument that miracles are impossible in a uniform world, C. S. Lewis points out that this is something we cannot know:

Now of course we must agree with Hume that if there is absolutely "uniform experience" against miracles, if in other words they have never happened, why then they never have. Unfortunately we know the experience against them to be uniform only if we know that all the reports of them are false. And we can know all the reports to be false only if we know already that miracles have never occurred. In fact, we are arguing in a circle.[17]

In effect, Hume is saying, "Miracles have not occurred because such things are not possible." Hume's conclusion is just his premise restated. That's what Lewis means by arguing in a circle. By definition, though, a miracle is something that breaks out of our ordinary experience. Otherwise we would never know that it was a miracle in the first place.

But let's move on to Hume's four "in fact" arguments and see if they are persuasive in making his case.

First, Hume said that "no historical miracle has been sufficiently attested by honest and reliable men who are of such social standing that they would have a great deal to lose by lying." But as Sean McDowell and Jonathan Morrow note, the gospel writers were, in fact, capable of writing accurate historical accounts and were willing to stake their lives on what they wrote. At the very least, this demonstrates the depth of their sincerity. "Liars make poor martyrs," they say.[18]

Second, Hume said, "People crave miraculous stories and will gullibly believe absurd" things. Yes, some people are gullible and believe improbable things, but it does not follow from this that no improbable things have ever occurred.

Third, Hume said that "miracles only occur among barbarous people." This, however, is not true in the case of Jesus. "Jesus's miracles did not occur among a barbarous people, but among the Jews who were a highly educated and sophisticated people," say McDowell and Morrow.[19]

Fourth, Hume said, "Miracles occur in all religions and thus cancel each other out, since they espouse contradictory doctrines." But the miracles in the Bible and throughout Christian history seem to be of a different character from those reports from other traditions. Poor, nonhistorical examples of miracles from other religions do not rule out the well-attested miracles common to Christian experience, most notably, as we will see, the resurrection of Christ.

> Poor, nonhistorical examples of miracles from other religions do not rule out the well-attested miracles common to Christian experience, most notably, as we will see, the resurrection of Christ.

This section is not, obviously, intended to completely refute David Hume's arguments about miracles. But as more and more evidence is collected, it becomes clear that human experience on this planet is far from uniform, as Hume asserted. Several years ago, New Testament scholar Craig Keener, skeptical of accounts of miraculous occurrences, developed a detailed methodology for examining thousands of reported miracles. What he found was stunning. Apparently, supernatural events, including miracles, are much more common than people assume. Keener's two-volume work titled *Miracles* describes his findings in more than twelve hundred pages of painstaking documentation.[20]

In the end, what Hume thought he knew in theory has turned out to be wrong both in theory and in practical reality. There is, at the very least, good reason to believe that Hume's arguments do not account for reality.

Probably no one has put it better than the inimitable G. K. Chesterton, who took disbelievers in miracles to task in a lively, and lengthy, passage in his book *Orthodoxy*:

> Somehow or other an extraordinary idea has arisen that the disbelievers in miracles consider them coldly and fairly calm, while believers in miracles accept them only in connection with some dogma. The fact is quite the other way. The believers in miracles accept them (rightly or wrongly) because they have evidence for them. The disbelievers in miracles deny them (rightly or wrongly) because they have a doctrine against them.... It is we Christians who accept all actual evidence—it is you rationalists who refuse actual evidence being constrained to do so by your creed. But I am not constrained by any creed in the matter, and looking impartially into certain miracles of medieval and modern times, I have come to the conclusion that they occurred. All argument against these plain facts is always argument in a circle. If I say, "Medieval documents attest certain miracles as much as they attest certain battles," they answer, "But medievals were superstitious"; if I want to know in what they were superstitious, the only ultimate answer is that they believed in the miracles.... Iceland is impossible because only stupid sailors have seen it; and the sailors are only stupid because they say they have seen Iceland.[21]

Saying that people in the past were gullible and easily fooled into believing insufficient evidence for miracles may be an indictment against being gullible and easily fooled, but it is insufficient evidence against believing in miracles themselves.

Materialism/Naturalism Presumes Too Much of Science

Scientific Method: a process of empirical inquiry that seeks to understand the phenomena of the physical world through hypothesizing, observing, measuring, experimenting, predicting, and testing.

Our second response to materialism/naturalism is that the **scientific method** is not actually as powerful as materialists/naturalists assume it to be. The scientific method makes sense of only a material world, where the things observed can be explained by natural processes. To say that anything outside of what science can study does not exist is like saying that a lake is only twenty feet deep because that's how long our measuring tape is. In fact, if only what can be measured using the scientific method exists, then wouldn't we have to say that the scientific method itself doesn't exist, as it cannot itself be measured, observed, or repeated?

Explaining all of reality is a burden far too heavy for science to carry. Even Julian Huxley, one of the twentieth century's leading evolutionists, recognized the limited nature of the scientific method:

SUPERNATURAL GOOD AND EVIL

Science has removed the obscuring veil of mystery from many phenomena, much to the benefit of the human race: but it confronts us with a basic and universal mystery—the mystery of existence in general, and of the existence of mind in particular. Why does the world exist? Why is the world-stuff what it is? Why does it have mental or subjective aspects as well as material or objective ones? We do not know.[22]

Very few scholars today would agree that we can know only that which can be studied with the scientific method. Historical facts, logical arguments, sociological observations, and aesthetic judgments are also accepted as evidence. And, as we will see, evidence of all of these sorts has been shown to lend credibility to many key Christian beliefs.

Materialism/Naturalism Explains Too Little about Reality

Our third response to materialism/naturalism is that even if we assume that science could do all that materialists/naturalists say it can, it has very little to say about what makes life worth living or societies worth living in. It cannot explain why humans want to be free or why society should preserve liberty. It cannot explain why we find life valuable or why the law should protect it. It cannot explain human happiness or why "the pursuit of happiness" should be considered an inalienable right, as the American Declaration of Independence says.

Still, people often just assume that materialism and naturalism are true. They live with what philosopher Charles Taylor refers to as an "immanent frame": if I can't see it, hear it, or feel it, it doesn't exist. In his massive and acclaimed text *A Secular Age*, Taylor points out that this modern bias toward materialism/naturalism is an unquestioned assumption, not a justified conclusion.[23] Materialism/naturalism prizes the kind of knowledge that we can individually possess, but as Taylor points out, if we begin our inquires with "I" rather than "we" or "God," we will arrive at very different, and not necessarily better, conclusions.

Clearly, science has dramatically increased human knowledge, and it offers a useful and powerful means for knowing a good many things, but it is not effective in explaining *all* of reality. Science simply does not replace religion as many materialists/naturalists suppose. Someone who says, "Science replaces religion," isn't making a statement of fact but rather is revealing how narrow his or her framework is for understanding reality. According to professor of political science Hunter Baker, "What happened in the matter of science and religion was the creation of a legend."[24]

> **Monism:** the belief that reality is ultimately composed of one essential substance.

Dualism Explains the World Better

Our fourth response to materialism/naturalism is to call into question the very idea that believing that reality is only material and that it can be explained through natural processes alone is valid. **Monism** (*mono* is Greek for "one") is the belief that ultimately reality consists of one thing. For some this may be the world of "spirit," as in **pantheism**. For others it may signify that only

> **Pantheism:** the belief that everything in the universe is ultimately divine.

the material world exists. **Dualism** (*duo* is Greek for "two") holds that reality is ultimately composed of two essential substances. **Mind/body dualism** says that human beings are composed of immaterial minds and material bodies.[25] According to this species of dualism, a soul or other immaterial entity is just as real as the physical body to which it is united. What happens in the mind has physical consequences and vice versa.

Dualism: the belief that reality is ultimately composed of two essential substances.

Mind/Body Dualism: the belief that human beings are composed of immaterial minds and material bodies.

Theism: the belief in the existence of a God or gods.

Atheism: the belief that God does not exist.

For most of the twentieth century, materialists/naturalists believed their viewpoint to be the only correct one, but this is changing. Contrary to materialists/naturalists' triumphant proclamations, the world is becoming more religious, not less.[26] And although materialists/naturalists may count among their ranks those who have jumped ship from **theism** to **atheism**, there have been many prominent conversions the other way, including one of the world's most notorious atheists, Antony Flew, who recanted his atheism in *There Is a God: How the World's Most Notorious Atheist Changed His Mind.* And in his book *Mind and Cosmos*, renowned atheist philosopher Thomas Nagel stunned the academic world by announcing his newfound skepticism of materialism: "It is prima facie highly implausible that life as we know it is the result of a sequence of physical accidents together with the mechanism of natural selection."[27] Too, we can hardly dismiss the anthology of essays from leading experts called *Rethinking Secularism*.[28] In it, several authors question the validity of the assumption that God is irrelevant to what's important in life, which is one thing nearly all materialists/naturalists believe.

Verifiable Experiences Demonstrate the Insufficiency of Materialism/Naturalism

Our fifth response to the materialist/naturalist challenge is that many things seemingly occur in the world for which materialist/naturalist arguments simply do not account for the data that has, and is continuing to be, collected by reasonable observers. The evidence for Near-Death Experiences (NDEs) is a surprising area of research challenging the belief that only the natural world exists. Recently, Eben Alexander, a respected neurosurgeon, wrote of having personally experienced a disease through which, according to hospital records, he suffered brain death but then revived. His experiences during that time caused Alexander to reexamine the evidence for NDEs, after which he concluded that materialist/naturalist explanations are simply insufficient.[29] Philosopher Gary Habermas has also rigorously studied such experiences and concluded that when it comes to explaining such things as NDEs, naturalism is the odd man out.[30]

NDE stories are often sensational accounts that result in significant life changes for people who experience them.[31] Profound life changes ought to get our attention, but often their sensational nature causes skeptics to immediately dismiss them. NDE researchers have

SUPERNATURAL GOOD AND EVIL

learned not to be so quick to scoff. Rather, separating out the "traveling through a tunnel and seeing a bright light" kind of stories and focusing instead on the well-documented cases in which people who experienced brain death reported going places and seeing things they simply could not have known in their "death" state—such as what meal was being cooked at their home or what objects were on the roof of the hospital.[32]

NDE claims have their doubters, as you might expect.[33] One person actually created a "God helmet" to simulate experiences people say they have when encountering God.[34] Just because it is possible to stimulate the brain to perceive God experiences, however, does not mean such experiences never have a supernatural origin. Scientists can stimulate the brain to experience sexual desire, but this does not mean there is no such thing as genuine love. Doubtless, the brain is a part of our experiences, but this does not sufficiently demonstrate that our experiences are only brain activity.

In this section, we've introduced responses to materialist/naturalist assumptions. But belief in the supernatural does not prevail just because the arguments for materialism/naturalism are inadequate. And Christianity in particular needs to show that we ought not just believe in the "generically" supernatural but in Jesus Christ as the God-man whose very life showed that God is active in the world and whose conquering of death and evil releases humanity from the fear of both. In this, it would be helpful to have evidence that can be explored with the tools of inquiry accepted among scholars. As it turns out, just such evidence is available for one of the most extraordinary events in all of history: the resurrection of Jesus.

4. Positive Evidence for the Supernatural: The Resurrection of the Son of God

As we have already seen, the biblical account is remarkably well supported for having been recorded so long ago. When it comes to the life of Christ, leading scholars, such as early twentieth-century archaeologist William F. Albright, were convinced that the New Testament books were written soon after the events they described and by people matching the characteristics of those said to have written them.[35] Further, the books of the Bible survived through time remarkably uncorrupted. Gleason L. Archer Jr., for example, reported that even though copies of Isaiah discovered in Qumran Cave 1 near the Dead Sea in 1947 were a thousand years earlier than the oldest dated manuscript previously known, they were word-for-word identical with our standard Hebrew Bible in more than 95 percent of the text. The 5 percent of variation consisted chiefly of obvious slips of the pen and variations in spelling.[36]

Though it is not necessary for the Bible to have been transmitted accurately for the miracles it reports to have been true,[37] it is comforting to Christians to see how Bible writers took great care in transmitting their heritage faithfully. Harvard's Simon Greenleaf, still respected as a great nineteenth-century expert on the common law, believed "that the competence of the New Testament documents would be established in any court of law."[38]

Many of the Bible's claims are also established by completely secular sources. Jesus is treated as a historical figure even by early secular historians, including Josephus, who wrote about Jesus at least twice in his *Antiquities of the Jews* (AD 93).[39] Another early historian, Publius Cornelius Tacitus, wrote circa AD 112 about "the persons commonly called Christians" and also stated, "Christus, the founder of the name, was put to death by Pontius Pilate, procurator of Judea in the reign of Tiberius: but the pernicious superstition, repressed for a time broke out again, not only through Judea, where the mischief originated, but through the city of Rome also."[40] According to American biblical scholar Bruce Metzger,

> The early non-Christian testimonies concerning Jesus, though scanty, are sufficient to prove (even without taking into account the evidence contained in the New Testament) that he was a historical figure who lived in Palestine in the early years of the first century, that he gathered a group of followers about himself, and that he was condemned to death under Pontius Pilate. Today no competent scholar denies the historicity of Jesus.[41]

Even secular historian Will Durant accepted the historicity of Jesus and called him in the spiritual sense "the greatest revolutionist in history."[42]

Too, we must remember what we learned in chapter 3, that the miracles reported in the Bible have stood up under empirical examination. Extensive studies of the gospel miracles have found that between half and three-fourths of the miracle accounts include enough detail to conclude that the historical scene they described could, in fact, have occurred as reported.[43] Enough evidence exists that it would be irresponsible to dismiss claims of the miraculous out of a mere bias against supernaturalism.

For the purposes of this chapter, though, let's turn our attention to the one miracle central to the Christian faith: the resurrection of Jesus of Nazareth. The apostle Paul, Christianity's earliest and most successful evangelist, treated the resurrection as the basis of Christianity's validity:

> Now if Christ is proclaimed as raised from the dead, how can some of you say that there is no resurrection of the dead? But if there is no resurrection of the dead, then not even Christ has been raised. And if Christ has not been raised, then our preaching is in vain and your faith is in vain. We are even found to be misrepresenting God, because we testified about God that he raised Christ, whom he did not raise if it is true that the dead are not raised. For if the dead are not raised, not even Christ has been raised. And if Christ has not been raised, your faith is futile and you are still in your sins. Then those also who have fallen asleep in Christ have perished. If in Christ we have hope in this life only, we are of all people most to be pitied. (1 Cor. 15:12–19)

Paul was not alone in emphasizing the resurrection's centrality. Among the gospel writers, Luke carefully situated the crucifixion and resurrection narrative in a "current events" context, mentioning people whose existence and testimony could have been easily verified, such as Pilate, Caesar, Herod, Barabbas, and Joseph of Arimathea. Luke is very concerned with this sort of historical approach (Luke 3:1–2)[44] and describes Christ's resurrection as a real event in history (Luke 24:36ff.).

5. EVIDENCE FOR THE RESURRECTION: THE MINIMAL FACTS APPROACH

So was the resurrection a real event? Many scholars think so, and their careful examination of the resurrection seems to have led to an abandonment of serious efforts to disprove it.

Much of this is due to the persistent lifelong work of a philosopher referenced earlier, Gary Habermas. Habermas, a professor at Liberty University, calls his methodology the *minimal facts approach* and presents it in a book coauthored with Michael Licona:

> When presenting the evidence for the Resurrection, let's stick to the topic of Jesus' resurrection. This means that we do not digress into a side discussion on the reliability of the Bible. While we hold that the Bible is trustworthy and inspired, we cannot expect the skeptical nonbeliever with whom we are dialoguing to embrace this view. So, in order to avoid a discussion that may divert us off of our most important topic, we would like to suggest that we adopt a "minimal facts approach." This approach considers only those data that are so strongly attested historically that they are granted by nearly every scholar who studies the subject, even the rather skeptical ones.... Most facts we use meet two criteria: They are well evidenced and nearly every scholar accepts them. We present our case using the "lowest common denominator" of agreed-upon facts. This keeps attention on the central issue, instead of sidetracking into matters that are irrelevant. This way we can present a strong argument that is both supportable and compelling.[45]

> ***Minimal Facts Approach:*** **a method formulated by Gary Habermas for investigating the resurrection of Jesus that concentrates only on the historical facts that are so well evidenced that they are accepted by nearly every scholar who studies the topic.**

So although Habermas does not reject the truth of the Bible as a whole, when it comes to studying the resurrection, he moves beyond questions of the Bible's inspiration or trustworthiness in order to focus on evidence and basic facts that even skeptics acknowledge as legitimate.

Habermas's approach is different from the "appeal to the majority" approach of asking what a majority of biblical scholars might believe. After all, just because a bunch of people believe something doesn't make it true. However, if there are facts that the majority of scholars accept, and if these facts, when taken together, point to a conclusion, then we should take that evidence seriously.

So what are these minimal facts?

First, Jesus died by crucifixion. Michael Licona points out that many sources, both Christian and non-Christian, report Jesus's execution, including the four gospels and the works of Josephus, Tacitus, Lucian, and Mara bar Serapion.[46] Each of these authors was familiar with crucifixion and knew the chances of surviving it were, at best, extremely bleak. Licona concludes, "The unanimous professional medical opinion is that Jesus certainly died due to the rigors of crucifixion, and even if Jesus had somehow managed to survive crucifixion, it would not have resulted in the disciples' belief that he had been resurrected."[47]

Second, Jesus's disciples believed that he rose and appeared to them. Paul testifies to the fact that the disciples believed and claimed it:

> I delivered to you as of first importance what I also received: that Christ died for our sins in accordance with the Scriptures, that he was buried, that he was raised on the third day in accordance with the Scriptures, and that he appeared to Cephas [Peter], then to the twelve. Then he appeared to more than five hundred brothers at one time, most of whom are still alive, though some have fallen asleep. Then he appeared to James, then to all of the apostles. Last of all, as to one untimely born, he appeared also to me. (1 Cor. 15:3–8)

In this passage, Paul seems to recite a sort of creed that probably dated back to before his conversion, in the immediate aftermath of Christ's resurrection.[48] Scholars agree that 1 Corinthians was an early book, probably written in the AD 50s at a time when there were potentially many hundreds of people alive who could verify its core truths.

Clearly, the disciples underwent a radical transformation following Jesus's resurrection. They believed so deeply that Jesus had risen from the dead that they devoted the rest of their lives to testifying about it. Lots of people have died for their convictions, but as Habermas points out, "Jesus's disciples were in the right place to know the truth or falsity of the event for which they were willing to die."[49] People often die for what they believe to be true, but it is a rare thing indeed for someone to willingly die for what he *knows* to be false.

Third, the apostle Paul was radically converted. What explained the transformation of Paul from highly esteemed persecutor of Christians to promoter of the Christian message?[50] Only one thing: he believed he had seen Jesus.[51] Of course, people convert from one belief to another all the time, but Paul's case was different. Habermas and Licona explain:

> People usually convert to a particular religion because they have heard the message of that religion from a secondary source and believed the message. Paul's conversion was based on what he perceived to be a personal appearance of the risen Jesus. Today we might believe that Jesus rose from the dead based on secondary evidence, trusting Paul and the disciples who saw the risen Jesus. But for Paul, his experience came from primary evidence: the risen Jesus appeared directly to him. He did not merely believe based on the testimony of someone else. Therefore, the difference is primary versus secondary sources. For most, belief is based on secondary sources. And even when religious belief is based on primary grounds, no other founder of a major religion is believed to have been raised from the dead, let alone have provided any evidence for such an event.[52]

Fourth, the skeptic James, brother of Jesus, was suddenly changed. Gospel accounts indicate that Jesus's brothers, including James, were unbelievers who did not hold to the truth of Jesus's message.[53] In the book of Acts, however, James is mentioned as one of the leaders of the church in Jerusalem.[54] What happened? The ancient creed we referred to earlier mentions Jesus's appearing to James. Simply put, James apparently converted to Christianity because he believed that Jesus appeared to him after rising from the dead. How much did he believe this? According to Habermas and Licona,

His beliefs in Jesus and his resurrection were so strong that he died as a martyr because of them. James's martyrdom is attested by Josephus, Hegesippus, and Clement of Alexandria. We no longer have any of the works of Hegesippus or the writings of Clement where the event is mentioned. However, sections have been preserved by Eusebius. Therefore, his martyrdom is attested by both Christian and non-Christian sources.[55]

It is difficult to explain these facts apart from the resurrection. Where did Jesus's body end up? Why were so many changed? And why did they all risk their lives? There simply isn't a sufficient naturalistic answer.

6. ADDITIONAL EVIDENCE FOR THE RESURRECTION

There are also other compelling arguments scholars have advanced that, although not meeting the minimal facts criteria, are nonetheless intriguing.

First, the tomb was empty. This conclusion is slightly less attested by the majority of scholars but is still a powerful piece of evidence because Jesus's execution was a public event. If Jesus's body had still been in the tomb, it would have been easy for his enemies to display the corpse and expose the claims of resurrection to be a hoax.[56]

Also, it's not only Jesus's friends who report the empty tomb but also Jesus's enemies (though they thought the disciples stole the body). From all the available evidence, the tomb was empty.[57] Here's something more: the emptiness of the tomb was first witnessed by women. In the Near Eastern culture of Jesus's time, in both Jewish and Roman traditions, the testimony of women was not considered strong evidence.[58] William Lane Craig says,

> If Jesus's body had still been in the tomb, it would have been easy for his enemies to display the corpse and expose the claims of resurrection to be a hoax.

> If the empty tomb story were a legend, then the male disciples would have been made to be the ones who discover the empty tomb. The fact that women, whose testimony was deemed worthless, were the chief witnesses to the fact of the empty tomb can only be plausibly explained if, like it or not, they actually were the discoverers of the empty tomb, and the gospels faithfully record what for them was a very embarrassing fact.[59]

New Testament scholar N. T. Wright examined the evidence for the empty tomb and said, "We are left with the secure historical conclusion: the tomb was empty.... I regard this conclusion as coming in the same category, of historical probability so high as to be virtually certain, as the death of Augustus in AD 14 or the fall of Jerusalem in AD 70."[60] This is a powerful statement from a respected scholar whose book *The Resurrection of the Son of God* is must reading for anyone wanting to seriously examine the evidence for the resurrection.[61]

Second, more than five hundred people witnessed the resurrected Christ (1 Cor. 15:6),[62] **including Mary, Peter, and ten other apostles, and it changed their lives.** These witnesses were so moved by the resurrection that they committed their lives to it and to the One whose divinity and righteousness it vindicated. The disciples did not abandon Christ (as they might have, because death by crucifixion was, according to their expectations, a sure sign of a failed messiah) but instead were willing to die for the gospel they were proclaiming because the resurrection absolutely defied their expectations. Indeed, the resurrection of Christ took a group of scared (Mark 16:8; John 20:19)[63] and skeptical (Luke 24:38; John 20:25)[64] men and transformed them into courageous evangelists who proclaimed that resurrection in the face of threats on their lives (Acts 4:21; 5:18).[65] It must have taken quite a life-shaping event to do that.

How do nonbelievers respond to this evidence? The most common response is that the disciples genuinely believed all this because they were hallucinating. But as Licona points out, this explanation simply does not hold water:

> Since a hallucination is an event that occurs in the mind of an individual and has no external reality, one person cannot participate in another's hallucination. In this sense, they are like dreams. I could not wake my wife in the middle of the night and say, "Honey, I'm having a dream that I'm in Hawaii. Go back to sleep. Come join me in my dream and let's have a free vacation!" We might go back to sleep and both dream that we are in Hawaii. But we would not be participating in the same dream, doing the same activity, in the same location, and carrying on the same discussion with precisely the same words. This is because a dream occurs in the mind of an individual and has no corresponding external reality. Hallucinations are similar in that sense as a psychological phenomenon.[66]

In fact, Licona points to the research of Dr. Gary Sibcy, a clinical psychologist who has studied the possibility of group hallucinations. Sibcy says,

> I have surveyed the professional literature (peer-reviewed journal articles and books) written by psychologists, psychiatrists, and other relevant healthcare professionals during the past two decades and have yet to find a single documented case of a group hallucination, that is, an event for which more than one person purportedly shared in a visual or other sensory perception where there was clearly no external referent.[67]

Still, even if the disciples hallucinated, faulty sight doesn't change the facts:[68] the tomb was empty and hundreds of people apparently saw Jesus alive.

Third, the theology of the disciples was drastically changed. Apart from the resurrection, the disciples' theology makes no sense at all. Nothing short of a miracle could have so radically altered the theology they had grown up with all their lives. William Lane Craig explains:

> Jews had no conception of a Messiah who, instead of triumphing over Israel's enemies, would be shamefully executed by them as a criminal. Messiah was supposed

to be a triumphant figure who would command the respect of Jew and Gentile alike and who would establish the throne of David in Jerusalem. A Messiah who failed to deliver and to reign, who was defeated, humiliated, and slain by His enemies, is a contradiction in terms. Nowhere do Jewish texts speak of such a "Messiah." Therefore, it's difficult to overemphasize what a disaster the crucifixion was for the disciples' faith. Jesus' death on the cross spelled the humiliating end for any hopes they had entertained that He was the Messiah. But the belief in the resurrection of Jesus reversed the catastrophe of the crucifixion.[69]

Clearly, something immensely powerful happened, that the disciples immediately developed a whole new theological tradition for which they were mocked, persecuted, and even put to death by both Jewish and Roman authorities. The Bible is clear about what this "something" is: Christ had risen from the dead. As New Testament scholar N. T. Wright puts it,

> The widespread belief and practice of the early Christians is only explicable if we assume that they all believed that Jesus was bodily raised, in an Easter event something like the stories the gospels tell: the reason they believed that he was bodily raised is because the tomb was empty and, over a short period thereafter, they encountered Jesus himself, giving every appearance of being bodily alive once more.[70]

The resurrection of Christ seriously challenges those who attempt to explain all reality through materialism, and it provides enticing evidence of a supernatural event that changed hundreds of lives instantly and billions more ever since.

> **The resurrection of Christ seriously challenges those who attempt to explain all reality through materialism, and it provides enticing evidence of a supernatural event that changed hundreds of lives instantly and billions more ever since.**

Let's take a moment to review. So far we've seen that the bias against miracles is an assumption about the way the world works that simply does not hold up. The evidence for miracles, especially in the miracle of the resurrection of Jesus, is strong.

What is the impact of all of this evidence? Like the disciples, we are enabled to be more firmly committed to believing that the gospel is true and spreading its good news. But it is more than that. Having confidence in the miraculous accounts of the Bible enables us to see with complete clarity that God is powerful *today* and operating in the world to empower us to live like Christ and resist evil.

As we'll discuss in a future chapter, I have found as a teacher that whenever the subject of miracles comes up, the question of evil follows quickly on its heels. People ask, "What about supernatural evil, such as Satan and demons?" Although it is not a central issue we are covering in this book, the reality of the existence of supernatural evil and Jesus's power over it is too big of a topic to ignore. First we need to understand what it is, then see how Jesus conquers it, and finally discern how we ourselves might pursue good and resist evil in our own world today.

7. THE REALITY OF SUPERNATURAL EVIL

Many of Jesus's miracles were the healing of physical ailments. Uncomfortably for modern people, the Gospels clearly record several instances in which these ailments were the result of supernatural evil. One account, recorded among others in Luke 8:26–29, reports how Jesus and the disciples sailed to a region called the Gerasenes and met a demon-possessed man whom Jesus subsequently healed.[71] Another such incident, recorded in Luke 13:10–11, is of a woman with a disabling spirit that left her body hunched and crooked.[72]

The biblical account clearly assumes that Satan is at work in the world. This very thought drives materialists/naturalists to scorn. For people who believe, as evolutionist Julian Huxley did, that "modern science must rule out special creation or divine guidance,"[73] possession by evil spirits is simply beyond the pale.

We talked earlier about how people in the past had more of a sense of spiritual connection with one another, God, and nature. It is as if they lived in a world we would now refer to as "enchanted": permeated with the supernatural in everyday life. Many people today think unbelief is a step forward and should be our default position. As philosopher Charles Taylor frames it,

> **Many people today think unbelief is a step forward and should be our default position.**

> Unbelief for great numbers of contemporary unbelievers, is understood as an achievement of rationality. It cannot have this without a continuing historical awareness. It is a condition which can't only be described in the present tense, but which also needs the perfect tense: a condition of "having overcome" the irrationality of belief. It is this perfect-tensed consciousness which underlies unbelievers' use of "disenchantment" today.[74]

For materialists/naturalists, the residue of enchantment is a serious problem: society cannot advance until people become sufficiently disenchanted with spiritual things.

Many Christians, in an attempt to meet the challenge of materialism/naturalism, try to explain things such as demon possession in terms that seem more scientifically acceptable, such as mental illness. Other Christian counselors, such as Jay Adams, strongly resist this approach:

> Organic malfunctions affecting the brain that are caused by brain damage, tumors, gene inheritance, glandular or chemical disorders validly may be termed mental illnesses. But at the same time a vast number of other human problems have been classified as mental illnesses for which there is no evidence that they have been engendered by disease or illness at all.[75]

Adams believes that proper biblical teaching and repentance can help people heal: "The fundamental bent of fallen human nature is away from God.... Apart from organically generated difficulties, the 'mentally ill' are really people with unsolved personal problems."[76] This is obviously a controversial position even among Christians in the mental health professions. But even if it does not account for more common approaches to mental illness, it at least highlights the fact that if what the Bible says about our rebellion against

God is true, reconciling with him is critical to healthy functioning. Christian counselor Larry Crabb Jr. explains, "An appreciation of the reality of sin is a critically necessary beginning point for an understanding of the Christian view of anything. A psychology worthy of the adjective 'Christian' must not set the problem of sin in parallel line with other problems or redefine it into a neurosis or psychological kink."[77]

If supernatural evil actually exists but isn't easily explained as mental illness, then what is it? We need to know what we're up against. As pastor and author Karl Payne says in his respected book on spiritual warfare, "Ignorance of a competitor is not an advantage in athletics, business, or spiritual warfare."[78]

Theologian C. Fred Dickason explains what we're up against. A theologian who has carefully studied what the Bible says about supernatural evil, he describes demon possession based on the meaning of the terms used in the original New Testament Greek:

> If supernatural evil actually exists but isn't easily explained as mental illness, then what is it? We need to know what we're up against. As pastor and author Karl Payne says in his respected book on spiritual warfare, "Ignorance of a competitor is not an advantage in athletics, business, or spiritual warfare."

> The verb *daimonizomai* means "to be possessed by a demon." The participle from the same root, *daimonizomenos*, is used twelve times in the Greek New Testament. It is used only in the present tense, indicating the continued state of one inhabited by a demon, or demonized. This participle has components to its structure. First there is the root, *daimon*, which indicates the involvement of demons. Second is the causative stem, *iz*, which shows that there is an active cause in this verb. Third is the passive ending, *omenos*. This conveys the passivity of the person described as demonized. Putting it all together, the participle in its root form means, "a demon caused passivity." This indicates a control other than that of the person who is demonized; he is regarded as the recipient of the demon's action. In other words, demonization pictures a demon controlling a somewhat passive human.[79]

To Dickason, when people are passive in the face of supernatural evil, they actually put themselves in the position of being controlled by it. In other words, it isn't just actively doing the wrong thing that is the problem; it is the failure to do the *right* thing that also constitutes sin. Why do people such as the apostle Paul and the gospel writers treat Satan's influence so seriously? This is where the theology of the gospel really comes to life in an exciting way. Let's take a look.

8. THE PRESENCE OF SUPERNATURAL EVIL HIGHLIGHTS THE POWER OF JESUS

In our own day, people have many superstitions. For example, even though every building more than twelve stories tall has a thirteenth floor, often the number thirteen is skipped so those riding the elevator can blissfully go straight to the "fourteenth floor." Why? The number thirteen is so widely considered to be bad luck that very few people would agree to have offices or stay in a hotel room on the thirteenth floor.

The people of Israel had superstitions too, but they were much more involved with the worship of a god named **Baal**. Baal worship fills the Old Testament. He was the main false god people worshipped, and the prophets constantly warned that this kind of worship would weaken people spiritually so much that they would lose everything, including their freedom as a nation. This is exactly what happened.

> *Baal:* meaning "Lord" or "ruler"; a false god worshipped by the people of Israel who was purported to control nature.

In the New Testament, the references to Satan are from the word **Beelzebub** in the Greek, a variation on the name Baal, which refers to the prince of the demons.[80] *Beelzebub* literally means "Lord of the flies," which is interesting to those who have read William Golding's book by that title. To the Hebrews, it was an ironic reference: Satan was Lord over the dung heap.

> *Beelzebub:* a Greek word meaning "Lord of the flies"; references Satan and is a variation of the false god Baal.

Because the word *Baal* really meant "Lord" or "ruler," the name seems to refer in ancient Near East literature to many different local deities and thus many diverse traditions. For our purposes, we should understand that people's *impressions* of Baal were all the scarier for being vague. He was widely believed in, if not worshipped. His power was thought to be real. By piecing together various Baal traditions, we can see the attributes Baal was thought to have:

- Baal is the one who made things grow. He was in charge of fertility.[81]

- Baal was the god of storms and ruler of the seas.[82]

- Baal worship was thought to involve the sacrifice of pigs.[83]

- Worshippers of Baal would scream and cut themselves and stay among the tombs.[84]

- Baal was the son of the great god El. He was son of the "Most High God."[85]

> Understanding the superstitions about Baal is crucial to seeing how Jesus's miracles directly confronted the dominant, but mistaken, belief that supernatural evil was more powerful than supernatural good.

Understanding the superstitions about Baal is crucial to seeing how Jesus's miracles directly confronted the dominant, but mistaken, belief that supernatural evil was more powerful than supernatural good.

Returning to the story referenced at the beginning of this section, when Jesus traveled to the country of the Gerasenes (modern-day Jordan), we see that Jesus's miracles surrounding this trip directly confronted the power of Baal. In Mark chapter 4, Jesus fed a crowd of many thousands of people by multiplying a small lunch. The lesson was clear: Jesus, not Baal, makes things grow. He can feed people out of thin air if he chooses to do so.

SUPERNATURAL GOOD AND EVIL

Immediately after this mass feeding, Jesus traveled with his disciples across the Sea of Galilee. Mark 4 recounts how the sea grew tempestuous and the disciples were afraid. Perhaps, as they were headed to the mysterious Gerasenes, they wondered in the back of their minds whether Baal-the-storm-god had anything to do with it. Given their fear, the storm must have seemed like a bad omen. When Jesus caused the storm to cease, the disciples became even more overwhelmed. Mark 4:41 says, "They were filled with great fear and said to one another, 'Who then is this, that even the wind and the sea obey him?'" The lesson? Jesus, not Baal, controls the weather.

Finally the disciples arrived in the Gerasenes and, according to Mark 5:1–20, experienced a terrifying sight: a wild man living among the tombs who could not be subdued and who cried out and cut himself with stones. Seeing Jesus, the man cried out with a loud voice, "What have you to do with me, Jesus, Son of the Most High God? I adjure you by God, do not torment me." Jesus asked his name and he replied, "My name is Legion, for we are many." These spirits implored him not to send them out of the country but to have them enter a herd of two thousand pigs, which subsequently stampeded and drowned in the sea. Hearing of this, the townspeople came and saw the demoniac "clothed and in his right mind" and were terrified.

Put yourself in the place of the disciples, the people of the Gerasenes, or even the demoniac himself. Everyone was terrified. They were in the presence of evil things they had heard about all their lives but probably didn't imagine they would personally witness. Perhaps they were thinking of the account in 1 Kings 18, in which the prophets of Baal tried to make it rain by running around, screaming, and cutting themselves just as the Gerasene demoniac did.[86] Or perhaps they were thinking of Isaiah condemning those who lived among the tombs and worshipped false gods, like the demon-possessed man at Gerasene.

But when the demons plaguing the tormented man called Jesus the "Son of the Most High God," the disciples must have just about come apart. Even the *demons* knew that Baal wasn't the true God; Jesus was. When Jesus sent the demons into the pigs, it was an almost ghastly but humorous action. It's as if Jesus was saying, "Baal, you like pigs? I'll give you pigs." The poor of the Gerasenes simply did not know what to do about all this. What truly frightened them was not that demons had killed their pigs but that the demoniac who could not even be chained for his own good had been set free from all that chained him to evil. He was clothed. He was in his right mind, but they nearly lost theirs.

> When the demons plaguing the tormented man called Jesus the "Son of the Most High God," the disciples must have just about come apart. Even the *demons* knew that Baal wasn't the true God; Jesus was.

In explanation of the convergence of the biblical text with the superstitions of Jesus's day, Bible teacher Paul T. Penley comments, "When Jesus performed the exorcism, he was not just casting out a bunch of demons to demonstrate his own authority. He was challenging the mythical authority that Baal claimed to have acquired over the inhabitants of the underworld. Jesus is showing himself to be the true Lord over all in place of Baal."[87]

But there is one more reference of great significance: the Gerasene demoniac became an *evangelist*. According to the text, the man asked to go with Jesus and the disciples. Instead, Jesus sent him to proclaim the gospel in the Decapolis, which means "ten cities." We know the names of these cities because a Roman historian named Pliny the Elder (AD 23–79) wrote about them. One is a city called Philadelphia, which is now Amman, the capital of Jordan. Another is Damascus, the capital of Syria. Both cities figure prominently in Middle Eastern politics to this day. The Gerasene demoniac must have been quite an evangelist, or maybe his converts were. From the second century AD to modern times, the Decapolis has been known as a thoroughly Christian region.[88]

So supernatural evil is real, but Jesus is more powerful than all its forces. As Martin Luther wrote, Satan's "doom is sure. One little word will fell him."[89] That word is Jesus, the very one who, in instantly converting the demoniac into an evangelist, turned evil against itself. This is the hope of which Paul speaks when he says that God will crush Satan under *our* feet (Rom. 16:20).[90] "Our feet" seems like an ever-present reference, something that continues to this day. So what does supernatural evil—and its being crushed by God's people—look like today?

9. How Supernatural Evil Manifests Today

When they hear stories of supernatural activity in other countries, Westerners often ask, *Why don't we see more of that here?* Given the extensive research of such people as Craig Keener, who documents encounters with supernatural evil, including many that can be verified with scientific evidence, it would appear that miracles and demonic activity are taking place all over the world today. If we don't see it, maybe we just aren't paying attention. At a deeper level, though, the materialist assumption that only the physical world exists is so much a part of our everyday lives that it conditions us to "not see" things that don't fit our preconceived notions. If everything can be explained through natural causes, then we might just assign some natural cause to it without even stopping to think about it.[91]

> The materialist assumption that only the physical world exists is so much a part of our everyday lives that it conditions us to "not see" things that don't fit our preconceived notions. If everything can be explained through natural causes, then we might just assign some natural cause to it without even stopping to think about it.

When we encounter a disruptive phenomenon, our human tendency is to try to make sense of it based on what we already know.[92] Often we simply fail to notice things we do not think can happen. Once a skeptic said to me, "If God is so powerful, why doesn't he just get a huge megaphone and announce his existence to the whole world?" The person seemed serious, so I gave a serious reply: "First of all, God doesn't operate that way. Second, you seem so predisposed to naturalism that I don't even think you would grasp what was happening if God did that. You'd probably interpret it as an odd burst of thunder." This is exactly what happened in Jesus's day when God spoke aloud (John 12:27–36). The people were predisposed not to hear God's voice, so they interpreted it as thunder.

C. S. Lewis incorporated this point into his book *The Magician's Nephew*. Stumbling into Narnia and captured by the Narnian animals, Uncle Andrew hears only barks and howls when they are speaking, and snarling when they are laughing. Lewis writes, "What you see and what you hear depends a great deal on where you are standing. It also depends on what sort of person you are."[93] It is true in our understanding of God as well.

Christians can also unknowingly trivialize the presence of evil. At a camp I directed, two students had been telling one another stories of demonic activity, when all at once the faucet in their room turned on. They were terrified. Upon further examination, though, the faucet had not been turned all the way off, and vibrating pipes from water flow in nearby rooms exerted just enough pressure to allow a small stream of water to pass through. With their scary talk, these students had convinced themselves that they were under demonic attack, and they interpreted everything they saw and heard from that perspective. Just as Uncle Andrew found himself unable to witness the supernatural anywhere, the students seemed to observe it everywhere.

> **Perhaps we don't see more demonic activity in the West because Satan doesn't need drama in order to succeed.**

But there is one more possibility: perhaps we don't see more demonic activity in the West because Satan doesn't need drama in order to succeed. Karl Payne claims, "The bottom line is that subtle covert attacks in our society are usually more effective than aggressive overt attacks that could possibly wake up even the most religious skeptics to question the reality, relevance, and correctness of spiritual faith, doctrinal presuppositions, and theistic worldviews."[94]

Don't forget, though, that demon influence does not need to manifest through wild-eyed screams or guttural voices. Demonic activity wearing the ordinary garb of doubt, irrational fear, and self-accusation would almost never be perceived as such and could spread like a virus. Payne thinks this is exactly what is happening: "I personally believe that demonic deception is increasing, even within the Christian church, and that the worst of this deception is still to come."[95]

Deception. It's the most common garb of the demonic. As C. S. Lewis wrote in *The Screwtape Letters* (from the Devil's perspective), "It is funny how mortals always picture us as putting things into their minds: in reality our best work is done by keeping things out."[96] Or, to quote Kevin Spacey's character in *The Usual Suspects*, "The greatest trick the devil ever played was to convince the world he didn't exist."[97] Materialism, self-sufficiency, even a denial of Satan's existence can be demonic.

The scriptural response to the enemy of our souls is to resist him and he will flee (James 4:7).[98] The New Testament, according to Dr. Dickason, regards demons as usurpers, squatters, thieves—those who do not own anything and have no right to any territory but act as if they do.[99] Christians are bought with a price by God (1 Cor. 6:20),[100] and demons can't change that. They can, however, make Christians miserable and cause them to be ineffective ambassadors for God's kingdom.

Asking, "Why don't we see more demonic activity here?" is sort of like asking, "Why isn't life more like a horror movie?" It's the wrong question. The right question is "How do we recognize demonic activity for what it is and resist it?"

10. CONCLUSION

Admittedly, this chapter has been a bit unusual. We began with the question of whether supernatural good and evil actually exist. We identified the materialist/naturalist bias that prevents us from recognizing the supernatural and responded to the claims of such philosophers as David Hume that miracles cannot occur and therefore do not. We saw that evidence for miracles is strong and that the miracle of Jesus's resurrection serves as an example of a miracle that can be confidently asserted to have actually occurred.

We also looked at the existence of supernatural evil and realized that even though many people are uncomfortable with discussions of Satan, demons, and demon possession, we have good reason to take supernatural evil seriously. Fortunately, as we also saw, Jesus is the Lord over all and has shown himself to be more powerful than any evil we might encounter.

Choosing to believe in the supernatural, then, does not make us second-class thinkers. As William Lane Craig states,

> Fortunately, the Christian faith does not call for us to put our minds on the shelf, to fly in the face of common sense and history, or to make a leap of faith into the dark. The rational person, fully apprised of the evidence, can confidently believe that on that first Easter morning a divine miracle took place.[101]

But confidence is not the only goal. If the supernatural world actually exists, it must color our whole understanding of reality, including what we think about the power of evil. As the Old Testament prophet Elisha told his terrified servant, "Do not be afraid, for those who are with us are more than those who are with them" (2 Kings 6:16). Similarly, Romans 8:31 says, "What then shall we say to these things? If God is for us, who can be against us?"

> If the supernatural world actually exists, it must color our whole understanding of reality, including what we think about the power of evil.

At the end of the day, it is hard to see the supernatural because we find ourselves incapable of paying attention to things that don't fit our preconceived notions of what's possible. The Bible encourages us to be unafraid and yet deeply aware that the world, the flesh, and the Devil tempt us to ignore or avoid what God says is good for us.

Five actions are called for to counter "the desires of the flesh and the desires of the eyes and pride of life" (1 John 2:16):[102]

1. Pursue good. Matthew 6:24 says, "No one can serve two masters, for either he will hate the one and love the other, or he will be devoted to the one and despise the other." So we must say, "I choose to see this from God's perspective rather than from my own."

2. Resist evil. Second Timothy 2:22 tells us to "flee youthful passions and pursue righteousness, faith, love, and peace, along with those who call on the Lord from a pure heart." We have to change our habits and intentionally avoid situations in which we might experience temptation.

3. Renew our minds. Ephesians 4:22–24 says, "Put off your old self, which belongs to your former manner of life and is corrupt through deceitful desires, and to be renewed in the spirit of your minds, and to put on the new self, created after the likeness of God in true righteousness and holiness." When we are tempted to believe things about ourselves that God says are not true or to perform actions that are not godly, our response needs to be "This is not me. I belong to God. I do not need to comply with Satan's thinking or agenda."

4. Walk controlled by the Spirit. Galatians 5:16 says, "I say, walk by the Spirit, and you will not gratify the desires of the flesh." As Payne says, "Part of the Holy Spirit's job is to convict us of sin so that we can get back to serving Jesus Christ."[103] It is appropriate to listen to these convictions and be restored to the way God wants us to walk.

5. Repent. Although temptation is not itself sin, succumbing to it is, as is believing we are invulnerable to it. As the apostle Peter told a man who wanted to buy spiritual power with money, "Repent, therefore, of this wickedness of yours, and pray to the Lord that, if possible, the intent of your heart may be forgiven you" (Acts 8:22). Repentance clears away sin's power over us.

To have victory over evil, we need a heightened sense of awareness to what's actually going on around us. Psychiatrist Curt Thompson encourages us to ask, "How well am I paying attention to what I am paying attention to?"[104] If we merely absorb the culture's messages or if we believe we're stuck in our past and its patterns of life, we'll probably never experience genuine spiritual success. As Thompson says, "Your memory creates your future."[105]

In order to pay attention to God's power, we have been given the mind of Christ. The apostle Paul said in 1 Corinthians 2:10–16,

> We have received not the spirit of the world, but the Spirit who is from God, that we might understand the things freely given us by God. And we impart this in words not taught by human wisdom but taught by the Spirit, interpreting spiritual truths to those who are spiritual. The natural person does not accept the things of the Spirit of God, for they are folly to him, and he is not able to understand them because they are spiritually discerned…. But we have the mind of Christ.

Therein is victory: that we see the world as God sees it, that we respond as he responds. We must remember this as we turn our attention in the next chapter to a subject that has bothered many people in the modern world: no matter how interesting we find claims about the supernatural, isn't it true that science has pretty much won the battle with Christianity over what is actually true?

> **Therein is victory: that we see the world as God sees it, that we respond as he responds.**

ENDNOTES

1. Letter from Thomas Jefferson to John Adams (October 12, 1813), www.encyclopediavirginia.org/Letter_from_Thomas_Jefferson_to_John_Adams_October_12_1813.
2. Timothy Keller, *The Reason for God: Belief in an Age of Skepticism* (New York: Dutton, 2008), 95.
3. Consider some passages in the Quran (A. Yusuf Ali, *The Holy Qur'an*) regarding Moses: "[Pharaoh] said: 'If indeed thou hast come with a Sign, show it forth, if thou tellest the truth.' Then [Moses] threw his rod, and behold, it was a serpent, plain (for all to see)! And he drew out his hand, and behold, it was white to all beholders!" (7:106–7). "Said Moses [to the sorcerers of Pharaoh's court]: 'Throw ye (first).' So when they threw, they bewitched the eyes of the people, and struck terror into them: for they showed a great (feat of) magic. We put it into Moses' mind by inspiration: 'Throw (now) thy rod': and

behold, it swallows up straightaway all the falsehoods which they fake! Thus truth was confirmed and all that they did was made of no effect" (7:116–18). "Then we sent Moses and his brother Aaron, and with Our Signs and Authority manifest" (23:45; see also 7:106–8).

4. The Quran states, "Then will God say: 'O Jesus the son of Mary! Recount My favour to thee and to thy mother … and thou healest those born blind, and the lepers, by My leave. And behold, thou bringest forth the dead by My leave. And behold, I did restrain the Children of Israel from (violence to) thee when thou didst show them the Clear Signs'" (5:110, A. Yusuf Ali, *The Holy Qur'an*).

5. The Quran says, "And the unbelievers say: 'Why is not a Sign sent down to him [Muhammad] from his Lord?' But thou art truly a warner and to every people a guide" (13:7, A. Yusuf Ali, *The Holy Qur'an*).

6. Oliver Leaman, *An Introduction to Classical Islamic Philosophy* (Cambridge, UK: Cambridge University Press, 2002), 102.

7. Blaise Pascal, *Pensées*, no. 600, www.ccel.org/ccel/pascal/pensees.x.html.

8. Eric Metaxas, *Miracles: What They Are, Why They Happen, and How They Can Change Your Life* (New York: Dutton, 2014), 16.

9. Stephen T. Davis, "God's Actions," in *In Defense of Miracles: A Comprehensive Case for God's Action in History*, ed. R. Douglas Geivett and Gary R. Habermas (Downers Grove, IL: InterVarsity, 1997), 165.

10. Mark Twain, *Following the Equator: A Journey around the World*, vol. 5 (New York: Harper and Brothers, 1906), 132.

11. Generally speaking, materialism is in the realm of metaphysics, the philosophical study of being. It hypothesizes about what exists. Naturalism is in the realm of epistemology, the philosophical study of knowing. These terms have been discussed and debated in one form or another for millennia, so any one definition of them risks being overly simplistic. Those interested in delving more deeply may find a good starting point in Robert Audi, ed., *Cambridge Dictionary of Philosophy* (Cambridge, UK: Cambridge University Press, 1999). See specifically the definition of *materialism* provided under the definition of *metaphysics* (p. 563) and the definition of *naturalism* (p. 596).

12. Richard C. Lewontin, "Billions and Billions of Demons," *The New York Review of Books*, January 9, 1997.

13. Edward O. Wilson, "Biology's Spiritual Products," *Free Inquiry* (1987): 14.

14. Rebecca Hamilton, "Dawkins: Mock Them. Ridicule Them. In Public. With Contempt." Patheos, July 31, 2013, www.patheos.com/blogs/publiccatholic/2013/07/dawkins-mock-them-ridicule-them-in-public-with-contempt/.

15. I recognize that this is one of many prominent interpretations of what Hume was doing in his essay on miracles, but for our purposes, it is not possible to discuss each one and decide among them.

16. Sean McDowell and Jonathan Morrow, *Is God Just a Human Invention? And Seventeen Other Questions Raised by the New Atheists* (Grand Rapids, MI: Kregel, 2010), 48–49.

17. C. S. Lewis, *Miracles* (New York: Macmillan, 1947), 105.

18. McDowell and Morrow, *Is God Just a Human Invention?*, 49.

19. McDowell and Morrow, *Is God Just a Human Invention?*, 49.

20. Craig Keener, *Miracles: The Credibility of the New Testament Accounts* (Grand Rapids, MI: Baker, 2011).

21. G. K. Chesterton, *Orthodoxy* (New York: John Lane Company, 1908), 278.

22. Julian Huxley, *Essays of a Humanist* (New York: Harper and Row, 1964), 107.

23. Specifically, Taylor found that it is only in the last five hundred years or so that people have gotten the sense of a "self" that is "'buffered" and clearly distinct from others. In other words, the focus on knowledge that is individually developed and individually held is a relatively recent phenomenon. This is important because the bias toward the individual is one thing that convinces us that what we used to know together is no longer relevant. Disenchantment rises as individualism replaces community. Charles Taylor, *A Secular Age* (Cambridge, MA: Belknap, 2007), 38–39.

24. Hunter Baker, *The End of Secularism* (Wheaton, IL: Crossway, 2009), 153.

25. We use the term *dualism* for the sake of simplicity. The precise term philosophers use for this is *substance dualism*.

26. See, for example, the work of the esteemed sociologist Peter L. Berger. Early in his career, Berger predicted the rise of Secularism and the death of religion. Through time, Berger now admits, the evidence has demonstrated precisely the opposite of what he originally supposed. A well-known article from Berger on the subject is "Secularization Falsified," *First Things*, February 2008. A recent interview with Berger can be found at thecresset.org/2014/Lent/Thuswaldner_L14.html.

27. Thomas Nagel, *Mind and Cosmos: Why the Materialist Neo-Darwinian Conception of Nature is Almost Certainly False* (New York: Oxford University Press, 2012), 6. On pages 14 and 15 he says, "If evolutionary biology is a physical theory—as it is generally taken to be—then it cannot account for the appearance of consciousness and of other phenomena that are not physically reducible."

28. Craig Calhoun, Mark Juergensmeyer, and Jonathan VanAntwerpen, eds., *Rethinking Secularism* (New York: Oxford University Press, 2011).

29. Eben Alexander, *Proof of Heaven: A Neurosurgeon's Journey into the Afterlife* (New York: Simon & Schuster, 2012).

30. This is the conclusion reached by Gary Habermas, a theologian and philosopher who has collected and examined Near-Death Experiences that he believes are impossible to explain by materialism and naturalism alone. Dr. Habermas's website, www.garyhabermas.com, features dozens of well-documented articles as well as audio and video interviews.

31. Although a changed life is not proof of an idea's truth, it can be powerful evidence that makes us stop and think about

what an experience with God can be like. That people seem to be changed forever when they encounter the supernatural inspired Robert J. Spitzer to include Near-Death Experiences among the new proofs for God he discusses in his book *New Proofs for the Existence of God: Contributions of Contemporary Physics and Philosophy* (Grand Rapids, MI: Eerdmans, 2010). Intriguingly, he says, "One might think that the experience of God would lead to fear of the immense, uncontrollable Creator-Other; but in fact the experience of the divine seems to be quite different. Despite the immensity and uncontrollable otherness of God, there seems to be a joy, love, and quieting of the human heart so profound that they transform what might have been an alienating otherness into a sense of perfect Home" (285).

32. Alex Tsakiris, "112: Christian Apologist Dr. Gary Habermas Skeptical of Near Death Experience Spirituality" (includes an interview with Gary Habermas), Skeptiko, August, 31, 2010, www.skeptiko.com/112-gary-habermas-skeptical-of-near -death-experience-spirituality/.

33. It is worth noting that some Christians are skeptical because some reports include things that seem inconsistent with biblical testimony. Although we ought respectfully to listen to such reports, we needn't accept them as valid. As Habermas puts it, "Just because there's a supernatural world it doesn't mean that everything that's supernatural has equally good data in its favor" (Tsakiris, "112: Christian Apologist Dr. Gary Habermas"). As with all experiences, we need to measure every-thing against a reliable standard of truth. See also Gary R. Habermas, "Near Death Experiences and Worldview Concerns: Addressing Difficult Questions," *Areopagus Journal* 11, no. 4 (Fall, 2011).

34. Molly Edmonds, "Is the Brain Hardwired for Religion?," *How Stuff Works*, http://science.howstuffworks.com/life /inside-the-mind/human-brain/brain-religion2.htm.

35. Albright said, "In my opinion, every book of the New Testament was written by a baptized Jew between the forties and the eighties of the first century (very probably sometime between about A.D. 50 and 75)" (W. F. Albright, "Toward a More Conservative View," in *Christianity Today* [January 18, 1963]: 4).

36. Gleason L. Archer Jr., *A Survey of Old Testament Introduction* (Chicago: Moody, 1968), 1.

37. This is called the minimal facts approach, and it is explained in greater detail later in this chapter.

38. John Warwick Montgomery, *Human Rights and Human Dignity* (Dallas: Probe, 1986), 137.

39. In one instance, Josephus recorded that the high priest Annas "assembled the Sanhedrim of the judges, and brought before them the brother of Jesus, who was called Christ, whose name was James." Flavius Josephus, *Antiquities of the Jews; A History of the Jewish Wars; and Life of Flavius Josephus, Written By Himself*, trans. William Whiston (Philadelphia: Jas. B. Smith, 1858), 439.

40. Cornelius Tacitus, Annals XV. 44, quoted in Josh McDowell, *Evidence That Demands a Verdict: Historical Evidence for the Christian Faith* (San Bernardino, CA: Campus Crusade for Christ International, 1972), 84.

41. Bruce M. Metzger, *The New Testament: Its Background, Growth, and Content* (Nashville: Abingdon, 1965), 78.

42. Will Durant, *Caesar and Christ: A History of Roman Civilization and of Christianity from Their Beginnings to A.D. 325*, Story of Civilization, bk. 3 (New York: Simon & Schuster, 1944), 566.

43. See John P. Meier, *A Marginal Jew: Rethinking the Historical Jesus*, vol. 2 (New York: Doubleday, 1994); Graham H. Twelftree, *Jesus the Miracle Worker: A Historical and Theological Study* (Downers Grove, IL: IVP Academic, 1999).

44. Luke 3:1–2: "In the fifteenth year of the reign of Tiberius Caesar, Pontius Pilate being governor of Judea, and Herod being tetrarch of Galilee, and his brother Philip tetrarch of the region of Ituraea and Trachonitis, and Lysanias tetrarch of Abilene, during the high priesthood of Annas and Caiaphas, the word of God came to John the son of Zechariah in the wilderness."

45. Gary R. Habermas and Michael R. Licona, *The Case for the Resurrection of Jesus* (Grand Rapids, MI: Kregel, 2004), 44–45.

46. Michael R. Licona, "Can We Be Certain That Jesus Died on the Cross?," in *Evidence for God: 50 Arguments for Faith from the Bible, History, Philosophy, and Science*, ed. William A. Dembski and Michael R. Licona (Grand Rapids, MI: Baker, 2010), 165.

47. Licona, "Can We Be Certain," 167.

48. Habermas expands on this point: "His explicit statement here is important, due to the respect that scholars have for Paul's testimony. Further, his claim has been vindicated because there are many textual indications that the words that follow were not composed by him. For example, this list of appearances exhibits a parallel structure, as if it were an ancient catechism whose purpose was to be passed on and learned. Moreover, to identify a few other characteristics, the Greek sen-tence structure, diction, and some of the words are not Paul's, judging from his other epistles. Most scholars who address the subject think that Paul received this material about AD 35 just three years after his conversion, when he made his first trip to Jerusalem. Paul explains that he visited Peter and James the brother of Jesus (see Gal. 1:18–19). In the immediate context both before and after, Paul is discussing the nature of the gospel (see Gal. 1:11–2:10). Additionally, Paul's choice of words in verse 18 shows that he was interviewing or questioning the two apostles in order to gain information." Gary Habermas, "The Resurrection Appearances of Jesus," in *Evidence for God: 50 Arguments for Faith from the Bible, History, Philosophy, and Science*, ed. William A. Dembski and Michael R. Licona (Grand Rapids, MI: Baker, 2010), 173–74.

49. Habermas, "The Resurrection Appearances of Jesus," 174–75.

50. See 1 Corinthians 15:9; Galatians 1:13–14; Philippians 3:4–7.

51. See 1 Corinthians 9:1; 15:8; Galatians 1:16.

52. Habermas and Licona, *The Case for the Resurrection of Jesus*, 65.

53. See Mark 3:21, 31; 6:3–4; John 7:52.

54. See Acts 15:12–21; Galatians 1:19.

55. Habermas and Licona, *The Case for the Resurrection of Jesus*, 68.

56. Habermas and Licona, *The Case for the Resurrection of Jesus*, 70.

57. See Matthew 28:12–13; Justin Martyr, *Dialogue with Trypho*, 108; Tertullian, *De Spectaculis*, 30; Habermas and Licona, *The Case for the Resurrection of Jesus*, 71.

58. Habermas and Licona, *The Case for the Resurrection of Jesus*, 72–73.

59. William Lane Craig, *On Guard: Defending Your Faith with Reason and Precision* (Colorado Springs, CO: David C Cook, 2010), 228–29.

60. N. T. Wright, *The Resurrection of the Son of God: Christian Origins and the Question of God*, vol. 3 (Minneapolis: Fortress, 2003), 710.

61. Wright, *The Resurrection of the Son of God*.

62. 1 Corinthians 15:6: "He appeared to more than five hundred brothers at one time, most of whom are still alive, though some have fallen asleep."

63. Mark 16:8: "They went out and fled from the tomb, for trembling and astonishment had seized them, and they said nothing to anyone, for they were afraid"; John 20:19: "On the evening of that day, the first day of the week, the doors being locked where the disciples were for fear of the Jews, Jesus came and stood among them and said to them, 'Peace be with you.'"

64. Luke 24:38: "He said to them, 'Why are you troubled, and why do doubts arise in your hearts?'"; John 20:25: "The other disciples told him, 'We have seen the Lord.' But he said to them, 'Unless I see in his hands the mark of the nails, and place my finger into the mark of the nails, and place my hand into his side, I will never believe.'"

65. Acts 4:21: "When they had further threatened them, they let them go, finding no way to punish them, because of the people, for all were praising God for what had happened"; Acts 5:18, "They arrested the apostles and put them in the public prison."

66. Michael R. Licona, "Were the Resurrection Appearances of Jesus Hallucinations?," in *Evidence for God: 50 Arguments for Faith from the Bible, History, Philosophy, and Science*, ed. William A. Dembski and Michael R. Licona (Grand Rapids, MI: Baker, 2010), 178.

67. Licona, "Were the Resurrection Appearances," 178.

68. Licona, "Were the Resurrection Appearances," 178.

69. Craig, *On Guard*, 241–42.

70. Wright, *The Resurrection of the Son of God*, 710.

71. Luke 8:26–29: "Then they sailed to the country of the Gerasenes, which is opposite Galilee. When Jesus had stepped out on land, there met him a man from the city who had demons. For a long time he had worn no clothes, and he had not lived in a house but among the tombs. When he saw Jesus, he cried out and fell down before him and said with a loud voice, 'What have you to do with me, Jesus, Son of the Most High God? I beg you, do not torment me.' For he had commanded the unclean spirit to come out of the man. (For many a time it had seized him. He was kept under guard and bound with chains and shackles, but he would break the bonds and be driven by the demon into the desert.)"

72. Luke 13:10–11: "He was teaching in one of the synagogues on the Sabbath. And behold, there was a woman who had had a disabling spirit for eighteen years. She was bent over and could not fully straighten herself."

73. Julian Huxley, *Evolution: The Modern Synthesis* (New York: Harper and Brothers, 1942), 457.

74. Charles Taylor, *A Secular Age* (Cambridge, MA: Belknap, 2007), 269.

75. Jay E. Adams, *Competent to Counsel: Introduction to Nouthetic Counseling* (Grand Rapids, MI: Baker, 1970), 28.

76. Adams, *Competent to Counsel*, 29.

77. Lawrence J. Crabb, *Basic Principles of Biblical Counseling: Meeting Counseling Needs through the Local Church* (Grand Rapids, MI: Zondervan, 1975), 48–49.

78. Karl I. Payne, *Spiritual Warfare: Christians, Demonization, and Deliverance* (Washington, DC: WND Books, 2011), 34.

79. C. Fred Dickason, *Demon Possession and the Christian: A New Perspective* (Wheaton, IL: Crossway, 1987), 37.

80. The references to Satan as the prince of the demons is translated in Greek as *Beelzeboul*, which is a reference to Baal, with *zeboul* meaning "flies." So Beelzebub is "Lord of the flies." See Matthew 12:24, 27; Mark 3:22; Luke 11:15, 18ff. See F. F. Bruce, "Bal-Zebub, Beelzebul," in *New Bible Dictionary*, 3rd ed., ed. I. Howard Marshall, A. R. Millard, J. I. Packer, and D. J. Wiseman (Downers Grove, IL: InterVarsity, 1996), 108.

81. W. E. Vine, Merrill F. Unger, and William White, *Vine's Expository Dictionary of Biblical Words* (Nashville: Thomas Nelson, 1985), 12.

82. Robert T. Boyd, "Baal Worship," in *Boyd's Bible Handbook* (Eugene, OR: Harvest House, 1983), 106–14.

83. Ray Vander Laan, "Fertility Cults of Canaan," Follow the Rabbi, followtherabbi.com/guide/detail/fertility-cults-of-canaan.

84. Isaiah 65:4 condemns the worshippers of false gods—namely, Baal—"who sit in tombs, and spend the night in secret

places; who eat pig's flesh, and broth of tainted meat is in their vessels."

85. The most thorough treatment of the exploits of the Canaanite god El and his family is probably Mark S. Smith, *The Ugaritic Baal Cycle* (Leiden, NL: E. J. Brill, 1994). For a popular treatment, see Paul T. Penley, *Reenacting the Way (of Jesus)* (Colorado Springs, CO: Re-enacting the Way, 2013), 120–31.

86. We know that this thought probably occurred to some of them because when Jesus asked his disciples who people thought he was, one of the views offered was that he was the reincarnation of Elijah (Matt. 16).

87. See Ray Vander Laan, "A Far Country—Decapolis," Follow the Rabbi, followtherabbi.com/guide/detail/a-far-country-decapolis. Vander Laan's insights are based on Bargil Pixner, *With Jesus through Galilee according to the Fifth Gospel* (Rosh Pina, Israel: Corazin Publishing, 1992). For a popular treatment, see Penley, *Reenacting the Way*, 129.

88. For more information, Vander Laan, "A Far Country—Decapolis."

89. Martin Luther, "A Mighty Fortress Is Our God," trans. Frederick H. Hedge, www.hymnsite.com/lyrics/umh110.sht.

90. Romans 16:20: "The God of peace will soon crush Satan under your feet. The grace of our Lord Jesus Christ be with you."

91. Charles H. Kraft, *Christianity with Power: Your Worldview and Your Experience of the Supernatural* (Eugene, OR: Wipf and Stock, 1989), 28.

92. See, for example, Jeremy Roschelle, "Learning in Interactive Environments: Prior Knowledge and New Experience," Institute for Inquiry, www.exploratorium.edu/ifi/resources/museumeducation/priorknowledge.html.

93. C. S. Lewis, *The Magician's Nephew* (New York: HarperCollins, 1994), 134.

94. Payne, *Spiritual Warfare*, 115.

95. Payne, *Spiritual Warfare*, xxii.

96. C. S. Lewis, *The Screwtape Letters* (New York: HarperOne, 2009), 16.

97. *The Usual Suspects*, directed by Bryan Singer (Metro-Goldwyn-Mayer, 1995).

98. James 4:7: "Submit yourselves therefore to God. Resist the devil, and he will flee from you."

99. Dickason, *Demon Possession and the Christian*, 37.

100. 1 Corinthians 6:20: "You were bought with a price. So glorify God in your body."

101. William Lane Craig, "Did Jesus Rise from the Dead?," in *Jesus Under Fire: Modern Scholarship Reinvents the Historical Jesus*, ed. Michael J. Wilkins and J. P. Moreland (Grand Rapids, MI: Zondervan, 1995), 166.

102. 1 John 2:16: "All that is in the world—the desires of the flesh and the desires of the eyes and pride of life—is not from the Father but is from the world."

103. Payne, *Spiritual Warfare*, 89.

104. Curt Thompson, *Anatomy of the Soul: Surprising Connections between Neuroscience and Spiritual Practices That Can Transform Your Life and Relationships* (Carol Stream, IL: Tyndale, 2010), 53.

105. Thompson, *Anatomy of the Soul*, 83.

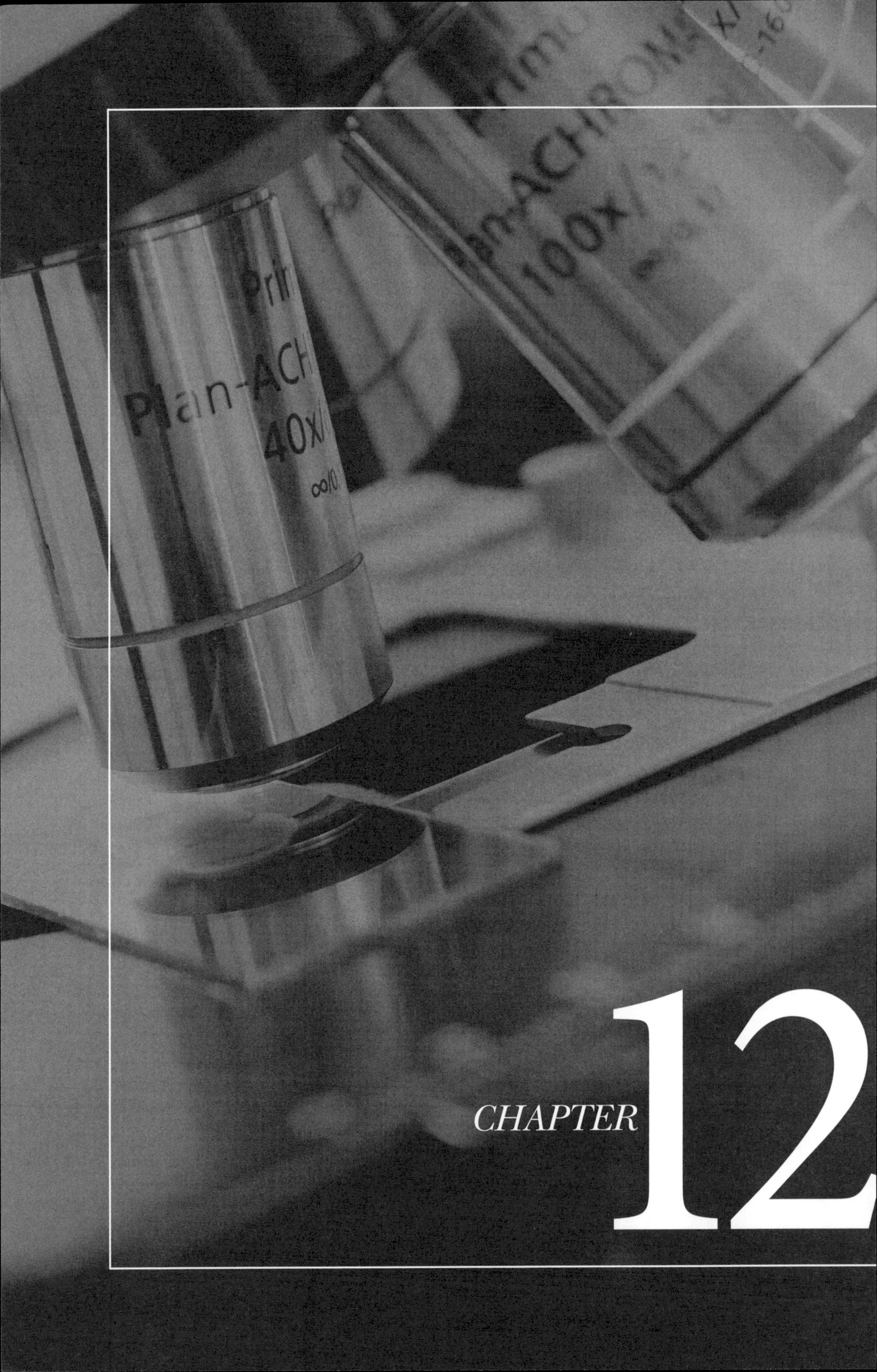

CHAPTER 12

ISN'T CHRISTIANITY ANTI-SCIENCE?

1. THE BATTLE BETWEEN CHRISTIANITY AND SCIENCE

In "Cosmos in Theological Scriptures"—a scholarly article published in a journal dealing with space, science, and law—Indian attorney Gurbachan Singh Sachdeva asserts the following:

Christian interpretations of the origin of the universe, as per the Christian Bible, are generally well known.... Christianity believes that the Earth is the stationary center of our solar system and everything else revolves around it, including the Sun. Man, the supreme earthly being, came to inhabit the Earth as the progeny of Adam, who was expelled from Heaven for his sin of having tasted the forbidden fruit that impelled him to commit the sin of fornication. In punishment, he was dropped onto the Earth to live in loneliness so that he could repent for his cardinal sin. Later, in compassion, God created Eve out of the rib of Adam to give him company and as consort. Cohabitation followed and the result has been mankind on Earth.[1]

Sachdeva has nearly every aspect of the biblical creation narrative wrong, but one wonders how many of his readers, in accepting the larger point of his article, also unthinkingly accept his account of Scripture.

That Sachdeva's account made it into a scholarly journal presumably concerned with accuracy may be a rather odd illustration of the tension between science and Christianity, but it serves to highlight a larger debate over whether science is supreme and Christianity is merely a quaint superstition. To many scientists, one cannot be both religious and intelligent at the same time. Famed biologist Edward O. Wilson puts it this way: "The human mind evolved to believe in the gods. It did not evolve to believe in biology.... The uncomfortable truth is that the two beliefs are not factually compatible. As a result those who hunger for both intellectual and religious truth will never acquire both in full measure."[2]

> **DNA (deoxyribonucleic acid):** a self-replicating, double strand of nucleic acid located in the nucleus of a cell; the storehouse for the genetic instructions used to build every protein within an organism.

Of course, there are scientists who dispute this "science versus religion" framing. Francis Collins, director of the National Institutes of Health and the scientist who headed up the Human Genome Project, which mapped the entire human deoxyribonucleic acid (**DNA**) sequence, said, "Science is not threatened by God; it is enhanced. God is most certainly not threatened by science; He made it all possible."[3]

So which point is closer to the truth? Are science and religion (specifically Christianity, in this case) compatible, or are they going to forever be at odds?

Some faith systems are incompatible with science, but Christianity is not one of them. The Bible describes a God who is orderly and knowable and who made a world that consists of knowable reality (Ps. 8:3–5).[4] Jesus Christ is presented as the creator of everything both visible and invisible (Col. 1:16).[5] As we will see, modern science was founded on these assumptions. Only in the past two centuries or so has science come to be seen as incompatible with and superior to Christianity.

It is possible that those who view Christianity and science as incompatible have observed something that somehow escaped the notice of everyone who has lived in the last two thousand years. But is it also possible that modern assumptions have somehow colored people's perceptions and caused them to miss a greater truth? To answer this question, we need to closely examine what science actually is, its history, the contributions of Christians to the field, the limits of science, and whether the supposed conflicts between the Bible's claims and the claims of science can be reasonably explained.

2. A Straightforward Way to Think about the Bible and Science

The National Academy of Sciences defines **science** as "the use of evidence to construct testable explanation and prediction of natural phenomena, as well as the knowledge generated through this process" and holds that "scientists gather information by observing the natural world and conducting experiments."[6] Science assumes that nature operates in a predictable, stable manner and

> *Science:* the process of using observable evidence to construct testable explanations and predictions for natural phenomena.

that the results we obtain in any given case will yield similar results under similar conditions. This assumption about the orderliness and predictability of nature—indeed a great many of science's underlying assumptions—is based on principles that early scientists believed *because* they believed in the God of the Bible.

This is not to say that the Bible is a book of science. It's bigger than that. The Bible, as we saw in earlier chapters, presents an overarching story—a metanarrative about the world and everyone in it from the perspective of a sovereign God and his plan for the world.

Though the Bible is not a book of science, it is not against science either. The relationship of science to the Bible is similar to the relationship between photography and the study of history. Just as science helps clarify our observations of nature, photography enables accurate pictures to be made. Accuracy does help tell better stories, but photographs themselves are not the story, nor are they the only or best way of telling it. Just as it would be foolish to say that there was no history before there was photography, it is foolish to say that people's prescientific thoughts were ignorant and now irrelevant.

"But this is an unfair analogy," some might protest. "Science makes our observations more accurate, which enables us to make superior decisions to those made in more Christian times." This is a serious point and one worth examining. It is true that there are many examples of how people in more Christian times made bad or bizarre decisions. But people have done bad and bizarre things in the name of science, too. Physics and engineering made possible weapons that are far deadlier than those used in previous centuries. And sometimes scientists even distort the truth for their own purposes, as happened with Soviet scientist T. D. Lysenko, who "outlawed" dissent from his theory of genetics because he believed that contrary thought would pose a threat to Marxism and upset the Soviet leader Joseph Stalin.[7]

As we will see, the relationship between Christianity and science is not what people imagine. It certainly does not fit the "We're smarter than we used to be, so we need to reject Christianity" narrative. The truth is much more complex—and much more fascinating.

3. How Christianity Brought About Modern Science

Everyone has heard the story of Isaac Newton (1643–1727) sitting under an apple tree, thinking deep thoughts, when all of a sudden an apple fell on his head and inspired him to discover the law of gravity. The story is so popular that descendants of the purported tree have been replanted in significant locations, including at Trinity College of Cambridge University outside the window of the room where Newton lived and studied.

Unfortunately, what really happened hardly keeps our interest: Newton did report a falling apple, and he did muse about why the fall of apples is perpendicular, rather than sideways, to the ground, but it took two decades for Newton to work out his subsequent thoughts about planetary motion and propose the law of gravity in *The Principia*, a tome of more than 450 pages.

Clearly, though, stories have immense power. According to British social scientist Philip J. Sampson, people tend to remember and believe well-told stories, even if false,[8] which might explain why so many believe that it was scientists who bravely rejected church authority and exalted reason and thus set people free from superstitious ignorance. Christianity, by this narrative, is illicitly grasping for control in the face of scientific truth. Sampson traces this narrative back to Thomas Huxley, "Darwin's bulldog," who thought that religious beliefs threatened acceptance of Charles Darwin's theory.[9] But is this a battle of truth or a battle of stories *about* truth? Was Huxley stating things as they actually were or glossing over complexities in order to replace one set of stories with another? Huxley did seem to resent Christianity, even forming the Sunday Lecture Society as an alternative to church to promote learning free of what he considered to be religious dogma.

After Huxley, late nineteenth-century historians such as John W. Draper and Andrew D. White promoted science by writing derisively of Christianity. They invented and used stories to perpetuate the myths that supported scientific progress,[10] such as Christopher Columbus's conquering religious superstition about the earth being a flat disc with Jerusalem at the center by fearlessly sailing toward the earth's supposed edge. White gleefully repeated the story of Pope Callixtus III, horrified at the arrival of Halley's Comet, excommunicating it as an agent of the Devil. Neither account has any factual basis. All educated people at the time of Columbus knew the earth was round, and the story of the pope excommunicating a comet was made up.[11] Both stories have nonetheless been trumpeted as evidence of Christianity being anti-science.

Another example often enlisted to portray Christianity as anti-science is that of Galileo Galilei's (1564–1642) interrogation at the hands of the Catholic Church in 1633. Secularist philosopher and mathematician Bertrand Russell, for instance, said, "Galileo, as everyone knows, was condemned by the Inquisition…. He recanted, and promised never again to maintain that the earth rotates or revolves. The Inquisition was successful at putting an end to science in Italy … and did considerable damage to the Church by its stupidity."[12]

> People tend to remember and believe well-told stories, even if false, which might explain why so many believe that it was scientists who bravely rejected church authority and exalted reason and thus set people free from superstitious ignorance.

Contrary to Russell's telling, Sampson quotes prominent Galileo scholars in labeling the "Galileo versus the Inquisitors" story a "simplistic myth." More accurately, he says, Galileo's interrogation resulted from "complex intrigues of politics and patronage" and "wounded pride" rather than a conflict over whether the earth revolves around the sun, or the sun around the earth.[13] Basically, what happened is this: Galileo's research confirmed some central aspects of

ISN'T CHRISTIANITY ANTI-SCIENCE?

Nicholas Copernicus's theory that the earth revolved around the sun rather than the other way around. Galileo sent his results to Pope Paul V, who responded warmly and offered to support the theory provisionally, pending further evidence. Rather than doing additional research to provide such evidence, though, Galileo picked fights with his fellow scientists, who he thought were questioning his brilliance by proving some aspects of his thesis wrong. He also quarreled with Vatican theologians by attempting to interpret the Bible in ways that Roman Catholic Church leaders found to be rebellious. At a time when the Protestant Reformation was in full swing, this was a definite no-no.

And still the church responded to Galileo in mild and restrained ways until he published a parable that included a character, Simplicio (simpleton), into whose mouth he put the words of the new pope, Urban VIII. Brought on trial for heresy, the church still tried to treat the now aging and sickly Galileo with kindness by providing a luxurious apartment at the Vatican and a personal valet during the trial. Mocking the Vatican court during his trial, Galileo was eventually sentenced to live out his days at a country house in Florence, cared for by his daughter.[14] Even Alfred North Whitehead, Russell's onetime coauthor, pointed out that contrary to tales of Galileo being imprisoned in a dank dungeon and threated with torture, he "suffered an honourable detention and a mild reproof, before dying peacefully in his bed."[15]

When all the facts are known, the Galileo story is not one of science versus religion. Galileo himself didn't believe that religion and science were in conflict. Rather, he wrote admiringly of God's design for the mind: "When I consider what marvelous things and how many of them men have understood, inquired into, and contrived, I recognize and understand only too clearly that the human mind is a work of God's, and one of the most excellent."[16]

> When all the facts are known, the Galileo story is not one of science versus religion. Galileo himself didn't believe that religion and science were in conflict.

The story of an age of ignorance in which religious superstition suppressed the development of science now appears to be a false history designed to make Christianity look villainous. As C. Warren Hollister, a distinguished medievalist, said, "Anyone who believes that the era that witnessed the building of Chartres Cathedral and the invention of parliament and the university was 'dark' must be ... deeply, deeply, ignorant."[17]

Although some may find the Christianity-as-villain-and-science-as-savior narrative compelling, the truth is actually more interesting. Science assumes an orderly universe. If the universe were disorderly or chaotic, we couldn't expect it to behave in a predictable, comprehensible, meaningful manner. For instance, we could not reasonably assume that Newton's apple would always fall down. Perhaps it would hit a pocket of chaos and fall up or travel sideways or aim directly for a neighbor's plate-glass window. But *why* should we assume that our universe is orderly and predictable? To distinguished scholar of science and religion John Hedley Brooke, early scientists assumed that "there were laws of nature only because there had been a Legislator."[18]

Indeed, a great deal of modern science was born out of Christian beliefs. Theologian Francis Schaeffer wrote, "Since the world had been created by a reasonable God, [scientists] were not surprised to find a correlation between themselves as observers and the thing observed—that is, between subject and object.... Without this foundation, modern Western science would not have been born."[19] Holmes Rolston III, distinguished professor of philosophy at Colorado State University, likewise explains,

> It was monotheism that launched the coming of physical science, for it premised an intelligible world, sacred but disenchanted, a world with blueprint, which was therefore open to the searches of the scientists. The great pioneers in physics—Newton, Galileo, Kepler, Copernicus—devoutly believed themselves called to find evidences of God in the physical world. Even Einstein, much later and in a different era, when puzzling over how space and time were made, used to ask himself how God would have arranged the matter. A universe of such beauty, an Earth given over to life and to culture—such phenomena imply a transcending power adequate to account for these productive workings in the world.[20]

American scholar Ian Barbour points out that the world's oldest scientific society, the Royal Society of London, "instructed its fellows to direct their studies 'to the glory of God and the benefits of the human race'" and notes that these early scientists "identified themselves with the Christian tradition in which they were nourished, and many of them seem to have experienced a personal response of reverence and awe toward the marvels they beheld."[21] He explains,

> Expressions of awed surprise and admiration of the skill of the Creator dot the pages of their writings. The sense of the grandeur and wisdom of God was evidently a very positive experience for many of them and not just an abstract intellectual formula or a concession to cultural respectability.[22]

> Philosopher and historian of science Stanley Jaki noted that the belief in creation and the Creator "formed the bedrock on which science rose."

Similarly, philosopher and historian of science Stanley Jaki noted that the belief in creation and the Creator "formed the bedrock on which science rose."[23] Jaki's perspective is especially noteworthy because, as a Catholic priest and influential philosopher, he was well-versed in both religion and science. Jaki maintained that

> the belief in a personal rational Creator … as cultivated especially within a Christian matrix … supported the view for which the world was an objective and orderly entity investigable by the mind because the mind too was an orderly and objective product of the same rational, that is, perfectly consistent Creator. [24]

Rolston, Barbour, and Jaki are by no means uneducated observers, and their conclusion is clear: science is possible because God was believed by early scientists to be as the Bible describes him: a God of reason and order. Christianity, then, was "the mother of modern science."[25] Skeptics may scoff, but today's scientific breakthroughs are possible because of tools forged in a faith-based belief system.

So who were these early scientists so committed to a Christian view of the world? We've already mentioned Isaac Newton. Another was Robert Boyle (1627–1691), a founder of modern chemistry and the discoverer of Boyle's Law, which describes the relationship between the pressure and volume of a gas. Boyle wrote a book called *The Christian Virtuoso*, in which he described what it would take for a Christian to be an outstanding scientist, or, as he termed it, "experimental philosopher." His criteria included being without material ambition, truth focused, humble, honorable, devout, and in submission to the authority of nature and not of other men.[26] Boyle was well known for trying to live up to this code, and it is hard to imagine other scientists in Oxford and in the Royal Society being uninfluenced by his views. John Hedley Brooke thus observes of Boyle and his contemporaries,

> Robert Boyle and Isaac Newton saw the study of nature as a religious duty. A knowledge of God's power and wisdom could be inferred from the intelligence seemingly displayed in the designs of nature. Newton affirmed that the natural sciences had prospered only in monotheistic cultures.... He believed the universality of his laws was grounded in the omnipresence of a single divine Will.[27]

Boyle and Newton, however, were hardly the only self-proclaimed Christians who became revered scientists.

Another example, English philosopher Francis Bacon (1561–1626) is credited with establishing the scientific method as the ruling method for investigation. Committed to his craft and his faith, he used distinctly biblical language to describe the "idols" that could corrupt science, such as self-deception, prejudice, misuse of words, and false persuasion. Summarizing Bacon's view, Harvard historian of science Steven Shapin says, "We are human, all-too-human; we are fallen and fallible; and such is our fate."[28] Bacon's theology, rooted in the biblical idea that humans are subject to sin, was the basis of the careful, studious approach to discovery that he pioneered.

So what caused the breakup between science and Christianity? Apparently, as science moved into the eighteenth century, those promoting the Enlightenment came to believe that rationality and systematic thinking could cure humanity's fall into sin and restore virtue.[29] Faith in rationality began to replace faith in God. Science became a form of worship. Famous historian of science George Sarton admitted as much when he described science as "the very anchor of our philosophy, of our morality, of our faith."[30]

> *Age of Enlightenment:* an eighteenth-century intellectual movement that emphasized reason, science, and individualism over tradition and religious authority.

Today, we are still experiencing vibrations from the earthquake that we now know as the **Age of Enlightenment**. And some of those vibrations opened a rift between science and Christianity that seems to be widening to this day.

4. ARE FAITH AND SCIENCE LOCKED IN MORTAL COMBAT?

David Berlinski is a mathematician and brilliant writer. Jewish by heritage and secular by conviction, he is nonetheless critical of those who pit faith against science. Both are necessary, he says, quoting Albert Einstein: "Science without religion is lame, religion without science is blind."[31]

Voices like Berlinski's, though, seem to be getting drowned out. Victor Stenger, a leading atheist who died in 2014, asserted, "Faith is belief in the absence of supportive evidence and even in the light of contrary evidence.... Science makes no such assumptions on faith."[32] He said, "Using the empirical method, science has eliminated smallpox, flown men to the moon, and discovered DNA.... Relying on faith, religion has brought us inquisitions, holy wars, and intolerance."[33] To Stenger it is clear that not only is there a battle between belief (represented by religion and philosophy) and knowledge (represented by science) but that science has won a clear victory. All that remains is for religious people to have the good sense to surrender.

In this chapter, we will suggest that the "science versus faith" battle Stenger outlined is much more nuanced than he seemed to believe, for two reasons.

First, science is consistent with the Christian faith. We must keep in mind that saying that science "has eliminated smallpox, flown men to the moon, and discovered DNA" is a kind of shorthand that makes science appear to be more powerful than it really is. In fact, "science" is not a force of nature but rather the result of the work of individuals who create breakthroughs by practicing the disciplines of repeatedly observing, measuring, and experimenting.[34] To do this, scientists must assume that the universe operates in observable, measurable, and repeatable ways—assumptions that are entirely consistent with the testimony of Scripture if not derived directly from a Christian worldview.

Still, many feel comfortable with near-worship of science. Physicist Stephen Hawking has crowed, "Scientists have become the bearers of the torch of discovery in our quest for knowledge."[35] But as Oxford mathematician John Lennox points out, Hawking's assertion is a philosophical statement, not a scientific one.[36] Scientists might be proud of their achievements, but most recognize the limits of their craft. A few—such as Stenger, Hawking, and Dawkins—seem to enjoy cutting loose with the occasional victory howl, but most just keep their heads down and continue their work.

> Christians should have no problem embracing scientific as well as philosophical, religious ways of knowing. After all, if one starts with a designer, a person expects to find design in the world.

Christians should have no problem embracing scientific as well as philosophical, religious ways of knowing. After all, if one starts with a designer, a person expects to find design in the world. This is why scholars such as Rodney Stark say it is precisely *because* of their religious convictions about design and order, not in spite of them, that the world's greatest scientists succeeded. Moreover, it was Christianity in particular (rather than Islam, New Age spirituality, or any of the atheistic humanisms) that was most responsible for this success.[37] Christians founded chemistry, paleontology, bacteriology, antiseptic surgery, genetics, thermodynamics, computer science, and many other fields.[38] If these breakthroughs come because of the faith of scientists rather than in spite of it—and strong evidence indicates that they do—then to pit faith against science is to misunderstand both faith and science.[39]

Second, naturalistic science is *based* on faith. Physicist and bestselling author Paul Davies, a respected scientist who is not a Christian believer, makes an interesting claim: "Science has its own faith-based belief system."[40] When Davies asked colleagues why the laws of physics are what they are, they replied, "That's not a scientific question" or "Nobody knows" or (and most revealing), "There is no reason they are what they are—they just are."[41] In short, science cannot account for the underlying truths that make it work. Scientists, Davies concludes, operate by faith. Until science comes up with a testable theory of the laws of the universe, he says, "Its claim to be free of faith is manifestly bogus."[42]

The next time someone implies that science is somehow "the good guy" while religion is "the bad guy," you might consider pressing forward with such questions as these:

- "What is science?"

- "If the universe is the product of chance, why is it reasonable to expect it to function as if it were designed, in a way that we can understand?"

- "What evidence do you have that only scientists who lack faith in design accomplish anything?"

At the very least, such questions can spark an interesting conversation. Perhaps they'll also leave the other person thinking more deeply about both faith and science.

So if science is a faith-based enterprise, based on faith in the orderliness of the world and operating by principles about the world for which it cannot account, what *are* those principles? We've addressed one already: how the lawfulness of the universe, without which scientific investigation is not possible, derives from a belief in a divine Creator. Yet the lawfulness of the universe is not the only scientific principle made uniquely possible by the Christian worldview. In their book *The Soul of Science*, Nancy Pearcey and Charles Thaxton list seven more:

1. Nature is valuable enough to study (as opposed to the ancient Greek belief that nature was transient and therefore relatively unimportant).

2. Nature is good but not god (as opposed to animistic religions that leave nature alone because it is the exclusive abode of the gods).

3. Nature is orderly (as opposed to religions that taught that the world is unpredictable because it is ruled by a pantheon of unruly and unpredictable gods).

4. Nature's laws can be precisely stated and understood (as opposed to ancient religions that taught that creation was too mysterious to be consistently known).

5. Humans can discover nature's order (as opposed to the ancient eastern belief that nature was not the product of a rational mind and therefore not subject to rational thinking).

6. Detailed observation is possible and important (as opposed to Aristotle's thinking that if an object's purpose was understood, detailed observation of it is was unnecessary).

7. The universe is rationally intelligible because God is rationally intelligent (as opposed to philosophies that trust limited human intelligence as the only kind that really exists).[43]

These assumptions, consistent with biblical revelation, inspired some of the world's greatest scientists to develop the enterprise we call modern science.

Today, though, there are many disagreements among Christians themselves about what the Bible teaches regarding science. Let's take a look at these differences and see if we can find common ground.

5. The Consistency of the Bible's Claims with Scientific Observation

The Bible is not, as we have already discussed, primarily a book of science. Often people critique it as *anti*-science, though, because they lack an understanding of how to properly interpret Scripture's various genres. For example, we would not read David's plea in Psalm 17:8 for God to shelter him under his wings to mean that God has wings. In a poetic genre, under which Psalm 17 falls, the appropriate question is not "What does this say about God's literal, physical characteristics?" but rather "What truth does this poem speak about God's nature?"

Skeptics eager to disprove the Bible's purported scientific claims have often scoured its pages to find claims they know to be wrong. Most of them understand that writings of a poetic nature are not to be taken literally, but what about those passages that make literal historical claims? Those are fair game, are they not? This is why such critics usually zero in on the creation account in Genesis chapter 1. Using the tools of science, there are many things about Genesis 1 that, at first blush, don't make sense, such as how it was possible for there to have been light on earth before the sun was created. To say that "God could make it happen" is unsatisfying to these critics, and they are all too happy to use their findings to conclude that Christianity is, in fact, anti-science.

We shouldn't dismiss such concerns too quickly. A thoughtful reading of Genesis 1 clearly depicts a very literal-sounding creation story. It mentions the sun, moon, and stars along with birds in the air and fish in the sea. These physical objects and living creatures actually exist, of course. The use of the word *day* in the creation account to denote a cycle of evening and morning sounds like the sorts of days we actually experience. Adam and Eve are depicted as actual people whose descendants can be traced through the biblical narrative down through the generations, even to the birth of Jesus. Jesus himself talked about Adam and Eve as if they were specially created by God (Matt. 19:4; Mark 10:6–9).[44]

So do the days of creation describe literal history? Is the Genesis 1 narrative intended to communicate a sequence of events as they actually happened? If so, scientists say, Genesis 1 gets the facts wrong, and this casts suspicion on other biblical claims.

There are four main ways Christians respond to the criticism of the claim that Genesis is factually inaccurate and unscientific.[45]

- **Young-age creationism:** Young-age creationists say that as recently as six thousand years ago, God created the universe in six twenty-four-hour days. Living organisms were created distinct and separate in much their present forms. Young-age creationists respond to their critics by saying that Christians ought to interpret science from the standpoint of the Bible rather than the Bible from the standpoint of science. If we do this, they say, we will see that scientists have misunderstood the data of the physical world. A handful of young-age creationists are currently developing and testing hypotheses about the young age of the earth that they believe will explain this data better than an old-earth hypothesis.

- **Progressive creationism:** Progressive creationists say God created basic kinds of living organisms separately (in something like their present forms) with the capacity to change and adapt to their circumstances over time (though within limits). Human beings were created separately by God at a much later time. This viewpoint holds that the days of creation were not literal twenty-four-hour days and accepts mainstream scientific beliefs about an "old" age of the earth and the universe, though it rejects Darwinian claims about the evolution of all life from the first self-replicating molecule.

- **Theistic evolution:** Theistic evolutionists generally grant that evolutionary theory is true but say God somehow initiated and oversaw the evolutionary process. Some believe that God sparked the first life and then worked through the natural process of evolution to bring about the diversity of life we see today. Others believe that the origin and evolution of life were completely natural events. In fact, some theistic evolutionists think God works only through natural causes. At some point, many theistic evolutionists believe, God gave human beings souls, setting them apart from other creatures.[46] Sometimes it's hard to distinguish the scientific views of theistic evolutionists from their atheistic counterparts except for their qualifier, "And by the way, God did it."

- **Intelligent design:** The fourth view has emerged in recent years to take insights about design and bring them into the scientific dialogue without commenting on the theological controversy among young-age creationism, progressive creationism, and theistic evolution. According to advocates of intelligent design (ID), from the cosmic architecture of the universe down to nanoscale molecular machines inside of cells, we find the marks of a designer. Many features of life are irreducibly complex—meaning they could not have evolved through chance-based, Darwinian evolutionary processes—and require an intelligent cause. Many scientists fail to see this, ID proponents believe, because they begin with a bias that says that only natural causes may be considered by science. They think the design hypothesis could check this naturalistic bias and yield greater scientific understanding. ID advocates take various positions on the age of the earth, though most recognize ID as consistent with an old-earth viewpoint and even with universal common ancestry.

As you can see, young-age creationism, progressive creationism, and theistic evolution are quite different. They all employ insights from ID, but they make assumptions that contradict the assumptions of the others. They cannot all be equally true. Knowing this, organizations have developed around each viewpoint, hoping to recruit theologians, philosophers, and scientists to their way of thinking.

If you listen to debates among Christians on the origins issue, you might find yourself thinking, *Can't we all get along?* Well, yes and no: "no" in the sense that some of the viewpoints, such as theistic evolution, take substantial theological liberties with the biblical text, leaving it difficult to see what about God's Word might actually be true (for example, denying that God specially created the first man and woman); "yes" in the sense that all these viewpoints affirm that God exists, that he is a creator outside of and transcendent over his creation, that creation is good, that God's work brings him glory, and that humans bear God's image and are stewards of creation. These are theological claims on which orthodox Christians agree.

If we step outside the controversy for a moment, we'll see that several of the Bible's claims are consistent with the scientific observations of our day: evidence of design in nature, something outside the universe bringing the universe into being, life arising from life and not from nonlife, intention and order in creation, humanity being at the apex of creation, and the limits to change in nature. Let's take a look at each of these in turn.

There is evidence of design in nature. Anglican clergyman William Paley's 1802 book *Natural Theology* was so widely respected that even Charles Darwin admitted, "I do not think I hardly ever admired a book more."[47] Paley offered what is now known as the **watchmaker argument**: a person chancing upon a watch in the wilderness could not conclude that the watch had simply always existed. Rather, the obvious design of the watch, including not only its internal makeup but also the fact that it exists for a purpose, would necessarily imply the existence of its designer and not the product of natural processes. Paley went on to substitute the universe for the watch and contend that a mechanism so obviously designed as the universe could only be the product of a grand designer.[48]

> *Watchmaker Argument:* an argument for God's existence that compares the design of a watch to the design found within the cosmos and concludes that the universe, like a watch, can be best explained by the existence of an intelligent designer.

As more details about the universe and living organisms are uncovered, the more we confirm the sort of design Paley saw with his limited scientific instruments. As Albert Einstein, who was certainly no creationist, said, "The harmony of natural law … reveals an intelligence of such superiority that, compared with it, all the systematic thinking and acting of human beings is an utterly insignificant reflection."[49] More recently, physicist Paul Davies, who, as mentioned earlier, does not profess to be a Christian, said, "Every advance in fundamental physics seems to reveal yet another facet of order."[50]

Biochemist Michael Behe, in his book *Darwin's Black Box*, coined the phrase **irreducible complexity** to describe the way molecular "machines" (such as the bacterial flagellum) and biochemical processes (such as blood clotting) exhibit design. Irreducibly complex features are those that, if reduced to simpler or fewer parts, could not still perform their required

ISN'T CHRISTIANITY ANTI-SCIENCE?

function. Take a mousetrap, for example. All of the parts must exist and be assembled at once if you want to catch mice. One cannot start with the wooden base and then, after catching a few mice, add the bait and then a spring. According to Behe, a gradual step-by-step evolutionary process cannot explain a biological system in which all of the parts either work together in harmony or don't work at all.[51] Darwin taught that natural selection works on small improvements in function. But if a basic set of components must be in place before there even *is* function, then Darwinism has little to say about how complex organisms arose in the first place.

Irreducible Complexity: a concept that considers the complexity of integrated systems such that if any part is removed, the system ceases to function, and that when applied to biology, challenges the notion that complex biological systems (such as the eye) could have gradually evolved through a series of intermediary steps.

Particularly among those scientists who have examined the tiny building blocks of life, there is growing suspicion of chance processes explaining the complexity they see. Australian biochemist Michael Denton explains,

> Although the tiniest bacterial cells are incredibly small, weighing less than 10-12 gms [grams], each is in effect a veritable micro-miniaturized factory containing thousands of exquisitely designed pieces of intricate molecular machinery, made up altogether of one hundred thousand million atoms, far more complicated than any machine built by man and absolutely without parallel in the non-living world.[52]

Even committed evolutionists recognize the unparalleled complexity of cellular systems. Former US National Academy of Sciences president Bruce Alberts wrote in the prominent journal *Cell*,

> The entire cell can be viewed as a factory that contains an elaborate network of interlocking assembly lines, each of which is composed of a set of large protein machines.... Why do we call the large protein assemblies that underlie cell function protein machines? Precisely because, like machines invented by humans to deal efficiently with the macroscopic world, these protein assemblies contain highly coordinated moving parts.[53]

Likewise, University of Chicago geneticist James Shapiro observes that "no human contrivance operates with either the degree of complexity, the precision, or the efficiency of living cells."[54]

Evidence for design has only grown since Paley wrote about it almost two centuries ago.[55] We now know that life is based upon an information-rich code in our DNA that provides building instructions for molecular machines inside our cells, which are full of coordinated, interacting parts that can operate at near 100 percent energy efficiency. But where in our experience do such things as language-based codes, computer-like programming commands, and irreducibly complex machines come from? They have only one known cause: intelligent beings.

Something outside the universe brought it into being. One of the greatest discoveries of modern cosmology is that the universe began with an unimaginably powerful explosion from an infinitely small and densely compacted point of matter and energy. The evidence shows that the universe is finite in space and time, and this requires that the universe had a beginning. Philosophically, everything that begins to exist has a cause. No causal chain we know of or can imagine is infinitely long, so there must have been a first cause. Theists call this uncaused cause God.

Science has something to say about this as well. In chapter 10, we briefly discussed the **second law of thermodynamics**, which posits that although the amount of energy in the universe remains constant, it does move from useful to less useful states, so there must have been a time when the energy "clock" began ticking.[56] The implication is that the universe must have had a beginning. Just like a grandfather clock that is winding down, there must have been a point at which it was originally wound up.

Second Law of Thermodynamics: a scientific law that states that the amount of usable energy in a closed system will decrease over time.

As philosopher and former atheist Antony Flew observes, "The universe is something that begs an explanation," and therefore, "if the universe had a beginning, it became entirely sensible, almost inevitable, to ask what produced this beginning."[57] Not only that, but as Christian theologians and philosophers are quick to point out, whoever began the universe must be capable of possessing the variety of characteristics we see in the world today. For example, moral force, intelligence, love, justice, and so forth are immaterial concepts that could not have plausibly arisen from material conditions alone.

Mutation: a change in the genetic makeup of an organism.

Natural Selection (aka Survival of the Fittest): the process by which organisms better adapted for their environment tend to survive longer, reproduce, and pass along more favorable biological traits.

Spontaneous Generation: the belief that nonliving matter produced living matter through purely natural processes.

Life does not come from nonlife. Naturalists believe that nothing exists except that which has a natural origin. Materialists believe in only the world of matter. Both naturalists and materialists share the belief that somewhere, somehow, at some time, life arose from nonlife and that it managed to survive and increase in complexity and organization through mechanisms such as **mutation** and **natural selection**. These resulted in the variety of life we see today, including human beings.

But how did this process begin? Life has never been observed to arise from nonlife. Even laboratory experiments under carefully controlled conditions have produced nothing more than a small handful of the dozens of chemical building blocks essential for life. Unless something alive and outside the universe brought life into existence, naturalists and materialists are stuck with only one option: at some point, life must have arisen from nonlife, a notion called **spontaneous generation**.

The authors of one of today's most popular biology textbooks admit that Francesco Redi and Louis Pasteur's

ISN'T CHRISTIANITY ANTI-SCIENCE?

mid-nineteenth-century experiments unequivocally disproved spontaneous generation and says that "those who had believed in the spontaneous generation of microorganisms gave up their fight."[58] Four pages later, however, this same text suggests that research by Soviet biochemist Alexander Oparin and others makes it "possible" to "believe" (note the faith-based language) that life can arise from nonlife.[59] Steven Garber's *Biology: A Self-Teaching Guide*, possibly the most popular biology text available (with more than two million copies sold), uses the same arguments.[60]

Although modern evolutionary scientists would no longer endorse "spontaneous genera-tion" in the way it was upheld in centuries past, they still believe in a version of Oparin's hypothesis, claiming that life arose from inanimate matter via unguided chemical reactions on the early earth some three to four billion years ago. According to this view, there were many steps involved in the origin of life, but the very first was probably the production of a **primordial soup**—a water-based sea of simple organic molecules—out of which life arose. While the existence of this "soup" has been accepted as unquestioned fact for decades, even this first seemingly simple step in most origin-of-life theories faces numerous scientific difficulties.

> *Primordial Soup:* a theory that proposes that life arose from a water-based sea of simple, organic molecules.

In 1953, a graduate student at the University of Chicago named Stanley Miller, along with his faculty adviser Harold Urey, performed experiments hoping to produce the building blocks of life under natural condi-tions on the early earth.[61] The **Miller-Urey experiments** intended to simulate lightning striking the gases in the early Earth's atmosphere. After running the experiments and letting the chemical products sit for a period of time, Miller discovered that amino acids—the building blocks of proteins—had been produced.

> *Miller-Urey Experiment:* a 1952 experiment conducted by Stanley Miller and Harold Urey that produced amino acids through the combination of electricity and gases thought to be present in Earth's atmosphere around three to four billions year ago.

For decades, these experiments have been hailed as a demonstration that the "building blocks" of life could have arisen under natural, realistic earthlike conditions,[62] cor-roborating the "primordial soup" hypothesis. However, it has also been known for decades that the earth's early atmosphere was fundamentally different from the gases used by Miller and Urey.

The atmosphere used in the Miller-Urey experiments was primarily composed of *reducing gases*, such as methane, ammonia, and high levels of hydrogen. (Reducing gases are those which tend to donate electrons during chemical reactions.) Geochemists now believe that the atmosphere of the early earth did not contain appreciable amounts of these components and lacked the "reducing atmosphere" used in Miller and Urey's experiments.[63] An article in the journal *Science* put it bluntly: "The early atmosphere looked nothing like the Miller-Urey situation."[64] Consistent with this, geological studies have not uncovered evidence that a primordial soup once existed.[65]

Because of these difficulties, some leading theorists have abandoned the Miller-Urey experiment and the "primordial soup" theory it is claimed to support. In 2010, University College of London biochemist Nick Lane stated the primordial soup theory "doesn't hold water" and is "past its expiration date."[66] Instead, he proposes that life arose in undersea hydro-thermal vents. But this isn't a clear-cut solution either. Assume for a moment that there was some way to produce simple organic molecules in a "primordial soup" or that these molecules arose near some hydrothermal vent. Either way, origin-of-life theorists must then explain how simple organic molecules (monomers) linked up to form long chains (polymers) such as proteins (or ribonucleic acid [RNA]).

Chemically speaking, however, the last place you'd want to link amino acids into chains would be a vast water-based environment like the "primordial soup" or underwater near some hydrothermal vent. As the National Academy of Sciences acknowledges, "Two amino acids do not spontaneously join in water. Rather, the opposite reaction is thermodynamically favored."[67] In other words, water breaks protein chains back down into amino acids (or other constituents), making it very difficult to produce proteins (or other polymers) in the primordial soup. Materialists lack good explanations for these first, simple steps necessary to the origin of life. Chemical evolution is literally dead in the water.

But even if a primordial sea filled with life's building blocks did exist on the early earth, and even if it did somehow form proteins and other complex organic molecules, and even if more and more complex molecules formed until some began to self-replicate, and even if natural selection favored those that were better able to make copies, how would these mole-cules evolve into complex machinery—such as that used in today's genetic code—to survive and reproduce? Theorists are nowhere near an explanation.

RNA World Hypothesis: a theory that proposes that early life was based on RNA instead of DNA and protein.

The most prominent option for the origin of the first life is called the ribonucleic acid world hypothe-sis (**RNA world hypothesis**), in which some theorists postulate that the first life might have used RNA instead of DNA (deoxyribonucleic acid) and proteins. But there are many problems with this hypothesis.

First, the first RNA molecules would have to arise by unguided, nonbiological chemical processes. But RNA won't assemble without the help of a skilled laboratory chemist intelligently guiding the process. New York University chemist Robert Shapiro critiqued the efforts of those who tried to make RNA in the lab, stating, "The flaw is in the logic—that this experimental control by researchers in a modern laboratory could have been available on the early Earth."[68] Second, although RNA has been shown to perform many roles in the cell, there is no evidence that it could perform all the necessary cellular functions currently carried out by proteins.[69] Third, the RNA world hypothesis does not explain the origin of genetic information.

RNA world advocates suggest that if the first self-replicating life was based upon RNA, it would have required a molecule between two hundred and three hundred nucleotides in length.[70] However, there are no known chemical or physical laws that dictate the order of those nucleotides.[71] To explain the ordering of nucleotides in the first self-replicating RNA molecule, materialists must rely on sheer chance. But the odds of specifying, say, 250 nucleo-tides in an RNA molecule by chance is about 1 in 10150—10 with 150 zeros. This is well below the universal probability boundary, below which events are not remotely possible to occur within the history of the universe.[72] Robert Shapiro puts the problem this way: "The sudden appearance of a large self-copying molecule such as RNA was exceedingly improbable....

ISN'T CHRISTIANITY ANTI-SCIENCE?

[The probability] is so vanishingly small that its happening even once anywhere in the visible universe would count as a piece of exceptional good luck."[73]

Fourth—and most fundamentally—the RNA world hypothesis does not explain the origin of the genetic code itself. In order to evolve into the DNA/protein-based life that exists today, the RNA world would need to evolve the ability to convert genetic information into proteins. However, this process of transcription and translation requires a large suite of proteins and molecular machines, which themselves are encoded by genetic information. This poses a chicken-and-egg problem, where essential enzymes and molecular machines are needed to perform the very task that constructs them.

To appreciate this problem, consider the origin of the first DVD and DVD player. DVDs are rich in information, but without the machinery of a DVD player to read the disk, process its information, and convert it into a picture and sound, the disk would be useless. But what if the instructions for building the first DVD player were found encoded on only a DVD? You could never play the DVD to learn how to build a DVD player. So how did the first disk and DVD player system arise? The answer is obvious: a goal-directed, intelligent process created both the player and the disk at the same time.

Life faces a similar conundrum. In living cells, information-carrying molecules (e.g., DNA or RNA) are like the DVD, and the cellular machinery that reads that information and converts it into proteins are like the DVD player. Just like the DVD analogy, genetic information can never be converted into proteins without the proper machinery. Yet in cells, the machines required for processing the genetic information in RNA or DNA are *themselves encoded by those same genetic molecules*. The machines perform and direct the very task that builds them. This system cannot exist unless both the genetic information and transcription/translation machinery are present at the same time and both speak the same language. Some sort of intelligence was required to provide the foresight needed to produce this complex system all at once.

Despite decades of work, origin-of-life theorists are still at a loss to explain how life arose. In 2007, Harvard chemist George Whitesides was given the Priestley Medal, the highest award of the American Chemical Society. During his acceptance speech, he offered this stark analysis: "The Origin of Life. This problem is one of the big ones in science. It begins to place life, and us, in the universe. Most chemists believe, as do I, that life emerged spontaneously from mixtures of molecules in the prebiotic Earth. How? I have no idea."[74]

Dr. Whitesides is welcome to believe that the chemical origin of life occurred through unguided mechanisms, but we should not pretend his belief is anything but faith based. The evidence, in contrast, suggests that a goal-directed scientific explanation such as intelligent design is necessary to produce the information and complexity we see in life.

Because of the lack of evidence for the chemical origin of life, some biology texts compensate with a short section on **panspermia**, the idea that life arrived from outer space. This idea has attracted a few prominent supporters, including molecular biologist Francis Crick, who co-won a Nobel Prize for discovering the

> *Panspermia:* the belief that life exists throughout the universe and has been dispersed by interstellar bodies such as asteroids, meteoroids, and comets.

structure of DNA. He explains why he gave up on the origin of life on earth: "An honest man, armed with all the knowledge available to us now, could only state that in some sense, the origin of life appears at the moment to be almost a miracle, so many are the conditions which would have had to have been satisfied to get it going."[75]

Crick's panspermia hypothesis, of course, only shifts the problem a few thousand light years away. Now the question becomes, how did life begin in outer space? It is odd for scientists to place their faith in something they cannot observe, measure, or repeat, like that life mysteriously arose from an extraterrestrial source that would had to have been spontaneously generated from inanimate matter. Even stranger still is that many of these scientists are quite critical of Christians for being "unscientific."

> *Design Argument (aka Teleological Argument):* an argument for God's existence that begins with the premise that design requires an intelligent designer and ends with the conclusion that God is the best explanation for the observable design within the universe.

There is intention and order in creation. The move from design to designer is called the **design argument** because things may *appear* to human observers to have been designed but may actually be without intention and order.[76] This is why deoxyribonucleic acid (DNA) is such a fascinating subject of study. Chemist Charles Thaxton believes DNA is the most powerful indicator of intelligent design: "Is there any basis in experience for an intelligent cause for the origin of life? Yes! It is the analogy between the base sequences in DNA and alphabetical letter sequences in a book.... There is a structural identity between the DNA code and a written language."[77] That is, we can assume that DNA is the product of intelligence because it is analogous to human languages, which are without exception products of intelligent minds.

When Francis Crick and James Watson discovered the structure of DNA, they trumpeted it as a condemnation of the "god hypothesis" and a debunking of religious myths. More recent research in genetics, though, indicates the presence of intention and order. The scientist who led the process to map the human genome, Francis Collins, says, "DNA can be thought of metaphorically as the language of God."[78] This is an astounding thing to have been said by someone who led the effort to solve the mysteries of DNA.

In fact, DNA research is one factor that led Antony Flew, the legendary British philosopher, to renounce atheism.[79] Flew writes, "The most impressive arguments for God's existence are those that are supported by recent scientific discoveries." He came to this conclusion because "the findings of more than fifty years of DNA research have provided materials for a new and enormously powerful argument to design."[80]

Humanity is at the apex of creation, both its final act and its caretaker. If you've ever taken time to look at the stars and consider the vastness of the universe, you may have found yourself thinking, *How is it possible for life on this earth to be significant when the universe is so big?* This is the very question raised by King David in a poem we now know as Psalm 8:

ISN'T CHRISTIANITY ANTI-SCIENCE?

When I look at your heavens, the work of your fingers,
    the moon and the stars, which you have set in place,
what is man that you are mindful of him,
    and the son of man that you care for him? (vv. 3–4)

In reflection on this question, some scientists find themselves compelled by the **anthropic principle** (*anthro* means "pertaining to man"). Physicists John Barrow and Frank Tipler wrote about this argument in a book titled *The Anthropic Cosmological Principle.*[81] In one of its forms, the anthropic principle says we can observe the universe only because it exists in a way that allows us as observers to exist. In other words, the universe must have properties that make the existence of intelligent life inevitable.

> *Anthropic Principle:* the theory that the universe contains all the necessary properties that make the existence of intelligent life inevitable.

Robert Jastrow—a highly regarded astronomer, physicist, and cosmologist—says, "The anthropic principle is the most interesting development next to the proof of the creation, and it is even more interesting because it seems to say that science itself has proven, as a hard fact, that this universe was made, was designed, for man to live in. It is a very theistic result."[82] Likewise, Nobel Prize–winning physicist Charles Townes explains, "Intelligent design, as one sees it from a scientific point of view, seems to be quite real. This is a very special universe: it's remarkable that it came out just this way. If the laws of physics weren't just the way they are, we couldn't be here at all. The sun couldn't be there, the laws of gravity and nuclear laws and magnetic theory, quantum mechanics, and so on have to be just the way they are for us to be here."[83]

There are limits to change in nature. Evolutionists who believe that all life arose from nothing beginning with spontaneous generation believe that mechanisms such as mutation and natural selection can explain all the variety of life we see today. Obviously, for this to be true, species must have been able to evolve into entirely different and more complex species over time. Mutation and natural selection can, according to evolutionists who take their theory all the way back to the origin of life, explain the production of and all the change in a vast array of structures—even a human eye—given enough time.

> *Microevolution:* the belief that small, adaptive changes are capable of producing variations within the gene pool of a species.

The biblical account suggests a subtler approach. Genesis claims that God created creatures according to their "kind," which implies groupings of animals. As we can observe through experimentation, many changes are possible within these groupings, but there seems to be a barrier beyond which they can no longer produce change in succeeding generations. This is the difference between **microevolution** (small changes within a species) and **macroevolution** (changes that lead to new species).

> *Macroevolution:* the belief that small, adaptive changes are capable of accumulating over time to produce entirely new species.

If a species can evolve only so far before it hits a barrier and is forced to remain the same species, then the idea of all species arising from one organism is problematic. Science simply has not been able to demonstrate that these barriers to change can be transcended. Zoologist Pierre-Paul Grassé, after studying mutations in bacteria and viruses, concluded, "What is the use of their unceasing mutations if they do not change? In sum, the mutations of bacteria and viruses are merely hereditary fluctuations around a median position; a swing to the right, a swing to the left, but no final evolutionary effect."[84] Similarly, US National Academy of Sciences member biologist Lynn Margulis maintained that "new mutations don't create new species; they create offspring that are impaired."[85] Her explanation:

> Mutations, in summary, tend to induce sickness, death, or deficiencies. No evidence in the vast literature of heredity changes shows unambiguous evidence that random mutation itself, even with geographical isolation of populations, leads to speciation [new species].[86]

Tree of Life: a metaphor used to illustrate the belief that all of life originated from a common ancestor and gradually branched out into the wide variety of species seen within the fossil record.

Universal Common Ancestry: the belief that all life originated from a common, single-celled organism.

In recent years, other core tenets of Darwinian theory, such as the **tree of life** supposition that all of life had a common ancestor, have also come under attack. A 2012 paper in *Annual Review of Genetics* challenged **universal common ancestry**, instead suggesting that "life might indeed have multiple origins."[87] Likewise, in a 2009 article in *New Scientist* titled "Why Darwin Was Wrong about the Tree of Life, " Graham Lawton wrote, "Many biologists now argue that the tree concept is obsolete and needs to be discarded." The article quoted scientists saying such things as "We have no evidence at all that the tree of life is a reality" or "We've just annihilated the tree of life."[88]

The fact that change in nature seems limited to *within* species does not *prove* that the biblical idea of kind is a valid scientific concept, of course, but it does provide affirmation and make the biblical account seem less unscientific than many naturalists and materialists have assumed.

Although those determined to reject any supernatural explanation of the world may remain unconvinced, the biblical account is closer to what we actually observe than is philosophical naturalism, which says that only nature exists and therefore everything came from nature. For the believer wondering whether he or she is obligated to reject the biblical account because of scientific advances, this kind of evidence helps restore balance and perspective.

By restoring balance and perspective, we mean that it is more reasonable to focus on these larger issues when considering the relationship between science and the Bible than on minor issues, such as whether the ancient Hebrew understanding of what it means for a rabbit to "chew its cud" is the same as our understanding of what rabbits do when they move their mouths in a way that looks like a cow when chewing its cud.[89]

For a moment, let's return to the idea of theistic evolution, the belief that evolution *can* explain the variety of life on the planet today but that God somehow guided the process. Is it the reasonable compromise position it appears to be on the surface?

ISN'T CHRISTIANITY ANTI-SCIENCE?

6. PROBLEMS WITH THEISTIC EVOLUTION

Students who learn about evolution these days are usually taught that life evolved from inorganic chemicals to the human race within a period of some 3.5 billion years. Because this is stated as science-based fact, Christians who believe in a creator are made to feel ignorant, backward, and unintelligent. They shouldn't feel this way. Rather, they should understand that when the theory of evolution moves beyond science and into the realm of philosophy, it becomes nothing more than a story that materialists and naturalists tell one another to affirm their rejection of the supernatural.

The story of materialism and naturalism *appears* true to people because it enlists what biologist Jonathan Wells calls "icons" that are used to make it seem true. These icons include pictures of peppered moths and finches, drawings of horse fossils of various sizes, Ernst Haeckel's inaccurate drawings that make the embryos of vertebrate species appear more similar than they actually are, and drawings of the progression from primate to human. In his book *Icons of Evolution*, Wells provides compelling evidence that these icons lack scientific rigor and are, in fact, misleading.[90]

Critics argue that Wells is asking too much of these icons and that he has nothing to replace them with.[91] Such critics miss the point. If the evidence supporting the evolutionary story is flawed, then these icons are leading people to believe a story that simply has not been proved true.

Christians suspect there is intelligence behind the universe, but they aren't the only ones. Paul Davies rejects the idea that everything in existence came about by chance: "I cannot believe that our existence in this universe is a mere quirk of fate, an accident of history, an incidental blip in the great cosmic drama. Our involvement is too intimate.... We are truly meant to be here."[92] Similarly, atheist cosmologist Fred Hoyle states, "A common sense interpretation of the data suggests that a superintellect has monkeyed with physics, as well as with chemistry and biology."[93] Christians who study the Bible find such comments affirming. The idea of a living God who created all things and who maintains them by his immense nature and character makes a lot of sense in light of comments such as these.

In spite of this, many Christian theologians and philosophers—the "theistic evolutionists"—have felt the need to reconcile their faith with evolution by proposing that God set up the universe but then somehow allowed inanimate matter to naturally evolve into human beings. It is a controversial view among atheists and theists alike. Is it enough to say that God is behind evolution, and does that even make sense with the way we understand evolution to work, as an unguided process?

This is particularly the case with the seeming contradiction between the evolutionary account that humans evolved through purposeless, chance-based processes and the biblical account that Adam and Eve were specially created. Many biblical authors treated Adam and Eve as if they were historical people, not mere allegories to help explain our earliest human ancestors. Jesus did too. In Mark 10:6, Jesus declared, "At the beginning of creation God 'made them male and female.'" Throughout the Bible, Adam is presented as a man who actually existed and whose sin brought condemnation and corruption upon all mankind, atoned for by Christ's death and resurrection (Rom. 5:12–19).

Denying Adam and Eve's existence creates a number of serious theological problems. Theistic evolution encourages us to drop that egg, but once we do, it is hard to put it together again. This is a difficult question for many believers, and it is one that is very much at the heart of the debate in our own time. Given that the scientific evidence for human evolution is weak[94] and Darwinism undermines key Christian doctrines, one might wonder why some Christians are rushing to embrace an evolutionary viewpoint.

There is perhaps common ground. In spite of very real and very serious differences, all of the various theistic perspectives on how creation took place can at least agree that humans are morally culpable creatures in a broken but privileged relationship with their Creator.

7. Conclusion

In the end, when people say that Christianity is anti-science, they show they understand neither Christianity nor science. Finding himself in the midst of a debate over the mechanisms of evolution, atheist and evolutionist Paul Lemoine wrote, "Evolution is a kind of dogma which the priests no longer believe, but they maintain for their people."[95] In other words, scientists are just as prone as anyone else to convincing themselves with wrong stories told repeatedly.

Earlier in this volume, we learned that what makes faith valid is not that we have it but that the object of our belief is actually worthy of belief. As we've examined the supposed conflict between faith and science, we can see that the battle is not at all what it first seems. Faith has its reasons, as authors Kenneth Boa and Robert Bowman say.[96] Science as a way of knowing can help inform biblical faith, and a biblical faith can help scientists be better at what they do. As C. S. Lewis puts it, "In science we have been reading only the notes to a poem; in Christianity we find the poem itself."[97]

Still, many critics of Christianity are not impressed. They believe that *arguments about the Bible's truth are just word games. No religion is more or less true than any other, and it is intolerant to suggest otherwise.* How to respond is the subject we'll tackle in chapter 13.

Endnotes

1. Gurbachan Singh Sachdeva, "Cosmos in Theological Scriptures," *Astropolitics* 10 (2012): 269.
2. Edward O. Wilson, *Consilience: The Unity of Knowledge* (New York: Vintage, 1999), 286.
3. Francis Collins, *The Language of God: A Scientist Presents Evidence for Belief* (New York: Free Press, 2006), 233.
4. Psalm 8:3–5: "When I look at your heavens, the work of your fingers, the moon and the stars, which you have set in place, what is man that you are mindful of him, and the son of man that you care for him? Yet you have made him a little lower than the heavenly beings and crowned him with glory and honor."
5. Colossians 1:16: "By him all things were created, in heaven and on earth, visible and invisible, whether thrones or dominions or rulers or authorities—all things were created through him and for him."
6. National Academy of Sciences, *Science, Evolution, and Creationism* (Washington, DC: National Academies Press, 2008), 10.
7. If you're interested, here's a more detailed account of how the Lysenko affair came about: Marxists long believed that communism was to society what evolution was to nature, a way of removing God from the equation of what happened in the past and bolstering a faith in future perfection (which they believed to be a communist society). Unfortunately, the mechanisms of evolution are terribly slow at producing change in nature, and their ultimate outcome is unpredictable by definition: they can move backward as well as forward. T. D. Lysenko, the leading Soviet biologist from the early 1930s into the 1950s and president of the Academy of Sciences, decided to customize evolutionary theory so it would better fit the Marxist view. Lysenko's ideas immediately ran up against the work of Gregor Mendel, the father of genetics, who demonstrated through his work with pea plants that living things reproduce by passing on inherited characteristics to their

offspring (implying that change in nature would be very slow). Marxists found this unsatisfactory. Consequently, Lysenko resolved the issue by political dictate. He declared, "It is time to eliminate Mendelism in all its varieties from all courses and textbooks." Textbooks were changed. Soviet biologists who disagreed with him either repented or met untimely deaths. The new party line: "Any little particle, figuratively speaking, any granule, any droplet of a living body, once it is alive, necessarily possesses the property of heredity." Lysenko's notions about heredity eventually led him to embrace Lamarckism, a theory that states that characteristics acquired during an organism's lifetime can be passed from one generation to the next as inheritable changes. Although Lamarckism has seen a very limited resurgence in recent years (see R. Bonduriansky, "Rethinking Heredity, Again," *Trends in Ecology and Evolution* 27, no. 6 [June, 2012]: 330–36), most of its claims are viewed by scientists as utterly impossible. If a person "acquires" an amputated arm, will his offspring be born without an arm? If he works hard to develop musical ability, will his offspring be more musical? Probably Lysenko was "encouraged" to embrace Lamarckism because the Soviet leader Joseph Stalin had once done so, and no one could oppose Stalin and survive. But based on Lysenko's confidence, other Soviet biologists came in line with it as well. After Stalin died, the truth had to be admitted. In the end, it was a conflict of rival faiths: science versus Marxism. Marxists went to war against legitimate science and ended up looking silly in the eyes of the world. For more information, see David Joravsky, *The Lysenko Affair* (Cambridge, MA: Harvard University Press, 1970), 210.

8. For a fuller explanation of how this is so, see "Introduction," in Philip J. Sampson, *6 Modern Myths about Christianity and Western Civilization* (Downers Grove, IL: InterVarsity, 2001), 7–26.

9. Sampson, *6 Modern Myths*, 20.

10. John W. Draper's book was published in 1890 under the title *History of the Conflict between Religion and Science*. Andrew D. White's *A History of the Warfare of Science with Theology in Christendom* was published in 1896.

11. The story of how this happened is complicated. Basically, an unreliable historian named Bartolomeo Platina mentioned something about the pope asking for prayers against a portending invasion by the Turks. Later, a scientist named Pierre-Simon Laplace embellished the story by saying the pope "conjured" against the comet. François Arago, in his pamphlet on comets, embellished even further by saying the pope "excommunicated" the comet. None of the papal documents of that time mentions anything about a comet factoring into concern over war with the Turks, so the entire story is now accepted as pure fiction by historians. A thorough explanation may be found in one of many Catholic encyclopedias, such as John Stein, "Bartolomeo Platina," *The Catholic Encyclopedia*, vol. 12 (New York: Robert Appleton Company, 1911).

12. Bertrand Russell, *The History of Western Philosophy* (New York: Simon & Schuster, 1967), 534.

13. Sampson, *6 Modern Myths*, 39.

14. For a brief and lively retelling of what actually happened to Galileo, see Joe Carter, "The Myth of Galileo: A Story with a (Mostly) Valuable Lesson for Today," *First Things*, September 8, 2011, www.firstthings.com/blogs/firstthoughts/2011/09/the-myth-of-galileo-a-story-with-a-mostly-valuable-lesson-for-today.

15. Sampson, *6 Modern Myths*, 38.

16. Galileo Galilei, *Dialogue concerning the Two Chief World Systems*, trans. Stillman Drake (New York: The University of California Press, 2001), 119–20, www.math.dartmouth.edu/~matc/Readers/renaissance.astro/7.1.DialogueFirstDay.html.

17. Quoted in Rodney Stark, *The Triumph of Christianity: How the Jesus Movement Became the World's Largest Religion* (New York: HarperCollins, 2011), 250.

18. John Hedley Brooke, "Science and Theology in the Enlightenment," in *Religion and Science: History, Method, Dialogue*, ed. W. Mark Richardson and Wesley J. Wildman (Oxford, UK: Routledge, 1996), 9.

19. Francis A. Schaeffer, *How Should We Then Live? The Rise and Decline of Western Thought and Culture* (Old Tappan, NJ: Revell, 1976), 134.

20. Holmes Rolston III, *Science and Religion: A Critical Survey* (San Diego: Harcourt Brace, 1987), 39.

21. Ian G. Barbour, *Religion and Science: Historical and Contemporary Issues* (San Francisco: HarperSanFrancisco, 1997), 19–20.

22. Barbour, *Religion and Science*, 19–20.

23. Stanley L. Jaki, *The Road of Science and the Ways to God* (Chicago: University of Chicago Press, 1978).

24. Jaki, *The Road of Science*, 242. We also recommend Norman L. Geisler and J. Kerby Anderson, *Origin Science: A Proposal for the Creation-Evolution Controversy* (Grand Rapids, MI: Baker, 1987), and J. P. Moreland, *Christianity and the Nature of Science* (Grand Rapids, MI: Baker, 1989).

25. Jaki, *The Road of Science*, 242; Geisler and Anderson's *Origin Science* contains a chapter titled "The Supernatural Roots of Modern Science." Many non-Christians, such as highly regarded scientists Alfred North Whitehead and J. Robert Oppenheimer, defend this view as well. Stark's *For the Glory of God* offers a great summary of the Christian roots of modern science for those who wish to know more.

26. Steven Shapin, *Never Pure: Historical Studies of Science as If It Was Produced by People with Bodies, Situated in Time, Space, Culture, and Society, and Struggling for Credibility and Authority* (Baltimore: Johns Hopkins, 2010), 197–99.

27. Brooke, "Science and Theology in the Enlightenment," 8.

28. Shapin, *Never Pure*, 48.

29. Shapin, *Never Pure*, 48–50.

30. Shapin, *Never Pure*, 4.

31. David Berlinski, *The Devil's Delusion: Atheism and Its Scientific Pretensions* (New York: Basic Books, 2009), 1–2.

32. Victor Stenger, *God and the Folly of Faith: The Incompatibility of Science and Religion* (Amherst, NY: Prometheus Books, 2012), 25.

33. Stenger, *God and the Folly of Faith*, 25.

34. John Lennox, *God and Stephen Hawking: Whose Design Is It Anyway?* (Oxford, UK: Lion Hudson, 2011), 18.

35. Stephen Hawking and Leonard Mlodinow, *The Grand Design* (New York: Bantam, 2010), 5.

36. John Lennox states, "Apart from the unwarranted hubris of this dismissal of philosophy … it constitutes rather disturbing evidence that at least one scientist, Hawking himself, has not even kept up with philosophy sufficiently to realize that he himself is engaging in it throughout his book," in *God and Stephen Hawking*, 19.

37. See Stark, *For the Glory of God*.

38. For a detailed list, see David F. Coppedge, "The World's Greatest Creation Scientists: From Y1K to Y2K," Creation Safaris, creationsafaris.com/wgcs_toc.htm.

39. This point has been well illustrated already, but additional supporting evidence comes from the eminent historian of science Ronald Numbers: "The greatest myth in the history of science and religion holds that they have been in a state of constant conflict," *Galileo Goes to Jail and Other Myths about Science and Religion* (Cambridge, MA: Harvard University Press, 2010), 1. See also David C. Lindberg, former president of the US History of Science Society, who wrote, "There was no warfare between science and the church" in "Medieval Science and Religion," in *The History of Science and Religion in the Western Tradition: An Encyclopedia*, ed. Gary B. Ferngren (New York: Garland, 2000), 266.

40. Paul Davies, "Taking Science on Faith," *New York Times*, op-ed (November 24, 2007).

41. Davies, "Taking Science on Faith."

42. Davies, "Taking Science on Faith."

43. This brief list is wonderfully explained, illustrated, and footnoted in Nancy Pearcey and Charles Thaxton, *The Soul of Science: Christian Faith and Natural Philosophy* (Wheaton, IL: Crossway, 1994), 21–37.

44. Matthew 19:4: "He answered, 'Have you not read that he who created them from the beginning made them male and female'?"; Mark 10:6–9: "From the beginning of creation, 'God made them male and female.' 'Therefore a man shall leave his father and mother and hold fast to his wife, and the two shall become one flesh.' So they are no longer two but one flesh. What therefore God has joined together, let not man separate."

45. See Norman L. Geisler, *Systematic Theology* (Minneapolis: Bethany, 2005), 2:632ff, for a good summary of the issue. Geisler says, "There are many scientific arguments for an old universe, some of which one may find persuasive. However, none of these is foolproof, and all of them may be wrong" (2:649). Those advocating an older universe include Hugh Ross, *Creator and the Cosmos*; Norman Geisler, *When Skeptics Ask*; Walter C. Kaiser Jr., *Hard Sayings of the Bible*; Don Stoner, *A New Look at an Old Earth*; and Francis A. Schaeffer, *No Final Conflict*. Those presenting a younger earth include Walt Brown, *In the Beginning*; Larry Vardiman, Andrew Snelling, and Eugene F. Chaffin, ed., *Radioisotopes and the Age of the Earth*; Jonathan Sarfati, *Refuting Compromise*; and Henry Morris, *The Long War against God*.

46. See Geisler, *Systematic Theology*, 2:632ff, for a good summary of the issue. *Creation and Time: A Biblical and Scientific Perspective on the Creation-Date Controversy*, by Hugh Ross (Colorado Springs, CO: NavPress, 1994), presents the case for an older universe, while *Refuting Compromise: A Biblical and Scientific Refutation of "Progressive Creationism" (Billions of Years) as Popularized by Astronomer Hugh Ross*, by Jonathan Sarfati (Powder Springs, GA: Creation Book Publishers, 2011), presents the case for a younger universe, along with Walt Brown, *In The Beginning* (Phoenix: Center for Scientific Creation, 2003) and volumes 1 and 2 of Larry Vardiman, Andrew A. Snelling, and Eugene F. Chaffin, ed., *Radioisotopes and the Age of the Earth* (El Cajon, CA: Institute for Creation Research, 2005).

47. Charles Darwin, *Autobiography* (New York: Dover, 1958), 59.

48. See Geoffrey Simmons, *What Darwin Didn't Know: A Doctor Dissects the Theory of Evolution* (Eugene, OR: Harvest House, 2004) for an up-to-date argument for creation from design.

49. Albert Einstein, *Ideas and Opinions* (New York: Crown, 1982), 40, quoted in Norman L. Geisler, *Systematic Theology* (Minneapolis: Bethany, 2003), 2:666.

50. Paul Davies, *Superforce* (New York: Simon & Schuster, 1984), 223.

51. See Michael J. Behe's *Darwin's Black Box: The Biochemical Challenge to Evolution* (New York: Free Press, 1996) for a full discussion on the complexity of the cell. Also, David Berlinski, "On the Origins of Life," *Commentary* 121, no. 5 (May 2006): 16. "Darwinian evolution," says Berlinski, "begins with self-replication, and self-replication is precisely what needs to be explained" (29).

52. Michael Denton, *Evolution: A Theory in Crisis* (Bethesda, MD: Adler & Adler, 1986), 250.

53. Bruce Alberts, "The Cell as a Collection of Protein Machines: Preparing the Next Generation of Molecular Biologists," *Cell* 92 (February 6, 1998): 291.

54. James A. Shapiro, "21st Century View of Evolution: Genome System Architecture, Repetitive DNA, and Natural Genetic Engineering," *Gene* 345 (2005): 91–100.

55. For more detail, see Norman L. Geisler and Frank Turek, *I Don't Have Enough Faith to Be an Atheist* (Wheaton, IL:

ISN'T CHRISTIANITY ANTI-SCIENCE?

Crossway, 2004) and Berlinski, "On the Origins of Life."

56. J. P. Moreland and William Lane Craig, *Philosophical Foundations for a Christian Worldview* (Downers Grove, IL: InterVarsity, 2003), 478.

57. Antony Flew and Roy Abraham Varghese, *There Is a God: How the World's Most Notorious Atheist Changed His Mind* (New York: HarperOne, 2007), 136, 145.

58. John H. Postlethwait and Janet L. Hopson, *Modern Biology* (New York: Holt, Rinehart and Winston, 2009), 281.

59. Postlethwait and Hopson, *Modern Biology*, 285.

60. Steven D. Garber, *Biology: A Self-Teaching Guide*, 2nd ed. (New York: Wiley, 2002), 3–5.

61. See Stanley L. Miller, "A Production of Amino Acids under Possible Primitive Earth Conditions," *Science* 117 (May 15, 1953): 528–29.

62. See Jonathan Wells, *Icons of Evolution: Why Much of What We Teach about Evolution Is Wrong* (Washington, DC: Regnery, 2000); Casey Luskin, "Not Making the Grade: An Evaluation of 19 Recent Biology Textbooks and Their Use of Selected Icons of Evolution," Discovery Institute, September 26, 2011, www.evolutionnews.org/DiscoveryInstitute_2011TextbookReview.pdf.

63. David W. Deamer, "The First Living Systems: A Bioenergetic Perspective," *Microbiology & Molecular Biology Reviews* 61 (1997): 239.

64. Jon Cohen, "Novel Center Seeks to Add Spark to Origins of Life," *Science* 270 (December 22, 1995), 1925–26.

65. Antonio C. Lasaga, H. D. Holland, and Michael J. Dwyer, "Primordial Oil Slick," *Science* 174 (October 1, 1971): 53–55.

66. Deborah Kelley, "Is It Time to Throw Out 'Primordial Soup' Theory?," NPR, February 7, 2010.

67. Committee on the Limits of Organic Life in Planetary Systems, Committee on the Origins and Evolution of Life, National Research Council, *The Limits of Organic Life in Planetary Systems* (Washington, DC: National Academies Press, 2007), 60.

68. Richard Van Noorden, "RNA World Easier to Make," *Nature*, May 13, 2009, www.nature.com/news/2009/090513/full/news.2009.471.html.

69. See Stephen C. Meyer, *Signature in the Cell: DNA and the Evidence for Intelligent Design* (New York: HarperOne, 2009), 304.

70. Jack W. Szostak, David P. Bartel, and P. Luigi Luisi, "Synthesizing Life," *Nature* 409 (January 18, 2001): 387–90.

71. Michael Polanyi, "Life's Irreducible Structure," *Science* 160 (June 21, 1968), 1308–1312.

72. See William A. Dembski, *The Design Inference: Eliminating Chance through Small Probabilities* (Cambridge, UK: Cambridge University Press, 1998).

73. Robert Shapiro, "A Simpler Origin for Life," *Scientific American* (June, 2007): 46–53.

74. George M. Whitesides, "Revolutions in Chemistry: Priestley Medalist George M. Whitesides' Address," *Chemical and Engineering News* 85 (March 26, 2007): 12–17.

75. Francis Crick, *Life Itself: Its Origin and Nature* (New York: Simon & Schuster, 1981), 88.

76. The design argument is also called the teleological argument (*telos* is the Greek word for "final cause").

77. Charles Thaxton, "In Pursuit of Intelligent Causes: Some Historical Background" (unpublished essay presented at Sources of Information Content in DNA, an interdisciplinary conference in Tacoma, Washington, June 23–26, 1988), 13.

78. Quoted in Eric Metaxas, *Socrates in the City: Conversations on "Life, God, and Other Small Topics"* (New York: Dutton, 2011), 316.

79. Antony Flew and Roy Abraham Varghese, *There Is a God: How the World's Most Notorious Atheist Changed His Mind* (New York: HarperOne, 2008).

80. Antony Flew and Gary Habermas, "My Pilgrimage from Atheism to Theism: A Discussion between Antony Flew and Gary Habermas," *Philosophia Christi* 6, no. 2 (2004): 201.

81. Barrow and Tipler do not believe that their arguments lead to a theistic result, but in the end, they seem to have two options: a designer or an infinite number of multiple universes from which evolution might have proceeded. See John D. Barrow and Frank J. Tipler, *The Anthropic Cosmological Principle* (New York: Oxford University Press, 1986). To read philosopher William Lane Craig's analysis of this dilemma, go to www.leaderu.com/offices/billcraig/docs/barrow.html.

82. Robert Jastrow, "A Scientist Caught between Two Faiths," *Christianity Today*, August 6, 1982, quoted in Norman L. Geisler, *Systematic Theology* (Bloomington, MN: Bethany, 2011), 28.

83. Charles Townes, quoted in Bonnie Azab Powell, "'Explore as Much as We Can': Nobel Prize Winner Charles Townes on Evolution, Intelligent Design, and the Meaning of Life," *UC Berkeley NewsCenter*, June 17, 2005.

84. Pierre-Paul Grassé, *Evolution of Living Organisms: Evidence for a New Theory of Transformation* (New York: Academic Press, 1977), 87.

85. Lynn Margulis, quoted in Darry Madden, "UMass Scientist to Lead Debate on Evolutionary Theory," *Brattleboro (Vt.) Reformer* (February 3, 2006). Some have wondered whether *superbugs* (bacteria that are resistant to antibiotics) and *super-viruses* (lethal viruses that occasionally emerge) might be proof of evolution. It is a complex question, but essentially antibacterial medicine works by getting bacteria to produce an enzyme that turns the antibiotic the bacteria uses to fight off other bacteria into a poison that kills itself. A *superbug* is a bacterium that has lost the ability to produce that enzyme. So, in a way, it is a bacterium that has lost complexity. Viruses are different from bacteria in that they require a host to live and survive by "hijacking" the cellular production system of the host and using it to produce the virus. *Superviruses*, such

as Ebola, are viruses that have probably been around as long as other viruses but are unable to spread as rapidly. Though more lethal (unless humans "weaponize" them through creating mutations in the laboratory, which is an obvious example of intelligent intervention), they tend to be confined to the host and perhaps those in closest contact with the host.

86. Lynn Margulis and Dorion Sagan, *Acquiring Genomes: A Theory of the Origins of the Species* (New York: Basic Books, 2003), 29.

87. Michael Syvanen, "Evolutionary Implications of Horizontal Gene Transfer," *Annual Review of Genetics* 46 (2012): 339–56.

88. Graham Lawton, "Why Darwin Was Wrong about the Tree of Life," *New Scientist*, January 21, 2009.

89. This is a reference to Leviticus 11:3–6 and Deuteronomy 14:7, which permit the children of Israel to eat animals that "chew the cud" but only if they have certain kinds of hooves. Animals such as camels and cows are classified as ruminants, which means they regurgitate their food and chew it once it has been partially digested. Rabbits do not meet this classification. For an explanation of what the rabbit does do, see www.answersingenesis.org/contradictions-in-the-bible/do-rabbits-really-chew-the-cud/.

90. Jonathan Wells, *Icons of Evolution: Science or Myth?* (Washington, DC: Regnery, 2000). Judith Hooper, in *An Evolutionary Tale of Moths and Men: The Untold Story of Science and the Peppered Moth* (New York: Norton, 2002), spends a whole book on the peppered moth, the insect that has been used as scientific proof for evolution. Few could read what really happened and call this science.

91. See, for example, Alan D. Gishlick's article "Icons of Evolution?" on the website for the National Center for Science Education, ncse.com/creationism/analysis/icons-evolution. Gishlick received his PhD in vertebrate paleontology from Yale University. Jonathan Wells, who holds a PhD in molecular and cellular biology from the University of California at Berkeley and a PhD in religious studies from Yale University, has written a response to Gishlick's criticisms at the following link: www.discovery.org/a/1320.

92. Paul Davies, *The Mind of God: The Scientific Basis for a Rational World* (London: Simon & Schuster, 1992), 232, quoted in John Lennox, *Seven Days That Divide the World: The Beginning according to Genesis and Science* (Grand Rapids, MI: Zondervan, 2011), 99. For a discussion of atheists and nonreligious skeptics of neo-Darwinism and proponents of intelligent design, see Casey Luskin, "Are There Non-Religious Skeptics of Darwinian Evolution and Proponents of Intelligent Design?," *Christian Research Journal* 36, no. 2 (2013): 42–47.

93. Quoted in Paul Davies, *The Accidental Universe: The World You Thought You Knew* (Cambridge, UK: Cambridge University Press, 1982), 189.

94. See Casey Luskin, "Human Origins and the Fossil Record," in *Science and Human Origins* (Seattle: Discovery Institute Press, 2012), 45–83.

95. Paul Lemoine, "Introduction: De L'Evolution?," in *Encyclopedie Francaise*, vol. 5, ed. Anatole de Monzie, Lucien Paul Victor Febvre, and Gaston Berger (Paris: Société de gestion de l'Encyclopédie française, 1937–1966).

96. Kenneth Boa and Robert M. Bowman Jr., *Faith Has Its Reasons: Integrative Approaches to Defending the Christian Faith* (Downers Grove, IL: IVP Books, 2012).

97. Quoted in Clyde S. Kilby, ed., *A Mind Awake: An Anthology of C. S. Lewis* (New York: Harcourt, Brace & World, 1968), 240.

CHAPTER 13

13

ISN'T CLAIMING TRUTH INTOLERANT?

1. CAN'T WE ALL JUST GET ALONG?

"Hey, what's new?"

My friend and his neighbor had always gotten along well, but this time my friend's heart pounded when asked the question. "Well," he said, swallowing hard, "I've had something spiritual happen."

"What?"

"I've become a Christian."

"Well, that makes sense. You're not Muslim or Hindu, after all," the neighbor joked.

"No. I mean, it's more than that. I don't just mean that my culture has changed. I had a conversion. I trusted Jesus Christ as my Savior."

"Oh, cool. I'm happy for you."

"Thank you."

"But I have a question. Does this mean you now believe I am a bad person and am going to hell?"

Somehow my friend managed to make it through the conversation, but he wasn't at all happy with how it turned out. In an email to me, he asked, "What am I supposed to say?" It *is* confusing because it was not his spiritual state that bothered the neighbor as much as the fact that, from his neighbor's viewpoint, my friend had embraced intolerance.

But who was *really* being intolerant in this situation? Was it my friend, for letting it be known that he had embraced new convictions, or the neighbor for assuming that these new convictions were intolerant because they claimed to be right? By confronting my friend over this, the neighbor made it clear that any views that make others *feel* bad *are* bad.

Such is the confusing world of belief these days. People can be touchy about what others believe. One example I came across recently is of a blogger who is a professor in his day job but uses his blog www.iloveyoubutyouregoingtohell.org to express how bad Christians are merely bad for claiming that they are right. The author simply will not tolerate what he perceives to be others' intolerance.

As someone who has spent much of my life working with college students, I understand why both my friend and his neighbor felt a sense of hurt: we naturally want to be at peace with people, even those with whom we strongly disagree. Brian Jones, a pastor from Philadelphia, phrases it nicely:

> The reality is that I want to live like religion doesn't matter too; I want to live like what I actually believe isn't that important. I like being liked. I don't like making waves. I don't like making people feel awkward. But I can't back down from what I know to be true. Sheer logic will not let me do that.[1]

As we've already seen, neighborly Christians display their love for God. Being neighborly, however, doesn't make disagreements over beliefs disappear. For example, Christians believe in an afterlife. Buddhists reject this belief and say that life is a cycle of rebirths. Both beliefs cannot both be true at the same time (though they could both be false at the same time, which is what the atheist believes). This disagreement between the two will hang over the relationship of a Christian and a Buddhist, at least if they take their respective beliefs seriously.

Today, though, many people call into question the idea that religious beliefs necessarily conflict with one another, or they say that even if they do conflict, it does not really matter. We each have a bit of insight into the world, it is believed, and if we work together, we can figure out the whole truth. Often this belief is expressed through parables such as that of six blind men who come into contact with an elephant: one handles the tail and exclaims that an elephant is like a rope, another grasps a leg and describes the elephant as a tree trunk, a third feels the tusk and says the animal is similar to a spear, and so on. Because each feels only a

ISN'T CLAIMING TRUTH INTOLERANT?

small portion of the whole elephant, all six men give correspondingly different descriptions of their experience. Only by putting all of their observations together can they arrive at a complete picture of the elephant.

In other words, by this analogy, we only *think* we are right because we don't see the big picture.

2. What It Means to Claim to Know the Truth

But as with all analogies, the elephant example is limited, and limited in such a way that the supposed truth it illustrates is questionable as well. The story assumes that there actually is an elephant as well as someone—the person telling the story perhaps—who knows the elephant well enough to see that each blind man has only a partial picture.

The heart of Christianity's claim is that someone exists who is not blind, who has complete knowledge, and who has, throughout the course of history, revealed some of this knowledge to us. The Bible, Christians say, is the record of God's creation and his plan for redemption through Jesus Christ. The Bible describes Jesus as the true and living way.[2] He is the key to reality itself.[3] So, although humans are fallen creatures and cannot know the truth *exhaustively*, Christianity says we can know *truly* that which God has revealed.

This leads inevitably to conflict. Either Christians correctly describe reality when they speak of a loving, wise, just, personal, creative God or they are talking nonsense. If they are talking nonsense, they may even be hurting other people by saying they know the full truth when they don't.

When it comes to God, the idea of claiming to have truth means those claims must be grounded in knowledge. In order for someone to claim truth about any given subject, he or she must have reasons for claiming that truth. Mere belief, even sincere belief that rings true to many people, isn't enough. We saw earlier in this text that to really know something, a person must have a "justified true belief."[4] A **belief** is an idea one has about reality, and this idea can be true or false; that is, the idea either corresponds to reality or it doesn't. But having only a "true belief" doesn't count as knowledge, as we might sometimes be lucky enough to

> *Belief*: an idea someone holds about the nature of reality.

"guess correctly" about reality every now and then (and guessing correctly, we know, isn't really knowing). So we need to have *warrant* for our beliefs too, which means having good reasons to have a belief. Some ways to justify our beliefs are reason, observation, experience, introspection, or authority. I am justified, for example, to believe that the chair in which I am sitting will hold me up because I have sat in it many times and it's always held me up, something I know through experience. I am justified in believing that I am angry or happy by introspecting, by looking inside myself. I am justified in believing I will do well on my driver's test because I have studied and understood the material and practiced. When my justified beliefs are true, then and only then can I call them **knowledge**.

Insofar as it is possible to have justified true beliefs about God, it is possible to have knowledge about him.

Of course, Christianity recognizes that other religions have discovered some truths about God. We find

> *Knowledge*: justified true belief.

---

many grains of truth on the shores of almost all world religions. Still, biblical Christianity claims to have true knowledge about God by which we can assess claims about his existence and what he requires of us. When Christians proclaim this, many dismiss them as intolerant, a label that is appropriate for anyone, including Christians, who arrogantly shuns people or makes hurtful comments. It's wrong, however, to think that all Christians are intolerant because some have behaved badly. It's like saying that Mozart is a bad composer because your nine-year-old sister plays his compositions poorly. Also, the label "intolerant" is often thrown at Christians not for their behavior but for their beliefs. Is the mere act of claiming to know truth intolerant?

To see if the "intolerant" label actually fits, we should outline a working definition of truth, learn whether religious truth claims count as knowledge, understand the meaning of tolerance, and respond thoughtfully to those who believe that claiming the truth is intolerant. In this chapter, we hope to accomplish this and one other goal: to develop a curious, determined, and humble spirit that enables others to see through our faults and focus on the truth.

3. The Reigning Idea of Tolerance

Tolerance means recognizing and respecting the dignity of people you think are wrong. Today, tolerance is defined as *accepting* the views of others as equally true and valid. Christian author Dallas Willard says, "No longer is tolerance a matter of saying 'I disagree with you and I believe you're wrong.' That's not enough. We're now in the situation where everyone must be equally right, where you cannot claim that people are wrong and still love them."[5]

> *Tolerance:* the willingness to recognize and respect the dignity of those with whom one disagrees.

Traditional Christians are often accused of being the worst offenders. Teresa Whitehurst, a liberal Christian commentator, says, "Conservative Christians have adopted the warrior mentality of Onward Christian Soldiers, and intolerance is nothing to be hidden under a white robe and pointed white hood: it's to be waved proudly as a flag demonstrating Christian rigor and personal rightness."[6]

Wow. By referring to white robes and pointed white hoods, Whitehurst is making a bigoted comparison between Christians with firm beliefs and Ku Klux Klan members who terrorized and even killed those they disagreed with, even fellow Christians. It's not only a harsh, unfair comparison but also a false one. Sadly, it's common. In researching for their book *unChristian,* David Kinnaman and Gabe Lyons asked young adults ages sixteen through twenty-nine who did not regularly attend church which characteristics were descriptive of the church "a lot" or "some." "Judgmental" was used by 87 percent to describe the church, and 70 percent described it as "insensitive to others." In fact, 84 percent of these non-church-attenders said they knew a Christian personally, but only 15 percent said they saw any lifestyle differences in those Christians.[7]

The realization that people see Christians primarily as hypocritical judgers rather than truth bearers should give us pause. If we are participating in demeaning behavior or are devaluing others, we ought to repent and seek to be conformed to the image of Christ. However, does the fact that people find biblical truth offensive mean we should stop proclaiming it?

According to three popular viewpoints, the answer is yes. Let's look at each of these viewpoints to see if they are correct to say that religious truth cannot be known and therefore should not be proclaimed.

4. POSTMODERNISM: RELIGIOUS TRUTH CANNOT BE KNOWN

The influence of **Postmodernism** has resulted in people believing that religious knowledge differs from "actual" knowledge because Postmodernists maintain that reality cannot be known by us—that what we call knowledge is just our use of language to give ourselves and others the impression that we know what is going on.

Postmodernists, then, dismiss any viewpoint as being characterized as true. The words we use to make this case are just words, they say. No necessary relationship exists between words describing religious knowledge and reality. That is, talk about "God" is *just talk*; it doesn't actually refer to God.

Postmodernists say that no religion's story of God, humans, or salvation is true. In other words, they reject all metanarratives. If no metanarratives can describe reality, then of course Christianity is doomed, as are all other religions that try to make sense of life. Further, if no metanarrative is true, then we can't "all have sinned and fall short of God's glory" (Rom. 3:23),[8] nor could God love the human race (John 3:16),[9] nor could Christ have died for our sins (1 John 2:2).[10] Christianity, then, is implausible.

> *Postmodernism:* a skeptical worldview, founded as a reaction to modernism, that is suspicious of metanarratives and teaches that ultimate reality is that inaccessible, knowledge is a social construct, and that truth claims are political power plays.

Usually Postmodernists don't present their cases so bleakly. They don't want to be the Grinch who stole Christmas; they just want people to stop believing that Christmas has any connection to truth. But maybe the Postmodernist is wrong. After all, if our language does not point to any truth, then the claim that "Christians are intolerant" can't be true. Nor can the claim that no one can know whether God exists because that, too, is a claim about reality.

Christian philosophers J. P. Moreland and Garrett DeWeese argue that at the end of the day, we can know things based on good reasons: "We don't trust a plumber who diagnoses our stomachache as appendicitis just because he believes it is, no matter how sincere his belief; we go to a doctor who knows about the appendix.... When it comes to our religious faith, it is no different."[11]

Christians believe that atheists are wrong, but they don't think atheists' words are meaningless. So if language can be used in moral judgments about tolerance and God's existence when it comes to views hostile to Christianity, surely such language can be used in moral and theological judgments about God in support of Christianity.

It is better to assume that thoughts are *about* real things and are *intended* to be about real things.[12] So the next time someone says that "no religious belief can be known to be true," don't be shocked into silence. Just say, "That sounds like a belief about religion. How do you know it is true?"

5. Pluralism 1.0: Religious Truth Is Individual

Perhaps someone has said to you, "That may be true for you, but not for me. Truth is relative." Francis Beckwith and Greg Koukl, in their book *Relativism: Feet Firmly Planted in Mid-Air*, say, "Today we've lost confidence that statements of fact can ever be anything more than just opinions; we no longer know that anything is certain beyond our subjective preferences. The word truth now means 'true for me' and nothing more. We have entered an era of dogmatic skepticism."[13] Beckwith and Koukl have hit on something important. Polls show that a very high percentage of people—in some surveys, as high as 90 percent—believe that truth and morality are relative to our situation.[14] For people who believe this, our claims to "know" something comes across as arrogant and presumptuous.

> Polls show that a very high percentage of people—in some surveys, as high as 90 percent—believe that truth and morality are relative to our situation.

Part of the problem is that people assume that religious experiences are completely individual and that no one has an objective enough standpoint from which to say that certain experiences are tied to perceptions that are evidentially verifiable.

Some people insist that it is offensive to claim to have true knowledge about religion. To them, saying that one's beliefs are true and other peoples' are not is like saying, "I'm sorry you're not smart enough to see what I see," or, "If you were a good person, you would abandon that belief." In this view, claiming to know *the* truth is the kind of thing bullies do when trying to hurt other people's feelings.[15]

Pluralism 1.0 says, how could anyone else say they know the truth for *me*? It's offensive and counterintuitive to say *you* know the truth for *me*. After all, my experiences are personal in the sense that *my* eyes can only bring visual images into *my* brain, where they are interpreted based on *my* own thinking.

> If truth is actually out there, my perceptions might affect how I understand it, but they do not affect the nature of truth itself.

But these objections can be sustained only if, in fact, there is no actual truth to perceive. If truth is actually out there, my perceptions might affect how I understand it, but they do not affect the nature of truth itself. A blue plush suede cushioned chair, for example, does not change its nature to become a brown oak hardback chair just because you and I perceive it differently.

> Our *internal* experiences are *externally* validated when we can see they are held in common, providing a compelling warrant for the belief that God is working all over the world.

If, on the other hand, truth actually exists, then it is possible for each person to perceive it individually and also experience it in a similar way as other people. We in the West tend to believe that we each experience God differently. But if I, a Christian, compared my experiences with God to the experiences of other Christians around the world, I would see that my experiences are more similar to theirs than I imagined.[16] We all experience God's presence, a sense of remorse over sin, a call to accept God's offer of forgiveness, and relief that he has healed us and is preparing us for a new kind of life. Our *internal*

ISN'T CLAIMING TRUTH INTOLERANT?

experiences are *externally* validated when we can see they are held in common, providing a compelling warrant for the belief that God is working all over the world.

Other religions are not like Christianity in this respect. Most religions are tied directly to an ethnic identity. In spite of massive publicity campaigns and the conversion of a handful of well-known actors and actresses, Buddhism remains mostly in the Far East. (Plus, Buddhism in China looks far different than Buddhism in California). Hinduism is the religion of India. Islam is prevalent in the Middle East and Indonesia, where people raised in its principles have gained influence.

Christianity may sometimes seem to be the religion of the West, but Christianity transcends ethnic identity. Christian conversions have taken place and are taking place all over the world and across all racial, ethnic, and age groups.

How might this be explained?

Of course, some people say Christianity initially grew through force. This is true of Islam and Marxism, but the evidence for Christianity spreading this way is slim. As we will see, where Christianity has taken root and spread, it is largely because Christians moved into an area and attracted followers through a winsome lifestyle and moral persuasion.[17]

In the case of Christianity, the simplest theory is that Christian conversions are genuine experiences of people encountering some kind of reality that people all over the world—regardless of cultural background, race, national identity, or language—can discern.[18] As Cambridge philosopher C. D. Broad suggested, we should treat these experiences as truthful unless we have positive evidence that they are delusional.[19]

Certainly, people are more likely to embrace whatever religion dominates the culture in which they are raised. But the fact that people all over the world have willingly converted to Christianity, making it the largest religion in the world, is a phenomenon unprecedented in history.

> As we will see, where Christianity has taken root and spread, it is largely because Christians moved into an area and attracted followers through a winsome lifestyle and moral persuasion.

> Certainly, people are more likely to embrace whatever religion dominates the culture in which they are raised. But the fact that people all over the world have willingly converted to Christianity, making it the largest religion in the world, is a phenomenon unprecedented in history.

> If someone says that our religious beliefs come from our cultural or historical situations and are thus not actually true, he or she is also saying to all world religions, "Your truth claims are not valid, but mine are." It seems to be an intolerant thing to say for someone who claims to be advancing the cause of tolerance.

6. PLURALISM 2.0: RELIGIOUS TRUTH IS CULTURAL

Although some believe that truth is relative to individuals, others believe it is relative to cultures. One such individual was philosopher of religion John Hick, whom we discussed earlier. Hick grew up as an evangelical Christian, but through his exposure to people of different religions at his university, he became convinced that each culture has its own religious truths and that all of these truths are equally valid.

Yet, as Alvin Plantinga points out, people all over the world seem to have always assumed that their own religion is the true one, and it is only in our own age that people began to widely embrace the idea that no one religion is actually true for everyone. If Hick had been born in another culture or time, Plantinga argues, it probably never would have occurred to him to believe that no religion has a legitimate claim to ultimate truth.[20]

If someone says that our religious beliefs come from our cultural or historical situations and are thus not actually true, he or she is also saying to all world religions, "Your truth claims are not valid, but mine are." It seems to be an intolerant thing to say for someone who claims to be advancing the cause of tolerance.

The idea that each religious viewpoint is true for those who hold it may seem to resolve the tensions among religious viewpoints, but it also creates all kinds of problems. As we asked in an earlier chapter, are religions that hold that women are of a lower status than men—that women may be beaten or killed without penalty—as valid as those that hold that women should be protected? Are religions that hold that it is good to kill and eat one's enemies as valid as those that say we ought to love them?

Christians who wish to be tolerant—according to the new definition of tolerance—must forfeit the belief that Jesus died for everyone and that he is the true way to God. The world's view of tolerance guts the gospel and removes the heart of the historic Christian worldview.

So who can meaningfully participate in the global conversation about religious belief? Could anyone qualify? What about those who have no meaningful beliefs? Wouldn't it be better for each of us to make the case for what is *true* regardless of time and culture rather than forfeiting our knowledge out of deference to other beliefs? To answer these questions, we need an understanding of what truth actually is.

7. What Is Truth Anyway?

"Peanut butter milkshakes are awesome" differs from "Five plus five equals ten," as one statement makes a claim about one's opinion, and the other claims something about reality. The first is based on a **subjective truth claim**, a kind of claim shared by those who greatly enjoy peanut butter milkshakes.[21] The second is an **objective truth claim**, a claim that all thinking people will rightly embrace. It corresponds with reality. Something is true if and only if it lines up with the way things actually are.

Subjective Truth Claim: a claim regarding a dependent fact about a subject.

Objective Truth Claim: a claim regarding an independent fact about the world.

Subjective truth claims deal with matters of preference or taste, while objective truth claims deal with the way the world actually is for all people everywhere. Subjective truth claims are about the "subject" (i.e., person) who is making the claim, not about the properties of what they're talking about. For example, "Fall is the best season," "Blue is the best color," and "Coke is better than Pepsi" are subjective truth claims. Objective truth claims attempt to accurately name properties of the "object," things that can be known to be true or false. Examples of objective truth claims include things such as, "Murder is against the law in Kansas," "The boiling point of water is 212 degrees Fahrenheit,"

ISN'T CLAIMING TRUTH INTOLERANT?

"James Garfield was assassinated by Charles Guiteau in 1881," and "Jesus is the Son of God, who offers salvation to any who would believe in him."

I bet I caught you on that last one. To Postmodernists and religious pluralists of the types I described earlier, the statement about Jesus falls into a category of things that are spiritual and cannot actually be known rather than the category of what counts as true knowledge. But keep in mind our definition of truth— that something is true if and only if it lines up with the way things actually are in the world. The **correspondence theory of truth** is described by authors Norman Geisler and Joseph Holden as follows:

> *Correspondence Theory of Truth:* **the view that the truth of a proposition is determined by how accurately it describes the facts of reality.**

> Remember, a distinction between our statements and the facts as they are in the real world must exist or else there could be no way of discovering which statements are true and which are false. The fancy name for this definition of truth is the "correspondence theory" because truth corresponds or relates to reality (the real world) as it actually is.[22]

Would it be reasonable for you to respond to my comment "It is raining outside" by saying, "It may be raining outside for you, but it isn't raining outside for me"? Couldn't my claim be verified? If we both understand what rain is, we could look out the window to see if my claim corresponds to reality. My claim "It is raining outside," is true if and only if it lines up with the way things actually are—if it *corresponds* to reality.

This is all well and good, but here's the big question: Are religious claims knowable in the same way as facts about rain or the boiling point of water? Let's have a look.

8. Is It Possible to Know the Truth about Religious Claims?

In the case of a claim about the natural world or historical events, we must examine evidence to see if the claims correspond to reality. In the natural world, we might use the scientific method to observe, measure, and, if possible, repeat experiments to see what happens under stable conditions. For claims about historical events, we might examine newspaper accounts, listen to the testimonies of witnesses, or perhaps look at pictures or watch film footage. In either case, it would be silly to say, "Well, maybe water boils at 212 degrees Fahrenheit for *you*, but in my culture it is different," or, "Perhaps it is true for *you* that Martin Luther King Jr. was shot on April 4, 1968, but how dare you impose that belief on me!" We can *know* these things. We don't label people as intolerant if they proclaim them. The question is, Can we claim religious knowledge in the same way that we claim scientific or historical knowledge?

If you've read the earlier chapters in this book, you can probably guess that the answer is yes. We can examine the biblical record, philosophical arguments, historical works from those living in Bible times, and so forth to come to an understanding that the biblical record corresponds to reality.

But what about such claims as "It is a bad thing to steal"? Is such a moral claim subject to knowledge? We think it is, and here's why: no matter what one's background or beliefs, everyone in the world must answer a few basic questions to live in the real world. Here is Christian author and speaker James Sire's list of such questions:

1. What is prime reality—the really real? (Is God the prime reality, or multiple gods, or the universe?)

2. What is the nature of external reality (the world around us)? (Was the world created, has it always existed, is it chaotic or orderly?)

3. What is a human being? (A highly complex machine, a sleeping god, a person made in the image of God, an animal?)

4. What happens to persons at death? (Are we reincarnated, simply cease to exist, go to heaven or hell?)

5. Why is it possible to think anything at all? (Were we made by an intelligent, all-knowing God, or did our consciousness develop through the long process of evolution?)

6. How do we know right from wrong? (Is morality determined by our own choice and whatever feels good? Is it based on what society says is moral? Is it based on the character of God?)

7. What is the meaning of human history? (Is it based on the purposes of a god or the gods, or is it to create some type of paradise on earth?)[23]

As soon as a religion makes a truth claim about one of these questions, it is making a claim about the nature of reality. Such statements are not mere preferences or opinions. They cannot be true for one person and false for someone else, especially if they are contrary to one another.[24]

Let's illustrate this with a silly example. Imagine a person were to tell you she believes that the world's troubles will be solved when we are all rescued by pink flying elephants. Imagine further that this is a deeply held belief and that she is willing to endure the mockery of others because of her belief. Could we evaluate such a truth claim? Of course. At the very least, we can say that there is no good reason to hold such a belief because pink flying elephants have never been observed to exist.

Some people view statements about God similarly. No one has seen God, so how is belief in God fundamentally different than belief in pink flying elephants? The only way to answer this question is to point out, as we have seen in earlier chapters, that there is strong warrant for belief in God's existence.

Moreland and DeWeese put it this way: "What should matter in matters of faith is knowledge, not merely sincere belief; good reasons, not mere hunches; truth, not feelings. We can rightly say that Christianity is a knowledge tradition, meaning it is more than ritual or emotions. Christianity claims certain things can be known."[25] This has a tremendous impact on

ISN'T CLAIMING TRUTH INTOLERANT?

how we view matters of religious faith. Faith has to do with certain claims about reality that are not in the realm of the subjective but in the realm of the objective. Although experiences and feelings can certainly bolster our faith, faith itself cannot be reduced to emotions and opinions no matter how sincere they may be. Faith may flower in emotional expression, but it is rooted in the soil of knowledge and reality.

Good arguments about God have been articulated by scholars for millennia, and these arguments have never been adequately refuted. The remaining question is this: Is Christianity the best way of knowing about God?

9. Christian View of Truth: Knowable, Sharable, Exclusive

To say that the Christian worldview is true is to say that it best describes the contours of the world *as it actually exists*.[26] For example, Christianity says that the universe is a product of design and that this fact is observable by everyone, whether or not that truth has been suppressed by other commitments.

Christianity's correspondence with the observable moral order of the world is another aspect of Christianity's justified true belief. As Francis Schaeffer pointed out, "If there is no absolute beyond man's ideas, then there is no final appeal to judge between individuals and groups whose moral judgments conflict. We are merely left with conflicting opinions."[27] To paraphrase C. S. Lewis, if moral judgment is impossible, then whether we like certain values is just a preference for certain impulses based on how strongly we feel them rather than based on whether they are actually real.[28] In a world of merely conflicting opinions, those best able to muster the power to get their way will always win. The biblical idea is that **moral absolutes** are not around to benefit the stronger and meaner but rather to protect the weak. Bullies are not right just because they are mightier. Common sense tells us that only bullies disagree with this claim.

> *Moral Absolute:* an objective, unchanging, and universal standard of right and wrong.

So far every culture in the world has understood and embraced moral absolutes to buffer society from the influence of raw power. Richard H. Beis, professor emeritus of philosophy at St. Mary's University in Nova Scotia, collected a list of moral absolutes that seem to be true in every culture that anthropologists have studied:

- Prohibition of murder or maiming without justification

- Prohibition of lying, at least in certain areas such as oaths, etc.

- Right to own property such as land, clothing, tools, etc.

- Economic justice: reciprocity and restitution

- Preference of common good over individual good

- Sexual restriction within all societies[29]

- Reciprocal duties between children and parents: parents care for and train children, and children respect, obey, and care for parents in old age

- Loyalty to one's social unit (family, tribe, country)

- Provision for poor and unfortunate

- Prohibition of theft

- Prevention of violence within in-groups

- Obligation to keep promises

- Obedience to leaders

- Respect for the dead and disposal of human remains in some traditional and ritualistic fashion

- Desire for and priority of immaterial goods (knowledge, values, etc.)

- Obligation to be a good mother

- Distributive justice (fairness)

- Inner rather than external sanctions considered better

- Recognizing courage as a virtue

- Identifying justice as an obligation[30]

People who believe there are moral absolutes think moral rules are universal because they are universally true, revealed to everyone. Yes, they work, and, in that, they are good. But they are not good because they work; they work *because they are good*. They are sensible, yes. But they are sensible because they are true, not the other way around. Christians can think this way because they believe the Bible's revelation of God's nature and character. From a biblical viewpoint, it is not that the truth is *unknowable* or that we are confused; it is that truth is *knowable* and we have *rebelled*. Even fallen humans can know the truth, and we ought to encourage one another to embrace it.

10. How Different Worldviews Respond to Christian Truth Claims

Although some insist that Christianity is intolerant because they do not think it is right for anyone to claim his or her religion as true, they likely believe that at least one religion—Christianity—is actually making a *false* claim and that they know better. This rejection almost always springs from one of two perspectives.

You may remember that **monism** means a belief in "one substance" and **dualism** means a belief in "two substances." Whereas Christianity (as well as Islam and other theistic religions) believes that both the material and immaterial worlds exist, most nontheistic worldviews believe in one or the other. Worldviews such as **Secularism** and **Marxism** choose **materialism**, saying that only the material world exists. Worldviews lining up with "New Spirituality," on the other hand, choose **spiritual monism**, saying that reality is ultimately divine—that the physical world is an illusion. If someone says that Christianity is intolerant, find out whether the person actually believes that the spiritual world is real. If he doesn't, then obviously he is going to disagree with Christianity as well as with just about all other world religions. If the person thinks the physical world is an illusion, he is also going to object to Christianity, but because he believes that the tools of knowledge can never reveal ultimate truth.

Just so you're prepared to deal with each of these viewpoints, let's examine them in a little more detail.

> *Monism:* the belief that reality is ultimately composed of one essential substance.

> *Dualism:* the belief that reality is ultimately composed of two essential substances.

> *Secularism:* an atheistic and materialistic worldview that advocates for a public society free from the influence of religion.

> *Marxism:* an atheistic and materialistic worldview based on the ideas of Karl Marx that promotes the abolition of private property, the public ownership of the means of production (such as socialism), and the utopian dream of a future communistic state.

> *Spiritual Monism:* the belief that reality is ultimately divine.

The First Kind of Monism: Only the Material Exists

In the television series *The Day the Universe Changed*, science historian James Burke says, "There is no metaphysical, super-ordinary, final, absolute reality. There is no special direction to events. The universe is what we say it is. When theories change, the universe changes. The truth is relative."[31] What *is* just *is*. If we perceive any special meaning, it is because we are making it up to explain the world better to ourselves. And over time, such explanations change. As German social psychologist Erich Fromm asserts, "Man creates himself in the historical process."[32]

People who think that truth is relative and based on societal consensus usually bristle when religious and political authorities imply that *their* perception of reality is actually *true*. Well-known philosopher Richard Rorty, for example, was fond of quoting the French revolutionary Denis Diderot in his speeches: "Man will never be free until the last king is strangled with the entrails of the last priest."[33] Rorty, whose particular viewpoint is called *pragmatism*, thought that the world just *is* and that people who claim to know the truth are merely trying to trick people into going along with their agendas.

Ironically, although Rorty was probably just attempting to be witty with the quote about kings and priests, other materialists have developed entire worldviews justifying violent opposition to those who express truth claims contrary to their own. Vladimir Lenin, the leader of the Russian revolution and founder of Soviet communism, stated flatly, "The philosophical basis of Marxism, as Marx and Engels repeatedly declared, is … a materialism which is absolutely atheistic and positively hostile to all religion."[34] Elsewhere, Lenin made it clear that fighting religion was an essential ingredient in a materialistic reality. "We must combat religion;" he said, "that is the ABC of all materialism, and consequently of Marxism."[35] Lenin didn't just object to religion; he openly promoted atheism.[36] "Every religious idea, every idea of God, even flirting with the idea of God, is unutterable vileness … vileness of the most dangerous kind, 'contagion' of the most abominable kind," he said.[37]

Judging by their rhetoric, it would appear that many materialists believe that supernatural religion is *dangerous*, not just *wrong*. Harvard's Edward O. Wilson broadly accuses people who believe in the Bible of practicing an aggressive "fundamentalist religion," which he describes as "one of the unmitigated evils of the world."[38]

Even more moderate materialist voices, such as the pragmatist philosopher Sidney Hook, insist that we can have a good society only if religious people give up their claims to truth: "The democratic open society must be neutral to all religious overbeliefs; but no matter how secular it conceives itself to be, it cannot be neutral to moral issues. It seeks to draw these issues into the area of public discussion in the hope that a reasonable consensus may be achieved."[39] Of course, this consensus must be based on some set of beliefs. But whose, and on what basis?

The Second Kind of Monism: Only the Spiritual Exists

A second kind of monism exists that denies the material world and says that only the spiritual world exists. My broad label for this is **New Spirituality**, which is a worldview held by people who see truth as known by feeling or experience, not by scientific, logical, or even religious knowledge, at least of the Christian kind. Author and speaker Marilyn Ferguson states, "We need not postulate a purpose for this Ultimate Cause nor wonder who or what caused whatever Big Bang launched the visible universe. There is only the experience."[40] Author Eckhart Tolle agrees: "The Truth is inseparable from who you are. Yes, you *are* the Truth. If you look for it elsewhere, you will be deceived every time."[41]

> **New Spirituality:** a pantheistic worldview that teaches that everything and everyone are connected through divine consciousness.

In New Spiritualist writings, it is clear that most New Spiritualists reject the personal God of the Bible as a dangerous myth separating people into religious factions. No one approach to God is correct. Bestselling New Spiritualist author Neale Donald Walsch claims that God revealed to him personally, "No path to God is more direct than any other path. No religion is the 'one true religion.'"[42] In an interview with journalist Bill Moyers, filmmaker George Lucas said, "The conclusion I've come to is that all the religions are true."[43] Lucas and Walsch's conviction is shared in the wider population, even among many Christians. According to George Barna, 63 percent of the teenagers surveyed agree that "Muslims, Buddhists, Christians, Jews, and all other people pray to the same god, even though they use different names for their god."[44] So, the claim continues, if we don't have peace on earth yet, it is only because some wrongly persist in their exclusionist beliefs.

Next we move on to how to defuse the most common slogans people raise against Christians in the name of tolerance.

11. Is Tolerance a Virtue?

People disagree all the time—in politics, science, philosophy, and virtually every other academic subject—but when it comes to issues of faith, embracing all beliefs as equally valid is considered a high moral virtue. To disagree is seen as a grave moral error.

Popularly, embracing all beliefs as valid is called "tolerance." But as noted earlier, this isn't tolerance. Authors Brad Stetson and Joseph Conti pose some interesting thoughts:

> There is widespread feeling today that something is very wrong with the way we think about tolerance. We have intuition that in our diverse society tolerance is very important to practice, but at the same time we are unable to agree on what exactly it means to be tolerant. Does tolerance require the acceptance of all views on a given subject as equally true? Does it mean that I must not believe too strongly that my views are right about a given subject? Can I be tolerant and still believe in objective truth about religion, ethics and politics?[45]

Stetson and Conti conclude that the commonly accepted definition of tolerance misses the mark. So what should we replace it with? J. Warner Wallace, a cold-case detective and Christian apologist, simply points to the YourDictionary.com definition, which says that tolerance is "a tolerating or being tolerant, especially of views, beliefs, practices, etc. of others that differ from one's own." When asked what it is to tolerate something, the same source says that we tolerate someone when we "recognize and respect [others' beliefs, practices, and so forth] without sharing them." According to TheFreeDictionary.com, *tolerate* can be defined as "to put up with" or "endure" something.[46]

As Wallace notes, for there to be tolerance, the following is necessary:

- Two or more people must exist.

- These folks must hold divergent views, beliefs, or practices. In other words, they must *DISAGREE.*

- These same folks must endure one another. In other words, they cannot eliminate each other even though they don't embrace each other's beliefs, but must instead find a way to peacefully co-exist.[47]

Professor of philosophy Paul Copan makes an excellent point about this: "If disagreement didn't exist, then tolerance would be unneeded. It's the existence of real differences between people that make tolerance necessary and virtuous."[48]

To reach a point of true tolerance, we must recognize that each of us has the freedom to believe what we want, whether true or false. However, the right to hold these beliefs does not mean they are equally true or valid or that to disagree with another's choice is somehow evil. *True tolerance* is the ability to disagree with someone and yet still live in peace. *False tolerance* is the intellectually dishonest practice of pretending that all beliefs are equally true and valid while actually believing that only one view—such as materialism or New Spirituality—is really the only true view.

Perhaps a word about living in peace is in order here. Because the Bible so often uses the metaphor of war to describe the spiritual conflict between good and evil, some Christians believe they are justified in using insulting language to put down those who do not hold to Christian beliefs. Harsh language, name-calling, and insults, though, are the weapons the world uses to exercise control over those who do not toe the party line. Christians' weapons should be different. Second Corinthians 10:4 says, "The weapons of our warfare are not of the flesh but have divine power to destroy strongholds."

What are "weapons of the flesh"? Galatians 5:19–21[49] says they include, among other things, "enmity [hostility], strife, jealousy, fits of anger, rivalries, dissensions, divisions, [and] envy." The works of the Holy Spirit, on the other hand, are "love, joy, peace, patience, kindness, goodness, faithfulness, gentleness, [and] self-control" (vv. 22–23). It is one thing to disagree with people; it is another thing entirely to disagree with them and do so as God desires.

Mere tolerance pales in comparison to these admirable virtues. J. Budziszewski writes,

> Our most gifted thinkers no longer treat tolerance as a queenly virtue to be guarded among many others equally precious, but as a shrewish virtue that excludes all the rest. For now we are told that the meaning of tolerance is ethical neutrality about which things are worth the love of human beings and which traits of character are worth praising.[50]

Perhaps we should raise our sights above mere tolerance and seek to act virtuously, hold as many true beliefs as possible, and enter into a dialogue of ideas where truth can be sought after and discovered. Here are three ways to do this.

12. Response 1: Defuse False Ideas of Tolerance

Two common errors often committed by those who claim that Christians are intolerant are (1) self-refuting claims and (2) weak slogans meant to stop Christians in their tracks.

Self-Refuting Claim: a statement that attempts to affirm two opposite propositions at the same time and in the same sense.

Self-Refuting Claims

Many statements about truth, according to Greg Koukl, commit suicide. In other words, they self-destruct because they contradict themselves. **Self-refuting claims** attempt to affirm two opposite propositions. If they are true, they are false. Here some examples:

ISN'T CLAIMING TRUTH INTOLERANT?

- "There is no truth." (Is this statement true?)

- "There are no absolutes." (Is this an absolute?)

- "No one can know any truth about religion." (And how, precisely, did you come to know that truth about religion?)

- "You can't know anything for sure." (Are you sure about that?)

- "Talking about God is meaningless." (What does this statement about God mean?)

- "You can know truth only through experience." (What experience taught you that truth?)

- "Never take anyone's advice on that issue." (Should I take your advice on that?)[51]

Often these statements are made to imply that anyone who believes another to be wrong is being intolerant. When we hear someone make a statement like this, we should graciously point out the contradiction.

Weak Slogans

Some slogans are repeated in religious conversation in order to stop Christians in their tracks. Although these slogans may be worded differently, the goal is the same: to portray Christians as intolerant, judgmental people who think they are right and everyone else is wrong. Following are some slogans along with examples of how to respond drawn from a book I strongly recommend by Paul Copan, *True for You, but Not for Me*.

"Who are you to judge others?" The first response when someone says this is to ask, "Is it wrong for me to judge?" If the person says yes, ask, "Is that your judgment?" Many people confuse making judgments with being judgmental. We certainly should not look down on others but rather have an attitude of humility (Gal. 6:1).[52] But this does not mean that we refrain from seeking the truth. Rather, as Copan reminds us, "In your interactions, remember your own sinfulness and the other's humanness—not vice versa. Speak the truth in love."[53]

"That's just your opinion." By informing us that our statement is one of opinion rather than knowledge, the person using this slogan is unwittingly claiming to *know* something true—namely, that what you are saying is *false*. Although it is certainly true that some people are not in touch with reality and their opinions ought to be taken with a grain of salt, to say, "That's just your opinion," simply does not answer the point you're making.[54]

"All religions are basically the same." Anyone who claims that all religions are basically the same has never studied what other religions teach. Copan puts it this way: "All religions aren't basically the same. They differ profoundly, in major ways. What they have in common is that they are so different."[55] As we have seen throughout this volume, we do well to affirm truth wherever we find it, even if we find it in other religions. We have to be careful, of course, because when truth and error are mixed together, the result can be even bigger error. But we ought to be on the lookout for glimpses of truth where we find them—for films that display the destructive consequences of sin and the power of redemption, for example, or that lift up the value of people as God's image bearers. As Copan phrases it, "Some aspects of various religions may help pave the way to the gospel, which is the fulfillment of all religions' and philosophies' highest ideals, aspirations and hopes."[56]

> We ought to be on the lookout for glimpses of truth where we find them—for films that display the destructive consequences of sin and the power of redemption, for example, or that lift up the value of people as God's image bearers.

"If you grew up in Iran, you would be a Muslim." Many people use this argument to show that Christians are intolerant because they impose their beliefs on others and say that other religions are wrong. They will argue that what someone believes is greatly determined by where he or she is born. However, location of birth is not a determining factor of objective truth. We would not say, for example, that repressive political regimes are good because some people grow up under them. It isn't arrogant to point out that some worldviews focus more on human flourishing than others. Rather, it is arrogant to say that differences among religions are meaningless or, worse, that every viewpoint is equally focused on the good. It just isn't true.[57]

"Saying Jesus is the only way to heaven is exclusive and discounts every other religion." If something is true, it excludes contrary beliefs. The very idea that truth is exclusive does not make it false. Jesus claimed to be the only way to heaven (John 14:6),[58] so it is not Christians who are exclusive, it is Jesus. The only ones excluded are those who choose not to believe him and receive his offer of salvation. So when people from another religion says that Christianity discounts their explanation of life and plan of salvation, they're right. However, their religion excludes Christianity too. In fact, those who object to all religions are likewise exclusivist when they say that religious truth claims cannot be known. Everyone is exclusivist; the question is what evidence they can bring to bear to show that their exclusiveness constitutes justified true belief.

13. RESPONSE 2: ASK GOOD QUESTIONS

Francis Scott Key, the man who penned the words to "The Star-Spangled Banner," was also a Christian interested in displayed Christianity's truth. He once wrote,

> I don't believe there are any new objections to be discovered to the truth of Christianity, though there may be some art in presenting old ones in a new dress. My faith has been greatly confirmed by the infidel writers I have read. Men may argue ingeniously against our faith, as indeed they may against anything—but what can they say in defense of their own. I would carry the war into their own territories, I would ask them what they believe—if they said they believed anything, [and] I think that they might be shown

ISN'T CLAIMING TRUTH INTOLERANT?

to be more full of difficulties and liable to infinitely greater objections than the system they oppose and they were credulous and unreasonable for believing it.[59]

Mr. Key understood a profound yet little-known principle of defending the Christian faith (1 Pet. 3:15).[60] It is simply this: the best defense is a good offense.

If you find it difficult to stand up for what you believe, start by asking questions. A few strategic questions can get your conversational partner thinking in short order. Good questions show thoughtfulness. They help us get to know others and gather information about what they believe.[61] Second, they compel others to think through beliefs they may have accepted without realizing it. Third, asking questions enables us to "level the playing field" and avoid sneaky argument strategies from a conversational partner. Plus, question asking is low risk. If a conversational partner gets upset, we can simply stop asking questions or change the subject. Years ago I learned a series of questions from a friend named Andrew Heister. Over time I've adapted Andrew's lengthier list into four basic questions for any conversation on just about any topic:[62]

> If you find it difficult to stand up for what you believe, start by asking questions.

"What do you mean by _____?" Always ask for a definition of the key terms. Arguments often employ fuzzy definitions of terms. When someone makes a truth claim, remember how Socrates, perhaps the world's most famous arguer, always required his opponents to define their terms, whether their topics were justice, the good life, or even what makes a valid argument in the first place. He understood that defining the terms is paramount to discovering the truth. For example, if someone says, "There is no God," ask, "What do you mean by God?"

"How did you come to that conclusion?" Always question how a particular fact came to be known. Most people miss this step because they assume that "facts" are always true. Surprisingly, most people believe things for which they have little or no evidence. Try this question out when someone expresses strong opinions, such as "Miracles are impossible" or "Christianity is for fools."

"Where do you get your information?" What is the source of the fact in question, and how can it be verified? Much of what passes as factual is based on dubious information or hearsay. Good facts should be backed up by citing evidence. When someone makes a difficult-to-believe claim, such as "Those who question whether global warming is human caused are victims of a conspiracy by big oil companies" or "Humans simply aren't made to be faithful to one person in marriage," ask detailed questions about how they know what they know. Before long you will get to the root of the issue and be on even terms in the discussion.

"What happens if you are wrong?" Most people don't like to think that they might be wrong, but it is important to understand what's at stake when we choose to believe something. It is one thing to claim a belief and yet another to stake one's life on it. The most important question that can be asked in life is "Where do you go when you die, and what happens if you are wrong?"[63] Of course, you must be prepared to receive this question as well as ask it. You don't have to know all the answers *right now*, nor should you expect others to know them. The goal is, instead, to spark conversation.

To see how these questions can work, consider the following imaginary conversation:

Friend: "It is intolerant to think that someone can know the truth about God."

You: "What do you mean by intolerant?"

Friend: "Intolerance is being judgmental about what other people think and believe by saying they are wrong."

You: "That is an interesting perspective. How did you come to that conclusion?"

Friend: "What do you mean?"

You: "Do you think it is possible to know anything about God?"

Friend: "Yes, I think people can know things about God, but no one can be certain they are right."

You: "Where did you get your information on that?"

Friend: "My religious studies professor said that we should appreciate what every religion has to say because each religion teaches us something about God. However, no one should be too dogmatic about what they think is true."

You: "So, let me see if I understand what you are saying. You believe it is wrong to tell other people they are wrong for thinking they know something about God, right? However, by saying Christians are wrong, aren't you doing the very thing you say is wrong? Aren't you saying that you know something to be true about God that Christians have missed? Isn't that being intolerant of Christians?"

Friend: "Well … I think what I am saying is different because I am accepting of all religious faiths and think they all have something to say about God."

You: "Do you accept what Christians believe about God?"

Friend: "No, because they think everyone else is wrong!"

You: "But what happens if you are wrong about that?"

In the end, the goal of such conversations is not to play mind games or be tricky; it is to discern how what others say matches up with reality as well as help them think through their assumptions.

14. Response 3: Have a Good Attitude

Understanding the truth isn't all we need to do. First Peter 3:15 says that we are "always being prepared to make a defense to anyone who asks you for a reason for the hope that is in you … with gentleness and respect." We need to learn to communicate the truth in the way Jesus would. Here are some ideas about how to do it.

Embrace humble transparency. Humble transparency means recognizing that our understanding of the truth is valid, but that in our sin nature we lack knowledge, misunderstand things, and sometimes even use God's truth to further our own personal agendas. We see now dimly, as in a mirror (1 Cor. 13:12). This leaves room to be honest about our own struggles without being dangerously wishy-washy. Here's how to articulate it:

- "We certainly cannot know everything. But there are some things we can be sure of. Let's talk about what some of those things might be."

- "I am a fallen creature, so my ability to reason is far from perfect, but here is what I understand to be true."

Our attitude counts for a great deal in this. As the Chuck Colson Center's John Stonestreet says, "Young adults have reacted to seeing certainty with no humility by choosing humility with no certainty. We need to offer them certainty with humility."[64]

Trust God's sovereignty. Most Christians would say their spiritual growth has involved honestly wrestling with significant issues. The people we talk to about God might also need to wrestle with such issues. Trusting God means surrendering the outcome to him, walking faithfully with others, and avoiding manipulating the situation. Here's how to articulate it:

- "This is a big issue and I'm glad you're not taking it lightly. I'll pray and ask God to give you insight."

- "I'm so glad you're interested in asking the tough questions, and I hope we have the chance to talk more about this."

- "I've wrestled a lot with that issue myself. Here are some resources that I found helpful."

Avoid indoctrinating. My friend Ken Van Meter found through his dissertation research that people become resistant when they believe that Christianity is being forced upon them.[65] Therefore, we ought to give people time and intellectual space to reason things through. Here's how to articulate it:

- "If you're like me, I would guess you have genuine questions and doubts. I want to hear your honest questions."

- "May I share with you how Christians throughout history have come to grips with this issue?"

Listen in an engaged fashion. A friend of mine once commented on why Christians need to learn how to listen: "Listening to another's beliefs before speaking makes the listener credible and compassionate. However misguided the other's beliefs may be, why should he or she listen to me if I cannot listen to them? Is my faith so small that I have to cover my ears?"

Here's how to articulate it:

- "Tell me more about that." (Nothing says, "I'm listening!" as clearly as a question that honestly solicits further communication.)

- "I want to hear what is important to you."

- "Can we take some time to share our points of view with one another?"

- "Thank you for trusting me with your thoughts on these real-life matters."

As much as we value openness and encourage conversation, we *never* want to give the impression that God's truth is up for debate. It is not. God's nature and character are revealed in Scripture, and he means for us to know what is true. John Stonestreet suggests, "Look them in the eye and say that you're willing to stand on these ideas. But when you don't know something, you have to be humble enough to say 'Good question.'"[66]

15. CONCLUSION

Claiming to know truth is not intolerant. It is not intolerant to say that we can have knowledge about God, just as it is not intolerant to say we can have knowledge about what we had for dinner last night or about the solar system. True tolerance gives people the opportunity to hold differing views and still accept each other as human beings. True *intolerance* is treating a person with disdain and disrespect because of a belief he or she holds. In the end, Christians should be able to practice tolerance of the best sort, valuing other people as human beings enough to take them seriously, asking thought-provoking questions, and together moving closer to an understanding of the truth.

> True tolerance gives people the opportunity to hold differing views and still accept each other as human beings. True *intolerance* is treating a person with disdain and disrespect because of a belief he or she holds.

There is perhaps no topic on which a compassionate and inquisitive attitude is more important than the topic we will discuss in the next chapter: why God would allow evil and suffering. People's experiences of pain are very real and their questions deserve serious answers, especially when their life experiences call into question God's goodness.

ENDNOTES

1. Brian Jones, *Hell Is Real: But I Hate to Admit It* (Colorado Springs, CO: David C Cook, 2011), 141.

2. John 14:6: "Jesus said to him, 'I am the way, and the truth, and the life. No one comes to the Father except through me.'"

3. Colossians 1:16: "By him all things were created, in heaven and on earth, visible and invisible, whether thrones or dominions or rulers or authorities—all things were created through him and for him"; Hebrews 1:1–3: "Long ago, at many times and in many ways, God spoke to our fathers by the prophets, but in these last days he has spoken to us by his Son, whom he appointed the heir of all things, through whom also he created the world. He is the radiance of the glory of God and the exact imprint of his nature, and he upholds the universe by the word of his power. After making purification for sins, he sat down at the right hand of the Majesty on high"; John 1:1–3: "In the beginning was the Word, and the Word was with God, and the Word was God. He was in the beginning with God. All things were made through him, and without him was not anything made that was made."

4. J. P. Moreland and Garrett DeWeese, *Philosophy Made Slightly Less Difficult* (Downers Grove, IL: IVP Academic, 2005), 56.

5. Dallas Willard, quoted in Brad Stetson and Joseph G. Conti, *The Truth about Tolerance: Pluralism, Diversity, and the Culture Wars* (Downers Grove, IL: IVP Academic, 2005), 139.

6. Teresa Whitehurst, "The Intolerance of Christian Conservatives," *CounterPunch*, http://www.counterpunch.org/2005/01/25/the-intolerance-of-christian-conservatives/.

7. David Kinnaman and Gabe Lyons, *unChristian* (Grand Rapids, MI: Baker, 2012).

8. Romans 3:23: "All have sinned and fall short of the glory of God."

9. John 3:16: "For God so loved the world, that he gave his only Son, that whoever believes in him should not perish but have eternal life."

10. 1 John 2:2: "He is the propitiation for our sins, and not for ours only but also for the sins of the whole world."

11. Moreland and DeWeese, *Philosophy Made Slightly Less Difficult*, 53.

12. Edmund Husserl makes precisely this point about reality in a devastating critique of Postmodernist epistemology in *Logical Investigations*, vol. 2, trans. J. N. Findlay (London: Routledge and Kegan Paul, 1970), 603.

13. Francis Beckwith and Gregory Koukl, *Relativism: Feet Firmly Planted in Mid-Air* (Grand Rapids, MI: Baker, 1998), 20.

14. The Barna Group regularly polls people on the question of whether there is such a thing as moral truth. See www.barna.org.

15. If you are this kind of person, please do not tell anyone you are a Christian.

16. Kai-man Kwan, professor of religion and theology at Hong Kong Baptist University, in studying verbal reports of people's conversion experiences concludes that such people are not having isolated, delusional experiences. Man-Kwan says religious experiences can be studied for their validity if they are (1) shared experiences that happen over and over again, across cultures and time, (2) common in their ontology in that the experiences reported by people occur around certain things, processes or properties, and (3) conceptually coherent in that they are describable in a coherent way. See Kai-man Kwan, "The Argument from Religious Experience," in *The Blackwell Companion to Natural Theology*, ed. William Lane Craig and J. P. Moreland (Malden, MA: Wiley-Blackwell), 511.

17. This claim may seem grand, but there is voluminous evidence for it. I suggest consulting books written by reputable scholars such as David Bentley Hart, *Atheist Delusion: The Christian Revolution and Its Fashionable Enemies* (New Haven, CT: Yale University Press, 2010) and Rodney Stark, *Cities of God: The Real Story of How Christianity Became an Urban Movement and Conquered Rome* (New York: HarperOne, 2007).

18. The simplest theory, according to Richard Swinburne, professor emeritus at Oxford University, is the one most likely to be correct. Richard Swinburne, *The Evolution of the Soul* (Oxford: Clarendon, 1986), 13–15, quoted in Kwan, "The Argument from Religious Experience," 508.

19. C. D. Broad, *Religion, Philosophy and Psychical Research* (London: Routledge and Kegan Paul, 1953), 197, quoted in Kwan, "The Argument from Religious Experience," 502.

20. Alvin Plantinga, "Pluralism: A Defense of Religious Exclusivism," *The Philosophical Challenge of Religious Diversity*, ed. Kevin Meeker and Philip Quinn (New York: Oxford University Press, 1999), 172–92.

21. Francis Beckwith and Greg Koukl put it this way: "My statement about Häagen-Dazs ice cream is subjective truth. It is true for me, the subject, but not for the object, the ice cream itself. The ice cream doesn't 'taste'; I taste it. The experience of flavor pertains to me as a subject, not to the ice cream as an object. Tastes are personal. They're private. They're individual." Beckwith and Koukl, *Relativism*, 27.

22. Norman Geisler and Joseph Holden, *Living Loud: Defending Your Faith* (Nashville: Broadman, Holman, 2002), 29.

23. James Sire, *Naming the Elephant: Worldview as a Concept* (Downers Grove, IL: InterVarsity, 2004), 20.

24. Philosophers J. P. Moreland and Garrett DeWeese provide us with a definition of the law of noncontradiction: "For any property F, nothing can be both F and not-F at the same time in the same way." Something cannot be both true and false at the same time. For example, if someone looked at an apple and said the apple is red, then looked at the same apple and said the apple is not red, this person is contradicting himself. However, if he judged the apple to be green and then later judged it to be red, he would not necessarily be contradicting himself because the apple might not have fully ripened and still had a green coloring to it when viewed earlier. See Moreland and DeWeese, *Philosophy Made Slightly Less Difficult*, 13.

---

25. Moreland and DeWeese, *Philosophy Made Slightly Less Difficult*, 54.

26. In other places, we go into more detail about tests for truth and how the Christian worldview meets them. Understanding Christian truth is not just an intellectual exercise; it involves both understanding what is true with our minds (Romans 12:2: "be transformed by the renewal of your mind") as well as with our hearts (Hebrews 4:12: "The word of God is … discerning the thoughts and intentions of the heart"). W. Gary Phillips, William E. Brown, and John Stonestreet expand on the correspondence criterion for truth and suggest a four-part test: (1) test of reason: Is it reasonable? Can it be logically stated and defended? (2) test of the outer world: Is there some external, corroborating evidence to support it? (3) test of the inner world: Does it adequately address the "victories, disappointments, blessings, crises, and relationships of our everyday world"? (4) test of the real world: Are its consequences good or bad when applied in any given cultural context? In *Making Sense of Your World: A Biblical Worldview* (Salem, WI: Sheffield, 2008). See chapter 3, "Putting Worldviews to the Test," 61–90.

27. Francis A. Schaeffer, *How Should We Then Live?* (Old Tappan, NJ: Revell, 1976), 145.

28. C. S. Lewis, *The Abolition of Man* (New York: Macmillan, 1973), 78.

29. In this particular list, Richard Beis includes incest prohibition within nuclear family, prohibition of rape, some form of marriage demanded, prohibition of adultery (with only a few strictly limited legal exceptions), opposition to promiscuity in the sense of having a large number of partners, lifelong union of the spouses is the ideal, exogamy (marriage outside the family) as a further determination of the incest rule, and disrespect for illegitimate children. By this last point, Beis does not mean a disrespectful attitude toward such children but rather a society-wide recognition that birth in such circumstances is less than ideal.

30. Richard H. Beis, "Some Contributions of Anthropology to Ethics," *The Thomist* 27, no. 2 (April 1964): 174–223, quoted in William D. Gairdner, *The Book of Absolutes* (Montreal: McGill-Queen's University Press, 2008), 198–200.

31. James Burke, *The Day the Universe Changed* (Boston: Little, Brown, 1985), 337.

32. Erich Fromm, *You Shall Be as Gods* (New York: Rinehart and Winston, 1966), 88.

33. Denis Diderot, quoted in "Diderot, Denis (1713–1784)," *The Encyclopedia of Libertarianism*, ed. Ronald Hamowy (Thousand Oaks, CA: Sage, 2008), 125.

34. V. I. Lenin, *Selected Works* (New York: International Publishers, 1938), 15: 402.

35. Lenin, *Selected Works*, 15: 405.

36. Lenin, *Selected Works*, 10: 86.

37. Lenin, *Selected Works*, 35: 122.

38. Edward O. Wilson "The Relation of Science to Theology," *Zygon* 15, no. 4 (1980): 433.

39. Sidney Hook, *Religion in a Free Society* (Lincoln, NE: University of Nebraska Press, 1967), 36.

40. Marilyn Ferguson, *The Aquarian Conspiracy* (Los Angeles: J. P. Tarcher, 1980), 383.

41. Eckhart Tolle, *A New Earth* (New York: Plume, 2005): 71.

42. Neale Donald Walsch, *The New Revelations: A Conversation with God* (New York: Artia Books, 2002), 97.

43. "Bill Moyers, 'Of Myth and Men: A Conversation between Bill Moyers and George Lucas on the Meaning of the Force and the True Theology of Star Wars," *Time*, April 26, 1999, 92.

44. George Barna, *Third Millennium Teens* (Ventura, CA: Barna Research Group, 1999), 48. It should be noted that of the teenagers surveyed, 70 percent were active in a church youth group and 82 percent identified themselves as Christians.

45. Stetson and Conti, *The Truth about Tolerance*, 11.

46. Quoted in J. Warner Wallace, "Is Christianity Intolerant?" http://coldcasechristianity.com/2015/is-christianity-intolerant/.

47. Wallace, "Is Christianity Intolerant?" (emphasis in the original).

48. Paul Copan, *True for You, but Not for Me* (Minneapolis: Bethany, 2009), 45.

49. Galatians 5:19–21: "The works of the flesh are evident: sexual immorality, impurity, sensuality, idolatry, sorcery, enmity, strife, jealousy, fits of anger, rivalries, dissensions, divisions, envy, drunkenness, orgies, and things like these. I warn you, as I warned you before, that those who do such things will not inherit the kingdom of God."

50. J. Budziszewski, *True Tolerance: Liberalism and the Necessity of Judgment* (New Brunswick, NJ: Transaction Publishers, 2000), xi.

51. Greg Koukl, *Tactics: A Game Plan for Discussing Your Christian Convictions* (Grand Rapids, MI: Zondervan, 2009), 108.

52. Galatians 6:1: "Brothers, if anyone is caught in any transgression, you who are spiritual should restore him in a spirit of gentleness. Keep watch on yourself, lest you too be tempted."

53. Copan, *True for You, but Not for Me*, 43.

54. Copan, *True for You, but Not for Me*, 60.

55. Copan, *True for You, but Not for Me*, 118.

56. Copan, *True for You, but Not for Me*, 118.

57. Copan, *True for You, but Not for Me*, 135.

58. John 14:6: "Jesus said to him, 'I am the way, and the truth, and the life. No one comes to the Father except through me.'"

59. Hugh A. Garland, quoting Francis Scott Key letter to John Randolph, January 20, 1814, in *Life of John Randolph of Roanoke* (New York: D. Appleton, 1874), 30.

60. 1 Peter 3:15: "In your hearts honor Christ the Lord as holy, always being prepared to make a defense to anyone who asks you for a reason for the hope that is in you; yet do it with gentleness and respect."

61. Recall the Bible story of Jesus's visiting the temple as a twelve-year-old boy. The Bible says that his parents found him asking questions of the religious leaders (Luke 2:41–52). In the Hebrew culture, asking intelligent questions showed that one understood the issues at stake.

62. My friend Bill Jack has created a similar list of questions, which he illustrates by asking them of people who hold different worldviews from his. His filmed interactions are compiled in a clever video titled *Simple Tools for Brain Surgery*.

63. Be warned: this question often draws a strong response. The anti-theist author Richard Dawkins once was asked this question in a public forum. How he responded comprises one of his most viewed videos on YouTube: www.youtube.com /watch?v=6mmskXXetcg. Unfortunately, because it was a public forum, Dawkins's response could not be easily debated. But note that rather than answering the question, he deflected it by creating imaginary views that people could not hold with good reasons and then mocking them. This is called the Straw Man fallacy.

64. John Stonestreet, interview with the author, October 21, 2009.

65. Kenneth G. Van Meter, "The Order of Importance of Component Parts of the Biblical Worldview in Christian High School Students" (dissertation, George Fox University School of Education, 2009).

66. Stonestreet, interview with the author.

CHAPTER 14

┌─────────┐
│   │
│   *14* │
│   │
└─────────┘

WHY IS THERE EVIL AND SUFFERING?

1. THE WORLD IS A MESS

For many people, the existence of evil poses a problem for belief in a good God. In his book *The Innocence of God*, Christian author Udo Middelmann states the problem frankly: "Reality is such a mess. If there is a God in charge of this, God should be held accountable for a monstrous experience....

Someone in heaven must be behind all this, in the same way that there was always some evil ruler behind everything bad on earth."[1]

Evil: that which deviates from good; the privation of good.

Good: that which embodies or reflects God's original design.

Suffering: pain or discomfort that results from such things as disease, injury, oppression, fatigue, old age, loneliness, and betrayal.

Moral Evil: evil brought about by the actions of human beings (for example, rape, murder, and genocide).

Natural Evil: evil brought about by acts of nature, such as fires, earthquakes, and diseases.

Not only does **evil** exist, it's everywhere. It trickles and soaks and floods into every aspect of our existence like nuclear waste from a burst storage container, contaminating everything in its wake. Can't God stop it? If he can't, is he truly as powerful as the Bible claims he is? If he *can* but doesn't, what kind of God is he?

It seems that the only way to approach this question, as difficult as it is, is to begin with clear, biblical definitions of good and evil. **Good** is the way things ought to be; **evil** is what deviates from the good. Evil is not a "thing" in itself, the early Christian philosopher Augustine of Hippo explained; rather, it exists *in* things as a corruption or a cancer. As we saw in chapters 5 and 6, evil cannot exist unless that which is good has an actual essence or substance that can be corrupted, starved, sucked dry, or abused.[2]

Suffering is pain or discomfort "that results from disease, injury, oppression, overwork, old age, sorrow for one's sins, disappointment with oneself or with one's lot in life (or that of persons close to one), the pain of loneliness, isolation, betrayal, unrequited love, and awareness of the suffering of others."[3]

Evil seems to be of two sorts. First, there is human-caused evil, or **moral evil**. Moral evil is committed by people, so it is hard to fully blame God. Still, couldn't God do at least *something* to alleviate the pain? Couldn't he step in and stop the really bad people from doing the worst evil? Why didn't he stop Hitler or a shooter who kills children at school, for example?

The second kind of evil is **natural evil**, which includes fires, floods, earthquakes, tsunamis, animal attacks, and anything that results from nature and causes pain and death. In Colorado Springs, Colorado, very near to where the publisher of this book is headquartered, massive wildfires in the summers of 2012 and 2013 scorched thousands of acres of spectacular mountain vistas. Even worse, the firestorms destroyed the homes and earthly possessions of hundreds of people.

And that wasn't the end of it. The burn from one of the fires left a scar that does not absorb water. Now when it rains, millions of gallons of water rush down the mountainside creating terror and destruction. Lives have been snuffed out, property has been destroyed, businesses built over a lifetime ruined. And the floods will continue for a decade, residents are told, until new plants grow and the soil can absorb water again. Meanwhile, the burn scar stands as a silent reminder of how little control we have over nature.

Compared to other natural disasters around the world, what we faced in Colorado was minor. Each year disasters around the world disrupt the lives of tens of millions of people and

WHY IS THERE EVIL AND SUFFERING?

claim tens of thousands of lives.[4] This raises perplexing questions. Why doesn't God protect people from disasters they have no control over? Why does he allow suffering to multiply through drought, disease, flood, and fire?

In this chapter, we'll see that although we don't have a God's-eye view of the universe and therefore cannot know all the answers, only a biblical worldview truly grapples with evil and suffering. It offers a coherent view of the past, meaning to the present, and hope for the future. In the end, the cross of Jesus Christ stands as God's ultimate answer to the problem of evil, offering hope for redemption and restoration.

Obviously, not everyone embraces a biblical worldview. As we will see, this does not exempt them from having to explain evil and suffering.

2. Everyone Has a "Problem of Evil"

Many who reject Christianity—and even God's existence—because of the problem of evil overlook something very important: by rejecting one worldview, they must embrace another, and *that* new worldview must deal with evil and suffering as well. Because evil exists, *every* worldview must explain it. Do other worldviews offer more rationally or emotionally satisfying solutions? Let's look at how several address this issue.

How Atheists and Naturalists Deal with the Problem of Evil

Atheism (the belief that there is no God) and naturalism (the belief that everything can be explained through natural processes) contend that the problem *of* evil is that we have a problem *with* evil. Because there is no higher cause or plan, life is tough and bad things happen. That's just the way it is, according to these worldviews. As Richard Dawkins coldly states,

> In a universe of blind physical forces and genetic replication some people are going to get hurt, other people are going to get lucky, and you won't find any rhyme or reason in it, nor any justice. The universe we observe has precisely the properties we should expect if there is, at the bottom, no design, no purpose, no evil and no other good. Nothing but blind pitiless indifference. DNA neither knows nor cares. DNA just is. And we dance to its music.[5]

As Dawkins sees it, there is no higher meaning. Life is painful; then you die. Deal with it.

Some think that if evil just *is* and there is no way to explain it, then the problem of evil vanishes. Not so. The problem of evil isn't merely that it exists but rather that we *know* it exists and *recognize* it as evil. If the atheist and naturalist story of the world is true, where did the idea of evil come from in the first place? This dilemma was, according to C. S. Lewis, what led him to reject his atheism:

> My argument against God was that the universe seemed so cruel and unjust. But how had I got this idea of just and unjust? A man does not call a line crooked unless he has some idea of a straight line.... Of course I could have given up my idea of justice by saying it was nothing but a private idea of my own. But if I did that, then

my argument against God collapsed too—for the argument depended on saying the world was really unjust, not simply that it did not happen to please my fancies. Thus, in the very act of trying to prove that God did not exist—in other words, that the whole of reality was senseless—I found I was forced to assume that one part of reality—namely my idea of justice—was full of sense. If the whole universe has no meaning, we should never have found out that it has no meaning: just as, if there were no light in the universe and therefore no creatures with eyes, we should never have known it was dark. Dark would be without meaning.[6]

We humans sense evil because we sense that good has been violated. As Douglas Groothuis says, "In order for objective evil to exist, objective goodness must exist as well, and good must exist in a more fundamental way."[7] Just as we can know we are sick because we know what it means to be healthy, we can see evil at work because we have some sense of the good corrupted by it.

Of course, not all atheists and naturalists detach themselves from the problem of evil in a Dawkins-like fashion. Many truly want life to be more comfortable for themselves and others, and they genuinely believe that human reasoning can minimize suffering—that the world can be made a better place. Yet if we become obsessive about minimizing suffering through reasoning, we can short-circuit our experience of a fully meaningful life. Psychologist Paul Vitz calls the attempt to minimize suffering at all costs "selfist" psychology that "trivializes life by claiming that suffering (and by implication even death) is without intrinsic meaning. Suffering is seen as some sort of absurdity, usually a man-made mistake which could have been avoided by the use of knowledge to gain control of the environment."[8] In the end, you either laugh or cry, so you might as well laugh, like Sisyphus in the ancient Greek myth, who laughed at the gods while carrying out his absurd sentence (pushing a boulder up a hill each day and having it roll back down again, for all of eternity).

Yet even if this psychological approach *did* make suffering more meaningful, it is still an unsatisfactory solution. As professor William Kirk Kilpatrick points out,

> What good does it do to the billions who have already passed through this life in wretchedness, that scientific humanism will one day create a world without suffering? For that matter what good does it do to those who are right now dying miserable and lonely deaths all over the world? All that a strict humanism has to say to most of the human race living and dead is "Too bad you were born too early," and "Too bad about your suffering." The bulk of the world's pain is written off as a bad expense.[9]

In the end, the atheist and naturalistic response to evil amounts to little more than feathering the nest, adding a bit of comfort here and there, numbing the pain. The "why" question, though, still goes unanswered, perhaps even unasked.

How Marxists Deal with the Problem of Evil

Marxism marries atheist and naturalist assumptions to revolutionary class struggle, and it is a worldview dominating political life for roughly 20 percent of the world's population.[10] As the

WHY IS THERE EVIL AND SUFFERING?

founder of the Soviet Union, Vladimir Lenin, put it, "According to the theory of **socialism**, i.e., of Marxism … the real driving force of history is the revolutionary class struggle."[11] Evil is human caused, Marxists believe, and the responsible party is the **bourgeoisie** (pronounced booze-wah-ZEE), the business owners. These people must be overthrown by the **proletariat**, the working class. As Marx phrased it in *The Communist Manifesto*, the communists' ends "can be attained only by the forcible overthrow of all existing social conditions.… The proletarians have nothing to lose but their chains. They have a world to win. Proletarians of all countries, unite!"[12]

> *Socialism:* an economic system based on governmental or communal ownership of the means of production and distribution of goods and services.

To Marx, the workers were cleansed of evil through their hard work. Stop the domination of the bourgeoisie, and most evil goes away. Of course the bourgeoisie class presumably includes those who embrace the supernatural because they encourage the proletariat to drown its terrible economic plight in the "spiritual booze" of a mythical heaven rather than rising up against their oppression.[13] The God-intoxicated make lousy revolutionaries. Unless they are cut off from God, they'll never sober up enough to revolt, and humanity's chance of creating a human-centered heaven on earth will be ruined.

> *Bourgeoisie:* a term used in Marxist theory to describe those who own the means of production.

But by denying the evil in the hearts of the workers, Marxism made things worse. Infinitely so. In their revolutionary zeal, Marxists discounted the suffering of the business owners, the wealthy, and the religious leaders as

> *Proletariat:* a term used in Marxist theory to describe the working-class wage earners who do not own the means of production.

necessary bloodletting for their cause. Eventually those who "resisted" Marxism, even the workers who were supposedly cleansed of evil through their work, became victims as well. Political scientist R. J. Rummel estimates that Marx's ideas led to the deaths of about 110 million people in the twentieth century.[14] Marxism became one of history's greatest sources of human-caused evil. In a sad irony, Marxist countries ended up destroying the people they set out to save: the working class.

In universities today, Marx's ideas have spread beyond economics to literature, sociology, and philosophy. Neo-Marxists teach that those in power always manage government and culture in a way that serves their own interests and marginalizes others. Evil is whatever those in power do; good is whatever those who neo-Marxists judge to be the oppressed do.

How Eastern Religions and New Spiritualists Deal with the Problem of Evil

Eastern religions (such as Buddhism, Hinduism, Taoism, Shinto, and Confucianism) share basic worldview beliefs with their Western counterparts (such as New Age thought, **Wicca**, neopaganism, and Scientology). Together, we can group them under the heading of

> *Wicca:* a neopagan, religious form of witchcraft.

New Spirituality, primarily because of their belief in **pantheism** (from two Greek words, *pan*, which means "all," and *theos*, which means "god"). All is god. All reality is one thing, and that thing is spiritual, not physical. The physical world is an illusion. Evil or any kind of physical suffering is also, therefore, an illusion. It doesn't actually exist.[15]

> *New Spirituality:* a pantheistic worldview that teaches that everything and everyone are connected through divine consciousness.

> *Pantheism:* the belief that everything in the universe is ultimately divine.

The idea that evil doesn't exist seems baffling to those who see evil and suffering as a universal aspect of the human experience. Haven't humans all over the world and throughout all of history suffered? What are we to do with this? In the Eastern world, it's really not much of an issue. The *Bhagavad Gita*—a treasured section of the *Mahabharata*, India's national epic poem—has Lord Krishna responding to Arjuna's grief by saying,

> Although you mean well, Arjuna,
> Your sorrow is sheer delusion.
> Wise men do not grieve
> For the dead or for the living.[16]

If sorrow over pain and suffering is delusional, the antidote is to stop grieving. Krishna's statement represents the general tenor of Hindu writing on evil and suffering, though Hinduism is a very diverse religion and not all Hindus hold this view of suffering.[17]

Among most who follow Hindu tradition, though, compassion toward the suffering is explicitly frowned upon. Whole classes of "untouchables" are ignored by those who believe that alleviating suffering is wrong because it cuts short the atonement for the sins of past lives. It was not devout Hindus but devout Christians such as Mother Teresa and the Sisters of Charity who sought to alleviate suffering as a way of displaying Christ's love, offering a warm heart rather than a cold shoulder.

Buddhism's approach to suffering runs along a parallel path. Finding an end to suffering is the whole point of Buddha's teaching.[18] In his first sermon, Buddha outlined several different kinds of suffering, including birth, aging, sickness, death, sorrow, pain, grief, and despair. The cause of this suffering, he said, was attachment. We are like a monkey who finds himself captured because he refuses to let go of the treat that is holding his hand inside a trap. Releasing attachment is the only way to be free. The end of suffering, Buddha said, is "the complete cessation of that very thirst, giving it up, renouncing it, emancipating oneself from it, detaching oneself from it."[19]

> *New Spirituality:* a pantheistic worldview that teaches that everything and everyone are connected through divine consciousness.

So in the Hindu and Buddhist traditions, the right response to suffering is not to sympathize with a person experiencing it but to remind that person that sorrow over suffering is delusional. Rather than grieve, the individual ought to let go of the attachment that causes the suffering in the first place.

WHY IS THERE EVIL AND SUFFERING?

In contrast to their Eastern counterparts, Western pantheists of the New Spiritualist mold tend to focus on the pursuit of health and success. Sickness and disease occur because people are not sufficiently in tune with what pantheists call the **higher consciousness**. Bestselling New Spiritualist author Marilyn Ferguson explains, "Health and disease don't just happen to us. They are active processes issuing from inner harmony or disharmony, profoundly affected by our states of consciousness, our ability or inability to flow with experience."[20]

To Shakti Gawain, another New Spiritualist writer, we experience pain because we don't trust ourselves to overcome it: "Every time you don't trust yourself and don't follow your inner truth, you decrease your aliveness and your body will reflect this with a loss of vitality, numbness, pain, and eventually, physical disease."[21]

The Western version of New Spirituality—that evil is an illusion we permit into our lives by not properly pursuing our interests—still doesn't answer the question, "Why evil?" Rather, it makes people wonder, *If evil is an illusion, why does it seem so real?*

For the Eastern version of New Spirituality, based on the twin ideas of **karma** and **reincarnation**, the evil we experience is payback for things we did in previous lives. This is unsatisfying as well. Think of a child suffering from disease. Think of a beloved grandparent getting cancer. Think of the victims of sex trafficking who are condemned to misery for the transitory pleasure of those who overpower them. According to Douglas Groothuis, the doctrines of reincarnation and karma do not really solve the problem of evil because they cannot explain the *reality* of evil. "One of the engines of the problem of evil is innocent suffering," he says. "This is a vexing conundrum for any worldview, but karma does nothing to solve or alleviate it. According to karma, there is no unjust suffering. Everyone gets what he or she deserves, even supposedly innocent children."[22]

> *Higher Consciousness:* the supposed state of awareness wherein individuals realize their divinity and the divine interconnectedness of all things.

> *Karma:* a concept found in Eastern religions that states that good is returned to those who do good, and evil is returned to those who do evil (either in this life or the next).

> *Reincarnation:* the belief that after biological death, the soul is reborn in a new body—either animal, human, or spirit—to continue its quest for enlightenment.

How Muslims Deal with the Problem of Evil

Of the major worldviews, Islam's approach to dealing with evil is closest to Christianity's. Yet, though Islam and Christianity (along with Judaism) share a belief in one God, there are major differences between Islam's and Christianity's approaches. **Islam** is Arabic for "submission." As a religion, Islam focuses on obedience to God and complete submission to him. "Such a life of obedience brings peace of the heart and establishes real peace in society at large," writes Khurshid Ahmad.[23]

> *Islam:* a theistic worldview centered on the life of the prophet Muhammad that derives its understanding of the world through the teachings of the Quran, Hadith, and *Sunnah.*

Muslims acknowledge humans as rulers over the earth but reject the *imago Dei* ("image of God"), seeing humans instead as slaves of God rather than as his image bearers.[24] The difference between the Christian and Muslim views on this point affects how Muslims deal with the problem of evil. As Udo Middelmann observes, Islam requires the "unquestioning submission to and acceptance of a … divine destiny."[25]

To Muslims, *why* evil exists is the wrong question. God need not explain himself; humans must simply obey, and in so doing they will find meaning in life and peace in death.[26] So in the end, Islam's answer to the problem of evil is unsatisfactory as well. If God causes it, and we can never really know why, the only real answer to the question of "Why evil?" is to stop asking the question.

Obviously, there are dozens of religious perspectives in the world. We've surveyed a few of the biggies and found that they offer little in actually addressing the questions of evil and suffering. For atheists and naturalists, it is a meaningless question. For Marxists, evil results from economic conditions and can be atoned for only by inflicting vengeance on the rich. In the case of Eastern religions and New Spirituality, evil is an illusion and should thus be ignored. To Muslims, asking why evil occurs is disrespectful to God.[27] None of these views explains why evil feels wrong or why we feel compelled to do something about it.

But even if other worldviews do not have a sufficient answer to the problem of evil, this does not mean that Christianity "wins" by default. Christians must still grapple with the problem, both rationally and personally. Let's start with the rational aspect.

3. Dealing with Evil Rationally

Sean McDowell and Jonathan Morrow aptly summarize the problem of evil from an intellectual standpoint: "When you encounter the vast literature on evil, two intellectual problems of evil emerge. First, it seems logically contradictory for a good God and evil to coexist, and second, given the magnitude, duration, and intensity of evil in the world, it is highly improbable that God exists."[28] If God is really good, then he would abolish evil—unless he is incapable of doing so. Thus, either God is not good or he is not powerful. You can't have it both ways, at least according to the popular argument.

It will take some time and patience to delve into the rational arguments about what evil is, how it came into existence, and how theologians in the past have explained a biblical approach to it. But it's worth it. Along the way, we'll discover that the Christian answer to the problem of evil not only explains the past but also gives meaning to the present and hope for the future.

The Christian Answer to the Problem of Evil Explains the Past

What is evil, anyway? Maybe you've seen a fallen tree with a rotten core or a car rusted out from underneath. Without the tree, there would be no rot. Without the car, there would be no rust. As we saw earlier in this volume, evil is like that rot and rust: it exists only by attacking that which is whole.

Most people have no problem seeing human-caused evil as a result of sin. We've seen married people who were blissfully happy at their wedding fall into a pattern of abuse or unfaithfulness.

The destructive actions of a married couple (or the corrective actions they neglect) cause emotional and physical pain, sadness, and fear. Sin is, as author Cornelius Plantinga bluntly puts it, "a parasite, a vandal, a spoiler" and a "ludicrous caricature of a genuine human life."[29]

Theologically speaking, evil is the loss of **shalom**. As we saw in our earlier chapter on the metanarrative of Scripture, *shalom* is a Hebrew word describing peace with God, peace from war, and peace with one's neighbors. To wish another person *shalom* is to wish that person completeness, safety, wellness, prosperity, tranquility, contentment, and friendship.

> **Shalom:** from the Hebrew for "peace, prosperity, and wellness"; implies harmony in creation and with one's neighbors as well as a right relationship with God.

God originally created human beings in a state of *shalom*. Their existence was one of wholeness in their relationship with God, with each other, and with creation. In the fall, each of these relationships was ruptured. We now live in a world that is truly not the way it's supposed to be.[30]

We read in chapters 5 and 6 that the flow of history is the process of God setting things to rights. At the very heart of the Christian gospel is a God, rich in grace, dealing with evil and suffering *personally*. God's answer to the problem of evil is not as much a set of logically stated answers as it is a life offered up in our place. Hebrews 4:15 says, "We do not have a high priest who is unable to sympathize with our weaknesses, but one who in every respect has been tempted as we are, yet without sin." Christ came to be with us, to suffer with us, and to accept the brunt of evil on our behalf.

Where did evil come from? One key biblical question is "Where did evil come from?" Did God make it? If so, isn't that an evil thing to do, sort of like Dr. Frankenstein creating a monster and unleashing it on the world? It's a simple question of negligence, and God ought to take responsibility. And if God did *not* make evil but permitted it to exist, isn't that a sign of weakness? Neither of these options is good. It appears, at first glance at least, that either God is sadistic and likes to see us suffer or he's a hapless bumbler who pushed over a cosmic domino and set the universe to tumbling.

As is often the case, though, what we see at first glance is not the whole story. To understand this, we need to look at how sin actually entered the universe and what happened as a result.

Though the Bible is not explicitly clear on this, there are good reasons to think that sin got "kicked off" when an archangel named Lucifer (Satan) tried to overthrow God.[31] Satan then inhabited a serpent in the garden of Eden and tempted Adam and the woman, Eve, to sin (Gen. 3). In Revelation 12:9[32] and 20:2,[33] this "ancient serpent" is described as "the devil and Satan." So how could a creature such as Satan fall into sin and cause humanity to fall in his wake? Perhaps, as Norman Geisler suggests, no one caused Lucifer to sin: he caused his own sin.[34]

Did God create evil? As we will see shortly, by creating free creatures, God made evil possible. These creatures chose either to withhold good or act contrary to it, thus taking potential evil and making it actual.[35] For example, if God makes a world with stones in it, people might pick up some of those stones and fling them at one another. The *potential* evil of having stones as a part of the material world becomes *actual* evil when misused.

But if God is all-knowing, would he not have stopped this process before it got out of control? To answer we must clearly understand what it means for God to be all-knowing. As we saw earlier in this volume, the word **omniscient** is used to describe God's all-knowingness. God knows everything possible and actual. He possesses complete knowledge of the past, present, and future.[36] Knowing all truths and believing no falsehoods, he is perfect in knowledge. We see this throughout Scripture, such as in Romans 11:33: "Oh, the depth of the riches and wisdom and knowledge of God!" As Gordon Lewis puts it, "God's intellectual capabilities are unlimited, and God uses them fully and perfectly."[37]

We humans, on the other hand, are severely limited. We cannot see the full scope of history or figure out the relationship between people and events in the past and in the future. God has no such limitation. Hebrews 4:13 says, "No creature is hidden from his sight, but all are naked and exposed to the eyes of him to whom we must give account."

To say God is **sovereign**, though, is not to say that he maintains *absolute* control, as an engineer running a machine seeks to do. Rather, he is the *ruler* of the universe. He is in charge and has created a world of laws in which we can act in a meaningful way.[38]

Philosopher William Lane Craig wrote an entire book about God's knowledge titled *Divine Foreknowledge and Human Freedom*.[39] In it, Craig argues for a position called **Molinism**, which was first articulated by a Jesuit priest named Luis de Molina (AD 1535–1600). Molina proposed a **middle knowledge** view of God that avoided the idea that God directly causes every single action in the universe (**divine determinism**) and also its opposite extreme, **Open Theism**—that although God is knowledgeable enough to make very accurate guesses about what will or won't happen in the future, he does not know with certainty.

What makes the problem of "what God knew and when he knew it" especially sticky is that some Christians hold such a strong view of God's sovereignty that there is little to distinguish it from the Muslim perspective that everything that happens comes into being from *God's* will, not ours.[40] However, if we recognize a difference between what God is *capable* of doing and what he *chooses* to do, we can see that the Christian perspective on God is quite different from the Muslim perspective. As R. C. Sproul, a well-known Reformed theologian, writes in

Omniscient: God's unique ability to know everything that can be known.

Sovereign: possessing supreme authority.

Middle Knowledge (aka Molinism): first proposed by the Jesuit priest Luis de Molina; the belief that God knows all future contingent possibilities and that through his omniscience can accomplish his divine will through the lives of free human beings.

Divine Determinism: the belief that God directly determines and causes every single action in the universe.

Open Theism: the belief that God does not have divine foreknowledge but that through his omniscience is able to deduce the most probabilistic future.

WHY IS THERE EVIL AND SUFFERING?

reference to sin coming into the world, "[God] ordained the Fall in the sense that he chose to allow it, but not in the sense that he chose to coerce it."[41]

Here is how Craig frames the middle knowledge view of God. Because God knows all things, he knows the choices free creatures make under every possible circumstance. And yet he still leaves them free to make those choices. As we make choices, God knows what will happen as a result and is working things out so that when we arrive at the place where our free choices take us, we will see that he has worked in such a way that his good, desired end is achieved.[42]

A biblical example of this is when Jesus replied to Peter's boast about his loyalty, "Truly, I tell you, this very night, before the rooster crows, you will deny me three times" (Matt. 26:34). Peter then did just as Jesus had said. But that is not the end of the story. After his resurrection, Jesus forgave Peter in a tender exchange and recommissioned him for faithful service (John 21:15–17).[43]

Jesus knew ahead of time what Peter would do, yet he permitted him to do it and forgave him once it was done. He even gave Peter the opportunity to affirm his love for Jesus three times, just as he had denied it three times. So why, if Jesus knew that Peter would deny him, did he not stop it? Perhaps because a Peter who had fallen and been redeemed was a better Peter than the one whose bravado had gotten him into so much trouble beforehand. Indeed, perhaps all creation is this way: it is better to be redeemed than to have never fallen.

Is evil necessary? If we program a computer to say, "I love you," we know it isn't real love. The computer is just doing what it is told to do. But God did not create humans to be computers. We can be truly loving only by choosing to love. And in order to choose to love, we must be free to reject love and choose hate.

To explain the relationship of freedom and evil, Christian philosopher Alvin Plantinga articulated what has been called the **free will defense**. It goes like this:

> *Free Will Defense:* an argument developed by Alvin Plantinga that contends there is no logical contradiction between the coexistence of evil and God because it is at least *possible* that evil exists because even an omniscient deity could not create a world in which human beings simultaneously possess free will yet never choose to do evil.

A world containing creatures who are significantly free (and freely perform more good than evil actions) is more valuable, all else being equal, than a world containing no free creatures at all. Now God can create free creatures, but He can't cause or determine them to do only what is right. For if He does so, then they aren't significantly free after all; and they do not do what is right freely. To create creatures capable of moral good, therefore, He must create creatures capable of moral evil; and He can't give these creatures the freedom to perform evil and at the same time prevent them from doing so. As it turned out, sadly enough, some of the free creatures God created went wrong in the exercise of their freedom; this is the source of moral evil. The fact that free creatures sometimes go wrong, however, counts neither against God's omnipotence nor against His goodness; for He could have forestalled the occurrence of moral evil only by removing the possibility of moral good.[44]

A key phrase is "He can't give these creatures the freedom to perform evil and at the same time prevent them from doing so." The freedom to choose good, therefore, entails the freedom to choose evil. Unfortunately, many make that choice or back into it by neglecting what is good.[45]

But wouldn't it be possible for God just to say, "Enough!" and put a stop to the bad things that happen? On this point, author Mark Mittelberg muses,

> When I hear someone say this, I like to ask them which freedoms they think God ought to take away from us right now. Usually people get a bit more reflective when they realize that "stopping all the evil" in this fallen, sinful world would entail taking away our human liberty as well as stopping all of us in our tracks—the people who to one degree or another are right now actively participating in that evil that "must be stopped."[46]

We may hate the painful effects of our actions, Mittelberg points out, but we humans continue to take the freedom-abusing actions that bring them about.

We've just taken a look at what evil is, how it came to be, whether God created it, and how it is necessary for the human freedom that allows us to genuinely love and serve. The biblical view of evil makes sense of the past, but it also, as we will see, gives meaning to the present.

The Christian Answer to the Problem of Evil Makes Sense of the Present

Those who reflect even briefly on the problem of evil can see how pointless it seems that evil and suffering exist. Although other worldviews say evil is a meaningless concept or an illusion or that it is disobedience to God to ask the question in the first place, the biblical worldview of the problem of evil helps us make sense of our lives right now. Let's examine this issue theologically, considering our own limited perspective and God's unlimited perspective. Let's also consider that in spite of the pain we experience, this is the best possible world, and then let's ask what we humans ought to be doing about evil.

> Let's consider that in spite of the pain we experience, this is the best possible world, and then let's ask what we humans ought to be doing about evil.

God is purposeful and unlimited in understanding. Our perspective of the world and everything in it is quite limited. I cannot know what is going on at any moment outside my own sphere of influence. Even *within* that sphere, I have little ability to make things go my way. I cannot know the future and how the various people yet to be born will act. However, God is not like us. Isaiah 46:9–11 says,

> I am God, and there is none like me,
> declaring the end from the beginning

and from ancient times things not yet done,
saying, "My counsel shall stand,
    and I will accomplish all my purpose,"
calling a bird of prey from the east,
    the man of my counsel from a far country.
I have spoken, and I will bring it to pass;
    I have purposed, and I will do it.

So if God has a larger perspective, is it possible that he has a good *reason* for allowing evil to enter the world, a reason we might not be able to see? If he does have a good reason, it would break the logjam between God being either well-meaning and powerless, or powerful but ill intentioned.[47]

We've already seen how evil must be possible in order for human freedom to exist. But how probable is it that God has good *reasons* for permitting suffering? Skeptics might say, "Look around you. So much suffering seems pointless. Couldn't a powerful God figure out a way to at least reduce the suffering, even a little bit?"

In order to make this argument, skeptics would need an objective standard for good and evil as well as a standard by which to show that suffering is, in fact, indefensible. Their own worldview precludes this, however. If Richard Dawkins is correct in saying, "DNA just is, and we dance to its music," then little can be done about suffering aside from anesthetizing it. Because nothing can be done about evil, the atheist or naturalist argument here isn't as much about the problem of evil as it is about attacking the character of a God they don't believe in.

As humans, we do have a sense that evil is meaningless and that suffering is pointless. If bad people simply got what was coming to them, we might be less concerned. But when seemingly innocent people get hurt, especially our loved ones, our questions multiply. It's important to note, though, that biblical authors were not immune to this, nor did they try to hide it. The prophet Jeremiah implores, "Why does the way of the wicked prosper? Why do all who are treacherous thrive?" (Jer. 12:1).

As hard as this seems to bear, we simply may never know this side of eternity why bad things happen to good people. But as William Lane Craig says,

> As finite persons, we're limited in space and time, in intelligence and insight. But God sees the end of history from its beginning and providentially orders history to His ends through people's free decisions and actions. In order to achieve His purposes God may have to allow a great deal of suffering along the way. Suffering that appears pointless within our limited framework may be seen to have been justly permitted by God within His wider framework.[48]

This does not mean we should stop asking questions of God. The biblical authors, operating under God's authority and the inspiration of the Holy Spirit, certainly didn't stop asking questions. But our mind-set and attitude matter. Arguments against God's goodness—such as those posed by William Rowe, philosophy professor and author of a popular argument against God based on the problem of evil—assume that what we know is sufficiently representative of what God knows, and therefore we are justified in saying that pointless suffering indicates there is no God.[49] As philosopher Greg Ganssle points out, saying, "I can't think of a good reason for allowing this evil, so there isn't one," is a weak argument if we aren't as smart as God or even as smart as we think we are.[50]

Ganssle illustrates this from the life of Christ himself:

> Let's take the case of Lazarus's death in John 11. Lazarus was likely in the prime of his life. He's a good man and a close friend of Jesus. Lazarus becomes ill and dies. The citizens of his village, Bethany, could see such an evil and after three days of mourning come to the conclusion that there is no reason for this. Therefore, God doesn't exist. Then Jesus comes to Bethany. Lazarus's sisters, Mary and Martha, chastise Jesus for not getting there sooner. As we read John's account, we see that unbeknownst to Mary and Martha, Jesus had reasons for delaying. Moreover, there were reasons Lazarus was permitted to die in the prime of his life. When Jesus arrived at Lazarus's tomb, He prayed and then called Lazarus to come out of the tomb four days after his death. The reason for Lazarus's sickness, death, Jesus's delay, and Lazarus's resuscitation was that God's glory might be seen. Some of the citizens might have thought they had a strong case against the existence of God the three days after Lazarus died. But subsequent events place the evil of Lazarus's death in a much different context. In light of this context, Lazarus's death is seen to be part of a much greater good than anyone in Bethany could imagine.[51]

When we see evil things happen, it may not be that God is unaware or helpless but rather that larger factors than we can see with our human eyes are at play.

So rather than denying that evil exists, or denying that it has meaning, God-followers through the ages have recognized that evil *does* exist, that it hurts, and that we might go to our graves with our most pressing questions unanswered. And yet we will pray for patience and perseverance in the confidence that God knows what we do not know and that he will redeem our suffering to good purposes.

Best of All Possible Worlds, the: a theory by Gottfried Wilhelm von Leibniz that states that the best of all possible worlds is the belief that the world we inhabit has been structured by God to maximize good and minimize evil.

This is the best possible world: A response to natural evil. As we have seen, sin causes humans to do bad things to one another. But what about such things as earthquakes and tsunamis and floods for which humans simply cannot be held responsible? Even if humans could have taken action to limit their destructiveness, these natural events still cause suffering. Clearly, natural evil differs from wicked acts committed by morally responsible people.[52]

Some philosophers, starting with the German mathematician and philosopher Gottfried Leibniz in 1710, have made a very interesting point about natural evil: perhaps God has created **the best of all possible worlds**, and although bad things happen, the world itself has been structured by God to maximize good and minimize evil to the greatest possible extent. This view was articulated by Leibniz in a work titled *Essais de Théodicée sur la bonté de Dieu, la liberté de l'homme et l'origine du mal (Attempts at a Theodicy on the Goodness of God, the Freedom*

WHY IS THERE EVIL AND SUFFERING?

of Man, and the Origin of Evil). Leibniz described the subject of his work as **theodicy**, which is a combination of two Greek words, *theos* ("God") and *dike* ("judgment"). Theodicy is the attempt to show that God's ways are justified.

Garrett DeWeese, a professor at the Talbot School of Theology, has expanded on Leibniz's point by positing that there are an infinite number of possible worlds that contain goods and that God has created a world in which goods such as creativity exist and in which new things can actually happen.[53] More specifically, DeWeese argues that God created a *dynamic* world, which is a great good but can be subject to disturbances that cause it to behave erratically. Obviously, this is a controversial view. After all, if the garden of Eden was designed to be a place of *shalom*, and if it was sin—not natural evil—that ruptured that *shalom* (Rom. 5:12ff),[54] we face a question of whether the initial conditions on the earth were really idyllic, as many assume they were. This point will probably be debated long after our lives end.

> **Theodicy:** a rational justification for why God would allow evil.

Norman Geisler, perhaps the most prolific author on Christian apologetics in our age, is one who finds the "best of all possible worlds" argument compelling. He points out that some physical evil is the by-product of good things we enjoy in the world today:

> Drowning is a byproduct of having water at our disposal to enjoy. Unintentional shooting deaths occur with guns meant for sport or food gathering. Rain that nourishes the soil also causes floods. Winds renew the air, but tornados sometimes spin up. Earthquakes recycle minerals needed for life but also cause death and destruction. Both hurricanes and tsunamis are byproducts of good natural processes. The greater enjoyment of flying, boating, or mountain climbing are the occasion of accidents that are byproducts of a good practice.[55]

Every step we take risks a fall, says Geisler. Does this mean we should never try to walk? If Leibniz, DeWeese, and Geisler have it right, natural evil is hurtful and disruptive, but it is part of life that is the best possible good. Still, as we saw earlier, the "best of all possible worlds" argument must be taken in the context of the goodness of God's creation and the reality of human fallenness. Sin infected what was once good and perfect. Someday the goodness of creation will be restored. Revelation 21:4 says, "He will wipe away every tear from their eyes, and death shall be no more, neither shall there be mourning, nor crying, nor pain anymore, for the former things have passed away."

Is there anything we humans ought to do about evil? In 2011, an earthquake in Japan, measuring 9.0 on the Richter scale, killed nineteen thousand people. The year prior, an earthquake of a much lesser magnitude, about one-quarter as strong, killed around two hundred thousand people in Haiti. Both were unspeakable tragedies, but the magnitude of suffering was altogether different. How did an earthquake in Haiti that was one-quarter the strength of the earthquake in Japan nonetheless kill ten times the people? The answer, unfortunately, has much to do with the misuse of human freedom. Corruption, government incompetence, poverty, economic mismanagement, and the embrace of wrong worldviews all play a role.[56]

Mark Mittelberg estimates in his book *The Questions Christians Hope No One Will Ask* that as much as 90 percent of nonnatural deaths (those not related to dying naturally from old age) result from human causes such as wars, crime, human trafficking, racial genocide, and sexually transmitted diseases such as HIV/AIDS. Human-caused pollution alone is said to cause 40 percent of the deaths worldwide.[57]

Governments, charged with protecting their people from abuse, cause a shocking amount of the world's evil as well. Historian R. J. Rummel said that more human beings in the twentieth century died at the hands of their governments, committed to Marxist or fascist ideology, than in all previous centuries combined. The murder of more than one hundred million innocent people created unimaginable suffering for the victims, their families, their friends, and their communities.[58]

If we remain apathetic about human fallenness, we will have missed history's most significant lesson: sin devastates, but a commitment to justice and human dignity has led to many profound efforts to alleviate suffering. According to researcher Scott Todd, extreme poverty has dropped by half in just the last generation, from 52 percent of the world's population to 26 percent.[59] One billion more people have access to improved water supplies than in 1990.[60] Though tuberculosis is still a major killer, the death rate from the disease is down 40 percent from twenty years ago.[61] Polio cases have decreased 99 percent since 1988.[62] Significant progress is being made in the fight against malaria as well.[63] These remarkable advances came from people using their God-given gifts and opportunities to bring redemption to the suffering. Christian artist Matthew West summarizes it well: "I shook my fist at heaven and said, 'God, why don't you do something?' He said, 'I did. I created you.'"[64]

So far we have seen that Scripture explains the past and gives meaning to the present. But that is not all. It also gives us hope for the future.

The Christian Answer to the Problem of Evil Gives Us Hope for the Future

Some people become so discouraged by evil and suffering that they stop trying to take action to secure a better future. They lose hope. But a biblical view of the problem of evil helps restore hope.

In his sovereignty, God directs us to take responsibility. The more we contemplate God's character, the more we can see his wisdom in not strictly controlling everything that happens. This ought to bring alive our own sense of responsibility. We are not bound by fate to what happens; we can choose to act. As Udo Middelmann says, "Christians are not drugged into faith by an opiate of religion that makes them see no evil and resign themselves to their present experience."[65]

Knowing that God expects us to take responsibility—and that our actions will have real consequences—might actually draw us closer to him. As professor of ethics and apologetics R. Scott Smith puts it,

> Knowing that God expects us to take responsibility—and that our actions will have real consequences—might actually draw us closer to him.

This God invites all people to come and reason together with him, to even enjoy him, and to know that they have been endowed by their creator with real freedom and responsibility to act in the world in ways that should bring about goodness, not evil, thereby benefiting others and giving glory to their good, holy God. It is this view that I think best describes the reality of good and evil, right and wrong, and our being moral agents.[66]

So is God the cause of evil? It depends on what is meant by the word *cause*. As Geisler summarizes, "God is the author of everything, including evil, in the sense that He permits it, but not in the sense that He produces it. Evil happens in His permissive will, but He does not promote evil in His perfect will. God allows evil yet does not encourage it."[67] Most people who argue that God is responsible for evil reason that if God created everything and evil exists, God is responsible for the creation of evil. But as we have seen, evil is *not* a thing. It is the absence of a good, not a thing in itself. It is not part of creation.

But still, why would God allow his creation to be tampered with by evil? As a father, I believe I have a glimpse of why God might not jump in and intervene in every situation in which evil is corroding that which is good. When my children were younger, I found myself on many occasions tempted to direct their minute-by-minute actions. I wanted the best for them, and I told myself that it would be best if I met all their needs. But it didn't take long to realize that they needed the freedom to make mistakes and learn from them. Growing up involves the freedom to experience needs and the freedom to figure out how to meet them.

We should not, therefore, talk about God's "sovereignty" as implying that he is dictating the actions of every atom in the universe. Rather, we should clarify that God is *in charge* in the sense that he rules the universe and yet permits evil actions in human history even as he moves us toward the consummation of his sovereign plan.[68] Michael Bauman explains this distinction with the analogy of a director and a play. God does not dangle us from strings like puppets; rather, he directs us as in a play. God is such a magnificent director that even though he allows the actors to ad-lib as they desire, the play is coming together exactly as God wishes. It's his play, after all.[69]

> We should clarify that God is *in charge* in the sense that he rules the universe and yet permits evil actions in human history even as he moves us toward the consummation of his sovereign plan.

There is hope. Author Randy Alcorn reminds us that "evil is temporary; God's goodness and our joy will be eternal."[70] Elisabeth Elliot, whose husband Jim Elliot was killed by an Ecuadorian tribe with whom he was trying to share the gospel, writes, "When our souls lie barren in a winter which seems hopeless and endless, God has not abandoned us. His work goes on. He asks our acceptance of the painful process and our trust that He will indeed give resurrection life."[71] Alcorn summarizes, "One day, evil will end. Forever. Suffering and weeping are real and profound, but for God's children, they are temporary. Eternal joy is on its way."[72] A biblical response to evil shapes evil's meaning and transforms its awful power into hope.

Perhaps this is why the Bible focuses so much on hope. Job said, "Though he slay me, I will hope in him" (Job 13:15). Psalm 33:22 says, "Let your steadfast love, O LORD, be upon us even as we hope in you." Psalm 78:7 admonishes the children of Israel to teach their children well so they would "set their hope in God." Proverbs 23:18 says, "Surely there is a future, and your hope will not be cut off." Romans 5:4 says, "Endurance produces character, and character produces hope."

Hope possesses enormous power. William Damon, a professor at Stanford University, has shown that having a personal sense of purpose—a sense of what life is all about—radically alters how people cope with their circumstances. Those without purpose report anxiety, disappointment, discouragement, and despair. Those with purpose report joy in spite of sacrifices they must make, a sense of energy, satisfaction, and persistence when they run into obstacles.[73]

These are remarkable findings. Everyone experiences trials, but some grow stronger through them, and others weaker. What makes the difference? For the non-Christian, suffering is a harsh reality that must be avoided at all costs, but for the Christian, suffering may be used by God to discipline and strengthen one's faith. Christians are sometimes called to plunge joyously into suffering in obedience to God (Heb. 12:7–11;[74] Acts 6:8–7:60). And the deeper the pain, the more this is so. As professor William Kirk Kilpatrick says, "The real test of a theory or way of life, however, is not whether it can relieve pain but what it says about the pain it cannot relieve.… In Christianity it has great meaning."[75]

> For the non-Christian, suffering is a harsh reality that must be avoided at all costs, but for the Christian, suffering may be used by God to discipline and strengthen one's faith.

Time magazine spoke to this matter of suffering some years ago with an edition titled "Special Mind and Body Issue."[76] In one article, researchers looked at why "religious people are less stressed and happier than nonbelievers." After describing the setbacks in the life of forty-one-year-old Karen Granger (husband laid off, a miscarriage, cousin's breast cancer, two hurricanes, and her best friend's brain tumor), *Time* reports that Granger, a Christian, claims to have relied on her faith, saying, "As a consequence, I haven't lost my joy."[77]

Time asks the question "So, what has science learned about what makes the human heart sing?"[78] Although wealth, education, and good weather do not make the heart sing, faith truly consoles although "it's tough to tell whether it's the God part or the community aspect that does the heavy lifting."[79] Interesting question, but it's a false choice. In reality it is both. Through Jesus, God became flesh and initiated a community that is his body. It is this body of Christ—the church—that brings hope into a suffering world.

Clearly, people can experience meaning and purpose without religious faith. Still, it is more than a little interesting that the academic research so strongly parallels the biblical account of what life is about and what to do when bad things happen. Although many people in this sinful world are born into purposeless lives through no fault of their own—born into famine, forced into child prostitution, born with drug addictions because of their parents' drug use, and so forth—Jesus has promised, "In the world you will have tribulation. But take heart; I have overcome the world" (John 16:33). Hope has arrived and is rallying the hopeless to God's banner of love.

4. DEALING WITH EVIL PERSONALLY

When people ask, "Why would God allow bad things to happen?" they are usually asking, "Why would God allow bad things to happen to *me*?" We feel sad that people suffer, but the philosophical crisis becomes acute when suffering finds *us*. And suffering does find us. Perhaps you have been abused or abandoned; perhaps you have lost people who were important to you; maybe your trust was violated or you were cheated. If you are human, you have been hurt. Even we in a relatively pampered and developed world still suffer.

Much of our indignation in light of our suffering might come from our belief that God is like a kindly grandfather who loves us and wants us to be happy. We have come to believe, as William Lane Craig muses, that "God's role is to provide a comfortable environment for His human pets."[80]

The message of Scripture, though, is that God is not primarily interested in our comfort. Craig continues,

> We are not God's pets, and the goal of human life is not happiness per se, but the knowledge of God—which in the end will bring true and everlasting human fulfillment. Much of the suffering in life may be utterly pointless with respect to the goal of producing human happiness; but it may not be pointless with respect to producing a deeper knowledge of God.[81]

The chief end of humanity is not temporal happiness but deep knowledge of and intimate relationship with God. That Craig would make this argument is interesting because he personally lives daily with a neuromuscular disorder that slowly atrophies his muscles and could lead to terrible disability. Each morning, he chooses to bear up under suffering and stay focused on knowing God more.

As we saw earlier, the Bible does not dismiss the reality of suffering. In Psalm 13:1–2, David cries out, "How long, O LORD? Will you forget me forever? How long will you hide your face from me? How long must I take counsel in my soul and have sorrow in my heart all the day? How long shall my enemy be exalted over me?" Even the God-man Jesus Christ felt anguish over suffering. In the garden of Gethsemane, he says, "Father, if you are willing, remove this cup from me" (Luke 22:42).

But the Bible does counsel a particular kind of response to suffering: an unshakable confidence in God's goodness. "I will sing to the LORD, because he has dealt bountifully with me," David says in Psalm 13:6. And even though Jesus is preparing to face unspeakable agony, he concludes his prayer with complete trust in God: "Nevertheless, not my will, but yours, be done" (Luke 22:42).

For Randy Alcorn, these passages show David's and Jesus's determination not to bury themselves in their sorrows but to cry out to God to deliver them, fully believing he has their best in mind. As Alcorn studied the Old Testament book of Job, he learned a great deal about the reality of suffering and how to see it from God's perspective:

> Through Job's story, God offers paradigm-shifting insights to face suffering. Job has taught me many valuable lessons, including these: Life is not predictable or

---

formulaic. Most of life's expectations and suffering's explanations are simplistic and naïve, waiting to be toppled. When the day of crisis comes, we should pour out our hearts to God, who can handle our grief and even our anger. We should not turn from God and internalize our anger, allowing it to become bitterness. We should weigh and measure the words of friends, authors, teachers, and counselors, finding whatever truth they might speak without embracing their errors or getting derailed by their insensitivities. We should not insist on taking control by demanding a rational explanation for the evils and suffering that befall us. We should look to God and ask him to reveal himself to us; in contemplating his greatness we will come to see him as the Answer above all answers. We should trust that God is working behind the scenes and that our suffering has hidden purposes that one day, even if not in this life, we will see. We should cry out to Jesus, the mediator and friend whom Job could only glimpse, but who indwells us by grace.[82]

About Job, author Philip Yancey says, "Job clung to God's justice when he was the best example in history of God's apparent injustice. He did not seek the Giver because of his gifts; when all gifts were removed he still sought the Giver."[83]

5. CONCLUSION

When it comes to understanding evil and suffering, we now see that God has created a world in which moral good is actually possible. We can *know* good and recognize when it is being attacked by evil. We can *do* good that is meaningful because it is possible for us to do otherwise.[84]

If someone asks you how God could allow evil, ask them in turn, "What do you mean by evil?" Is evil something that actually exists, or is it just a category into which we put things we prefer not to have happened? To know that something is evil, we have to know that it is not the way it is supposed to be. Where do we get this sense of "oughtness"? Why do we have the sense that reality ought to be good? If there is no God, there is no reason to expect it to be.[85]

> Without a normative sense of "oughtness," there is really no such thing as good and therefore no point in our noting when it is being violated.

To put it in philosophical terms, we cannot make sense of the problem of evil without a normative sense of "oughtness." If people who parachuted out of airplanes occasionally went up instead of down, we would say the law of gravity is not normative. Because they know the law of gravity *is* normative, though, jumpers carefully check their chutes before leaping out of the plane. Going up or down is not a matter of preference. In the same way, without a normative sense of "oughtness," there is really no such thing as good and therefore no point in our noting when it is being violated.

But our humanity demands more than philosophical explanations. The universal realization that something is wrong in the world that needs to be fixed leads us to better understand the meaning behind Jesus's own suffering on the cross. As Yancey says, "Any discussion of how pain and suffering fit into God's scheme ultimately leads back to the cross."[86] It is at the cross that God declared victory. The apostle Paul wrote in 1 Corinthians 15:54–58,

WHY IS THERE EVIL AND SUFFERING?

When the perishable puts on the imperishable, and the mortal puts on immortality, then shall come to pass the saying that is written: "Death is swallowed up in victory." "O death, where is your victory? O death, where is your sting?" The sting of death is sin, and the power of sin is the law. But thanks be to God, who gives us the victory through our Lord Jesus Christ. Therefore, my beloved brothers, be steadfast, immovable, always abounding in the work of the Lord, knowing that in the Lord your labor is not in vain.

Respected theologian and Anglican pastor John Stott related his experience in Asian temples, standing respectfully before the statue of Buddha, eyes closed and detached from the world's agonies:

I could never myself believe in God, if it were not for the cross.… In the real world of pain, how could one worship a God who was immune to it?… In imagination I have turned … to that lonely, twisted, tortured figure on the cross, nails through hands and feet, back lacerated, limbs wrenched, brow bleeding from thorn-pricks, mouth dry and intolerably thirsty, plunged in Godforsaken darkness. That is the God for me![87]

This is a hugely important insight. Philosophical approaches to the problem of evil are important, but if we remain at that level—that is, if we remain merely philosophical—then we miss the mark. As speaker John Stonestreet says, "Applying logical answers for the existence of evil to the emotional and personal struggles associated with a particular evil is to miss how Jesus Himself confronted it."[88]

A person in pain is experiencing not a philosophical problem but a personal problem. We ought to think carefully about the intellectual problem of evil, but as Alcorn says, "The answer to the problem of evil and suffering is not a philosophy, but a Person; not words, but the Word."[89]

We do not have a God who is aloof or incomprehensible. We do not have a God who encourages us to ignore evil or treat it as an illusion. We do not have a pantheon of gods who are reckless or incapable of solving great problems. We have, instead, a God who is with us. As poet Edward Shillito says in his poem "Jesus of the Scars,"

> *Through* Christ, meaning emerges out of meaninglessness. *In* Christ, we have a model for what to do in the midst of pain. *Because* of Christ, God not only makes good possible, he makes good happen.

The other gods were strong; but Thou wast weak;
They rode, but Thou didst stumble to a throne;
But to our wounds only God's wounds can speak,
And not a god has wounds, but Thou alone.[90]

God-with-us is the sun of righteousness breaking through the clouds of confusion and pain. *Through* Christ, meaning emerges out of meaninglessness. *In* Christ, we have a model for what to do in the midst of pain. *Because* of Christ, God not only makes good possible, but he makes good happen.[91]

For our part, in the light of the cross, we can see clearly what is right and wrong, what is good and evil. We can—and must—walk with those who suffer. Says Douglas Groothuis, "Fighting against injustice, unbelief, prejudice, poverty, violence and stupidity is not done in vain if it is done 'in the Lord.'"[92]

And *because* of the cross, we have hope that God *will* conquer evil. In fact, the entire story of the Bible is how he is doing just that. Evil persists because God is patient in waiting for people to turn to him. Second Peter 3:9 says, "The Lord is not slow to fulfill his promise as some count slowness, but is patient toward you, not wishing that any should perish, but that all should reach repentance."

In the end, the problem of evil may be the greatest objection to God's existence, but God's existence is the problem of evil's only solution. As William Lane Craig puts it, "If God does not exist, then we are locked without hope in a world filled with pointless and unredeemed suffering. God is the final answer to the problem of suffering, for He redeems us from evil and takes us into the everlasting joy of an incommensurable good: fellowship with Himself."[93] This has given meaning to the lives of millions of Christians throughout the ages and enables us in our own uncertain times to be people who live with hope and then inspire it in others.

> The problem of evil may be the greatest objection to God's existence, but God's existence is the problem of evil's only solution.

There is, however, one aspect of God's answer to the problem of evil that has generated a great deal of controversy: the doctrine of hell. Is hell real, and would a God of love actually send people there? That's what we'll explore in the next chapter.

ENDNOTES

1. Udo Middelmann, *The Innocence of God: Does God Ordain Evil?* (Colorado Springs, CO: Paternoster, 2007), 1–2.

2. Norman L. Geisler, *If God, Why Evil? A New Way to Think about the Question* (Minneapolis: Bethany, 2011), 19. Augustine discusses the problem of evil at length in *Confessions*, Book 7, which is available free online at www.ccel.org/a/augustine/confessions/confessions.html.

3. Alvin Plantinga, "Supralapsarianism, or 'O Felix Culpa,'" in *Christian Faith and the Problem of Evil*, ed. Peter van Inwagen (Grand Rapids, MI: Eerdmans, 2004).

4. "Annual Disaster Statistical Review 2012: The Numbers and Trends," Reliefweb, August 31, 2013, reliefweb.int/report/world/annual-disaster-statistical-review-2012-numbers-and-trends.

5. Richard Dawkins, *River out of Eden: A Darwinian View of Life* (New York: Basic Books, 1995), 133.

6. C. S. Lewis, *Mere Christianity* (San Francisco: Harper, 2009), 39.

7. Douglas R. Groothuis, *Christian Apologetics: A Comprehensive Case for Biblical Faith* (Downers Grove, IL: IVP Academic, 2011), 617–18.

8. Paul Vitz, *Psychology as Religion: The Cult of Self-Worship* (Grand Rapids, MI: Eerdmans, 1985), 103.

9. William Kirk Kilpatrick, *Psychological Seduction: The Failure of Modern Psychology* (Nashville: Thomas Nelson, 1983), 185.

10. The world's five communist countries (China, Vietnam, Laos, North Korea, and Cuba) account for approximately one of five people on the planet. They are not, however, the only ones dealing with Marxism's implications. Socialism is the official policy of many other nations (Bangladesh, India, Sri Lanka, Portugal, Tanzania, and Guyana). Countries with powerful socialist parties include France, Greece, Venezuela, Sweden, Zambia, Syria, Norway, and Algeria, among others. We could also add to this list countries that pursue socialist policies as a matter of practice or that are bent on destroying the right to private property, such as Zimbabwe.

11. V. I. Lenin, *Complete Collected Works*, 45 vols. (Moscow, USSR: Progress, 1980), 11:71.

12. www.marxists.org/archive/marx/works/1848/communist-manifesto/.

13. Lenin, *Complete Collected Works*, 10:83.

14. www.hawaii.edu/powerkills/COM.ART.HTM.

WHY IS THERE EVIL AND SUFFERING?

15. Jonathan Morrow, *Welcome to College: A Christ-Follower's Guide for the Journey* (Grand Rapids, MI: Kregel, 2008), 119.

16. Stephen Mitchell, trans., *Bhagavad Gita* (New York: Three Rivers, 2000), 47.

17. Hinduism is actually a religious culture that, according to Taylor University professor of philosophy and religion Winfried Corduan, "has moved back and forth through various phases of monotheism, henotheism, polytheism and animism, with each stage retaining at least a vestigial presence in the ensuing one. There is no set of core beliefs that remain constant throughout. The name itself, actually a label devised by Westerners, simply means 'the religion of India.'" Winfried Corduan, *Neighboring Faiths: A Christian Introduction to World Religions* (Downers Grove, IL: IVP Academic, 2012), 267. See also R. C. Zaeher, *Hinduism* (New York: Oxford University Press, 1983). Hinduism is primarily spread today through the practice of yoga, a meditational exercise. Whether this is harmful or not is the subject of much debate in the Christian community. For more information, see Albert Mohler's podcast "The Meaning of Yoga: A Conversation with Stephanie Syman and Doug Groothuis," www.albertmohler.com/2010/09/20/the-meaning-of-yoga-a-conversation-with-stephanie-syman-and-doug-groothius/.

18. "A View of Buddhism: The Four Noble Truths," viewonbuddhism.org/4_noble_truths.html.

19. "The First Sermon of the Buddha," www.tricycle.com/new-buddhism/teachings-and-texts/first-sermon-buddha.

20. Marilyn Ferguson, *The Aquarian Conspiracy: Personal and Social Transformation in Our Time* (Los Angeles: J. P. Tarcher, 1980), 257.

21. Shakti Gawain, *Living in the Light: Follow Your Inner Guidance to Create a New Life and a New World, with Laurel King* (San Rafael, CA: New World Library, 1986), 156. Vera Alder goes even further, explaining that criminals who cause others to suffer should be celebrated because such suffering forces us to seek more urgently a connection with a higher consciousness: "A criminal or an idler will be recognized as a sick individual offering a splendid chance for wise help. Instead of being incarcerated with fellow unfortunates in the awful atmosphere of a prison, the future 'criminal' will be in much demand." Vera Alder, *When Humanity Comes of Age* (New York: Samuel Weiser, 1974), 82.

22. Groothuis, *Christian Apologetics*, 624.

23. Khurshid Ahmad, *Islam: Our Choice*, comp. and ed. Ebrahim Ahmed Bawany (1961), 2.

24. The Quran consistently refers to people as "servants" or "slaves" of Allah. See, just as a starting point, 2:23, 2:90, 2:186, 3:15, 3:20, 7:128, 7:194, 8:51, 10:107, 14:11, and 15:49. The Arabic word is *abd*, which means one who is totally subordinated, a slave. Badru Kateregga says, "The Christian witness, that man is created in the 'image and likeness of God,' is not the same as the Muslim witness." See Badru D. Kateregga and David W. Shenk, *Islam and Christianity: A Muslim and a Christian in Dialogue*, electronically available on The World of Islam: Resources for Understanding CD-ROM, published by Global Mapping International, 5350.

25. Middelmann, *The Innocence of God*, 197.

26. The Quran states, "Those who believe, and whose hearts find satisfaction in the remembrance of God: for without doubt in the remembrance of God do hearts find satisfaction. For those who believe and work righteousness, is (every) blessedness, and a beautiful place of (final) return" (13:28–29, A. Yusuf Ali, *The Holy Qur'an*).

27. I am by no means an expert on the Quran or its interpretation, but the teaching of the Quran seems clear about the complete control of Allah over creation: "Those whom Allah (in His plan) willeth to guide, He openeth their breast to Islam; those whom He willeth to leave straying, He maketh their breast close and constricted, as if they had to climb up to the skies: thus doth Allah (heap) the penalty on those who refuse to believe" (6:125); "If We had so willed, We could certainly have brought every soul its true guidance: but the Word from Me will come true, "I will fill Hell with Jinns and men all together" (32:13, A. Yusuf Ali, The Holy Qur'an); "But ye will not, except as Allah wills; for Allah is full of Knowledge and Wisdom" (76:30); "But ye shall not will except as Allah wills, the Cherisher of the Worlds" (81:29). Muzammil H. Siddiqi, president of the Islamic Society of North America says, in response to the question of why Allah allows evil, "Let us ask this question to understand Allah's ways in His creation. The Qur'an tells us that good, evil and whatever happens in this world happens by Allah's Will (mashi'at Allah). Only Allah knows fully His Will. We finite beings cannot grasp fully His infinite Will and Wisdom. He runs His universe the way He deems fit. The Qur'an tells us that Allah is Wise and everything that Allah does is right, just, good and fair. We must submit and surrender to His Will. The Qur'an has not given us all the details about Allah's Will, but it has enlightened us with the guidance that is useful and sufficient for us." "Why Does Allah Allow Suffering and Evil in the World?," interview with Muzammil H. Siddiqi, www.onislam.net/english/ask-the-scholar/muslim-creed/muslim-belief/174982-why-does-allah-allow-suffering-and-evil-in-the-world.html.

28. Sean McDowell and Jonathan Morrow, *Is God Just a Human Invention? And Seventeen Other Questions Raised by the New Atheists* (Grand Rapids, MI: Kregel, 2010), 213.

29. Cornelius Plantinga, *Not the Way It's Supposed to Be: A Breviary of Sin* (Grand Rapids, MI: Eerdmans, 1995), 199.

30. This reference plays off the title of Plantinga's *Not the Way It's Supposed to Be*.

31. The references to this are slim, making it hard to figure out exactly what happened. Isaiah 14:12 says, "How you are fallen from heaven, O Day Star, son of Dawn! How you are cut down to the ground, you who laid the nations low." The account continues to explain that the archangel in question sinned by wanting to displace God. In the King James Bible, the name "Day Star" is translated "Lucifer." The immediate reference is to the king of Babylon, but many Christians compare this account to that in Revelation 12, which describes a heavenly battle in which the "coup" leader and his followers,

one-third of the angels ("stars"), are cast out of heaven. Ezekiel 28:11–19 describes the wisdom and beauty of the king of Tyre and his subsequent fall into corruption. Some think this is a reference to Lucifer as well.

32. Revelation 12:9: "The great dragon was thrown down, that ancient serpent, who is called the devil and Satan, the deceiver of the whole world—he was thrown down to the earth, and his angels were thrown down with him."

33. Revelation 20:2: "He seized the dragon, that ancient serpent, who is the devil and Satan, and bound him for a thousand years."

34. Norman Geisler says, "Many consider this an insoluble mystery. But is it? Not really, not once we understand what free choice entails. The best way to comprehend the basis of a free act is to examine the three possible alternatives. A free act is either uncaused, caused by another, or self-caused; that is, it is undetermined, determined by another, or self-determined. No action can be uncaused (undetermined); that would be a violation of the law of causality (every event has a cause). Neither can a free act be caused by another; for if someone or something else caused the action, then it is not ours (not from our free choice) and we would not be responsible for it. Hence all free actions must be self-caused (that is, caused by oneself). Now we can answer the question, 'What caused Lucifer to sin?' No one did. He is the cause of his own sin. Sin is a self-caused action, one for which we cannot blame anyone or anything else. Who caused the first sin? Lucifer. How did he cause it? By the power of free choice, which God gave him." Geisler, *If God, Why Evil?*, 30–31. It should be noted that Geisler's point is highly disputed. Do angels have free will? Did they once but no longer? Scripture doesn't tell us. If angels are free, we'd expect more to be failing since, but we have no scriptural record of this happening. Also, if Lucifer was the cause of Adam and Eve's sin, was there an agent who caused his own sin? Because Scripture says little about these questions, we are left with pondering them in humility, which is not a bad thing.

35. Geisler, *If God, Why Evil?*, 30–31.

36. For a helpful explication of this doctrine amid challenges of Open Theism, see William Lane Craig's very readable book, *What Does God Know? Reconciling Divine Foreknowledge and Human Freedom* (Norcross, GA: RZIM, 2002).

37. Gordon Lewis, "Attributes of God," in *Evangelical Dictionary of Theology*, ed. Walter A. Elwell (Grand Rapids, MI: Baker Academic, 2001), 494.

38. Thanks to R. Scott Smith for articulating this point. R Scott Smith, *In Search of Moral Knowledge: Overcoming the Fact/Value Dichotomy* (Downers Grove, IL: InterVarsity, 2014). See also Middelmann, *The Innocence of God*, 134.

39. William Lane Craig, *Divine Foreknowledge and Human Freedom: The Coherence of Theism* (Leiden, NJ: Brill, 1991).

40. Although there is disagreement among Muslims about the nature of free will, just as there is among Christians, the primary teaching of Islamic theologians seems to be that God is in control to the extent that free will is an illusion. One source for this theology is in the "Hadith," a collection of the sayings of the Prophet Muhammed. In *Sahih al-Bukhari*, vol. 4, bk. 54, hadith 430, we are given the narration of Abdullah bin Mus'ud who recorded Muhammed saying the following: "(The matter of the Creation of) a human being is put together in the womb of the mother in forty days, and then he becomes a clot of thick blood for a similar period, and then a piece of flesh for a similar period. Then Allah sends an angel who is ordered to write four things. He is ordered to write down his (i.e. the new creature's) deeds, his livelihood, his (date of) death, and whether he will be blessed or wretched (in the Hereafter). Then the soul is breathed into him. So, a man amongst you may do (good) deeds till there is only a cubit between him and Paradise and then what has been written for him decides his behavior and he starts doing (evil) deeds characteristic of the people of the (Hell) Fire. And similarly a man amongst you may do (evil) deeds till there is only a cubit between him and the (Hell) Fire, and then what has been written for him decides his behavior, and he starts doing deeds characteristic of the people of Paradise," p. 40. Sayyid Mujtaba Musavi Lari, in "Lesson 19: Free Will," explains, "Just as all creatures in the world lack independence in their essence, all being dependent on God, they also lack independence in causation and the production of effects. Hence, we have the doctrine of unity of acts, meaning perception of the fact that the entire system of being, with its causes and effects, its laws and its norms, is the work of God and comes into being from His will; every factor and cause owes to Him not only the essence of its existence, but also its ability to act and produce effects." See http://www.al-islam.org/god-and-his-attributes-sayyid-mujtaba-musawi-lari/lesson-19-free-will.

41. R. C. Sproul, *Chosen by God* (Carol Stream, IL: Tyndale, 1986), 74–75.

42. Craig, *Divine Foreknowledge and Human Freedom*, 134.

43. John 21:15–17: "When they had finished breakfast, Jesus said to Simon Peter, 'Simon, son of John, do you love me more than these?' He said to him, 'Yes, Lord; you know that I love you.' He said to him, 'Feed my lambs.' He said to him a second time, 'Simon, son of John, do you love me?' He said to him, 'Yes, Lord; you know that I love you.' He said to him, 'Tend my sheep.' He said to him the third time, 'Simon, son of John, do you love me?' Peter was grieved because he said to him the third time, 'Do you love me?' and he said to him, 'Lord, you know everything; you know that I love you.' Jesus said to him, 'Feed my sheep.'"

44. Alvin Plantinga, *God, Freedom, and Evil* (Grand Rapids, MI: Eerdmans, 1977), 30.

45. Note that Plantinga is not trying to justify why God would allow evil. To do that, he would have to know the mind of God. Rather, he is offering a defense, an explanation for why it might be so. To those who say, "There is no explanation," Plantinga is replying, "Here is a possible one." Even if his explanation is faulty, it nonetheless demonstrates that the argument that "there is no explanation" is invalid.

WHY IS THERE EVIL AND SUFFERING?

46. Mark Mittelberg, *The Questions Christians Hope No One Will Ask (with Answers)* (Carol Stream, IL: Tyndale, 2010), 143–44.

47. See the essay by Greg Ganssle, "How Can God Have All Power and Be Loving and Yet There Be Evil?," in Ted Cabal et al., eds., *The Apologetics Study Bible* (Nashville: B&H, 2007), 736.

48. William Lane Craig, *On Guard: Defending Your Faith with Reason and Precision* (Colorado Springs, CO: David C Cook, 2010), 158.

49. In his interview with graduate student Nick Trakakis, Rowe not only reveals why he believes the problem of evil disproves God's existence but also explains how he went from being a fundamentalist Christian enrolled in Bible college to being an atheist. See "Interview: William Rowe," by Nick Trakakis, *Philosophy Now*, April/May 2015, philosophynow.org /issues/47/William_Rowe.

50. Ganssle, "How Can God Have All Power," 736–37.

51. Ganssle, "How Can God Have All Power," 736–37.

52. Garrett DeWeese, "Natural Evil: A 'Free Process' Defense," in *God and Evil: The Case for God in a World Filled with Pain*, ed. Chad Meister and James K. Dew Jr. (Downers Grove, IL: IVP Books, 2013), 53.

53. Gary DeWeese is careful to point out that he does not see his efforts as a theodicy, which he sees as a claim of an authoritative argument, as much as a defense, or an exploration of the logical possibilities for why God would allow natural evil. "I think my argument is not only logically possible but also quite plausible, with considerable empirical support," he says. "But I'll stop short of claiming it is precisely the (or the only) reason God may have for allowing natural evil." DeWeese's argument has six steps: "(1) the natural world is a dynamic world composed of a vast number of interacting nonlinear dissipative dynamical systems which are sensitively dependent on initial conditions"; (2) "nonlinear dissipative dynamical systems may, given a very slight disturbance in initial conditions, lose equilibrium and behave in wildly erratic ways"; (3) "wildly erratic systems in the natural world cause natural evil"; (4) "a dynamic world in which free creatures can exercise genuine creativity, thereby bringing about truly novel effects, is better than a static world"; (5) "God would want to create a dynamic world"; (6) "even God cannot make a dynamic world in which natural evil could not occur." See DeWeese, "Natural Evil," 54–61.

54. Romans 5:12: "Just as sin came into the world through one man, and death through sin, and so death spread to all men because all sinned."

55. Geisler, *If God, Why Evil?*, 75.

56. Lucy Rodgers, "Why Did So Many Die in Haiti's Quake?," news.bbc.co.uk/2/hi/8510900.stm.

57. Cornell University, "Pollution Causes 40 Percent of Deaths Worldwide, Study Finds," *ScienceDaily*, February 14, 2010, http://www.sciencedaily.com/releases/2007/08/070813162438.htm.

58. See R. J. Rummel, *Death by Government* (New Brunswick, NJ: Transaction Publishers, 1994).

59. Scott Todd, *Fast Living: How the Church Will End Extreme Poverty* (Colorado Springs, CO: Compassion International, 2011), 37.

60. "Health through Safe Drinking Water and Basic Sanitation," World Health Organization, www.who.int/water_sanitation _health/mdg1/en/.

61. Carol Pearson, "Tuberculosis Cases Down, Disease Still a Major Killer," *Voice of America*, October 18, 2012, www.voanews.com/content/tb-cases-down-but-disease-still-a-major-killer/1528710.html.

62. "Poliomyelitis," World Health Organization, www.who.int/mediacentre/factsheets/fs114/en/.

63. "World Malaria Report 2011," World Health Organization, www.who.int/malaria/world_malaria_report_2011/en/.

64. Matthew West, "Do Something," on *Into the Light*, Sparrow Records, a division of Universal Music Group, 2012.

65. Middelmann, *The Innocence of God*, 211.

66. R. Scott Smith, *In Search of Moral Knowledge: Overcoming the Fact/Value Dichotomy* (Downers Grove, IL: InterVarsity, 2014).

67. Geisler, *If God, Why Evil?*, 23–24.

68. Geisler, *If God, Why Evil?*, 23–24.

69. See Michael Bauman's lecture "Augustine and Pelagius," given at Summit Ministries during the student conferences.

70. Randy C. Alcorn, *If God Is Good: Faith in the Midst of Suffering and Evil* (Colorado Springs, CO: Multnomah, 2009), 449.

71. Elisabeth Elliot, *A Path through Suffering: Discovering the Relationship between God's Mercy and Our Pain* (Ann Arbor, MI: Vine, 1990), 43.

72. Randy C. Alcorn, *If God Is Good*, 449.

73. William Damon, *The Path to Purpose: How Young People Find Their Calling in Life* (New York: Free Press, 2008).

74. Hebrews 12:7–11: "It is for discipline that you have to endure. God is treating you as sons. For what son is there whom his father does not discipline? If you are left without discipline, in which all have participated, then you are illegitimate children and not sons. Besides this, we have had earthly fathers who disciplined us and we respected them. Shall we not much more be subject to the Father of spirits and live? For they disciplined us for a short time as it seemed best to them, but he disciplines us for our good, that we may share his holiness. For the moment all discipline seems painful rather than

pleasant, but later it yields the peaceful fruit of righteousness to those who have been trained by it."

75. Kilpatrick, *Psychological Seduction*,181.

76. *Time*, January 17, 2005.

77. Pamela Paul, "The Power to Uplift," *Time*, January 17, 2005, A4–6.

78. Paul, "The Power to Uplift," A5.

79. Paul, "The Power to Uplift," A5–6.

80. Craig, *On Guard*, 163.

81. Craig, *On Guard*, 163.

82. Alcorn, *If God Is Good*, 455–56.

83. Philip Yancey, *Where Is God When It Hurts?* (Grand Rapids, MI: Zondervan, 1990), 91.

84. This summary necessarily leaves out many nuances of the free-will argument. Readers wishing to study the argument in more detail are directed to, in addition to the other resources from this chapter, Plantinga's *God, Freedom, and Evil*.

85. For an extended version of this argument, see Greg Ganssle, "Evil as Evidence for Christianity," in *God and Evil: The Case for God in a World Filled with Pain*, ed. Chad Meister and James K. Dew Jr. (Downers Grove, IL: IVP Books, 2013), 214–24.

86. Yancey, *Where Is God When It Hurts?*, 232.

87. Quoted in Alcorn, *If God Is Good*, 217.

88. John Stonestreet, "Why Evil? Why This Evil?," Breakpoint Commentaries, July 24, 2012, http://www.breakpoint.org/bpcommentaries/entry/13/19912.

89. Alcorn, *If God Is Good*, 216.

90. Edward Shillito, "Jesus of the Scars," *The Christian Century*, April 28, 1921, 9.

91. Alvin Plantinga, "Supralapsarianism, or 'O Felix Culpa.'"

92. Groothuis, *Christian Apologetics*, 646.

93. Craig, *On Guard*, 173.

15

WHAT'S THE DEAL WITH HELL?

1. THE PROBLEM WITH HELL

For many, Christianity would be far more attractive if it didn't include the doctrine of hell. Bertrand Russell—mathematician, philosopher, and author of *Why I Am Not a Christian*—said,

There is one very serious defect to my mind in Christ's moral character, and that is that He believed in hell. I do not myself feel that any person who is really profoundly humane can believe in everlasting punishment…. [The doctrine of hell] put cruelty into the world and gave the world generations of cruel torture; and the Christ of the Gospels, if you could take Him as his chroniclers represent Him, would certainly have to be considered partly responsible for that.[1]

The Bible presents hell as a small but significant part of God's answer to the problem of evil. Judgment eventually comes to the wicked. To Russell, though, the doctrine of hell is a cruel and unjust source of evil in the world.

Jesus had compassion on the suffering, died for the sins of the world, and taught widely admired moral principles. In this light, the harshness of his teaching on hell does seem to be at odds with his other teachings. So is Russell right? Are Jesus's teachings on hell morally defective and cruel?

Let's start with this: one's discomfort with an idea or teaching has no bearing on how well grounded or true the idea actually is.[2] Still, Christians who take Jesus's teachings on hell seriously are often rewarded with ridicule. One of my university professors assigned us to read Jonathan Edwards's sermon "Sinners in the Hands of an Angry God," in which Edwards pleads with his hearers to recognize the precariousness of their state before God and seek redemption. To my professor, the actual content of Edwards's sermon was of little significance because it "proved" that Edwards was mean-spirited and hated for people to have a good time. Without expressly saying so, my professor implied that people who believe like Edwards should be similarly written off.

Edwards should not be so easily dismissed. A leading intellectual of his day, and for a brief time the president of what is now Princeton University, Edwards based his teaching on eternal punishment on the awesomeness of God, not any kind of vengeful spirit:

God is a being infinitely lovely, because he hath infinite excellency and beauty. To have infinite excellency and beauty, is the same thing as to have infinite loveliness. He is a being of infinite greatness, majesty, and glory; and therefore he is infinitely honourable. He is infinitely exalted above the greatest potentates of the earth, and highest angels in heaven; and therefore he is infinitely more honourable than they. His authority over us is infinite; and the ground of his right to our obedience is infinitely strong; for he is infinitely worthy to be obeyed himself, and we have an absolute, universal, and infinite dependence upon him. So that sin against God, being a violation of infinite obligations, must be a crime infinitely heinous, and so deserving of infinite punishment.[3]

To Edwards, the Bible's teachings on eternal punishment were proof of mercy, not meanness. According to apologist Douglas Groothuis, this should ground our thinking on hell today also:

Only by understanding hell can we grasp the immensity of God's love. God's love took his Son to the hell of the cross for our sake. This is a costly love, a bloody love that has no parallel in any of the world's religions. Although other religions (particularly Islam) threaten hell, none offer the sure deliverance from it that Christianity offers through the sacrificial love of God himself. In this sense Jesus Christ suffered hell for his people.[4]

Nonbelievers and believers alike may find this difficult to grasp, but hell's seriousness serves best to underscore the immensity of God's mercy. What the human race needs is not just a cosmic pat on the head before being sent out to play; we need saving, and we know we can't rescue ourselves.

As we have seen throughout this book, the scriptural picture of God is of a mighty deliverer, not a grumpy old man. The apostle Peter wrote, "The Lord is not slow to fulfill his promise as some count slowness, but is patient toward you, not wishing that any should perish, but that all should reach repentance" (2 Pet. 3:9). This was true in the Old Testament, even of Israel's enemies. As scholar Old Testament scholar Walter Kaiser Jr. pointed out, God wanted even the Egyptians, those who enslaved his chosen people, to come to know him as Lord (Exod. 8:22, 29–30).[5] Some of Pharaoh's servants did, in fact, come to worship God (Exod. 9:20),[6] and it's possible that some even joined the Israelites when they left Egypt, which would account for the "mixed multitude" described in Exodus 12:38.[7]

Even in view of God's mercy, however, many people still recoil at the doctrine of hell. Most Christians find it uncomfortable to discuss. Still, diminishing hell's importance also diminishes the love and justice of God. Therefore, trying to uncouple the doctrine of hell from the train of gospel thought would be a serious mistake.

To see how this is so, we need to investigate what the Bible says about hell, the purpose of hell, the justice of hell, and the common questions people ask about hell. Our goal, whether or not the outcome feels comfortable, is to see if this doctrine is reasonable, consistent with God's character, and taught by Scripture.

2. What the Bible Says about Hell

As with most topics, we are tempted to approach the topic of hell based on what *we* think rather than what *God* thinks. We ought not do this. C. S. Lewis was once reading a periodical in which the author claimed that "the fundamental thing is how we think of God." Lewis replied indignantly, "By God Himself, it is not! How God thinks of us is not only more important, but infinitely more important."[8]

Lewis was right. What we think about God is important, as we have noted before, but if he actually exists as described in the Bible, his perspective is higher than ours and what he reveals is of utmost importance. If we begin with the belief that the Bible accurately describes the contours of the world as it actually is (a belief that we defended earlier), then our journey will be quite different from having begun with the belief that it cannot be true unless it meets the test of human pleasantry. As I quoted

> People don't like seeing themselves as sinners who deserve wrath, so they cast Christianity as a primitive fable invented by superstitious, unscientific people whose faith helped them deal with fear and uncertainty.

Flannery O'Connor before, "Truth does not change by our ability to stomach it emotionally."[9]

The issues of truth and authority are exactly the sticking point for most people, who have no problem acknowledging Christianity's power in helping people overcome addictions, leave anger behind, reunite with their spouses, and be kinder to their children. Of course, many believe that Buddhism, Hinduism, and atheism can do that too. "It doesn't matter what you believe," we often hear, "as long as you believe in something." In other words, religions may be *useful*, but they aren't really *true*.

Regeneration: God's making people new through his Holy Spirit.

Conversion: a turning from idolatry to the one true God.

Justification: being declared righteous by God through the work of Jesus Christ.

Adoption: being included as a rightful member of God's eternal family.

Sanctification: the process whereby believers advance in holiness.

Glorification: the point at which believers become closely identified with Christ.

This belief about beliefs, of course, assumes that the biblical narrative, from creation to the fall to redemption, is *simply untrue*. People don't like seeing themselves as sinners who deserve wrath, so they cast Christianity as a primitive fable invented by superstitious, unscientific people whose faith helped them deal with fear and uncertainty. Just like all religions, Christianity would at best be interesting, but not true.

If Christianity is nothing more than a primitive superstition, the doctrine of hell must be seen in that light, and Christianity's answer to the question "What happens when we die?" becomes just as incomprehensible as every other answer. As we have seen throughout the earlier chapters of this book, the claim that "Christianity is a primitive superstition" simply does not fit the facts. We have good reason to believe in God's revelation in Scripture. Because this is the case, let's examine several Scripture passages in both the Old and the New Testaments to see exactly what the doctrine of hell entails.

What Do We Mean by "Saved"?

First Thessalonians 1:10 describes Jesus as the one who delivers us from the wrath to come.[10] Exactly what it means to be delivered, or saved, has been the subject of theological discussions for two thousand years, and we don't presume to offer the final word in this chapter. We can at least say that Scripture describes several things that happen in salvation: **regeneration** (God's making people new through his Holy Spirit—see Titus 3:5),[11] **conversion** (a turning from idolatry to the one true God—see Acts 15:3),[12] **justification** (being declared righteous by God—see Rom. 3:24),[13] **adoption** (being included as a rightful member of God's eternal family—see Rom. 8:15, 23),[14] **sanctification** (advancing in holiness—see Rom. 15:16),[15] and **glorification** (becoming closely identified with Christ—see Rom. 8:17).[16]

Scripture does not teach that these are distinct steps or anything we can accomplish ourselves. They are described as the work of the Holy Spirit, saving people from the just penalty that would otherwise accompany sin.

Does the Bible Actually Teach the Doctrine of Hell?

The answer is yes. In Matthew 5:22, Jesus said, "I say to you that everyone who is angry with his brother will be liable to judgment; whoever insults his brother will be liable to the council; and whoever says, 'You fool!' will be liable to the hell of fire." In Matthew 23:33, Jesus strongly condemned certain religious leaders of his day when he said, "You serpents, you brood of vipers, how are you to escape being sentenced to hell?"

The biblical teaching of hell is usually presented in the context of **judgment**. In Matthew 25:46, Jesus describes the different fates of the wicked and the righteous. The wicked "will go away into eternal punishment, but the righteous into eternal life." Eternal punishment is an expression of God's wrath (Col. 3:6),[17] but whatever wrath is to come is exactly what Jesus delivers us from (1 Thess. 1:10).[18]

> *Judgment:* the act of ruling or sentencing based on the careful deliberation of evidence and circumstances.

According to the apostle John's writing in Revelation 6:16–17, this **wrath** is something from which every right-thinking person will want to be saved. It is so terrible that those who face it will call to the mountains and rocks, "Fall on us and hide us from the face of him who is seated

> *Wrath:* retributive punishment for an offense.

on the throne, and from the wrath of the Lamb, for the great day of their wrath has come, and who can stand?" Christopher W. Morgan and Robert A. Peterson say that this final judgment, anticipated both in Daniel 12:1–2[19] and Isaiah 66:24,[20] is taught in the Gospels and the letters of the apostles Paul and Peter as well as in the apocalyptic writing of the apostle John.[21] John's writings are particularly graphic, as seen in this passage from Revelation 20:11–15:

> Then I saw a great white throne and him who was seated on it. From his presence earth and sky fled away, and no place was found for them. And I saw the dead, great and small, standing before the throne, and books were opened. Then another book was opened, which is the book of life. And the dead were judged by what was written in the books, according to what they had done. And the sea gave up the dead who were in it, Death and Hades gave up the dead who were in them, and they were judged, each one of them, according to what they had done. Then Death and Hades were thrown into the lake of fire. This is the second death, the lake of fire. And if anyone's name was not found written in the book of life, he was thrown into the lake of fire.

Clearly, the Bible refers to hell a great deal. To strip away its teaching about hell would fundamentally alter the message of much of the New Testament, especially the Gospels. The very idea that Jesus died on the cross to reconcile us to God so we would not spend eternity apart from him would become meaningless.

How Does the Bible Describe Hell?

Although there are many passages thought to refer to eternal punishment, here are some that describe what hell is like:

- A place of outer darkness (Matt. 8:12; 22:13)[22]

- "Outside" the gate of the city of God (Rev. 22:14–15)[23]

- Away from the "presence of the Lord" (Matt. 25:41)[24]

- Outside in the dark forever (Matt. 8:12; Jude v. 13)[25]

- A perpetually burning dump (Mark 9:43–48)[26]

- A place of anguish and regret (Luke 16:28)[27]

- An eternal separation from God (2 Thess. 1:7–9)[28]

In chapter 16 of Luke's gospel, Scripture records a parable told by Jesus about a poor man named Lazarus who died and went to heaven while the rich man from whom Lazarus begged during his lifetime died and went to a "place of torment." In the parable, Jesus describes the rich man as being in a place of anguish and regret (Luke 16:23–28). "A great chasm ha[d] been fixed" (v. 26) between where Lazarus and the rich man found themselves. Because Jesus told the story as a parable, it is unclear whether he meant it to describe what heaven and hell are actually like or to make the larger point that people who are stubborn in their rejection of God will continue to be stubborn regardless of how much instruction they receive.

As Norman Geisler points out, though, "terms like 'down' and 'outside' are relational terms, not necessarily spatial ones. God is 'up' and hell is 'down.' God is 'inside' and hell is 'outside.' Hell is the other direction from God."[29] J. P Moreland and Gary Habermas summarize what Scripture's references to hell, taken together, imply:

> The Bible's picture of hell, therefore, indicates that upon death some people will be translated into a different, nonspatial mode of existence. They will be conscious, and they will await a resurrection of their bodies, at which time they will be banished from heaven and secured in hell where they will experience unending, conscious exclusion from God, his people, and anything of value. This banishment will include conscious sorrow, shame, and anguish to differing degrees, depending on the person's life on earth.[30]

Did Jesus Teach about Hell?

Bertrand Russell, mentioned at the beginning of this chapter, rejected Christianity for reasons that, as we have seen in this book, are unwarranted. But he was right about one thing: Jesus did teach about hell. In fact, Jesus is quoted speaking about hell more than anyone else in the Bible. According to authors Sean McDowell and Jonathan Morrow, "He saw no contradiction between the offer of love and forgiveness on the one hand and the reality of hell as a place of eternal punishment on the other. Whatever your ultimate verdict on Jesus as the

Son of God, the fact that he practiced what he preached is beyond reasonable doubt, giving him substantial moral credibility."[31]

Not only did Jesus teach about hell, but he is the one who used the figures of speech of fire, darkness, punishment, banishment from God's presence, and God's wrath.[32] Jesus mentioned hell in the Sermon on the Mount and in many parables. As authors Kenneth Boa and Robert Bowman argue,

> Impartial tests of authenticity prove that the teaching about Hell in the Gospels does indeed originate from Jesus himself. Given that Jesus said the kinds of things about Hell recorded in the Gospels, some people today need to revise their view of Jesus. The idea of Jesus as an easy-going fellow who just loved everybody and said only positive, uplifting things is a complete myth. Christian faith, if it is to be faithful to Christ, must acknowledge the reality of Hell.[33]

Many people just can't fathom Jesus talking about, much less believing in, hell. But if hell is real, failing to warn people about it would be callous. Yet many find it inconsistent for Jesus to teach about hell and also teach about mercy. They fail to see that this is precisely the point: the one who is quoted the most about hell is also the one who gave his own life so that no one would have to go there. As we will see, the work of Christ was an expression of God's justice and mercy, which delicately and beautifully intertwine like the two strands in a DNA double helix.

Is Suffering in Hell Physical or Spiritual?

When people read the biblical passages about hell and judgment, they tend to think of it as something a person would experience with the kind of bodies we have now. As Geisler notes, Scripture says that after this life is over, people still have imperishable physical bodies (John 5:28–29; Rev. 20:13–15).[34] Yet if we take the figures of speech about hell as completely physical, they seem confusing. Hell has flames yet is complete darkness. It is a place where people remain but is also bottomless so that those who go there—physically, anyway—would never stop falling. Geisler believes that these references are intended as figures of speech to describe hell's torment rather than its physical conditions. "While everything in the Bible is literally true, not everything is true literally," he says. "For instance, God is not a literal rock (Psalm 18:2),[35] since He is Spirit (John 4:24),[36] but it is literally true that He is a solid, rocklike foundation we can trust."[37] So does this mean that hell is as much a form of spiritual as physical suffering? Boa and Bowman seem to think so:

> Jesus says that wicked people will be sent away "into the eternal fire prepared for the devil and his angels" (Matt. 25:41). Since the Devil and his angels are spiritual beings, not physical beings, Jesus' statement can only mean that the "eternal fire" is a form of punishment designed for spiritual beings. The implication is that the suffering of the condemned human beings in Hell will also be a spiritual type of suffering. It will consist of spiritual or mental anguish, perhaps in the form of regret, an abiding sense of loss, and the devastation of permanent exile from God, the world, and all that is good, beautiful, whole, and meaningful.[38]

Though we have physical bodies and apparently will for all of eternity, the worst part of punishment in hell might be spiritual, not physical, pain.

Is Hell Forever?

The Bible describes hell as a place that is everlasting, or eternal. Daniel 12:2 says, "Many of those who sleep in the dust of the earth shall awake, some to everlasting life, and some to shame and everlasting contempt." In Matthew 25:41–46, Jesus explains in a parable what will happen at the end of all things:

> He will say to those on his left, "Depart from me, you cursed, into the eternal fire prepared for the devil and his angels. For I was hungry and you gave me no food, I was thirsty and you gave me no drink, I was a stranger and you did not welcome me, naked and you did not clothe me, sick and in prison and you did not visit me." Then they also will answer, saying, "Lord, when did we see you hungry or thirsty or a stranger or naked or sick or in prison, and did not minister to you?" Then he will answer them, saying, "Truly, I say to you, as you did not do it to one of the least of these, you did not do it to me." And these will go away into eternal punishment, but the righteous into eternal life.

Of course, the words *eternal* and *everlasting* are used a number of different ways in Scripture, so it isn't always easy to discern what they mean in reference to hell, but the passage from Matthew 25 indicates that eternal punishment for those who did evil and failed to act righteously is paralleled with eternal life for the righteous. Whatever hell is, it is an experience that continues for an unimaginably long time.

3. What Is the Purpose of Hell?

Throughout the New Testament, we see God's *love* presented in context with God's *wrath*. Ephesians 2:4–5 says, "God, being rich in mercy, because of the great love with which he loved us, even when we were dead in our trespasses, made us alive together with Christ." Even the beloved verse John 3:16 ("For God so loved the world that he gave his only Son") is followed by verse 19, "And this is the judgment: the light has come into the world, and people loved the darkness rather than the light because their works were evil." So what are the implications of this for the doctrine of hell? Is God mad?

The biblical diagnosis for the human condition is not that we have been sinned against and are therefore justified in creating a god in our own image; rather, it's that we've rejected the God in whose image we are made and have fallen into sin. From a spiritual standpoint, we need salvation from our sin and its consequences.

Adherents to a Christian worldview recognize how difficult it is to fully understand the nature and character of a transcendent God. Through the biblical narrative, however, we can clearly see that God is described as a creator, a ruler, and a redeemer. His attributes include truth, justice, and love. For many, this seems like a contradiction: How can God be loving, just, compassionate, and wrathful at the same time?

When you think about it, however, we often see these traits together among humans in a perfectly natural way:

- A mother shows her love for her child by forcefully opposing a would-be molester.

- A missionary demonstrates his love for the oppressed by offering a no-holds-barred testimony against those who kidnap children and force them to be soldiers.

- A district attorney expresses her love for justice by passionately arguing for strict punishment for a criminal who terrorized a neighborhood.

How can a God who doesn't exercise justice ever truly express love? Imagine a Nuremberg judge saying to Nazi Rudolf Höss, who murdered so many concentration-camp victims, "Because of love, I overlook your offense." It would be an outrage because **justice** involves setting things right. The failure to do so is called *injustice*, not love. The point of Scripture is not that God fails to exercise justice but that he laid on Christ the iniquity of us all (Isa. 53:6).[39] As author Randy Alcorn puts it, "To fear and dread Hell is understandable, but to argue against Hell is to argue against justice."[40]

> *Justice:* the act of making things legally and morally right.

Yet God goes a step further: he expresses both love and wrath *toward the same people.* Why? Because Scripture indicates that all human beings are self-righteous, thinking we can bear our own image rather than God's. To this point, theologian D. A. Carson says,

> God's wrath is not an implacable blind rage. However emotional it may be, it is an entirely reasonable and willed response to offenses against His holiness. At the same time His love wells up amidst His perfections and is not generated by the loveliness of the loved. Thus there is nothing intrinsically impossible about wrath and love being directed toward the same individual or people at once. God in His perfections must be wrathful against His rebel image-bearers, for they have offended Him; God in His perfections must be loving toward His rebel image-bearers, for He is that kind of God.[41]

So how can God's love and his wrath be reconciled? Scripture is clear: God is unalterably wrathful against anything that mars his image in those who should bear it.

With this background in mind, we can see a purpose for hell. As Kenneth Boa and Robert Bowman phrase it,

> The purpose of Hell is not to make those who go there better people or to help them see the error of their ways and come to repentance. Hell is not like the Betty Ford Clinic [a treatment center for those with addictions]. It is not even like a modern prison, where most prisoners are encouraged to become rehabilitated so that they may reenter society as useful citizens. The purpose of Hell is to punish sinners. It is about retribution, not restoration. The evidence for this thesis in the New Testament

is beyond reasonable challenge. God's final disposition toward the wicked is consistently described throughout the New Testament as one of anger and wrath (Matt. 3:7; 18:34; Luke 3:7; John 3:36; Rom. 2:5, 8–9; 5:9; 9:22; Eph. 2:3; 5:6; Col. 3:6; 1 Thess. 1:10; 5:9; Rev. 6:16–17; 14:10; 19:15).[42]

This assessment seems harsh, but in reality it is good news. In fact, it is *the* good news. It's laudable when someone is saved from a poor self-image or a wretched upbringing or suddenly feels God's presence or is able to overcome an addiction. But the good news of the gospel is much more than this. The good news of the gospel is that Jesus died to satisfy God's wrath so that his decaying image bearers, and the creation they brutalized, may be restored. *The* good news is that by trusting in that sacrifice, we may know Christ and reflect his character in all of culture.

> The good news of the gospel is that Jesus died to satisfy God's wrath so that his decaying image bearers, and the creation they brutalized, may be restored. *The* good news is that by trusting in that sacrifice, we may know Christ and reflect his character in all of culture.

In short, I can't atone for the sin of the kid who beat me up in grade school, but I am accountable for my bitterness, pent-up anger, lack of forgiveness, and resentment. He threw a punch, but in my mind I wished him dead. I don't know where he stands with God, but I know I stand in desperate need of salvation, for I have been, and am, desperately wicked.

Still, hell seems like overkill. Most people just aren't that bad. Is the biblical teaching on hell just?

4. Is Hell Just?

Most people understand that sin must be punished, but the punishment of hell may seem too severe for the crime. How can someone's seemingly minor sins in a finite lifetime earn an eternity in hell? Couldn't God arrange for people's souls to be annihilated after just a brief punishment or even give them a chance to repent after they see how bad hell is?

Pastor Tim Keller addresses the misunderstanding from which these questions proceed:

> Modern people inevitably think hell works like this: God gives us time, but if we haven't made the right choices by the end of our lives, he casts our souls into hell for all eternity. As the poor souls fall through space, they cry out for mercy, but God says "Too late! You had your chance! Now you will suffer!" This caricature misunderstands the very nature of evil. The Biblical picture is that sin separates us from the presence of God, which is the source of all joy and indeed of all love, wisdom, or good things of any sort. Since we were originally created for God's immediate presence, only before his face will we thrive, flourish, and achieve our highest potential.[43]

The desire to be free of God's immediate presence is what sin is all about. We cannot assume that those who reject Christ will come to their senses and change once in hell. People continue to sin there. Their rebellion has not ceased. They still don't want God. Carson says, "Perhaps we should think of hell as a place where people continue to rebel, continue to insist on their own way, continue societal structures of prejudice and hate, continue to defy the living God. And as they continue to defy God, so he continues to punish them. And the cycle goes on and on and on."[44]

Whether or not people continue rebelling against God for all of eternity, their sin—and ours—does constitute an eternal debt. English poet and cleric John Donne said, "When all is done, the hell of hells, the torment of torments, is the everlasting absence of God, and the everlasting impossibility of returning to his presence.… To fall out of the hands of the living God, is a horror beyond our expression, beyond our imagination."[45]

> Whether or not people continue rebelling against God for all of eternity, their sin—and ours—does constitute an eternal debt.

To the Christian worldview, anything good we have or understand is because of God's constant presence in our lives. Yet we are constantly tempted to believe we are the ones who make our lives good, so our minor indiscretions should be seen in this context. We think we're like the football quarterback who throws an interception but who also completes several touchdown passes: an interception is bad, but touchdowns make up for it. Similarly, we think that because of all the good we've done, our rebellion against the creator and redeemer of the universe isn't all that serious. But Randy Alcorn states bluntly,

> We hate Hell precisely because we don't hate evil. We hate it also because we deserve it. We cry out for true and lasting justice, then fault God for taking evil too seriously by administering eternal punishment. We can't have it both ways. Sin is evil; just punishment of sin is good. Hell is an eternal correction of and compensation for evil. It is justice.[46]

It is a human temptation to think that we are good because we are not as bad as some other people we can think of. This view obscures the truth and makes our need for redemption seem like a choice of drinks at Starbucks: "You have a cup of Buddhism, and I'll take the Christianity—no big deal." Hell is the bracing reminder that the choice is ultimately not ours. As British theologian Lesslie Newbigin said, "It is one of the weaknesses of a great deal of contemporary Christianity that we do not speak of the last judgment and of the possibility of being finally lost."[47]

5. Ultimately, Those Who Go to Hell Know Why They're There

When all of the scriptural evidence and analysis is woven together, we arrive at a conclusion that startles many. Hell is not something foisted upon unsuspecting innocents but a place where the unrepentant finally get what they want: to be apart from God. A drowning person who refuses a life ring will have no righteous cause for blaming the lifeguard for his predicament. As Christian philosopher Dallas Willard put it,

> No one chooses in the abstract to go to hell or even to be the kind of person who belongs there. But their orientation toward self leads them to become the kind of

person for whom away-from-God is the only place for which they are suited. It is a place they would, in the end, choose for themselves, rather than come to humble themselves before God and accept who he is. Whether or not God's will is infinitely flexible, the human will is not. There are limits beyond which it cannot bend back, cannot turn or repent. One should seriously inquire if to live in a world permeated with God and the knowledge of God is something they themselves truly desire. If not, they can be assured that God will excuse them from his presence. They will find their place in the "outer darkness" of which Jesus spoke. But the fundamental fact about them will not be that they are there, but that they have become people so locked into their own self-worship and denial of God that they cannot want God.[48]

> We do not know at what age or due to what level of sinfulness people establish their destiny in this way, but it does seem that over the course of their lives, people establish their destination much as a railroad building crew lays down railroad track.

We do not know at what age or due to what level of sinfulness people establish their destiny in this way, but it does seem that over the course of their lives, people establish their destination much as a railroad building crew lays down railroad track. With each bit of track, the destination becomes nearer and the willingness to change course diminishes. It's not that they can't turn around and come back; it's that they just don't want to.

Tim Keller says that "hell is simply one's freely chosen identity apart from God on a trajectory into infinity."[49] He likens this choice to that of an addiction to alcohol, gambling, or pornography. People first choose addictions, but then those addictions take control and life disintegrates into a frantic obsession for sustaining the same level of high. At first, addicts see themselves as in control of their behavior ("I can quit any time"). Gradually, they submit control to the addiction and feel more isolated and sorry for themselves ("No one understands!"). "Personal disintegration happens on a broader scale," says Keller. "In eternity, this disintegration goes on forever. There is increasing isolation, denial, delusion, and self-absorption."[50]

Alcorn reminds us, "Hell is not pleasant, appealing, or encouraging. But Hell is morally good, because a good God must punish evil. Hell will not be a blot on the universe, but an eternal testimony to the ugliness of evil that will prompt wondrous appreciation of a good God's magnificence."[51] Evil, disintegration, and the obsession with self-salvation simply have no place in the new heavens and the new earth, covered as these are with the personal presence of God.

6. Why Can't God Just Forgive Everyone?

Many people will say, "All right, I can see how people who go to hell choose to go there. But surely because God knows this is a bad choice and we are too limited to see the full implications of what we are deciding, why doesn't he just forgive us?"

Again, we need to go back to understanding what good and evil actually are and therefore what it means to condone evil as opposed to forgiving it. In *The Problem of Pain*, C. S. Lewis said, "To condone an evil is simply to ignore it, to treat it as if it were good. But forgiveness needs to be accepted as well as offered if it is to be *complete*: a man who admits no guilt can accept no forgiveness."[52]

Our human dilemma is clear: although we want to believe that good and evil actually exist, and that God cares enough to deal with the desperately evil people such as Hitler and Stalin, we want God to overlook our own offenses. We each tend to draw the line between good and evil in such a way that we always fall on the "good" side. But this makes *us* the ones who decide the differences between good and evil. The distinction between good and evil either exists objectively or it does not. If it does, it exists according to God's terms, not ours. If it does not exist, then we are never in a position to say with certainty that other people, even evil dictators who killed millions, are evil and worthy of judgment. Our desire for judgment would be just a matter of preference. Mao Tse-tung was responsible for the deaths of seventy-two million people. Who's to say this was a bad thing? Maybe those people needed to die. The necessary implication of denying the objective difference between good and evil is that the concepts lose their meaning completely.

> The necessary implication of denying the objective difference between good and evil is that the concepts lose their meaning completely.

Even if we do not like the implications, we are far better off acknowledging the existence of objective good and evil even if it means we need to repent. As authors Sean McDowell and Jonathan Morrow put it, "The final proof that God is a perfect moral being, not indifferent to questions of right and wrong, is the fact that he has committed himself to judge the world. Since all of us expect this level of moral integrity and consistency from human judges, shouldn't we at least expect the same from God?"[53]

But if God is loving, how can he also be so angry at the bad things we do? We ask this question because we struggle with understanding exactly how God's love and his justice perfectly coexist in his nature. Tim Keller's explanation is helpful:

> In Christianity God is both a God of love and of justice. Many people struggle with this. They believe that a loving God can't be a judging God. Like most other Christian ministers in our society, I have been asked literally thousands of times, "How can a God of love be also a God ... filled with wrath and anger? If he is loving and perfect, he should forgive and accept everyone. He shouldn't get angry." I always start my response by pointing out that all loving persons are sometimes filled with wrath, not just despite of but because of their love. If you love a person and you see someone ruining them—even they themselves—you get angry.[54]

The coexistence of love and justice in God's nature makes it so that he can *forgive*, not just *ignore*, our sin. The apostle Paul proclaims in Romans 3:23–25, "All have sinned and fall short of the glory of God, and are justified by his grace as a gift, through the redemption that is in Christ Jesus, whom God put forward as a propitiation by his blood, to be received by faith." How is this so? Paul continues with an allusion to the Passover in Egypt, when God *withheld* judgment from those who deserved it by an act of his divine will: "This was to show God's righteousness, because in his divine forbearance he had passed over former sins. It was to show his righteousness at the present time, so that he might be just and the justifier of the one who has faith in Jesus" (Rom. 3:25–26).

7. Answers to Tough Questions about Hell

If you've ever been in a discussion about hell, you've probably heard a lot of questions raised—good questions. Good people who love God have examined these questions and have arrived at different answers, so we need to reason carefully and prayerfully on each question.

Does God Send Children to Hell?

If everyone who has lived since the fall of humanity possesses a sin nature, babies are sinners from the moment of conception. Even adults who are mentally disabled are still sinners in need of Christ's redemption. Are such people bound for hell? To answer this question, we need to distinguish between what it means to have a sin nature and what it means to be capable of sinful deeds of the sort that would lead to eternal judgment.

Theologian and pastor John MacArthur believes that this distinction is important and that it implies that those who are innocent of willful sin and rebellion will be saved. He says,

> Yes, all children who die before they reach a state of moral awareness and culpability in which they understand their sin and corruption—so that their sins are deliberate—are graciously saved eternally by God through the work of Jesus Christ. They are counted as elect by sovereign choice because they are innocent of willful sin, rebellion, and unbelief, by which works they would be justly condemned to eternal punishment.[55]

What is the biblical basis for this position? Well, first, it is clear from Scripture that if we call on God for salvation in Christ, we are judged according to Christ's work on the cross. Titus 3:5–7 says,

> He saved us, not because of works done by us in righteousness, but according to his own mercy, by the washing of regeneration and renewal of the Holy Spirit, whom he poured out on us richly through Jesus Christ our Savior, so that being justified by his grace we might become heirs according to the hope of eternal life.

When we rely on our own works to save us, we are judged by our own criterion. Revelation 20:13 says, "The sea gave up the dead who were in it, Death and Hades gave up the dead who were in them, and they were judged, each one of them, according to what they had done."

That people will be judged according to what they have done is a theme running throughout Scripture. Psalm 62:12 says of God, "You will render to a man according to his work." Proverbs 24:12 says, "Will he not repay man according to his work?" Speaking of his own return, Jesus says, "He will repay each person according to what he has done" (Matt. 16:27). The apostle Paul is also clear: "He will render to each one according to his works" (Rom. 2:6) and "We must all appear before the judgment seat of Christ, so that each one may receive what is due for what he has done in the body, whether good or evil" (2 Cor. 5:10).

How do these passages relate to the question of whether children or the mentally disabled will be saved? The answer, at least as far as can be discerned from the handful of Scripture passages we have to go by, is that there is an age at which children become capable of believing in the redemptive work of Christ or demonstrating their rejection of it. This is *not* to say that belief *causes* salvation but that it is a medium through which salvation occurs.[56] The Holy Spirit enables us to turn from idolatry, be declared righteous by God, and advance in holiness as we become like Christ. But it *is* to say that for a person to be punished for sin, he must be capable of embracing evil and also understanding of the reason for the punishment.

Bible scholars assume that such a distinction exists between those who are guilty because they are capable of choosing evil and knowing that this choice implies punishment and those who are not. Deuteronomy 1:39[57] refers to children qualifying for the Promised Land as grown-ups because they "have no knowledge of good or evil." Isaiah 7:15–16[58] refers to a timeline of destruction that would occur before the one referred to in the passage "knows how to refuse the evil and choose the good." In Romans 9:11,[59] Paul refers to Isaac's children who were chosen by God "though they were not yet born and had done nothing either good or bad." When King David's son died, David expressed confidence that his son would go to wherever the righteous dead go: "I shall go to him, but he will not return to me" (2 Sam. 12:23).

> Bible scholars assume that such a distinction exists between those who are guilty because they are capable of choosing evil and knowing that this choice implies punishment and those who are not.

Perhaps a better way to understand what happens to children who die is to return to what the Bible says about God's character, specifically his grace. According to the apostle Paul, sin proceeds from our nature, not just from our acts (see, for example, Rom. 14:14–20).[60] Salvation comes through grace (Eph. 2:8–9).[61] Does God's grace apply to children and others who are incapable of spiritual reasoning? Of course. And throughout the Gospels, we see signs of Jesus's special grace for those of childlike innocence. Jesus had a special place for children in his ministry (see Matt. 19:14; also Luke 17:2, where Jesus harshly condemned anyone who would lead little ones into sin).[62]

Except for the passage from David, none of the passages we've quoted is about eternal destiny. But writing under the inspiration of the Holy Spirit, these authors offer a picture of how God approaches children that gives us reason to hope. Children rely on God's grace; so does everyone else.

What about Those Who Have Never Heard about Jesus?

"So what about those who have never heard?" It may be one of the most asked questions about the doctrine of hell and the one that worries people the most. It just doesn't seem fair that people who have never had the opportunity to hear the gospel would be condemned to an eternity in hell.

Before I attempt to answer the question, I always try to figure out the questioner's motivation: "Do you really want to know, or are you just offering this question as an accusation against Christianity?" The actual answer is quite simple: We can't know what God will do in every circumstance because the mind of God is a mystery. But Scripture tells us that God is gracious and just, so whatever the gracious and just thing is, that is what he will do. Still, Jesus commands us to go and tell the good news throughout the earth, and when he says go, he means go. It is exciting to see how in our own time, God works directly as well as through ease of travel and technology to enable the spreading of the good news. Many have come to faith through visions and dreams, and millions have come to faith through missionary outreaches, radio programs, Bible distributions, television, and the Internet.[63]

Jonathan Morrow helps us think through the issue of "those who have never heard" by looking at what the Bible says about God's nature and character:[64]

- God is compassionate and just (Gen. 18:25; Deut. 32:4; Pss. 7:9; 85:11; 89:14; 145:8–9; Rev. 16:7).

- The basis of our condemnation is sin, and all are in need of a savior (Rom. 3:10–18, 23; 5:12–21; 6:23; Eph. 2:1–3).

- Jesus Christ is the only means of salvation (John 14:6; Acts 4:12; 1 Tim. 2:5; 4:10; 1 John 2:2) and the only way to God.

- Since the time following the resurrection of Jesus, no one can be saved apart from the knowledge of Christ (Acts 16:31; Rom. 10:14; Acts 17:30-31).

- God genuinely desires all to be saved (Ezek. 18:23; John 3:16; 1 Tim. 2:3–6; 2 Pet. 3:9).

- God has revealed himself to the whole world both in creation (Ps. 19:1–2; Acts 14:15–17; Rom. 1:19–20) and human conscience (Eccles. 3:11; Rom. 2:14–16) so that people are without excuse.

- God's Spirit is at work convicting the world of sin, righteousness, and judgment (John 16:8–11).

- Christians are commanded to take the gospel to the whole world (Matt. 28:19–20; Acts 1:8).

- God has providentially arranged the world so that people might seek him and that everyone who seeks him will find him (Acts 17:24–28; cf. Heb. 11:6; Jer. 29:13; Acts 10:35).

- There will be people from every tribe, tongue, and nation in God's eternal kingdom (Rev. 7:9).

- The awful reality of hell indicates that not everyone is saved in the end (Matt. 10:28; 25:31–46; 2 Thess. 1:7–9).

- There is no second chance after death to accept the gospel (Heb. 9:27).[65]

These references display a fairly clear pattern: all humans stand condemned before God, and this condemnation is based on their *sins*, not on what they do or do not know.

Once a person asked me, "But if people aren't condemned until they have knowledge of God, aren't they better off to remain without knowledge?" Initially, the question struck me as arrogant and racist, as if the person were saying, "As an 'enlightened Westerner,' I think we should not help the poor natives. They're happier the way they are and are best just left alone." First, people who have not heard the gospel are not like little children who are safe in their ignorance. Christianity says that everyone needs to know the gospel. It is the only way to God. And Jesus specifically commands us to share it throughout the entire world. To use a theological nuance—that we aren't sure who are condemned or not based on what they do or do not know—is to ignore an explicit command of Jesus and is gross misuse of Scripture and dangerously disobedient to God.

The more I thought about it, however, I realized that the person was asking a genuinely valid question. So my answer was this: we do not know whether people who have never heard the gospel will be saved. We do know two things: God is just and no one is beyond his reach, and God is gracious in saving many who deserve to be condemned. As Morrow phrases it, "We are left with some mystery when it comes to saying exactly how God will work out His plan of salvation among the nations. Therefore we trust ultimately in His goodness and justice. Will not the judge of the earth do right?"[66]

Second, we are commanded by Jesus to spread the good news, not because we have superior knowledge but because all authority in heaven and on earth has been given to him and, in this authority, he has commanded us to do it (Matt. 28:18–20).[67] Our mission is not to enlighten the ignorant but rather to call everyone in the world to repentance (Acts 17:30).[68] Dallas Willard expands on this point: "We should be very sure that the ruined soul is not one who has missed a few more or less important theological points and will flunk a theological examination at the end of life. Hell is not an 'oops!' or a slip. One does not miss heaven by a hair, but by constant effort to avoid and escape God."[69] We can see in creation that God exists as creator, but without specific revelation from God, each will remain, as Willard puts it, "disastrously in error about their own life and their place before God and man."[70] It is this error Jesus confronts, not a lack of theological knowledge.

Doesn't Everyone Eventually Escape Hell?

A few years ago, an evangelical pastor named Rob Bell wrote a book that was propelled to bestseller status by the controversy it ignited. *Love Wins: A Book about Heaven, Hell, and the Fate of Everyone Who Ever Lived* was discussed on television, in the pages of *USA Today*, and on the cover of *Time* magazine, a publication that called Rob a "rock star" among evangelicals.

Bell is an excellent communicator. With a quick wit and a gift for bringing the Bible to life for both seekers and longtime believers, he relishes charging straight into its mouth of controversy. This has earned him a reputation as a fearless, though sometimes prickly, voice of a new generation of Christians.

In his book, Bell says that the main thing that keeps people away from Christianity is that they don't feel good about a God who would condemn the unrepentant to hell. To help people feel better, he argues that God's love will eventually woo everyone, and because that isn't (to his way of thinking) happening here on earth, God must have some kind of plan for saving people after they die. This is a form of **universalism**: the belief that everyone will ultimately be saved, even if salvation takes place after death.

> *Universalism:* the belief that all human and angelic beings will eventually be restored to a right relationship with God, either while alive or sometime after death.

Bell gives the strong impression that the doctrine of hell is the main thing evangelical churches emphasize today. Through carefully chosen, shocking examples, Bell takes his stand against what he sees as heartless and socially inept yahoos who get a perverse pleasure out of knowing that others will get punished in the afterlife. Though the subtitle implies that his book is about who goes to heaven and who goes to hell, it is really about whether people who have rejected Christ will be wooed to salvation after they die. Bell develops this theory to remove the excuses people use to dismiss Christianity.

That Jesus satisfies God's justice is one of the key themes of Scripture and one that Bell explicitly rejects ("We do not need to be rescued from God"). In fact, he blames "inquisitions, persecutions, trials, book burnings, blacklisting" on those who disagree with his stated position, calling them "misguided" and "toxic."[71]

The idea that God will eventually convert people beyond the grave is hopeful but also at odds with virtually everything we understand to be true from Scripture about death, salvation, and judgment. It's also confusing. How can we say that people are free to reject God in this lifetime but somehow after death they are no longer free? Is it consistent with God's nature and character to take no for an answer during a person's lifetime but force that person to "love" him after death, sort of like a cosmic stalker to whom no really means yes? As William Lane Craig says,

> No orthodox Christian likes the doctrine of hell or delights in anyone's condemnation. I truly wish universalism were true, but it is not. My compassion toward those in other world religions is therefore expressed, not in pretending that they are not lost and dying without Christ, but by supporting and making every effort myself to communicate to them the life-giving message of salvation through Christ.[72]

The apostle Paul says, "Knowing the fear of the Lord, we persuade others" (2 Cor. 5:11). Bell's *Love Wins* shows how far one kindhearted pastor is willing to go to avoid acknowledging the fear of the Lord or to avoid persuading others that they themselves are evil and need redemption. It is compassionate and well intentioned, but the scriptural evidence we have seen in this chapter simply does not support it.

Aren't People's Souls Just Annihilated after Going to Hell?

Some Christians believe that lost souls are annihilated rather than tormented forever. Historically, early Christian apologist Justin Martyr seemed to believe this, and in our own day it has been defended by respected scholar John Stott.[73]

The problem with this idea, called **annihilationism**, is that it doesn't fit Scripture very well. John 5:28–29[74] refers to the resurrection of the just and the unjust, which would be hard if the unjust had been annihilated. Also, the apostle Paul describes the punishment for the wicked as "eternal destruction," an active, ongoing state in 2 Thessalonians. This eternal destruction is "away" from God's ongoing glory: it is an eternal destruction of a relationship rather than an annihilation.[75] Those who do not believe seem to be missing out in some conscious fashion from what those who accepted the gospel are experiencing.

> *Annihilationism:* the belief that damned souls are utterly destroyed rather than tormented in hell for eternity.

The idea that hell involves conscious suffering seems consistent with the passages on hell we explored earlier (Matt. 8:12; 22:13; 25:41; Mark 9:43–48; Jude v. 13; Rev. 22:14–15; and others).[76] Although we might hope that the suffering in hell would quickly come to an end, especially for those we personally love and care for, such a view is hard to square with scriptural teaching.

8. HOW TO RESPOND TO THOSE WHO ARE OFFENDED

How should we respond to those who question the biblical doctrine of hell? My friend Sue Bohlin, from Probe Ministries in Dallas, demonstrates a thorough and yet compassionate approach in response to a letter she received from a sixteen-year-old Wiccan practitioner. Here is the letter:

> I am a 16. I was searching through the web when I found your web site on the Occult. Naturally I was interested so I read through it. I found all of the information to be quite intriguing. I am a practitioner of Wicca. I am a Wiccan. I have been for the past year. I am not a worshiper of Satan nor do I inflict bodily harm upon myself through rituals. I do not believe in one all mighty god, rather I believe in many gods and goddesses. I am a believer of faith, I worship all things, the dead, trees, inanimate or not. I do not use rituals to gain, or hinder others. I simply use them to help or support things I love, like a protection spell while a loved one is on a trip and away from the family. I also ask the Lord and Lady to look over a loved one as they make their last journey. I do not believe in Heaven or Hell. I believe in personal "heavens" and personal "hells." Your site has given me the impression that your view is that if you are not a pure Christian you are going to "hell." You must worship a certain way and do certain things to be "saved." Am I right in saying this? I was just wondering your personal views on Wiccanism. I am curious about your opinions. Please feel free to e-mail me back. I would greatly appreciate it.[77]

And here is Sue's reply:

> Thank you for taking the time to write us.
> Yes, you read our views correctly. What we believe is definitely not politically correct. We believe that there is one God, that He has interacted with our world (which He created), and that He communicated true truth to us. Part of that truth is that there is only one way to be reconciled to Him, and that is by trusting in His Son Jesus to save us from our sin problem and to equip us for life as He intended it in this world, and for heaven when we die.

We do realize that it is far more appealing to believe that there are many ways to God or god, however one defines him/her/it, all equally valid. However, just as you can't live in the real world under that type of "all preferences are equally valid, all truths are equally true" misbeliefs, we believe that spiritual reality doesn't abide by those lies either. For instance, many people say they believe that physical reality is mere illusion, but you don't find them meditating on railroad tracks. And many people say they create their own truth, but they all seem to agree that "red means stop" or they don't live too long!

Let me try to reframe a common misunderstanding of hell. When Jesus was on earth, He claimed to be God. He said, "I am the way, the truth, and the life." One of the implications of that statement is that life is found in a relationship with Him. Apart from Jesus, there is no life, only death, which means separation from the source of life. Heaven isn't so much a place as it the fullness of relationship with a real Person—God. So being "saved" is not about jumping through religious hoops; it is about being rescued from an eternity of destruction and death where people are separated from life, which is only found in Jesus.

You said you don't believe in one almighty God, but various gods and goddesses. Are they real? What evidence do you have that they exist? If you are trusting in imaginary friends, wouldn't you want to know that? On the other hand, Jesus was a real, historical Person who made astounding claims that are ridiculous if they are not true, and the only way to be reconciled to God if they are. (He also said He was the only way to the Father. Again, that is an arrogant and presumptuous thing to say—unless it's true.)

So hell is not a place where an angry, vengeful God laughs as he sends people who wouldn't jump through his hoops. Hell exists because God made us to be in a love relationship with Him, and He will not, cannot, force us to love Him. It has to be freely chosen. Since life is only found in God, hell is the place for people who would not accept His offer of love and friendship. And since there is no life apart from God, hell is a place of everlasting death and destruction because there is no life where there is no relationship with God.

You asked about our view of Wicca: it is not the same as Satanism, but it is another false religion based on lies and misbeliefs that are designed to draw people away from the true God. We believe that Wicca ultimately comes from the mind of the literal, evil being called Satan who hates God and hates people and lies to them so that they will suffer like he does. And while you may well be a gentle, kind and wonderful person, the kind of person that all of us at Probe would love to have as our next-door neighbor, we believe that without a personal relationship with the one true God through His Son Jesus Christ, you cannot experience life as He intended for you to live in this life, your sins will separate you from a holy God forever, and you cannot go to heaven when you die.

I do pray that because God loves you as much as He does, He will do whatever it takes to show Himself to you in a way that is sufficiently intimate to your heart that you will KNOW that it is Him pursuing you with a strong but gentle divine love.

And I pray you will experience His blessing on your life.[78]

Notice what Sue did and did not do. She did not mock her young correspondent's view. She did not avoid the distinct teaching of Scripture. She did, however, communicate clearly and compassionately. This is a model for how we ought to talk with people about hell.

9. Conclusion

As we have seen, people reject Christ because their hearts are desperately wicked. They *prefer* a counterfeit form of salvation because it maintains the illusion that they control their own destiny. Rejecting Christianity because one is offended by often clumsy arguments is an *excuse*, not a reason.

Those who will go to hell will know why they are there. They are in rebellion against God to the very end. C. S. Lewis put it this way: "I willingly believe that the damned are, in one sense, successful rebels to the end; that the doors of hell are locked on the *inside*."[79]

So how should we respond? First, recognize that most people don't take hell as seriously as they should. According to a survey by George Barna, only 1 percent of Americans actually think they're going to hell.[80] Why this low of a percentage? Because people don't think they're very bad. If they are trusting in themselves for salvation, however, they are making a tragic mistake.

Second, we as Christians need to become familiar with the biblical doctrines of heaven and hell. We need to demonstrate loving community and pray that the Holy Spirit will work in people's lives to bring about repentance.

So although the doctrine of hell seems like very bad news at first glance, it is actually part of God's very good news: love does indeed win. God's perfect love wins. Good triumphs over evil. Humanity is not doomed after all. This good news, based on the authority of Jesus, must be shared with everyone in the world.

> Although the doctrine of hell seems like very bad news at first glance, it is actually part of God's very good news: love does indeed win. God's perfect love wins. Good triumphs over evil.

We'll expand on this theme of God's goodness and the relationship between his love and his justice in the next chapter as we consider another common objection to the Bible: If God is love, why does he seem like such a mean bully in the Old Testament?

Endnotes

1. Bertrand Russell, *Why I Am Not a Christian and Other Essays on Religion and Related Subjects* (New York: Simon & Schuster, 1957), 17–18.
2. Douglas Groothuis, *Christian Apologetics: A Comprehensive Case for Biblical Faith* (Downers Grove, IL: InterVarsity, 2011), 656.
3. Jonathan Edwards, "The Justice of God in the Damnation of Sinners," in *Works of President Edwards*, 4 vols. (New York: Leavitt & Allen, 1852), 4:228.
4. Groothuis, *Christian Apologetics*, 660.
5. Exodus 8:22: "On that day I will set apart the land of Goshen, where my people dwell, so that no swarms of flies shall be there, that you may know that I am the LORD in the midst of the earth"; Exodus 8:29–30: "Moses said, 'Behold, I am going out from you and I will plead with the LORD that the swarms of flies may depart from Pharaoh, from his servants, and from his people, tomorrow. Only let not Pharaoh cheat again by not letting the people go to sacrifice to the Lord.' So Moses went out from Pharaoh and prayed to the LORD."
6. Exodus 9:20: "Whoever feared the word of the LORD among the servants of Pharaoh hurried his slaves and his livestock

into the houses."

7. Walter Kaiser, *Toward an Old Testament Theology* (Grand Rapids, MI: Zondervan, 1978), 103–4. Exodus 12:38: "A mixed multitude also went up with them, and very much livestock, both flocks and herds."

8. *C. S. Lewis: Readings for Meditation and Reflection* (New York: HarperOne, 1996), 37. See also www.articles.sfgate.com/2002-07-06/news/17553634_1_evangelical-churches-portions-of-christian-theology.

9. Flannery O'Connor, *The Habit of Being: Letters of Flannery O'Connor* (New York: Farrar, Straus & Giroux, 1979), 100.

10. 1 Thessalonians 1:10: "… to wait for his Son from heaven, whom he raised from the dead, Jesus who delivers us from the wrath to come."

11. Titus 3:5: "He saved us, not because of works done by us in righteousness, but according to his own mercy, by the washing of regeneration and renewal of the Holy Spirit."

12. Acts 15:3: "Being sent on their way by the church, they passed through both Phoenicia and Samaria, describing in detail the conversion of the Gentiles, and brought great joy to all the brothers."

13. Romans 3:24: "… are justified by his grace as a gift, through the redemption that is in Christ Jesus."

14. Romans 8:15, 23: "You did not receive the spirit of slavery to fall back into fear, but you have received the Spirit of adoption as sons, by whom we cry, 'Abba! Father!'… And not only the creation, but we ourselves, who have the firstfruits of the Spirit, groan inwardly as we wait eagerly for adoption as sons, the redemption of our bodies."

15. Romans 15:16: "… to be a minister of Christ Jesus to the Gentiles in the priestly service of the gospel of God, so that the offering of the Gentiles may be acceptable, sanctified by the Holy Spirit."

16. These six aspects of salvation come from Robert A. Webb, *The Theology of Infant Salvation* (Harrisonburg, VA: Sprinkle Publications, 1992). Romans 8:17: "… if children, then heirs—heirs of God and fellow heirs with Christ, provided we suffer with him in order that we may also be glorified with him."

17. Colossians 3:6: "On account of these the wrath of God is coming."

18. 1 Thessalonians 1:10: "… to wait for his Son from heaven, whom he raised from the dead, Jesus who delivers us from the wrath to come."

19. Daniel 12:1–2: "At that time shall arise Michael, the great prince who has charge of your people. And there shall be a time of trouble, such as never has been since there was a nation till that time. But at that time your people shall be delivered, everyone whose name shall be found written in the book. And many of those who sleep in the dust of the earth shall awake, some to everlasting life, and some to shame and everlasting contempt."

20. Isaiah 66:24: "They shall go out and look on the dead bodies of the men who have rebelled against me. For their worm shall not die, their fire shall not be quenched, and they shall be an abhorrence to all flesh."

21. Morgan and Peterson reference dozens of verses they say constitute the doctrine of hell, including Matthew 5:22; 29–30; 7:13, 23; 8:12, 29; 10:28; 13:42, 49–50; 18:6–9; 22:13; 23:33; 24:51; 25:30, 41, 46: 26:24; Mark 1:24; 5:7; 9:43, 45, 47–48; Luke 3:17; 4:34; 12:5; 13:3, 5; 16:23–25, 28; John 3:16–18, 36; 5:28–29; 8:21, 24; Acts 10:42; 17:31; Romans 2:5, 8–9, 12; 6:23; 9:3, 22; 1 Corinthians 11:32; 2 Corinthians 2:15–16; 4:3; Galatians 1:8–9; 6:8; Ephesians 5:6; Philippians 1:28; 3:19; Colossians 3:6; 1 Thessalonians 1:10; 5:3, 9; Hebrews 6:2; 9:27; 10:27, 39; James 4:12; 2 Peter 2:1, 3, 4, 9, 12, 17; 3:7; Jude vv. 4, 6, 7, 13; and Revelation 2:11; 6:16–17; 11:18; 14:10–11, 19; 16:19; 17:8, 11; 18:8, 9, 18; 19:3, 15, 20; 20:10, 14–15; 21:8; 22:15. See Christopher W. Morgan and Robert A. Peterson, eds., *Hell Under Fire: Modern Scholarship Reinvents Eternal Punishment* (Grand Rapids, MI: Zondervan, 2004), 168.

22. Matthew 8:12: "The sons of the kingdom will be thrown into the outer darkness. In that place there will be weeping and gnashing of teeth"; Matthew 22:13: "The king said to the attendants, 'Bind him hand and foot and cast him into the outer darkness. In that place there will be weeping and gnashing of teeth'"

23. Revelation 22:14–15: "Blessed are those who wash their robes, so that they may have the right to the tree of life and that they may enter the city by the gates. Outside are the dogs and sorcerers and the sexually immoral and murderers and idolaters, and everyone who loves and practices falsehood."

24. Matthew 25:41: "He will say to those on his left, 'Depart from me, you cursed, into the eternal fire prepared for the devil and his angels.'"

25. Matthew 8:12: "The sons of the kingdom will be thrown into the outer darkness. In that place there will be weeping and gnashing of teeth"; Jude v. 13: "… wild waves of the sea, casting up the foam of their own shame; wandering stars, for whom the gloom of utter darkness has been reserved forever."

26. Mark 9:43–48: "If your hand causes you to sin, cut it off. It is better for you to enter life crippled than with two hands to go to hell, to the unquenchable fire. And if your foot causes you to sin, cut it off. It is better for you to enter life lame than with two feet to be thrown into hell. And if your eye causes you to sin, tear it out. It is better for you to enter the kingdom of God with one eye than with two eyes to be thrown into hell, 'where their worm does not die and the fire is not quenched.'"

27. Luke 16:28: "I have five brothers—so that he may warn them, lest they also come into this place of torment."

28. 2 Thessalonians 1:7–9: "… to grant relief to you who are afflicted as well as to us, when the Lord Jesus is revealed from heaven with his mighty angels in flaming fire, inflicting vengeance on those who do not know God and on those who do not obey the gospel of our Lord Jesus. They will suffer the punishment of eternal destruction, away from the presence of the Lord and from the glory of his might."

29. Norman L. Geisler, *If God, Why Evil? A New Way to Think about the Question* (Minneapolis: Bethany, 2011),103.

30. J. P. Moreland and Gary R. Habermas, *Beyond Death: Exploring the Evidence for Immortality* (Eugene, OR: Wipf and Stock, 2003), 291.

31. Sean McDowell and Jonathan Morrow, *Is God Just a Human Invention? And Seventeen Other Questions Raised by the New Atheists* (Grand Rapids, MI: Kregel, 2010), 160.

32. Kenneth D. Boa and Robert M. Bowman, *Sense and Nonsense about Heaven and Hell* (Grand Rapids, MI: Zondervan, 2007), 99–100.

33. Boa and Bowman, *Sense and Nonsense*, 99–100.

34. John 5:28–29: "Do not marvel at this, for an hour is coming when all who are in the tombs will hear his voice and come out, those who have done good to the resurrection of life, and those who have done evil to the resurrection of judgment"; Revelation 20:13–15: "The sea gave up the dead who were in it, Death and Hades gave up the dead who were in them, and they were judged, each one of them, according to what they had done. Then Death and Hades were thrown into the lake of fire. This is the second death, the lake of fire. And if anyone's name was not found written in the book of life, he was thrown into the lake of fire."

35. Psalm 18:2: "The LORD is my rock and my fortress and my deliverer, my God, my rock, in whom I take refuge, my shield, and the horn of my salvation, my stronghold."

36. John 4:24: "God is spirit, and those who worship him must worship in spirit and truth."

37. Geisler, *If God, Why Evil?*, 104.

38. Boa and Bowman, *Sense and Nonsense*, 115.

39. Isaiah 53:6: "All we like sheep have gone astray; we have turned—every one—to his own way; and the LORD has laid on him the iniquity of us all."

40. Randy C. Alcorn, *If God Is Good: Faith in the Midst of Suffering and Evil* (Colorado Springs, CO: Multnomah, 2009), 309.

41. D. A. Carson, "God's Love and God's Wrath," *Bibliotheca Sacra* 156 (1999): 388–90.

42. Boa and Bowman, *Sense and Nonsense*, 102.

43. Timothy J. Keller, *The Reason for God: Belief in an Age of Skepticism* (New York: Dutton, 2008), 76.

44. D. A. Carson, *How Long, O Lord? Reflections on Suffering and Evil* (Grand Rapids, MI: Baker Academic, 1990), 102.

45. John Donne, quoted in D.A. Carson, *The Gagging of God: Christianity Confronts Pluralism* (Grand Rapids, MI: Zondervan, 1996), 532.

46. Alcorn, *If God Is Good*, 309.

47. Lesslie Newbigin, "Confessing Christ in a Multi-Religion Society," *Scottish Bulletin of Evangelical Theology* 12 (1994): 130–31.

48. Dallas Willard, *Renovation of the Heart: Putting On the Character of Christ* (Colorado Springs, CO: NavPress, 2002), 57–59.

49. Keller, *The Reason for God*, 76.

50. Keller, *The Reason for God*, 76.

51. Alcorn, *If God Is Good*, 309.

52. Quoted in McDowell and Morrow, *Is God Just a Human Invention?*, 166–67 (emphasis mine).

53. McDowell and Morrow, *Is God Just a Human Invention?*, 166–67.

54. Keller, *The Reason for God*, 71.

55. John MacArthur, *Safe in the Arms of God: Truth from Heaven about the Death of a Child* (Nashville: Thomas Nelson, 2003), 90.

56. See Webb, *The Theology of Infant Salvation*.

57. Deuteronomy 1:39: "As for your little ones, who you said would become a prey, and your children, who today have no knowledge of good or evil, they shall go in there. And to them I will give it, and they shall possess it."

58. Isaiah 7:15–16: "He shall eat curds and honey when he knows how to refuse the evil and choose the good. For before the boy knows how to refuse the evil and choose the good, the land whose two kings you dread will be deserted."

59. Romans 9:11: "They were not yet born and had done nothing either good or bad—in order that God's purpose of election might continue, not because of works but because of him who calls."

60. Romans 14:14–20: "I know and am persuaded in the Lord Jesus that nothing is unclean in itself, but it is unclean for anyone who thinks it unclean. For if your brother is grieved by what you eat, you are no longer walking in love. By what you eat, do not destroy the one for whom Christ died. So do not let what you regard as good be spoken of as evil. For the kingdom of God is not a matter of eating and drinking but of righteousness and peace and joy in the Holy Spirit. Whoever thus serves Christ is acceptable to God and approved by men. So then let us pursue what makes for peace and for mutual upbuilding. Do not, for the sake of food, destroy the work of God. Everything is indeed clean, but it is wrong for anyone to make another stumble by what he eats."

61. Ephesians 2:8–9: "By grace you have been saved through faith. And this is not your own doing; it is the gift of God, not a result of works, so that no one may boast."

62. Matthew 19:14: "Jesus said, 'Let the little children come to me and do not hinder them, for to such belongs the kingdom

of heaven"'; Luke 17:2: "It would be better for him if a millstone were hung around his neck and he were cast into the sea than that he should cause one of these little ones to sin."

63. "The Bible clearly teaches that people are judged for their willful sins (Rev. 20:12–15; cf. Isa. 64:6–7; Matt. 5:48; 12:36; 2 Tim. 4:14; James 2:10–11) according to the standard of revelation they have received (Rom. 2:4–16; James 4:17). They are not condemned because a missionary never made it to them and they never heard the name of Jesus." Jonathan Morrow, "What about Those Who Have Never Heard about Jesus?" www.thinkchristianly.org/what-about-those-who-have-never-heard-about-jesus/.

64. Morrow, "What about Those."

65. Morrow, "What about Those."

66. Morrow, "What about Those."

67. Matthew 28:18–20: "Jesus came and said to them, 'All authority in heaven and on earth has been given to me. Go therefore and make disciples of all nations, baptizing them in the name of the Father and of the Son and of the Holy Spirit, teaching them to observe all that I have commanded you. And behold, I am with you always, to the end of the age.'"

68. Acts 17:30: "The times of ignorance God overlooked, but now he commands all people everywhere to repent."

69. Willard, *Renovation of the Heart*, 57–59.

70. Willard, *Renovation of the Heart*, 57–59.

71. Rob Bell, *Love Wins: A Book about Heaven, Hell, and the Fate of Every Person Who Ever Lived* (New York: HarperOne, 2012), 183, viii.

72. William Lane Craig, "No Other Name: A Middle Knowledge Perspective on the Exclusivity of Salvation through Christ," in *The Philosophical Challenge of Religious Diversity*, ed. Philip L. Quinn and Kevin Meeker (New York: Oxford University Press, 2000), 52.

73. John Stott defends annihilationism but in an extremely cautious way. He says, "I find the concept [of eternal conscious punishment in hell] intolerable and do not understand how people can live with it without either cauterizing their feelings or cracking under the strain. But our emotions are a fluctuating, unreliable guide to truth and must not be exalted to the place of supreme authority in determining it. As a committed Evangelical, my question must be—and is—not what does my heart tell me, but what does God's word say?" See David L. Edwards and John R. W. Stott, *Essentials: A Liberal-Evangelical Dialogue* (London: Hodder & Stoughton, 1988), 314–15.

74. John 5:28–29: "Do not marvel at this, for an hour is coming when all who are in the tombs will hear his voice and come out, those who have done good to the resurrection of life, and those who have done evil to the resurrection of judgment."

75. 2 Thessalonians 1:9: "They will suffer the punishment of eternal destruction, away from the presence of the Lord and from the glory of his might."

76. Matthew 8:12: "The sons of the kingdom will be thrown into the outer darkness. In that place there will be weeping and gnashing of teeth"; Matthew 22:13: "The king said to the attendants, 'Bind him hand and foot and cast him into the outer darkness. In that place there will be weeping and gnashing of teeth'"; Matthew 25:41: "He will say to those on his left, 'Depart from me, you cursed, into the eternal fire prepared for the devil and his angels'"; Mark 9:43–48: "If your hand causes you to sin, cut it off. It is better for you to enter life crippled than with two hands to go to hell, to the unquenchable fire. And if your foot causes you to sin, cut it off. It is better for you to enter life lame than with two feet to be thrown into hell. And if your eye causes you to sin, tear it out. It is better for you to enter the kingdom of God with one eye than with two eyes to be thrown into hell, 'where their worm does not die and the fire is not quenched'"; Jude v. 13: "Wild waves of the sea, casting up the foam of their own shame; wandering stars, for whom the gloom of utter darkness has been reserved forever"; Revelation 22:14–15: "Blessed are those who wash their robes, so that they may have the right to the tree of life and that they may enter the city by the gates. Outside are the dogs and sorcerers and the sexually immoral and murderers and idolaters, and everyone who loves and practices falsehood."

77. "I Am a Wiccan: Are You Saying I'm Going to Hell?," May 27, 2002, www.probe.org/i-am-a-wiccan-are-you-saying-im -going-to-hell/. Spelling errors have been altered for the sake of readability.

78. "I Am a Wiccan."

79. C. S. Lewis, *The Problem of Pain* (New York: HarperSanFrancisco, 2001), 130 (emphasis in the original).

80. "Americans Describe Their Views about Life after Death," October 21, 2003, www.barna.org/barna-update/5-barna -update/128-americans-describe-their-views-about-life-after-death.

CHAPTER 16

16

IS GOD A MEAN BULLY?

1. IS GOD GOOD?

Richard Dawkins, a former zoology professor at Oxford University, has made a name for himself as the world's most famous, most vocal critic of Christianity. At the beginning of the second chapter of his book *The God Delusion*, Dawkins writes,

> The God of the Old Testament is arguably the most unpleasant character in all fiction: jealous and proud of it; a petty, unjust, unforgiving control-freak; a

vindictive, bloodthirsty ethnic cleanser; a misogynistic, homophobic, racist, infanti-cidal, genocidal, filicidal, pestilential, megalomaniacal, sadomasochistic, capriciously malevolent bully.[1]

Dawkins quotes this line in his speeches and always gets a cheer from university students, presumably because it summarizes well what many students perceive to be the evils of Judaism and its largest offshoot, Christianity.

In this quotation, Dawkins is calling into question not so much whether the title "God" is appropriately applied to any being as whether God as named in the Old Testament is actually a moral being. It isn't a question of whether God exists but rather whether he is good.[2]

If what Dawkins says is true, it is certainly an embarrassing set of facts for Christians. On the other hand, is it possible he is overstating—or even misstating—the case and that his attack is just a smug, culturally insensitive applause line?

Obviously, Christianity's truth does not rest on what one seemingly cranky atheist writes, even if he is clever, and even if he writes it in a bestselling book. If there is any truth to these kinds of criticisms of Scripture, however, we need to know. If they are untrue, we ought to be able to explain why this is so.

Each of Dawkins's accusations condenses complex assumptions into apparently simple, self-evidently true words. But we have only one chapter in this volume in which to respond to these objections. Entire books have been written on the content of virtually every section in this chapter, and I encourage you to look at the authors and books cited in the references if you are interested in a more complete analysis.

In this chapter, we'll look at the implications of what we understand to be true about God in relation to four questions:

- Did God command genocide?

- Does God hate homosexuals?

- Does the Bible endorse slavery?

- Is the Bible oppressive to women?

In tackling these questions, we need to be careful not to reply to Dawkins with insults. We'll seek instead to approach each question in a culturally sensitive, historically informed manner that takes the Bible seriously. This might not stop critics in their tracks, but perhaps it will bring us nearer to the truth and remove a few barriers to genuine confidence in Scripture.

2. Understanding the God of the Old Testament from His Own Perspective

The Bible, as we've seen, presents God as having created a good world and a very good plan for his image bearers. Adam and Eve were given the significant calling of turning the entire earth into a garden while working in the loving, caring presence of their creator, yet, as we saw in our chapters on the metanarrative of Scripture, our first parents strayed. All of history from that point to this is of God seeking, finding, and winning back his image bearers.

One of the fall's consequences is self-centeredness. It's tempting to view everything—even God's redemptive work—from our own perspective rather than from God's. Not only does self-centered thinking distort our grasp of the truth but, as authors Michael Goheen and Craig Bartholomew point out, "It is treason—not against a rightful yet distant authority but rather against a loving, generous, ever-present Father. It is life turned away from God's loving intention."[3]

Because humans cannot obtain a God's-eye view of the world, some think seeing things from our own perspective is all we can do. This is like trying to discover the extent of the Gobi Desert while we're in the middle of it rather than while viewing it through satellite photos. We're too close to see the big picture.

What if, through some kind of revelation from one who *can* see the big picture, we were able to rethink our questions about the world and our place in it? This is exactly what the Bible claims to do, and we've already seen an impressive amount of evidence that this claim is valid. But before we present robust answers to difficult questions, we should seek to understand what the Bible says God is like.

The Old Testament begins with what we call the **Pentateuch** (*penta* meaning "five," and *teuch* meaning "scroll"): Genesis, Exodus, Leviticus, Numbers, and Deuteronomy. These five books show how God created, called out, taught, organized, and established a people holy for himself.

> *Pentateuch:* the first five books of the Bible (Genesis, Exodus, Leviticus, Numbers, and Deuteronomy).

So what was God up to? Well, as we saw in our chapters on the metanarrative of Scripture, God rescued his people from slavery in Egypt and resettled them to form a nation. The early books of the Bible form their history lesson so they would know where they came from and how they were set free from Egypt. In them, we also find the civil, cultural, and religious laws by which God directed them to live. The people were called Israelites after a man, Israel, who, before God changed his name, had been called Jacob. Israel/Jacob was the son of Isaac, Isaac was the son of Abraham, and Abraham was the patriarch of the Jewish race.

So who is this God? As revealed in the Old Testament, the God of Abraham, Isaac, and Jacob is vastly different from the regional gods worshipped in the ancient Near East. According to authors Wayne House and Dennis Jowers, all of these nations had developed systems of worship to explain why seasons change, why weather seems beyond our control, why people are born, and why, in spite of our hopes, we all die.[4] For most of history, each generation of adults transmitted the received stories to the younger generation. According to writings we have from this time period, many of these gods displayed the characteristics of which Dawkins accuses the God of the Bible.

But the God of Israel was a complete contrast to these regional gods. Isaiah 40:18 asks, "To whom then will you liken God, or what likeness compare with him?" We can see this in at least five ways:

1. The God of the Bible is portrayed as the God of all peoples of the earth and not merely an ethnic or regional deity (Ps. 46:8–9, 1 Kings 8:60).[5]

In the ancient Near East, gods operated in community—in a **pantheon**, a divine assembly, or with a consort. By contrast, the biblical God works alone and doesn't share his power or glory with another.[6]

Pantheon: the collection of gods belonging to a particular religion or mythology.

2. As opposed to inanimate statues worshipped by pagan cultures of gods who were found in the cycles of nature and incapable of revealing themselves, the God of the Bible reveals himself as a *living* God—fifteen times in the Old Testament and thirteen times in the New Testament.[7]

3. Although other gods were incomprehensible to the people who worshipped them, the God of the Old Testament is portrayed as the Lord of history (Dan. 4:25, Isa. 41:1–10) who actually communicates truthfully with his worshippers. Habakkuk 2:18 asks, "What profit is an idol when its maker has shaped it, a metal image, a teacher of lies?"[8]

4. In contrast to lifeless idols, the God of the Bible desires conversation with his chosen people and reveals himself in miraculous events, divine speech, and incarnational acts. Isaiah 1:18 says, "'Come now, let us reason together,' says the LORD."[9]

5. The God of Israel also is the creator-God, not hiding himself but making himself known in all of his works. Romans 1:19 says, "What can be known about God is plain to them, because God has shown it to them."[10]

In light of these differences, it is no wonder that the ancient Israelites were told not to worship other gods or make images of them. Unlike other gods worshipped in the ancient Near East, the one true God did not need his image to be awakened, fed, washed, and put to bed to ensure his continued presence. Nor would God allow his name to be harnessed for the selfish purposes of his worshippers, as was common with regional deities.[11]

Clearly, the Bible's revelations about God stand in stark contrast to the fantastical tales of heavenly power struggles and misbehavior told of the other gods of other nations. As Wayne House and Dennis Jowers put it, "God was willing to *prove* His existence, power, and faithfulness to His covenant to those who were believers in Him and those who were not."[12]

Yahweh: from the Hebrew for "I Am"; the personal and covenantal name of God used in the Old Testament.

So who did this God reveal himself to be? Scholar Walter Kaiser Jr. says that the primary name by which he reveals himself in the Old Testament is **Yahweh**, which means "I am." In other words, as Kaiser puts it, he was "the God who would be dynamically, effectively present when He was needed and when men called on Him."[13] In other words, God was known by his *character*: his attributes and qualities. This was not a static god about whom we tell outlandish stories but rather a dynamic, active, involved, *personal* God.[14]

The people of Israel were special to him. He describes them as follows:

1. His family (Exod. 4:22–23; Deut. 14:1).[15]

2. His people; they had a national identity (Exod. 6:7; 19:6).[16]

3. His congregation; they were his flock (Exod. 12:3).[17]

4. His treasured possession (Exod. 19:5).[18]

5. Those he made holy (Deut. 7:6; 14:2; 26:18–19).[19]

6. A kingdom of priests, a holy nation (Exod. 19:3–6).[20]

Kaiser's summary is powerful: "Israel was to be separate and holy; she was to be separate and as no other people on the face of the earth. As an elect or called people now being formed into a nation under God, holiness was not an optional feature."[21] The Israelites had a special status. In essence, they were God's priests to the world.[22]

In a way, God set the children of Israel apart in the same way husbands and wives are set apart for one another, by marriage covenant, pledging to put their energy into the relationship rather than into other things and maintain the purity and integrity of the relationship as a means of bringing good to one another and to the world. Physically, nothing stops them from wasting their energy elsewhere or entering into sexual relations with others, but they refuse because of their commitment to their marriage covenant. Abiding by this choice cultivates the soil in which it is possible for lifelong love to grow.[23]

Seeing how Israel was set apart clears some of the fog away from the Old Testament. This is especially true with certain difficult passages in which Israel was commanded to kill those in the surrounding nations.

3. WHY WOULD GOD COMMAND HIS PEOPLE TO WIPE OUT ENTIRE PEOPLE GROUPS?

Killing an entire people group is called **genocide**. If any person committed genocide, we would think it to be a heinous act. It's as simple as that. So why, many wonder, wouldn't God be judged accordingly? In fact, to this way of thinking, God's bigness only magnifies the cruelty. He's a bully.

> *Genocide:* the systematic killing of a particular racial, ethnic, or religious group.

Understanding the historical context may help us grapple with the question this section asks. As we discussed earlier, God brought his people out of Egypt and resettled them in an area that is occupied today by the modern nation of Israel and the territory of Palestine. For the people to settle and live there in peace, they first had to deal with two people groups, the Canaanites and the Amalekites, whose settlements and way of life posed a threat to their security and stability.

How were these surrounding nations a threat? God had promised Abraham a land where his people could settle so they could bring blessing to the nations. After leaving Egypt, they had no place to call their own. They were a minority culture in that land surrounded by wicked people who were morally and spiritually destructive. If the Israelites became like them, it would undermine God's saving purposes for the world. For Israel, idolatry and sexual immorality would be tantamount to acts of treason that would threaten the very identity of Israel itself. This created problems with the Canaanites and Amalekites. Let's look at each in turn.

The Canaanites and Amalekites

From history, we know that the Canaanites openly lived the kind of lifestyle God wanted his chosen people to avoid. The Canaanites were given over to sexual deviance such as temple prostitution, incest, and bestiality as well as child sacrifice—acts which are serious, punishable crimes, not mere lifestyle variations. They worshipped deities such as Anath, patroness of sex and war, who was described as wading in blood up to her neck and washing her hands in human gore, all with a heart full of joy.[24]

Moloch is another god worshipped by the Canaanites. Here's how the *International Standard Bible Encyclopedia* describes Moloch worship:

> The image of Moloch was a human figure with a bull's head and outstretched arms, ready to receive the children destined for sacrifice. The image of metal was heated red hot by a fire kindled within, and the children laid on its arms rolled off into the fiery pit below. In order to drown the cries of the victims, flutes were played, and drums were beaten; and mothers stood by without tears or sobs, to give the impression of the voluntary character of the offering.[25]

These are not the kind of people who make good neighbors. It would be like moving to a community in which all the surrounding homes were occupied by sexual predators and serial killers.

The Amalekites, the other people group in the region, did more than just conduct wicked practices. They also dedicated themselves relentlessly to Israel's destruction. This dedication continued long after the Israelites were settled in their new territory. The Amalekites were like a neighborhood gang, always waiting around the corner to hurt the Israelites however they could. Haman, the man who wanted to destroy Esther's relative Mordecai (as recorded in the book of Esther) was an "Agagite," which means he was of the line of King Agag, who was an Amalekite (Esther 3:1; 1 Sam. 15). Continuing the tradition of his forefathers, Haman aimed to utterly wipe out the Jews.[26]

In 1 Samuel 14:48, we are told that Israel's king, Saul, responded to the Amalekites' plundering of Israel with a defensive military action in which the battle account (1 Sam. 15:8, 20)[27] says that Saul utterly destroyed all the people.

What Does It Mean to "Utterly Destroy" a People?

But then Amalekites appear in 1 Samuel 27, 1 Samuel 30, and even 250 years later in 1 Chronicles 4:43. Clearly, the utter destruction of the Amalekite people did not literally happen. Similarly, in the tenth chapter of Joshua, we read how Joshua led the Israelites to attack the city of Makkedah and "left none remaining" (v. 28).[28] He then went to Libnah, where he also "left none remaining" (v. 30).[29] Same thing in Lachish, Eglon, Hebron, Debir, and so forth. Deuteronomy chapters 7 and 20 include similar language. The phrase for utterly wiping out someone, **haram** ("ban" or "consecration to destruction"), is used thirty-seven times of the Canaanites and ten times of the Amalekites.[30]

Confusingly, in other passages, we read that the Canaanites and the Amalekites were to be *driven* out, not *wiped* out. As theologian and blogger Matthew Flannagan notes,

> *Haram:* a Hebrew word translated as "total destruction" often used hyperbolically to communicate a strong defeat.

> The books of Deuteronomy and Exodus, in numerous places, state that the Canaanites are to be slowly driven out and expelled from the land, which is not the same thing as killing them. In fact, legislation is cited in the texts which clearly assumes that the Canaanites will survive Joshua's invasion. Immediately after stating that the Israelites should "destroy them totally" the text reads, "make no treaty with them, and show them no mercy. Do not intermarry with them. Do not give your daughters to their sons or take their daughters for your sons." If they were all supposed to be dead then why bother issuing instructions regarding treaties and intermarriage?"[31]

So how do we explain this? Well, for one thing, these accounts were written in a similar fashion to other epic stories of that time, according to certain historical and legal conventions that are unfamiliar in our own time.[32] Old Testament scholar Kenneth Kitchen writes,

> The type of rhetoric in question was a regular feature of military reports in the second and first millennia…. In the later fifteenth century BC Tuthmosis III could boast "the numerous army of Mitanni, was overthrown within the hour, annihilated totally, like those [now] non-existent" whereas, in fact, the forces of Mitanni lived to fight many another day, in the fifteenth and fourteenth centuries. Some centuries later, about 840/830 BC, Mesha king of Moab could boast that "Israel has utterly perished for always,"—a rather premature judgment at that date, by over a century! And so on, *ad libitum*. It is in this frame of reference that the Joshua rhetoric must also be understood.[33]

A simple reading of the text reveals that the Canaanites were not, in fact, wiped out. Flannagan notes,

> Over and over the text affirms that the land was still occupied by the Canaanites, who remain heavily armed and deeply entrenched in the cities. Astute readers will note that these are the same regions and the same cities that Joshua was said to have "destroyed all who breathed," left "no survivors" in just a few chapters earlier.[34]

So what is going on? Perhaps these accounts were, as was standard in battle accounts of the time, written with hyperbole (intentional exaggeration). Retired Notre Dame philosophy professor Alvin Plantinga compares it to a boxing fan yelling, "Knock his head off!" or a football fan rejoicing in the way his team "destroyed the defense."[35] As Paul Copan, a professor at Palm Beach Atlantic University and author of *Is God a Moral Monster?*, puts it, "Some might accuse Joshua of being misleading, or of getting it wrong. Not at all. He was speaking the language that everyone in his day would have understood. Rather than trying to deceive, Joshua was just saying he had fairly well trounced the enemy."[36]

This language of promised destruction was used in relation to not only Israel's enemies but Israel itself. In Jeremiah 25:9,[37] God promised to "utterly destroy" (*haram*) Judah and leave its cities "an everlasting desolation." But when we get to the end of Jeremiah, we see that although Judah's religious, political, economic, and military structures were incapacitated by the Babylonians, the people themselves were very much alive.

Is Aggression Ever Justified?

Based on what we have just seen, it seems that Israel's enemies were wicked, dangerous, and aggressive. They refused ample opportunities to change their ways.[38] Knowing what we know, it's not easy to classify these passages as a strong nation whipping up on a weaker one just because it is more powerful. Instead, Copan says that "we should think more along the lines of the Sicilian police invading a Mafia stronghold to remove a corrupting network of crime so that citizens can live in peace rather than in fear."[39]

The foregoing analysis does not answer all our questions, but it does help us see many of the Old Testament accounts in a new light. There will always be people who retort, "Oh yeah? Well what about 'X' or 'Y'?" When faced with these challenges, we need to learn to ask—as Peter Williams, warden of Tyndale House, Cambridge, suggests—"Do you think that's the whole story?" Framing the issue from a twenty-first-century progressive mindset is what C. S. Lewis called **chronological snobbery**.[40] Good Bible scholars try to approach their tasks with sensitivity to the cultural nuances and historical realities of the time rather than assuming that their way of thinking is superior just because it is newer.

> **Chronological Snobbery:** a term used to identify the fallacious thinking that ideas of an older time are inherently inferior to present ideas simply by virtue of their temporal priority.

> **Homophobia:** the fear of homosexuals.

One fact, though, changes our deliberations entirely. If God is the all-knowing, all-loving, all-powerful creator of the universe, then his perspective on this world's events is by necessity higher than our perspective as mere humans. If God has complete foreknowledge, which Scripture claims he does, he would know what we couldn't: that a particular group needs to be subdued and that failing to drive them out would over the long term generate unthinkable harms.

Today, though, the charge that God is genocidal isn't as emotionally explosive as the charge that he is homophobic. **Homophobia**, strictly speaking, means the fear of homosexuals. Today, though, it is taken to mean an intense dislike of homosexuals or even the failure to approve of the homosexual lifestyle. God, according to Richard Dawkins, is insensitive and cruel to gay people and ought to be considered a homophobe. Let's take up this topic and see what we can make of it.

IS GOD A MEAN BULLY?

4. Does God Hate Homosexuals?

The most quoted passage about sexuality in the Old Testament is probably Leviticus 18:6–23, which refers to "uncovering nakedness," a euphemism for sexual relations that literally means "dis-covering the sex of."[41] The passage prohibits people from having sexual relationships with their parents, with a parent's spouse, with their siblings or their siblings' spouses, with their children or grandchildren or with their spouses, with close relatives, with married neighbors, with someone of the same sex, or with animals. God promised that if people did these things, the land itself would "vomit" them out (Lev. 18:24–30).[42] Those who refused to pursue sexual purity or to repent of their sexual sin were to be "cut off," or made to leave the community. In some cases, Levitical law called for the death penalty. Although it seems extreme today, capital punishment for sexual offenses was not uncommon in history. In fact, in Muslim nations following sharia law, sexual offenses such as adultery and homosexuality are considered *hudud* crimes—crimes against God himself—and are punishable by stoning or mutilation.

While the Levitical law focuses on all kinds of sexual sin, some believers have narrowly emphasized those prohibiting homosexual behavior, giving the impression that the Bible cruelly and insensitively targets those who experience same-sex attraction. Bearing down on only one kind of sexual sin not only seems hypocritical but also distracts from the true biblical focus, which is on protecting people from sexual corruption and abuse and providing a way for people who have wrongly acted on their sexual impulses to be redeemed.

In this section, we will consider the question of homosexuality in the larger context of what key biblical passages say about marriage and sexuality in general. First, though, we must understand where modern views of sexuality come from and why they cause so many people to recoil when they read passages such as Leviticus 18–20. Much of what people believe about sexuality today can be traced to an Austrian psychoanalyst named Sigmund Freud, who hypothesized that our conscious behavior is shaped by our unconscious recollection of our past experiences. Through **psychoanalysis**, he believed he could uncover people's unconscious thoughts and motivations and then identify the stage of human development in which people were stuck so they could be freed.[43]

Freud thought the suppression of sexual desire hurt people. This is so widely believed today that sexual immorality is now defined as the failure to permit people to pursue sexual pleasure any way they see fit. In the 1950s, a researcher named Alfred Kinsey issued two reports, *Sexual Behavior in the Human Male* (1948) and *Sexual Behavior in the Human Female* (1953), which challenged traditional views on sex and marriage. Kinsey's reports seemed scientific, and who can argue with science?

To those convinced of Freud's and Kinsey's arguments, it is difficult to imagine that God is the one who designed sex and that he made it to be normal and healthy. Rather, God is seen as the enemy of freedom and it's believed that restricting sexual freedom makes people unhealthy, abnormal, and mean.[44]

To Freud and Kinsey, sex is something we do with our bodies; to God, sex is something we do with our souls as well as our bodies. Our sexual behavior reflects our internal understanding of

> *Psychoanalysis:* an approach to psychology developed by Sigmund Freud whereby a psychologist attempts to resolve a patient's psychological problems by uncovering and discussing the patient's unconscious, unfulfilled, and repressed desires.

who we are as people and how we ought to treat others. Professor G. A. Cooke frames it this way: "The ancient mind fastened on the outward acts revealing the inward state. While the modern mind goes directly to the internal condition."[45] The biblical passage assumes that people have the ability to avoid acting on destructive feelings and to fail to do so leads to corruption and abuse.

Having a whole section in the law on sexual activity underscores a simple point: God views sexual immorality as a tipping point toward idolatry. As Michael Goheen and Craig Bartholomew express it,

> The close connection between idolatry and adultery in Scripture helps us to see the religious and relational nature of sin. A husband has the right to the exclusive loyalty of his wife, and the wife to that of her husband. Marriage is an exclusive relationship that admits no third party. Sin is portrayed in Scripture as religious adultery: a third party (some idol) has insinuated itself into that exclusive relationship and adulterated it. Sin is religious and relational: it is against God.[46]

To God, sexual sin is not just those innocent, private acts between two people for which God enjoys punishing people. Jeremiah 7:19 says, "'Is it I whom they provoke?' declares the LORD. Is it not themselves, to their own shame?" Sexual sin is an act of rebellion against God's design for his image bearers. It is saying, in essence, "I am so intent on satisfying my sexual passions that I am willing to break down my community, destroy relationships, shatter trust, forego God's plan for my life, and choke off the blessing God intends for those around me." Sexual sin takes many of the *very good* aspects of creation and turns them into a source of hurt and diminishment. Such impudence always hurts those most vulnerable: women and children. This understanding explains why sexual impurity mattered so greatly to the first group of people to receive the Levitical commands about sexual ethics, the ancient nation of Israel. It threatened to unravel the most delicate threads holding the community together. No one *had* to remain a member of this community, but if one chose as much, he was to act the part of those *set apart*.

Still, should sexual purity mean so much that people who violate it should be *killed*? The penalty listed in Leviticus 18 was that the offenders were to be "cut off," or made to leave the community. Under what circumstances were they to be killed instead? We don't know. Perhaps it was just a strongly worded warning, akin to what we saw earlier with the wording of battle victory reports. Or perhaps there were circumstances in which sexual offenders who refused to repent and refused to leave would actually lose their lives, not just their place in the community.

> The sacrificial system made it clear that God's goal was not to create a nation of vigilantes who roamed around finding people to stone but rather to create a people who pursued purity in every area of life.

Christians who have used the Levitical passages to unfairly target homosexuality and those who are offended by this are both missing the point, which is that God does not express his mercy by overlooking sin but by providing a way of repentance. Leviticus makes provisions for sacrifices that will atone for sin of various kinds (Lev. 6:1–7), and the most common phrase in the instructions relating to the Levitical sacrifice was forgiveness (Lev. 1:4; 4:20, 26, 31, 35; 5:10, 16; 16:20–22). Even in the Old Testament, we see that God arranged for a substitute, a ransom, in the form of an animal to be sacrificed. This was a very costly thing that underscored how seriously God took Israel's purity. As Walter Kaiser puts it, "Forgiveness was not and could not be cheap, just as human forgiveness necessitated that someone pay if the reality of forgiveness were ever to be more than a cliché."[47] The sacrificial system made it clear that God's goal was not to create a nation of vigilantes who roamed around finding people to stone but rather to create a people who pursued purity in every area of life.

To summarize, the children of Israel were a set-apart community. If they failed to act as those set apart, provision was made for them to repent and be forgiven. If they refused to repent, they forfeited their right to live in the community and possibly risked being put to death. The big question, then, is not specifically how homosexuality was treated in the Old Testament, for all sexual impurity was treated equally. God expected self-discipline, and we have every indication that the nation was healthy and prosperous when it was and dysfunctional and abusive when it was not.

The question for us today is different than it was for Israel. We do not live in a nation that was chosen by God in the same way Israel was. Just as there were **sojourners** who joined Israel's community, Christians today are sojourners in society. As sojourners, Christians are to bring biblical standards of purity to bear by their behavior. First Peter 2:11–12 says, "Beloved, I urge you as sojourners and exiles to abstain from the passions of the flesh, which wage war against your soul.

> *Sojourner:* someone who lives in a particular place for an extended period of time but whose home is somewhere else.

Keep your conduct among the Gentiles honorable, so that when they speak against you as evildoers, they may see your good deeds and glorify God on the day of visitation."

Living pure, set-apart lives in a society given over to evil is not an easy thing to do. It is much easier to give in to society's values than to live in a way that challenges them. It can be done, though, as the early Christians living in Rome demonstrated. When Christianity first arose, Rome was a shockingly perverse society, even by today's standards. Everything was fair game sexually, including preying sexually on children.[48] It is fashionable to think that sexually permissive cultures offer more freedom. The truth is, women and children end up as victims. Women live in fear of being raped. Wives are afraid of being discarded. Mothers worry that their kids will be molested. Beneath the airbrushed image is an ugly reality that treats women as objects and children as dispensable.

The Bible's call to faithfulness is not anti-sex. Quite the opposite. Biblical sexual mores break the shackles of false freedom and bring those imprisoned by it into the light of Christ, where there is true freedom (John 8:36).

Sometimes evidence of the biblical truth about sexuality arises in unexpected places, such as in a class at Harvard University. For many years, Dr. Armand Nicholi has taught a popular class at Harvard comparing the worldviews of Sigmund Freud, whose views of sexuality helped spark the sexual revolution, and C. S. Lewis, the famous author and scholar who was one of Freud's critics.[49] Lewis does not so much refute Freud's ideas but rather shows how anemic they are in comparison to a biblical view of sexuality. According to Nicholi, "Lewis goes beyond Freud to argue that people who control their sexual impulses understand their sexuality *more* than people who fail at controlling. 'Virtue—even attempted virtue—brings light; indulgence brings fog.'"[50]

Interestingly, Nicholi, who plays the role of an impartial observer in the discussions with his students, says in his capacity as a psychiatrist,

> From my clinical practice of many years and my research on young adults who come from divorced families, I can say unequivocally that a great deal of the unhappiness in our society results from failure to understand the distinction between being in love (Eros) and loving in the deeper sense (Agape).[51]

Referencing Lewis, he concludes that "the intense feeling of being in love ought to change to a deeper, more comfortable and mature kind of love based on the will as well as on feeling."[52] Put simply, to be sexually mature is to restrain ourselves from acting on our sexual impulses outside of man/woman marriage, whether those impulses are heterosexual or homosexual. The best love is based on our wills, not just our feelings. This is how God made us. Nicholi's studies of Harvard students who had experienced a Christian conversion shows how profound this sort of love can be. Before their conversions, students described their sexual relationships as "less than satisfactory and as contributing little to providing the emotional closeness they desired."[53] Afterward, though, even though the biblical standard of chastity inside of marriage seems strict by modern standards, "they found these clear-cut boundaries less confusing than no boundaries at all and helpful in relating to members of the opposite sex 'as persons rather than sexual objects.'"[54]

> Inside the marriage bond, though, what would otherwise be using another person as an object becomes two people breathing life into each other.

This is an awesome realization, and it helps us better understand God's viewpoint. To violate God's sexual standards diminishes us as image bearers of God. It sounds harsh, but it's as if we say to our sexual partners, "By following my own rules rather than God's, I am making my desires my idol, and you must participate in the sacrifice by allowing me to use you as an object by which I can achieve satisfaction." The other person's willingness to be used doesn't make it any less selfish. In fact, it makes both individuals selfish: two people complicit in using one another.

Inside the marriage bond, though, what would otherwise be using another person as an object becomes two people breathing life into each other. In Rome, it was this aspect of Christian morality that seemed to have the most influence. Of Christians, it was said that "they share their table with strangers, but not their spouses with strangers."[55] The morality of Christian families gave them such an advantage in society that Galen, a Greek physician, said that Christians had such an "intense desire to attain moral excellence that they are in no way inferior to true philosophers."[56] Ultimately, the whole society began to see the wisdom of Christian sexual morality and passed laws protecting marriage and prohibiting the sexual exploitation of children.

As we have seen throughout Scripture, God and his people are in a covenant relationship, and the marriage relationship between a man and a woman mirrors how we relate to God in this way. So does this mean God hates homosexuals? No. Those who struggle with homosexual attraction are just as much covenant members of the bride of Christ—the church—as anyone else. Their will to remain faithful to God by refraining from homosexual

IS GOD A MEAN BULLY?

behavior, as with those who experience heterosexual attraction also refrain from sexual behavior outside of man/woman marriage, breathes life into the church as it breathes into them through Christ.

To summarize, when we see what the Old Testament really claims about sexuality, it becomes clear that these passages are not targeting homosexuals for discrimination. This explanation may not satisfy those who lodge the criticism in the first place, but Christianity is not a viewpoint that becomes more popular the less it claims to be true. As Chuck Colson, who went from working for a US president to prison to launching the world's largest Christian ministry to prisoners, phrases it,

> Orthodoxy often requires us to be hard precisely where the world is soft, and soft where the world is hard. It means condemning the homosexual lifestyle and being labeled bigots. It means caring for AIDS patients though many think us fools. It means respecting the life of law though our culture is increasingly lawless. It means visiting the prisoners who offend that law though our culture would prefer to forget them. In every way that matters, Christianity is an affront to the world; it is countercultural.[57]

D. A. Carson agrees, pointing out that "the plurality of errors and heresies that our generation confronts demands that lines be drawn—thoughtfully, carefully, humbly, corrigibly, but drawn nonetheless."[58]

5. DOES THE BIBLE ENDORSE SLAVERY?

Slavery is in the Bible. Abraham had slaves and even had a child by one of them, Hagar, when his wife insisted on it.[59] We need to be careful, though, not to associate the word *slavery* in the Old Testament with the abusive slavery of the antebellum South in America. The term translated "slave" or "servant" (*ebed*) is really emphasizing a dynamic relationship of dependency, not ownership.[60]

> *Ebed:* a Hebrew word translated as "servant" or "slave"; communicates a relationship of dependency, not ownership.

Slavery has been common everywhere and at all times throughout history. What is different is the Bible's emphasis on the creational norm that *everyone* bears the image of God (Gen. 1:26–27).[61] We see this where Job recognized that his bondservants were just as much image bearers of God as he was and that he would have to answer to God if he mistreated them (Job 31:13–14).[62] The Old Testament law makes provisions for the care and protection of slaves in Leviticus 19, 22, 25, and Deuteronomy 5, 15, 16, and 21.

In the New Testament, slaves are mentioned as well, but not in the way we might expect if Christianity by its nature endorsed slavery. For example, in Romans 16:9, Paul greets slaves by referring to them using terms of equality such as *kinsmen, fellow prisoners,* and *fellow workers.* Believers were to worship together and even "greet one another with a holy kiss" (v. 16, in the context of giving greetings to certain believers by name, including those known to be slaves).[63] Equality with slaves was a deeply radical belief for that time. More common was the view of Aristotle, who believed that some humans were slaves by nature.[64]

The radical equality of slaves in the New Testament is everywhere in the text, and clear: *all* are one in Christ Jesus no matter their role in life (Gal. 3:28; 1 Cor. 12:13; Col. 3:11).[65] Paul commanded that the slave Onesimus be treated as a brother by Philemon (Philem. v. 16).[66] Revelation 18:11–13[67] condemns trading humans as "cargo," echoing Ezekiel 27:13.[68] First Timothy 1:9–10[69] condemns "kidnappers," people who forced humans into slavery.

But if God created everyone with equal dignity and in his image, why would the Bible not expressly and universally condemn slavery? Let's look at this question from five perspectives:

First, Christianity did not invent slavery. Virtually every society at that time had slaves. It was universal. It would not have been the case that someone would pick up the Torah and think, *Hey, this thing called slavery is pretty cool. I think I'll get a slave for myself.*

Second, we should put the biblical discussion in its cultural context. The ancient Near Eastern cultural context is different from our modern postcolonial context. The two biggest causes of slavery in the ancient world were war and poverty, not skin color. According to Old Testament scholar Christopher J. H. Wright, the slavery found in ancient Israel was

> qualitatively vastly different from slavery in the large imperial civilizations—the contemporary ancient Near Eastern empires, and especially the latter empires of the Greeks and Romans. There the slave markets were glutted with captives of war and displaced peoples, and slaves were put to degrading and dehumanizing labour. And, of course, Israelite slavery was even more different from the ghastly commercialized and massive-scale slave trade that Arabs, Europeans and Americans perpetrated upon Africa.[70]

How was slavery in Israel qualitatively different? First, people could actually enter into slavery in order to achieve their financial objectives. Because there was no bank to which they could go to get a loan to buy a piece of property, they would go to work as a "slave" to the property's owner for an agreed-upon period of time. This kind of slavery was not "chattel" slavery (forced servitude and treatment as an object rather than as a person). In fact, banning this kind of slavery would have made it impossible for poor people to advance economically. Second, the laws of Israel were very specific in how to treat slaves with dignity, which must have been a great relief to those who had been slaves elsewhere.

Please understand: this is not a justification of chattel slavery, nor is it some kind of absolution for Christians who participated in this type of slavery in the West or those who justified dehumanizing slaves by twisting Scripture. It is simply to point out the fact that slavery in ancient Israel was different, even though we use the same word to describe it.[71]

Third, just because slavery is mentioned and provisions are made for it does not mean that Scripture endorses slavery. Rather, it acknowledges slavery's existence and makes specific provisions to protect slaves from the abuse and the stripping away of their rights that was common in the ancient Near East. As we saw earlier, the humane laws outlined in the Torah were a vast improvement over the laws of other ancient Near East nations.

Fourth, we need to remember that Israel was not God's ideal society. Israel came out of slavery and was already corrupt and broken just like the rest of the peoples of the world. God's redemptive work with them was a progressive work. Even though slavery in ancient Israel differed markedly from slavery in other cultures, it was still far from representing God's ideal of people who would steward the earth as his image bearers.

An uncomfortable question, but one that must be addressed, is how fast should we expect such a society to progress? Surely some people say "We need to change slowly," because they benefit from things being the way they are and don't really want them to change at all. But this does not mean that the "Change everything *now*" approach is therefore correct. As author John Mark Reynolds observes, "Economic slavery is evil, but immediate abolition could have been a worse evil, possibly leading to violence, starvation, and total societal collapse."[72] Immediate abolition would have created lots of problems; a moral tipping point had to be reached over time. Instant, destabilizing change almost always ends in misery, whereas gradual change based on right principles stands a good chance of producing long-term good.

> Even though slavery in ancient Israel differed markedly from slavery in other cultures, it was still far from representing God's ideal of people who would steward the earth as his image bearers.

Fifth, when it comes to the New Testament, Jesus was not silent on slavery. Jesus was about setting spiritual captives free, and this freedom had real-world effects. When Jesus began his public ministry, he stood in the synagogue to read the following passage: "The Spirit of the Lord is upon me, because he has anointed me to proclaim good news to the poor. He has sent me to proclaim liberty to the captives and recovering of sight to the blind, to set at liberty those who are oppressed" (Luke 4:18). Because Jesus was quoting Isaiah 61:1–2[73]—which seems to deal with literal captives, not just spiritual captives—we can see the relationship between humanity's spiritual and physical condition in a new way. Being no longer helplessly bound to sin, our lives begin to change. Society begins to change. The conditions in which people find themselves, whether through their own sin or the sin of others, begins to change.

In later times, the foundation laid down in the Old Testament and continued through the ministry of Christ galvanized Christian opposition to chattel slavery. In some cultures, such as in America, it took a shamefully long time. Still, before Christianity influenced cultures, every civilization thought slavery was normal and acceptable. Christians inspired by Jesus's proclamation of freedom for the captives changed that.[74]

> Before Christianity influenced cultures, every civilization thought slavery was normal and acceptable. Christians inspired by Jesus's proclamation of freedom for the captives changed that.

We must also keep in mind that slavery is still an issue today. This is particularly the case with sex trafficking, which results from a refusal to live by the ethic of sexual integrity established in the Bible. In the end, the most stable opposition comes from acknowledging and practicing that all humans are made in the image of God and have inherent dignity. The Judeo-Christian worldview—and not others, including

Secularism—laid this foundation. As Sean McDowell and Jonathan Morrow put it, "If you remove God from the equation, you also remove inherent human dignity and equality."[75]

6. Isn't the Bible Oppressive to Women?

We take women's rights so much for granted today that it is easy to forget how the Judeo-Christian worldview made them possible. Ideas have consequences for people, and the biblical idea of human dignity has led to an about-face in which women are treated as equally valuable to men in areas influenced by Christianity. This is not the case in most other places in history, even today.

> *Misogyny:* the hatred or dislike of women.

The dislike of women or girls is called **misogyny**. Many people in history, including Christians, have acted in misogynistic ways by abusing or diminishing women. Does this mean, as Richard Dawkins seems to think, that the Bible is inherently misogynistic? From our modern perspective, it might seem that the Bible, especially the Old Testament, is domineering or unfair toward women. At the time it was written, however, the commands in the Old Testament provided women unprecedented protection from and even legal recourse against men's anger, pride, lust, and jealousy.

Even today, equal treatment for women is a pipe dream in most of the world. So when Dawkins characterizes God as a misogynist, he is comparing the Bible to his notion of an ideal state, which does not exist and for which, as an atheist, he has no rational basis. In a fallen world, we should not ask why the Christian worldview is not being lived perfectly but whether, in spite of the flaws of its adherents, the Christian worldview best describes the contours of the world as it actually is. When viewed from this perspective, we can see that the Christian worldview gives unparalleled dignity to women. In short, Jesus is good news for women.

Being a woman in the ancient world would have been extremely challenging. Canaanite and Amalekite civilizations were shockingly abusive to women. Greek and Roman cultures were also difficult for women. According to scholar Rodney Stark,

> Women were in relative short supply owing to female infanticide, practiced by all classes, and to the additional deaths caused by abortion. The status of women was very low. Girls received little or no education ... were married at puberty and often before. Under Athenian law a woman was classified as a child, regardless of age, and therefore was the legal property of some man at all stages of her life. Males could divorce by simply ordering a wife out of the household.[76]

In Rome, as author Alvin Schmidt points out, *patria potestas* and *pater familias* gave the husband and father "supreme, absolute power over his children and grandchildren, even when they were grown. He alone had the power to divorce his wife, and he also possessed the power to execute his children. He could even execute his married daughter if she committed adultery in his or her husband's house."[77]

The Old Testament treats women very differently from other cultures of that time, starting with the affirmation in Genesis that men and women *both* bear God's image, and Levitical law, which provided unprecedented protection of women. For example, Israelites were not

IS GOD A MEAN BULLY?

to treat female prisoners of war as sex objects. They were to be either married or released (Deut. 21:10–14).[78] Leviticus chapter 12 says that women who have recently given birth or who are in their monthly cycle are to be considered unclean, which gave them a break from daily chores, ensured proper hygiene, and protected them from sexual advances during the period of menstruation.

In Jesus's ministry, women gained a stature unheard of even in the context of Israel. Jesus healed several women of diseases, interacted with women of different races, and extended forgiveness to women who had committed sexual sin. All of these acts were radically progressive (and, many have argued, even feminist) for his time and context. Women followers supported Jesus's ministry, were the last to leave the cross, and were the first to arrive at the empty tomb. Jesus treated women with the dignity of their inherent value as image bearers.

The apostle Paul, although he's often attacked for his perceived low view of women, considered at least twelve women coworkers in his ministry (Acts 16:14–15, 40;1 Cor. 1:11; Phil. 4:2–3; Col. 4:15).[79] This would have been unprecedented because women were either ignored or shunned in religious conversation at that time. Moreover, Paul calls husbands to love their wives "just as Christ loved the church and gave himself up for her" (Eph. 5:25). He even instituted new respect for children, teaching fathers to "not provoke your children to anger, but bring them up in the discipline and instruction of the Lord" (Eph. 6:4).

Paul emphasized that the gospel is good news to all, and available to all, regardless of gender or status:

> In Christ Jesus you are all sons of God, through faith. For as many of you as were baptized into Christ have put on Christ. There is neither Jew nor Greek, there is neither slave nor free, there is no male and female, for you are all one in Christ Jesus. And if you are Christ's, then you are Abraham's offspring, heirs according to promise. (Gal. 3:26–29)

Similarly, the apostle Peter reminds Christian husbands to treat their wives with "honor" because "they are heirs with you of the grace of life" (1 Pet. 3:7).

In light of all of this, is it any wonder that "the ancient sources and modern historians agree that primary conversion to Christianity was far more prevalent among females than males"?[80] Christianity that was properly understood and applied was very good news for women.

Obviously, other worldviews call Christianity's goodness for women into question. New Spiritualist Eckhart Tolle says that the story of history is the story of the male form dominating the female form, which led to the Inquisition and witch burning (a not-so-subtle accusation against Christianity). "Males who denied the feminine even within themselves were now running the world, a world that was totally out of balance," he says. "The rest is history or rather a case history of insanity."[81]

> Human sinfulness of all kinds has caused all manner of moral evil, with women and children often being targeted. Christianity, when properly understood and practiced, does not lead to the oppression of women. Any such oppression has occurred in spite of Christian convictions, not because of them.

Some feminist historians, in trying to bolster claims that Christianity was a force for evil, claim that millions were killed in witch hunts perpetrated by the church.[82] Feminist Mary Daly accepts reports of nine million people being killed as witches, most of whom were women.[83] Scholars examining the issue have arrived at a still appalling but drastically lower number of around 150 to 300 hundred people per year in Europe and North America (three-quarters of whom were women) over the course of three hundred years.[84] Such witch trials ended in the aftermath of nineteen accused witches being executed in Salem, Massachusetts. Governor Sir William Phips, horrified at how things had gotten out of hand, joined respected ministers such as Deodat Lawson, Increase Mather, and Samuel Willard in bringing the Salem trials to an end.[85] Today we see such trials and executions as an example of the bizarre excess that can occur when people become exercised about demonic activity. Tragic as these deaths were, it is a case of rhetorical excess to call them a holocaust, a term implying slaughter on a massacre and that is properly applied to the eleven million killed by the Nazis, the tens of millions starved to death in the USSR under Stalin, the seventy-two million killed under Mao in China, or even the forty thousand or so who had their heads lopped off during a two-year period of the French Revolution.

Human sinfulness of all kinds has caused all manner of moral evil, with women and children often being targeted. At the same time, if we are to be intellectually honest, Christianity, when properly understood and practiced, does not lead to the oppression of women.[86] Any such oppression has occurred in spite of Christian convictions, not because of them.

7. What Kind of God Is This, Really?

Our examination of Richard Dawkins's accusations—that Christianity upholds genocide, homophobia, slavery, and misogyny—shows that his claims are exaggerated, culturally insensitive, and factually wrong. Moreover, his assumption that his atheistic worldview has produced or is capable of producing better results is a conclusion for which there is no evidence.

> **Megalomania:** a psychopathic condition characterized by delusions of grandeur.

Still, as we draw this chapter to a close, we should tackle one more problem. Dawkins claimed that God is megalomaniacal. The term **megalomania** refers to a delusional condition in which someone considers himself to be worthy of worship. I have heard people say (and you probably have too), "*I just can't love or worship a God who is so self-centered.*" But again, in our sin nature, we assume that *we* are viewing the world properly and that *God* is not. It is hardly different from the approach to the world we saw our first parents take in the garden of Eden. Author and speaker Alex McFarland addresses this issue:

> Worship does relate to God's own self-knowledge and His comprehensive understanding of us. God must treat Himself as the greatest good because He is the greatest good. He is the perfect being based on His nature, apart from any function related to us. If God treats anything else as the greatest good, then He is not affirming the truth about Himself. It is wrong for us to treat ourselves as the greatest good because we are not. It is not wrong for God to treat Himself as the greatest good because He

is. He is not the one who benefits from our worship; rather worship allows us to see Him as He is and so continues the extension of His love and goodness in creation.[87]

In order to assume that God is megalomaniacal, we would have to assume that he is not who he claims to be and that we are somehow in a special position to know this. In other words, we can reduce God only by being megalomaniacal ourselves. As pastor Tim Keller puts it, "Without the gospel, our hearts have to manufacture self-esteem by comparing our group with other groups. But the gospel tells us we are all unclean without Christ, and all clean in Him."[88]

The desire to diminish God and elevate ourselves is not just a problem for Richard Dawkins; it's also a problem for you and me. This problem is called **idolatry**. When we judge God, we usually judge him from the standpoint of power: "If I were in charge, I would do it differently." But we don't have that kind of power, nor do we know the things God knows. Our delusions of power, then, are actually idols. As attorney and author Ken Sande notes, once we embrace an idol, even if it is an utterly false god, it still changes us. First we *desire*

> *Idolatry:* the act of worshipping or valuing something above God; entertaining thoughts about God that are unworthy of him.

things to be the way we want them, then we *demand* that they are that way, then we judge those we think are keeping things from being the way we want them, and then ultimately we seek to punish those who do not conform to our expectations.

Idols always demand sacrifices, and what we end up sacrificing are our own best interests. I remember being a child in a grumpy mood during an ice cream stop. Instead of ice cream, I wanted a hamburger. My parents said no. To "punish" them, I refused to order any ice cream. It didn't occur to me until years later that my refusal to eat ice cream was not a punishment to my parents. It saved them a couple of bucks, and they happily enjoyed their ice cream while I sat in the backseat and pouted. Similarly, our attempts to "punish" God always end up hurting us more.

Let's return to a theme repeated throughout this volume. The Christian insists that the good news of Jesus Christ is that he became the sacrifice for sin so grievous it called for our own deaths. Brian Jones says,

> The older translations of the Bible such as the King James, American Standard, and New American Standard versions all use the word *propitiation* as a translation of *hilasterion* [a propitiatory gift for the gods], while the newer English translations have opted to translate it with phrases like 'sacrifice of atonement' or 'sacrifice for sin.' The meaning is the same, regardless. *Hilasterion* was used to describe offerings made in pagan temples. Surprisingly, Paul chose this exact word to capture the essence of the work of Christ on the cross.[89]

In many pagan religions, the gods are manipulated and soothed and even fed by sacrifices. Two things, however, make the Christian idea very different. First, God provided the gift himself through Christ. He *became* the gift.[90] As Tim Keller states,

> If your fundamental is a man dying on the cross for his enemies, if the very heart of your self-image and your religion is a man praying for his enemies as he died

for them, sacrificing for them, loving them—if that sinks into your heart of hearts, it's going to produce the kind of life that the early Christians produced. The most inclusive possible life out of the most exclusive possible claim—and that is that this is the truth. But what is the truth? The truth is a God become weak, loving, and dying for the people who opposed him, dying forgiving them.[91]

Second, God did this to demonstrate his justice. In other words, God is not like the gods of history, restless through unsatisfied lusts. God's anger is justified *because true injustice has occurred*. To us, anger is usually a sign of losing control, as in road rage. To God, anger is a determination to do what is right, whatever the cost, and according to the Bible the cost was self-sacrifice. Romans 3:21–26 says,

> The righteousness of God has been manifested apart from the law, although the Law and the Prophets bear witness to it—the righteousness of God through faith in Jesus Christ for all who believe. For there is no distinction: for all have sinned and fall short of the glory of God, and are justified by his grace as a gift, through the redemption that is in Christ Jesus, whom God put forward as a propitiation by his blood, to be received by faith. This was to show God's righteousness, because in his divine forbearance he had passed over former sins. It was to show his righteousness at the present time, so that he might be just and the justifier of the one who has faith in Jesus.

8. Conclusion

It's practically impossible for our human imagination to conceive of a love so deep that the lover would sacrifice everything for his beloved. In fact, we could not conceive of it without specific revelation from God. This kind of love is like a judge who, in pronouncing the death penalty for a guilty killer, steps down and accepts the sentence himself. We can't conceive of this. But the biblical record describes that it did happen almost just that way, and in paying our penalty himself, God demonstrated a kind of love we can only hope that people like Richard Dawkins someday come to discover.

> It's practically impossible for our human imagination to conceive of a love so deep that the lover would sacrifice everything for his beloved.

Endnotes

1. Richard Dawkins, *The God Delusion* (New York: Houghton Mifflin, 2006), 51.

2. For a thorough analysis of the goodness of God from a theological and philosophical perspective, see David Baggtett and Jerry L. Walls, *Good God: The Theistic Foundations of Morality* (New York: Oxford University Press, 2011).

3. Michael W. Goheen and Craig G. Bartholomew, *Living at the Crossroads: An Introduction to Christian Worldview* (Grand Rapids, MI: Baker Academic, 2008), 47.

4. H. Wayne House and Dennis W. Jowers, *Reasons for Our Hope: An Introduction to Christian Apologetics* (Nashville: B&H Academic, 2011), 123.

5. House and Jowers, *Reasons for Our Hope*, particularly chap. 9: "Apologetics in the Old Testament." Psalm 46:8–9: "Come, behold the works of the LORD, how he has brought desolations on the earth. He makes wars cease to the end of the earth; he breaks the bow and shatters the spear; he burns the chariots with fire"; 1 Kings 8:60: "All the peoples of the earth may

know that the LORD is God; there is no other."

6. See John H. Walton, "Interpreting the Bible as an Ancient Near Eastern Document," *Israel: Ancient Kingdom or Late Invention?*, ed. Daniel I. Block (Nashville: B&H Academic, 2008), 313–18.

7. House and Jowers, *Reasons for Our Hope*, particularly chap. 9: "Apologetics in the Old Testament."

8. House and Jowers, *Reasons for Our Hope*, particularly chap. 9: "Apologetics in the Old Testament."

9. House and Jowers, *Reasons for Our Hope*, particularly chap. 9: "Apologetics in the Old Testament."

10. House and Jowers, *Reasons for Our Hope*, particularly chap. 9: "Apologetics in the Old Testament."

11. In an ancient Near Eastern setting, the third commandment would have been understood as a prohibition against misusing God's name in an attempt to manipulate or harness his power for one's own selfish purposes. The "name" of a given pagan deity was frequently invoked as a technique—a magical incantation—to master supernatural forces to pursue earthly or material success. This third commandment prohibits using the name Yahweh ("the LORD") for this type of purpose. See Walton, "Interpreting the Bible as an Ancient Near Eastern Document," 313–18.

12. House and Jowers, *Reasons for Our Hope*, 129 (emphasis mine).

13. Walter Kaiser, *Toward an Old Testament Theology* (Grand Rapids, MI: Zondervan, 1978), 100.

14. Kaiser, *Toward an Old Testament Theology*, 106–7.

15. Exodus 4:22–23: "Then you shall say to Pharaoh, 'Thus says the LORD, Israel is my firstborn son, and I say to you, "Let my son go that he may serve me." If you refuse to let him go, behold, I will kill your firstborn son'"; Deuteronomy14:1: "You are the sons of the LORD your God. You shall not cut yourselves or make any baldness on your foreheads for the dead."

16. Exodus 6:7: "I will take you to be my people, and I will be your God, and you shall know that I am the LORD your God, who has brought you out from under the burdens of the Egyptians"; Exodus 19:6: "And you shall be to me a kingdom of priests and a holy nation. These are the words that you shall speak to the people of Israel."

17. Exodus 12:3: "Tell all the congregation of Israel that on the tenth day of this month every man shall take a lamb according to their fathers' houses, a lamb for a household."

18. Exodus 19:5: "If you will indeed obey my voice and keep my covenant, you shall be my treasured possession among all peoples, for all the earth is mine."

19. Deuteronomy 7:6: "You are a people holy to the LORD your God. The LORD your God has chosen you to be a people for his treasured possession, out of all the peoples who are on the face of the earth"; Deuteronomy 14:2: "You are a people holy to the LORD your God, and the LORD has chosen you to be a people for his treasured possession, out of all the peoples who are on the face of the earth"; Deuteronomy 26:18: "The LORD has declared today that you are a people for his treasured possession, as he has promised you, and that you are to keep all his commandments"; Deuteronomy 26:19: "He will set you in praise and in fame and in honor high above all nations that he has made, and that you shall be a people holy to the LORD your God, as he promised."

20. Exodus 19:3–6: "Moses went up to God. The LORD called to him out of the mountain, saying, 'Thus you shall say to the house of Jacob, and tell the people of Israel: You yourselves have seen what I did to the Egyptians, and how I bore you on eagles' wings and brought you to myself. Now therefore, if you will indeed obey my voice and keep my covenant, you shall be my treasured possession among all peoples, for all the earth is mine; and you shall be to me a kingdom of priests and a holy nation. These are the words that you shall speak to the people of Israel.'"

21. Kaiser, *Toward an Old Testament Theology*, 109.

22. Kaiser, *Toward an Old Testament Theology*, 109.

23. As a set-apart nation, Israel "could not be consecrated any further to any thing or person (Leviticus 27:26) or enter into any rival relationships (Leviticus 18:2–5)." Kaiser, *Toward an Old Testament Theology*, 111.

24. Paul Copan, *Is God a Moral Monster? Making Sense of the Old Testament God* (Grand Rapids, MI: Baker Academic, 2011), 159.

25. *International Standard Bible Encyclopedia*, s.v. "Molech; Moloch," www.biblestudytools.com/encyclopedias/isbe/molech -moloch.html.

26. It could be that Haman was, as was the custom of the day, using hyperbole to describe the extent of his intentions. The book of Esther, though, displays details of a conspiracy at the highest levels of society that aimed to carry out genocide.

27. 1 Samuel 15:8: "He took Agag the king of the Amalekites alive and devoted to destruction all the people with the edge of the sword"; 1 Samuel 15:20: "Saul said to Samuel, 'I have obeyed the voice of the LORD. I have gone on the mission on which the LORD sent me. I have brought Agag the king of Amalek, and I have devoted the Amalekites to destruction.'"

28. Joshua 10:28: "As for Makkedah, Joshua captured it on that day and struck it and its king, with the edge of the sword. He devoted to destruction every person in it; he left none remaining. And he did to the king of Makkedah just as he had done to the king of Jericho."

29. Joshua 10:30: "The LORD gave it also and its king into the hand of Israel. And he struck it with the edge of the sword, and every person in it; he left none remaining in it. And he did to its king as he had done to the king of Jericho."

30. Copan, *Is God a Moral Monster?*, 174.

31. Matt Flannagan, "Contra Mudum: Did God Command Genocide in the Old Testament?," August 1, 2010, www.mandm .org.nz/2010/08/contra-mundum-did-god-command-genocide-in-the-old-testament.html.

32. Flannagan, "Contra Mudum."

33. Quoted in Flannagan, "Contra Mudum."

34. Flannagan, "Contra Mudum."

35. Flannagan writes, "In a comprehensive comparative study of ancient Near Eastern conquest accounts, Old Testament scholar, K. Lawson Younger documents stylistic and literary similarities between Joshua and reports of wars written by some of these surrounding cultures. He concludes that the Old Testament uses the same literary conventions. He notes, 'the composition and rhetoric of the Joshua narratives in chapters 9–12 are compared to the conventions of writing about conquests in Egyptian, Hittite, Akkadian, Moabite, and Aramaic texts, they are revealed to be very similar.' He substantiates with numerous examples in his book." See "Contra Mudum."

36. Copan, *Is God a Moral Monster?*, 171.

37. Jeremiah 25:9: "Behold, I will send for all the tribes of the north, declares the LORD, and for Nebuchadnezzar the king of Babylon, my servant, and I will bring them against this land and its inhabitants, and against all these surrounding nations. I will devote them to destruction, and make them a horror, a hissing, and an everlasting desolation."

38. Keep in mind that God had provided ample evidence that he was the one true God. The plagues on Egypt, the parting of the Red Sea, the provision of manna to keep the Israelites alive, and the presence of a cloud by day and fire by night over Israel's camp. Some in the surrounding nations saw these signs and aligned themselves with Israel (for example, Rahab and the Shechemites at Mount Ebal (Josh. 2:8–13; 8:33, 35). Those who chose instead to attack Israel were justly repelled.

39. Copan, *Is God a Moral Monster?*, 167.

40. C. S. Lewis, *Surprised by Joy: The Shape of My Early Life* (New York: Harcourt, 1955), 206–16.

41. For more on the Hebrew *erva galah*, see John S. Borgsma and Scott W. Hahr, "Noah's Nakedness and Curse on Canaan (Genesis 9:20-27)," *Journal of Biblical Literature* 124, no. 1 (2005): 25–40.

42. Leviticus 18:24–30: "Do not make yourselves unclean by any of these things, for by all these nations I am driving out before you have become unclean, and the land became unclean, so that I punished its iniquity, and the land vomited out its inhabitants. But you shall keep my statutes and my rules and do none of these abominations, either the native or the stranger who sojourns among you (for the people of the land, who were before you, did all of these abominations, so that the land became unclean), lest the land vomit you out when you make it unclean, as it vomited out the nation that was before you. For everyone who does any of these abominations, the persons who do them shall be cut off from among their people. So keep my charge never to practice any of these abominable customs that were practiced before you, and never to make yourselves unclean by them: I am the LORD your God."

43. For more information on Freud, including the shortcomings of his research, see James W. Kalat, *Introduction to Psychology* (Belmont, CA: Wadsworth, 2011), 500–506.

44. C. S. Lewis calls a lie the idea that "any sexual act to which you are tempted at the moment is also healthy and normal." C. S. Lewis, *Mere Christianity* (New York: HarperOne, 1952), 100. Armand M. Nicholi Jr., *The Question of God: C. S. Lewis and Sigmund Freud Debate God, Love, Sex, and the Meaning of Life* (New York: Free Press, 2002), 137.

45. G. A. Cooke, *The Book of Ezekiel*, International Critical Commentary (Edinburgh: T&T Clark, 1967), 199, quoted in Kaiser, *Toward an Old Testament Theology*, 112.

46. Goheen and Bartholomew, *Living at the Crossroads*, 47.

47. Kaiser, *Toward an Old Testament Theology*, 117.

48. See Alvin Schmidt, *How Christianity Changed the World* (Grand Rapids, MI: Zondervan, 2004). See chapter 3: "Christianity Elevates Sexual Morality."

49. Nicholi, *The Question of God*.

50. Nicholi, *The Question of God*, 137.

51. Nicholi, *The Question of God*, 141–42.

52. Nicholi, *The Question of God*, 142–43.

53. Nicholi, *The Question of God*, 158.

54. Nicholi, *The Question of God*, 158.

55. Schmidt, *How Christianity Changed the World*, 83.

56. See Schmidt, *How Christianity Changed the World*, 83.

57. Charles Colson, *Against the Night: Living in the New Dark Ages* (Ann Arbor, MI: Servant, 1989), 151–52.

58. D. A. Carson, *The Gagging of God: Christianity Confronts Pluralism* (Grand Rapids, MI: Zondervan, 1996), 365.

59. See Genesis 16. It was the custom at the time for a woman who could not conceive to give her servant to her husband and claim the child as her legal heir.

60. It is interesting that in the exodus, Israel went from one state of servitude to another. Exodus 4:23 says, "Let my son go that he may serve me." The Israelites were to be let go, not so that they would no longer serve but that they would serve God rather than the Pharaoh (see Exod. 7:16; 8:1, 20; 9:1, 13; 10:3, 7, 8, 11, 24, 26). The issue was less where they were coming from than what they were going to: as God's son and servant, the Israelites should be free from Pharaoh because they belonged to God.

61. Genesis 1:26–27: "God said, 'Let us make man in our image, after our likeness. And let them have dominion over the

fish of the sea and over the birds of the heavens and over the livestock and over all the earth and over every creeping thing that creeps on the earth.' So God created man in his own image, in the image of God he created him; male and female he created them."

62. Job 31:13–14: "If I have rejected the cause of my manservant or my maidservant, when they brought a complaint against me, what then shall I do when God rises up? When he makes inquiry, what shall I answer him?"

63. Romans 16:16: "Greet one another with a holy kiss. All the churches of Christ greet you."

64. See Aristotle, *Politics* 1.3–6 and *Nicomachean Ethics* 8.11.

65. Galatians 3:28: "There is neither Jew nor Greek, there is neither slave nor free, there is no male and female, for you are all one in Christ Jesus"; 1 Corinthians 12:13: "In one Spirit we were all baptized into one body—Jews or Greeks, slaves or free—and all were made to drink of one Spirit"; Colossians 3:11: "Here there is not Greek and Jew, circumcised and uncircumcised, barbarian, Scythian, slave, free; but Christ is all, and in all."

66. Philemon v. 16: "… no longer as a bondservant but more than a bondservant, as a beloved brother—especially to me, but how much more to you, both in the flesh and in the Lord."

67. Revelation 18:11–13: "The merchants of the earth weep and mourn for her, since no one buys their cargo anymore, cargo of gold, silver, jewels, pearls, fine linen, purple cloth, silk, scarlet cloth, all kinds of scented wood, all kinds of articles of ivory, all kinds of articles of costly wood, bronze, iron and marble, cinnamon, spice, incense, myrrh, frankincense, wine, oil, fine flour, wheat, cattle and sheep, horses and chariots, and slaves, that is, human souls."

68. Ezekiel 27:13: "Javan, Tubal, and Meshech traded with you; they exchanged human beings and vessels of bronze for your merchandise."

69. 1 Timothy 1:9–10: "The law is not laid down for the just but for the lawless and disobedient, for the ungodly and sinners, for the unholy and profane, for those who strike their fathers and mothers, for murderers, the sexually immoral, men who practice homosexuality, enslavers, liars, perjurers, and whatever else is contrary to sound doctrine."

70. Christopher J. H. Wright, *Old Testament Ethics for the People of God* (Downers Grove, IL: InterVarsity, 2004), 333.

71. Sean McDowell and Jonathan Morrow, *Is God Just a Human Invention? And Seventeen Other Questions Raised by the New Atheists* (Grand Rapids, MI: Kregel, 2010), 150.

72. John Mark Reynolds, "Does the Bible Endorse Slavery?," in *The Apologetics Study Bible for Students*, ed. Sean McDowell and the Holman Bible Staff (Nashville: Holman, 2014), 1322.

73. Isaiah 61:1–2: "The Spirit of the Lord GOD is upon me, because the LORD has anointed me to bring good news to the poor; he has sent me to bind up the brokenhearted, to proclaim liberty to the captives, and the opening of the prison to those who are bound; to proclaim the year of the LORD's favor, and the day of vengeance of our God; to comfort all who mourn."

74. See Rodney Stark, *For the Glory of God: How Monotheism Led to Reformations, Science, Witch-Hunts, and the End of Slavery* (Princeton, NJ: Princeton University Press, 2003), chap. 4.

75. McDowell and Morrow, *Is God Just a Human Invention?*, 154–55.

76. Rodney Stark, *The Rise of Christianity: A Sociologist Reconsiders History* (Princeton, NJ: Princeton University Press, 1996), 102.

77. Schmidt, *How Christianity Changed the World*, 100.

78. Deuteronomy 21:10–14: "When you go out to war against your enemies, and the LORD your God gives them into your hand and you take them captive, and you see among the captives a beautiful woman, and you desire to take her to be your wife, and you bring her home to your house, she shall shave her head and pare her nails. And she shall take off the clothes in which she was captured and shall remain in your house and lament her father and her mother a full month. After that you may go in to her and be her husband, and she shall be your wife. But if you no longer delight in her, you shall let her go where she wants. But you shall not sell her for money, nor shall you treat her as a slave, since you have humiliated her."

79. Acts 16:14–15: "One who heard us was a woman named Lydia, from the city of Thyatira, a seller of purple goods, who was a worshiper of God. The Lord opened her heart to pay attention to what was said by Paul. And after she was baptized, and her household as well, she urged us, saying, 'If you have judged me to be faithful to the Lord, come to my house and stay.' And she prevailed upon us"; Acts 16:40: "They went out of the prison and visited Lydia. And when they had seen the brothers, they encouraged them and departed"; 1 Corinthians 1:11: "It has been reported to me by Chloe's people that there is quarreling among you, my brothers"; Philippians 4:2–3: "I entreat Euodia and I entreat Syntyche to agree in the Lord. Yes, I ask you also, true companion, help these women, who have labored side by side with me in the gospel together with Clement and the rest of my fellow workers, whose names are in the book of life"; Colossians 4:15: "Give my greetings to the brothers at Laodicea, and to Nympha and the church in her house."

80. Stark, *The Rise of Christianity*, 100.

81. Eckhart Tolle, *A New Earth: Awakening to Your Life's Purpose* (New York: Plume, 2005), 156.

82. Carl Sagan, *Demon-Haunted World: Science as a Candle in the Dark* (New York: Ballantine, 1997), 122.

83. Mary Daly, *Gyn/Ecology: The Meta-Ethics of Radical Feminism* (Boston: Beacon, 1990), 183.

84. Philip J. Sampson, *6 Modern Myths about Christianity and Western Civilization* (Downers Grove, IL: InterVarsity, 2000), 137.

85. The full account of the Salem witch trials is complex and at times baffling, involving a perfect storm of war, economic uncertainty, disease, paranoia, and political calculation. What seems undisputed now is that witch trials came to an end after the people of Salem awakened to the evil they had carried out. See the account by a professor of history at Salem State University, Emerson W. Baker, *A Storm of Witchcraft* (New York: Oxford University Press, 2015), particularly chap. 7, "An Inextinguishable Flame."

86. McDowell and Morrow, *Is God Just a Human Invention?*, 229.

87. Alex McFarland, *Ten Answers for Skeptics* (Ventura, CA: Regal, 2011), 173–74.

88. Timothy Keller, *Galatians for You: For Reading, for Feeding, for Leading* (Surrey, England: The Good Book Company, 2013), 55.

89. Brian Jones, *Hell Is Real: But I Hate to Admit It* (Colorado Springs, CO: David C Cook, 2011), 147.

90. Jones, *Hell Is Real*, 148.

91. Tim Keller, "Reason for God," *The Explorer*, Veritas Forum, Fall 2008, quoted in Copan, *Is God a Moral Monster?*, 222.

CHAPTER

17

17

IF CHRISTIANITY IS TRUE, WHY DO PEOPLE WALK AWAY?

1. CRISIS OF FAITH

As a teenager, my friend Sean McDowell had a crisis of faith. And because Sean's dad is the world-renowned evangelist Josh McDowell, this event might have morphed into a family crisis. But instead of panicking about his reputation or Sean's faith, Josh told him, "Son, I'm excited for you. It's great to explore answers to these questions. I just ask one thing: don't reject Christianity without *knowing* that it is untrue." Instead of ignoring Sean's doubts, his dad took them seriously, giving Sean space to search for answers. As a result, Sean's faith grew stronger.

Sean's dad was right when he said it's great to explore the answers to ultimate questions. Too many people make decisions without good reasons or even blame others for their own failure to think things through. People say such things as "My friends *caused* me to reject my faith" or "My parents got divorced and that *caused* me to walk away." Even when someone says something like "I was raised Hindu, which is what *causes* me to be a Hindu," that person is not giving reasons for his or her actions but is acting as if she had no choice in the matter. *Causes* are not necessarily *reasons.*

According to worldview scholar James Sire, talking about what we were *caused* to do is a way of evading responsibility.[1] On the other hand, if a person responds to the question "Why do you believe as you do?" by saying, "This worldview explains reality and answers my tough questions," this person is giving reasons and showing clear thinking. It's a way of taking responsibility; it is a mature thing to do.

As we've seen throughout this volume, Christianity has good reasons on its side. It is reasonable to believe that a supreme mind has always existed, that he created the universe, and that we might come to know this creator personally.

> The truth of Christianity does not depend on whether we know it, admit it, agree about it, follow it, or grasp it. If something is true, it is true when we don't like it as well as when we do.

Yet we may still wonder, *If Christianity is really true, why don't more people believe it, and why do some people who profess belief walk away at some point in their lives?*

We should note, though, that we're *not* asking whether people's level of belief determines Christianity's truth. As professor Paul Copan points out, the truth of Christianity does not depend on whether we know it, admit it, agree about it, follow it, or grasp it.[2] If something is true, it is true when we don't like it as well as when we do.

What we *are* asking is, *Why do people not find compelling the reasonable arguments for the Christian faith we've discussed in this book?*

Well, for one thing, there are reasonable-sounding arguments for other viewpoints. But as we will see, there is something besides reason at work in most peoples' decision-making processes. People find evidence persuasive only if they are *willing* to be informed, *willing* to abandon conflicting commitments, and *willing* to align their lives with God's revealed truth. These acts of the will are often very difficult for people to achieve.

Scripture tells us in Romans 1:21 that people will turn away from perfectly good reasons: "For although they knew God, they did not honor him as God or give thanks to him, but they became futile in their thinking, and their foolish hearts were darkened." It's like a person with a disabling brain tumor trying to self-diagnose his own malady: the very faculty by which he would try to think clearly about his problem is the very faculty whose injury prevents him from doing so.

How much of a problem is it that people walk away from the Christian faith? Although church attendance isn't *everything*, it is a helpful and accurate indicator of who identifies as Christian, and today more and more people experience crises of faith and drop out of church. Such crises of faith are pandemic: one study found that 70 percent of those who regularly attended youth group in their teens stopped attending church regularly for at least a year when they left home.[3]

Probably the most helpful way to think about crises of *faith* is to view them as crises of *trust*. As author Dave Sterrett explains, in the midst of relationship problems, spiritual dilemmas, and intellectual doubts, people commonly look around, find nonbelievers getting along okay, and ask, *Can I really trust God to help me with these difficulties?*[4]

There are, of course, different kinds of disbelief. For example, some people say their disbelief is due to cultural differences. Others disbelieve because they were talked out of faith. Others just stop believing because of some kind of doubt. The questions we will address are *Why do people stop believing? What should we do with our personal doubts? And what is God's answer to doubt and disbelief?* Let's dig in to see if we can find answers.

2. Doubts Come from Lack of Foundational Knowledge

Some people stop believing in Christianity because they just don't know enough to do any differently. Their beliefs are not based on knowledge to begin with. In America, around 85 percent of people say they believe in God. Because around three-fourths of Americans identify with a Christian denomination,[5] most of these would say they are Christian. However, around half of Americans (53 percent) see God as a "cosmic force."[6] God clearly reveals himself in Scripture as a person, so people who describe him primarily as a force have either embraced a non-Christian theology or are uninformed. Christians are not immune to ignorance. According to a Pew Research Center study, atheists as a group knew the most and Christians as a group knew the least on a basic test of religious knowledge.[7]

> Some people stop believing in Christianity because they just don't know enough to do any differently. Their beliefs are not based on knowledge to begin with.

Being uninformed can itself be a source of doubt. English author Os Guinness says that when people embrace a wrong view of God, they end up blaming God for their own faulty picture of reality. "Unable to see God as he is, they cannot trust him as they should, and doubt is the result," he says.[8]

I saw this kind of distrust firsthand when a lady approached me at a conference to say, "I don't want to teach my children that God is always there. It sounds creepy." To her, God is like Santa Claus, who, as the old song says, "knows if you've been bad or good, so be good *for goodness' sake.*"[9] I'm sure creepiness was not on the minds of John Frederick Coots and Haven Gillespie when they wrote the song featuring those lyrics, "Santa Claus Is Coming to Town."[10] But the upbeat melody disguises a vaguely threatening theology that Santa's watching you to punish or reward you. Uninformed people believe that God is like Santa. No wonder they feel freedom in giving up belief in him.

Giving up belief in God is not like switching a light from "on" to "off." Unbelief represents shakiness in a person's answers to life's ultimate questions. Think of a set of building blocks. If the blocks at the base are unstable, the blocks at the top will wobble. Often people experience a crisis of belief when they have an inadequate foundation and their "knowledge blocks" pile up faster than their foundation can support. If people start with an inadequate understanding of God, they'll grow more confused with every piece of unintegrated information they gain. Proverbs 18:17 says, "The one who states his case first seems right, until the other comes and examines him." Those who grow up in church but never grapple with hard questions often find themselves on the receiving end of this proverb.

I experienced this myself as a university student. I heard a psychology professor parrot Sigmund Freud's idea that people believe in God because of wish fulfillment. In other words, Freud taught that weak-minded people are fearful of the world and wish for a great father figure to protect them, so they invent God. "Thus the benevolent rule of a divine Providence allays our fear of the danger of life," Freud said.[11]

At the time, it sounded like a good theory. Who hasn't felt a sense of fear and wished for protection from someone bigger? Fortunately, a professor named Paul Vitz helped me see that it could be the reverse—that perhaps Freud's strained relationship with his own father led him to attack the idea of God as a father. After all, Freud's argument isn't really an argument; it's an assertion purporting to explain why we have a desire for God, with no particular bearing on whether God actually exists. It's a fairly simple observation on Vitz's part, but it helped shore up my basis for belief.

But be careful to shore up your faith with strong arguments, not just slogans. When young Christians come across arguments against Christianity, they are tempted to shore up their thinking with whatever little bits of knowledge they find compelling at the time rather than develop a deep understanding of the problem and a humble, articulate response. As Basil Mitchell, a professor of philosophy at Oxford, put it, "Many ordinary people, particularly young people, [are] quite happy to adopt a pragmatic, utilitarian attitude to society at large, and to meet the crises of personal life with odd and often inconsistent scraps of 'philosophy' picked up from anywhere and claiming no universal truth or even relevance."[12]

> One reason people walk away from their faith is that they lack a proper knowledge base and grow more unstable through time.

So one reason people walk away from their faith is that they lack a proper knowledge base and grow more unstable through time. Often this lack of knowledge is compounded by a misunderstanding of what belief actually is. This leads us to a second reason people walk away.

3. Doubts Come from a Misunderstanding of What Belief Is About

Many people turn away from Christianity when their understanding of belief itself breaks down. People embrace one of what my friend Mark Mittelberg describes as different "faith paths." There are six such paths:

1. The "relativistic faith path" says that truth is *what you make it*.

2. The "traditional faith path" says that truth is *what you've always been taught*.

3. The "authoritarian faith path" says that truth is *what you've been told to believe*.

4. The "intuitive faith path" says that truth is *what you feel in your heart.*

5. The "mystical faith path" says that truth is *what you think God told you personally.*

6. The "evidential faith path" says that truth is *what logic and evidence point to.*[13]

Of these six, Mittelberg says, only the last one accurately represents the biblical idea of a believing faith. His intent in focusing on logic and evidence is not to diminish the work of the Holy Spirit in securing salvation (Eph. 1:13) but rather to point out that other paths have the most potential for distorting belief by making it a matter of personal preference, tradition, or feeling. People who walk along one of the other faith paths are more likely to question Christianity's uniqueness to the point of changing their convictions.

If you find yourself objecting to the idea that only one of these paths is legitimate, you're not alone. Most people think of faith as believing in something without good reasons.[14] As we saw earlier in this volume, though, the Christian view of **faith** is trusting in what we have good reason to believe is true.[15] Christian faith is not opposed to knowledge, but acting—indeed, *trusting*—in accordance with what we know.

> *Faith:* **firm trust or confidence in someone or something.**

The Bible does not discourage *knowing* things as a foundation of belief. In fact, it encourages it. Isaiah 43:10–11 says, "'You are my witnesses,' declares the LORD, 'and my servant whom I have chosen, that you may *know* and *believe* me and *understand* that I am he. Before me no god was formed, nor shall there be any after me. I, I am the LORD, and besides me there is no savior.'" John 20:30–31 says, "Jesus did many other signs in the presence of the disciples, which are not written in this book; but these are written so that you may believe that Jesus is the Christ, the Son of God, and that by believing you may have life in his name." The Bible itself encourages us to believe based on the presence of knowledge and evidence rather than its absence.

Yet even if people understand what belief is all about and acknowledge that Christianity is based in a real understanding of the world, they still might refuse to believe because they're holding on to something they don't want to give up. This leads us to a third reason people walk away.

4. Doubts Come from Conflicting Commitments

Some people don't want to embrace Christianity because they are committed to ideas or lifestyles they don't want to abandon. They think, *If the Bible is true, then I'm in trouble. I don't want to change my lifestyle or behavior, so instead I'm going to try to ignore what the Bible says.* If you meet someone who opposes Christianity, you might ask, "What are you afraid would happen to you if you became a Christian?" Often it isn't about good reasons at all; it's about not wanting to pay the cost in lifestyle, reputation, or family harmony.[16]

"Not wanting to pay the cost" happens more often than you might think, even among atheists, who we might not expect to admit it. In chapter 11, we heard from Harvard biologist Richard Lewontin, who admits that his unwillingness to "allow a Divine Foot in the door" led him to embrace science "in spite of the patent absurdity of some of its constructs, *in spite* of its failure to fulfill many of its extravagant promises of health and life, *in spite* of the tolerance of the scientific community for unsubstantiated just-so stories."[17]

Thomas Nagel, professor of philosophy at New York University, is even more pointed: "It isn't that I don't believe in God and naturally hope that I'm right in my beliefs, it's that I hope there is no God. I don't want there to be a God. I don't want the universe to be like that."[18]

You'll run into a lot of professors like Lewontin and Nagel at secular colleges, where Christian belief is rare among faculty.[19] This high level of unbelief, in turn, creates strong pressure for students to avoid beliefs of which their respected professors might disapprove. To paraphrase the late journalist Upton Sinclair, it is difficult to get a person to believe something when his grade depends upon his not believing it.[20]

The Bible itself acknowledges that many will turn away simply because they are unwilling to pay the cost. In Luke 14:27–30, Jesus said,

> Whoever does not bear his own cross and come after me cannot be my disciple. For which of you, desiring to build a tower, does not first sit down and count the cost, whether he has enough to complete it? Otherwise, when he has laid a foundation and is not able to finish, all who see it begin to mock him, saying, "This man began to build and was not able to finish."

Some don't count the cost. Others count it, and realize they don't want to pay it. Either way, their reasons for walking away have less to do with intellectual consideration than with a desire to hold on to a particular lifestyle or maintain the respect of people they want to have like them. The focus on personal comfort leads us to a fourth reason for walking away: people simply have become comfortable living as if God does not exist.

5. Doubts Come from Practical Atheism

Research by the Pew Research Center shows that among people eighteen to twenty-nine years of age, one-third claims no religious affiliation.[21] This figure has tripled in the last three decades. According to professor Craig Gay, the central problem is not the high number of atheists but rather the high number of those who live as if God has no bearing on their lives. Gay calls this **practical atheism** and says, "Under modern conditions the question of God is simply irrelevant to so much of what we do on a daily basis that it eventually drops out of mind and heart. God is simply forgotten."[22]

> *Practical Atheism:*
> believing in the existence
> of God but living as
> if he doesn't exist.

Many people, when asked about questions of faith, say, "Everything is going just fine; I don't need faith." However, people who make this point probably do not realize what they're actually saying:

- To say things are "fine" is usually to say that one's own life is relatively trouble free. But is this a good criterion for a meaningful life?

IF CHRISTIANITY IS TRUE, WHY DO PEOPLE WALK AWAY?

- Is the person saying that everything is fine in the *world* or just in his or her own life? It seems selfish to make life about personal satisfaction rather than about making life better for others.

- Why would a person think that Christianity is only for times of trouble? That's a misunderstanding of what the gospel is all about.

Many embrace practical atheism because they either will not or cannot see the world from God's perspective and so embrace the culturally approved way of living because it just seems like the acceptable thing to do.[23]

But how do people arrive at the idea of a culturally approved way of living? Christian apologist Charles Kraft theorizes that it is a matter of what we train ourselves to pay attention to. Of all the things that happen, he says, we acknowledge only that which we believe to be possible. Of what we believe to be possible, we acknowledge only those things we can directly experience. Of the things we experience, we acknowledge only those things we can analyze. Out of this, we form our view of reality.[24]

Here's what this constrained view of reality looks like visually:

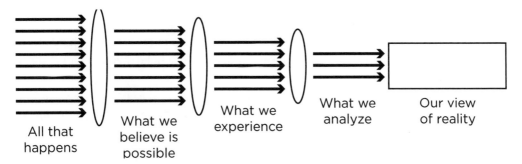

Before explaining how this truncated way of seeing relates to faith, let's try to understand the concept itself through a baseball example. The Chicago Cubs baseball team is known as the "lovable losers" because they have not won a World Series in 104 years, the longest losing streak of any North American team in any professional sport. Let's say that someone rushed up and announced, "The Chicago Cubs have won the World Series!" Assuming you had no contradictory evidence, you might reason this way:

1. The Cubs did *not*, in fact, win the World Series.

2. The Cubs *cannot* win in the regular season, so clearly they *cannot* win in the World Series.

3. I have never *seen* the Chicago Cubs win a World Series, so it didn't happen.

4. It is impossible to *imagine* the Cubs winning the World Series, so it didn't happen.

5. Therefore, I know you think the Cubs won the World Series, *but you must be mistaken.*

Now let's apply this thinking to something supernatural, such as a miraculous healing. Here's how someone who believes that miracles cannot occur might make sense of such a claim:

1. The miracle didn't happen.

2. I do not believe that miracles are possible, so this particular miracle didn't happen.

3. I have never seen a miracle, so it didn't happen.

4. Miraculous healings are scientifically impossible, so this particular miracle didn't happen.

5. Therefore, I know you think a miraculous healing occurred, but it did not.

Can you see how this kind of thinking might lead to practical atheism? Rather than try to make sense of all of life, practical atheists confine their analysis to their own personal spiritual experiences, which in turn shapes their wills. Conveniently, living this way avoids rocking the boat. Unfortunately, it also avoids thoughtful reflection. As C. S. Lewis said in his sermon "The Weight of Glory," "We are half-hearted creatures, fooling about with drink and sex and ambition when infinite joy is offered us, like an ignorant child who wants to go on making mud pies in a slum because he cannot imagine what is meant by the offer of a holiday at the sea. We are far too easily pleased."[25]

Practical atheism, then, is not so much a rebellion against God as it is a very small view of what is really going on in the world.[26] It's not merely a failure of reason; it is a failure of imagination.

Practical atheism can be hereditary. In a widely discussed article about the impact of families on faith, Catholic priest Robbie Low analyzed a report from Switzerland about church attendance habits reported by parents and their adult children. Here's Low's stunning conclusion: "There is one critical factor. It is overwhelming, and it is this: It is the religious practice of the father of the family that, above all, determines the future attendance at or absence from church of the children."[27] The study further revealed that where neither parent practices their religion faithfully, "only 4 percent of children will become regular attenders and 15 percent irregulars. Eighty percent will be lost to the faith."[28]

Practical atheism has long roots that grow deeper with each passing generation. Perhaps the longest root, though, is in the area of morality. This leads us to a fifth reason people walk away from the faith: personal sin.

6. Doubts Come from Sin's Effects

The word *moral* comes from the Greek *moralis*, which author Steven Garber says, referencing Scottish philosopher Alasdair MacIntyre, is "about the formation of character, about developing dispositions 'to behave systematically in one way rather than another.'"[29] People's moral stances come from their view of God and in turn affect their views on everything, from science to government to issues such as adultery, gay marriage, and abortion.[30] In a

IF CHRISTIANITY IS TRUE, WHY DO PEOPLE WALK AWAY?

moment of brutal honesty, the author of *Brave New World*, Aldous Huxley, openly revealed the relationship between his view of reality and his moral choices:

> I wanted to believe the Darwinian idea. I chose to believe it not because I think there was enormous evidence for it, nor because I believed it had the full authority to give interpretation to my origins, but I chose to believe it because it delivered me from trying to find meaning and freed me to my own erotic passions.[31]

Huxley's comments about his erotic passions are more than just incidental to his argument. The effects of sin are particularly potent when it comes to sexuality. Our sexual choices deeply affect our worldview and thus our lives. A study of Christian young men, for example, found that those who reported using pornography also reported lower levels of religious practice, lower self-worth, lower identity development regarding dating, and higher levels of depression.[32]

> A study of Christian young men found that those who reported using pornography also reported lower levels of religious practice, lower self-worth, lower identity development regarding dating, and higher levels of depression.

Sin is a distortion of love. We sin when we love things wrongly at the wrong time in the wrong way. In a study of the faith of twentysomethings, sociologists Jeremy Uecker, Mark Regnerus, and Margaret Vaaler found that although young people can return to faith from just about every life circumstance, certain life habits—such as cohabitation, fornication (sexual intercourse outside of marriage), drug use, and alcohol abuse—all accelerate diminished religiosity.[33] This is further evidence that our lifestyle choices affect our relationships with God.

Let's return to the question of sexual sin for a moment. Because almost all humans experience sexual desire, and because this desire is tangled up with our understanding of love, sexual sin is a common area in which the biblical idea of love gets distorted. As we saw earlier in this volume, God's love for us and our love for him is the central plotline of the entire human story. As theologian and pastor John MacArthur affirms, "God's love is the single central principle that defines the Christian's entire duty."[34]

How does sexual sin cut against true love? In both Romans 13:8–10 and Galatians 5:14,[35] the apostle Paul says that the commandments are summed up in the command to love our neighbors. This kind of love involves kindness, tenderheartedness, and forgiveness (Eph. 4:32).[36] As MacArthur emphasizes, "True love is always sacrificial, self-giving, merciful, compassionate, sympathetic, kind, generous, and patient."[37]

> True love gives. Counterfeit love takes. True love builds up. Counterfeit love tears down. True love takes a long-term view. Counterfeit love focuses on only short-term pleasure. True love treats people as persons. Counterfeit love treats people as objects.

To truly love, one must reject love's counterfeits, which include the following:

- Immorality: the Greek word *porneia* includes every kind of sexual sin.

- Impurity: the Greek word *akatharsia* refers to filth, crudeness, and perversion.

- Covetousness: a narcissistic focus on self-gratification.[38]

True love gives. Counterfeit love takes. True love builds up. Counterfeit love tears down. True love takes a long-term view. Counterfeit love focuses on only short-term pleasure. True love treats people as persons. Counterfeit love treats people as objects. For these reasons, habitually indulging a distorted idea of love has serious consequences.

Many people never get to the place where they can think deeply about sin in this way. Why? They're not attentive. This leads us to a sixth reason people walk away from faith.

7. Doubts Come from Distraction

The average American sees as many as five thousand advertising messages per day, from billboards to T-shirts to web pop-ups to television ads.[39] Advertisers roll beaches with indentations of their logos, project ads onto walls at sporting events, wrap buses and buildings with product pictures, and even use parking stripes, streetlights, manhole covers, toilets, mirrors, and floors as advertising spaces.

And it's not just visual ads. Every move you make online is tracked by advertisers who then target you with things they want you to buy. New breakthroughs even make it possible to identify your age, race, and gender when walking through the mall and to instantly customize electronic billboards to feature ads that people like you have found compelling. This new technology can, for example, discern whether a shopper is a teenage girl and feature a special price on something teen girls like that is available in a store just a few steps ahead. Very soon advertisers will even be able to merge the virtual and real worlds, using your social media profiles to recognize your face when you go shopping and offer you special deals from nearby stores.[40]

Some people find this kind of advertising an annoying invasion of privacy. Others appreciate the convenience. Either way, we might easily get the impression that life is about buying things, shifting our identities from being producers to being consumers.

> We can concentrate on only so much. If we pay too much attention to our consumer appetites, we can't pay attention to more meaningful pursuits.

We can concentrate on only so much. If we pay too much attention to our consumer appetites, we can't pay attention to more meaningful pursuits. Life today is, as the Chuck Colson Center's John Stonestreet puts it, "the drowning of truth in perpetual noise."[41] Journalist Maggie Jackson sees tremendous danger in a culture "increasingly shaped by distraction":

This is why we are less and less able to see, hear, and comprehend what's relevant and permanent, why so many of us feel that we can barely keep our heads above water, and our days are marked by perpetual loose ends. What's more, the waning of our powers of attention is occurring at such a rate and in so many areas of life, that the erosion is reaching critical mass. We are on the verge of losing our capacity as a society for deep, sustained focus. In short, we are slipping toward a new dark age.[42]

Distraction makes selfishness and laziness easy. The Internet slang expression "tl;dr" ("too long, didn't read") reveals much, emphasizing, *You must make yourself instantly accessible to me. If not, I will ignore you.*

Just about every form of knowledge, religious or otherwise, requires our careful attention. In fact, God has designed our brains such that our sustained attention best ensures our joy and sense of meaning. Here's a brief summary of some of the research:

> Just about every form of knowledge, religious or otherwise, requires our careful attention.

- **Organizing your thoughts can bring pleasure.** The frontal lobe of your brain helps you plan and strategize. In your brain's limbic system, called the *nucleus accumbens*, a collection of neurons are activated when you experience pleasure. Stimulating activity in your frontal lobe in turn stimulates the limbic system, bringing a sense of pleasure, which is why you can occasionally find yourself working hard on something and enjoying it even though the work is difficult. The brain is actually designed to *work* and enjoy it.

- **Meditating and praying can bring pleasure.** Andrew Newberg, from the Thomas Jefferson University and Hospital in Pennsylvania, has conducted studies measuring blood flow as people meditate or pray. He has found that the more that people meditate and pray, the more activity there is in the frontal lobe and the limbic system (which give a person a feeling of pleasure). During this activity, the parietal lobe of the brain, which is sensitive to space and time, goes dim.[43] Perhaps you've had the experience of concentrating hard on something and losing track of time and space. The brain is actually designed to *concentrate* and enjoy it.

- **Communicating our thoughts can bring pleasure.** David Caplan, a neurologist from Massachusetts General Hospital, discovered that the mechanisms that trigger language use require motivation and arousal.[44] In other words, if you're thinking hard and enjoying it, you'll be able to communicate more vividly about it. The brain is actually designed to *communicate* and enjoy it.

Today's media-saturated culture makes it difficult to give the kind of sustained attention that leads to this kind of joy. In fact, some technology can actually have a counterproductive effect. For example, medical doctor and psychologist Leonard Sax reviewed a study of boys ages seven to fourteen years old who played a lot of video games. He found that video games shut off blood flow to the brain's executive center while stimulating the brain's pleasure center. This gave the players a feeling of reward at having achieved great objectives without actually accomplishing anything in the real world.[45]

In other words, being distracted through mediated experiences—not just advertisements but also movies, video games, or other technology—can actually have the effect of diminishing thoughtfulness, communication, and the capacity for spiritual reflection. When people lose their ability to think well, this leads them to stop paying attention to the textured, often complex world where truth resides. Distracted people have a hard time focusing on what is really true and worth believing. They may even question whether there is anything worth believing.

---

8. Dealing with Doubt

Even without such distractions, doubt is normal.[46] According to Christian educator Ben Williams, "Doubt is not a Christian problem; it's a human problem."[47] If you're experiencing doubt, you might be comforted by knowing that practically every scriptural hero experienced doubt, from Abraham to Job to Moses to David to Jeremiah to the disciples.

The sheer number of people in our culture today who doubt Christianity's truth can make Christians feel that their doubt is more real than the truth. The solution to doubts both simple and complex is that *we must doubt our doubts as much as we doubt the truth we doubt*.

When he speaks on doubt, Brett Kunkle asks audiences to write down their top three intellectual questions or objections to God, Jesus, the Bible, or Christianity; their top three hurts; and the top three sins they currently struggle with. As his audience members complete the exercise, they often realize that their intellectual questions, hurts, and sins are related. To see how, let's look at each in turn.

Intellectual Doubt

Many Christian believers look around the world and say to themselves, *Most people don't believe what I believe, so either I am wrong or they are wrong. How could so many people, especially smart people I know, be wrong?* Ironically, a humble desire not to proclaim our "rightness" may lead us to accept arguments against Christianity we otherwise might not find compelling.

The first response to **intellectual doubt**—or entertaining intellectual reasons for rejecting faith, such as wondering whether evolution proves that no God created the universe—is, Kunkle says, to write down your doubts. Second, go through them one by one, praying for God to tear down the strongholds of doubt and enable you to live a life pleasing to Christ (2 Cor. 10:3–5).[48] Third, search out the matter by reading books and talking with mature, informed Christians.

> **Intellectual Doubt:** spiritual doubt brought about by rational questions regarding God's existence.

If you find yourself in conversation with others who are expressing intellectual doubts, especially if they are being sarcastic or mean, remember that behind almost all "intellectual" doubts are personal areas of pain or resistance. Keep this in mind: "Love is patient and kind; love does not envy or boast; it is not arrogant or rude" (1 Cor. 13:4–5).

Emotional Doubt

> **Emotional Doubt:** spiritual doubt brought about by pain, anger, or angst.

Intellectual doubt is often tied to **emotional doubt**, such as questioning God's goodness or doubting one's salvation. Sometimes, Kunkle says, unresolved pain leads to anger and thus doubt. About these kinds of doubts, author Os Guinness says,

> Out-voted, out-gunned, faith is pressed back and hemmed in by the unruly mob
> of raging emotions that only a while earlier were quiet, orderly citizens of the

personality. Reason is cut down, obedience is thrown out, and for a while the rule of emotions is as sovereign as it is violent. The coup d'etat is complete.[49]

We deal with emotional doubts in much the same way that we deal with intellectual doubts. First, we recognize our doubts and pray through them, acknowledging that emotions, although good, can also turn negative and take over our lives. Second, we practice replacing negative, harmful emotions with biblically rooted, healing ones. Romans 12:21 says, "Do not be overcome by evil, but overcome evil with good." For example, despair must be replaced with hope, anger with forgiveness, anxiety with prayer, selfishness with self-control, and so on. Third, and most important, we lean on others—especially older people in the faith—to listen to and guide us.

Moral Doubt

The third kind of doubt, according to Kunkle, is **moral doubt**. This is the kind of doubt we experience as a result of personal sin, rebellion, and wrongly placed motivation. Psalm 14:1 says, "The fool says in his heart, 'There is no God.' They are corrupt, they do abominable deeds, there is none who does good." This verse is often used as a hammer to criticize nonbelievers, but notice its true intent: corruption, evil, and refusal to do good are associated with a denial of God's existence. This does not mean that atheists are closet ax murderers but instead that a strong correlation exists between someone's personal habits and his or her state of belief.

> *Moral Doubt:* spiritual doubt brought about by personal sin and rebellion.

What should we do if our personal habits are moving us further from God? According to Scripture, we should first confess the moral failing to God and ask for his help in repenting and obtaining forgiveness. First John 1:8–9 says, "If we say we have no sin, we deceive ourselves, and the truth is not in us. If we confess our sins, he is faithful and just to forgive us our sins and to cleanse us from all unrighteousness." Second, we should confess to others, asking forgiveness. James 5:16 says, "Confess your sins to one another and pray for one another, that you may be healed. The prayer of a righteous person has great power as it is working."

It can be embarrassing at first to admit that we have sin in our lives, but confession to others brings our secrets out into the open. Once it is out in the open, sin loses its controlling power over us. As part of repentance, Williams encourages his students to mediate on Psalm 73:21–26. This passage summarizes how God brings us out of bitterness, evil, and ignorance, and into his strengthening presence:

> When my soul was embittered,
>   when I was pricked in heart,
> I was brutish and ignorant;
>   I was like a beast toward you.
>
> Nevertheless, I am continually with you;
>   you hold my right hand.

You guide me with your counsel,
    and afterward you will receive me to glory.
Whom have I in heaven but you?
    And there is nothing on earth that I desire besides you.
My flesh and my heart may fail,
    but God is the strength of my heart and my portion forever.

Doubt your doubts as much as you doubt the truth you're doubting. And remember that even in your doubt, God cares for you and guides you. There's one more thing to mention, and it is the very thing that ties everything else together.

9. GOD'S ANSWER TO UNBELIEF: THE CHURCH

Many young Christians struggle in their faith because they've never seen what it looks like for someone to fully live out a Christian worldview. One college student confided in me, "I've been going to the same church my whole life and there are people there who have attended for forty years and it has never made any difference in their lives. Why should I continue going?"

I shared with this young man what he probably already knew: that we shouldn't measure the truth of God's plan for the world based on how fallen people live. This would be like blaming a car designer for my poor driving or faulting the design of a piece of furniture when I fail to assemble it according to the instructions. It's true that people are flawed. God wants us to focus on his Son more than on the flawed people around us. When the apostle Peter asked Jesus about God's plan for another person, Jesus said to him, "What is that to you? You follow me!" (John 21:22). Each person has to answer the question "What do you do with Jesus?" I can't answer that question for you, nor can you answer it for me. As C. S. Lewis said through the Aslan character in *The Horse and His Boy*, "No one is told any story but their own."[50]

> As C. S. Lewis said through the Aslan character in *The Horse and His Boy*, "No one is told any story but their own."

At the same time, I share the student's frustration. We know that what we *believe* connects with what we *do*. Garber was once asked by an anxious twentysomething, "But what does this have to do with where I work?"[51] It's a valid question. Who would want a worldview that can't be lived out in daily life?[52] "For individuals to flourish they need to be part of a community of character," Garber insists, "one which has a reason for being that can provide meaning and coherence between the personal and the public worlds."[53]

Where should we look to find a worldview robust enough for a fruitful, victorious life? There is one answer and one answer only: in the church. Not just in *a* church, as in a particular church building, but also in the universal church, the body of Christ. As odd as it seems, God works through flawed people all over the world, each of whom is flailing like a child learning to walk, steadied by an ever-patient God.

Sociologists Peter Berger and Thomas Luckmann have noted that being together with other believers is one of the key factors that makes a serious faith plausible: "To have a conversion experience is nothing much. The real thing is to be able to keep taking it seriously; to retain a sense of its plausibility. This is where the religious community comes in."[54] The church serves as an "authoritative community" that gives people of all generations a sense of place, nurtures them, helps them grow spiritually, and teaches them to treat those inside and outside the community with dignity and love.

Recent studies have shown the power of authoritative communities in people's lives, helping children and adults live mentally, emotionally, and spiritually healthy lives.[55] Churches ought to be the most purposeful authoritative communities. No church is perfect, but every church ought to consider itself a key to human flourishing, not just a place to go on Sundays.

Let me state it even more strongly: church is not a place to practice listening to sermons. It is where we practice the life of the kingdom, which is ours now and forever. This is why it is so important not to just look for a church you find entertaining but to find a place where you can participate fully as a member of the body of Christ in the following areas.

Reconciliation

If we are to love God and love our neighbors, our first duty is to be reconciled to our maker and those others he has made. We will be incomplete as long as we are unable to do this. In *The Problem of Pain*, C. S. Lewis said, "To condone an evil is simply to ignore it, to treat it as if it were good. But forgiveness needs to be accepted as well as offered if it is to be complete: a man who admits no guilt can accept no forgiveness."[56]

Reconciliation with our neighbors takes many forms. For example, many Christians have allowed racial, cultural, generational, and political differences to divide them from their brothers and sisters in Christ. Also, when it comes to dealing with doubt and unbelief, resolving the divide between generations may be of special importance. My own research has found that when the older and younger generations interact with one another in a positive way, it has the effect of reinvigorating the older generation and providing the younger generation with motivation, engagement, prosocial behavior, a healthier lifestyle, and greater spiritual development.[57] It is a shame when such interactions are rare.

In one study, the number one factor explaining the continued church involvement of young people in their twenties was their having had mentors in high school.[58] You need an older mentor if you want to grow.[59]

Worship

In one of America's longest-running academic studies, researchers examined generations of adults to better understand the factors leading to heart disease. Social environment has been found to play a huge role in physical health, and the expression of contentment and happiness is especially important. Researchers found that every *contented* person you know increases your likelihood of being contented by 2 percent. For every *discontented* person you know, your likelihood of being discontented rises 4 percent. In other words, unhappy people are twice as damaging to your state of mind as happy people are good for it.[60]

How does this apply to worship? It's simple. You need to be around contented, happy people who experience the joy of the Lord and worship with all of their hearts. Just as others affect you, you affect them. Your expression of joy, happiness, and contentment is just as contagious as theirs (a negative, shy, or distant attitude is also contagious).

Worship is an offering to God, so worship with your all. Worship leader Matt Redman says that true worshippers "gather beneath the shadow of the Cross, where an undying devotion took the Son of God to His death. Alive now in the power of His resurrection, they respond to such an outpouring with an unquenchable offering of their own."[61]

Worshipping together with other believers ought to be like a family reunion. Of course, reunions are painful for some families, but it is up to each person to bring healing. Our attitudes make an enormous difference.[62]

> Worshipping together with other believers ought to be like a family reunion. Of course, reunions are painful for some families, but it is up to each person to bring healing.

Another aspect of worship is the act of communion, which should never be treated as just another ritual. Orthodox theologian Alexander Schmemann says, "The liturgy of the Eucharist is best understood as a journey or procession. It is the journey of the Church into the dimension of the Kingdom."[63] Christian traditions surrounding communion vary significantly, so talk with your pastor about how you might be able to participate more fully in this life-giving act.

Community

Earlier in this volume, we discovered that Scripture considers God's plan for humans "very good" and that the "very goodness" of creation, *tob meod* in Hebrew, means that God's plan is richly and heartbreakingly good. God seeks abundance, and we experience the best of God's abundance in our with-ness—our being *with* others.

The Inklings club provides an intriguing example of with-ness. As a group of authors in Oxford in the 1940s and '50s, the Inklings gathered for friendship and to help improve one another's writing. Twice a week they got together, on Tuesday mornings at the Eagle and Child pub and on Thursday evenings at Magdalen College. Among those in the group were C. S. Lewis and J. R. R. Tolkien. Out of these meetings came Lewis's *Narnia* series and Tolkien's *Lord of the Rings* trilogy, among dozens of other fictional, nonfictional, and poetic works. Without the Inklings, might the world be bereft of some of its most beloved stories?

The Inklings were a form of companionship but also a form of spiritual support for people working in a university where brilliant people routinely mocked God. As Lewis said in a letter to his friend Arthur Greeves, "O for the people who speak one's own language."[64] Although we now think of such people as Lewis and Tolkien in heroic terms, they were in one sense ordinary men with ordinary problems. They helped each other through many personal difficulties. In the throes of a troubled marriage, Tolkien wrote in his diary, "Friendship with Lewis compensates for much."[65]

The particular kind of community represented by the Inklings is not a form of worship or communion but rather one of hospitality. It is inviting other people into a comfortable space where they can feel both personally challenged and safe. As Paige Gutacker, alumni director for Summit Ministries, says, hospitality tells others, "Come on in and get a glimpse of what is real." This is the church in action: "The front door of the home is the side door of the church."[66]

Hospitality is so important that the apostle Paul listed it as one of the required characteristics for church leaders (1 Tim. 3:2–7).[67]

Hospitality means creating an environment where people can go beneath the surface, where—without fear of abandonment—they feel free to share what is really going on. Gutacker puts it this way: "The hospitable reception of a guest is more than just the opening of one's door to another. It is also—and perhaps more fundamentally—about opening one's self to another. The type of hospitality that truly matters is one that is about the creation of a space, a free space within and around the host."[68]

Although being in groups of people is something that comes naturally to humans, true, hospitable community takes practice because to participate we must take off our masks and put others first.

Community is based on friendship, but there is a vital, deeper level as well. It's called accountability.

Accountability

Ted Haggard was the pastor of a large, successful church that started with a Bible study in his basement but grew to include many thousands of people. Haggard's position of leadership enabled him to speak to millions of people through books, television programs, speeches, and news appearances. All of this made Haggard one of the most influential evangelical leaders in America. Sadly, Haggard's entire life unraveled when a male prostitute came forward with credible claims that he had participated in homosexual sex with Haggard and sold him drugs.

Admitting to most of the allegations, Haggard wrote a wrenching letter to his congregation in which he said, "The public person I was wasn't a lie; it was just incomplete. When I stopped communicating about my problems, the darkness increased and finally dominated me. As a result, I did things that were contrary to everything I believe."[69] Haggard's story is not as rare as you might think. Seminary professor Bobby Clinton believes, based on his research, that 70 percent of Christian leaders do not finish well.[70] This should shake us to the core and call us to repentance.

If we hope for good accountability, we must prepare for frequent repentance. As Haggard attested, without others keeping us accountable, we're unlikely to be honest with ourselves or with God. Chuck Colson says, "There is no limit to the human capacity for self-justification." We need others to call us to repentance.

Some churches call people to repentance through tearful altar calls. Those who feel emotionally touched respond, while those who are not emotionally touched do not. How we feel, however, should not determine whether we engage in regular repentance. As John Stonestreet says, "Classic Christianity is not to repent *when* you feel like it, but repent *so* you will feel like it."

Repentance involves soul-searching. Is there rebellion in your heart? Are you hiding from God's presence in any area of life? Have you acted toward your neighbor in a way that was ungodly?

In addition to taking time to talk to God in prayer about your hurts and sins, schedule time to meet with a mentor with whom you can share what you are going through. Meeting often with a spiritual director helps one heal more quickly and rest in the assurance that God *wants* us to be restored in our relationships with him.

Service

Scripture describes the church as a body (Rom. 12; 1 Cor. 12), and just as each part plays a role in a body's survival and health, so each individual participates in the meaning of the church, building others up, which then returns energy to the individual, making him or her feel more alive.

And we, the body of Christ, must also apply all the gifts of God to every area of life. We must not separate what we bring to the body from how we exercise our gifting outside the body. Everyone's gifts—even those that are not usually deemed "spiritual"—have enormous value. Authors Ralph T. Mattson and Arthur F. Miller Jr. put it this way:

> A big goal makes a group more disciplined. It is easier to say no to the merely good when there is something truly great to which to say yes. The power of yes—of yes said together—makes it easier to tackle bad habits, shake off laziness, and strengthen one's willpower.

The Body can get into trouble by failing to embrace the gifts of its members when the exercise of those gifts occurs mainly in the world. If I am a lawyer, a merchant, a dentist, a farmer, or a machinist with gifts appropriate to those vocations, the Body makes my life of work irrelevant to my life of faith unless it includes all of me when we are together.[71]

This does not mean we should demand a place based on what we think our gifts might be. "You do not announce your gift to the fellowship and create a place for yourself," say Mattson and Miller. "As opportunities arise, you demonstrate your gift and allow the fellowship to confirm your gift and to supply increased opportunities for its use."[72]

10. Conclusion

Overcoming doubt and disbelief calls for more than just intellectual solutions. We need other people. We need the kind of community that enables us to grow stronger and flourish.

The church, like a sports team with its heart set on the state championship, thrives in community. When one falls, others pick him up. When another flags in his enthusiasm, he is buoyed by the enthusiasm of the others. Because of its members' unifying goal, the team grows stronger, not weaker, through difficulty.

A big goal makes a group more disciplined. It is easier to say no to the merely good when there is something truly great to which to say yes. The power of yes—of yes said together—makes it easier to tackle bad habits, shake off laziness, and strengthen one's willpower.

> Be one whose focus gives you something to say yes to, and see what God will do.

Here's another example. For many years, my family and I lived in a home near the Tennessee River, a major

IF CHRISTIANITY IS TRUE, WHY DO PEOPLE WALK AWAY?

route for barge traffic. We spent hours in our kayaks watching tugboats push massive barges of grain, coal, and other products down the river. Occasionally, we heard reports of barges coming loose from one another. Adrift from their guidance system, these barges posed a serious threat to other river traffic and to bridge supports.

When we come loose from our anchoring to God and our anchoring to the guidance and companionship of others, we lose our way and pose a danger to ourselves and others. I urge you, as an older brother in Christ, to find mentors. Become involved in Christian community, seek accountability, repent of sin, and be reconciled to God and others. Ask God to strengthen your vision and give you courage to live faithfully with your calling, great or small. Be one whose focus gives you something to say yes to, and see what God will do.

ENDNOTES

1. James W. Sire, *Why Good Arguments Often Fail: Making a More Persuasive Case for Christ* (Downers Grove, IL: InterVarsity, 2006), 48–49.

2. Paul Copan, *True for You, but Not for Me: Overcoming Objections to Christian Faith* (Minneapolis: Bethany, 1998), 18.

3. Scott McConnell, "LifeWay Research Finds Reasons 18- to 22-Year-Olds Drop Out of Church," August 7, 2007, www.lifeway.com/Article/LifeWay-Research-finds-reasons-18-to-22-year-olds-drop-out-of-church.

4. Dave Sterrett, *Why Trust Jesus* (Chicago: Moody, 2010), 23.

5. Frank Newport, "In U.S., 77% Identify as Christian," Gallup, http://www.gallup.com/poll/159548/identify-christian.aspx.

6. Quoted in Paul Froese and Christopher Bader, *America's Four Gods: What We Say about God and What That Says about Us* (New York: Oxford, 2010), 5.

7. "U.S. Religious Knowledge Survey," September 28, 2010, Pew Research Center's Forum on Religion and Public Life, www.pewforum.org/2010/09/28/u-s-religious-knowledge-survey/.

8. Os Guinness, *God in the Dark: The Assurance of Faith beyond a Shadow of Doubt* (Wheaton, IL: Crossway, 1996), 58–59.

9. John Frederick Coots and Haven Gillespie, "Santa Claus Is Coming to Town," 1934 (emphasis mine).

10. Coots and Gillespie, "Santa Claus Is Coming to Town."

11. Sigmund Freud, "The Future of an Illusion" in *The Freud Reader*, ed. Peter Gay (New York: Norton, 1989), 703–4.

12. Basil Mitchell, *How to Play Theological Ping-Pong: Essays in Faith and Reason* (Grand Rapids, MI: Eerdmans, 1990), 32–33, quoted in Steven Garber, *Fabric of Faithfulness: Weaving Together Belief and Behavior* (Downers Grove, IL: InterVarsity, 2007), 102.

13. See Mark Mittelberg, "Faith Path: Helping Friends Find Their Way to Christ," *Christian Research Journal* 33, no. 3, 2010, www.equip.org/articles/faith-path/.

14. For example, Steven Pinker, "Less Faith, More Reason," *The Harvard Crimson*, October 27, 2006, www.thecrimson.com/article/2006/10/27/less-faith-more-reason-there-is/.

15. Sean McDowell and Jonathan Morrow, *Is God Just a Human Invention? And Seventeen Other Questions Raised by the New Atheists* (Grand Rapids, MI: Kregel, 2010), 267.

16. For more on this point, I recommend Abdu Murray, *Grand Central Question: Answering the Critical Concerns of the Major Worldviews* (Downers Grove, IL: InterVarsity, 2013).

17. Richard Lewontin, "Billions and Billions of Demons," *The New York Review*, January 9, 1997, 31 (emphasis in the original).

18. Thomas Nagel, *The Last Word* (New York: Oxford University Press, 1997), 130.

19. Statistically speaking, your chances of running into a professor who believes in God are two in three. But only half of professors who believe in God express any kind of Christian belief. And among professors who claim to be Protestant or Catholic, the chance that the person will be religiously conservative—that he or she will actually believe the Bible is true, for example—is about one in twenty. In other words, only two out of every one hundred professors is likely to be an evangelical Christian who embraces traditional moral beliefs, whereas twenty-six out of every hundred will be committed Secularists, atheists, or agnostics. See Neil Gross and Solon Simmons, "The Religiosity of American College and University Professors," *Sociology of Religion* 70, no. 2 (2009): 114–18.

20. Upton Sinclair's actual quotation is "It is difficult to get a man to understand something, when his salary depends upon his not understanding it!" *I, Candidate for Governor: And How I Got Licked* (Berkeley: University of California Press, 1935), 109.

21. www.pewforum.org/Unaffiliated/nones-on-the-rise.aspx.

22. Craig M. Gay, *The Way of the Modern World: Or, Why It Is Tempting to Live As If God Does Not Exist* (Grand Rapids, MI: Eerdmans, 1998), 239.

23. Charles H. Kraft explains this temptation thoroughly in his book *Christianity with Power: Your Worldview and Your Experience of the Supernatural* (Eugene, OR: Wipf and Stock, 1989), 18–19.

24. Kraft, *Christianity with Power*, 18–19.

25. C. S. Lewis, *The Weight of Glory: And Other Essays*, originally published in 1949 (New York: HarperCollins, 2001), 26.

26. This "smallness" is often referred to as *reductionism*.

27. Robbie Low, "The Truth about Men and the Church," *Touchstone*, June 2003, www.touchstonemag.com/archives/article .php?id=16-05-024-v.

28. Low, "The Truth about Men and the Church."

29. Garber, *Fabric of Faithfulness*, 149.

30. See Froese and Bader, *America's Four Gods*, 90–91, 104. Froese and Bader, Baylor University sociologists, found there are four common views of God and that peoples' views of God affect everything else in their lives. For example, political conservatives are more likely to believe in an authoritative God, whereas liberals are more likely to believe in a distant God (60). Those who believe in an authoritative God are more likely to say that adultery, gay marriage, and abortion are always wrong, whereas those who believe in a distant God are more likely to say such activities are not wrong at all (66). People who believe that God is authoritative or benevolent are less likely to believe that science can solve human problems and less likely to see humans as evolved from primates but also more likely to view science as revealing God's glory (90–91, 104).

31. Aldous Huxley, *Ends and Means: An Inquiry into the Nature of Ideals* (London: Chatt & Windus, 1946), 310.

32. Larry J. Nelson, Laura M. Padilla-Walker, and Jason S. Carroll, "I Believe It Is Wrong But I Still Do It: A Comparison of Religious Young Men Who Do Versus Do Not Use Pornography," *Psychology of Religion and Spirituality* 2, no. 3 (August 2010): 137–47.

33. The other condition was drug use. Jeremy E. Uecker, Mark D. Regnerus, and Margaret L. Vaaler, "Losing My Religion: The Social Sources of Religious Decline in Early Adulthood," *Social Forces* 85, no. 4, June 2007, 1667–92.

34. John MacArthur, "God's Word on Homosexuality: The Truth about Sin and the Reality of Forgiveness," *The Master's Seminary Journal* 19, no. 2 (Fall 2008), 154.

35. Romans 13:8–10: "Owe no one anything, except to love each other, for the one who loves another has fulfilled the law. For the commandments, 'You shall not commit adultery, You shall not murder, You shall not steal, You shall not covet,' and any other commandment, are summed up in this word: 'You shall love your neighbor as yourself.' Love does no wrong to a neighbor; therefore love is the fulfilling of the law"; Galatians 5:14: "The whole law is fulfilled in one word: 'You shall love your neighbor as yourself.'"

36. Ephesians 4:32: "Be kind to one another, tenderhearted, forgiving one another, as God in Christ forgave you."

37. MacArthur, "God's Word on Homosexuality," 154.

38. MacArthur, "God's Word on Homosexuality," 154–55.

39. Caitlin Johnson, "Cutting through Advertising Clutter," *CBS News Sunday Morning*, September 17, 2006, www.cbsnews.com /8301-3445_162-2015684.html.

40. Judith Grey, "Inside the Orwellian World of Ad-Funded Face-Recognition Technology," *Business Insider*, May 21, 2013, www.businessinsider.com/advertisers-using-facial-recognition-technology-2013-5.

41. John Stonestreet, talk given at Teach for Eternity, Orlando, Florida, October 13, 2013.

42. Maggie Jackson, *Distracted: The Erosion of Attention and the Coming Dark Age* (Amherst, NY: Prometheus, 2008), 14.

43. Newberg's research covers both chanting-type meditation and intercessory prayer. You can find more information at his website, http://www.andrewnewberg.com/research/.

44. David Caplan, "Language and the Brain" in *Handbook of Psycholinguistics*, ed. Morton Ann Gernsbacher (San Diego: Academic Press, 1994), 1023–53.

45. Leonard Sax, *Boys Adrift: The Five Factors Driving the Growing Epidemic of Unmotivated Boys and Underachieving Young Men* (New York: Basic Books, 2007), 91.

46. When I say doubt is normal, I mean to say that lots of people doubt what they believe. Even atheists experience doubt. Louis Menand tells a moving story of Oliver Wendell Holmes Jr., who ultimately became a respected justice of the US Supreme Court. As a young man, Holmes fought in the Civil War and was injured nearly to the point of death. At that point, Holmes began entertaining serious doubts and wondered whether he should recant his atheism. Ultimately, he decided not to but, with great irony, drifted off to sleep with a prayer: "God forgive me if I'm wrong." Louis Menand, *The Metaphysical Club: A Story of Ideas in America* (New York: Farrar, Straus & Giroux, 2001), 38.

47. Ben Williams, "Dealing with Doubt," Summit Ministries Lecture Series.

48. 2 Corinthians 10:3–5: "Though we walk in the flesh, we are not waging war according to the flesh. For the weapons of our warfare are not of the flesh but have divine power to destroy strongholds. We destroy arguments and every lofty opinion raised against the knowledge of God, and take every thought captive to obey Christ."

49. Os Guinness, *God in the Dark: The Assurance of Faith beyond a Shadow of Doubt* (Wheaton, IL: Crossway Books, 1996), 126.

50. C. S. Lewis, *The Chronicles of Narnia, Book 3: The Horse and His Boy* (New York: HarperTrophy, 1954), 216.

51. Garber, *Fabric of Faithfulness*, 100.

52. John Stonestreet paraphrases Dorothy Sayers on this point, asking, "Why would anyone want a worldview that applies

to only 10% of life?" See Stonestreet, "Worldview at Work: Running Companies More Truly," Breakpoint Commentaries, May 2, 2013, www.breakpoint.org/bpcommentaries/entry/13/22119.

53. Garber, *Fabric of Faithfulness*, 159.

54. Peter L. Berger and Thomas Luckmann, *The Social Construction of Reality: A Treatise in the Sociology of Knowledge* (New York: Doubleday, 1966), 163.

55. See Commission on Children at Risk, *Hardwired to Connect: The New Scientific Case for Authoritative Communities* (New York: Broadway Publications, 2003), 8. This crucial report was produced jointly by the YMCA of the USA, the Commission on Children at Risk, Dartmouth Medical School, and the Institute for American Values. The report's website provides ten characteristics of an authoritative community as one that is "warm and nurturing," "multi-generational," and inclined "toward the principle of love of neighbor" along with seven other criteria. Although it is possible for business and civic organizations to fulfill this function, by design they can almost never fulfill all ten. Churches, by definition, almost always do (obviously some churches do better than others). For all ten of the criteria, see www.cgie.org/blog/resources/papers-publications/project-summary-hardwired-connect-new-scientific-case-authoritative-communities/.

56. Quoted in McDowell and Morrow, *Is God Just a Human Invention?*, 166–67.

57. See Monika Ardelt, "Effects of Religion and Purpose in Life on Elders' Subjective Well Being," *Journal of Religious Gerontology* 14, no. 4 (2003). Ardelt reports that activities that increase a person's sense of well-being may have a profound effect on fundamental aspects of his or her psychology. In turn, a high level of purpose in life was associated with a reduced risk of mortality among older persons. When it comes to the power of mentoring, there are many studies demonstrating these effects. See, for example, Andrew J. Martin and Martin Dowson, "Interpersonal Relationships, Motivation, Engagement, and Achievement: Yields for Theory, Current Issues and Educational Practice," *Review of Educational Research* 79, no. 1 (2009): 344; Kathryn R. Wentzel, "Social-Motivational Processes and Interpersonal Relationships: Implications for Understanding Motivation at School," *Journal of Educational Psychology* 91, no. 1 (1999), 76–97; Andrew J. Martin, Herbert W. Marsh, Dennis M. McInerney, Jasmine Green, and Martin Dowson, "Getting Along with Teachers and Parents: The Yields of Good Relationships for Students' Achievement Motivation and Self-Esteem," *Australian Journal of Guidance and Counseling* 17, no. 2 (2007): 109–25; and Barbara Fresko and Cheruta Wertheim, "Learning by Mentoring: Prospective Teachers as Mentors to Children at Risk," *Mentoring and Tutoring* 14, no. 2 (2006): 149–61. Keith A. King, Rebecca A. Vidourek, Beth Davis, and Warren McClellan, "Increasing Self-Esteem and School Connectedness through a Multidimensional Mentoring Program," *Journal of School Health* 72, no. 7 (2002): 294–99; Rachel C. Vreeman and Aaron E. Carroll, "A Systematic Review of School-Based Interventions to Prevent Bullying," *Archives of Pediatric and Adolescent Medicine* 161, no. 1 (2007): 86.

58. This is one of many conclusions reached by Jason Lanker, "The Relationship between Mid-Adolescent Natural Mentoring and the Christian Spirituality of North American First-Year Christian College Students" (Unpublished dissertation, Talbot School of Theology, Biola University, May 2009), 141, 147.

59. Barna Group has found that among young adults who stayed faithful to church, as opposed to those who left, those who stayed were significantly more likely to have an older adult in the church who cared for them personally and to have that care extend even to helping them in their vocation and education. See "5 Reasons Millennials Stay Connected to Church," www.barna.org/barna-update/millennials/635-5-reasons-millennials-stay-connected-to-church.

60. The study is called the "Framingham Heart Study" (after the name of the town in Massachusetts whose residents have been studied). It has been carried on by generations of academics since 1948. Its main focus has been to examine the causes of cardiovascular disease. For more information, see www.framinghamheartstudy.org.

61. Matt Redman, *The Unquenchable Worshipper: Coming Back to the Heart of Worship* (Ventura, CA: Regal, 2001), 18.

62. Researcher Sigal Barsade found that whether our spirit is positive or negative affects those around us without our ever saying a word. See "The Ripple Effect: Emotional Contagion and Its Influence on Group Behavior," *Administrative Science Quarterly* 47, no. 4 (December 2002): 644–75.

63. Alexander Schmemann, *For the Life of the World: Sacraments and Orthodoxy* (Crestwood, NY: St. Vladimir's Seminary Press, 1973), 26.

64. Humphrey Carpenter, *The Inklings: C. S. Lewis, J. R. R. Tolkien, Charles Williams and Their Friends* (London: HarperCollins, 1978), 22.

65. Carpenter, *The Inklings*, 32.

66. An unnamed Los Angeles pastor quoted in Christine D. Pohl, *Making Room: Recovering Hospitality as a Christian Tradition* (Grand Rapids, MI: Eerdmans, 1999), 57.

67. 1 Timothy 3:2–7: "An overseer must be above reproach, the husband of one wife, sober-minded, self-controlled, respectable, hospitable, able to teach, not a drunkard, not violent but gentle, not quarrelsome, not a lover of money. He must manage his own household well, with all dignity keeping his children submissive, for if someone does not know how to manage his own household, how will he care for God's church? He must not be a recent convert, or he may become puffed up with conceit and fall into the condemnation of the devil. Moreover, he must be well thought of by outsiders, so that he may not fall into disgrace, into a snare of the devil."

68. Paige Lewis Gutacker, "Welcome Home: The Art and Practice of Hospitality," unpublished paper.

69. "Ted Haggard: I Am a Deceiver and a Liar," Beliefnet, November 5, 2006, www.beliefnet.com/News/2006/11/Ted-Haggard -I-Am-A-Deceiver-And-A-Liar.aspx#ted.

70. Referenced in Bill Thrall, Bruce McNicol, and Ken McElrath, *Ascent of a Leader: How Ordinary Relationships Develop Extraordinary Character and Influence* (San Francisco: Jossey-Bass, 1999), 14.

71. Ralph Mattson and Arthur F. Miller Jr., *Finding a Job You Can Love* (Phillipsburg, NJ: Presbyterian and Reformed, 1982), 172.

72. Mattson and Miller, *Finding a Job You Can Love*, 36–37.

IF CHRISTIANITY IS TRUE, WHY DO PEOPLE WALK AWAY?

CHAPTER 18

18

CONCLUSION

1. LOOK HERE FOR LIFE'S DIRECTIONS

Wow. We've covered a lot of ground since you parachuted into New York City's Central Park. Remember the story? You were told by a mysterious stranger about a five-thousand-dollar diamond necklace, yours free, provided that you claimed it within twenty minutes at Tiffany & Co. And to win the prize, you needed to know where you were, where you were going, and the best route to take.

Life offers few free diamond necklaces but lots of opportunities to pursue fulfilling lives. If we embrace false beliefs about life and the world, though, we'll find ourselves lost. We need help from the One who can see the end from the beginning and who knows the path we ought to take.

In this book, we've examined the Bible's claim that the good life is a God life. Along the way, we've encountered many big questions: Is God even real? What is he like? Is the Bible a trustworthy source? And what about biblical teachings that seem to counter the Bible's claim that God is good? We shouldn't settle for hit-or-miss answers. The last thing we need is a shallow worldview that can't provide solid guidance on life's most important questions.

Understanding the Faith was written to explore the foundation of a biblical worldview: how the Bible reveals the truth about God, humanity, and life in this world. As our odyssey comes to a close, let's review where we've been and end on a clear note about how to live our lives differently.

2. According to the Bible, We Can Know the Way to Live

Every day we make thousands of decisions, big and small. Our biggest decisions have to do with such things as how to nurture lifelong relationships. Our smaller ones include such things as what kind of vegetables to have with dinner. Even if we do succeed in making the small decisions well, no one five years from now will remember or care. But the decisions we make about whom to be friends with, what to study in college, where to live, and what kind of community to be involved with have consequences that will affect us all our days. Good decisions create synergy with other good decisions, but bad decisions add up too. Just as a boulder rolling down a hillside can trigger an avalanche, bad decisions can cascade into unthinkable consequences.

Given the weight of our decisions, some people would rather avoid deciding anything important. They may even tout the virtues of opting out of the rat race. After all, as actress Lily Tomlin says, "The problem with the rat race is that even if you win, you're still a rat." If the biblical account is true, we are far more than rodents running on life's treadmill. Our lives on this planet, including difficult decisions and trying circumstances, are part of an everlasting journey of bearing the image of the Creator of the universe.

Here's the rub: when it comes to discovering the purpose for life, the clock is ticking.

> Our lives on this planet, including difficult decisions and trying circumstances, are part of an everlasting journey of bearing the image of the creator of the universe.

Every worldview offers ideas of how to make the most of our limited time on earth. Each offers ideas that grapple with ultimate questions, such as where we came from (origin), who we are (identity), what is real (meaning), what the good life is (morality), and where are we going for now and for eternity (destiny). Some people think very little about these questions. Others gravitate toward complex and mysterious answers. Either way, our responses form patterns that shape how we live, for better or for worse.

The Bible does not promote escapist answers to life's ultimate questions; rather, it upholds as positive examples those who understand the times and know what to do (1 Chron. 12:32).[1] There is a good way and a bad way to live, a way of wisdom and a way of foolishness, a way of life and a way of death. The Scriptures are clear that *we can and should know the difference* (Isa. 30:21).[2] We can choose life (Deut. 30:19).[3] We can be set free by truth (John 8:32).[4]

Yet the Bible is also clear that walking in the right way is impossible without divine guidance. Twisted in our thinking by original sin and apt to embrace inadequate or wrong answers to life's ultimate questions, we find ourselves loving the wrong things in the wrong way. To paraphrase Augustine, disordered loves lead to lives of disorder. Fortunately, the Bible's story doesn't end in our futility. It offers hope: salvation through the death and resurrection of Jesus Christ, who is the only way.

Complicating our own internal struggle is the common belief that there are no answers "out there" in the world. We often hear from various sources in our culture that thoughts about spiritual things are private, subjective, and relative, not public, objective, and universal.[5] This sacred/secular split makes the search for spiritual truth seem pointless. As a result, says Christian philosopher J. P. Moreland, "The life of the mind is thus separated, broken off, and compartmentalized as a function of the 'secular' life instead of more naturally being integrated with the spiritual."[6]

But in this volume, we've seen that this sacred/secular split is a false notion. Christianity is a deep knowledge tradition that says the Bible reveals who God is as well as the truth about humanity and reality. The Bible does not call for blind faith; rather, it provides reliable assurance that God is worthy of our belief. But does the Bible actually have the authority to reveal God, as it claims?

> The Bible does not call for blind faith; rather, it provides reliable assurance that God is worthy of our belief.

3. Where the Bible's Authority Comes From

It is one thing to see that Christianity is true and yet another to recognize the authority the Bible claims over our lives. We looked at two kinds of authority in this book, *soft* and *hard*. The Bible's authority is both *soft* authority, promising peace with God and flourishing on earth through a relationship with Christ, and *hard* authority, with Jesus being presented as "King of kings and Lord of lords" (Rev. 19:16)[7] who will someday render judgment.

The Bible is God's story. It's both by God and about God. It reveals who he is and what he has done, is doing, and will do in the world and for all eternity. Even more, the Bible is *from* God and *for* humans. So, it's our story too. It is a compass, directing what takes place in the world as it daily turns and makes its way around the sun. The Bible's message is that God in his justice stands firmly against evil but in his grace desires all to come to repentance (2 Pet. 3:9).[8]

More than two billion people on the planet embrace the Bible's message, at least insofar as they claim the moniker "Christian." Not surprisingly, then, the Bible is the world's bestselling book. It has been enormously influential in the United States, where, as French sociologist Alexis de Tocqueville wrote in the 1830s, belief in the Bible had made it "both the most enlightened and the freest" of nations.[9] The Bible's place in world literature is also unrivaled. Even atheist Richard Dawkins once said that a person who has not read the Bible, the King James Version at least, is "verging on the barbarian."[10] The Bible is important. But its importance is not where its authority comes from.

The Bible promises blessing, insight, freedom from spiritual bondage, direction in life, and the ability to grasp truth and defeat error. The Bible is remarkably coherent for a book containing sixty-six separate books of history, poetry, prophesy, gospels, and letters penned by about forty authors over a time span of approximately fifteen hundred years. But the Bible's authority does not come from its promises or coherence, either.

> If the Bible is a compass for life, Jesus Christ is true north.

So *on what basis* do we say the Bible has authority? It is on the basis of **revelation** that the Bible makes known something that was previously unknown.[11] Revelation is God's way of making the infinite finite, the unknowable knowable, and the complex plain. Certainly, there are things that can be known about God without the Bible, such as his virtues as the Creator. As Psalm 19:1 says, "The heavens declare the glory of God, and the sky above proclaims his handiwork." However, what we humans need to know about salvation, God's nature as Trinity, the unfolding of God's plan through the nation of Israel, and Jesus's death and resurrection could not be known without Scripture.

If the Bible is a compass for life, Jesus Christ is true north. Jesus claimed to be the

> Jesus considered all of Scripture to be authoritative.

"I am" of the Old Testament. He said that he and God were "one" **essence** and told his followers that those who had seen him had seen God.[12] The gospel writers were clear about what Jesus was claiming, and they seemed certain—and became more certain after Jesus's resurrection—that he was telling the truth.

Jesus considered all of Scripture to be authoritative. In referring to the Old Testament, Jesus consistently said, "As it *is* written," implying that he believed the Scriptures not to be something from the past but to be the present and eternal truth of God. Jesus treated Scripture as final in authority and leaned on the Old Testament in his personal spiritual anguish.[13]

Jesus also conferred authority on his disciples and indicated that this authority extended far beyond the time boundaries of his own earthly ministry. On the night before going to the cross, Jesus prayed, "I do not ask for these only, but also for those who believe in me through *their* word" (John 17:20). In what we now call the Great Commission, Jesus claimed all authority in heaven and on earth and commissioned the disciples to spread his teachings to the whole world (Matt. 28:18–20).[14]

To summarize, the Old Testament Scripture is considered by Jesus to accurately portray God and tell the truth about reality. In his own ministry, Jesus claimed the authority of God, and he imparted that authority to those who would spread his message. The whole of Scripture, then, tells a single story, with Jesus at the center and its words conducted by the Holy Spirit, who "breathed out" what God wanted said (2 Tim. 3:16).[15] As professor Gordon R. Lewis explains, "The Holy Spirit supernaturally motivated and superintended the prophetic and apostolic recipients of revelation in the entire process of writing their scriptural books."[16] To paraphrase theologian Carl F. H. Henry, the Bible is a collection of writings through which God directed the authors to communicate exactly what he wanted, without overriding their personalities.

Jesus's claims of authority, as well as his recognition of the Old Testament's authority and his giving of authority to the apostles, constitute *internal* evidence for the Bible's authority. But external evidence also reinforces that authority.

4. Can We Know the Bible's Claims to Be True?

Is there evidence *outside* the Bible that shows it to be true? By "true," we mean that which corresponds to reality (i.e., the **correspondence theory of truth**).[17] The biblical account is that God created us to be knowers and gave us language to facilitate communication between himself and us and with one another. To *know* things is not just to conduct experiments about them. **Knowledge** is what philosophers call "justified true belief." Yes, people have their biases, but this does not mean that truth cannot be known. By this criterion, there are two kinds of external evidence showing the Bible to be reliable. The first is the accuracy with which it was transmitted through time, and the second is its accuracy in describing historical times and places that can be verified, as well as factual events occurring in those times and places.[18]

> Knowledge is what philosophers call "justified true belief."

> Many of the places and events of the Bible have been verified through historical and archaeological methods.

In criticism of the Bible's reliability, some cite **textual variants**, including spelling and unclear readings, word order changes, and obvious errors. Yet of the four hundred thousand variants scholars have found, fewer than four thousand have any real significance at all for the meaning of a verse, and none of these affects core doctrines. What we have today, in the New Testament at least, is a text that reproduces with 99 percent accuracy what was written nearly two millennia ago. Not only has the Bible been accurately transmitted through time but many of the places and events of the Bible have been verified through historical and archaeological methods, providing the kind of converging evidence one would expect a divinely authoritative book to possess.

> Humans are capable of writing the truth, and the documents claiming God's existence are historically reliable.

Of course, there are many who do not think the Bible is trustworthy. *The Bible was written by men*, they object. This is obviously true. Christians have never claimed that the Bible descended from heaven in its complete form. But as we saw throughout the text of this volume, humans are capable of writing the truth, and the documents claiming God's existence are historically reliable. So saying the Bible is false just because it was written down by human beings is not a sufficient reason to reject its claims.

A second objection is that the Bible has been corrupted through time and is therefore untrustworthy. As is the case with all ancient documents, no original manuscripts of the Old and the New Testaments are known to exist. Scholars have worked to reconstruct accurate versions of these original texts, and they have plenty of source material with which to work: more than ten thousand Old Testament manuscripts of various passages, more than fifty-seven hundred Greek New Testament manuscripts from all over the world, and through the ages more than twenty thousand versions and more than one million quotations of the text by ancient writers.[19] The abundance of evidence gives us reason to believe that the Bible we have today is substantially faithful to what was originally written.

A third objection to the Bible's trustworthiness is that it leaves out a number of Scripture-like books, the so-called **Lost Gospels**. Though the Lost Gospels may be historically interesting, they far from meet the careful criteria used by church fathers to decide which books should be included in the **canon**, the body of Scripture considered authoritative.

Lost Gospels: a collection of fifty-two gnostic texts discovered in 1945 in Nag Hammadi, Egypt, and written sometime between the second and fourth centuries AD.

If the Bible has both internal and external validity, and if it has been accurately transmitted through time, it is reasonable to take its claims of authority seriously. If the Bible is indeed from God to us, nothing escapes its scope. Cultures, governments, life, death, family, and entertainment are all to be understood in the light of what the Bible reveals of God and his authority. So what does the Bible's authoritative revelation say about who God is?

Canon: from the Greek word for "standard"; the collection of biblical writings commonly accepted as genuine and authoritative.

5. WHAT THE BIBLE SAYS ABOUT GOD

More than eight out of every ten people in the United States believe in God, but how they define God differs.[20] Some view him as a judgmental authority figure; others view him as a good and kind guide in life; others see God as distant and critical; and still others view him as more of a cosmic force who isn't really a person at all.[21] How people understand God seems to have an effect on many other areas of their lives, including how they raise their families and their views on the social and political issues of our day.

Elohim: from the Hebrew for "deity"; the generic name used in the Old Testament for the creator-God.

Can God's nature and character be known beyond mere opinion? The Bible assumes yes. Although the biblical revelation of God shows that he is bigger than our ability to comprehend, the question for Christians is not whether we can know him *completely* but whether we can know him *truly* through what Scripture says. Further, Scripture itself encourages us to know God. We are to bask in, and enjoy his glory.[22] And the best

Yahweh: from the Hebrew for "I Am"; the personal and covenantal name of God used in the Old Testament.

way of knowing God, according to Hebrews 1:1–2,[23] is to know Jesus. Through the death and resurrection of Jesus, we can truly come to know God.

So who does God reveal himself to be? The names used to describe God in Hebrew, the language of God's covenant people, are **Elohim**, which focuses on God as the creator of the whole world, and **Yahweh**, or "the Lord," the personal and covenantal name of God, embodying how he redeemed his people and brought them into relationship with himself. The Bible says God is holy, eternal, **omniscient**, **omnipotent**, **omnipresent**, unchanging, wise, righteous, loving, and mercifully gracious.[24]

Scripture also shows God to be three persons in one—a Trinity of Father, Son, and Holy Spirit—one divine being with three equal, distinct centers of consciousness in a personal, indwelling relationship.[25] Scripture does not use the word *Trinity*, but it does clearly communicate that God is one essence, the Father is God, Jesus is God, and the Holy Spirit is God. It also contains several passages that refer to the Father, Son, and Holy Spirit together.[26]

The **doctrine of the Trinity** distinguishes biblical Christianity from other theistic religions. Knowing that God is both eternally personal and in relationship transforms our understanding of what it means to be persons in relationship. The relationship among the Father, Son, and Holy Spirit shows us how to be in relationship with God. Unity with one another also becomes possible; we understand what harmony in relationships looks like because of the Trinity.

> The doctrine of the Trinity distinguishes biblical Christianity from other theistic religions.

God's attributes are unified in his nature. God doesn't *become* these things by doing them, nor does any aspect of his character take second place to any other aspect. His justice and mercy, for example, are not in conflict. This is an important realization as we look at the Bible's metanarrative: its story of history, life, and the world to come.

6. The Bible as a Metanarrative

All good stories have a theme, a tension arising and being resolved, and diversity within unity. The Bible is such a story. All of its little stories combine into one big story that moves from the creation to the end of time and even hints at what life is like *beyond* time. The Bible claims to be the true story that makes sense of all other stories. This is what we mean when we say the Bible is a **metanarrative**. It is the narrative of narratives. A metanarrative is not true just because people fervently believe in it. Some metanarratives are made-up stories; others describe events that actually took place.

> A metanarrative is not true just because people fervently believe in it.

The sheer coherence of the Bible's metanarrative adds to its credibility, demonstrating how unlikely it is that it was manufactured for someone's selfish purposes. Seeing Scripture as a metanarrative also blunts the impact of our self-interested reading of the Bible, clearing up the confusion that often comes from relying on selective verses or personal hunches about what a given passage means. It also helps resolve some things in the Bible we find confusing, such as God being, at the exact same time and without conflict, both a God of justice and a God of love. God's love threads through the entire story of the Bible, even in times when his people experienced the just consequences of their defiance of God's commands.

In chapters 5 and 6, we examined the Bible's metanarrative in six acts.

Act 1: Creation. The Bible celebrates God's creation of the heavens most notably in Genesis chapters 1 and 2. These accounts of creation offer the big picture and the close-up and are alternately formal and informal, dignified and earthy, general and specific, big-picture and personal. Creation showcases God's glory, explains how he establishes order, confronts the pagan creation myths, establishes humans as the climax of creation, explains humanity's purpose, and clears up confusing issues such as the purpose and place of sexuality.

> In defying God, Adam and Eve displace shalom with unbelief, irresponsibility, and rebellion.

Act 2: Fall. God originally creates human beings in a state of **shalom**: peace, prosperity, goodness, and order. In defying God, Adam and Eve displace *shalom* with unbelief, irresponsibility, and rebellion. Sin says, "God, I don't think your plan is as good as you say it is." It results in ever-increasing arrogance, abuse, and death. In Genesis, sin multiplies to the point where people *crave* evil (Gen. 6:5).[27] Each person did—and continues to do—what was right in his own eyes (Judg. 17:6).[28] We are not sinners because we sin; we sin because we are sinners.

Act 3: Redemption Initiated. The nation of Israel is sent on a mission from God. The Old Testament of the Bible tells this part of the story in three stages: God initiates redemption, Israel fails, and God continues his work of redemption even in the midst of that failure. Although many people look at the Old Testament and see only God's judgment, a closer look reveals that God's grace is the subtle subtext of the curse on Adam and Eve, promising that their seed would ultimately triumph over Satan's work. In this situation, as in many

> God interacts with his people through covenants.

others, God interacts with his people through covenants. The word **covenant** refers to an agreement secured by God in which he expressed his will based on a larger vision of life rather than merely giving a list of instructions. God makes covenants with Adam and Eve in creation, with Noah and his descendants, with Abraham and his descendants, with Moses and the nation of Israel, with David and his descendants, and finally with Israel that promised to restore *shalom*.

Act 4: Redemption Accomplished. The prophets of the Old Testament envisioned a messiah who would drive out death and humiliation. Yet, after God's initiation of the new covenant with Israel, a four hundred–year silence follows. Punctuating this silence is the good news of God's gospel through Jesus Christ, the God-man who fulfills the Abrahamic and Davidic covenants and establishes a kingly dynasty to fulfill prophecy, save his people, and establish his kingdom. Much to the surprise of the nation of Israel, though, the kingdom established by Jesus Christ is not a *place* but a *reality*: God is king. It is not a military triumph but a victory over everything that plagues us: sin, sickness, death, and unfaithfulness. And it is for us—all of us—because as we saw in chapter 6, Jesus Christ extends the new covenant to all people, both Jews and non-Jews (Gentiles).

Act 5: Redemption Applied. Through Jesus's ministry, the New Testament announces that God's kingdom is at hand (Matt. 4:17)[29] and that it will bring blessing to the nations of the earth (Gal. 3:6–9).[30] The vehicle by which this good news is carried to the world is the church, the *ecclesia*, a community united by God's Spirit and charged with proclaiming Christ's kingdom. The early church was very diverse: Jews and non-Jews, men and women, slaves and free people. Drawing from Old Testament imagery, the church is described as a bride, an army, a nation, a body, a family, a team, a temple, a flock, and a hospital.

Act 6: Redemption Completed. To those who think that all the good stuff is "up there" in heaven, Act 6 of God's story comes as quite a surprise. It does not culminate with an emptying out of the earth; rather, at the end of all things, the book of Revelation explains, God comes to "tabernacle" among us in a new heaven and new earth. The experience of his presence will be even better than creation because a world that was fallen and redeemed is a greater testament to God's glory than creation itself. The parallels between the creation account in Genesis 1–3 and the end of all things in Revelation 20–22 demonstrate that the entirety of Scripture is one story: a story of Christ renewing all things and reversing sin, suffering, and brokenness.

Taken together, these six acts show God as wisely and patiently instructing, chastening, delivering, and restoring his people. He is faithful when they are not and continually woos them, providing a strong counterpoint to the common impression that God is brooding, grumpy, mean, and distant. Actually, all through the pages of Scripture, we see a God of grace, whose story is the whole story—the true story of the world and everyone in it. And it calls forth two very specific responses: loving God and loving our neighbors.

7. THE ROLE HUMANS PLAY IN THE BIBLE'S METANARRATIVE

When asked about the greatest commandment, Jesus said, "You shall love the Lord your God with all your heart and with all your soul and with all your mind. This is the great and first commandment. And a second is like it: You shall love your neighbor as yourself. On these two commandments depend all the Law and the Prophets" (Matt. 22:37–40).

In other words, with every aspect of our beings, we are to pledge allegiance to God, the one whose image we bear. In the ancient Near Eastern culture in which the Bible was written, kings set up images of themselves in conquered cities to remind people who was in charge. When God decided to set up his image, he formed living, breathing humans who would represent him with purpose, trust, confidence, decisiveness, creativity, and responsibility.

We bear God's image in our function as rulers on the earth. The **doctrine of the fall** describes how our first parents tried to slough off their image-bearing capacity but found underneath only nakedness and shame. Irresponsibility, paranoia, and blame replaced responsibility, trust, and purpose. By trying to take matters into their own hands, Adam and Eve transmuted pleasure into pain and fruitfulness into barrenness. They experienced what it was like to be cast out of God's presence.

> *Doctrine of the Fall:* the orthodox Christian belief that sin entered the natural world when Adam and Eve chose to disobey God and ate from the Tree of Knowledge of Good and Evil.

The Bible's word for this rebellion is *sin.* Sin is a parasite that survives by living off its human hosts. Like rust, sin eats away at us, corroding our image-bearing capacity even as we crown ourselves kings and queens of our stolen domain. Ultimately, we become like what we worship: mute and lifeless yet cruel and insatiably demanding. The theological term for what happened is *original sin*, the biblical doctrine that we are thoroughly and absolutely fallen.

The antidote to sin is God's glory. His glory reveals our hidden idols and scours away our illusions. The white-hot hum of God's glory ignites within us a burning determination to declare war against *anything* standing in the way of fully bearing the image of the always-good, always-merciful, and always-faithful God. This restoration occurs through **repentance**, the biblical word for "changing one's mind."

> Restoration occurs through repentance, the biblical word for "changing one's mind."

It is like waking up to a new world, to a realization that we have accepted counterfeits, and finding new joy in discovering a way of life far superior.

In this climate of repentance, we can see that sins such as wrath, greed, sloth, pride, lust, envy, and gluttony are parasites that attack something good. The good path is finally open to us, and through the Holy Spirit, we can see beyond sin's obstacles to a life of wisdom and flourishing. We can learn to love the right things at the right time and avoid the path of foolishness. In the end, the gospel of God is not merely a plan by which to avoid hell but also a way to live differently now.

The life of repentance changes the way we love our neighbors from just *getting along* with the people around us to actively seeking their genuine good. Whereas sin breaks relationships with God, one another, ourselves, and even creation, redemption transforms our relationships, enabling us to seek *shalom* for those around us so we may find *shalom* for ourselves (Jer. 29:7).[31]

If the Bible has authority, if it clearly reveals who God is and what he is doing in the world, being able to read and understand it becomes one of the most important things we can do. Yet most people don't know how to read the Bible well. They're easily distracted by the search for things that speak to them personally. They're sometimes bogged down in details. With a little help, they can learn to see God's nature and character more clearly in a life-changing fashion.

8. HOW TO READ THE BIBLE

Though we want to know God personally, we often filter our reading of Scripture through our own desires and cultural understandings, as though our personal search for meaning is what makes Scripture meaningful. But as we have seen, the Bible is about God, not us. It does not bend to our thoughts or desires. It expresses what God thinks and wants to see happen. Scripture itself calls us to be "transformed by the renewal of [our] mind[s]" because by doing that, we may "discern what is the will of God, what is good and acceptable and perfect" (Rom. 12:2). For anyone struggling with a sense of direction in life, that is very good news.

Often believers miss the fullness of this blessing by making several common reading mistakes such as assuming that the Bible doesn't need to be interpreted, misapplying the text, selectively applying the Bible's teaching to certain agendas, treating the Bible as mainly a collection of "life lessons," getting bored with not always discovering new truths, taking the Bible out of context, and trying to make the Bible fit contemporary moral standards and politically correct notions.

These mistakes may be remedied by interpreting biblical texts more faithfully. Reading the Bible well involves selecting a good study Bible and committing to seriously getting into the text. Read chapters, not just verses. As you read Scripture, seek to understand the genre (poetry, history, proverbs, and so forth), the context (the historical and literary basis), the content (the meaning of the words), and the relationships among passages in different books and different parts of the Bible (a study Bible will help you do this by listing cross-references). Then courageously pursue a response: we are to be "doers of the word, and not hearers only" (James 1:22).[32] Personally, I like to *journal* about what I am learning, *share* with others what I'm learning, and find ways to *live* the text out practically *that day*.

Through the Bible, God is shaping us into the image of his Son. It's not a mechanical process like flipping a light switch; it's more like blowing on the embers of a fire to kindle it into flame so that we may be on fire for understanding who God is and how we are part of the great story he is telling.

Although Christians find God's story deeply compelling, there are others who find it to be a negative influence, and possibly even dangerous. Their objections are numerous, and one of the key goals of *Understanding the Faith* is to address those objections in a way that allows us to see God's story even more powerfully than before.

9. What External Evidence Demonstrates That God Actually Exists?

As we examined the biblical metanarrative of creation, fall, and redemption in this text, and as we dealt with questions about the authority of Scripture, we assumed that we will better understand the flow of history—indeed, the character of God himself—if we take the Bible as seriously as it takes itself. What evidence or reasoning apart from Scripture supports the Bible's claims about God? If God made everything, who made him? Why is belief in God so important when unbelievers seem capable of living just as morally as believers? Isn't belief in God a matter of cultural preference?

People want to know whether the biblical story about God is anything more than an interesting historical artifact. It's not just that people want evidence; it's that they want to test the Christian idea of God to see if it stands up to scrutiny. Scripture says that the evidence for God's existence is clearly seen (Rom. 1:20).[33] Although Scripture's truth does not rise or fall on whether "God meets the test" of evidence or reasoning, we saw in this book three different sets of reasons that enable us to logically understand God's existence.

Cosmological Argument. Cosmology is the study of the order, structure, and design of the universe. The **cosmological argument** says that everything that exists has an explanation for its existence. The universe obviously exists. The only sufficient explanation for its existence is God. A variation of the cosmological argument called the

> The cosmological argument says that everything that exists has an explanation for its existence. The universe obviously exists. The only sufficient explanation for its existence is God.

kalam cosmological argument was developed by Islamic philosophers who sought to explain how they could know about the supernatural when our tools of understanding seem to work only inside of nature. These philosophers reasoned that whatever begins to exist has a cause. The universe began to exist; therefore, the universe has a cause.

> *Kalam Cosmological Argument:* an argument for God's existence that begins with the premise that something caused the universe to exist and ends with the conclusion that God is the best explanation for that cause.

Of course, many object to these cosmological arguments, saying that they make an unsupportable assumption of how God came to exist: "If God made the universe, who made God?" they ask. We saw in chapter 10, though, that there must be one eternal uncaused causer or nothing would have ever come into existence. And although such scientists as Stephen Hawking point out that it is possible for particles to emerge out of a pure vacuum, a vacuum isn't really "nothing," and neither are the laws of physics by which such a process would take place.

Design Argument. According to the **design argument**, the world appears to be the product of design. A design requires an intelligent designer. That designer is God. Just as we can see that Mount Rushmore's rock formations resembling George Washington, Thomas Jefferson, Teddy Roosevelt, and Abraham Lincoln were not caused by natural processes, so too can we observe specified complexity in the natural world. Not only does there appear to be fine-tuning in the universe, but we see complex biological information that cannot be explained by Darwinian mechanisms. We live on "a privileged planet."

> *Design Argument (aka Teleological Argument):* an argument for God's existence that begins with the premise that design requires an intelligent designer and ends with the conclusion that God is the best explanation for the observable design within the universe.

Some say that the extreme odds of the universe coming into existence exactly as needed to support life on earth can be overcome if there are an infinite number of universes. Unfortunately, for proponents of this multiverse theory, there has yet to emerge a scientifically credible, plausible mechanism for generating these many worlds. Not only that, but no scientist has proposed a way we could ever check to see if these other universes actually exist. Multiverse theory is little more than a guess, and one that people seem to make primarily to avoid acknowledging a designer.

Moral Argument. Objective morality—morality that is always true across all times and cultures—exists because there is a moral law giver, and that lawgiver is God. Humans have a sense of right or wrong, of "oughtness," that is deeper than mere personal preference. The **moral argument** says that if God does not exist, objective moral values and duties do not exist.

> The moral argument says that if God does not exist, objective moral values and duties do not exist.

Objective moral values and duties *do* exist; therefore, God exists.

CONCLUSION

Of course, there are objections to the moral argument. The first is that objective morality doesn't exist. But with few exceptions, every person seems to have a sense of what's right and wrong, of what's good and evil. We humans view right and wrong as being objectively real, which means that rightness and wrongness depend on something far deeper and more solid than human opinion. Very few people would say that the very bad things that have happened in this world are only wrong for people who *say* they are wrong. A more serious objection to the moral argument is that nonbelievers can live good lives without God. The issue, though, isn't whether atheists can be moral but whether atheism can *explain* morality apart from God. It is not whether we *believe* in God that makes morality objective but whether he actually exists. If he does, objective moral truths are explainable and defensible. If he does not, they are mere cultural or individual preferences.

> We humans view right and wrong as being objectively real, which means that rightness and wrongness depend on something far deeper and more solid than human opinion.

10. Isn't Belief in God a Cultural Phenomenon?

Some object, "You find those reasons for God's existence plausible only because you grew up in a culture where belief in God is normal." The argument that religious beliefs are just cultural phenomena, artifacts of where we grew up, makes sense on the surface. After all, a person growing up in India is more likely to be Hindu than Christian. The only way we could hold this view, though, is if we were in a position to know that there is no real substance to religious claims beyond the fact that they are culturally situated. But this in itself is a claim to know something about religion to be true.

The biblical view, which is widely accepted across all cultures, is not that other religions are devoid of truth but rather that biblical Christianity accurately describes the contours of the world as it actually is better than other religious systems. Christians base this claim on what the Bible says about God, humanity, and reality and how this understanding has worked itself out since Bible times.

Others will say, "Your arguments about God's existence are just word play." This argument, based on the idea of **Postmodernism**, says that when we claim to know objective reality, we are just using language to construct our own meaning shaped by our culture and life experiences. The argument states that books such as the Bible are just words connected to subjective experiences, not true statements about reality. It seems like a powerful argument until we realize that objects and thoughts have qualities that present themselves consistently to the mind, no matter who is thinking about them. Even people who believe that love is a social construction still know the difference between loving a person and killing that person. Christians do not disagree that we can use talk to create concepts that can be acted on to create real things in the world. But Scripture views talk about God in a different way than other kinds of talk. The talk of Scripture is intended to communicate truth that applies to all people at all times in all cultures.

An extreme version of Postmodernism goes even further, though, asserting that trying to change a culture through a worldview such as Christianity is a form of genocide that destroys that culture's history and practices. But as we saw earlier, careful research into the history of missions has shown that although many non-Christian ways of "civilizing" the natives (some of which were practiced by professed Christians) have done harm, Christian missionaries have, on balance, done a great deal of good in bringing freedom, health, and peace to cultures around the world as well as preserving native music, culture, and language.

At the end of the day, there is strong evidence that God exists, that the sort of God whose existence we can deduce through reasonable arguments matches the description of the God of the Bible, and that this understanding goes beyond cultural practices and how we use words. The good news of the gospel is that our salvation is not just for "us"; it is for the world, enabling us to share the good news—in both word and deed—with everyone everywhere.

When people insist that God does not exist or that our understanding of him is culturally bound and not actually true, they're doing so based on two assumptions about the world that, in the end, are unsupported by evidence. Perhaps we should turn the spotlight on these unwarranted assumptions as part of making sense of the Bible's claims.

11. Shining the Spotlight on Critics' Unwarranted Assumptions

Theoretically, it is possible to believe in a God from whom the universe proceeds, who designed the world, and who established a moral law yet still doubt whether God is active in the world today. The Bible indicates very strongly that God not only exists but also superintends the world he has made and even intervenes miraculously in it. Some are embarrassed by the Bible's claims. They see them as, at best, a distraction from Jesus's moral teachings and, at worst, a silly fantasy produced by overactive imaginations. One philosopher who articulated this objection was David Hume (1711–1776), who said that miracles are by definition the suspension of the natural order, that nature develops in a uniform fashion, that miracles cannot occur in such a world, and that therefore they most likely have not occurred.

> *Miracle:* a supernatural sign or event that is intended to highlight the power and goodness of God.

Theologically, the Bible presents a **miracle** as an event that *restores*, rather than *suspends*, the natural order. Miracles are presented in the Bible as having freed the Hebrews from slavery, displayed God's power over evil, restored sick people to health, and showed God's love of abundant provision. But aside from this theological point, the argument Hume articulates against miracles has been criticized as being a circular argument. Saying that miracles have never happened because our experience in the world is of uniformity is to say that all reports of miracles are false. The reason for believing them to be false, though, is that no such miracles are possible. That's like saying, "I'm full because I'm not hungry," or, "The only reason she is so popular is because she is a celebrity." It uses one of the premises as the conclusion and, in effect, says nothing.

The circular nature of Hume's argument against miracles highlights critics' two unwarranted assumptions: **materialism** and **naturalism**. To say, "Only the natural world exists; therefore, the supernatural does not exist," does not prove that only the natural world exists: it *assumes* that only the natural world exists and bases its criticisms of the supernatural on that assumption. Similarly, to *proclaim* that only the material world exists is not to *prove* that it does but to *assume* that it does. The best an honest person can say is "I believe only the material world exists" or "In my experience, I have no basis on which to say anything but the material world exists" or "I have not encountered evidence that anything outside the material world exists."

In my experience, it is rare for people who hold to materialism and naturalism to qualify or defend their assumptions. Many times, they don't even realize they're making assumptions at all. They think they're just being scientific. But materialism/naturalism are unwarranted assumptions for at least two reasons. First, they presume too much of science and seek to make **Secularism** absolute. Saying that science replaces religion isn't making a statement of fact but rather is revealing a narrow framework for understanding reality. Instead, we ought to seriously consider the idea that both the material and immaterial world exist (i.e., an acceptable form of **dualism**). We have brains, but we also have minds. Ideas such as justice and love and liberty are not just social constructs; they are categories of meaning that exist whether or not we have trained our senses to perceive them. A growing amount of reasoning and evidence is showing that the materialist/naturalist assumption that "what we see is all there is" is simply insufficient to explain the data of how the mind functions and how humans experience life and death.

Second, credible reports of miracles also show materialism/naturalism to be unwarranted assumptions. In *Understanding the Faith*, we have examined the claims that the Bible's accounts of miracles are unsupportable and found that, in addition to credible claims of thousands of miracles that have been catalogued, the biblical account is remarkably well supported for having been recorded so long ago.[34] The Bible writers took great care in transmitting their heritage, and many of its claims are supported by completely secular sources. The biblical accounts are specific enough in detail to conclude that the historical scenes in which miracles occurred could, in fact, have occurred just as reported.

Naturalism: the belief that all phenomena can be explained in terms of natural causes.

Secularism: an atheistic and materialistic worldview that advocates for a public society free from the influence of religion.

Dualism: the belief that reality is ultimately composed of two essential substances.

Minimal Facts Approach: a method formulated by Gary Habermas for investigating the resurrection of Jesus that concentrates only on the historical facts that are so well evidenced that they are accepted by nearly every scholar who studies the topic.

One miracle in particular commands attention because it is so central to the Christian faith: the resurrection of Jesus of Nazareth. The **minimal facts approach** that the vast majority of scholars accept as valid points to the following facts: Jesus died by crucifixion, his disciples believed he rose and appeared to them, the apostle Paul was radically converted by what he claimed was a personal encounter with Jesus, and the skeptic James (Jesus's brother) was suddenly changed. But there is other intriguing evidence as well: the tomb was empty, and more than five hundred people witnessed the resurrected Christ and were forever changed. This strong historical evidence led the respected theologian N. T. Wright to say, "The widespread belief and practice of the early Christians is only explicable if we assume that they all believed that Jesus was bodily raised."[35]

If the grave cannot keep him, then evil certainly cannot. The Gospels show Jesus's power over evil. Jesus did not treat demonic manifestation or the existence of Satan as vain superstitions but instead used them as opportunities to put Satan and his minions in their place and lay bare Israel's false gods. Materialism/naturalism tempts us to trivialize evil, but the biblical account warns us not to be deceived or fall prey to evil through doubt, irrational fear, or self-accusation.

When we open our minds and hearts to the possibility that materialism and naturalism are inadequate ways of seeing the world, we become capable of seeing the world as God sees it and responding to Christ as one who has authority over everything in heaven and on earth. Giving up materialist/naturalist assumptions is harder than it looks, though, because of the steady drumbeat of the message that "science shows Christianity to be nothing more than a primitive superstition." Fortunately, as we have seen, the relationship between Christianity and science is nothing like we are learning from today's culture.

12. The Battle between Christianity and Science

In spite of the flawed reasoning of those arguing against miracles—and even the evidence that the supernatural, immaterial world actually exists—materialists/naturalists are not prepared to concede the battle. The "Christianity is defeated by science" refrain dies hard. True, some faith systems are incompatible with modern science, but Christianity is not one of them. Scientists operating out of a Christian framework, such as Isaac Newton and Robert Boyle, are responsible for a great deal of modern science. In fact, of the fifty-two active scientists who made the most significant contributions during the Scientific Revolution, only one was an atheist. Sixty percent were devout Christians.[36] In spite of this, many otherwise-intelligent people still believe the now discredited notion that Christianity is a superstition that led to an age of ignorance and that the world was rescued by science.

Indeed, as authors Nancy Pearcey and Charles Thaxton point out, science's underlying assumptions can be derived only from a belief in a divine creator. These assumptions include not only the orderliness and lawfulness of the universe but also the beliefs that nature is valuable enough to study, nature is good, nature's laws can be precisely stated and understood, humans can discover nature's order, and it is possible—and good—to observe nature and describe it in a rationally intelligent fashion.[37]

Even more intriguing, although the Bible is not a book of science, it is consistent with many things scientists have discovered about the world, including the inherent design in the natural world, that something outside the universe brought it into being, that life does not come from nonlife, that there is intention and order in creation, the nature of humanity as a self-reflective species capable of symbolic communication and higher levels of social organization, and that there are limits to change in nature. Although differences over biblical interpretation and the age of the earth are real and serious, most Christians agree that God is the Creator and that humans are morally culpable creations in a broken-but-privileged relationship with him. As C. S. Lewis puts it, "In science we have been reading only the notes to a poem; in Christianity we find the poem itself."[38]

So far in this chapter, we've summarized what we've learned in *Understanding the Faith* about the internal and external evidence for the Bible, the coherence of its metanarrative, the logic of its postulates, and the unwarranted assumptions of those who question its authority. In view of this evidence, one would think that critics might at least grudgingly acknowledge that belief in the Bible is not unreasonable. Instead, a whole new line of argument has developed saying that the very act of claiming truth is intolerant and that the bigotry and violence of Scripture ought to serve as a warning against biblical thinking. What, if anything, ought we to say about this?

13. Isn't Claiming the Truth Intolerant?

In the last couple of decades, people who oppose God's authority have begun arguing that the very act of *claiming* to be right is what is wrong with Christianity. The word **tolerance** means recognizing and respecting the dignity of people you think are wrong. A new view of tolerance has arisen, though, that pegs Christians as intolerant people who demean other beliefs and threaten harmony in our world. To this view, tolerance means accepting each religious viewpoint as no more or less true than any other. The only way for Christians to be viewed as tolerant, accordingly, is to forfeit the belief that Jesus died for everyone and is the true way to God. This, of course, guts the gospel at the heart of historic Christianity.

> The word tolerance means recognizing and respecting the dignity of people you think are wrong.

At the risk of being shut out of today's public dialogue, Christians need to identify and respond to the two sources of the "Christianity is intolerant" attack. The first source is Postmodernism. Postmodernism is the worldview that says language is so culturally bound that it cannot adequately describe reality. Postmodernism rejects all metanarratives (except for the metanarrative that says that no metanarrative is objectively true). But if our language does not point to any truth, then the claim that "Christians are intolerant" can't be true. Nor can the claim that God's existence is unknowable be true because it, too, is a claim about reality. The second source of the "Christianity is intolerant" claim is **prescriptive religious pluralism**, the idea that all religious viewpoints are equally valid. Pluralism comes in two forms. "Pluralism 1.0" says that religious truth is individual: we all have our own truths and should not judge

> *Prescriptive Pluralism:* the belief that we should be tolerant of other religions because no single religion can be universally true for everyone.

the truth claims of others. "Pluralism 2.0" says that religious truth is cultural and that we are each raised in certain religious traditions and can't help believing in them, so we must tolerate the claims of other cultures.

What gets lost in the discussion about tolerance is what is actually meant by truth. Pluralists mean by truth what a given person or most of the people in the culture think of as true. But something is true if and only if it lines up with the way things actually are. To make a truth claim, we must know the difference between facts and opinions. Claiming that Bill Clinton was president of the United States in 1993 is different from claiming that medium-rare steak is best. One is a fact; the other is an opinion. As soon as any worldview posits answers to questions about humanity, death, thinking, morality, or the meaning of history, it is claiming to know something about the nature of reality. Such claims cannot be true for one person and false for someone else, especially if they are contrary to one another.

As we saw earlier, Christianity claims that the Bible describes the contours of the world as it actually exists more accurately than other religions. Further, Christianity says, this truth is observable by anyone who has not suppressed his or her understanding by other commitments. It is justifiably believed. Christianity's moral commands, such as "Thou shalt not murder" and "Thou shalt not bear false witness," work to produce a good society, but this is not what makes them good. They are good because they reflect God's nature and character, and this is why they work.

There are three ways to defuse wrong ideas of tolerance. First, point out how tolerance claims commit suicide, so to speak. For example, if someone says, "Who are you to judge others?" the response should be "Is it your judgment that I should not judge?" If someone says, "There is no truth," the response is "Is that statement true?" A **self-refuting claim** kills itself. Second, ask questions such as "What do you mean by that?" "How did you come to that conclusion?" and "What happens if you are wrong?" Third, have a good attitude. Be humble and transparent and listen well. Having a good attitude does not mean that God's truth is up for debate; rather, it shows openness and a willingness to converse in the hope that God will "grant them repentance" and lead them to the truth (2 Tim. 2:25–26).[39]

At root, people who question whether Christianity is intolerant are asking a deeper question: Is the God of the Bible *good*? After all, in spite of the Bible's moral teachings, it sometimes seems as if God is not playing by his own rules. If God is truly good and powerful, why does evil exist, and why is suffering such a part of reality?

14. WHY IS THERE EVIL AND SUFFERING?

Every worldview must grapple with the problem of evil. Some worldviews do so by saying, "Bad things happen. That's just the way it is." Other worldviews say, "Evil is an illusion," "Evil is what you get for having done bad things in past lives," "Evil happens because rich people take money away from the poor," or even "Evil is punishment for not living a life pleasing to the deity [or deities]." The question is not just how a good God could allow evil but whether, if evil actually exists, the Bible's explanation of it is the most sensible one.

If someone asks you how God could allow evil, ask, "What do you mean by evil?" Is evil something that actually exists, or is it just a category for things we prefer not to happen? To know that something is evil, we have to know that it is not the way it is supposed to be. Where do we get this sense of "oughtness"? If what the Bible says about God is untrue, there is no reason to expect that our sense of what ought to be is reasonable.

The biblical answer to evil and suffering is not *what* but *who*. Through his Son, Jesus Christ, God has entered into our suffering, has conquered death and hell, and will set the world to rights. It is Christianity that makes sense of the past, explaining how humans created for *shalom* chose to go their own way and were permitted by God to do so, even though they were miserable. It makes sense of the present, showing how a God who is purposeful and unlimited in understanding knows the choices of free creatures and works things out so that his good, desired end is achieved. It also makes sense of the future. We are not bound by fate: God is in charge and moving the world toward the consummation of his sovereign plan.

Through suffering, we are forced to realize that the chief end of humanity is not temporal happiness but an intimate relationship with God. Nothing in the Bible denies or explains away the reality of suffering. In fact, many biblical authors cry out to God in pain. But the Bible does counsel in response to suffering an unshakable confidence in God's goodness.

God is not aloof or incomprehensible. He does not encourage us to ignore evil or treat it as an illusion. We do not have a pantheon of reckless gods who are incapable of solving great problems. We have, instead, a God who is with us. In the light of the cross, we can see clearly what is right and wrong, good and evil. And *because* of the cross, we have hope that God will conquer evil. In fact, the entire story of the Bible is how he is doing just that.

Yet it seems that part of the Bible's answer to the problem of evil and suffering—the doctrine of hell—may catch many people unaware in its trap and actually make the problem worse. Is there a way to reconcile God's goodness with this severe doctrine?

15. What's the Deal with Hell?

Hell is part of God's answer to evil and suffering. Judgment eventually comes to the wicked. But this leads to a problem most Christians wish they didn't have. Jesus lavished compassion on the suffering, died for the sins of the world, and taught widely admired moral principles, yet he referred to hell more than anyone else quoted in the Bible. How could a loving God—and his loving, savior Son—condemn anyone to such a fate, especially those who have never heard?

The Bible clearly teaches the existence of hell. It describes hell as a place of outer darkness, away from the heavenly city, a perpetually burning dump, a place of anguish and regret, and an eternal separation from God. Hell is the other direction from God. Suffering in hell is both physical and spiritual and it goes on forever.

Hell's seriousness underscores the immensity of God's mercy. What we need is not a scratch behind the ear, like a pet. We need saving, and we can't rescue ourselves. But isn't hell too extreme of a punishment for those who try to save themselves? Aside from serial killers and mass murderers and child abusers, who could possibly deserve such a fate? Although we can sympathize with people who wonder about this, we must remember that the desire to be away from God's immediate presence is what sin is all about. Hell is not something foisted upon unsuspecting innocents but a place where people finally get what they want: to be apart from God. Ultimately, those who go to hell know exactly why they're there.

Even as we consider difficult questions such as "Does God send children to hell?" and "What about those who have never heard?" we can conclude that God is loving and just and will not act inconsistently with his character. So although the doctrine of hell seems like very bad news at first glance, it is actually part of God's very good news: love does indeed win. God wins. Good triumphs over evil. Humanity is not doomed after all. This good news, based on the authority of Jesus, must be shared with everyone in the world.

Yet those who doubt God's goodness point to something beyond the doctrine of hell: they point to passages in Scripture that seem to show God as a bully. Why would God command his people to wipe out entire people groups? Does God hate homosexuals? Doesn't the Bible endorse slavery? Isn't the Bible oppressive to women? If we want to communicate biblical truth to today's world, we need to figure out what the Bible actually teaches about such things.

16. Is God a Mean Bully?

The Bible reveals God as dynamic, active, involved, and personal. He describes his people as his family, his congregation, his treasured possession, those he made holy, and a kingdom of priests. If God is really like this, though, why would he seemingly command things that are so clearly evil? Let's take a look at several criticisms people make of the Bible in this regard.

Does God command genocide? According to Old Testament accounts, God commanded his people to wipe out entire people groups. How can this be justified? The question is not as simple as it first appears. It is clear from the Bible that God wanted his chosen people to avoid the lifestyle of the surrounding Canaanites, whose acts of child sacrifice, temple prostitution, incest, and bestiality were deeply corrupt and evil. Moreover, both the Canaanites and the Amalekites, another nearby people group, openly committed themselves to Israel's destruction. Is war justified in this case? Probably so.

But what about the killing of women and children—isn't that still evil? As we saw, the Israelite accounts of "banning" or "consecrating people to destruction" were written in the typical battle-report language of the time and clearly did not represent the actual killing of every person. Rather, it seems that it is a socially acceptable form of hyperbole, akin to sports fans cheering their team to "crush" the opponent in defeat, not demanding their actual killing.

Does God hate homosexuals? The Old Testament book of Leviticus displays a strong concern about sexual sin, especially sins that harm or demean women and children. To God, sexual sin is not just an innocent, private act between two people. It produces shame, breaks down relationships, shatters trust, and prevents people from being the kind of blessing God intended. It takes the *very good* aspects of creation and turns them into a source of hurt and diminishment. The children of Israel were a set-apart community, the likes of which does not exist today. No one *had* to stay there, but if they did stay, they agreed to follow the community's rules, including its rules about sexual purity. Homosexuals were not singled out.

Is God pro-slavery? Slavery has been common everywhere and at all times throughout history. What changed that is the Bible's emphasis that everyone bears the image of God. In the New Testament, the radical equality of slaves becomes clear. Slaves were treated as brothers, and those who traded humans as cargo or kidnapped others to bring them into slavery were condemned.[40]

Is God anti-woman? The Bible also is a book that—in a complete break from the norms of the time—gave unparalleled dignity to women. Especially in a Greek culture in which husbands and fathers had supreme, absolute power over their wives and children, Jesus is good news for women. In the ministry of Jesus, and later in the ministries of the apostles, women gained a stature unheard of in those times, even to the point where the gospel accounts of the resurrection acknowledge that women were the first to testify to Jesus's resurrection, even though their testimony would have been scorned in court. No wonder conversion to Christianity in ancient times was more prevalent among females than males.

In a fallen world, things often do not turn out as we expect. Good intentions go awry. People—indeed, entire cultures—fail to live up to their ideals. Evil exists. People suffer. How could a good God allow this? And how can we take the Bible seriously when it seems to *promote* suffering by condemning nonbelievers to an eternity in hell? Are these objections to the Bible simply too great to overcome? Let's review each in turn.

17. IF CHRISTIANITY IS TRUE, WHY DO PEOPLE WALK AWAY?

As we come to the close of this book, we believe that it is reasonable to acknowledge the validity of the Bible's case for itself, the case made for it in light of external evidence, and the answers it provides to life's ultimate questions. Yet many are skeptical: some because they are seeking the truth, and others because they are avoiding it. There seem to be six reasons people turn away from Christianity:

> **1. Lack of knowledge.** They haven't taken time to examine the claims of Christianity or the Bible, and they make assumptions about both that simply are unwarranted.

> **2. Misunderstanding of belief.** They assume that faith is what they make it or what they've always been taught or what they feel rather than what they are led to through wisdom and knowledge.

> **3. Conflicting commitments.** They're committed to a certain lifestyle or way of seeing things that they recognize is in conflict with biblical revelation, and they are unwilling to let those commitments go and embrace the truth.

> **4. Practical atheism.** They believe in God but live as if he doesn't exist or is irrelevant to most of life.[41]

> **5. Effects of sin.** Their bad habits erode sensitivity to the work of the Holy Spirit in their lives.

6. Distraction. They fill their lives with the intellectual equivalent of empty calories: food that makes them feel full even if it is of dubious nutritional value.

The common denominator in all six of these reasons is that they lead to doubt. Doubt itself is not shocking. Biblical heroes experienced doubt. Notable Christians throughout history experienced doubt.

Overcoming doubt and disbelief calls for more than just intellectual solutions, though such solutions have tremendous power when rightly understood. We need other people. We need community with believers. Such a community can help us develop patience as we work through our doubts. It can give us a hopeful way to live even when we sense there is much we do not understand. Its members can share answers they've found helpful. In the church, we find safety and perspective as well as teaching and repentance. Doubt may encourage us to shrink away, but if we let it move us *toward* God's people instead, we gain strength and the opportunity to flourish as we prepare to be a blessing to the nations of the earth.

18. CONCLUSION

It's not just that there are many worldviews and that people are content to take them or leave them. The reality is that certain worldviews seem to be discontent with anything less than dismantling the Christian worldview. If we do not seek to influence the world for what is good and true, the proponents of what is bad and false will compromise the church's influence on the world.

> If we do not seek to influence the world for what is good and true, the proponents of what is bad and false will compromise the church's influence on the world.

> It doesn't matter if you are outnumbered. It has been said that one person sincerely committed to a cause is more valuable than a thousand who are merely interested.

Our situation today is similar to when Israel was taken captive in Babylon. The Babylonians were militarily strong, but they sensed that if they wanted to win over the long term, they had to mentor the rising generations. They set about training the best of the Hebrew boys to embrace pagan philosophies and become leaders who would spread the Babylonian message throughout the world.

There was, however, a sticking point in the Babylonians' plan. Actually, there were four. Their names were Daniel, Shadrach, Meshach, and Abednego. They refused to bow the knee to false gods. They trusted God's Word and stood strong—so strong, in fact, that they became leaders in the Babylonian government. Rather than convert to Babylonian ways, they converted some of Babylon's leaders to God's way.

This is the kind of leader we need today. It doesn't matter if you are outnumbered. It has been said that one person sincerely committed to a cause is more valuable than a thousand who are merely interested.[42] What we need is not a crowd of people lurching toward the truth but instead a handful of brave souls who will embrace God's revelation in the Bible and stand for truth, whatever the odds. The world is crying out for a few to say, "By God's grace, here I stand." For those who rise, it will change everything. It might even change the world.

ENDNOTES

1. 1 Chronicles 12:32: "… of Issachar, men who had understanding of the times, to know what Israel ought to do, 200 chiefs, and all their kinsmen under their command."

2. Isaiah 30:21: "Your ears shall hear a word behind you, saying, 'This is the way, walk in it,' when you turn to the right or when you turn to the left."

3. Deuteronomy 30:19: "I call heaven and earth to witness against you today, that I have set before you life and death, blessing and curse. Therefore choose life, that you and your offspring may live."

4. John 8:32: "You will know the truth, and the truth will set you free."

5. Nancy Pearcey, *Saving Leonardo: A Call to Resist the Secular Assault on Mind, Morals, and Meaning* (Nashville: B&H, 2010), 26–27.

6. J. P. Moreland, *Love Your God with All Your Mind: The Role of Reason in the Life of the Soul*, rev. and updated ed. (Colorado Springs, CO: NavPress, 2012), 21–22.

7. Revelation 19:16: "On his robe and on his thigh he has a name written, King of kings and Lord of lords."

8. 2 Peter 3:9: "The Lord is not slow to fulfill his promise as some count slowness, but is patient toward you, not wishing that any should perish, but that all should reach repentance."

9. Alexis de Tocqueville, *Democracy in America*, ed. J. P. Mayer, trans. George Lawrence (New York: Harper Perennial, 1969), 291.

10. Dawkins specifically referenced the King James Version of the Bible, which was produced during a time of rich development for the English language. See Richard Dawkins, "Why I Want All Our Children to Read the King James Bible," *The Guardian*, May 19, 2012, www.guardian.co.uk/science/2012/may/19/richard-dawkins-king-james-bible.

11. As we saw earlier, the Hebrew word *galah* and the Greek word *apokalupto* "express the idea of uncovering what was concealed." Millard Erickson, *Christian Theology*, 2nd ed. (Grand Rapids, MI: Baker, 2001), 201.

12. Biblical references for these points include the following: Jesus asserted authority (Matt. 7:28–29; Mark 2:8–12), Jesus claimed to be the "I am" of the Old Testament (John 8:58), Jesus said that he and God were "one" essence (John 10:30), and Jesus told his followers that those who had seen him had seen God (John 14:7–9).

13. See Matthew 4:1–10.

14. The following passages support these claims: Jesus conferred authority on his disciples (Matt. 10:1; 11:27), and Jesus indicated that this authority extended far beyond the time boundaries of his own earthly ministry (John 14:25–26; 15:26–27; 16:12–15).

15. 2 Timothy 3:16: "All Scripture is breathed out by God and profitable for teaching, for reproof, for correction, and for training in righteousness."

16. Gordon R. Lewis, "What Does It Mean That God Inspired the Bible?," in Ted Cabal et al., eds., *The Apologetics Study Bible* (Nashville: B&H, 2007), 1812.

17. Douglas R. Groothuis, *Christian Apologetics: A Comprehensive Case for Biblical Faith* (Downers Grove, IL: IVP Academic, 2011), 124.

18. The theological doctrine that, with the Holy Spirit superintending it, the Bible is without error is called the doctrine of inerrancy. There are many versions of this doctrine, but all seem to agree that, as David Dockery puts it, the Bible is accurate in all it affirms "to the degree of precision intended by the author, in all matters relating to God and his creation." David S. Dockery, *Christian Scripture: An Evangelical Perspective on Inspiration, Authority, and Interpretation* (Nashville: B&, 1995), 64.

19. J. Ed Komoszewski, M. James Sawyer, and Daniel B. Wallace, *Reinventing Jesus: How Contemporary Skeptics Miss the Real Jesus and Mislead Popular Culture* (Grand Rapids, MI: Kregel, 2006), 82.

20. Frank Newport, "More than 9 in 10 Americans Continue to Believe in God," Gallup, June 3, 2011, www.gallup.com/poll/147887/americans-continue-believe-god.aspx.

21. For detailed descriptions of research in these four categories, see the work of Baylor sociologists Paul Froese and Christopher Bader, *America's Four Gods* (New York: Oxford, 2010), 33–34. It is worth repeating an observation from a footnote in chap. 4, that *authoritative* and *judgmental* are loaded terms in today's world. God certainly does have authority in his universe, but his love and authority work in concert, not in opposition. The Bible proclaims God to be a completely balanced being, exercising grace, mercy, and loving-kindness alongside authority and judgment, without contradiction. God *does* judge humans but does so as a just and all-knowing deity who has a right to judge and does so with understanding and mercy.

22. See Jeremiah 9:23–24 and Deuteronomy 29:29.

23. Hebrews 1:1–2: "Long ago, at many times and in many ways, God spoke to our fathers by the prophets, but in these last days he has spoken to us by his Son, whom he appointed the heir of all things, through whom also he created the world."

24. References for these attributes of God include the following: holy (Exod. 15:11; Rev. 4:8), eternal (Ps. 90:2; Deut. 33:27), all-knowing (Rom. 11:33; Isa. 46:8–11), all-powerful (Jer. 32:17; Mark 10:27), everywhere present (Jer. 23:23–24; Ps. 139:7–10), unchanging (Ps. 33:11; Mal. 3:6), wise (Rom. 11:33; Ps. 104:24), righteous (Deut. 32:4; Ps. 89:14), loving (John 17:20–23,

Deut. 33:12), and mercifully gracious (Ps. 103:8; Neh. 9:17).

25. J. Scott Horrell, "The Eternal Son of God in the Social Trinity," in *Jesus in Trinitarian Perspective: An Introductory Christology*, ed. Fred Sanders and Klaus Issler (Nashville: B&H Academic, 2007), 47–48.

26. Biblical references for these claims include the following: God is one essence (Eph. 4:4–6), the Father is God (1 Cor. 8:6), Jesus is God (Titus 2:13), and the Holy Spirit is God (1 Cor. 6:11). Scripture also contains several passages that refer to the Father, Son, and Holy Spirit together (for example, Matt. 3:16–17; 28:19–20; 2 Cor. 13:14; Heb. 9:14; and 1 Pet. 1:1–2).

27. Genesis 6:5: "The LORD saw that the wickedness of man was great in the earth, and that every intention of the thoughts of his heart was only evil continually."

28. Judges 17:6: "In those days there was no king in Israel. Everyone did what was right in his own eyes."

29. Matthew 4:17: "From that time Jesus began to preach, saying, 'Repent, for the kingdom of heaven is at hand.'"

30. Galatians 3:6–9: "… just as Abraham 'believed God, and it was counted to him as righteousness'? Know then that it is those of faith who are the sons of Abraham. And the Scripture, foreseeing that God would justify the Gentiles by faith, preached the gospel beforehand to Abraham, saying, 'In you shall all the nations be blessed.' So then, those who are of faith are blessed along with Abraham, the man of faith."

31. Jeremiah 29:7: "Seek the welfare of the city where I have sent you into exile, and pray to the LORD on its behalf, for in its welfare you will find your welfare."

32. James 1:22: "Be doers of the word, and not hearers only, deceiving yourselves."

33. Romans 1:20: "His invisible attributes, namely, his eternal power and divine nature, have been clearly perceived, ever since the creation of the world, in the things that have been made. So they are without excuse."

34. Most recently, see Eric Metaxas, *Miracles: What They Are, Why They Happen, and How They Can Change Your Life* (New York: Dutton, 2014).

35. N. T. Wright, *The Resurrection of the Son of God* (Minneapolis: Fortress, 2003), 710.

36. Stark outlines his methodology in chap. 2, "God's Handiwork: The Religious Origins of Science," in *To the Glory of God: How Monotheism Led to Reformations, Science, Witch-Hunts, and the End of Slavery* (Princeton, NJ: Princeton University Press, 2003), 160–63. Of the fifty-two scientists Stark examined, half were Catholic and half were Protestant. Only two, Edmund Halley and Paracelsus, qualified as skeptics, and Halley was probably, Stark concludes, an atheist.

37. This brief list is wonderfully explained, illustrated, and footnoted in Nancy Pearcey and Charles Thaxton, *The Soul of Science: Christian Faith and Natural Philosophy* (Wheaton, IL: Crossway, 1994), 21–37.

38. Clyde S. Kilby, ed., *A Mind Awake: An Anthology of C. S. Lewis* (New York: Harcourt, Brace & World, 1968), 240.

39. 2 Timothy 2:25–26: " … correcting his opponents with gentleness. God may perhaps grant them repentance leading to a knowledge of the truth, and they may come to their senses and escape from the snare of the devil, after being captured by him to do his will."

40. See Galatians 3:28; 1 Corinthians 12:13; Colossians 3:11; Philemon v. 16; Revelation 18:11–13; and 1 Timothy 1:9–10.

41. See Craig M. Gay, *The Way of the Modern World* (Grand Rapids, MI: Eerdmans, 1998), 239.

42. Attributed to William E. Brown.

GLOSSARY

Abad: from the Hebrew for "to serve"; to work and worship.

Adoption: being included as a rightful member of God's eternal family.

Agape: from the Greek word *agapé* for "selfless love."

Age of Enlightenment: an eighteenth-century intellectual movement that emphasized reason, science, and individualism over tradition and religious authority.

Agnosticism: the belief that knowledge of God is ultimately inaccessible or unknowable.

Allegory: a fictional narrative in which characters and events are presented as symbols for moral and spiritual truths.

Anarchy: a society that exists without government control.

Annihilationism: the belief that damned souls are utterly destroyed rather than tormented in hell for eternity.

Anthropic Principle: the theory that the universe contains all the necessary properties that make the existence of intelligent life inevitable.

Anthropology: the study of humanity's origins, cultures, and behavior.

Apartheid: government-enforced racial segregation.

Asceticism: the practice of avoiding all forms of indulgence.

Aseity: from the Latin word meaning "from oneself"; God's self-existent and self-sufficient nature.

Astrology: the belief that astronomical events affect human events and that human beings can gain insight by studying the movements and positions of celestial bodies.

Atheism: the belief that God does not exist.

Authority: the power to command or the expertise to influence others.

Baal: meaning "Lord" or "ruler"; a false god who was purported to control nature and was worshipped by the people of Israel.

Basar: from the Hebrew for "flesh"; implies the idea of clan or family.

Beelzebub: a Greek word meaning "Lord of the flies"; references Satan and is a variation of the false god Baal.

Belief: an idea someone holds about the nature of reality.

Best of All Possible Worlds, the: a theory by Gottfried Wilhelm von Leibniz that states that the best of all possible worlds is the belief that the world we inhabit has been structured by God to maximize good and minimize evil.

Bible Commentary: a verse-by-verse exposition of scriptural passages written to help people better understand the Bible.

Biblical Genre: a classification of literary styles used in Scripture, including poetry, historical narratives, legal prescriptions, prophesies, psalms, proverbs, parables, epistles, and apocalyptic literature.

Big Bang Theory: the theory that the universe arose around fourteen billion years ago from an extremely dense state that rapidly expanded and continues to expand today.

Bourgeoisie: a term used in Marxist theory to describe those who own the means of production.

Canon: from the Greek word for "standard"; the collection of biblical writings commonly accepted as genuine and authoritative.

Chronological Snobbery: a term used to identify the fallacious thinking that ideas of an older time are inherently inferior to present ideas simply by virtue of their temporal priority.

Communicable Attributes: qualities that God and human beings share, such as wisdom, righteousness, love, mercy, and grace.

Content: the meaning of words or passages; the subject matter of a written work.

Context: the discourse surrounding a passage that gives meaning to the content; the historical background and literary setting of a text that helps clarify meaning.

Conversion: a turning from idolatry to the one true God.

Correspondence Theory of Truth: the view that the truth of a proposition is determined by how accurately it describes the facts of reality.

Cosmological Argument (aka Casual Argument): an argument for God's existence that begins with the premise that something caused the universe to exist and ends with the conclusion that God is the best explanation for the existence of the universe.

Cosmology: the study of the structure, origin, and design of the universe.

Covenant: an agreement between two parties that involves both rights and responsibilities.

Cultural Imperialism: the belief that one's culture or race is superior to others.

Dead Sea Scrolls: the oldest surviving collection of Jewish canonical texts written three hundred to four hundred years before the birth of Christ.

Death of God Theology: a theological movement that believes in a god who transcends all being and thus technically does not exist.

Deconstruction: a method of literary analysis that questions the ability of language to represent reality adequately and seeks to discern and expose the purported underlying ideologies of a text.

Deism: the belief that God exists and created the world but currently stands completely aloof from his creation; the belief that reason and nature sufficiently reveal the existence of God but that God has not revealed himself through any type of special revelation.

Derek: from the Hebrew for "the way"; refers to the overall direction of a person's life.

Derived Authority: authority that has been ordained or permitted by God.

Descriptive Passage: a biblical passage that describes specific events.

Descriptive Pluralism: the belief that we should be tolerant of competing religions in order to get along with one another.

Design Argument (aka Teleological Argument): an argument for God's existence that begins with the premise that design requires an intelligent designer and ends with the conclusion that God is the best explanation for the observable design within the universe.

Dialogue: from the Greek for "through words"; the process of talking through thoughts.

Divine Determinism: the belief that God directly determines and causes every single action in the universe.

DNA (deoxyribonucleic acid): a self-replicating, double strand of nucleic acid located in the nucleus of a cell; the storehouse for the genetic instructions used to build every protein within an organism.

Doctrine of Original Sin: the orthodox Christian belief that Adam's first sin corrupted the nature of his descendants, leading to humanity's present propensity toward committing sin.

Doctrine of the Fall: the orthodox Christian belief that sin entered the natural world when Adam and Eve chose to disobey God and ate from the Tree of Knowledge of Good and Evil.

Doctrine of the Trinity: the orthodox Christian belief that God is one being in three persons: Father, Son, and Holy Spirit.

Doxology: a liturgical or poetic narrative of praise to God.

Dualism: the belief that reality is ultimately composed of two essential substances.

Ebed: a Hebrew word translated as "servant" or "slave"; communicates a relationship of dependency, not ownership.

Elohim: from the Hebrew for "deity"; the generic name used in the Old Testament for the creator-God.

Emotional Doubt: spiritual doubt brought about by pain, anger, or angst.

Epistemology: the branch of philosophy that seeks to understand the nature of knowledge.

Eros: the Greek word for "sexual love."

Essence: defining attributes that give an entity its fundamental identity.

Essenes: a first-century Jewish faction that lived a monastic and communal life in the desert, shared everything in common, practiced ritual cleansing, and produced the oldest known copies of the Old Testament (for instance, the Dead Sea Scrolls).

Eternal: always existing or existing outside of time; everlasting.

Eudaimonia: a term used in ancient Greek philosophy to describe a life of flourishing and happiness.

Eugenics: a social movement advocating the genetic improvement of the human race through such practices as selective breeding, compulsory sterilization, forced abortions, and genocide.

Evil: that which deviates from good; the privation of good.

Evolutionism: the belief that all life arose through random chance processes starting with the first self-replicating molecule.

Exegesis: from the Greek for "lead out"; the exposition or explanation of a biblical text based on careful study and analysis.

Faith: firm trust or confidence in someone or something.

Fatalism: the belief that all events are predetermined and inevitable.

Flow: a state in which a person works intently on something fascinating and is able to work in a smooth rhythm, be creative, and recognize afterward that it was a pleasurable experience.

Free Will Defense: an argument developed by Alvin Plantinga that contends there is no logical contradiction between the coexistence of evil and God because it is at least *possible* that evil exists because even an omniscient deity could not create a world in which human beings simultaneously possess free will yet never choose to do evil.

Functional View of Personhood: the belief that human beings become persons only after gaining particular abilities, such as sentience, higher-level thinking, and self-awareness.

General Revelation: God's universal revelation about himself (Ps. 19:1–6; Rom. 1:18–20) and morality (2:14–15) that can be obtained through nature.

General Theory of Relativity: Albert Einstein's geometric theory of gravitation, which proposes that space and time are interwoven and can be curved by the presence of massive objects, such as planets and black holes.

Genocide: the systematic killing of a particular racial, ethnic, or religious group.

Gerotranscendence: the stage in life when a person makes the shift from self-interest toward a genuine concern for others and society.

Glorification: the point at which believers become closely identified with Christ.

Gnosticism: a second-century heretical Christian movement that taught that the material world was created and maintained by a lesser divine being, that matter and the physical body are inherently evil, and that salvation can be obtained only through an esoteric knowledge of divine reality and the self-denial of physical pleasures.

Good: that which embodies or reflects God's original design.

Gospel: from the Old English for "good news"; the message of Jesus's saving work and God's present kingdom.

Grace: receiving what one does not deserve.

Haram: a Hebrew word translated as "total destruction" often used hyperbolically to communicate a strong defeat.

Hard Authority: the power or right to give orders and demand obedience with the threat of punishment.

Hellenization: the spread of Greek culture (language, arts, ideas, religion, government) throughout the conquered ancient world.

Heresy: any belief that is contrary to orthodox Christian doctrine.

Hermeneutics: from the Greek for "interpret"; the process of devising the best methods for understanding and interpreting Scripture.

Higher Consciousness: the supposed state of awareness wherein individuals realize their divinity and the divine interconnectedness of all things.

Historical Context: the time, place, culture, and audience of a text.

Historical Narrative: a story of historical events.

Holy: to be set apart.

Homophobia: the fear of homosexuals.

Horizontal Commands: commandments relating to humanity's social relationships.

Hubble's Law: based on Edwin Hubble's astronomical observations; the law that states that the universe is expanding, i.e., the galaxies within the universe are moving away from one another at a rate directly proportional to the distances between galaxies.

Identity: the set of characteristics, giftings, and convictions that uniquely define who a person is.

Idiot: from the Greek for "private"; a person who fails to be active in society.

Idolatry: the act of worshipping or valuing something above God; entertaining thoughts about God that are unworthy of him.

Imago Dei: from the Latin for the "image of God"; the idea that human beings were created in God's likeness.

Immanent: an attribute of God that describes him as being both within and among his creation.

Incommunicable Attributes: qualities that belong to only God, such as being holy, eternal, omniscient, omnipotent, omnipresent, and unchanging.

Inerrancy: the doctrine that the Bible is without error.

Intellectual Doubt: spiritual doubt brought about by rational questions regarding God's existence.

Intelligent Design: the study of information, complexity, and design in life and the cosmos; the theory that life could not have arisen by chance and random natural processes but was designed by an intelligent being.

Intertestamental Period: the four-hundred-year period between the completion of the Old Testament and the writing of the New Testament.

Intrinsic View of Personhood: the belief that human beings are inherently persons.

Irreducible Complexity: a concept that considers the complexity of integrated systems such that if any part is removed, the system ceases to function, and that when applied to biology, challenges the notion that complex biological systems (such as the eye) could have gradually evolved through a series of intermediary steps.

Islam: a theistic worldview centered on the life of the prophet Muhammad that derives its understanding of the world through the teachings of the Quran, Hadith, and *Sunnah*.

Judgment: the act of ruling or sentencing based on the careful deliberation of evidence and circumstances.

Justice: the act of making things legally and morally right.

Justification: being declared righteous by God through the work of Jesus Christ.

Kalam Cosmological Argument: an argument for God's existence that begins with the premise that something caused the universe to exist and ends with the conclusion that God is the best explanation for that cause.

Karma: a concept found in Eastern religions that states that good is returned to those who do good, and evil is returned to those who do evil (either in this life or the next).

Knowledge: justified true belief.

Koinonia: from the Greek for "community"; the role of fellowship within the Christian church.

Lexicon: an alphabetical dictionary that translates and defines words from another language, particularly Greek, Hebrew, and Latin.

Literary Context: the genre, structure, and grammar of a text.

Lost Gospels: a collection of fifty-two gnostic texts discovered in 1945 in Nag Hammadi, Egypt, and written sometime between the second and fourth centuries AD.

Love: a commitment to cherish others regardless of how one feels about them.

Macroevolution: the belief that small, adaptive changes are capable of accumulating over time to produce entirely new species.

Marxism: an atheistic and materialistic worldview based on the ideas of Karl Marx that promotes the abolition of private property, the public ownership of the means of production (such as socialism), and the utopian dream of a future communistic state.

Materialism: the belief that reality is composed solely of matter.

Megalomania: a psychopathic condition characterized by delusions of grandeur.

Mercy: not receiving what one deserves.

Metanarrative: a single, overarching interpretation, or grand story, of reality.

Microevolution: the belief that small, adaptive changes are capable of producing variations within the gene pool of a species.

Middle Knowledge (aka Molinism): first proposed by the Jesuit priest Luis de Molina; the belief that God knows all future contingent possibilities and that through his omniscience can accomplish his divine will through the lives of free human beings.

Miller-Urey Experiment: a 1952 experiment conducted by Stanley Miller and Harold Urey that produced amino acids through the combination of electricity and gases thought to be present in Earth's atmosphere around three to four billions year ago.

Mind/Body Dualism: the belief that human beings are composed of immaterial minds and material bodies.

Minimal Facts Approach: a method formulated by Gary Habermas for investigating the resurrection of Jesus that concentrates only on the historical facts that are so well evidenced that they are accepted by nearly every scholar who studies the topic.

Miracle: a supernatural sign or event that is intended to highlight the power and goodness of God.

Misandry: the hatred or dislike of men.

Misogyny: the hatred or dislike of women.

Modalism (aka Sabellianism): the belief that the Trinity is composed of one God who has presented himself in different modes, or forms (the Father in the Old Testament, the Son in the New Testament, and the Holy Spirit today) throughout time.

Modernism: a broad term used to describe a range of arts, attitudes, philosophies, and cultural moods that emerged following the eighteenth-century Enlightenment. It is characterized by a strong belief in rationalism, empiricism, science, and technological progress as well as skepticism toward the supernatural, special revelation, and the authority of religion.

Monism: the belief that reality is ultimately composed of one essential substance.

Moral Absolute: an objective, unchanging, and universal standard of right and wrong.

Moral Argument (aka Axiological Argument): an argument for God's existence that begins with the premise that objective morality exists and ends with the conclusion that God is the best explanation for the existence of an objective morality.

Moral Doubt: spiritual doubt brought about by personal sin and rebellion.

Moral Evil: evil brought about by the actions of human beings (for example, rape, murder, and genocide).

Moral Relativism: the belief that morality is relative to, or defined by, the individual or culture.

Multiverse Theory: a theoretical reality that postulates an infinite set of parallel and diverse universes, of which our own universe is just one instantiation.

Mutation: a change in the genetic makeup of an organism.

Natural Evil: evil brought about by acts of nature, such as fires, earthquakes, and diseases.

Natural Selection (aka Survival of the Fittest): the process by which organisms better adapted for their environment tend to survive longer, reproduce, and pass along more favorable biological traits.

Naturalism: the belief that all phenomena can be explained in terms of natural causes.

New Atheism: a contemporary form of atheism that not only denies the existence of God but also contends that religion should be vehemently criticized, condemned, and opposed.

New Spirituality: a pantheistic worldview that teaches that everything and everyone are connected through divine consciousness.

Nihilism: the view that the world and human existence are without meaning, purpose, comprehensible truth, or essential value.

Objective Morality: the belief that morality has a universal and unchanging standard that is independent from human opinion, culture, and sentiment.

Objective Truth Claim: a claim regarding an independent fact about the world.

Omnipotent: God's unique ability to do anything that can be done.

Omnipresent: God's unique ability to be present in all places and at all times.

Omniscient: God's unique ability to know everything that can be known.

Open Theism: the belief that God does not have divine foreknowledge but that through his omniscience is able to deduce the most probabilistic future.

Panentheism: the belief that God is in everything.

Panspermia: the belief that life exists throughout the universe and has been dispersed by interstellar bodies such as asteroids, meteoroids, and comets.

Pantheism: the belief that everything in the universe is ultimately divine.

Pantheon: the collection of gods belonging to a particular religion or mythology.

Parasite: an organism that survives at the expense of a host (for example, viruses, bacteria, tapeworms, flukes, fleas, ticks, and louses).

Pentateuch: the first five books of the Bible (Genesis, Exodus, Leviticus, Numbers, and Deuteronomy).

Perfect Being Theology: a view of God formulated by Anselm of Canterbury that defines God as "the greatest possible being" and "that than which none greater can be conceived."

Pharisees: a first-century Jewish faction that practiced a legalistic interpretation of the Torah, accepted the Talmud as authoritative, believed in the concept of an afterlife, and opposed the Roman occupation of Palestine.

Philos: the Greek word for "brotherly, familial love."

Polygenesis: the evolution of species from several independent sources.

Polytheism: the belief in a multitude of deities.

Postmodernism: a skeptical worldview, founded as a reaction to modernism, that is suspicious of metanarratives and teaches that ultimate reality is inaccessible, that knowledge is a social construct, and that truth claims are political power plays.

Practical Atheism: believing in the existence of God but living as if he doesn't exist.

Prescriptive Passage: a biblical passage that prescribes how people ought to live.

Prescriptive Pluralism: the belief that we should be tolerant of other religions because no single religion can be universally true for everyone.

Prime Mover (aka Unmoved Mover): Aristotle's conception of an utterly transcendent, impersonal, immortal, immaterial, necessary, and unchanging being that set the universe into motion.

Primordial Soup: a theory that proposes that life arose from a water-based sea of simple, organic molecules.

Progressive Creationism: the belief that God created the cosmos and all life in its present forms, in progressive stages, over a long period of time.

Proletariat: a term used in Marxist theory to describe the working-class wage earners who do not own the means of production.

Protevangelium: the first gospel or God's first promise of coming redemption through Jesus Christ (Gen. 3:15).

Psychoanalysis: an approach to psychology developed by Sigmund Freud whereby a psychologist attempts to resolve a patient's psychological problems by uncovering and discussing the patient's unconscious, unfulfilled, and repressed desires.

Quantum Physics: the branch of physics dealing with physical phenomena on the subatomic level, where particles behave in a fashion difficult to quantify and understand using the scientific method.

Real, the: defined by John Hick to be ultimate reality and the source of all world religions.

Recapitulation: a storytelling technique in which an overview of a story is given before the story is laid out in specific detail.

Red Shift: the expansion of the frequency of light toward the red end of the electromagnetic spectrum.

Regeneration: God's making people new through his Holy Spirit.

Reincarnation: the belief that after biological death, the soul is reborn in a new body—either animal, human, or spirit—to continue its quest for enlightenment.

Relativism: the belief that truth, knowledge, and morality are relative to the individual, society, and historical context.

Religious Pluralism: the acknowledgment that many different religions exist in today's diverse society.

Repentance: from the Greek for "changing one's mind"; the process of reviewing, regretting, and then changing direction with one's thoughts and actions.

Revelation: the act of making something known that was previously hidden or unknown.

Righteousness: the quality of being morally and spiritually right with God.

RNA World Hypothesis: a theory that proposes that early life was based on RNA instead of DNA and protein.

Sadducees: a first-century Jewish faction of priests and aristocrats who expressed complacency toward the Roman occupation, denied the concept of an afterlife, rejected the Talmud, and believed that only the first five books of the Torah were authoritative.

Sanctification: the process whereby believers advance in holiness.

Science: the process of using observable evidence to construct testable explanations and predictions for natural phenomena.

Scientific Method: a process of empirical inquiry that seeks to understand the phenomena of the physical world through hypothesizing, observing, measuring, experimenting, predicting, and testing.

Scientism: the philosophical belief that reliable knowledge is obtained solely through the scientific method.

Second Law of Thermodynamics: a scientific law that states that the amount of usable energy in a closed system will decrease over time.

Secular Humanism: a religious and philosophical worldview that makes humankind the ultimate norm by which truth and values are to be determined; a worldview that reveres human reason, evolution, naturalism, and secular theories of ethics while rejecting every form of supernatural religion.

Secularism: an atheistic and materialistic worldview that advocates for a public society free from the influence of religion.

Self-Refuting Claim: a statement that attempts to affirm two opposite propositions at the same time and in the same sense.

Sentience: the ability to feel and experience sensations.

Septuagint: the Greek translation of the Hebrew Scriptures.

Shalom: from the Hebrew for "peace, prosperity, and wellness"; implies harmony in creation and with one's neighbors as well as a right relationship with God.

Socialism: an economic system based on governmental or communal ownership of the means of production and distribution of goods and services.

Soft Authority: the power to influence and persuade others because of a person's knowledge or out of an earned respect.

Sojourner: someone who lives in a particular place for an extended period of time but whose home is somewhere else.

Sovereign: possessing supreme authority.

Special Revelation: God's unique revelation about himself through the Scriptures (Ps. 19:7–11; 2 Tim. 3:14–17), miraculous events (dreams, visions, prophets, prophecy), and Jesus Christ (John 1:1–18).

Specified Complexity: any event that is contingent, complex, and exhibits an independently given pattern.

Spiritual Monism: the belief that reality is ultimately divine.

Spontaneous Generation: the belief that nonliving matter produced living matter through purely natural processes.

Subjective Truth Claim: a claim regarding a dependent fact about a subject.

Suffering: pain or discomfort that results from such things as disease, injury, oppression, fatigue, old age, loneliness, and betrayal.

Systematic Theology: a form of theological inquiry that aims to arrange and categorize religious truths into an internally consistent system.

Textual Variants: differences between particular words, phrases, or passages within multiple copies of the same ancient manuscript.

Theism: the belief in the existence of a God or gods.

Theistic Evolution: the belief that God created the cosmos billions of years ago and then guided the process of biological evolution to produce the diversity of life seen today.

Theodicy: a rational justification for why God would allow evil.

Theological Context: the theological purpose of a text.

Theological Dictionary: a reference book of words and phrases found in the Bible.

Tolerance: the willingness to recognize and respect the dignity of those with whom one disagrees.

Tort Law: the area of law governing remedies for those wronged by others, such as through negligence.

Transcendent: an attribute of God that describes him as being both above and outside of his creation.

Tree of Life: a metaphor used to illustrate the belief that all of life originated from a common ancestor and gradually branched out into the wide variety of species seen within the fossil record.

Tritheism: the belief that the Trinity is composed of three separate and distinct Gods.

Ummah: from the Arabic word for "nation"; the collective community of Muslims around the world.

Universal Common Ancestry: the belief that all life originated from a common, single-celled organism.

Universalism: the belief that all human and angelic beings will eventually be restored to a right relationship with God, either while alive or sometime after death.

Vertical Commands: commandments relating to humanity's relationship with God.

Vocation: from the Latin for "to call"; the work to which a person is drawn or well suited.

Watchmaker Argument: an argument for God's existence that compares the design of a watch to the design found within the cosmos and concludes that the universe, like a watch, can be best explained by the existence of an intelligent designer.

Wicca: a neopagan, religious form of witchcraft.

Wisdom: the ability of thinking and acting with good judgment.

Wrath: retributive punishment for an offense.

Yahweh: from the Hebrew for "I Am"; the personal and covenantal name of God used in the Old Testament.

Young-Age Creationism: the belief that God created the cosmos and all life in its present forms, in six literal days, around six thousand years ago.

Zealots: a first-century Jewish faction that militantly opposed the Roman occupation of Palestine.

INDEX

- A -

abad, 218

The Abolition of Man (Lewis), 228

Abrahamic Covenant, 144, 145–46

abundance, 235

accountability, 447–48

achievement, identity, 202–3

Adams, Jay, 284

Adams, John, 36, 270

Adams, John Quincy, 36

Adams, Samuel, 35

Adler, Mortimer, 206

adoption, 382

adultery, 414

agape, 99–100, 234, 416

Age of Enlightenment, 262, 270, 303

agnostics and agnosticism, 11, 69, 125, 218

Ahmad, Khurshid, 358

Alberts, Bruce, 309

Albright, William F., 277

Alcinous, 206

Alcorn, Randy, 367, 369–70, 371, 387, 389, 390

Alexander, Eben, 276

Alfred P. Murrah Federal Building, Oklahoma City, 58

Ali, A. Yusuf, 104

All Faiths for One Race (AFFOR), 259

allegory, 172–73, 183

Allen, Scott D., 263

Amalekites, 409–10, 420

Amazing Grace (movie), 43

ambition, 205–6

anger, 223, 424

annihilationism, 397

Anselm, of Canterbury, 88

The Anthropic Cosmological Principle (Barrow & Tipler), 315

anthropic principle, 315

anthropology, 126

Antiquities of the Jews (Josephus), 277

Apocrypha, 60

Appleton, Frances, 192

Aquinas, Thomas, 250, 251

Archer, Gleason L., Jr., 277

Aristotle, 50, 70, 209, 246, 417

asceticism, 127

Aseity, 90

Asset-Based Community Development, 235

Astrology, 124

atheism, 86, 124, 195, 218, 256, 276, 314, 353–54, 382, 436–38, 475

atheists, 11, 16, 28, 37, 69, 86, 87, 94, 122–23, 139, 207, 221, 247, 254, 258, 262, 271, 272, 303, 310, 317, 318, 326, 329, 337, 338, 353–54, 358, 363, 406, 420, 422, 433, 435, 457, 467, 469, 470

Athenian law, 420

Atlas Shrugged (Rand), 38

Augustine, of Hippo, 89, 168, 209, 352, 457

authoritarian faith path, 434

authority, 20–23, 45, 57–67, 74–78, 211, 457–58

axiological argument, 254–58, 467

Ayala, Francisco, 250

- *B* -

Brown, William E., 59

Bruce, F. F., 66

Buddhism, 326, 331, 355, 356, 382

Budziszewski, J., 340

bullying, 474–75

Burke, James, 337

Buster, Bobette, 146

- *C* -

Callixtus III (pope), 300

Canaanites, 409–10, 420

Cannon, Amber, 236

canon, biblical, 60, 72–73, 460

Caplan, David, 441

Carson, D. A., 41, 170, 220, 387, 388–89, 417

The Case for a Creator (Strobel), 251

Casual Argument, 245–46, 249, 465

certainty, 48–49, 245, 345

Chan, Francis, 167

chattel slavery, 418, 419

Chesterton, G. K., 136, 274

Christian missionaries, 262, 468

Christian theism, 48, 104

The Christian Virtuoso (Boyle), 302

Christianity, 40, 44–45, 60

"Christmas Bells" (poem), 192–93

chronological snobbery, 412

church, 154–55

citizenship, 236–38

Clark, David, 23, 45

Cliburn, Van, 231–32

Clinton, Bobby, 447

Collins, Francis, 253, 298, 314

Collins, Robin, 251

Colson, Chuck, 42, 210, 417, 447

Columbus, Christopher, 300

Colvin, Geoff, 231–32

commitments, 435–36, 475

communicable attributes, of God, 92, 97–101, 118

The Communist Manifesto (Marx & Engels), 38, 355

community, 234–36, 446–47

compass, Bible as a, 39–40, 44, 51, 457, 458

Confessions (Augustine), 168

Confucianism, 355

conspiracy theorists, 22

Constitution of the United States, 236

content, of bible, 181–82

context, of bible, 179–81

Conti, Joseph, 339

conversation, 232–34

conversion, 382

Cook, Glen, 255

Cooke, G. A., 413–14

Coolidge, Calvin, 36

cooperation, 235

Coots, John Frederick, 433

Copan, Paul, 257, 340, 341–42, 412, 432

Copernicus, Nicholas, 300, 302

Cornish, Rick, 95

correspondence theory of truth, 50–51, 332, 333, 459

Cosmological Argument, 249, 465

cosmology, 126, 218, 245–46

Donne, John, 389

doubt, 23–24, 185–86, 435–44, 476

doxology, 122

Draper, John W., 300

dualism, 275–76, 337, 469

Durant, Will, 278

Dylan, Bob, 59, 78

Dyson, Freeman, 252

- E -

Eastern religions, 355–57

ebed, 417

Edwards, Jonathan, 380

Egyptian Memphite Creation text, 123

Ehrman, Bart, 71

Einstein, Albert, 247, 302, 303, 308

Eisenstein, Elizabeth, 168

Eliot, T. S., 225

Elliot, Elisabeth, 367

Elliot, Jim, 367

Elohim ("God"), 122, 194, 460

emotional doubt, 442–43

Engels, Friedrich, 338

Enlightenment rationalism, 262

Enuma Elish, 123, 218

epistemology, defined, 16

Erickson, Millard J., 43, 91, 92, 94, 98, 100

Erikson, Erik, 202

eros, 100, 416

essence, 61, 101, 102, 458

Essenes, 150

Eucharist, 446

eudaimonia, 209

evidential faith path, 435

evil, 94, 284–89, 352, 470, 472–74

evolution and evolutionary theory, 47–48, 125, 127, 218, 250, 254, 256, 284, 307–8, 312, 315–18, 354

excommunication temptation, 28

exegesis, 176

external evidence of bible's authority, 64–67, 459, 465–67

external, God as, 93

- F -

faith, 23–27, 435

faith paths, 434–35

fall, doctrine of, 197, 462, 463

Fant, Gene, 174, 176–77, 180–81

fatalism, 217

fear, of asking for help, 9–10

Feder, Kenneth L., 221

Fee, Gordon, 170–71, 173, 176, 178, 180, 181

Feinberg, John, 90

feminists, 422

Ferguson, Marilyn, 338, 357

fine-tuning, 251–52

Finkelstein, Israel, 64

Flannagan, Matthew, 411

Flew, Antony, 247, 276, 310, 314

flow, defined, 219

flow-producing activities, 225

foreclosure, identity, 202

forgiveness, 414–15

formal equivalence translations, 178

fortitude, 209

Frame, John, 97

Franklin, Benjamin, 59

free translations, 178

free will defense argument, 361

freedom, 38

Freud, Sigmund, 413, 415, 434

Froese, Paul, 86

Fromm, Erich, 139, 155, 337

functional equivalence translations, 178

functional view of personhood, 222

- G -

Galatians for You (Keller), 175

Galilei, Galileo, 300–301, 302

Ganssle, Greg, 364

Garber, Steven, 311, 438, 444

Gawain, Shakti, 16, 357

Gay, Craig, 436

Geisler, Norman, 359, 365, 367, 384, 385

Geldenhuys, Norval, 74

general revelation, 42–43, 74, 131, 244, 245

general theory of relativity, 247

genocide, 406, 409–12, 468, 474

genre, of bible, 179

George, Timothy, 105

gerotranscendence, 207

gifting, 230–31

Gill, Stewart, 262

Gillespie, Haven, 433

Girl with the Pearl Earring (Vermeer), 42

glorification, 382

gnosticism, 73, 125, 273

The God Delusion (Dawkins), 405

God Is Not a Christian (Tutu), 234

God Revelation, and Authority (Henry), 45–46

Goheen, Michael, 117, 136, 140, 181, 407, 414

Golden Rule of morality, 37

Golding, William, 286

Goldsworthy, Graeme, 173, 179

Gonzalez, Guillermo, 252

good, defined, 352

gospel, 151–52, 154

grace, 100–101, 141–44

Graham Lawton, 316

Granger, Karen, 368

Grasse, Pierre-Paul, 315

Great Commission, 63, 458

Greene, Brian, 253

Greenleaf, Simon, 277

Greeves, Arthur, 446

Groothuis, Douglas, 50–51, 253, 256–57, 259, 354, 357, 372, 380–81

Grudem, Wayne, 172

Grunwald, Henry, 225

Guinness, Os, 88, 433, 442

Gutacker, Paige, 446, 447

Gutenberg, Johannes, 168

- H -

Habermas, Gary, 276, 279–81, 384, 469

Habermas, Jürgen, 195

habits, 209–10

Haeckel, Ernst, 317

Haggard, Ted, 447

hallucination, 282

Haman, 410

haram, 411, 412

hard authority, 20, 457

Hawking, Stephen, 249, 304, 466

"I Heard the Bells on Christmas Day" (poem), 192–93

Heister, Andrew, 343

hell, doctrine of, 379–83, 386, 396, 399

hell, explanation of, 379–402, 473–74

Hellenization, 149

Henley, William Ernest, 58

Henry, Carl F. H., 45–46, 61, 62, 74, 75, 458

heresy, 102

hermeneutics, 170

Hick, John, 259–60, 331

higher consciousness, 357

Hinduism, 38, 149, 217, 331, 355, 356, 382

historical context, 120, 180

historical narrative, 113, 277–78

Hitler, Adolph, 391

Holbrooke, Richard, 192

Holden, Joseph, 332

Hollister, C. Warren, 301

holocaust, 422

holy, defined, 92

homophobia, 412

homosexuals, 413–17, 474

Honest to God (Robinson), 261

Hook, Sidney, 338

hope, 23, 191–94, 367–68

Hopkins, Gerard Manley, 112

horizontal commands, 148

Horrell, Scott, 101

The Horse and His Boy (Lewis), 444

hospitality, 446–47

Hoss, Rudolf, 387

House, Wayne, 407

How Christianity Changed the World (Schmidt), 37

Howard, Thomas, 227

Hoyle, Fred, 317

Hubble, Edwin, 247

Hubble's Law, 247

Human Nature in the Bible (Phelps), 37

The Humanist Manifesto, 38

humanity losing its way, 128–29

humans, 13–14, 125–28, 194–96, 218, 221–22, 334, 463–64

humble transparency, 345

Hume, David, 272–73, 289, 468

Husserl, Edmund, 261

Huxley, Aldous, 439

Huxley, Julian, 274, 284

Huxley, Thomas, 300

- I -

Icons of Evolution (Wells), 317

ideas, 12–13

ideas map, 13

identity, of humans, 202–4

idiot, defined, 222

idolatry, 199–201, 414, 423

image, 125–26, 196–97

imago Dei, 124, 196–97, 198–201, 358

immanent, 95, 121

immanent frame, 275

immorality, 439

impurity, 440

In Search of Ancient Israel (Davies), 64

incommunicable attributes, of God, 92–97, 118

indulgence, 415

inerrancy, 45–46

Ingolfsland, Dennis, 65

injustice, 92, 148, 370, 387

Inklings club, 446

The Innocence of God (Middelmann), 351

inspired, meaning of, 45

intellectual doubt, 442

intelligent design (ID), 250, 307, 315

internal evidence of bible's authority, 60–64, 458

internal experiences, 330–31

interpretation, 170–76

intertestamental period, 149

intrinsic view of personhood, 222

intuitive faith path, 435

intuitive knowingness, 16

"Invictus" (poem), 58

involvement, Gospel redemption and, 237

irreducible complexity, 308

Is God a Moral Monster? (Copan), 412

Isaacs, William, 232

Islam, 38, 69–70, 104–5, 114, 115, 124, 217, 246, 271, 304, 331, 337, 357–58, 381, 413, 466

Issachar (ancient tribe in Israel), 14, 25, 237

- J -

Jackson, Maggie, 440

Jaki, Stanley, 302

Jastrow, Robert, 315

Jay, John, 35

jealousy, 118

Jefferson, Thomas, 26, 270

The Jesus Storybook Bible (Lloyd-Jones), 34

Jones, Brian, 326, 423

Josephus, 277

Jowers, Dennis, 407

"Joy to the World" (hymn), 74

judgment, 383

justice, 209, 236–37, 387, 424

justification, 382

- K -

Kaiser, Walter, 415

Kaiser, Walter, Jr., 381, 408–9

kalam cosmological argument, 246–49, 466

karma, 357

Keener, Craig, 273, 288

Keller, Tim, 23–24, 103, 175, 204–5, 270, 388, 390, 391, 423–24

Kelly Monroe Kullberg, 52

Kennedy, D. James, 68–69

Key, Francis Scott, 342–43

Kilpatrick, William Kirk, 354, 368

King, Martin Luther, Jr., 223–24

kingdom of God, 153–57

Kinnaman, David, 328

Kinsey, Alfred, 413

Kirk, Russell, 28

Kitchen, Kenneth A., 64, 66, 411

knowledge, 46–47, 49, 327, 433–34, 459, 475

koinonia, defined, 223

Köstenberger, Andreas, 73

Koukl, Greg, 50, 68, 257, 330, 340

Kraft, Charles H., 96, 437

Kruger, Michael, 73

Kullberg, Kelly Monroe, 52

Kunkle, Brett, 442–43

Kurtz, Paul, 16–17, 139

Kuyper, Abraham, 211

- L -

Lamont, Corliss, 17

Lane, Nick, 311

Law, William, 229

Lawson, Deodat, 422

Leaf, Caroline, 219

Leaman, Oliver, 271

Leibniz, Gottfried Wilhelm von, 245–46, 364–65

Leithart, Peter J., 207

Lemoine, Paul, 318

Lenin, Vladimir, 338, 355

Lennox, John, 304

Levitical law, 413, 420–21

Lewis, C. S., 27, 28, 114, 210, 211, 228, 263, 272–73, 288, 289, 318, 335, 353–54, 381, 390, 399, 412, 415–16, 438, 444, 445, 446, 471

Lewis, Gordon R., 41, 45, 92, 93, 98, 99, 104, 360, 458

Lewontin, Richard, 272, 435–36

lexicon, 183

liberal whateverism, 27

Libertarians, 38

Licona, Michael, 279–81, 282

Life after God (Coupland), 226

The Life and Morals of Jesus of Nazareth (Jefferson), 270

Life at the Bottom (Dalrymple), 15

Lincoln, Abraham, 36, 192

Linton, Calvin D., 263

The Lion, the Witch, and the Wardrobe (Lewis), 211

listening, 346

literary context, 120, 180

Livingston, David, 262

Lloyd-Jones, Martyn, 76

Lloyd-Jones, Sally, 34, 35

Longfellow, Henry Wadsworth, 192, 193, 211

Nicomachean Ethics (Aristotle), 209

Nicomachus, 209

nihilism, 64, 125, 218

Noebel, David, 24–25, 37, 38, 49

- O -

objective knowledge, 49

objective morality, 254–58, 466–67

objective truth claims, 51, 332

O'Connor, Flannery, 16, 76, 381

Olim, Ellis G., 140

omnipotent, 94, 460

omnipresent, 95, 460

omniscient, 93, 360, 460

On the Reliability of the Old Testament (Kitchen), 66

Oparin, Alexander, 310, 311

Open Theism, 360

order, Gospel redemption and, 236

Origin of Species (Darwin), 262

original sin, 136, 139, 464
(See also sin)

Ortberg, John, 186

Orthodoxy (Chesterton), 274

otherworldly beliefs, 269–71

- P -

Packer, J. I., 47, 210

Paganism, 123–28

Paley, William, 308, 309

Palmer, Parker, 230

panentheism, 124, 218

panspermia, 313

pantheism, 96, 124, 218, 275, 338, 356

pantheon, 408

parasite, 197–98

Park, Michael Alan, 221

Pascal, Blaise, 271

Pasteur, Louis, 310

Paul V (pope), 301

Payne, Karl, 285, 289, 291

The Peacemaker (Sande), 234

Pearcey, Nancy, 19, 20, 44, 227–28, 305, 470

Penley, Paul T., 180, 287

Pentateuch, 407

Perfect Being Theology, 88

personhood, 221–22, 257

Peterson, Eugene, 178

Peterson, Robert A., 383

Pharisees, 150

Phelps, William Lyon, 37

Phillips, W. Gary, 59, 62, 156

Philo of Byblos, 123, 218

philos, 100, 234

philosophy, study of, 17–18

Phips, Sir William, 422

Pinker, Steven, 23

Pirsig, Robert, 222

Plantinga, Alvin, 47, 48, 259–60, 332, 361–62, 441

Plantinga, Cornelius, 137, 220, 359

Plato, 206

Pliny the Elder, 287

Plotinus, 206–7

Plummer, Robert L., 40, 174, 178–79

pluralism, 258–63, 330–32, 471–72

polytheism, 104, 124, 218

pornography, 224

Postmodernism, 329, 467, 468, 471

Postmodernist, 49, 75, 114, 115, 169–70, 173, 195, 258, 260–63, 333

practical atheism, 436–38, 475

pragmatism, 338

prayer, 27, 210–11

prescriptive passage, 184

prescriptive pluralism, 259, 471–72

prime mover, 209

prime reality, 334

primordial soup, 311, 312

The Principia (Newton), 300

privileged planet argument, 252

The Problem of Pain (Lewis), 390, 445

progressive creationists, 307

proletariat, 355

prophetic fulfillment, 152–53

Protestant Reformation, 168, 185, 301

protevangelium, 141

prudence, 209

psychoanalysis, 413

- Q -

quantum physics, 249

quarter-life crisis, 207

The Questions Christians Hope No One Will Ask (Mittelberg), 366

questions humans need help with, 10–12

Quran, 34, 38, 69–70, 104, 105, 271, 357

- R -

race relationships, 223

Reagan, Ronald, 36

the Real, defined, 259–60

recapitulation, 120

reconciliation, 235, 445

red shift, 247

redemption, 117, 131, 136–37

redemption accomplished, 150–54, 462

redemption applied, 154–55, 462–63

redemption completed, 146–47, 155–57, 463

redemption initiated, 145–46, 462

redemption predicted, 147–50

Redi, Francesco, 310

Redman, Matt, 446

Reenacting the Way (of Jesus) (Penley), 180

regeneration, 382

Regnerus, Mark, 439

reincarnation, 357

Reinventing Jesus (Komoszewski, Sawyer, & Wallace), 70

relationships, 182, 222–23

relativism, defined, 16, 51, 257

Relativism: Feet Firmly Planted in Mid-Air (Beckwith & Koukl), 330

relativistic faith path, 434

relativity, general theory of, 247

religious pluralism, 258–60, 471–72

renewal, of minds and spirit, 17

repentance, 204–5, 447, 464

Rescorla, Rick, 228

- S -

shalom, 137, 144, 181, 192, 217, 220, 359, 462, 464

Shapin, Steven, 303

Shapiro, James, 309

Shapiro, Robert, 312

sharia law, 413

Sheler, Jeffery, 64–65

Shillito, Edward, 371

Shinto, 355

Shop Class as Soulcraft (Crawford), 222

Sibcy, Gary, 282

sin, 136–39, 141, 148, 197–99, 205–6, 220, 359, 414–15, 438–440, 464, 475

Sinatra, Frank, 191–92

Sinclair, Upton, 436

Sire, James, 334, 432

slavery, 417–20, 475

slogans, 341–42

Smith, Christian, 27, 198

Smith, R. Scott, 300, 366–67

socialism, 355

society, 14–17, 25

Socrates, 343

soft authority, 20–21, 457

sojourners, 415

The Soul of Science (Pearcey & Thaxton), 305

sovereign, defined, 360

speaking, Gospel redemption and, 237–38

special revelation, 43, 74, 96, 125, 131, 260

specified complexity, 251

spiritual bondage, 38, 457

spiritual disciplines, 27

spiritual fruits, 38

spiritual monism, 337

spontaneous generation, 310, 311

Sproul, R. C., 361

Stalin, Joseph, 115, 299, 391

Stark, Rodney, 304, 420

Stenger, Victor, 303–4

Sterrett, Dave, 433

Stetson, Brad, 339

Stonestreet, John, 59, 210, 234, 345, 346, 371, 440, 447

Stott, John, 264–65, 371, 396

Strobel, Lee, 251

Stuart, Douglass, 170–71, 173, 176, 178, 180, 181

study, 17–18, 237

subjective truth claims, 51, 332

suffering, 351–76, 472–73

Summit Ministries, 24–27, 204, 237

supernatural evil, 284–89

superstitions, 285–86

survival of the fittest, 310

systematic theology, 172

- T -

Tacitus, Publius Cornelius, 277–78

Talent Is Overrated (Colvin), 231

Taoism, 355

Taylor, Charles, 275, 284

technology studies, 224

Tegmark, Max, 253

teleological argument, 249–54, 314, 466

Vermeer, Johannes, 42

vertical commands, 148

virtue, 209, 415

Vitz, Paul, 354, 434

vocation, 229–30

Voltaire, 122–23

voting, Gospel redemption and, 237

- W -

Wallace, Daniel, 71

Wallace, J. Warner, 339

Walsch, Neale Donald, 338, 339

Ward, Glenn, 195

Ward, Graham, 261

watchmaker argument, 308

Watson, James, 314

Watters, Wendell W., 139, 155

Watts, Isaac, 74

the way (*derek*), 14, 226

We Were Soldiers (book and movie), 228

Webster, Noah, 36

"The Weight of Glory" (Lewis), 438

Wells, Jonathan, 317

West, Matthew, 366

White, Andrew D., 300

Whitehead, Alfred North, 301

Whitehurst, Teresa, 328

Whitesides, George, 312, 313

"Why, Georgia?" (song), 207

Why I Am Not a Christian (Russell), 379

Wicca, 355, 397

Wilberforce, William, 43

Willard, Dallas, 47, 328, 389, 395

Willard, Samuel, 422

Williams, Ben, 442, 443

Williams, Joel, 14

Williams, Peter, 412

Wilson, Edward O., 221, 272, 298, 338

Wilson, Woodrow, 36

Winfrey, Oprah, 118

wisdom, 98, 206–8

Wolters, Albert, 197

Wolterstorff, Nicholas, 236

women, 402–22, 475

Wood, Peter, 223

Wooldridge, Adrian, 86

Woolman, John, 238

World Magazine, 237

worship, 105, 445–46

wrath, 383, 387

Wright, J. H., 418

Wright, N. T., 39–40, 43, 154, 168, 226, 281, 283, 470

- Y -

Yahweh ("the Lord"), 122, 194, 245–46, 408, 460

Yamauchi, Edwin, 66

Yancey, Philip, 370

young-age creationists, 306–7

- Z -

Zealots, 149

A Pivotal Book from Dr. Jeff Myers and Summit Ministries

Understanding the Times: A Survey of Competing Worldviews is a landmark guide to understanding the most significant religious worldviews operating in Western civilization: Christianity, Secularism, Marxism, Islam, New Spirituality, and Postmodernism. It equips today's generation to know and defend their Christian faith against the onslaught of skepticism and doubt.

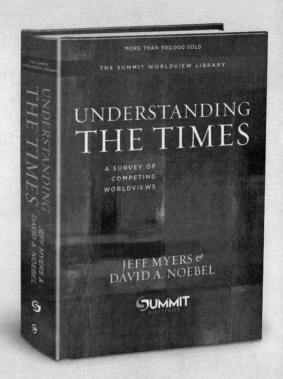

A GIFT TO YOU:

I'd like to give you a free 7-day devotional taken from my book *Understanding the Times: A Survey of Competing Worldviews*.

I want to share this devotional with you because Christians—especially students—are under constant attack for their faith and beliefs. Understanding what a worldview is, and having confidence that the true Christian worldview can stand up to the counterfeit worldviews of today, is extremely important in the battle for sharing and defending truth.

To start this free devotional, simply visit **bit.ly/understanding-the-times**

Sincerely,

Jeff Myers